Welcoming Ruin

Studies in Critical Social Sciences Book Series

Haymarket Books is proud to be working with Brill Academic Publishers (www.brill.nl) to republish the *Studies in Critical Social Sciences* book series in paperback editions. This peer-reviewed book series offers insights into our current reality by exploring the content and consequences of power relationships under capitalism, and by considering the spaces of opposition and resistance to these changes that have been defining our new age. Our full catalog of *SCSS* volumes can be viewed at https://www.haymarketbooks.org/series_collections/4-studies-in-critical-social-sciences.

WELCOMING RUIN

The Civil Rights Act of 1875

ALAN FRIEDLANDER
RICHARD ALLAN GERBER

Haymarket Books
Chicago, IL

First published in 2018 by Brill Academic Publishers, The Netherlands.

Published in paperback in 2020 by
Haymarket Books
P.O. Box 180165
Chicago, IL 60618
773-583-7884
www.haymarketbooks.org

ISBN: 978-1-64259-074-6

Distributed to the trade in the US through Consortium Book Sales and Distribution (www.cbsd.com) and internationally through Ingram Publisher Services International (www.ingramcontent.com).

This book was published with the generous support of Lannan Foundation and Wallace Action Fund.

Cover design by Jamie Kerry and Ragina Johnson.

Printed in United States.

10 9 8 7 6 5 4 3 2 1

Library of Congress Cataloging-in-Publication Data is available.

Contents

Appendices

Acknowledgements

This volume represents a collaboration of contributions. Our students at Southern Connecticut State University have challenged our ideas; the current project originated in a senior seminar in historical methodology. We have enjoyed multiple opportunities to present our findings to our faculty colleagues – at conferences of the Connecticut State University Research Foundation, to the Southern Connecticut State University Arts and Sciences faculty, to the New England Historical Association and before the Connecticut Academy of Arts and Sciences. CSURF provided generous funding for research in primary materials. The faculty awarded occasional research time. NEHA colleagues offered positive suggestions. The Academy first invited our public lecture and then published our preliminary work. From these colleagues we have benefited from occasional critical commentary and more than occasional encouragement.

We owe a huge debt of gratitude to the librarians and archivists who located manuscript materials and public records for our scrutiny. Lists of unpublished manuscripts, obscure newspapers and other primary documents that we consulted are noted. The professionals of Buley Library of SCSU, and in particular Beth Paris, inter-library loan expert, vastly facilitated our endeavors. Our research was enhanced by specialists at the Library of Congress and the National Archives, the Massachusetts Historical Society, the Houghton Library at Harvard University, at Smith College and at the Historical Society of Pennsylvania. Special thanks to Willie S. Maryland, recently of the Alabama Department of Archives and History, and to Lucille Houde of Yale University for their expertise and good will. We are extraordinarily grateful to Amy Wallace and Linda Larkin, our editors and proofreaders. Great thanks to Dawn Volkman for her technical expertise. They will go straight to heaven if we have anything to say about it.

We owe most to our families for their love and for knowing when to intervene. It is a wondrous occurrence that at the end of this historical journey we remain compadres as well as collaborators – but if there are errors in this volume, the other one is responsible.

Alan Friedlander
Richard Allan Gerber

List of Illustrations and Maps

Illustrations

Maps

CHAPTER 1

Prologue

The Speaker's gavel commanded order as James A. Garfield rose to the House floor. For that Friday, February 5, 1875, and for just one month more, the Ohio Republican Congressman and his political confreres would retain their majority in the House of Representatives. The term of the 43rd Congress was to expire on March 3, 1875. The House in the 44th would be dominated by Democrats, who had swept to electoral victory in the midterms of 1874. The Republicans were the lamest of lame ducks.

The galleries were packed. An anxious anticipation filled the room. At stake was the civil rights bill, a radical proposal to ban racial discrimination in places of public accommodation. The statute enacted equal racial access to "inns, public conveyances ... theatres and other places of public amusement," and to service on juries. Perhaps the most critical portion of the bill included integrated public schools, "all common schools and public institutions of learning" supported by general taxation.[1]

A significant version of that legislation had, indeed, passed the Senate on May 23, 1874, prior to the congressional recess and the 1874 congressional elections. Once the House Republicans gained passage of their own civil rights bill, the Senate must cast an aye or nay vote. There would not be time enough for amendments to be considered by the full Congress.

Garfield, the powerful chairman of the House Appropriations Committee, strongly supported the civil rights bill. Perhaps because of his Radical Republican proclivities he had been selected by his party to deliver the penultimate speech of this contentious debate. Garfield shared the continuing bitter partisanship of Civil War and Reconstruction issues even a decade after Appomattox. He understood especially the raw racial sensitivities of House members on both sides of the aisle. Garfield exhorted his Republican colleagues to enact the civil rights statute. During the past twelve years "it has often been rung in our ears that by doing justice to the negro we shall pull down the pillars of our political temple and bury ourselves in its ruins." But warnings of political disaster had failed to occur, Garfield observed, when the Republicans abolished slavery, and then enacted the Thirteenth, the Fourteenth and the Fifteenth Amendments. Passing this civil rights bill would not cause disaster either. As a matter of equity and fairness the new law would extend "equal enjoyment" of "public chartered privileges" granted by state statutes to all American citizens.

1 *Cong. Record,* 43rd Congress, 2nd Session: 1010.

> For this act of plain justice we are told that ruin is again staring us in the face!
>
> If ruin comes from this, I welcome ruin.[2]

Defiant words, given the outcome of the 1874 midterm congressional elections. Perhaps the threatened "ruin" of the Republican "political temple" had already begun. Looking around at his 199 Republican colleagues (of a total House of 292), he would have noticed that 94 of them would not be present when the 44th Congress convened on December 6, 1875. The Democratic contingent of 88 in the 43rd conclave would instead be augmented to 182 in the 44th.[3] Republicans had enjoyed a safe two-thirds majority in the 43rd. In the 44th the Democrats reversed the situation, gaining nearly a two-thirds majority. Certain of the losses were predictable, as "Redeemer" governments in many southern states voted themselves back into white Democratic power after years of angry refusal to participate in any political process that included freedmen. Northern Republicans, too, were defeated in substantial numbers. Garfield had survived. The sponsor of the civil rights bill in the House, Rep. Benjamin F. Butler of Massachusetts, lost his seat.

In the Senate, too, Republicans faced a rising tide of Democrats. While they managed to retain a majority in the 44th, eight Republicans had lost their seats. In large measure the elections of 1874 served as a referendum on the civil rights bill. Republicans had paid dearly. Those midterm elections, for two decades, tightly balanced political power between the two parties. There was no four-year period during which either Republicans or Democrats controlled both houses of Congress until 1896.

The 1874 midterms also "ruined" for nearly a generation the progressive stance of the Republican Party. Passage of the Civil Rights Act of 1875 was the last Republican victory of Reconstruction. After the elections of 1876 the GOP all but disappeared as the institutional advocate of equal rights through political reform. The organization which had originated as the party of free soil, and then of free men, and which had become the incubator of a postwar multiracial democracy in America, largely forsook its progressive outlook until nearly the end of the 19th century. The pro-business orientation of the party – prominent within Republican circles since the platform of 1860 – would

2 *Cong. Record,* 43rd Congress, 2nd Session: 1005. Totals may differ from *Cong. Record.*

3 The 43rd Congress: 199 Republicans, 88 Democrats represents party totals after election. The House total also included 4 Liberal Republicans, 1 Independent. Total House – 292. The 44th Congress: 182 Democrats, 105 Republicans, 5 Independents. *Office of the Clerk of the House of Representatives of the United States.*

dominate Republican ideology and Republican policy until once more balanced (or divided) by the advent of a new wave of reform symbolized by Theodore Roosevelt.[4]

Garfield's remarks were followed by those of Congressman Butler. Butler refused to admit the view that Republicans were defeated at the polls in 1874 because of their support for civil rights. To the contrary! "I say in the face of the country ... the reason why some here have not been sent back [to Congress] is because we did not pass this bill a year ago. The people turned from us because we were a do-nothing party, afraid of our shadows."[5]

Election defeat or not, the Republicans stuck to their ideological guns. The lame duck Republican House passed the Civil Rights bill on a strict partisan vote, 162 Republican ayes, 99 Democratic nays, with 28 not voting. The bill then went to the Senate, where it passed on February 27. President Grant signed the Civil Rights Act into law on March 1, 1875.

1 The Civil Rights Act of 1875 in the History of Reconstruction

Welcoming Ruin raises the stature of the Civil Rights Act of 1875 to a prominent position in the history of Reconstruction. The law rarely occupies a central location in current discussions of the postwar period. Our research fairly shouts that the narrative of Reconstruction – perhaps commencing as early as President Lincoln's plan for restoring Louisiana government in 1863 – remains incompletely told until this remarkable legislation can receive proper focus and emphasis. This book investigates and explicates the dramatic development of the Civil Rights Act of 1875. The research considers both national and state level sources, including scrutiny of 40 congressional districts in the 1874 midterm elections.

Moreover, comprehension of the importance of the Civil Rights Act serves to modify the primary current interpretations of Reconstruction. For nearly

4 Even civil service reform, enacted initially in 1883, following the assassination of now President Garfield in 1881, enhanced the power of business interests in the Republican Party. Prior to the Pendleton Civil Service Act of 1883, the primary source of money for Republican (and Democratic) political campaigning came from "donations" from appointed office holders at every level. Businessmen were customers who might pay handsomely for political favors. The 1883 Act, however, eliminated any requirement that political appointees contribute to a political organization in order to keep their jobs. Most ceased their contributions. Businessmen thereafter became the principal sources of party revenue; parties became the supplicants for funds. Business tended to determine policy preferences.

5 *Cong. Record*, 43rd Congress, 2nd Session: 1009.

the past two generations historians have tended to give the 1875 law short shrift. To appreciate the critical place of the Civil Rights Act would require substantial revision in the traditional examinations of the Reconstruction decade.

In a variety of interpretations historians have declared that Reconstruction began with a bi-racial democratic bang only to end with a whimper of surrender to white supremacy. That proposition loses strength, however, once the 1875 law gets a fair hearing. If Republicans for one reason or another abandoned the cause of racial equity in the early 1870s, how can we explain the results of the Congressional elections of 1874 and the subsequent passage of the Civil Rights Act by the lame ducks of 1875?[6]

Why were Republicans defeated so definitively in 1874? One oft-repeated viewpoint holds that a plethora of urgent issues dominated the politics of the mid-1870s. A severe depression, precipitated in September 1873, had buffeted the nation for a year. The corruption of the Grant Administration plagued the Republican Party; scandal had reached as high as Vice-President Schuyler Colfax. The continuing disgruntlement of "The Best Men" focused attention on patronage and civil service reform. A group of western policy questions, including dealing with Native American tribes, government financing of railroads, and public land distribution all concerned American voters. The rise of concentrated corporate power raised arguments about tariff rates, paper money, the lot of American workers, the capture of American natural resources, even the validity of government's role in the American economy. Thus the Democratic sweep of 1874 had little or nothing to do with civil rights. By 1874 the nation had moved beyond Reconstruction issues. The requirements of the day led Republicans to abandon the cause of the freed people. This scenario produces limited results. It might explain why Republicans in both congressional chambers suffered the shellacking of the 1874 midterms. But it cannot account for the oratory of Republican "ruin" declaimed by Congressman Garfield. It cannot explain why Republicans voted for the Civil Rights Act as the lame ducks of 1875.

We argue that one principal reason for Republican losses in 1874 was precisely their forceful advocacy of the equal public accommodations bill. Our research demonstrates that the Republicans of the 43rd Congress understood exactly that to campaign for equal public rights gambled their political futures – and they did it anyway! They knew that they faced increasing Democratic

6 A preliminary abridged version of this discussion may be found in Richard A. Gerber, Alan Friedlander, "The Civil Rights Act of 1875 A Reexamination," *Transactions of the Connecticut Academy of Arts and Sciences* (2005): 1–50.

strength. Even if they did not want to discuss civil rights, Democratic rivals on the stump and in the press compelled them to wear the civil rights albatross in any event. As Garfield's comments make clear Republicans knew that their political careers were at stake. Many had ended. If the Republican Party had abandoned the cause of protecting African Americans, would it not have been strategically preferable for House Republicans to say little or nothing about the Senate's civil rights bill or even oppose it altogether? Though many might have been defeated for reasons unrelated to racial equality, our research indicates that overt advocacy of civil rights in 1874 stood at the forefront of Republican ideals, "ruin" or not. Outright support for racial equity contributed significantly to electoral defeat. How frequently do incumbents insist on positions they must know will guarantee that they lose their seats? How rarely do politicians commit political suicide?

We might invoke the possibility that Republican veterans of past political wars were out of touch with the national mood and the attitudes of their constituents. They never saw the defeats of 1874 coming. Senate Republicans, of course, were already on the hot seat, having recorded their votes in passing their equal public accommodations bill. They must defend their positions; they could not escape Democratic wrath. For House Republicans the association with equal civil rights proved so politically unpalatable, North and South alike, that Democrats could hang it around their necks whether they campaigned actively for it or did not. Were House Republicans sufficiently detached from reality that they stumbled blithely into the electoral sandstorm? That option lacks a footing in reality.

We contend that the Republicans of the 43rd Congress, in both houses, were ideologically committed to the protection of the freed people in 1874 and in 1875. They retained the same ideology that had allowed them to legislate the Civil Rights Act of 1866 and enact the Fourteenth Amendment, and then initiate military rule in the South and secure ratification of the Fifteenth Amendment. In our view Republicans demonstrated ideological consistency in the 1874 elections and in the passage of the 1875 Act. Our examination of Republican ideology, which we label "Rights-for-Order," follows immediately.

We concur with the current historical viewpoint that the Republicans lost the war over Reconstruction, that the forces of white supremacy overcame the thrust of bi-racial democracy. Republicans in the South were defeated through violence, intimidation and racism. We resist, however, the reason ascribed to that defeat – that Republicans lost the postwar peace because they surrendered, retreated or abandoned the freedmen. The analysis of abandonment assumes that had Congressional Republicans persisted in their programs, or improved their implementation, they could ultimately have succeeded. The election campaigns of 1874 confound that argument. The enactment of the Civil Rights Act of 1875 refutes that interpretation.

We assert that Congressional Republicans lost a bi-racial Reconstruction to bigotry and white supremacy, but not because they shrank from their cause any more than Appomattox proved that Southerners had yielded theirs. Republicans were defeated, but they refused to sacrifice or surrender their ideology. They went down fighting for their wartime and post-war objectives. That is the meaning of the Civil Rights Act of 1875. It is the reason of this volume to clarify this substantial historical distinction.

2 Rights-For-Order

Welcoming Ruin advances the thesis that the Civil Rights Act of 1875 was driven by the fundamental ideological view that equal rights created stability in the social order. If the source of disorder in society was inequality, the remedy was equality, equal rights. The 1875 law thus stood consistently with the earlier Reconstruction acts – the Civil Rights Act of 1866, the 14th and 15th amendments – in seeking social order through equal rights. This book invents a short-cut phrase, Rights-For-Order, to identify this view not present in the historical literature. Rights-For-Order meant conferring and implementing legal and political power on the freed people, permitting them to protect themselves against their white neighbors. Over time white Southerners would adjust to this dramatic alteration in their behavior and their culture.

The Rights-For-Order approach to Reconstruction taken by Republicans stood as middle ground within a threesome of general approaches for dealing with the post-war South. On one end of the spectrum of strategies stood the "lenient" pro-southern version of Reconstruction embodied in the civil governments structured and encouraged by Presidents Abraham Lincoln and Andrew Johnson. Republicans generally rejected this option. Moderate and Radical Republicans alike refused to permit Southern whites to determine the nature of race relations in the postwar. Congressional Republicans in particular opposed any policy that would turn over to their former masters the fate of four-plus million persons so recently emancipated from chattel slavery. Republicans must deny to white southerners the power to overturn the results of civil war.

Alternatively, Republicans might maintain an army of occupation in the rebel territory until whites had learned to alter their behavior toward blacks. To expect revisions of "hearts and minds" might be considered a stretch, but enforcement of civil equality might be managed. But how long would troops be required before the goals were met? A decade? A generation? Armed force, though, was unthinkable except to the very most radical Republicans. Northern families wanted their veterans to come home. Demobilization on the broadest scale was a (fulfilled) expectation of northern society. Even if some military force might be utilized to achieve temporary measures, such as serving as a relief agency or establishing new southern state constitutions, troops in the streets ran against the American grain. If the United States was genuinely a Union, with the government defeating insurrection, not fighting any sovereign nation, no set of circumstances could possible justify a large-scale military force over a long period of time – in peacetime – against Americans. That option could gain no traction.

Rights-For-Order stood as the significant middle position on this tripartite continuum of Reconstruction strategies. Congress could enact measures that embodied civil equality – equality before the law – and thereby empower the freed people to protect themselves through the justice system and the political process. The conservative mechanisms of inclusion into the governance system of African-American freed people could be launched by enacting uniform free institutions in the South. Free institutions, implanted and implemented, would establish over time a peaceful southern social order. Inclusion would prevent the risk of renewed sectional conflict, preclude any long-term military presence in the South, and reflect the values of democracy and equality. The conferral and implementation of equality before the law for freed people offered an orderly social environment. Civil equality would remove the dangers caused by continuing inequality.

Stated differently, Congressional Republicans perceived the greatest threat to the southern social environment – and thus to the permanent results of the Union victory – as the continuing festering condition of race relations. Southern whites were determined to restore in the aftermath of war their historical culture and the local institutions and mores of white supremacy, even if they could not exactly re-impose chattel slavery. Republicans could not permit them to succeed. Southern blacks, emancipated from the shackles of bondage, would not submit to anything like the renewal of their former status. They would fight to prevent the prospects of re-enslavement. Republicans must guarantee that the freed people overcame inequality. They must prevent race conflict, whether by open warfare or covert behavior.

The Civil Rights Act of 1875 was the final episode by which the Republicans of the 43rd Congress sought to achieve Rights-For-Order. The initial statement of that essentially counter-revolutionary ideology had occurred nearly a decade earlier with the Republicans of the 39th. The sectional drama of Reconstruction opened with the Civil Rights Act of 1866 and continued with the 14th and 15th amendments to the Constitution. The establishment of Republican dominated new civil southern state governments were classic Rights-or-Order enactments. Republicans who attempted to implant bi-racial democracy in the former Confederate states sought to enact a homogenous set of national free-labor values encapsulated in the ideal of equality before the law. The notion of Rights-For-Order is unique in the historical writing about Reconstruction.

3 Historiographical Perspectives

This book challenges the prevailing interpretation of Reconstruction. The current conventional interpretation holds that Reconstruction, however idealistically, even nobly, begun ultimately failed because the Republicans did not provide sufficient guarantees for the freed people. Republicans who claimed to believe in justice for a people oppressed for centuries, and who believed in liberty and equality – and who had the votes – nonetheless abandoned their ideology and left the newly-freed former slaves to the tender mercies of the white South. What went wrong?

The most common contentions hold that congressional Republicans limited their programs to mild and less controversial enactments related to civil equality – the Civil Rights Act of 1866, the 14th and 15th amendments and analogous state-based programs. However, there were no public school integration programs. And no land reform – no forty acres, no mule. Alternatively, Republicans became distracted from Reconstruction efforts because of new issues: the rise of corporate power, a massive economic depression, westward expansion, corruption in government. Or further that many Republicans had already achieved their Reconstruction objectives with the ratification of the 15th Amendment. They had enacted the measures by which African Americans could protect themselves. It was time to let them do it!

Just a glance at a few titles of influential works about Reconstruction reveals the point.[7] Eric Foner of Columbia University, perhaps the most prominent

---

7 Eric Foner, *Reconstruction, America's Unfinished Revolution 1863–1877* (New York: 1988); Michael les Benedict, *A Compromise of Principle, Congressional Republicans and Reconstruction 1863–1869* (New York: 1974). On the elections of 1874 and the Civil Rights Bill, the best account remains William Gillette, *Retreat From Reconstruction, 1869–1879* (Baton Rouge: 1979): 211–258. See variously Heather Cox Richardson, *The Death of Reconstruction: Race, Labor and Politics in the Post-Civil War North 1865–1901* (Cambridge: 2001); Herman Belz, *Emancipation and Equal Rights* (New York: 1978); Hans Trefousse, *The Radical Republicans* (New York: 1969); David Herbert Donald, *Charles Sumner and the Rights of Man* (New York: 1970); recently Charles W. Calhoun, *Conceiving a New Republic: The Republican Party and the Southern Question 1869–1900* (Lawrence: 2006).

scholar of Reconstruction, called his book *Reconstruction: America's Unfinished Revolution.* William Gillette of Rutgers, another major student of the period, titled his book *Retreat from Reconstruction.* Michael Les Benedict of Ohio State named his work *A Compromise of Principle.* Heather Cox Richardson of Boston College titled her work *The Death of Reconstruction.* Reconstruction was unfinished, or a retreat, or a compromise, or dead. One cannot get much plainer than that!

Welcoming Ruin challenges those perspectives. There are two significant issues to note. A certain present-mindedness lurks in these historical attitudes. Perhaps historians are bound to view the world with post-1960s eyes! They grew up influenced by the Civil Rights revolution, in a time when progressive forces sought racial equality, and the "soul" liberty that found expression in free love and the peace movement. Given this experience the primary focus has rested on the plight of African Americans.

Historians have projected this set of values back onto Reconstruction. They demand that the Radical Republicans who claimed to share their ideology be held to account for not having implemented the guarantees of racial equality in the fallen South. They focus on what was left undone. It is the fault of 19th century Republicans for not enacting the racial equality of the civil rights era of the 1960s and since.

Present-mindedness also blocks appreciation of what the idea of reunion meant to the huge majority of Northerners who were not Radical Republicans. *Welcoming Ruin* asserts that victory included uniform institutions established in a reunited America. Could anyone imagine fighting for the Union only to bring the South back into the fold with the institution of slavery still intact, or with no protections for the freed people once the Union army stood down? Restore the South the way it was before all this carnage of 625,000 dead? Of course not!

Welcoming Ruin asserts that postwar civil rights, and particularly the Civil Rights Act of 1875, were indeed conservative objectives – Rights for Order – for the future security and peace of the nation. They would remove the seeds of discord between North and South. One nation, not two, inside the same constitutional system. The South could not be allowed to rebel again in the next crisis ten years down the road.

A further fundamental problem with the interpretations is that historians do not know what to make of the Civil Rights Act of 1875. The struggle for equal public accommodations, enacted ten years after Appomattox, is inconsistent with the theory that the Republicans enacted minimal guarantees for the freed people and then abandoned the freedmen. Historians who decry the failure of Reconstruction understand this contradiction. But rather than reexamine their basic assumptions about Reconstruction, they have instead disparaged the 1875 law. Eric Foner declares that the act may have represented "a broad assertion of principle" but not even "its sponsors expected it to be enforced in the South." For Foner the law had become "a dead letter." Similarly, William Gillette claims that "half-hearted Republicans" and Democrats, weary of filibuster, finally yielded to political compromise, to a law that would "do no good to anybody in the universe." An "insignificant victory," Gillette calls it.

Other historians have claimed that the Civil Rights Act was "more the product of political maneuvering than any serious civil rights concern." In *Emancipation and Equal Rights* Herman Belz declared that the sponsors did not expect the Act to apply to private businesses, but only to those which "occupied a special position by virtue of their legal franchise." The late Hans Trefousse of Brooklyn College of CUNY admitted in *The Radical Republicans*, that a few remaining Radicals in 1875 "bestirred themselves" to enact the public accommodations law, but because of the conservative reaction against Radical Reconstruction the Republicans as a party "had proved most reluctant." Heather Cox Richardson explained that the law had no chance to succeed because it ran contrary to the temper of the times. Equal public accommodations was a contradiction of the free labor ideology of the time. For the national government to confer those rights upon a person, in an era of free labor and *laissez faire*, made the law of 1875 at best an empty gesture.

Harvard Professor David Herbert Donald, and so many since, have held that the Civil Rights Act was merely a gesture of tribute to the bill's original sponsor. In *Charles Sumner and the Rights of Man*, Donald relates that Sumner's deathbed wish, whispered to Massachusetts Congressman Ebenezer R. Hoar was about the passage of this legislation. "You must take care of the civil rights bill – my bill, the civil rights bill, don't let it fail." Sumner's congressional colleagues, according to Donald, simply nodded a farewell to the man who had been their leader for a generation.[8]

Those reasons lack historical stamina. What congressman would risk losing a seat in Congress for a policy that he already knew to be useless, or unenforceable, or unconstitutional, or otherwise meaningless? Would any congressman

8 Most recently Douglas R. Egerton has extended this reasoning, noting that African Americans, while pleased by the public accommodations aspects of the Civil Rights Act in its final form, were nonetheless significantly disappointed that the "mixed schools" clause, which would have integrated public schools, was stricken from the bill moments prior to its passage in the House. See Douglas R. Egerton, *The Wars of Reconstruction, The Brief, Violent History of America's Most Progressive Era* (New York: 2014), especially pp. 310–313. See also Barry Friedman, *The Will of the People* (New York: 2009); Mark Wahlgren Summers, *The Ordeal of the Reunion: A New History of Reconstruction* (Chapel Hill: 2014); A.J. Langguth, *After Lincoln: How the North Won the Civil War and Lost the Peace* (New York: 2014).

campaign for a law that his constituents would not support, when it would be easier to drop it and say nothing? Who would sacrifice a career to honor the memory of a fallen Senator?

The research for *Welcoming Ruin* indicates that the Republicans who enacted the Civil Rights Act of 1875 remained steadfast, consistently supportive of civil order for the South in an America far more conservative than it had been in 1866. Out of step in a nation struggling with economic depression, corporate greed, westward expansion, and corrupt government, in which seven of the eleven Confederate states had shifted from Republican to Democrat, and in which they – and many of their northern Republican colleagues had been ousted by Democrats – they remained committed to principles of social integration. An interpretive course correction must take place in the writing of Reconstruction history.

Welcoming Ruin arrays an arsenal of primary sources. These include newspapers, memoirs and analyses of electoral campaigns in forty congressional districts, South and North, in which the Civil Rights Act became an issue in the elections of 1874. This profusion of sources offers evidence for Republican motives and outcomes. In examining the development and significance of the Civil Rights Act of 1875 we chronicle the origins of the statute from Massachusetts Senator Charles Sumner's first proposal of late 1870, through the legislative history of the law, to signature by President Grant on March 1, 1875. We examine, albeit briefly, the post-passage implementation of the law until the declaration by the U.S. Supreme Court that the Act was unconstitutional in the *Civil Rights Cases* of 1883. We examine the partisan debates in Congress and in the press. We submit our findings as a contribution to the primary interpretations, to the historical literature of both the Civil Rights Act and more generally of Reconstruction. We suggest that our investigation of the continuing ideological commitment behind the 1875 Act adjusts the prevailing word on the historiographical street.

4 Precedent: The Civil Rights Act of 1866

The Civil Rights Act of 1875 itself had a precursor, the Civil Rights Act of 1866: "An act to protect all persons in the United States in their civil rights and furnish a means of their vindication." That measure, enacted in April 1866, two months prior to the passage of the Fourteenth Amendment, was deliberately designed to supersede the so-called Black Codes. To that end the Act defined American citizenship for the first time. "All persons born in the United States and not subject to any foreign power, excluding Indians not taxed, are hereby declared to be citizens of the United States." This citizenship clause bestowed the Bill of Rights and other constitutional rights upon four million people who had been slaves but a year ago. The Act went further. The heart of the 1866 law, written by Illinois Republican Senator Lyman Trumbull, prohibited racial discrimination in private property transactions between individuals:

> Citizens ... shall have the same right ... to make and enforce contracts, to sue, be parties and give evidence, to inherit, purchase, lease, sell, hold and convey real and personal property ... any law, statute, ordinance, regulation, or custom to the contrary notwithstanding.[9]

Section 2 announced how the law should be enforced:

> That any person who, under color of any law, statute, ordinance, regulation, or custom, shall subject, or cause to be subjected, any inhabitant of any State or Territory to the deprivation of any right secured or protected by this act ... shall be deemed guilty of a misdemeanor, and, on conviction, shall be punished by fine not exceeding one thousand dollars, or imprisonment not exceeding one year, or both, in the discretion of the court.

The 1866 Act eliminated racially-based systems of criminal justice. It removed to the federal courts "cognizance of all crimes and offenses committed against the provisions of this act," and also the appeals of any persons "who are denied or cannot enforce in the courts or judicial tribunals of the State or locality where they may be the rights secured to them by the first section of this act." It authorized United States attorneys, marshals and deputies to enforce the act's provisions; levied fines on officers who failed to perform their duties; imposed penalties of $1,000 and six months' imprisonment on persons who impeded implementation of the Act; permitted the president to employ the armed forces of the United States, "to prevent the violation and enforce the due execution of this act;" directed appeals ultimately to the United States Supreme Court.

His measure, said Senator Trumbull, enforced the Thirteenth Amendment. While officially emancipated, the freed people remained circumscribed by laws and customs and degraded by discrimination. "There is very little importance in the general declaration of abstract truths and principles, unless they can be carried into effect:"

9 Civil Rights Act, April 9, 1866, 14 Stat. 27–30. U.S. Code Sec.1982.

> We have a right to enact such legislation as will make them [black people] free, we believe; and that can only be done by punishing those who undertake to deny them their freedom. When it comes to be understood in all parts of the United States that any person who shall deprive another of any right or subject him to any punishment in consequence of his color or race will expose himself to fine and imprisonment, I think such acts will soon cease.[10]

On March 27, 1866, President Johnson vetoed the Civil Rights Act. His veto message was blunt: "I regret that the bill, which has passed both Houses of Congress, contains provisions of which I cannot approve."[11] He questioned congressional power to confer citizenship. He questioned the propriety of conferring citizenship, even if it could be done: "Four millions of them [black people] have just emerged from slavery into freedom. Can it be reasonably supposed that they possess the requisite qualifications to entitle them to all the privileges and immunities of citizens of the United States? Have the people of the several States expressed such a conviction?" It was, the President said, as it had been, a matter of capital and labor. How the possessors of means associated with their workforce – barring slavery – was not the affair of government. He worried that what began as simple "civil rights" might end with unlimited rights, rights of intermarriage, political rights, the right to hold office, or even the right to vote.

On April 9, 1866, Congress overrode President Johnson's veto – the first override in American history. The Fourteenth Amendment, ratified in 1868, settled the question of United States and state citizenship. It banned states from denying due process of law or equal protection of the law. And yet, the Act and the Amendment notwithstanding, citizens discriminated freely, without the slightest hesitation, without objection of the law, against their fellow citizens. State governments turned a blind eye. It was done in the north as in the south. Congressional action, many believed, was needed to enforce the protections of the Amendment and put teeth into the Civil Rights Act. A supplemental civil rights act, with particular reference to equal public accommodations, was in order. Discrimination, in transport, in inns, in places of public resort, whether

---

10 On the Civil Rights Act of 1866, Lyman Trumbull's remarks, and discussion, see Bernard Schwartz, *Statutory History of the United States. Civil Rights. Part I* (New York: 1970), 99–112. Mark Krug, *Lyman Trumbull Conservative Radical* (New York: 1965). The 1866 law was not challenged in court until 1968. The Supreme Court upheld it as constitutional. See Richard Allan Gerber, "Playing Tricks on the Dead: *Jones v. Alfred H. Mayer Company*, An Historical Inquiry," *Pace Law Review*, vol. 1, No. 1 (1980): 59–119.

11 President Johnson's veto message, Schwartz, *Statutory History*, 150–155.

decreed by state law or tolerated by state neglect, must end. A peremptory statute must put principles into practice.

5 Charles Sumner's Quest

One man took up the challenge: Charles Sumner, senior senator from Massachusetts. For two decades Sumner stood as the nation's most earnest and unshakable voice for emancipation and the rights of man.[12] His spirit animated the Supplemental Civil Rights Act. Sumner was 62 years old, silver-haired, elegant, eloquent, as the 43rd Congress opened its sessions in December, 1873. (see Illustration 1) Three months of life remained to him. For four years he had tried to secure some measure that would enforce the promises of the initial Civil Rights Act. This was his final try. Death robbed him of the pleasure of seeing its triumph in 1875 – and spared him the pain of witnessing its downfall in 1883. For the South Sumner personified aggressive abolitionism, the force that had precipitated the war. A decade after Appomattox that image had mellowed somewhat. His sympathetic call for amnesty for ex-Confederates softened some hard feelings. His call to remove from northern battle-flags the names of Union victories soothed other animosities. Animosities rekindled as the civil rights campaign caught fire.

Charles Sumner was a person not easily approached. He possessed a layer of frosty reserve, an intellectual arrogance. Those who disagreed with him felt the frostbite. So his biographer David Herbert Donald has portrayed him, "a man inflexibly committed to a set of basic ideas as moral principles.... In his speeches in Congress [he] assumed the faintly condescending air of a pedagogue instructing backward children, as he explained the rudimentary principles of justice to his colleagues ... his left hand on his hip, his right hand toying with an eyeglass."[13] Some colleagues found him insufferable. "A cold, haughty aristocrat who would not take much notice of ordinary men," one southern detractor declared.[14] To others he was transcendent. "Fond of power, fitted for its exercise, he chose the side of weakness," his friend George Frisbie Hoar remembered. "Surrounded by wealth, he chose the cause of the poor.

---

12 The definitive biography remains David Herbert Donald, *Charles Sumner and the Coming of the Civil War* (New York: 1960), and *Charles Sumner and the Rights of Man* (New York: 1970).

13 Donald, *Charles Sumner and the Coming of the Civil War*, vii–viii, 214.

14 Remarks of James M. Headon of North Carolina, see below, Chapter 6.

ILLUSTRATION 1 Charles Sumner
SOURCE: LIBRARY OF CONGRESS

Rich in friends, he became the defender of the friendless."[15] "His own pathway was illuminated by the light of his intense individuality," said Michigan Congressman Omar Conger. "All who traveled with him along that royal road were

15 *Memorial Addresses on the Life and Character of Charles Sumner (a Senator from Massachusetts,) Delivered in the Senate and House of Representatives, Forty-third Congress, First Session, April 27, 1874* (Washington: 1874), 100.

clothed in purple, and all who went by other ways were groping in darkness. To him the absolute equality of all human beings ... left no place for partiality, no room for prejudice." "John Brown," concluded Oregon's Congressman James Nesmith, "was Charles Sumner reduced to action."[16] His final monument, Sumner hoped, would be the new Civil Rights Act. "If my works were completed and my civil-rights bill passed," he said to Indiana Senator Daniel Pratt, "no visitor could enter the door that could be more welcome than death."[17] Death entered. The work was incomplete.

Charles Sumner commenced his quest to bequeath the nation a supplemental civil rights act in 1870. Four years of frustration followed.[18] Constitutional questions blocked his initial efforts in the 41st Congress. Lyman Trumbull, Chairman of the Senate Judiciary Committee, rejected a supplement to his own Civil Rights Act. In the 42nd Congress Sumner adopted a new strategy: civil rights coupled with amnesty. Democrats desperately wanted amnesty, the return of political rights to their wayward southern brethren. Republicans desired to assure civil rights to their faithful freedmen, now empowered by the Fifteenth Amendment with the ability to vote. Sumner tied the two elements together.

In December 1871 an Amnesty Bill, H.R.380, arrived in the Senate. Passed by the House of Representatives, the bill removed political disabilities imposed by the Fourteenth Amendment on those who had, from a northern perspective, committed treason: erstwhile federal congressmen and senators who had "gone South," officers who had commanded rebel forces, state officials who had voted for ordinances of secession. To this Sumner added a rider, a civil rights amendment. Grant amnesty to the southern people; ensure black people equality.

Sumner's amendment to the amnesty bill unleashed a swirl of political maneuvers. Republicans, New York's Roscoe Conkling, Vermont's George Edmunds, John Sherman of Ohio, Oliver Morton of Indiana, promoted it enthusiastically. It was a trap for Democrats. If Democrats wanted amnesty they would have to swallow civil rights. That, as Republicans well knew, they would not do. Amnesty would fail – yet no blame would attach to Republicans. Nevada Senator James Nye chided Democratic opponents.

16 *Memorial Addresses*, eulogies of Omar Conger, p. 107; James Nesmith, 93.

17 Eulogy of Daniel Pratt: *Mem. Add.*, 31.

18 On Sumner's early civil rights bill struggles, see Donald, *Charles Sumner and the Rights of Man*: 530–539, 544–547; Alfred Avins, *The Reconstruction Amendments' Debates: The Legislative History and Contemporary Debates in Congress on the 13th, 14th, and 15th Amendments* (Richmond: 1967), 577–630; Alfred H. Kelly, "The Congressional Controversy over School Segregation, 1867–1875," *American Historical Review*, 64 (1959): 546–552.

> All men, and women too, are equal before the law. What does that mean? Does it mean that I am to be kicked from the cars because I am not blessed with a white skin? No, sir; it does not mean any such thing. If these men read carefully, on the brow of every negro they will find the United States authority stamped for freedom, and if they will examine his uniform they will find that it is the uniform of a United States citizen.... If I had outraged the laws and Constitution of my land, if I had attempted to tear down the very temple of liberty here, and now, professing to be its friend, have not sorrow and regret enough in my heart for my bloody deeds to ask pardon, I do not deserve to be forgiven. So I take it that these [Democratic] friends who want to get immediately into a position to hold office had better conclude to let a negro ride in the cars with them.[19]

On February 9, 1872, Charles Sumner's amendment passed the Senate, a flat-footed tie broken by the affirmative vote of Vice-President Schuyler Colfax. Civil rights' success guaranteed the amnesty bill's failure. Democrats turned against their own proposal. The Amnesty Bill fell short of the two-thirds needed to satisfy the requirements of the Fourteenth Amendment. Three months later, on May 9, the drama replayed itself. A new amnesty bill arrived. Again Sumner attached his civil rights rider. Again the amendment passed on the vice-president's casting vote. Again the amnesty bill failed to acquire the two-thirds majority.

The presidential election of 1872 fractured the Republican Party. Disaffected Republicans broke away from President Grant to form a new organization, the Liberal Republican Party. The new party demanded an end to Reconstruction, a reconciliation of North and South. The Liberals also supported civil service reform and lower tariffs. They castigated the corruption of the Grant administration.[20] Their convention in Cincinnati in early May, 1872, nominated for president New York *Tribune* editor Horace Greeley. Democrats, convening at Baltimore, also endorsed Greeley, the only time in American history when a third party had strength enough to compel one of the two major parties to nominate its presidential candidate.

---

19 *Cong. Globe*, 42nd Congress, 2nd Session: 495; see Kelly, "School Segregation," 549.

20 On the Liberal Republican movement see Richard Allan Gerber, "Carl Schurz's Journey from Radical to Liberal Republican: A Problem in Ideological Consistency," *Mid-America*, vol. 82, (2000): 71–99; "The Liberal Republicans of 1872 in Historiographical Perspective," *Journal of American History*, 1975: 40–73; "Liberal Republicanism, Reconstruction, and Social Order: Samuel Bowles as a Test Case," *New England Quarterly*, 1972: 393–407.

Charles Sumner joined the Liberals.[21] On civil rights, however, he remained a Radical. Amnesty must be coupled with equality. Once more an amnesty bill reached the Senate floor. Sumner attached his amendment. Now Republicans backtracked. The Liberals' appeal cut into their southern support. Radical policies must recede for the moment. The Senate took up Sumner's proposal while he was absent from the chamber. He returned too late. The amnesty bill passed. But the civil rights attachment was gutted. The House, for its part, refused to take it up.

A new year offered new hope. In the elections of 1872 Grant had emerged victorious in a presidential landslide. The Republican Party platform of 1872 had called for the enactment of civil rights legislation. Ulysses Grant endorsed that call in his second inaugural address. Senators assured Charles Sumner. He would see his final monument rise.

Yet a cloud lurked on the horizon: the United States Supreme Court. On April 14, 1873, the Court delivered its decision in the Slaughter-House Cases: *The Butchers' Benevolent Association of New Orleans v. The Crescent City Live-Stock Landing and Slaughter-House Company*.[22] New Orleans' butchers protested an 1869 state law that prohibited their time-honored custom of setting up ramshackle riverside abattoirs, there to slaughter cattle and to dispense the offal, the fluids and putrescent particles into the stream, just above the intakes that supplied the city's water system. A new, consolidated slaughterhouse – a monopoly – was established, downstream. All tradesmen were required to apply there. Inspectors would monitor proceedings.

To those who framed the law it seemed a sensible regulation of public health. To the butchers and their lawyer, John Archibald Campbell, it was government tyranny. Campbell, a former Supreme Court Justice before adopting the Confederate side in 1861, loaded his legal brief with a lusty diatribe against the authors of this regulation, Louisiana's biracial legislature composed of carpetbaggers, "the foulest off-spring of the war," and blacks, soiled by "avarice, usurpation, servility, licentiousness." He turned the case into a test of the Fourteenth Amendment. Louisiana had violated his clients' privileges, their use of their private property, free enterprise.

Justice Samuel Freeman Miller wrote the Court's ruling. He upheld the slaughter-house law but in the process weakened the Fourteenth Amendment.

21 As chairman of the Senate Committee on foreign relations Sumner had split with the president over Grant's efforts to acquire Santo Domingo, a country offered for sale by its president, Buenaventura Báez.

22 *Butchers' Benevolent Association of New Orleans v. Crescent City Live-Stock Landing and Slaughter-House Company*, 83 U.S. 36 (1873).

The Amendment, according to Miller, had distinguished between the rights of U.S. citizens and those of state citizens. The rights of U.S. citizenship he defined narrowly, those of state citizenship broadly. States could regulate for public health and safety, to protect citizens from harm. States could regulate the operation of slaughter-houses. By implication they could regulate the rights of people. The ruling left civil rights in the very insecure realm of state government.[23]

Few Supreme Court pronouncements in Reconstruction have generated as much controversy and vituperation as did Justice Miller's ruling. "The only thing slaughtered in the Slaughterhouse cases," one critic suggested, "was the right of the Negro to equality."[24] Samuel Miller wrote with liberal intentions. His ruling nonetheless handed conservative opponents of any forthcoming Civil Rights Act a potent weapon.

The hand of death meanwhile, as Senator Pratt recalled, hovered over Charles Sumner. For a final twelve weeks of life he labored to bring to life his cherished supplemental civil rights bill. The Republican Party enacted it finally on March 1, 1875. Eight years were granted to Sumner's legislative child before the Supreme Court struck it down. Eighty years passed before the nation witnessed its return.

---

23 "[The Fourteenth Amendment] speaks only of privileges and immunities of citizens of the United States, and does not speak of those of citizens of the several States," Miller wrote. "The language is: 'No State shall make or enforce any law which shall abridge the privileges or immunities of citizens of *the United States*.' It is a little remarkable, if this clause was intended as a protection to the citizen of a State against the legislative power of his own State, that the term 'citizen of the State' should be left out when it is so carefully used in contradistinction to 'citizens of the United States,' in the very sentence which precedes it.... If, then, there is a difference between the privileges and immunities belonging to a citizen of the United States as such, and those belonging to the citizen of the State as such, the latter must rest for their security and protection where they have heretofore rested, for they are not embraced by this paragraph of the amendment." Slaughterhouse Cases 83 U.S. 36 (1873). For a review of the long, varied controversies, and the many varied opinions of the Slaughter-House Cases, see Michael A. Ross, "Justice Miller's Reconstruction: The Slaughter-House Cases, Health Codes, and Civil Rights in New Orleans, 1861–1873," *Journal of Southern History*, 64 (1998): 649–676. For a summary account see Peter Irons, *A People's History of the Supreme Court* (New York: 2006), 198–201.

24 Ross, "Justice Miller's Reconstruction," 650.

CHAPTER 2

A Muster of Moths: The Forty-Third Congress of the United States

Expectations for the 43rd meeting of Congress, high achievements that is to say, were hardly high. Observers accorded it one virtue: it was not the 42nd. That august body, expired on March 4, 1873, had excelled in exploits of graft, corruption and fraud. "If you are a member of Congress (no offense)," Mark Twain quipped.[1] Its successor seemed to offer similar prospects. The leadership remained the same; many of the same members returned. "Congress contains few men of a higher grade than fourth-rate," the Decatur, Illinois, *Magnet* observed. "The House, viewed from the gallery, forcibly reminds you of the deck of a convict ship."[2] The Galveston *News* preferred sarcasm: "The typical public servant of the present day is not addicted to the smaller vices, wrestling with bottles and decanters.... He scorns to be vicious below the lofty pursuits of public corruption. Let the public be congratulated."[3] Younger men, the New York *Mail* suggested, should be elected to Congress so they might learn the art of statesmanship. "A good idea," snapped the Altoona *Tribune*. "They would have twice the opportunity even that Oliver Twist had at old Fagin's."[4]

Southerners surveyed the large Republican majority, including a half-dozen Negro members, with deep distaste. "The dregs of humanity," one correspondent wrote to Kentucky's Senator John Stevenson.[5] Where, the Cincinnati *Commercial* wondered, were the great men of yore? "Massachusetts sends a pursy manufacturer [William Washburn] who was once a grocer," to fill the seat of Webster; New York replaces Seward with Roscoe Conkling and that inefficient, plausible nobody, Reuben E. Fenton."[6] The New York *Times* simply was appalled:

1 Mark Twain and Charles Dudley Warner, *The Gilded Age, A Tale of To-Day* (Hartford: 1899), vol. 1, 268.
2 Quoted in Chicago *Tribune*, January 3, 1874.
3 Galveston *News*, January 3, 1874.
4 Altoona, Pennsylvania, *Morning Tribune*, July 10, 1874.
5 Richard Vaux to Stevenson, December 17, 1872. John White Stevenson Papers, Library of Congress.
6 Cincinnati *Commercial*, February 6, 1875.

> People understand that a seat in a public hall was made to sit, not to lounge upon, and that their neighbors' desks were not intended as receptacles even for well-shod feet; that the frequent use of spittoons, and the flourishing of cigars are quite as much out of place in a debating assembly as at an evening reception in a lady's drawing room.... This nation is nearly one hundred years old, and its representatives, as a mass, are less decorous than when it was a yearling.[7]

Such platitudinous carping, of course, is commonplace. But it seemed especially apt in the changing times of Reconstruction. Too much democracy, a gift of the new constitutional amendments, had filled congressional seats with contemptible plebeians. Their ethics were unclean. But they kept their hands clean at taxpayers' expense. To wit, one reporter noted, the annual inventory of the Senate's Sergeant-at-Arms:

> Ready for senatorial use 122 dozen of toilet soap; one box Kitching's crystal soap; two boxes of castile soap; sixty-five soap and fifty-two nail brush dishes; three dozen nail brushes; four quarts each of bay rum and cologne, and thirty-two dozen towels.[8]

One item stood out: a golden toothpick provided for an unnamed senator. "Who got the gold tooth-pick?" demanded the Harrisburg *Patriot*. Who "picks his molars and incisors with a golden instrument paid for out of the taxes of the people?"[9]

Before they took their seats the 292 members of the House were requested to identify their occupations for the Directory. Fully 188 claimed the title of lawyer. Twelve identified themselves as bankers, 13 as journalists. There were 22 farmers (6 others preferred the designation planter). John Roy Lynch, black member from Mississippi, named the occupation of photographer. There were two lumbermen, two teachers and two doctors. Illinois' John B. Rice, ex-mayor of Chicago, once a music-hall performer, called himself actor. Marcus Ward, retired governor of New Jersey, inscribed "citizen."

Many carried titles of military distinction. "There are enough generals, colonels, majors, and captains in Congress to form a respectable army," joked

---

7 New York *Times*, June 27, 1874.

8 Chattanooga *Times*, January 4, 1874.

9 Harrisburg *Patriot*, January 30, 1874. Senator Patterson, South Carolina railroad magnate, scorned the accusation; he already owned a gilded toothpick. Senator Morrill of Maine denied it; no such item existed.

Georgia's Benjamin Hill, "but not enough statesmen to make a good committee." Generals John A. Logan and Stephen Hurlbut of Illinois, Carl Schurz of Missouri, Benjamin Butler of Massachusetts, and James Garfield of Ohio, Pennsylvanian James Negley among others, had fought for the Union. Generals John B. Gordon, Pierce Young and Philip Cook of Georgia, Robert Vance of North Carolina, and Eppa Hunton of Virginia had served the Confederacy.

Perhaps Congress' most colorful member was Democrat Samuel Sullivan Cox representing New York's 6th District, Manhattan's lower east side. Known as "Sunset," or, occasionally, "Dewdrop" Cox, he served first in his birth state of Ohio until unseated in 1864. Relocating to the big city, there he flourished, witty, urbane, a raconteur, admirer of Mark Twain.[10] Reporters delighted in describing his appearance on the House floor:

> A little, swinging, prancing man; when he makes a speech he often turns down his collar slightly, turns up his sleeves, swings a pocket-handkerchief in his hand, leaves his seat and comes down to the front aisle.... He throws back the skirt of his coat on the left side, thrusts his left hand into his jacket pocket in the pet American style, nods that remarkable head in emphatic bobs, looks as if a funny thought just now originated in his brain.[11]

Cox became, by universal acclaim, the House's resident humorist. His book, *Why We Laugh,* sold out through two editions.[12] Not everyone laughed. James Garfield found him tiresome: "He is fast losing his standing among men of education by his intellectual frivolity."[13] But his dissertations on humor filled lecture halls across the country. His speeches filled the House with deftly cultured, gentle wit.

Frivolity aside, Cox upheld political principles and loyalty to the Democratic Party, as he explained to newsman Manton Marble of the New York *World.* He decried economic injustice: "We have been waxing too rich and fat without fair distribution.... Parvenu pride turns up its aristocratic nose at plebeian vocations. We have theorists without sagacity, philanthropists without morality ... vaunting patriots whose patriotism, as of old, is scoundrelism."[14] He advocated increased wages, improved working conditions, shorter working hours for the

---

10 See David Lindsey, *Sunset Cox: Irrepressible Democrat* (Detroit: 1959).

11 Boston *Commonwealth,* June 27, 1874; Xenia, Ohio, *Torchlight,* March 31, 1875.

12 Samuel S. Cox, *Why We Laugh* (New York, 1969): 14.

13 James Garfield, *The Diary of James A. Garfield,* ed. Harry J. Brown and Frederick D. Williams (East Lansing: 1967), vol. 3, 230.

14 Samuel S. Cox, *Why We Laugh,* 39, 44.

immigrants filling his district. "But for injustices to the Negro," as his biographer has written, "Cox had a blind spot."[15]

That spot illuminates the struggle of the Civil Rights Act. The law faced the hardships of political calculation and the barriers of unthinking prejudice. It also faced the opposition of thoughtful men, men such as Samuel Cox. He regarded prejudice as instinctive, "as American as Plymouth Rock." Let civil rights advocates pause before they rushed ahead with schemes of social justice for which society was unprepared. Sunset Cox it was, before there was yet a civil rights bill to debate, who gave the country its first taste of a civil rights debate. June 6, 1862, he rose to speak about Emancipation.

> Prejudice, stronger than all principles ... has imperatively separated the whites from the blacks. In the school-house, the church or the hospital, the black man must not seat himself beside the white; even in death and at the cemetery the line of distinction is drawn. To abolish slavery the North must go still further and forget that fatal prejudice of race which governs it, and which makes emancipation so illusory. To give men their liberty, to open to them the gates of the city, and then say, "There, you shall live among yourselves, you shall marry among yourselves, you shall form a separate society in society," is to create a cursed caste and replace slaves by pariahs.... It has been said that we ought to free the African, even though we build a bridge of gold over the chasm from slavery to freedom! It will prove a Bridge of Sighs to both black and white.[16]

Cox's words proved prophetic. By 1874 multiple efforts to pass Charles Sumner's civil rights measures had failed. Violence raged, despite the several Enforcement Acts. The freed people remained, as Dr. Martin Luther King, Jr. would say a century later, exiled in their own land. Slaves had gone; pariahs remained. Now Sumner proposed legislating civil equality, to force the mingling of pariahs with those who despised them.

Sunset Cox himself had shed the more distasteful marks of prejudice, perhaps a refutation of his own argument. He joked on the House floor with the black congressman Joseph Rainey. He "extended the hand" to Rainey's colleague Robert Elliott after a memorable oration for the Civil Rights Bill. He dined with Frederick Douglass after the bill had passed. The New York *Times*

---

15 Lindsey, *Irrepressible Democrat*: 264.

16 Samuel S. Cox, *Emancipation and its Results – Is Ohio to be Africanized? Speech of Hon. S.S. Cox of Ohio, Delivered in the House of Representatives, June 6, 1862* (Washington: 1862), 10–11.

invited him to join the Republican Party "and live happily ever afterwards."[17] Cox would not switch parties. But on February 5, 1874, he offered the "Moth Speech." He immortalized the 43rd Congress, both parties impartially.

William Wheeler, Republican of New York, future Vice-President under Rutherford B. Hayes, held the floor for an amendment to the Army Appropriations Bill, H.R.1009. It aimed to cover the expense of moth-proofing the nation's stockpile of superfluous military uniforms.[18] Wheeler, in a jocular aside, suggested that if anyone were interested in the eradication of vermiform animals gnawing at the fabric of the public weal, the objectionable creatures perhaps were to be found rather in Congress than in nature. Had anyone "studied the history of the Party moth? It has fed on his party" – he turned to Cox – "and no chemical process has yet been invented, I believe, to stay its ravages. [Laughter]"[19]

Cox was ready (indeed, the dialogue must have been prearranged). He would, with the gentleman's permission, "read in the life and character of the moth some of those attributes which are making the people regard the Administration so carefully." Moths and politicians, Cox mused – not so very different:

> All moths you will find have a political, and destructive, significance. If you note how they are hatched; how they hide in cocoons; how they creep into dark places through crannies; how they go into closets where goods are stored; how they lie all summer quietly [Laughter].

Members left their seats to gather around the speaker. As if on cue the straightman appeared. Moses Field of Michigan (evidently not in on the joke): "I rise to a question of order. Let the House be brought to order." Laughter on all sides. "May I quote" – Cox raised from his desk a heavy tome – "from Harris' *Treatise on Insects* to illustrate the physical and political relations of the moth?"

> "The clothes moth in its natural state" – like the politician – "never leaves its cocoon until it emerges therefrom as a winged moth. Wherever it is seen as a naked worm it is because it has been disturbed and knocked out of its cocoon" – for example, by an election or otherwise – "and in

17 New York *Times*, March 18, 1874.

18 The moth appropriation eventually developed into a minor congressional scandal. The firm of Cowles & Brega, purveyors of the patented chemical moth-proofing process, "persuaded" assorted congressmen to endorse its product and to vote an expenditure in the military budget for its application. The process proved harmless to moths, but costly to taxpayers.

19 Sunset Cox, "Moth Speech," *Cong. Record*, 43rd Congress, 1st Session: 1241–1243.

> these instances the moth" – and just so the politician – "does not feed, and in a few days dies." How sad the thought, but how true the analogy! [Laughter]

Field: "Mr. Chairman, I insist on my point of order." Loud laughter on all sides.

James Platt rose. Republican of Virginia, his district, the Virginia 2nd, centered on the city of Norfolk with its great Navy Yard, vast source of patronage, and votes, for a sitting representative: "I would like to get the fullest information about the habits of the creatures the gentleman from New York is discussing and I wish him to mention, when these moths die, whether other moths take their places."

"That depends," Cox returned, "upon whether they have a navy-yard in their district. [Great laughter] 'The little whitish caterpillars or moth worms' (he continued to read) 'immediately begin to gnaw the substances within their reach and cover themselves with the fragments, shaping them into little hollow rolls and lining them with silk.'"

> "Some pass the summer within their rolls" – That is, I suppose, they go down to Long Branch, ride in free Pullman cars – "Concealed within their movable cases or in their lint cupboard burrows, they carry on the work of destruction through the summer" – That is when Congress is not in session – "and in the autumn" – That is just before elections [Laugher] – "they leave off eating, make fast their habitations, and remain at rest and seemingly torpid through the winter." – That is until committees of investigation get to work. [Laughter]

Field: "I insist upon my point of order. [Roars of laughter]."

Cox: "I will submit just one question ... whether the moths which we are called upon to appropriate against – and whose incursions upon our Army clothes are so wasteful – are the moths of the more numerous [political] branch of the *Lepidoptera,* or do they belong to the *Phalaena* family of Linnaeus? [Laughter]"

Wheeler: "To that question I answer in the affirmative. [Laughter]"[20]

All moths assembled, Republicans held 194 seats in the House. There were 94 Democrats and 4 Liberal Republicans. James G. Blaine of Maine took the

---

20 A sense of humor, even amid partisan and civil rights contention, remained with the 43rd Congress. Speaker James Blaine, not known for such sallies, also brought down a chorus of laughter as he solemnly announced two days' leave of absence for Michigan's Omar Conger; Congressman Conger, everyone knew, had been married that same afternoon. Harrisburg *Patriot*, May 15, 1874.

Chair for the third time. A troika of powerful committee chairmen stood as his closest advisers: James Garfield of Ohio; Henry Dawes of Massachusetts; Horace Maynard of Tennessee, dean of the southern Republicans.

Garfield was serving his sixth consecutive term from Ohio's 19th District. For the second time he sat as chairman of the Appropriations Committee. Congress held the purse-strings of the nation; Garfield held the purse-strings of Congress. His relations with the Speaker were close, politically and personally. The future President was 42. Kansas Senator John James Ingalls, his friend from college days, remembered him, "a cordial, effusive, affectionate manner … a splendid rusticity in his simple nature."[21] Garfield's "rusticity" belied an intellectual mind and classical education. He believed intellectually and naturally in the idea of civil rights.

Dawes, chairman of the Ways and Means Committee, had represented western Massachusetts, the 11th District, for fourteen years. Now 57, he had shaved his greying beard and returned to Congress with only a "close mustache." Still his face wore its expression of perpetual distress. "Careworn, sensitive, anxious, thoughtful and earnest," wrote the Boston *Commonwealth*, "the Jeremiah of the House," ready to "tear his hair to any extent over the iniquities of the people."[22] "The Springfield Ishmael with dyspepsia," one unsympathetic constituent retorted.[23] The contrast with Garfield, "gentle-voiced, scholarly, as jolly as old King Cole," struck reporters who observed them on the floor.[24]

Tennessee's Horace Maynard, currently his state's congressman at-large, had represented the Knoxville district for seven terms. Born in Massachusetts, he had come south prior to secession. Tall, gaunt, clean-shaven, long black hair falling to his shoulders, he brought to mind somehow the image of an Indian chief. Opponents, choosing a northern tribe, dubbed him "The Narragansett." The Narragansett chaired the Banking and Currency Committee. He also sat on the Rules Committee.[25]

---

21 John J. Ingalls, *A Collection of the Writings of John James Ingalls. Essays, Addresses, and Orations*, ed. William E. Connelly (Kansas City: 1902), 398.

22 Boston *Commonwealth*, June 27, 1874.

23 Charles H. Doe to George F. Hoar, January 4, 1874. George Frisbie Hoar Papers, Massachusetts Historical Society, Boston.

24 New York *World*, December 13, 1874.

25 Other committeemen included Indiana's Godlove Orth, chairman of Foreign Affairs, the amiable William Wheeler, head of the Commerce Committee, John Coburn of Indianapolis, chairman of Military Affairs, Ohio's James Monroe, chairman of the Committee on Education and Labor, Indiana's John Peter Shanks, chairman of the Committee on Indian Affairs. The Civil Service Reform Committee, an unenviable post, fell to Stephen Kellogg of Connecticut. The Judiciary Committee, responsible for all civil rights legislation, came under Massachusetts' Benjamin Franklin Butler.

Behind the chairmen sat the House's back-benchers. Among them were men of gaudy wealth, Maryland's Thomas Swann, Edwin Stanard of Missouri, New York's debonair though larcenous ex-mayor Fernando Wood.[26] There were men of modest means, David Mellish of New York, formerly a police-court stenographer, Indiana's Simeon Wolf, a cobbler born in a log cabin. Chicago's Charles Farwell reigned as the House's resident expert on poker. Few, it was said, could outdrink Vermont's Luke Poland. None, for sheer elegance, not to say arrogance, surpassed Republican William Walter Phelps of New Jersey – only 33, already a millionaire several times over, graduate of Yale class of '60 *summa cum laude*, his hair combed in "Prince of Wales bangs" parted dandily in the middle. To some he seemed a peerless presence, to others a preening popinjay. He was in either way, the press agreed, "a rising man of mark in Congress."[27] The rising man suffered a calamitous collapse, the most spectacular, though not the only, victim of the Civil Rights Bill.

Civil rights advocates placed great hope in the Forty-Third Congress with its overwhelming Republican majority. Louisiana's J. Hale Sypher and Henry Barry of Mississippi had commanded Negro regiments in the war. Kansan William Phillips had led the federal army's brigade of native-American troops. Once, as special correspondent of the New York *Tribune,* Phillips had thrilled the country with dispatches from his bleeding state. Such men had stood up for equality in the past. Would they do so again?

Massachusetts sent a full delegation of Republicans. Among them were the brothers Hoar, George Frisbie and Ebenezer Rockwood. Enlightenment accompanied them. Rockwood, distinguished judge, trustee of Harvard University, once United States Attorney-General, had been nominated (and barely defeated) for the Supreme Court. Frisbie shone as the advocate of education, champion of the common-school system.

Southerners disliked Frisbie, an unabashed Negrophile. "He is not content" one Democratic organ complained, "that the negro should enjoy equal rights with the white citizen, but insists that he shall belong to a preferred class.... [It is] the policy of hate, of persecution, and of a centralized government."[28] Rockwood, the closest friend of the very author of iniquity, held the dying Charles Sumner's hand and received his last request: "You must take care of the civil rights bill." Neither Hoar took care of the bill. Frisbie rose not once to speak on its behalf. Rockwood opposed it outright until the final moments of the final debate.

26 Satirist David Ross Locke saluted the suavely suspicious Democrat on his return to Congress: "Steel viggerusly, O Fernandywood, fer it's yer last chance." David Ross Locke, *The Struggles (Social, Financial, and Political) of Petroleum V. Nasby* (Boston, 1873): 121.

27 Boston *Commonwealth,* June 27, 1874.

28 Dayton *Democrat,* January 29, 1875.

Republicans dominated the powerful state delegations of New York, 23 of 33 seats; Pennsylvania, 23 of 28; Illinois, 14 of 19; Indiana, 10 of 13. They occupied 12 of 20 seats in Ohio, all 9 in Iowa and 6 of 7 in New Jersey. They populated every southern delegation except Kentucky and Texas. South Carolina, with its massive black population, filled all five districts with Republicans; four were black men. All five Louisiana congressmen were Republicans, both of Florida's, and five of Alabama's eight. They held seven of ten seats in Tennessee, five of nine in Virginia.

Southern Republican seats not held by freedmen belonged either to "carpetbaggers" or "scalawags." The civil rights measure enjoyed the support of carpetbaggers but suffered from the desertion of scalawags. Only two of Tennessee's six congressional scalawags, Horace Maynard and David Nunn of the 8th District, voted for the Civil Rights Bill. The lone "carpetbagger," Barbour Lewis of Memphis, supported it. Native Virginians James Sener, John Ambler Smith and Christopher Thomas opposed the bill. Immigrants James Platt and William Henry Harrison Stowell voted for it. Some native white southerners did support the Civil Rights Bill. Alabamians Charles Hays, Charles Pelham and Alexander White voted for it. In Georgia Richard Henry Whiteley endorsed it. In South Carolina it had the vote of Alexander Wallace. But the desertion of a dozen native southern white Republicans raised a serious obstacle.

Democrats opposed the bill without exception. Northerners spoke discreetly. New Jersey's Robert Hamilton recalled that he enjoyed occasionally to sit beside his coachman (a Negro) on the carriage seat. Should said person, however, presume to sit beside him in a first-class railway car or purchase a nearby seat in a theater, he would find it intolerable. Such action would be "to invade the circles of the refined and fastidious ... break down all the conventionalities of social life." Charles Eldredge of Wisconsin warned black people. By accepting the helping hand of government they forfeited their self-respect. Reaching for a crutch, they acknowledged they were cripples.

Southern Democrats were less subtle. They filled the hall with fervent cries. Virginia's John T. Harris dared anyone to state that black men were the equal of whites. Thomas Whitehead, another Virginian, concluded his speech by wishing civil rights fanatics all a swift passage to Hell. Southerners had lost their independence. They had lost their property (slaves). Now they would lose their dignity. "Except to hang our leaders and butcher our women and children, what could the enemy have done that they have left undone? Into what depth of humiliation have we not been plunged?"[29] North Carolina's Congressman William Robbins begged for mercy, and understanding.

29 Greeneville *American*, August 25, 1875.

> I earnestly appeal to the majority here to spare us, under all our misfortunes, the untold evils of this ill-devised measure.... We have been sorely tried, sorely humiliated.... Sport with our miseries no longer. Else you will break the spirit of a generous race ... you will doom one-half of this glorious land to perpetual blight, despair, and desolation.[30]

Southerners pleaded. They yielded strategic command to northerners. Democrats formed ranks behind their floor leader, future Speaker of the House Samuel Jackson Randall of Pennsylvania, and Wisconsin's Charles Augustus Eldredge, their senior member on the Judiciary Committee. Randall, the peerless parliamentarian, staved off the Senate's civil rights bill in the first session. In the second session he orchestrated the great filibuster that nearly stopped the House bill forever. Had civil rights failed, credit would surely have gone to Sam Randall. Southerners did not forget. Twenty years later their eulogies expressed deathless appreciation. "Every son and daughter of the South," said Kentucky's Joseph Blackburn, "owes a tribute to his memory, a flower to his grave." "The South owes him a lasting debt of gratitude," declared Virginian Charles O'Ferrall. "She loved Randall with a love that knew no bounds."[31]

Two southerners joined Randall and Eldredge in the command post. Kentuckian James Beck, at 52, began his fourth term in Congress. Craggy, dark bearded, he was a southerner by way of Scotland. He arrived a poor immigrant, labored as a farm hand, before becoming overseer of a plantation. "He was from the people," said Missouri's George Vest, "the uncompromising foe of class privilege." A class warrior, Frisbie Hoar agreed, "he used to pour out his denunciation of the greed of the capitalists." "An intense believer in the equality of manhood," Congressman William Breckinridge remembered.[32] Belief in the equality of manhood differed from belief in the equality of mankind. In black people Beck saw only inequality. In civil rights he saw the ultimate form of class privilege, legislative privilege on behalf of one class against another.[33]

---

30 Speech of William Robbins, 177–178.

31 *Memorial Addresses on the Life and Character of Samuel J. Randall, a Representative from Pennsylvania, Delivered in the House of Representatives and in the Senate, 51st Congress, 1st Session* (Washington: 1891), 27–28, 140.

32 *Memorial Addresses on the Life and Character of James B. Beck, (A Senator from Kentucky), Delivered in the Senate and House of Representatives, August 23 and September 13, 1890* (Washington: 1891), 36, 108; George F. Hoar, *Autobiography*, vol. 2, 73. Non-eulogistic opinions were harsher. "A slave-driver and a coward," was the verdict of Tennessee's Senator William Brownlow. E. Merton Coulter, *William G. Brownlow: Fighting Parson of the Southern Highlands* (Knoxville: 1937), 391.

33 Beck's argument did not go out of style. Georgia Senator Herman Talmadge reprised it in 1964: "Where are the civil rights in legislation which would make special classes favorites

From the House he moved on to denounce capitalists in the Senate until a heart attack felled him as he stepped from his train at Washington's 6th Street Station in 1890.

Lucius Q.C. Lamar, formerly professor of mathematics, metaphysics and law at the University of Mississippi, worried more about race than class. He pursued an agenda of white supremacy, quietly. Publicly he played the role of peacemaker, determined to bridge the "bloody chasm" and heal the wounds of civil discord. Lamar forged his reputation on April 27, 1874. He, alone among southern white Democrats, spoke a eulogy for Charles Sumner. Sumner's Civil Rights Bill did not appear in Lamar's celebrated overture. Sumner's concern for the rights of black people did. That solicitude, said Lamar, was misplaced. Sumner had failed to consider the right to servitude:

> It mattered not to him how humble in the scale of rational existence the subject of restraint [slavery] might be, how dark his skin, how dense his ignorance. It mattered not to him that the slave might be contented with his lot ... that the mixed social system of which he formed an element had been regarded by the fathers of the republic and by the ablest statesmen who had risen up after them as too complicated to be broken up without danger to society itself, or even to civilization.[34]

The estimable "mixed social system" (master and slave) no longer existed. Lamar forgave. Let Sumner's foibles be. His spirit bade Americans clasp hands: "My countrymen! Know one another, and you will love one another."[35] Lamar's saccharin soothed some. Others felt nausea. A snake, said Kansas' Senator Ingalls, "his venom was not secreted, but distilled."[36] Speaker Blaine was not a fan. "Mr. Lamar is the only man in public life who can be praised in New England

---

of the law? How can it be called civil rights to grant special privileges to certain citizens and take away the constitutional rights [the right to discriminate] of others?" *Cong. Record* 88th Congress, 2nd Session, 15,890–15,891.

34 *Memorial Addresses on the Life and Character of Charles Sumner, (A Senator of Massachusetts), Delivered in the Senate and House of Representatives, Forty-Third Congress, First Session, April 27, 1874* (Washington: 1874), 61–62.

35 Even Henry Adams fell under the charm. He recalled Lamar, "one of the calmest, most reasonable and most amiable Union men in the United States." Henry Adams, *The Education of Henry Adams* (New York: 1931), 185. Posterity preserved that image. John F. Kennedy awarded Lamar a "Profile in Courage." It was an artful impersonation. "From the date of his carefully planned Sumner eulogy," notes his biographer, "he kept up appearances as the harbinger of peace and slipped from the pose only in a few instances." James B. Murphy, *L.Q.C. Lamar: Pragmatic Patriot* (Baton Rouge: 1973), 272.

36 Ingalls, *Writings*: 360.

for a warm eulogy of Charles Sumner, and immediately afterward be elected to the Senate as the representative of the 'white line' Democrats of Mississippi."[37] Lucius Lamar rose finally to the Supreme Court. He moved in the shadows to extinguish the last hope of his eulogy's subject.

One genuine symbol of reconciliation did appear. Alexander Hamilton Stephens of Georgia, once United States congressman then Vice-President of the Confederacy, returned to Congress. "Aleck" Stephens, at 61, was an extraordinary sight: a shrunken man dressed in black, drifting white hair, weighing less than 80 lbs. Lifted daily from his wheeled chair, he drew all eyes to him. He hobbled on Congress' first day, balanced on his crutches through a silent House. Two southerners, Pierce Young of Georgia and Alfred Waddell of North Carolina, held him upright as he took the oath of office.[38]

Unlike his once-president Jefferson Davis, Stephens reintegrated into his former nation. He owed his front-row aisle seat, no. 12 east, to the indulgence of former enemies. By special agreement the House let him pick his place. "I expected kind treatment here," he remarked, "but nothing like what I have received."[39] Concerning the Civil Rights Bill Alexander Stephens had no intention of remaining mute. Projecting his shrill thin voice across the chamber he delivered the Democrats' principal oration against the bill.

In striking contrast to the old Confederate chieftain, seven African Americans sat in the 43rd Congress. Congress indeed was the first national institution to break the color barrier. South Carolina, with its decisive majority of black voters, supplied four representatives: Joseph H. Rainey, Alonzo Ransier, Richard Harvey Cain, and Robert Brown Elliott. Mississippi sent John Roy Lynch. Alabama's 2nd District elected James Rapier. Florida returned its black congressman Josiah Walls. A band of seven,[40] they might have been swallowed up in the throng of white men. They stood out nonetheless. Reporter George S. Merriam was inspired.

---

37 James G. Blaine, *Political Discussions, Legislative, Diplomatic, and Popular, 1856–1886* (Norwich: 1887), 287. Lamar was aghast, Henry Dawes recalled, finding that the House had scheduled him to speak his eulogy immediately after black representative Joseph Rainey. "I can't follow a nigger," he pleaded. Republicans kindly adjusted the order of speeches, allowing Lamar to go second, sandwiched between Ebenezer Hoar and another white speaker, Godlove Orth, who then yielded the floor to Rainey. Dawes himself followed next. Loren Schweninger, *James T. Rapier and Reconstruction* (Chicago: 1978), 129.

38 Alfred M. Waddell, *Some Memories of My Life* (Raleigh: 1908), 128.

39 Wilmington, Delaware, *Every Evening*, December 10, 1873.

40 There might have been nine. Samuel Peters, elected in the Louisiana 4th District, died before he could take office. Pinckney Pinchback, also in Louisiana, saw his election to an at-large seat contested.

> It is ten years since the war closed, and in our national House of Representatives we have the Vice-President of the Southern Confederacy, and three or four men who were formerly slaves – all treated with respect and courtesy, all bearing themselves as good citizens. Surely, with all our blunders and shortcomings, there are in this people great qualities of justice and magnanimity.[41]

Henry Watterson's Louisville *Courier-Journal* found it less inspiring. "It is curious to see them sit there, no one sympathizing, no one heeding.... No one does really either feel for them or notice them. Except in a disdainful way or for some unworthy purpose they are not consulted."[42]

Joseph Rainey, dean of the African-American delegation, was 42. Born a free person in Georgetown, South Carolina, he had followed the trade of barber until conscripted into forced labor for the Confederate army. He escaped, then returned to become the first black man to serve in the House. Elected to the 41st Congress, Rainey was also the first called, in the 43rd Congress, to sit in the Speaker's chair. Rainey expressed pride, and chagrin:

> We have been content to remain in the background and wait to see if justice would be done us, but we are tired of this dilly dallying.... Do you think it right that when I go forth from this capital, an honorable member of Congress, that I should be subjected to insults of the lowest fellow upon the street if he should happen to feel so inclined?... We know as well as anybody that you can't legislate a prejudice away, but we do want that when we are orderly and decently dressed, we shall be allowed to purchase for our needs the same as anyone else. We ask no more. Why, look at us, holding positions of members of Congress and voting upon important legislation having a direct effect upon the interest of the country, and yet when we go out it is with fear and trembling that we may be openly insulted when we are seeking only the common necessities of life.[43]

---

41 *The Christian Union*, February 17, 1875, 131.

42 Louisville *Courier-Journal*, February 12, 1874. Ninety years later five African Americans sat in the House of Representatives: Robert Nix of Pennsylvania, Augustus Hawkins of California, William Dawson of Illinois, Charles Diggs of Michigan, and New York's Adam Clayton Powell, Jr. Overtly, at least, the twentieth-century contingent was not disdained. "Why in the name of reason would I hate my friend Bob Nix, or my friend Bill Dawson? What difference, beneath the skin, is there between us?" Texas Congressman, future Speaker Jim Wright inquired. "I tell you I would be insane if I felt for them anything but kindliness and friendship. And that is what is wrong. The sane men have been silent, and the insane men have spoken." *Cong. Record*, 88th Cong. 1st Session: 19,802.

43 Pittsburgh *Leader*, quoted in Washington *New National Era*, June 18, 1874.

Rainey's South Carolina colleagues came to Congress with diverse backgrounds. Alonzo Ransier had been a clerk before the war. He served in the South Carolina House, as State Party chairman, and as lieutenant-governor. His first congressional term was his last. "Redemption" came to South Carolina in 1877. Ransier found work as a night watchman. He died forgotten in 1882.[44]

Richard Cain was born in Virginia, raised in Ohio, and settled first in Brooklyn as a minister of the African Methodist Episcopal Church. After service in the 43rd and 45th Congresses he returned to the ministry, becoming a bishop before his death in 1887. Cain spoke out most passionately for civil rights. His speeches scorched the House with the fire of the pulpit. Nonetheless it was Cain who fashioned the critical compromise, to abandon mixed schools. That compromise let the Civil Rights Bill pass.

Robert Elliott left the most dazzling impression. He was young, brash, combative, a polished orator. His Charleston district once had sent Preston Brooks to Congress. Now Republicans chose him, a black man. They also chose him to answer the Democrats' champion, Alexander Stephens. On January 6, 1874, Elliott delivered the party's principal civil rights speech. When he finished the House echoed with applause. "Supremely insolent, arrogant, and arbitrary," huffed the Charleston *News and Courier*.[45] In August Elliott resigned his seat to become Speaker of the South Carolina House of Representatives. From there he aimed to win a place in the United States Senate. He did not. "Redemption" ended his hopes. Robert Elliott died in obscurity in 1884, 42 years old. He died a failure, his biographer concluded oxymoronically, a "glorious failure."[46]

Josiah Walls had held Florida's sole congressional seat in the 42nd Congress. He returned as one of its two representatives in the 43rd. He had been born in Virginia, most probably enslaved, but escaped to freedom.[47] He enlisted in Pennsylvania as a sergeant of the Third Regiment, United States Colored Troops. His service took him to Florida. "A decent, youngish mulatto, of some

---

44 See Thomas C. Holt, *Black Over White: Negro Political Leadership in South Carolina during Reconstruction* (Urbana: 1977), 51, 105, 218–219.

45 Charleston *News and Courier*, November 25, 1874.

46 Peggy Lamson, *The Glorious Failure: Black Congressman Robert Brown Elliott and Reconstruction in South Carolina* (New York: 1973). Elliott's antecedents are murky. According to the official account he was born in 1842. He described a privileged upbringing in England, studies at the High Holborn Academy and Eton, the reading of law with Mr. Sergeant FitzHerbert. Lamson found no record of his presence at Eton, no record of a High Holborn Academy or the existence of a sergeant-of-law FitzHerbert. Elliott evidently padded his résumé. Yet somewhere, if not at Eton, he acquired a superior education. Sunset Cox himself praised his depth of literary knowledge.

47 See Peter Klingman, *Josiah Walls: Florida's Black Congressman of Reconstruction* (Gainesville: 1976).

education, not peculiarly offensive," was the offhand appraisal of the Savannah *News*. "As an overseer or porter he would probably be a success."[48] Walls did not dazzle. Yet his civil rights speech made solid points, some that his more colorful colleagues passed over in their rhetoric.

James Rapier, 36 years old, was born free in Florence, Alabama, and received his education in Canada. Rapier alone among his African-American colleagues had the benefit of foreign travel. For five months he toured Europe, experiencing respect in the most elegant resorts of white society. His speech for the Civil Rights Bill compared his unprejudiced treatment in foreign places with the discrimination he endured in his native country. His died in 1883, "disillusioned," his biographer concluded, "and embittered."[49]

Mississippi's John Roy Lynch, youngest of the African-American representatives, was the second youngest member of the 43rd Congress. Only 26 as he took his seat, he lived on into another era. When he died on November 2, 1939, *Gone With the Wind* was preparing to open in movie theaters. The Ku Klux Klan was enjoying a renaissance. Another civil rights movement approached on the horizon. Lynch left behind a memoir of his life. Those reminiscences all but ignore the civil rights struggle of 1874. Of all the black congressmen Lynch was the most reticent, the most reluctant to embrace the Civil Rights Bill. He declined to speak until the final debate. Even then he acknowledged that it was a distasteful task. Lynch was a pragmatist. He framed the matter in terms of political priorities. Protection must come first, protection from violence and protection of the vote. Without political safety exalted promises of civil rights would prove pointless.

Seven African Americans stood on the House floor. Another stood nearby: George T. Downing, a man of Congress but not in it. Downing belonged to the black bourgeoisie, "a satellite of upper-crust white society."[50] Oyster bars, restaurants and a fashionable hotel in Newport, Rhode Island, established his fortune. He clung desperately to his dignity. He threw himself into the campaign for integrated schools. He succeeded in 1866, when the Rhode Island legislature abolished its separate-school system. Now, at age 55, he threw himself into the fight for civil rights. From New England he moved to Washington, becoming proprietor of the Capitol restaurant. Caterer to Congress, he buttonholed hungry clients, senators and representatives. Downing was prickly. He quarreled with the Douglasses, Frederick Sr. and sons. They twitted his self-importance,

---

48 Savannah, *News*, January 8, 1875.

49 Schweninger, *James T Rapier* 182.

50 Lawrence Grossman, "George T. Downing and Desegregation of Rhode Island Public Schools," *Rhode Island History*, 36 (1997): 99–105.

"this pretended floor-manager of the House of Representatives."[51] Yet as Sumner's bill began its legislative journey Downing took the lead, lobbyist-in-chief, at the head of the National Civil Rights Council.

In the House, Downing's lobbying focused on the Judiciary Committee. That body of eleven white men, eight Republicans and three Democrats, had in charge the conduct of all civil rights legislation. Its chairman was Massachusetts' Benjamin Franklin Butler. No one in the 43rd Congress – or in congresses fore or since – achieved a record that greater endures: idolized and despised in equal measure. No one outdid him in attracting the nation's attention, no one in exciting its passions. His record as a Civil War general is mixed, yet he served ably as military governor at New Orleans. In Congress he advocated (scandalously to some) for women's rights, for a ten-hour workday, for workers' rights in the mill towns of New England. Chairman of the Judiciary Committee, he authored the House civil rights bill.[52] (see Illustration 2)

Southerners detested Benjamin Butler. During the war he refused to return their fugitive human property, "contraband of war." Then, as one of the first federal commanders to organize black troops, he armed that property against them. New Orleans, Confederates hoped, would be a deathtrap; plagues would decimate northerners unused to southern sun and malarial infestations. Butler cleaned up the city. Epidemics ceased. Most unpardonably, he insulted their women. New Orleans' ladies, to demonstrate disdain for the occupiers, spat upon and insulted his soldiers. He issued Order No. 28: any female pursuing such conduct shall be considered "a woman of the street plying her avocation," and treated accordingly. The insult was unforgivable. Multiple nicknames – "Spoons," "Old Cock-Eye," "Butcher of New Orleans," "The Beast" – testified to southerners' loathing.[53] "Beast, assassin, thief, he was to his enemies," wrote

51 Washington, *New National Era,* May 28, 1874. "He is impulsive, imperative, vain," San Francisco's black newspaper, the *Elevator,* agreed. "What great man who is not vain, and George has a right to be vain… [Yet] a purer, nobler man never lived." San Francisco *Elevator,* May 2, 1874.

52 Not all military historians have dismissed his abilities: "To adjudge Butler as nothing but the sum of bad traits is to distort the historical record…. He was loyal to favored subordinates and to his soldiers, and his solicitude for the often despised Negro troops probably surpassed that of any other major Union commander. Beyond these personal qualities he showed some military aptitude … a sense of strategic planning that would do credit to West Pointers…. [He was] an officer who could plan with some skill campaigns for his subordinates to execute." Richard J. Sommers, *Richmond Redeemed: The Siege at Petersburg* (Garden City: 1981), 20–21.

53 According to southern lore he had, while military governor of New Orleans, stolen everything not tied down, including the kitchen utensils from the mansion he occupied as headquarters; hence the reference to silverware in an unusually disparaging manner.

ILLUSTRATION 2 Benjamin Butler
SOURCE: LIBRARY OF CONGRESS

his biographer, "man of action, courageous champion of the poor and the oppressed, he seemed to his friends ... able to fight for reform ... He deserves to be remembered."[54] Even his physical appearance fascinated and repulsed: short, round, bald, a cast in one eye. He moved the Richmond *Dispatch* to flights of invective:

> When the golden waters of the Nile have receded the reptiles that crawl in the mud come to light. And of all reptiles Butler is the most noisome and the most hideous. Conceived in corruption and born in iniquity, he

54 Hans L. Trefousse, *Ben Butler: The South Called Him Beast!* (New York: 1974), 10–11.

> fills the whole atmosphere with a sickening stench, and emits a fetid poison which nauseates and destroys all with whom he comes in contact.... His repulsive features are an index of his debased soul.[55]

Southerners were not alone in their antipathy. Aristocratic northerners (the Hoars in particular) likewise despised him, and he them. He had risen from poverty. He harbored notions of class struggle. For Boston gentry he was unbearable.[56] To Frisbie Hoar he belonged among history's villains. Benedict Arnold, Aaron Burr, Robespierre, Catiline, were fit companions.[57] Black people conversely exalted Ben Butler. Frederick Douglass' *New National Era* praised him, among politicians second only to Sumner.

> We defy anyone to point to a general or public officer during the war or since, who has done more honestly and consistently for the good of the negro than this much-abused man.... It is all very well for journals to rail at the general, disparage his ability, cry "spoons," and mock at his personal defects. Very few of the politicians hold up cleaner hands than Butler. The only trouble with him has been that he sees further ahead than most men, has accepted the issues with an alacrity and earnestness which showed his sincere conversion and his determination to do the right thing by the negro.[58]

---

55 Richmond *Dispatch*, April 20, 1874. Virginia Congressman Thomas Whitehead invoked literary comparison, the image of Quilp, Dickens' ultimate villain, creeping lascivious dwarf perpetually stalking a virginal victim. Yet some southerners learned to love the Beast. Confederate Admiral Raphael Semmes thanked Butler for endorsing the bill to restore his political rights. "I thank you for this kindness to myself ... and still more for the kindly feeling which your conduct manifests toward our Southern people." Raphael Semmes to Benjamin Butler, June 1, 1874, Butler Papers, Library of Congress.

56 Margaret S. Thompson, "Ben Butler versus the Brahmins: Patronage and Politics in Early Gilded Age Massachusetts," *New England Quarterly*, 55 (1982): 167. "The Brahmins were an exceedingly and often self-consciously paternalistic group who viewed the masses as obligations, not as equals.... To such men as these, someone like Butler – earthy, Anglophobic, egalitarian, combative, unimpressed by their assertions of noblesse oblige ... was clearly anathema."

57 George F. Hoar, *Autobiography*, vol. 1, 329, 353. When Butler became Governor of Massachusetts in 1883 Harvard University cancelled its tradition of awarding each sitting governor an honorary degree, rather than award one to Benjamin Butler. Butler attended commencement anyway, riding onto campus surrounded by a glittering entourage, his magnificently-arrayed Governor's Guard. "An amusing incident," he recalled in his memoirs. Benjamin Butler, *The Autobiography of Benjamin Butler* (Boston: 1892), 735–6.

58 Washington *New National Era*, July 10, 1873.

He seemed impervious to invective. "Fire a whole battery of hard words in his face," the Paterson *Press* declared, "and he only cocks his belligerent eye and says 'Bully for you, my boy. It is my turn now.'"[59] Butler dismissed his critics.

> They [the people] will know where to look in time of public peril, calamity, or commotion, for a man upon whose fixedness of purpose and steadfastness in action they may surely rely, and I shall in so far have acquired that place in the good opinion of my countrymen, which most of all I desire in the present, as fitting me for service to the people, or as a name and fame to leave to my descendants as an incentive to duty well done.[60]

At the height of the congressional battle over civil rights, Butler's friend, black Massachusetts State Representative Joshua B. Smith, urged him on: "Start your great ship on the political sea, and watch what will fall in the wake."[61] To crew that ship Butler relied on the seven fellow Republican members of his Judiciary Committee. Four of those Republicans demanded full steam ahead; nothing must adulterate a proper civil rights bill. Two preferred a more cautious approach, wary of reefs and rocks ahead. One warned of shipwreck as they sailed into a civil rights maelstrom.

Pennsylvanian John Cessna led the radical four. He, like Butler, had been a pre-war Democrat and now a post-war Radical. He became, some said, Butler's closest congressional confidante and keenest political friend: "a nimble, sharp man, the very best aid Butler ever found."[62] Cessna seemed especially nimble while sticking his finger into the public pie. "Honest John," as the press dubbed him facetiously, was 52. He came to Washington from Pennsylvania's 16th District, surrounding the industrial towns of Altoona and Johnstown. Cessna cut an elegant figure. In an age of beards he went clean shaven. In an age of hard drinkers he abstained. When it came to civil rights he did not abstain. He demanded a bill precisely as Charles Sumner imagined it.

Alongside Cessna was Chicago's Jasper Delos Ward, former alderman, protégé of the powerful Senator and ex-Governor Richard Oglesby. Ward upheld

---

59 Paterson *Press*, March 10, 1874. He was the man you loved to hate. "How we shall miss him," wrote the correspondent of the New York *World* after Butler's defeat for the 44th Congress, "that slouching figure, strolling up the aisle after the morning hour has begun. He always comes in late, chewing his cigar; throws his overcoat to one page, his hat to another, sticks his hands in his pockets, and turns around to take a leisurely survey of the House." Congress would be a duller place. New York *World*, February 7, 1875.

60 Boston *Commonwealth*, August 16, 1873.

61 Joshua Smith to Benjamin Butler, December 15, 1874. Butler Papers, Library of Congress.

62 Springfield, Massachusetts, *Republican*, February 4, 1875.

the vision of radical equality. "I would obliterate all prejudices of race and birth," he declared. "I would wish to see this people made one, and Americans in principle, action, and ambition; and until just and equal laws secure to every citizen in all States every right which he may enjoy under the rule above stated, the work is not done, and the progressive people, the true men, must not rest."[63]

Jeremiah Wilson, the third radical, entered his third term in Congress. He represented a rural constituency in Indiana's southeast, the 4th District, formerly the bailiwick of George W. Julian. In May he announced he would not seek re-election. Even opposition papers were sorry to see him go. "In these days when the investigation of official misdoing and the punishment of official evil-doers is the most important branch of congressional service," wrote the St. Louis *Republican,* "Judge Wilson is the most valuable man in Congress. He is the right man in the right place and at the right time."[64]

William Frye, the last member of the quartet, was 43, the committee's youngest member. He was brilliant, graduate of Bowdoin College at age 19. He was rich. Already three times Attorney-General of Maine, he entered the second of six consecutive terms in the House. From there he rose to the Senate, chosen in 1881 to succeed James Blaine. For more than a year this band of four kept alive the Civil Rights Bill's most radical feature, the mixed school clause. Their insistence on purity, more than any other factor, delayed passage of the bill until the very last days of the 43rd Congress.

Two Republican committeemen charted a more cautious course. Lyman Tremain was 55, congressman at-large of New York. His reputation rested on the prosecution of Boss Tweed. But he was weary. His son had died in the war. His health was poor. His first term was also his last. He supported civil rights, but he thought Sumner's vision too bold. Concessions must be faced to push a bill through.

Vermont's Luke Poland at 58 was the committee's oldest member. He dressed quaintly, favoring a cerulean blue swallowtail coat with great brass buttons. He possessed, according to Frisbie Hoar, an uncanny ability to absorb alcoholic stimulants and never be drunk.[65] He possessed something else, an understanding of the passions that swirled around the idea of civil rights. He had served in the 42nd Congress as co-chairman of the Joint Investigative Committee on the Ku Klux. That commission traveled across the South documenting terrorism and violence, the relentless resistance of white people to an occupying regime.

---

63 Chicago *Tribune*, October 18, 1874.

64 St. Louis *Republican*, May 30, 1874.

65 George F. Hoar, *Autobiography,* vol. 1, 234.

Sudden mandates for social change risked unpredictable consequences. He counseled caution on behalf of wisdom.

The last Republican, Alexander White of Alabama, was 57, the only southerner on the Judiciary Committee. Beardless, slightly built, seemingly frail, "a sere and yellow leaf," the Montgomery *Advertiser* pictured him. "An oppressive gloom seems to overcast him.... His manner makes you feel that you are in the presence of one of those mysterious monopolists of all wisdom whom the ancients consulted on stormy nights and inaccessible heights."[66] He had traveled a twisty political path. A Whig in the 32nd Congress, he turned to serve the Confederacy. He opposed Reconstruction. Then he turned to support it. He pleaded for moderation, "the safest road." Both sides mistrusted him.[67] Perhaps for that reason Ben Butler trusted him.

The Judiciary Committee's Democrats watched their Republican colleagues with detached amusement. None had a positive word to say for the Civil Rights Bill. The Democrats' senior player was Charles Eldredge of Wisconsin, a veteran of six terms. He had served on the Judiciary Committee as far back as the impeachment of Andrew Johnson. James Blaine admired him, "one of the ablest parliamentarians of the House."[68] With full beard but bare upper lip, he looked the part of a Puritan preacher. He preached redemption for the South. He voted against the first Civil Rights Act in 1866. In 1868 he opposed the Fourteenth Amendment. In 1874 he urged black citizens to reject Congress' civil rights gift grafted on the Amendment. It was an acknowledgment of inferiority. By asking for help they admitted they could not help themselves.

Second in Democratic seniority was Clarkson Nott Potter, serving his third term from New Rochelle, New York's fashionable and wealthy 11th District. He was the fruit of a remarkable family tree, the Potters and the Notts. Their branches produced bishops, college presidents, architects and army generals. The congressman cut a striking figure. "Handsome, stylish, arrogant, as is the way of New Yorkers," wrote the New York *World*.[69] His magnificent side-whiskers alone parted the crowds as he passed: "the most beeyoutiful Dundreary in Congress."[70] Despite his family's Quaker ancestry and ecclesiastical bent, Potter never wavered from his party's principles. His urbanity won him Republican friends. Frisbie Hoar and James Garfield enjoyed his company.

66 Montgomery *Advertiser*, March 7, 1875.

67 "His political course has been eccentric, tortuous and vacillating," wrote the Mobile *Register*. "He has long since proved himself a disgrace to the whites. Now he is being looked upon as a fraud by the negroes." Mobile *Register*, September 9, 1874.

68 James Blaine, *Twenty Years of Congress*, vol. 1, 502.

69 New York *World*, December 13, 1874.

70 Indianapolis *Journal*, October 27, 1874.

When it came time to vote, however, he hewed the party line, opposed to all civil rights measures.

The committee's junior Democrat was Hugh Jewett of Zanesville, Ohio. Politics was his pastime, railroads his profession. He abandoned congressional service after one session to become general counsel and then President of the Erie Railroad. Thereupon he moved to New York City to enjoy unbridled affluence. It was hard to quarrel with his choice. In the boardroom of the Erie he collected $50,000 annually plus an immediate payout of $125,000 in the first year. Malcontents called it excessive, "illegal, fraudulent, unreasonable and exorbitant." It seemed reasonable enough to Hugh Jewett.

Jewett's successor in the second session, William E. Finck, replaced him in his Zanesville constituency and on the Judiciary Committee. Spare, balding, he might have been a model for Grant Wood. Judge Finck was a man of the law. He had served in the 39th Congress. There, as Eldredge, he voted against the Fourteenth Amendment. In the 43rd Congress he saw no cause to vote for a bill embodying an amendment he opposed.

Civil rights endured a monumental struggle in the House. The Senate proved easier ground. A mere twenty hours of debate sufficed to pass the measure before the end of the first session. Only a perfunctory discussion occurred in the second session. Seventy-three senators represented thirty-seven states. One vacant chair, Louisiana's second seat, remained contested. Republicans held 47 seats, Democrats 19. Seven senators entered as Liberal Republicans, among them Charles Sumner. The Liberals, all but Sumner, sided with the Civil Rights Bill's opponents.

Republicans covered all sections of the nation. The northeast remained the party's heart. Maine sent two Republicans. The senior was Lot Morrill. He had entered the Senate in 1861 to fill the seat of Hannibal Hamlin, elected as Lincoln's Vice-President. His colleague in 1874 was Hannibal Hamlin, who returned to his former pasture. Two Republicans represented New Hampshire, Aaron Cragin and the dapper, portly Bainbridge Wadleigh. Two arrived from Vermont. Justin Morrill came to the Senate in 1867, after 12 years in the House. His colleague George Edmunds was elected in 1866. In 1874 Edmunds held the critical post, Chairman of the Committee on the Judiciary.

Rhode Island and Connecticut each sent one Republican and one Liberal Republican. Henry Anthony, after Charles Sumner senior senator in continuous service, was Rhode Island's Republican. His colleague was the unhappy William Sprague. Once a golden boy of the Republican Party, he had jumped to the Liberals in 1872. Now he watched that party collapse, and his political fortunes with it. Sprague said little in his last term. He spoke no word on civil rights. He voted against it.

Connecticut's senior senator, Orris Ferry of Norwalk, also allied with the Liberals. Ferry, like Sumner, was a dying man. He appeared rarely on the Senate floor. Several times a day he injected himself, morphine drawn from a portable kit. "Day after day he sat here racked with physical pain," recalled Wisconsin's Timothy Howe, "but not a moan escaped him. His body was enfeebled by disease, but his spirit never languished."[71]

Massachusetts gave its second seat to George S. Boutwell, a Radical's radical. The more aristocratic Brahmin branch of Massachusetts Republicans disliked Boutwell. His political dalliance with Benjamin Butler confirmed their antipathy. They denied him a second term. He remained steadfast to the end of his long life, president of the Anti-Imperialist League and a defender of human rights.[72] Boutwell was a polarizing figure. Northerners, even Democrats, respected his sagacity. Southerners detested him. "He was without an exception, the most bitter, malignant, and offensive radical Republican in the whole body," Virginia's Robert Withers recalled. "He really seemed to entertain feelings of personal hatred towards every Southern man."[73] George Boutwell insisted that civil rights meant more than equal rights. It meant the end of prejudice. Commingling of the children, co-education of the races, would undo unnatural teachings. Society would emerge transformed.

New York sent one Republican of towering influence, Roscoe Conkling, and one Liberal Republican of fading fortunes, Reuben Fenton. New Jersey also split its seats. Republican Frederick Frelinghuysen was balanced by a Democratic colleague, John Stockton.

Four critical states to the west, Pennsylvania, Ohio, Indiana and Illinois, brought delegations dominated by Republicans. Pennsylvania's Simon Cameron had entered the chamber almost thirty years before, filling the place of James Buchanan. He took time out to serve as Lincoln's Secretary of War. Cameron's colleague John Scott was serving his only senatorial term. But he had acquired a deep appreciation of race issues as co-chair, with Luke Poland, of the Ku Klux Commission.

71 *Memorial Addresses on the Life and Character of Orris S. Ferry (a Senator from Connecticut,) Delivered in the Senate and House of Representatives, February 8, 1876* (Washington: 1876), 23. Massachusetts Congressman Julius Seelye, a boyhood friend, recalled his fortitude: "He would force his weak body to its work with a vigor and courage that it is not extravagant to call heroic." *Memorial Addresses*, 57–58.

72 See Thomas M. Brown, *George Sewell Boutwell, Human Rights Advocate* (Groton: 1989), 100–102.

73 "I have in my experience met with many bitter partisans of all political parties, but Senator Boutwell went a bow-shot beyond them all," wrote one southern colleague. Robert E. Withers, *Autobiography of an Octogenarian* (Roanoke: 1907), 334.

Ohio seated a Republican, John Sherman, and a Democrat, Allen Thurman. The great general's brother, chairman of the Committee on Finance, devoted his energies primarily to the nation's economy. Sherman supported the Civil Rights Bill. He voted for it. He campaigned for it. Allen Granberry Thurman, formerly chief justice of the Ohio Supreme Court, sat as the senior Democrat on the Judiciary Committee. From that post he led the fight against the Civil Rights Bill.

Indiana and Illinois produced two of the bill's most fervent advocates. Oliver H.P.T. Morton of Indiana, war-time governor and voice of radical Reconstruction, was to the Senate what Ben Butler was to the House, the bogeyman of southerners' fears. "The devil on two sticks," the Little Rock *Gazette* described the crutch-bound senator.[74] He possessed admirable qualities, said the Chicago *Tribune*, if one admired bloody revolutionaries, "the eloquence of Danton, the unscrupulousness of Marat, and the inexorableness of Robespierre."[75] Illinois' John A. Logan spoke for the Civil Rights Bill with less deviltry and more dash. "Black Jack" Logan, with great handlebar moustache and flowing dark hair, emerged from the war a popular idol, hero of the battle of Atlanta. A Democrat before the war, he turned decidedly radical after it.

Morton and Logan shared their states' seats with Republican colleagues, Daniel Pratt in Indiana and Richard Oglesby in Illinois. The other mid-western states also populated the Senate with Republicans: Matthew Carpenter and Timothy Howe of Wisconsin, Alexander Ramsay and William Windom of Minnesota, George Wright and William Allison of Iowa. Michigan seated Thomas Ferry and Zachariah Chandler, the latter also chairman of the Republican caucus. Kansas sent John J. Ingalls and James Madison Harvey. Only Nebraska included in its delegation persons of different parties: Phineas Hitchcock, Republican, and Thomas Tipton, Republican turned Liberal Republican. Tipton possessed a particularly mordant wit. He pointed it against Charles Sumner's bill. Democrats applauded. Civil rights' supporters were not appreciative. Tipton, wrote the New Orleans *Republican*, "is a babbling idiot.... It is a blessed chance for Nebraska that the term of a United States Senator is only six years"[76]

Republicans held four of six seats in the far western states. Both Nevada senators were Republicans, rugged men, conspicuous for their luxuriant beards

---

74 Little Rock *Gazette*, August 15, 1874. "The lovely Indiana Senator does not actually boast that his poor apology of a heart has been flinted over," the Shreveport *Times* conceded. "He hates from the innate meanness of the man." Shreveport *Times*, October 7, 1874.

75 Chicago *Tribune*, February 21, 1874.

76 New Orleans *Republican*, January 16, 1875.

and luxuriant bank accounts. "Two poor, impecunious miners," quipped the Atlanta *Constitution,* "with only a few millions apiece."[77] William Stewart, in his second term, had been a principal author of the Fifteenth Amendment. He supported Sumner's bill, but worried about the mixed-school clause. Integrated education, he feared, would destroy education. Stewart's colleague, John Percival Jones, supported civil rights bills, as long as they related to the civil rights of African Americans. When the subject turned to the Chinese his sympathy evaporated. "Cruel, licentious, dishonest from childhood, and liars by obligation, the Chinese possess none of the plastic traits of the adaptable negro."[78]

California sent one Republican and one Democrat. Democrat John S. Hager disagreed with Senator Jones. Science, said Hager, had demonstrated the fact: Asians placed far higher on nature's evolutionary scale than the African. Neither approached the pinnacle occupied by the whites. California's Republican was Aaron Sargent, champion of the railroads. While in the House in 1862 he had written the Pacific Railroad Bill, paving the way for construction of the first transcontinental line.[79] He was also the Senate's champion of women's rights, the author (though he did not live to see its fulfillment) of the Nineteenth Amendment. Domestic harmony, perhaps, obliged. His wife, Ellen Sargent, marched at the side of Susan B. Anthony as Treasurer of the National Women's Suffrage Association. On civil rights for black people, Sargent agreed with the Nevadan Stewart. He endorsed the bill, but he feared the impact of mixed schools.

Oregon elected one Democrat, James K. Kelly, and one Republican, John Hipple Mitchell. Mitchell, with chestnut hair and chest-sweeping beard, was acknowledged the Senate's "Adonis." Accordingly he found his life plagued by women. Oregonians petitioned Congress for the senator's expulsion as a bigamist and wife-deserter. He had abandoned one wife, changed his name and married another, "a man guilty of the worst social crimes."[80] The Senate declined to act. A member's morals were between him and his constituents. The immoral man supported the civil rights of man.

---

77 Atlanta *Constitution,* February 11, 1875.

78 Chicago *Tribune,* May 3, 1874. Mark Twain, once a Nevadan, remembered Jones kindly: "a big-hearted man with ninety-nine parts of him generosity – and that is the case to this day.... There are not many John P. Joneses in the world." Mark Twain, *The Autobiography of Mark Twain* (Berkeley: 2013), vol. 2, 56.

79 See Rhoda F. Milnarich, *The Public Career of Aaron Augustus Sargent* (El Paso: 1961). Railroaders appreciated Sargent. Those who found railroad magnates robber barons did not. "Nature intended him for a district school master or a village pettifogger," railed the San Joaquin *Republican,* "and Stanford made him a United States Senator." Quoted in Santa Clara *Argus,* May 4, 1874.

80 Frederick A. Arnold to Henry Dawes, Henry Laurens Dawes Papers, Library of Congress.

The South in 1874 solidified rapidly around the Democratic Party. Redemption progressed apace. Nineteen Democrats sat in the Senate. Only four came from anywhere outside the southern or border states. On the Civil Rights Bill Georgians led the way. Their senior member personified the Lost Cause: General John B. Gordon. Confederate hero, he played on wartime nostalgia; he fed on racial fear. "The chief of the Ku-Klux Klan in Georgia, if not in the South," Rebecca Felton recalled.[81] On civil rights Gen. Gordon delivered a clear message. It was slavery, white slavery.

> What an amazing spectacle is this country … a Republic conceived in the purest of hearts and formed in consummate wisdom – whose sons and daughters at its birth sang together like the heavenly hosts.… Yet this same Republic in less than the lapse of a single century holds in bondage the children of those very colonies who joined the chorus at its birth and ministered at its baptismal font. Palliate these circumstances who can – defend these acts who may, by all the arguments and sophistries the reasonings and plausibilities of men – they constitute the blackest record in all politics.[82]

Gordon's colleague Thomas Norwood, though of serviceable age, had sat out civil war. He did not sit out civil rights. It was the essence of evil. It was the essence of the North. The North, for Norwood it was an abode of fear, an alien land. There dwelt negrophiles, purveyors of racial pollution, of sin and degradation.

> A heterogeneous mass of humanity … millions of immigrants who were little better than slaves; who had no social rank; no pride of race, and who affiliate with negroes on perfect equality.… The North and the South! … While one is striving to keep pure the blood of the white race, the other has been striving for fifty years to force a mixture of white and negro blood.… He [the northerner] has murdered a million whites to free three million blacks, and signalized his venom, hate, malice, and brutality by trying to force the master to be servant under his slave.[83]

81 Rebecca Latimer Felton, *My Memories of Georgia Politics* (Atlanta: 1911), 161–162, 478, 493. On Gordon's oratorical gifts, see Cal M. Logue, "Restoration Strategies in Georgia, 1865–1880," in Waldo W. Braden, ed., *Oratory in the New South* (Baton Rouge: 1979), 53–55.

82 Santa Clara *Argus*, February 15, 1873.

83 Thomas M. Norwood, *A True Vindication of the South in a Review of American Political History* (Savannah: 1917), ix, 404–405, 422.

Worse, the North was the land of capitalists, vipers draining the people's lifeblood. But, said Norwood, revolution would come. The people would rise. Wall Street would fall.[84] Norwood possessed wit. He staked his claim to be the Senate's Sunset Cox. He did not succeed. His jokes caused only one side to smile. His civil rights oration nevertheless lived long, cherished in the South and preserved.

North Carolina also provided the Senate two Democrats, ex-soldier Matt Ransom, and civilian Augustus Merrimon. General Ransom professed kindly feelings for the enfranchised people. But he refused, as he said, to dilute that affection with the degradation of social equality. Judge Merrimon was more light-hearted. He wished Republicans all success with their civil rights measure. If they passed it, it would destroy them. Public revulsion would ensure the triumph of a Democratic majority. Then they could eliminate Sumner's legacy along with his old party.

Democratic senators arrived from Virginia – John Johnston, nephew of General Joseph E. Johnston; Alabama – George Goldthwaite, a southerner by way of Boston; and Tennessee in the person of Henry Cooper. Cooper was one of the Senate's silent men. "A solid thinker," declared the Memphis *Appeal,* "who has only spoken once in two years."[85] He woke from his slumbers to speak against the Civil Rights Bill. Two Democrats represented Kentucky: Thomas McCreery and John Stevenson.

Border state Democrats, Maryland's William Hamilton and Delawareans Eli Saulsbury and Thomas Bayard, took prominent anti-civil rights stands. Bayard emerged as a leader. With Allen Thurman he mapped the party's strategy. He nurtured presidential ambitions, positioning himself as the champion of the hard pro-Southern wing of his party. He would rather die, he told election crowds, he would rather be shot by firing squad, than live under the terms of Charles Sumner's iniquity.

Missouri sent the Senate one Democrat, Lewis V. Bogy, and one Liberal Republican, Carl Schurz. Bogy stood inevitably in the shadow of his extraordinary colleague. But he cast a shadow of his own. Bogy was a consummate politician. He prided himself on being a self-made man. Once, a poor and barefoot boy of sixteen, he went from his humble home to seek his fortune. Entrusted to his sainted mother he left a pledge. Before the age of 60, he vowed, he would sit

84 "The sound of revelry and the roar of commerce rushing through the streets drown the rising hungry growl of St. Germain just below their feet." *Ibid.*, vii–viii. On Norwood's career, see William H. Bragg, "The Junius of Georgia Redemption: Thomas M. Norwood and the 'Nemesis' Letters," *Georgia Historical Quarterly*, 77 (1993): 86–122.

85 Memphis *Appeal*, February 26, 1874.

in the United States Senate.[86] Now he owned the mines at Iron Mountain. His own railroad transported his ore. He took his Senate seat on March 4, 1873, just 36 days before his sixtieth birthday. Free enterprise, said Bogy, and freedom, inseparable: Sumner's measure was but another element in the ceaseless march of centralization suffocating the liberties of the people. If Congress could dictate one's companions on the trains, at hotel tables, in the theater, what freedom remained that it could not trample?[87]

Carl Schurz, the great German senator, once a fiery revolutionary of 1848, had mellowed. He founded the Liberal Republican movement in Missouri in 1870 and nationally in 1872. No one in the Senate claimed a closer friendship to Charles Sumner. No one disappointed his friend more. In the civil rights debate he maintained a total silence. In the final vote he joined the remaining Liberals – Ferry, Fenton, Sprague, Tipton and Morgan Hamilton of Texas – opposed to the Civil Rights Bill.

Republicans held 13 southern seats. South Carolina produced Thomas Robertson and John J. Patterson. Florida, Mississippi and Arkansas, though they teetered on the brink, also seated Republicans: Floridians Simon Conover and Abijah Gilbert; Arkansans Powell Clayton and Stephen Dorsey; Henry Pease and James Alcorn of Mississippi. Arkansas' Gen. Powell Clayton was the most forceful. He did everything possible to keep Redemption at bay. He worried about the impact of a civil rights measure. It would arouse hatred. It would bring bloodshed. It would ruin the Republican Party. Nevertheless he voted for the bill. His supreme moment came in October, when he orchestrated the Southern Republican Convention, a last, desperate attempt to stave off political disaster.

Pease of Mississippi was a Senate neophyte, a despised carpetbagger, once a schoolteacher from New Jersey. Democrats did not like Henry Pease. "Pease is bad," punned the Richmond *Dispatch*. "He exceeds the onions in exceptionable odor."[88] The Vicksburg *Vicksburger* was less witty: "He thinks that darkies are better than he is, and we think he is correct."[89] Equally disliked by their white constituents were Clayton's Arkansas colleague Stephen Dorsey and Alabama's George E. Spencer. Spencer, following a much-disputed election, entered his

86 *Memorial Addresses on the Life and Character of Lewis V. Bogy (a Senator from Missouri,) Delivered in the Senate, January 16, 1878, and in the House of Representatives, January 23, 1878* (Washington: 1878), 88. Bogy exuded a pompous air. But he earned his colleagues' respect. "I became attached to him," Oliver Morton recalled, "despite all our differences of opinion." *Memorial Address*, 23.

87 Cincinnati *Commercial*, July 21, 1874.

88 Richmond *Dispatch*, February 1, 1875.

89 Quoted in Monroe, Louisiana, *Ouachita Telegraph*, February 13, 1874.

second term. White League activists threatened to shoot him. The Mobile *Register* urged restraint: "If he ever rises to the dignity and worth of martyrdom, a rope would best supply the dignity of things."[90]

Spencer and Dorsey, along with Clayton, Pease, Conover, Gilbert and Patterson qualified as carpetbaggers. Six southern Republican senators were scalawags. Four, Louisiana's J. Rodman West, Robertson of South Carolina, James Alcorn of Mississippi and James Flanagan of Texas, supported the Civil Rights Bill.[91] Most vocal was Texan Flanagan. Sixty-nine years old, shrewd and caustic, he posed as the Senate's hay-seed. Various "whars and thars" punctuated his discourse. Occasionally, it was noted, "he relieves his feelings during his speeches by blowing his nose with his fingers to the admiration of the galleries."[92] His speech on the Civil Rights Bill rambled in rustic reflections. Yet Flanagan, alone, found conviction to face the ultimate consequence of social equality: mixed marriage. He faced it, and accepted it.

Two southern Republicans opposed their party's civil rights measures. Virginia's John Francis Lewis said little, Tennessee's William G. "Parson" Brownlow much. Even in a chamber filled with formidable figures, he stood out. Once a fiery post-war governor, now he seemed a shell of a man. Attendants carried him to his seat. Staring, immobile, the Atlanta *Constitution's* reporter described him: "There he sits, pale, attenuated, ghostly, never speaking, never smiling, save for the perpetual twitch of a terrible palsy. Such is Parson Brownlow of Tennessee."[93] In the grip of a wasting disease, his body had failed. The mind remained sharp. His antipathy to the Civil Rights Bill ran deep. Unable to orate, he delivered his words in print, setting off a spiral of controversy and violence.

The hierarchy of the upper chamber lacked the central dominating presence that Speaker Blaine provided for the House. Vice-President Henry Wilson presided, or ought to have presided. But his health was fragile, forcing prolonged absences. Late in November 1874 he seemed to improve. "Henry Wilson's health is becoming alarmingly good," remarked the Cincinnati *Commercial*. "He is suspected of a rapid tendency to robustitude."[94] He died one year later precisely.

90 Mobile *Register*, July 4, 1874.

91 New Orleans' black newspaper the *Louisianian* praised Rodman West: "We have not found occasion to lose confidence either in his integrity or discretion ... in his influence and strength, his capabilities to serve his State, and in the confidence of the citizens thereof." New Orleans *Louisianian*, June 6, 1874.

92 Charleston *News and Courier*, May 23, 1874.

93 Atlanta *Constitution*, February 11, 1875.

94 Cincinnati *Commercial*, November 21, 1874.

Taking the chair in Wilson's absence was Matthew Hale Carpenter, President Pro Tempore. "Our Matt," the St. Louis *Republican* winked at the adipose Wisconsin statesman, noted constitutional lawyer and colorful congressional crank: "the Bohemian of the Senate who wears an inflated shirt-front and makes inflation speeches, who sports a nose-gay in his button-hole and tumbles his hair about his Websterian head."[95] The "Webster of the West" joined the civil rights skeptics. The intent was good, the means bad. It violated the Constitution.

Charles Sumner hoped his measure, having been three times before the Senate, would come immediately to the floor. He presented it on the first day. It received the designation S.1. Sumner called for a vote, without objection. There were objections. S.1 passed to the Judiciary Committee for review. Before it emerged its author had died. It was left to the seven members of that panel to bring forth the Civil Rights Act of 1875.

The Committee boasted a distinguished cast. George Edmunds of Vermont held the chairmanship. His reputation as a constitutional lawyer was unsurpassed. Ben Butler, asked to name someone to argue a case in the Supreme Court, could think of no one better than Edmunds.[96] Forty-six, prematurely bald, Edmunds indulged an acerbic disposition. He seemed to revel in contradicting whatever proposition anyone cared to offer.[97] At times his fussiness tended to get lost in details. "Edmunds can see a fly on a barn door," one colleague quipped, "but sometimes he fails to see the door."[98] On civil rights, he saw clearly. The spirit of the law, he said in the final debate, was essential, "to safeguard those rights that belong to all men alike in the reason of things."

At Chairman Edmunds' side was the Senate's most dynamic personality, master politician and power broker, New York's Roscoe Conkling. Always impeccably arrayed, a carnation in the lapel, his hair arranged, one carelessly-curled forelock carefully set in place – his trademark emblem – he radiated brilliance and condescension. "There was something almost sublime in his disdain," Frisbie Hoar recalled.[99] "Egregious vanity," said Kansas' John Ingalls, "his habitual attitude was that of supercilious disdain. He advocated drastic

---

95 St. Louis *Republican*, May 4, 1874.

96 Butler, *Autobiography*: 955.

97 At the deadlocked Republican convention of 1880, Frisbie Hoar recalled, he tried to persuade him to become a candidate for the presidential nomination: "I said, 'But Edmonds, just think of the fun you would have vetoing bills.' He smiled, and his countenance beamed all over … and he replied with great feeling: 'Well, that would be good fun.'" George F. Hoar, *Autobiography*, vol. 1, 388.

98 Robert Withers, *Autobiography*: 328.

99 Hoar, *Autobiography*, vol. 2, 59.

measures for the protection of the negro and the assertion of the national authority. He trampled upon the sensibilities of his adversaries like a rhinoceros crashing through a tropical jungle."[100] In the civil rights jungle Conkling crashed through all adversaries. In May, 1872, as Sumner's Amnesty Bill amendment approached the Senate, he wrote his friend abolitionist Gerrit Smith: "I hope we shall not fail in obtaining final action on Civil Rights. We shall try."[101] That effort fell short. Two years later Roscoe Conkling stayed on the floor through a day and a night, twenty straight hours. He did not fail.

Iowan George Wright was the Republicans' junior member. Sixteen years a justice of the Iowa Supreme Court, he helped found the University of Iowa's school of law. His efforts on behalf of the Civil Rights Bill are least apparent among the Republican committeemen. He declined to speak on the floor. Nor did he record his thoughts in print. In the committee, however, he provided crucial support.

Matthew Carpenter likewise had a seat on the Judiciary Committee. He did not provide support. The bill, he insisted, was unconstitutional. His arguments, precise, legal, ultimately validated by the Supreme Court, impressed some wavering colleagues. They did not deter a sufficient majority.

The last Republican added that sufficient voice. He also inherited the most critical assignment. Charles Sumner died on March 11, 1874. To sponsor the bill, the Committee selected New Jersey's Frederick Frelinghuysen. The senator was 53. Tall, serious, he enjoyed a reputation for plain dealing and piety, guided by his Calvinist faith.[102] Frelinghuysen boasted a pedigree second to none, founded on his grandfather and namesake's service in the Revolution and Continental Congress. Yet he affected a simple manner. Between the cocky Conkling and the edgy Edmunds, he was a steadying presence. His greatest service, as President Arthur's Secretary of State, was yet to come. He served in 1874 to see the Civil Rights Bill through its first confrontation in the Senate.

The Judiciary Committee's Democrats were John Stevenson of Kentucky and Allen Thurman of Ohio. They could annoy the Republicans. They could not, even with Carpenter's help, block their majority. Stevenson, 61, silver-haired, antebellum congressman and former governor, was the committee's only southerner. Stevenson upheld his party. But he avoided partisan passions,

100 Ingalls, *Writings*, 352.

101 Roscoe Conkling to Gerrit Smith, May 17, 1872. Gerrit Smith Papers, Syracuse University.

102 See John W. Rollins, "Frederick Theodore Frelinghuysen, 1817–1885: The Politics and Diplomacy of Stewardship," Diss., University of Wisconsin, Madison, 1974.

a gentlemanly presence.[103] On civil rights he left command of the resistance to the bulldog, Allen Thurman.

Thurman accepted the challenge. Courtly, mannered, a devotee of opera and the theater, he celebrated in 1873 his 60th birthday. He enjoyed his colleagues' universal esteem. They respected him especially as the Senate's keenest constitutional expert. On that document Allen Thurman yielded reverence to no man.

> I know that with some gentlemen anything like a constitutional argument is only a subject of ridicule.... Here are some Senators who are tired of hearing of the Constitution, and who will continue to be tired of it just so long as there is any Constitution to think about. I for one am not tired of it.[104]

Even Roscoe Conkling, friend and friendly enemy, bowed deferentially. "When I speak of the law I turn to the Senator from Ohio," he declared, "as the Mussulman turns to Mecca ... as to the world's most copious fount of human jurisprudence."[105] As the civil rights debate unfolded it fell to Thurman to present the Democrats' strongest case. The Constitution was his battle-ground. Civil rights' proponents, Thurman said, relied on the Fourteenth Amendment. But that amendment did not suffice. It had but one function: to serve as a prohibition on the states. It did not interfere with individuals. Private persons could discriminate at will. Thurman made that argument his own. In the end the Supreme Court agreed. One fellow Democrat felt aggrieved. Ex-senator Eugene Casserly of California, chafing in unwanted retirement, wrote his friend Delaware's Thomas Bayard. He first, he said, had espied the legal loophole that gutted civil rights of the nineteenth century. Thurman, howbeit, accepted the praise.[106]

---

103 Even cantankerous George Edmunds enjoyed his friendship. Among his papers Stevenson preserved a note from the Chairman. In January 1875, as civil rights battles raged, he begged to "request the pleasure" of the Kentuckian's company – an informal dinner at home; no one would be more welcome. George Edmunds to John W. Stevenson, January 5, 1875. John Stevenson Papers, Library of Congress.

104 *Cong. Globe*, 42nd Congress, 2nd Session: 496.

105 Conkling, *Life and Letters*, 411,

106 "I had the other day his [Thurman's] Civil Rights Bill speech.... It is very able, tho' I do think he might have owned, en passant, that he was indebted to me for his key note – that the 14th amendment operates on States not on individuals. I first in the Senate – or out of it so far as I know – took that ground.... I told him first of it. He was greatly gratified and admitted that it was the solution of the question. I fear he is as cold as a frog, Tom." Eugene Casserly to Thomas Bayard, June 6, 1874. Thomas Bayard Papers, Library of Congress.

Congressmen meanwhile gathered to pursue their varied tasks. Civil rights was not the most urgent. Atop the agenda came the nation's finances, which Congress debated in the form of the Currency Bill. Foreign affairs remained quiet, after the threat of war with Spain over the Virginius Affair subsided. But final details of the Geneva Awards had yet to be resolved. Westerners demanded regulation of the railroads. The economy had tumbled into recession. An election approached. With a plate full of problems, members of the 43rd Congress settled into their quarters to prepare for the opening session.

Monday, December 2, 1873, pursuant to Article 1, Section 4 of the Constitution, the nation's representatives sallied forth to meet in Congress assembled.[107] In the House James Blaine, re-elected as Speaker, walked to the chair escorted by a Republican, Horace Maynard, and a Democrat, Fernando Wood. In the Senate Rev. E.D. Owen spoke the prayer: "Infinite Majesty, ever adorable Jehovah, accept our praises." War had ended. The guns had ceased firing. "This day we are free from the horrors of war." Let peace and reconciliation endure. "Lord, bless Thy servants. Infuse them with Thy grace and supply them with infinite wisdom in all their deliberations."[108]

107 Some members nested in opulent accommodations, others less posh. Ben Butler entertained friends at his residence on 15th Street. Carl Schurz repaired to his house at 10 Lafayette Square. His colleague Lewis Bogy could be found in a boardinghouse at 485 C Street NW. The Hoar brothers split up, Ebenezer rooming at 905 13th Street, George at 128 K Street. Three other Massachusetts members, Daniel Gooch, John Williams and Henry Pierce, settled in at Willard's Hotel. Henry Dawes and James Buffinton stopped at the Ebbitt House. Alexander Stephens chose the National Hotel. Wheeled through the lobby, he might have passed Virginia Republican William H.H. Stowell. Many members bunked as bachelors. New York's David Mellish, a poor man, took along his wife and two small daughters, whom he could not afford to leave behind. Kentuckian John Stevenson took along his wife and children, whom he could not bear to leave behind. Boston *Commonwealth*, December 13; Fredericksburg, Virginia, *Ledger*, December 16, 1873.

108 *Cong. Record*, 43rd Congress, 1st Session: 1.

CHAPTER 3

Charge at New Market Heights: Debate in the House of Representatives

January, 1874. Charles Sumner returned to the Senate. Still recovering from his illness, he wrote Michigan's Zachariah Chandler on the 20th: "Stronger & very hopeful to be in my seat soon. But my medicines are not pleasant."[1] Civil rights may have offered a more pleasant antidote. Congress hesitated; states acted. A rash of civil rights statutes broke out across the nation. Southern states still with Republican governments, and some northern states, framed their own bills.[2]

Louisiana's version of equality had already been written into its constitution of 1868. Article 13 of that document enshrined the public accommodations clauses. Article 135 integrated public schools. A civil rights law followed in 1869. It levied fines and loss of license upon those who discriminated in the use of railways, streetcars, steamboats, hotels, inns, and places of public entertainment. After an initial veto, Gov. Henry Clay Warmoth signed this supplementary act.[3] South Carolina's statute also passed in 1869.

In 1873 the wave broke through. Four states passed civil rights acts. Four more considered them. Florida's Governor Ossian Hart signed the law in January. In February Mississippi joined Florida. Governor James L. Alcorn had already signed a statute against discrimination in public transport. His successor Ridgley Powers put his name to a comprehensive act. Noting the momentum, the San Francisco *Elevator*, California's black newspaper, urged voters to press the case, "so that in every State there should be a Civil Rights Bill before the Legislature at their next session."[4] Bills did appear before the year was out in Arkansas, Alabama, North Carolina, Kansas, New Jersey and New York. They did not pass everywhere. But they put the nation on notice.

---

1 Charles Sumner to Zachariah Chandler, January 20, 1874. Charles Sumner Papers, Library of Congress.

2 See James M. McPherson, "Abolitionists and the Civil Rights Act of 1875," *Journal of American History*, 52 (1965): 495.

3 Henry Clay Warmoth, *War, Politics and Reconstruction: Stormy Days in Louisiana* (New York: 1930), 91–92; see also Ted Tunnell, *Crucible of Reconstruction: War, Radicalism, and Race in Louisiana, 1862–1877* (Baton Rouge: 1984), 117–134, 167–169; Roger A. Fischer, *The Segregation Struggle in Louisiana, 1862–1877* (Urbana: 1974), 64–69.

4 San Francisco *Elevator*, June 21, 1873.

The most spectacular success came in New York. The legislature passed its statute on April 9: "Chapter 186: An Act for the Protection of Citizens in their Civil and Public Rights." The vote was overwhelming – 90–11 in the Assembly; 24–3 in the Senate:

Section 1. No citizen of this State shall, by reason of race, color, or previous condition of servitude be excepted or excluded from the full and equal enjoyment of any accommodation, advantage, facility, or privilege furnished by inn-keepers, by common carriers, whether on land or water, by licensed owners, managers or lessees of theaters, or other places of amusement; by trustees, commissioners, superintendents, teachers, and other officers of common schools and public institutions of learning, and by cemetery associations.[5]

Section 3 annulled all statutes or regulations causing discrimination by use of the word "white." Governor John A. Dix signed the civil rights law. New York's black people celebrated. They tendered thanks to the governor, to Lieutenant-Governor John C. Robinson, and to Roscoe Conkling. They thanked State Senators William H. Robertson and James Wood, its sponsors in that chamber.[6] Assembly Speaker James W. Husted of Peekskill received special recognition. *Harper's Weekly* ran his engraved portrait. The "Bald Eagle of Westchester," his bald spot carefully combed over, became a civil rights icon.[7] New York City festivities included a grand procession led by regiments of Colored Militia. They concluded with a rally at the Cooper Institute. Messages arrived from Governor Dix, Senator Conkling, Gerrit Smith, Alonzo Cornell, William Lloyd Garrison, Wendell Phillips and Frederick Douglass.[8]

Across the Hudson River in New Jersey the outcome was less successful. A civil rights bill reached the legislature, sponsored by State Senator J. Henry Stone.[9] It stalled there. In Alabama and North Carolina efforts also fell short. The North Carolina bill, written by black State Senator Edward R. Dudley, appeared on November 21. It was voted down in December. At the same time delegates assembled in Washington for the opening of the National Civil Rights Convention. The drumbeat of state action did not lessen the urgency for federal legislation. Frederick Douglass' *New National Era* praised the new laws.

---

5 See David McBride, "Fourteenth Amendment Idealism: The New York State Civil Rights Law, 1873–1918," *New York History*, 71 (1990): 207–209.

6 Washington, *New National Era*, May 1, 1873.

7 *Harper's Weekly*, March 14, 1874, p. 232.

8 New York *Times*, May 16; San Francisco *Elevator*, May 31, 1873; McBride, "Idealism," 208–209.

9 Washington, *New National Era*, March 13, 1873.

But they did not suffice. An act with national scope was required.[10] States might pass statutes. Evasion or circumvention was readily accomplished.

The Arkansas statute took effect in March. Its provisions covered public transportation and accommodations. On March 7 the steamboat *Dardanelle* set out from Little Rock on the Arkansas River almost empty of passengers. Two black men presented tickets to the first-class cabin. White voyagers fled pell-mell to the safety of the shore.[11] This success turned to failure. Captains of vessels simply refused to book anyone into the cabin class. All voyagers boarded as deck passengers. Officers then invited the white people to dine and sleep in cabin accommodations, as their personal guests. "There is no law to regulate the hospitality of steamboat captains, and they generally find their white friends to be quite as many as they can afford to accommodate without charge."[12]

In Mississippi railroads posted a notice: "The officers of the road reserve the right to locate the seat of any person in this train." Conductors located black persons into the smoking cars.[13] As to public accommodations, hotel proprietors announced that their establishments no longer accommodated the public. They were boarding houses only, for "selected guests and personal friends." Theater managers reserved admission "for those who have special invitations, and a contribution will be expected ... towards defraying the expense of the entertainment." At Vicksburg one case made it to court in the law's first three months. The plaintiff sued after being excluded from a public lecture. The judge took the matter under advisement for six weeks, then dismissed the complaint.[14]

Some encouraging signs appeared. In Iowa Emily Coger brought suit against the Northwestern Union Packet Co. She had insinuated herself – as a "quadroon" her off-coloration was barely detectable – onto one of its steamboats at the town of Keokuk. She was detected. Despite her forceful objection (saluting the captain uncivilly as a "white-livered son of a b –"), she was propelled from the cabin table. Her suit asked for $5,000 in damages. Liberal-minded advocates, Republican Congressman George McCrary and attorney Daniel F. Miller, took up her cause. She won an award of $250. Northwestern Packet appealed. The State Supreme Court upheld Coger's case, citing, in the absence of

10 Washington, *New National Era*, May 22, 1873.
11 Washington, *New National Era*, March 13, 1873.
12 Thomasville, Georgia, *Times*, April 12, 1873.
13 Chicago *Inter Ocean*, October 12, 1874.
14 Washington, *New National Era*, May 29, 1873.

an Iowa civil rights law, the Fourteenth Amendment and the Civil Rights Act of 1866.[15] Lawyer Miller exulted: "We in Iowa are ahead of Mr. Sumner."[16]

In Louisiana, Governor Warmoth called the law operationally meaningless, a "dead letter."[17] An early test nonetheless resulted in a victory. Josephine DeCuir filed the complaint against John G. Benson, captain and owner of the steamboat *Governor Allen,* which carried passengers and cargo between New Orleans and Vicksburg, Mississippi. Mme. DeCuir, though armed with a first-class ticket, found herself refused a place in the cabin. The district court, applying the state's 1869 statute, awarded $1,000 damages for denial of her civil rights. Captain Benson appealed. The State Supreme Court, Chief Justice John T. Ludeling writing for the majority, upheld the decision.

But there was a jarring note. Justice William Wyly dissented. Louisiana's civil rights law, he said, was unconstitutional. The boat, even though the plaintiff went ashore inside Louisiana, traveled across state lines. Thus the law interfered with interstate commerce, a matter over which only Congress had jurisdiction. It violated Article I, Section 8, the commerce clause of the United States Constitution.[18] "Congress alone," Justice Wyly wrote, "has authority to regulate commerce among the several States … . Until the lawgiver speaks, it is our duty to remain silent."[19]

Judge Wyly's dissent did not prevail for the moment. It raised questions. What could apply to a steamboat could apply to a railway that crossed state lines, to a hotel that accommodated interstate travelers. It presented a legal argument capable of overturning local civil rights laws, in the absence of a federal act.[20] Lax enforcement within the states, restrictive constitutional limits among the states, all made the need for a national statute imperative. Civil rights supporters began the final push.

---

15 See Jonathan Lurie, "The Fourteenth Amendment: Use and Application in Selected State Court Civil Liberties Cases, 1870–1890 – A Preliminary Assessment," *The American Journal of Legal History,* 28 (1984): 308–310; Robert J. Kaczorowski, *The Nationalization of Civil Rights: Constitutional Theory and Practice in a Racist Society, 1866–1883* (New York: 1987), 291.

16 Washington, *New National Era,* February 27; San Francisco *Elevator,* November 15, 1873.

17 Warmoth, *War, Politics and Reconstruction:* 92.

18 New Orleans *Louisianian,* April 11, 1874.

19 Monroe, *Ouachita Telegraph,* April 17, 1874.

20 The DeCuir case did sabotage state civil rights laws. In Hall *v.* DeCuir of 1877, written by Chief Justice Morrison Waite with a lengthy concurrence by Mr. Justice Clifford, the Supreme Court validated Judge Wyly's objection. That ruling became a precedent, but a double-edged sword. It served first to undermine civil rights. Then it helped to overthrow segregation statutes, which could equally constitute meddling in the conduct of interstate commerce. See Sarah H. Lemmon, "Transportation Segregation in the Federal Courts since 1865," *Journal of Negro History,* 38 (1953): 176–193.

The National Civil Rights Convention opened on December 9, 1873. Delegates arrived early. On December 1 they trooped up F Street past the home of Charles Sumner. There they paused to serenade the senator. A band played airs. Sumner stepped out with a welcome to the Civil Rights Convention.[21] There was reason for optimism. The Republican Party had pledged itself to the cause. It had proclaimed the doctrine in its platform at the Philadelphia convention that re-nominated President Grant: "Complete liberty and exact equality in the enjoyment of all civil, political, and public rights should be established and effectually maintained throughout the Union by efficient and appropriate State and Federal legislation." The president promised again in his second inaugural address. He repeated it in his Annual Message to Congress. Elections had delivered Republicans an unassailable majority. What could go wrong?

William Nesbit of the Pennsylvania Equal Rights League called the sessions to order. The elite of African-American society sat in the hall: Virginia's John Mercer Langston; P.B.S. Pinchback, paramount black leader and ex-governor of Louisiana; North Carolinians Stuart Ellison and John Hyman; Robert Harlan of Ohio; Daniel Straker of Kentucky; Frederick Douglass; George Downing. All seven black congressmen reported present. By acclamation the convention chose Pinchback as president. Downing was elected first vice-president. Douglass wrote the call: "This convention earnestly and urgently prays Congress to enact into law a measure that will protect all classes of citizens in the enjoyment of their civil and public rights."[22]

On December 12 Pinchback withdrew to continue his efforts to validate a seat in the United States Senate. Downing led the delegates to the White House. Ulysses Grant received them in the Blue Room. Downing spoke:

> President Grant … we begin to feel that the country has nearly arrived at that state designed by our forefathers, that all men are created equal. The convention has assembled to express our grievances, and ask of Congress to give us relief, and from the expression of your sentiments, given by you in your inaugural address, we have no doubt that such relief will meet your approval.[23]

The President greeted each delegate as he advanced.

---

21 Boston *Commonwealth*, December 6, 1873.

22 Washington, *New National Era*, December 11, 12, 18; San Francisco *Elevator*, December 20, 27; Charleston *News and Courier*, December 11; Bainbridge, Georgia, *Weekly Sun*, December 17, 1873.

23 Washington, *New National Era*, December 12, 1873.

> I have always believed that enfranchisement and equal rights should accompany emancipation. These rights should have followed without legislation. It is unfortunate that any enactment is necessary to secure such rights, but existing prejudice seems to have rendered it necessary. I hope the present Congress will give you the relief you seek.[24]

The delegates also pressured their elected officials. Louisiana Rep. George L. Smith hosted a reception at Gray's Restaurant; the state's entire congressional delegation, including Senator West, attended.[25] New Jersey delegates warned their representatives. The "colored people" would vote, "only for those who are their true and tried friends." Senator Frelinghuysen pledged his loyalty. So did Congressman Phelps. He regarded the Civil Rights Bill as "just and right, and he should, whenever presented, give it his hearty approval and vote."[26] The dapper congressman from Englewood had occasion later to regret those impulsive words.

Delegates returned home. To ensure that senators and representatives did not lapse into forgetfulness, the National Civil Rights Convention left behind an offspring, the National Civil Rights Council. An executive board of forty members, George Downing at its head, took charge of sustaining the movement: the civil rights lobby. "Mr. Downing and his thirty-nine men of nerve," Sunset Cox dubbed them. Republicans must not forget the party's pledge.

Democrats, too, felt a tug upon their buttonholes. One was Alexander Stephens. Six councilmen, including Downing and Frederick Douglass, Jr., descended upon the ex-Confederacy's ex-vice-president for a personal meeting on December 24.[27] Outwardly it seemed an unlikely Christmas Eve mission. Yet Downing and Douglass were hopeful. Since his restoration to United States citizenship Alexander Stephens appeared to have recognized the new order of things.[28] In 1866 he addressed the Georgia legislature: "Accept the issues of the

---

24 *Cong. Record*, 43rd Congress, 1st Session: 618. The council surrounded Downing with a selection of the African-American community's foremost figures: Philip Bell of California; Mifflin Gibbs of Arkansas; J. Henri Burch of Louisiana; William D. Forten of Pennsylvania; Frederick Douglass, Jr. Norris Wright Cuney of Texas served as vice-president, George W. Mitchell of Virginia treasurer, Frederick Barbadoes and Florida's William U. Saunders as secretaries. *New National Era*, January 1; New York *Tribune*, January 16, 1874.

25 Washington, *New National Era*, December 18, 1873.

26 Washington, *New National Era*, December 25, 1873.

27 Charleston *News and Courier*, December 24, 1873.

28 See Thomas E. Schott, *Alexander H. Stephens of Georgia: A Biography* (Baton Rouge: 1988), 455–457.

war and abide by them in good faith," he counseled. "Slavery, as it was called … upon which all our institutions rested, is abolished forever."

> Wise and humane provisions should be made for them [the freedmen] … ample and full protection should be secured to them, so that they may stand equal before the law in the possession and enjoyment of all rights of person, liberty, and property.[29]

So mellow had Stephens' attitude grown that rumors spread he might switch to the Republican Party.[30] It was reported he intended to speak in favor of the Civil Rights Bill. He had been overheard at one of Fernando Wood's dinner parties telling General Sherman of his sympathetic regard for black people's aspirations.[31] Stephens hastened to deny this story, but its impression remained. The Chicago *Tribune* predicted he would endorse the bill.[32] "We are prepared to hear him take open grounds in favor of negro equality," fretted the Raleigh *Sentinel.*[33] The Mobile *Register* pronounced him a traitor.[34] His own Atlanta *Constitution* suggested the southern people find a better man to defend their honor, "to take that course which becomes a Patriot." When he should speak, Stephens retorted, "it will be time enough to form a proper judgment whether he truly represents her [the South's] interest, and faithfully 'defends her honor.'"[35]

In the end Stephens answered the black delegates evasively. "Colored men," he agreed, "were entitled to protection of their civil rights." But "it was the duty of the states, and not the federal government" to provide that protection: state rights, as always. Meanwhile the debate had begun. Charles Sumner introduced his bill, designated S.1, on the first day, December 2, 1873. The Senate hesitated. George Edmunds, Chairman of the Judiciary Committee, urged that S.1 be referred to that committee. Changes might be required in the senator's proposal. His interpretation of the constitution was bold, but not always pointedly legal. "Let the committee scrutinize this one carefully and send it back with no flaw that might make its passage futile."[36] Sumner was livid. He would

29 *Cong. Record,* 43rd Congress, 1st Session, 379. See Schott, *Stephens*, 463–464.
30 Indianapolis *Journal*, January 9, 1874.
31 Springfield, Massachusetts, *Republican*, January 5, 1874.
32 Chicago, *Tribune*, January 4, 1874.
33 Raleigh *Sentinel*, January 2, 1874.
34 Mobile *Register*, January 9, 1874.
35 Atlanta, *Constitution*, January 4, 1874.
36 *Cong. Record,* 43rd Congress, 1st Session: 2. See Ronald B. Jager, "Charles Sumner, the Constitution and the Civil Rights Act of 1875," *New England Quarterly*, 17 (1969): 355. "Although

stand for no review. The next day, with Edmunds absent, he moved for immediate consideration. Once again a senator objected. Orris Ferry of Connecticut asked for understanding:

> It is easy to charge upon those of us who stand in that position hostility to human rights, and therefore attempt, by casting opprobrium upon us, to invalidate our arguments; but the ground upon which I stand is simply the Constitution of the United States … . Remedy the wrongs of our people wherever they exist in conformity with, not in violation of, the Constitution of the United States.[37]

Charles Sumner replied, his feelings somewhat softened.

> Mr. President … the Senator is mistaken if he supposes that I charge upon him any indifference to human rights …. I know too well his heart, his excellent and abounding nature, his New England home, to attribute to him any such indifference …. But it seems to me – I may be mistaken, but I cannot help saying it – that the Senator has not yet recognized that greatest of all victories by which a new interpretation is fixed upon the national Constitution, so that hereafter all its sentences, all its phrases, all its words, shall be interpreted broadly and emphatically for human rights. How often have I been obliged to say this? But the Senator forgets that victory. There is his error.… Our colored fellow-citizens must be admitted to complete equality before the law. In other words, everywhere, in everything regulated by law, they must be equal with all their fellow-citizens. There is the simple principle on which this bill stands. Who can impugn it? Who can throw upon it the shadow of question? Sir, if the Constitution of the United States does not sanction a bill like this, then forthwith should we proceed to amend that Constitution.… Terrible war will have been, then, a beneficent parent.

Sumner's words left his fellow senators unmoved. His bill lay upon the table. Now Sumner's illness prostrated him. On January 27 he returned to the floor. He renewed his plea for a vote. Committees act as the Senate's eyes and ears, to shield it from dubious propositions. "But who wants eyes and ears for the

---

Sumner was a penetrating student of the law, his humanitarian zeal led him to believe that any measure for human rights was constitutional.… He believed that life should control the Constitution, rather than vice versa."

37 Ferry's speech and Sumner's reply, Cong. Record, 43rd Congress, 1st Session: 11.

appreciation of this measure? Its character is manifest; its justice is confessed." George Edmunds rose in a huff. He unsheathed his sarcastic streak. "I am for giving my friend from Massachusetts the full benefit of what he claims, that his zeal is strong, and that his heart is strong ... but it is just possible – I know it is a very remote possibility, but it is just possible – that a majority of his brother Senators might think he was too strong in his legislation, or so strong as to make his legislation absolutely weak." One last time Charles Sumner spoke:

> I do not know, sir, why my position on this question should justify the personalities which the Senator from Vermont considers so essential to debate ... why the Senator should, with personality of manner and allusion taunt me for the position that I occupy. Do I deserve it? ... My desire – the darling desire, if I may say so, of my soul – at this moment is to close forever this great question, so that it shall never again intrude into these Chambers; so that hereafter in all our legislation there shall be no such word as "black" or "white," but that we shall speak only of citizens and of men. Is not that an aspiration worthy of a Senator? Is such an aspiration any ground for taunt from the Senator from Vermont? Will he not, too, join in the aspiration and the endeavor to bring about that beneficent triumph?[38]

Even the crotchety Edmunds was moved. He apologized. Frederick Frelinghuysen intervened. If Sumner would be patient, all would be well: "I think we can give the Senator the assurance that a fortnight will not pass without the bill being reported."

Wisconsin's Timothy Howe urged Edmunds: "See that the bill will get back here in good season."

"And in good condition," added Sumner.

"Much better than it is now," Edmunds returned. There was some laughter.

Before the discussion ended a Democrat, Eli Saulsbury of Delaware, also gave an assurance. In whatever season the bill returned he would oppose it. Everlastingly the Senate dithered over the "equal rights" of black people, while white people suffered misery. "Let me ask the Senator," he looked at Edmunds, "whether, in the section of country which he represents, there are not hundreds and thousands of operatives to-day living upon the mere scanty pittance that is doled out to them by the large manufacturers, the rich men of that section, who use them worse than the slaves of the South were ever used?" For

38 Sumner's remarks and following colloquy, *Cong. Record*, 43rd Congress, 1st Session: 945–951.

Edmunds this was too much. Poor people suffered in Vermont. At least they had their rights.

> No task-master in New England has goaded them to toil with the whip, and has fed them as he does his cattle in the stable, according to the stock of wheat or fodder he might have on hand. Every poor man in New England has had always the equal rights of the citizen, the right to the school and the church and the cemetery, the right to make his own bargain for his own labor and the right to face the proudest and richest of his neighbors at the polls and in the ballot-box and in the jury-box and everywhere else. Now, when my friend finds a state of things in New England where about one-twentieth, perhaps one-thirtieth of the community have enslaved the rest ... made them as near brutes as it is possible for human malignity to make them, he may then undertake to draw parallels and comparisons between the condition of things.

The presiding officer, Thomas Ferry of Michigan, tapped his gavel. S.1 was referred to the Judiciary Committee. Initiative on civil rights passed to the House.

The House had already commenced. Benjamin Butler brought his measure forward directly. He found himself preempted. On December 8, Frank Morey, Republican of Louisiana, called up his own civil rights bill, H.R.473. Morey demanded a suspension of the rules of order so that measure could be read and passed at once.[39] Democrats objected. This hasty call denied them the opportunity to debate. Republican Charles Willard of Vermont urged Morey to refer his bill to the Judiciary Committee.

Josiah Walls rose, the first of the black representatives to engage in the contest. There was no need for consideration in committee, no need for discussion. Everyone knew the issue of civil rights as well as they knew the issue of amnesty. "We did not ask that the amnesty bill should be referred to a committee, and all we ask is that the same justice shall be done to us." The House sent Morey's bill to committee.

Ten days passed. On Thursday, December 18, Ben Butler's Civil Rights Bill – designated H.R.796 – advanced to the floor.[40] It received its first and its second reading. The next morning Butler moved the bill, urging swift passage.[41]

39 *Cong. Record*, 43rd Congress, 1st Session: 97. Morey's bill, H.R.473, repeated the form of Sumner's original S.1. For Butler's far less elaborate proposition H.R.796, see texts, Appendix B.

40 *Cong. Record*, 43rd Congress, 1st Session: 318.

41 *Cong. Record*, 43rd Congress, 1st Session: 340.

He proposed one hour for debate. Fifty minutes of that time he offered to opponents. Then he would call for the question, allowing one more hour to close debate. He yielded most of that hour to the gentleman from Georgia, Mr. Stephens, who had expressed a desire to speak.

Kentuckian James Beck rose. He intended to place no undue obstacles in the way of the Republicans' pet project. But his party demanded the chance to speak, to make its views known to the people. If the debate were cut down to a mere two hours' time, Democrats would resist. They would be compelled to filibuster, using dilatory motions to obstruct the whole proceeding. Stephens, too, appealed for at least two days of debate upon so important a question. In this first confrontation Butler yielded. He agreed to allow each member who wished to speak twenty minutes for his remarks. Debate would start at once. As this day's session was the last before Christmas break, it would continue when the House returned and conclude on the second day thereafter at four o'clock. He reserved the final hour for himself.

So Benjamin Butler began the discussion. His opening remarks briefly stated the case for civil rights and anticipated the case that would be raised against it. Private citizens, Butler agreed, engaged in private enterprise had the right to discriminate. The law could not deprive them of that privilege. The bill applied only to the public sphere. Public enterprises, licensed by the government, demanded that government protect the public rights of citizens. State government had failed in that task. National government must act. "State rights are one thing and State wrongs are another." Butler embraced the majesty of the Fourteenth Amendment. That amendment declared black people citizens of the United States. An obligation rested with the United States to defend its citizens. "It is not the duty of the State Legislatures to protect the interests of citizens of the United States." He denied the implication of social equality: the law applied to public institutions only, supported by public taxation or licensed by public authority.[42]

It was incumbent upon the Democrats to respond. Their frail paladin, Alexander Stephens, was unwell. James Beck, once a plantation overseer, stepped up to oversee the cause. Beck began with the constitutional argument. He invoked the opposition's heaviest weapon, the Supreme Court's Slaughter-House decision. That ruling, framed by a Republican court, invalidated any argument Republicans might make based on the Fourteenth Amendment, Beck argued. The Court had interpreted the amendment. It could not sustain a civil rights bill. The justices had distinguished two types of citizenship: United

42 Speech of Benjamin Butler, *Cong. Record* 43rd Congress, 1st Session: 340–341.

States citizenship and citizenship of a state. The amendment's prohibitions applied only to the former. Rights, privileges, immunities of citizens of states, as citizens of states, did not come within reach of the Fourteenth Amendment. Public corporations, licensed services, public schools, existing within a state were subject to regulation by that state. They could not be protected by an amendment restricted to rights of United States citizenship. Privileges and immunities invoked by the Civil Rights Bill – in railroad cars, in stage-coaches, steamboats, theaters, inns, and in public schools – were untouchable because they all operated under state license.[43]

Beck moved next to the ruin of the common schools. The matter was obvious. No decent white man would educate his children in proximity to Negroes. If Congress integrated public schools, whites would flee. States would withdraw financial support: no schooling but for the rich. The masses would grow up in ignorance.

> Our legislation will not affect the gentlemen in this hall. It does not affect me. I can send my children where I please to have them educated. When you undertake, by your legislation here, to force white and black, male and female, into the same school, the men who have wealth will not send their children; but the poor man will be compelled to send his, or let them grow up in ignorance and vice, which will be the alternative chosen in most instances.

Beck's twenty minutes neared its end. He introduced the ultimate horror, "social equality." Once the barriers were down the races would mingle. Mingling meant sex, a vortex of racial pollution, an inevitable, sequential chain of events: fraternization; miscegenation; mongrelization:

> I suppose there are gentlemen on this floor who would arrest, imprison, and fine a young woman in any State of the South if she were to refuse to marry a negro man on account of race, color, or previous condition of servitude, in the event of his making her a proposal of marriage, and her refusing on that ground. That would be depriving him of a right he had under the amendment, and Congress would be asked to take it up, and say, "This insolent white woman must be taught to know that it is a misdemeanor to deny a man marriage because of race, color, or previous condition of servitude"; and Congress will be urged to say after a while

43 Speech of James Beck, *Cong. Record*, 43rd Congress, 1st Session: 342–343.

> that that sort of thing must be put a stop to, and your conventions of colored men will come here asking you to enforce that right.[44]

Beck closed with a warning. Behind the bright painted façade of the Civil Rights Bill lurked a dark design. The law meant to cause unrest. Southern manhood, unable to bear the indignity of equality, would resist. The shackles once more would fasten.

> The purpose is, I fear, by this federal legislation, to impose laws so obnoxious in the States in which there are large numbers of colored persons that they will, whenever the proper occasion arises, be goaded on to demand their rights in the most offensive form. It will happen, of course, that in some localities those offensive demands will be resisted or grudgingly given. Arrests will be made; imprisonments will follow; fines will be inflicted; the cry will be raised that these men are disloyal ... the Army and Navy will be called into requisition upon statements made by spies and informers ... the people will be put under the ban, and their ballot-boxes closed, or they driven away and put into jails .... That is the meaning, the intent, the purpose, and the object of driving this legislation through now, and under these circumstances. Time will prove the truth of what I say.

Joseph Rainey took the floor. The first African American to sit in the House of Representatives spoke the first Republican response. He could not allow Beck's remarks to go unanswered. Rainey avoided the constitutional questions; the issue transcended petty points of law. "I view it in the light of humanity; I view it in the light of the progress and civilization which are now rapidly marching over this country." His people sought no special privileges. "We, sirs, would not ask of this Congress that they should legislate for us specifically as a class if we could only have those rights which this bill is designed to give us accorded us without this enactment."

> So long as he [the Negro] makes himself content with ordinary gifts, why it is all well; but when he aspires to be a man, when he seeks to have the rights accorded him that other citizens of the country enjoy, then he is asking too much.... States mete out to us what they think we ought to

44 Civil rights/miscegenation, for a recent discussion see Hannah Rosen, *Terror in the Heart of Freedom: Citizenship, Sexual Violence, and the Meaning of Race in the Postemancipation South* (Chapel Hill: 2009), 137–144.

> have, and we receive it without objection, [then] we are good, clever fellows, but just as soon as we begin to assert our manhood and demand our rights we are looked upon as men not worthy to be recognized, we become objectionable, we become obnoxious, and we hear this howl about social equality.[45]

Rainey rejected the social-equality howl. "The negro is not asking social equality ... that the two races should intermarry." Social dignity, not social equality:

> Why is it that colored members of Congress cannot enjoy the same immunities that are accorded to white members? Why cannot we stop at hotels without meeting objection? Why cannot we go into restaurants without being insulted? ... Why cannot we enjoy the same benefits that are accorded to our white colleagues on this floor?"

Rainey too finished with a warning.

> I tell you that the negro will never rest until he gets his rights.... Gentlemen, I say to you this discrimination must cease. We are determined to fight this question; we believe the Constitution gives us this right.... We say to you that if you will not obey the Constitution then the power is given by that Constitution for the enactment of such a law as will have a tendency to enforce the provisions thereof.

Rainey's remarks ended the first House discussion. The debate awaited its renewal in a new year. Members retired to celebrate Christmas and to consider, in the spirit of that charitable occasion, what they had heard.

January 5, 1874. Galleries were packed, a concourse of black people. "What a spectacle!" grumbled the Savannah *News*. "Caucasian humiliation, absurd and maudlin and mistaken philanthropy."[46] Debate reopened with the voice of the opposition. John T. Harris of Virginia took the floor. The congressman was 50, clean-shaven, a gentleman of the old school. He had served before, sitting in the 36th Congress. War had torn a hole in his career. He represented again his war-torn district, the Shenandoah Valley.

"Now, sir, what does this bill propose?" Harris inquired. Equality. "It proposes to put all upon an equality, and to force it upon the people of the country." Equality meant dictatorship. Government would dictate its citizens' lives,

---

45 Speech of Joseph Rainey: *Cong. Record*, 43rd Congress, 1st Session: 343–344.

46 Savannah *News*, January 9, 1874.

meddle with their affairs, control their modes of transport, their inns, their amusements, regulate their social contacts. America would be "in fact, if not in form, a monarchy or despotism."[47]

That point being made, Harris proceeded to clear up a misconception. The Civil Rights Bill rested upon a false assumption. "It seeks to enforce by law a doctrine not accepted by the minds nor received in the hearts of the people of the United States – that the negro in all things is the equal of the white man." To Congressman Harris it was obvious. He put it to the House: "I say there is not one gentleman upon this floor who can honestly say he really believes that the colored man is created his equal."

A voice cried out: "I can." Harris' challenge, clearly, was directed to the white members – to "gentlemen," in his eyes. But a black man had answered, Alonzo Ransier. Harris turned. "Of course you can. But I am speaking to the white men of the House; and, Mr. Speaker, I do not wish to be interrupted again, by him."

Murmurs rose from the floor, then settled down. Harris continued. Mixed schools. Indeed, not only schools but every useful system of public benevolence would suffer. They would come to ruin: poor-houses, shelters for the blind, asylums for the insane. Their inmates, be they destitute or desperate, homeless, witless, sightless, all would flee, terrorized by the presence of black persons.[48]

Harris had another bone to chew. Prejudice. That word served to defame his people, to stifle any attempt at rational discourse. Let a southern man merely presume to protest fanaticism, social leveling, and he was silenced with the cry of "Oh, prejudice!" It was hypocrisy. Prejudice existed. "It was born in the children of the South; born in our ancestors, and born in your ancestors in Massachusetts – that the colored man was inferior to the white."

"I deny that!" Alonzo Ransier, once again, could not contain his indignation. This time he called down chaos. Harris had worked his emotions raw: "I do not allow you to interrupt me," he cried. "Sit down; I am talking to white men; I am talking to *gentlemen*."

---

47 Speech of John T. Harris, *Cong. Record*, 43rd Congress, 1st Session: 375–378.

48 "A little strained," the New York *Times* commented, "that asylums of his State would be ruined if black and white lunatics and black and white blind persons were compelled to lie together." New York *Times*, January 7, 1874. The congressman's solicitude for the blind and the feeble-minded had a practical motive. His home town, Staunton, housed both the Virginia Institution for the Deaf, Dumb and Blind, and the Western District Asylum for the Insane. Harris had already introduced an amendment to counteract the menace to his constituency: "Amend, in lines 8 and 9, striking out the words 'or other benevolent institutions.'" *Cong. Record*, 43rd Congress, 1st Session: 339.

Members jumped to their feet. Rockwood Hoar: "I call the gentleman from Virginia to order. When a member ceases to address the whole House he ceases to have a right to the floor."

Speaker Blaine had left the hall. Henry Dawes sat in the chair. His perpetually worried countenance took on an expression of genuine alarm. His gavel sounded. "The rule requires a gentleman to address the Chair." Harris refused. Ransier, not he, was out of order, interrupting a speaker who had the floor. The Chair itself was out of order: "The gentleman from Massachusetts should begin correcting the evils on his right and not on his left." Dawes banged again. An uneasy calm returned. Harris plunged ahead.

> I say, sir, that prejudice may exist, but it is a natural prejudice that God himself placed in the hearts of southern children and the southern people, and it becomes us to consider that prejudice in our action here ... whether you will not only invade the asylums for the insane, but drive the poor children of Virginia and of the South from the public schools, expelling the little orphans with fair hair and blue eyes, because they have been taught by God and by their mothers that colored children are not their equals.

Ransier bit his tongue. Harris closed with a threat. War had ended. The South generously admitted defeat. Let the victors not presume upon that magnanimity. It was not a boundless virtue. "[Those who] have trifled with the liberties of a generous people, they will find revenge as rapid as the whirlwind and as merciless as the angel of death."

Harris' speech drew mixed reactions. Northern papers, even moderate sheets, disliked it. "Ill-tempered ... full of unseemly contempt," remarked the Chicago *Tribune*. "A display of plantation manners," wrote the New York *Tribune*.[49] Southerners disagreed. Harris' critics were ill-mannered: "treachery to their own race."[50]

With harsh sentiments ringing in its ears, jangled nerves, restlessness in the galleries and on the floor, the House prepared to hear the opposition's champion. The time had come for Alexander Stephens to speak his mind. Almost at once he drew a soft, soothing, sleep-inducing blanket over everyone. One might applaud or repudiate Stephens' message, but members and spectators exhaled. The scene became hushed.

---

49 Chicago *Tribune*, New York *Tribune*, January 6, 1874.

50 Richmond *Dispatch*, January 9, 1874.

The tiny, shriveled man, dressed all in black, silver hair falling to his collar, spoke in a thin shrill voice that penetrated the silence of the House. His regular seat was at the front, but Stephens had himself wheeled to a place at the very back row. A barricade of books propped him up. A glass of water stood nearby, and a silver mug containing some medicinal or other liquid stimulant. Members gathered to assist him. James Beck turned the pages of his manuscript. Tennessee's William Crutchfield guarded his crutches, which threatened continually to slide to the floor.[51] Stephens sat immobile. Only his burning eyes, said the New York *Times,* defied the emaciation of his body.[52]

The crowd that had filled the spectators' gallery left disappointed. The thin voice piped in a monotone. "Most members," noted the New York *Tribune,* "drifted away after the first half-hour and occupied themselves at their desks shuffling papers."[53] Alexander Stephens said little that had not already been said. He urged states to accord enfranchised people their rights. He simply could not accept enforcement of those rights by the hand of the United States government. Therein lay dictatorship. "Colored men, as citizens, were entitled to full protection in their civil rights without any individual proscription." But "it was the duty of the respective States, and not that of the federal government, to act in order to secure them." Beware centralization. Keep sacred respect for State Rights.

To some northern observers it seemed Stephens dreamed of the antiquated political doctrines of his youth. Absent from his words, however, was any note of racial animosity, of bitterness toward black people that had pervaded the speeches of Beck and Harris. He made no appeal to prejudice. He asserted no dogma of inequality. To that extent Frederick Douglass' hope that he might find in the old Confederate a sympathetic voice was not misplaced.

Stephens looked back to the days of secession and war. Slavery had unleashed the war. The South – he did not deny it – had fought for slavery. War had ended slavery. He proposed a paradox. "While I do not hold the doctrine of the equality of races of men, yet I do maintain the great truth … that all men are created equal."

> All men have an equal right to justice, and to stand, so far as governmental powers are concerned or exercised over them, perfectly equal before the law. This is the right of all classes of men, whether white, red, brown, or black. This American principle is as broad as our jurisdiction, and as

51 New York *Tribune,* January 6, 1874.

52 New York *Times,* January 6, 1874.

53 New York *Tribune,* January 6, 1874.

> catholic as the doctrines of Him who first announced to the world the true principle of justice; that is, "As ye would that men should do to you, do ye also to them likewise."[54]

All men are created equal. "This great truth was first enunciated on the 4th of July, 1776.... It came from the pen of Jefferson, the apostle of liberty upon this continent." But Jefferson had placed the operation of his great truth within the framework of a federated democracy. There it must remain. To the states let black people look for justice and for the safeguard of their equal rights. He reached his peroration.

> The old Jeffersonian democratic republican principles are not dead, and will never die so long as a true devotee of liberty lives.... Dead, indeed! When the tides of ocean cease to ebb and flow, when the winds of heaven are hushed into perpetual silence, when the clouds no longer thunder, when earth's electric bolts are no longer felt nor heard, when her internal fires go out, then, and not before, will these principles cease to animate and move the liberty-loving masses of this country.

Stephens slumped back in his chair. His effort had taken all his strength. Assistants wheeled him from the chamber. His health collapsed. In April he returned to Georgia. "I am going home to die," he told reporters.[55] He did not die. His seat in the House, however, remained vacant for the rest of the session.

Alexander Stephens had appealed for reconciliation. Was it from a shaken sense of guilt, or a conscience haunted by the memory and carnage of war? He extended the hand of compromise. Neither side took up the hand. Republicans condescended to laugh. "Poor old Rip Van Winkle did not drift further behind during his twenty years' sleep than Stephens has during his forced seclusion from public life," sneered the Indianapolis *Journal*.[56] Democratic papers, the kindly ones, offered him the favor of silence. "The fact is, Alex is slightly tedious," concluded the Nashville *Banner*, "and when he grows eloquent ... he is not impressive."[57] The Atlanta *Constitution*, which he had challenged to comment on his words, passed them by without comment. Unkind southern sheets

---

54 Speech of Alexander Stephens, *Cong. Record*, 43rd Congress 1st Session: 378–382.

55 Louisville *Courier-Journal*, April 30; Nashville *Banner*, May 2, 1874.

56 Indianapolis *Journal*, January 7, 1874. See Schott, *Stephens of Georgia*, 467: "Unreconstructed rebels came in many guises. Some, like Toombs, kicked and cussed till they died. Others simply could not or would not understand that the war had changed the nation, its Constitution, and the South irrevocably. Stephens was one of these."

57 Nashville *Banner*, January 10, 1874.

commented loudly. "So far as we have been able to observe," the Montgomery *Advertiser* snapped, "the only difference between Butler and himself was as to the mode of carrying into operation a theory of negro rights and social equality. Butler was of opinion that Congress should enforce negro social equality by penal statute. Mr. Stephens seemed to think that the State Legislature should execute the programme!"[58]

Back in Congress, Alonzo Ransier took the floor. Ignoring Stephens, he returned to the remarks of James Beck. Ransier's anger had cooled. But his words oozed sarcasm:

> It is feared by the gentleman from Kentucky and those he represents ... that if we colored people are put upon a plane of civil equality ... we, by virtue of our intellectual superiority and our moral and physical force, if not numbers, will absorb the race to which he and they belong. Let me thank him, in the name of the colored people of this country, for the compliment he has, perhaps unconsciously, paid them, but I must here deny that that would necessarily follow civil equality in this country, or that there is any serious intention on our part to thus destroy those for whom he speaks or the race to which he belongs. We are known, Mr. Speaker, to be too magnanimous for that. If we are powerful, we know how to be merciful.[59]

His people, Ransier said, requested only what the law accorded all citizens – common decency. "Mr. Speaker, all these people ask is an equal chance in the race of life." An equal chance in life, Ransier added, extended also to the rights of women:

58 Montgomery *Advertiser*, January 14, 1874.

59 Speech of Alonzo Ransier: *Cong. Record*, 43rd Congress, 1st Session: 382–383. Ransier's irony was sharp but not original. Satirist David Ross Locke had already developed the theme in a popular lecture: "It is firmly asserted that he [the black man] would not labor; yet the same men undertook the large job of conquering the North that they might continue to enjoy the fruits of his labor. He was said to be so stupid as to be incapable of receiving even the rudiments of an education, and yet we found it necessary, in our States, to put stringent laws with fearful penalties attached to prevent him from doing it. It was held by eloquent speakers that he would invade the North, and, as he was too indolent to work, he would fill our almshouses and jails; and the same speakers would assert a moment later, with equal eloquence, that, accustomed as he always had been to labor, he would work for less pay than white men, and throw them all out of employment.... Lower down on the scale of creation than the baboon, they were fearful he would, if not restrained by law, teach their schools, sit as judges, and be elected to Congress.... Immeasurably beneath them in every particular, they felt called upon to perpetually cry 'Protect us from nigger equality' – and so on." David Ross Locke, "Cussed be Canaan," in *The Struggles (Social, Financial, and Political) of Petroleum V. Nasby* (Boston:1873), 632–633.

> And may the day be not far distant when American citizenship in civil and political rights and public privileges shall cover not only those of our sex, but those of the opposite one also; until which time the Government of the United States cannot be said to rest upon the consent of the governed.

The afternoon drew on. The House heard from one more Democrat, Roger Q. Mills, congressman at-large of Texas. State rights, said Mills. That doctrine must prevail. "The States have always exercised the right to fix the status of their citizens, and they will continue to do so.... Whether the white people admit the black people to terms of social equality with them is a question that belongs to the people of the States, to be exercised by them or not in their own sovereign pleasure." Mills recalled Harris' warning. Do not presume upon the forbearance of the southern people. "I see ruinous and fearful mischief in this measure. He [the black man] cannot force association with an unwilling people."[60]

The floor belonged to Robert Elliott, designated by the Republicans to speak their principal address – a black man to give their answer to Alexander Stephens. Time was short. Members were restless. Republicans preferred that their champion should pronounce his words on a new day. Butler rose. He called for the House to adjourn. If the gentleman from South Carolina would consent to postpone his address, the House would hear him in the morning.

"I am willing," Elliott replied, "that the sense of the House shall be tested on a motion to adjourn."

"Then I renew the motion," replied Butler. "We have earned our salaries to-day."

Tuesday, January 6. Congress and the nation awoke to the prospect of a unique spectacle, a great speech on a matter of national importance to be spoken by a black man, on behalf of a national party and in reply to one who had been practically the leader of the Confederacy. Crowds filled the galleries in anticipation of a historic moment. Robert Elliott did not disappoint them. His oration struck the highest note achieved by an African American on the national stage since emancipation. His deep, earnest voice, wrote the New York *Times*, carried through the hall. "Every sentence closed with a musical cadence."[61] "A few extreme Democrats," one reporter observed, "pretended to be busy with letters and documents, but the eloquence of the speaker soon drew them away from their affected preoccupation and compelled them to

60 Speech of Roger Q. Mills, *Cong. Record*, 43rd Congress 1st Session: 382–386.
61 New York *Times*, January 7, 1874.

listen."[62] Senators crossed over. Dignitaries stepped inside to witness the scene. (see Illustrations 3 and 4)

ILLUSTRATION 3 Robert B. Elliott
SOURCE: LIBRARY OF CONGRESS

62 Cincinnati *Commercial*, January 6, 1874.

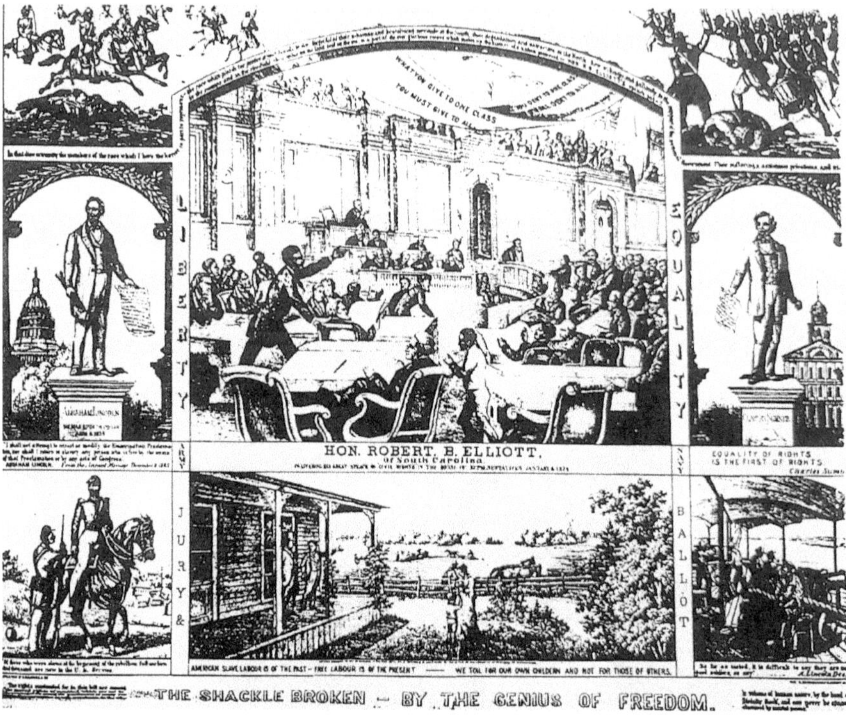

ILLUSTRATION 4 Speech of Robert Elliott
SOURCE: LIBRARY OF CONGRESS

"I regret, sir," Elliott began, "that the dark hue of my skin may lend a color to the imputation that I am controlled by motives personal to myself in my advocacy of this great measure of national justice.... I advocate it, sir, because it is right."

> The rights contended for in this bill are among the sacred rights of mankind, which are not to be rummaged for among old parchments or musty records; they are written as with a sunbeam, in the whole volume of human nature, by the hand of Divinity itself, and can never be erased or obscured by mortal power.[63]

Sunbeams did not blind Elliott to consideration of the legal points. The Slaughter-House ruling had been misinterpreted. The Court had not dismissed but rather

63 Speech of Robert Elliott, *Cong. Record*, 43rd Congress, 1st Session: 407–410. See also, Peggy Lamson, *The Glorious Failure*, 174–181.

confirmed the power of the Fourteenth Amendment. It declared that amendment a guarantee to all citizens of freedom, "not only their nominal freedom, but their complete freedom from those who had formerly exercised unlimited dominion over them." Let states control the operation of abattoirs. What did it matter? Who could compare the butchery of cattle with the slaughter of a people's rights? Who could equate the stigmatizing of a race with a regulation for improved municipal sanitation?

> Are the colored race to be assimilated to an unwholesome trade or to combustible materials? ... If we are to be likened in legal view to "unwholesome trades," to "large and offensive collections of animals," to "noxious slaughter-houses," to "the offal and stench which attend on certain manufactures," let it be avowed. If that is still the political doctrine of the party to which the gentlemen belong, let it be put on record. If State laws which deny us the common rights and privileges of other citizens, upon no possible or conceivable ground save one of prejudice, or of "taste," ... are to be placed under the protection of a decision which affirms the right of a State to regulate the police of her great cities, then the decision is in conflict with the bill before us. No man will dare maintain such a doctrine. Does the gentleman from Kentucky say that my good is promoted when I am excluded from the public inn? Is the health and safety of the community promoted?

James Beck's facetious thrust, that civil rights would force white girls to marry black men, struck Elliott badly. "Mr. Speaker, I have neither the time nor the inclination to notice the many illogical and forced conclusions, the numerous transfers of terms, or the vulgar insinuations which further incumber the argument of the gentleman from Kentucky. Reason and argument are worse than wasted upon those who meet every demand for political and civil liberty by such ribaldry as this."

Elliott turned to Alexander Stephens. He would not disparage the old Confederate chieftain. His venerable presence entitled him to respect, but not to immunity. His participation in this debate, or any debate on civil rights, was unacceptable. "When the honorable gentleman from Georgia lends his voice and influence to defeat this measure, I do not shrink from saying that it is not from him that the American House of Representatives should take lessons in matters touching human rights." Nor did Elliott spare Harris of Virginia:

> To the diatribe of the gentleman from Virginia who spoke on yesterday, and who so far transcended the limits of decency and propriety as to

> announce upon this floor that his remarks were addressed to white men alone, I shall have no word of reply. Let him feel that a negro was not only too magnanimous to smite him in his weakness, but was even charitable enough to grant him the mercy of his silence.

Robert Elliott reduced the civil rights debate to a sound-bite, one simple encapsulating phrase: "What you give to one class you must give to all; what you deny to one class you shall deny to all."[64] For his finale he turned to the Bible. He brought the House to a standing ovation. He recited the Prayer of Ruth.

> The Holy Scripture tells us of an humble hand-maiden who long, faithfully and patiently gleaned in the rich fields of her wealthy kinsman; and we are told further that at last, in spite of her humble antecedents, she found complete favor in his sight. For over two centuries our race has "reaped down your fields." The cries and woes which we have uttered have "entered into the ears of the Lord of Sabaoth," and we are at last politically free. The last vestiture only is needed – civil rights. Having gained this, we may, with hearts overflowing with gratitude, and thankful that our prayer has been granted, repeat the prayer of Ruth: "Entreat me not to leave thee, or to return from following after thee, wither thou goest, I will go; and where thou lodgest, I will lodge; thy people shall be my people, and thy God my God; where thou diest, will I die, and there will I be buried."

Shouts resounded on the floor and echoed across the galleries. They drowned out the banging of the Speaker's gavel. Members thronged Elliott. A solid column formed in the aisle, moving past his seat to offer congratulations.[65] Among those who "extended the hand" was Sunset Cox.[66] General William T. Sherman likewise clasped Elliott's hand.[67] Newspapers sang praises. "A champion, able and fearless, suddenly arose to wield the lance of freedom and carry dismay to the supporters of oppression," the *National Republican* exulted.[68] *Harper's Weekly* wrote the congressman's biography and posted his portrait for

---

64 A century later one congressman echoed Elliott's phrase: "What is granted to one will be granted to all.... It cannot be vanquished because its people have something to live by and to fight for." Speech of William St. Onge of Connecticut, *Cong. Record*, 88th Congress, 1st Session: 12,406 (1964).

65 New York *Tribune*, January 7, 1874.

66 Cincinnati *Commercial*, January 6, 1874.

67 New York *Times*, January 7, 1874.

68 Washington, *National Republican*, January 7, 1874.

posterity.[69] The Chicago *Tribune* disapproved of the Civil Rights Bill; it hailed Elliott's oration nonetheless.

> It is an eloquent monument to the human progress that has been wrought in discord, peril and civil war. It is the brilliant product of a fiery furnace.... He has proved to the world that our progress has not been in vain.... He has furnished an animate and speaking refutation to the effete and now almost extinct ideas upon which the people of the South foolishly and recklessly sought to found a nation.[70]

The contrast with Alexander Stephens did not pass unnoticed. "There stand in the House the same Stephens," wrote the Cleveland *Herald*, "and by his side one of his former cattle, now clothed in the dignity of a freeman, the political equal of him who was Vice President of a Confederacy whose corner stone was human bondage."[71] Even the New York *Herald* found Elliott's eloquence impossible to deny. "Men who still cling tenaciously to their old prejudices find themselves met in argument and overthrown by the very negroes whose inferiority they love to proclaim."[72]

Southern papers were less enthusiastic. "Elliott is a very black negro," the Louisville *Courier-Journal* observed. "He has the same hatred for the white race as that which inspired the negroes of San Domingo." Not eloquence but insolence was on display: "a speech full of insolence and malignity ... studied insolence to Messrs. Beck, Stephens and Harris, to try to provoke these gentlemen to an unseemly altercation with a negro."[73] The Montgomery *Advertiser* was disgusted. Elliott had no business in Congress. He belonged as a field hand. "It would be infinitely better for the 'Wards of the Nation' if they were allowed to cultivate cotton, corn and tobacco, which they would naturally do if they were left alone." The speech was "an exhibition of insolence and puerility."[74]

Insolence, the *Courier-Journal* agreed, but puerility? The speech was too good: "Their grand idea was to try to make it appear that a negro could be the peer of the white man in debate." Since that was impossible, clearly Elliott was a trained parrot taught to recite words written for him by a white man. The question was which white man. Ben Butler seemed a likely choice, or Rockwood Hoar. Reports named them one or the other as the presumed

69 *Harper's Weekly*, February 14, 1874, pp. 149–150.
70 Chicago *Tribune*, January 8, 1874.
71 Quoted in Indianapolis *Journal*, January 9, 1874.
72 New York *Herald*, January 8, 1874.
73 Louisville *Courier-Journal*, January 7, 1874.
74 Montgomery *Advertiser*, January 14, 1874.

ghost-writer.[75] James Beck favored the latter. "I suppose Judge Hoar has set up all night to write that nigger's speech for him," he remarked.[76]

African Americans were ecstatic. Congressman Charles Clayton shipped home to San Francisco a printing of 100 copies. The *Elevator* offered them, along with individually-wrapped copies of the paper, to its readers for the special price of 25¢.[77] The *New National Era* hailed Elliott: "Mr. Elliott can no longer be claimed by South Carolina as her representative alone; he belongs to us all and is the pride of us all."[78] On Saturday evening, January 10, at Elliott's boarding-house at 320 Second Street, NE, the elite of Washington's black citizenry assembled. Bands played airs. Richard Cain and John Roy Lynch offered tributes.[79] Daniel Straker spoke on behalf of the National Civil Rights Council: "We congratulate the African race all over the world, that, to its catalogue of great men, whose virtues and ability have shone in meridian splendor, it now adds the name of Hon. Robert B. Elliott."[80] That same evening, across town, Alexander Stephens joined a dozen of his particular friends for dinner at the National Hotel. No bands played. But the mood was upbeat. "The occasion was one of much interest, and sociability."[81]

The unenviable privilege of following Robert Elliott to the House floor, once the applause subsided, fell to Democrat James Blount of Georgia. He rejected the prayer of Ruth. "Whither thou goest" – in Pullman palace cars, steamboat cabins or stage-coaches – "where thou lodgest" – in first-class hotels – "where thou diest and are buried" – in public cemeteries – he wanted no black people to go. Otherwise there would be sex (as between the biblical Ruth and her smitten kinsman Boaz). Black persons had their own vehicles for going places: "they have railroad facilities, comfortable and satisfactory." They had access to lodging: "the negroes have their own inns." There was earth enough to dispose of their remains: "they have the same cemetery with the whites, divided between

75 Baltimore *Sun*, January 12; Richmond *Dispatch*, January 8; Savannah *News*, February 26; Chicago *Tribune*, February 3; Indianapolis *Journal*, January 28, 1874.

76 Boston *Commonwealth*, January 23, 1875. The *Commonwealth* refuted Beck's assertion. South Carolina's black lawyer Richard T. Greener recalled the genesis of the speech. Elliott, he related, composed the words as he traveled to Washington to face his great moment: "The entire speech, as it stands reported in the *Record*, with the exception of the impromptu excoriation of Harris and the legal argument, was written before he left Columbia from a skeleton, rather a germ, which he jotted down while on the cars."

77 San Francisco *Elevator*, January 24, February 21, 1874.

78 Washington, *New National Era*, January 8, 1874.

79 Washington, *Forney's Sunday Chronicle*, January 11, 1874.

80 Washington, *New National Era*, January 15, 1874.

81 Washington, *Forney's Sunday Chronicle*, January 11, 1874.

the races." What more did they need? "A kindly feeling exists between the races. Let our people alone."[82]

Speakers rose on both sides. John Bright, Democrat of Tennessee, exploited an inconsistency. Republicans claimed love for the Fourteenth Amendment, its rights and privileges. Yet they denied those rights and privileges to female persons born or naturalized in the United States. In the 42nd Congress the House had received a petition from Mrs. Victoria Woodhull asking for women's suffrage. Her plea had gone to Ben Butler's Judiciary Committee. The committee rejected it. "I invite the attention of the distinguished chairman of the committee to this argument, and I wish no evasion of it." Butler could only say that he had dissented from the committee's decision. "I made a minority report," Butler replied. "I know you did," said Bright. "I have it before me."

Things had gone too far, Bright concluded. They had gone too fast. "No nation of their race before has emerged from the broken chains of slavery, been habilitated, and raised to the grandeur of American citizens, in the same length of time." A little patience was wanted. "Sir, he can stand a little tobacco-smoke in a railroad car."[83]

Missouri Democrat John Glover argued a different hypocrisy. Republicans professed humanitarian ideals, but they disdained to live by them. They forced others to endure repugnant social contacts while they retreated behind walls of money and privilege, far from all distasteful things.

> When has President Grant chosen to take his children from a white school and send them to a colored school? When has he seen fit to leave his box at the theater and go to the pit or the gallery to get in contact with those who cannot come to him? ... Why have we never witnessed the "civil rights" advocates setting one solitary example of the propriety, the advantage, and the excellence of a law which they propose to enforce against their remonstrating countrymen with fire and sword?[84]

---

82 Speech of James Blount: *Cong. Record*, 43rd Congress, 1st Session: 410–412.

83 Speech of John Bright: *Cong. Record*, 43rd Congress, 1st Session: 414–416.

84 Speech of John Glover: *Cong. Record*, 43rd Congress, 1st Session, Appendix: 4–5. "Limousine liberals" was the phrase in 1964. "Wealthy white people have retreated to the splendid isolation of Georgetown," Louisiana's Senator Allen Ellender declared, "guarded by bridges not dissimilar to the drawbridges and moats of yore. Only the poor white people are affected by forced association.... The poor are always the ones who must submit." *Cong. Record*, 88th Congress, 2nd Session: 14,277. Or, as Tom Lehrer sang, "It's fun to eulogize/ The people you despise/ As long as you don't let 'em in your school." Tom Lehrer, "National Brotherhood Week," album: "That Was The Year That Was" [1965].

One more African-American Representative spoke. Florida's Josiah Walls did not enjoy Elliott's reputation for eloquence. Yet Walls put his finger on a pertinent point: the issue of state neglect. Democrats dismissed the Fourteenth Amendment. Unless states actively legislated to deny their citizens equal rights its protections could not be invoked. States, said Walls, did not need to pass discriminatory laws. Failure to protect civil rights was an act of omission as palpable as any act of commission. State sanctioned injustice, be it active or passive, called forth the powers of the Fourteenth Amendment.[85]

Prejudice, gentlemen insisted, could not be legislated away. So be it, said Walls. Punishment would do the job. "Public sentiment needs penal correction.... We will then hear no more of a public sentiment that feeds upon the remnants of the rotten dogmas of the past, and seeks a vitality in the exercise of a tyranny both cheap and unmanly."

Butler's original schedule called for speeches to conclude on the second day following the Christmas break. Then he would call for the vote. Extensions of time to several speakers and the postponement of Elliott's oration drew proceedings into a third day. On Wednesday, January 7, the Chairman took the floor. He delivered a bombshell. He did not call for a vote. He called for the bill to be recommitted, returned to the Judiciary Committee for further review.

Democrats professed amazement. New York's Fernando Wood rose. It was a farce. Republicans never intended to pass the bill. It was to be dangled before the eyes of their black constituents, but not to be consummated in law. Butler denied the accusation. Twelve different amendments had already been proposed. To debate each one would occupy another two days. Better to consider them in committee and return the bill purified: "then we shall not allow any more time to be spent in fruitless debate over it, but make it the law as speedily as due regard to legislative forms will permit."

Democrats smelled a rat. Butler's hesitation, in fact, did not surprise them. Diligent members of the press had anticipated it. All was not well within the

85 Speech of Josiah Walls: *Cong. Record*, 43rd Congress, 1st Session: 416–417. Walls' doctrine of state neglect had support. Justice Joseph Bradley wrote in 1871 to Judge William Woods: "The Fourteenth Amendment prohibits States from denying to all persons within its jurisdiction the equal protection of the laws. Denying includes inaction as well as action, and denying the equal protection of the laws includes the omission to protect, as well as the omission to pass laws for protection." North Carolina's Senator John Pool declared in 1870: "If a State, by omission, neglects to give to every citizen within its borders a free, fair, and full exercise and enjoyment of his rights," it should be the duty of the federal government to protect those rights. On the evolution of the argument of state neglect, see Pamela Brandwein, *Rethinking the Judicial Settlement of Reconstruction* (New York: 2011), 28–57, 161–183.

majority's ranks. On January 6, the day of Elliott's speech, both the Atlanta *Constitution* and the New York *Tribune* reported that the bill would not be put to a vote. "Timid Republicans seem to insist upon this action," wrote the *Constitution*. "Carlos," the Mobile *Register's* Washington correspondent, quoted a Republican source: "If that bill passes it will destroy the Republican party." Carlos rejoiced: "Some faint glimmer of truth has reached the Radical brain."

One factor, mixed schools, particularly disturbed the Republican equilibrium. Pressure to remove that incendiary provision was intense. Butler himself reportedly admitted that fear of that clause had caused him to pull the bill back.[86] The decision to recommit, the New York *Times* wrote, came from "motives of expediency." The most expedient solution seemed simply to eliminate the mixed-schools provision. Softening the Civil Rights Bill might make it easier to swallow for endangered Republicans. The *Times* reported it as a fact: mixed schools would go.[87] The Fredericksburg, Virginia, *Ledger* considered itself well posted. Its owner, James Sener, was a Republican member of Congress. He also predicted the school clause's demise.[88]

Supporters of integrated schools reacted with alarm. From Boston, Wendell Phillips wrote Butler: "I earnestly beg you not to drop the school clause. In the name of all your record – for the sake of all we hope from you and plan for you, I trust you will consent to no such treachery."[89] From the presidium of the National Civil Rights Council George Downing produced a manifesto, "An Address to the Colored People of the United States." Black folks must inform backsliding politicians where they stood. Politicians understood only one kind of pressure. They must not take the votes of black constituents for granted. "Organize; cause your power to be properly felt.... Come together; organize in every city and town ... every man and woman in every community."[90]

Downing and his colleagues awoke to a new realization. The struggle for civil rights would not be short. Up to now all seemed secure. The party had endorsed civil rights. The party held a monumental majority. The National Civil Rights Council had merely to monitor its progress. Now all had changed. The council prepared for a prolonged engagement.

---

86 Alfred H. Kelly, "The Congressional Controversy over School Segregation, 1867–1875," *American Historical Review*, 64 (1959): 553–554.

87 New York *Times*, January 8, 16, 1874.

88 Fredericksburg *Ledger*, January 9, 1874.

89 "Make no such sad misstep – We have been able to say hitherto that never in any critical moment for the negro, since 1861 have you done anything wrong – or given an uncertain sound. Save us the right to boast that still." Wendell Phillips to Benjamin Butler, January 24, 1874. Butler-Ames Papers, Smith College.

90 NCRC Manifesto: Washington *National Republican*, January 21, 1874.

> Money will be needed; *this council must have funds;* it will have to carry on an extensive correspondence, use the columns of newspapers, have a clerk or clerks, and agents.... Your council needs your co-operation. No effort, no matter how desirable and worthy, has succeeded without material support.[91]

Black people answered Downing's call. Atlanta on the night of January 26 witnessed a mass rally. The *Constitution* ran a humorous headline: "How Sambo Proposes to Get His Rights." But it recounted a serious affair. The rally overflowed City Hall, "a perfect mob of six or seven hundred negroes." The temper of the crowd was ominous, "showing their fixed determination to make trouble if the bill passes."[92] The Atlantans drew up a petition to Congress. They demanded the Civil Rights Bill in full. Fiery speeches followed. Richard H. Carter, student at Atlanta University (or, as per the *Constitution*, "a young mulatto"), addressed the assembly: "When this government takes care only of citizens of one color then this government will go to the devil. We say to Congress that we want this bill passed at once, and will have it." Another enthusiastic university scholar, George S. Smith, spoke next: "Anyone who would not shed his blood to procure his children their rights does not deserve the name of a man." Mr. Smith added further remarks. But, the *Constitution's* reporter concluded, they were unprintable, "too disgusting for publication."[93]

In Tennessee a meeting filled the City Hall of Chattanooga.[94] Black people rallied in the District of Columbia. Pinchback spoke. "He was tired of cringing and fawning; he thought it was time for the colored men to show that they duly appreciated their importance and the influence they ought to exert upon politics and politicians."[95]

Republicans and their black supporters danced a delicate pas de deux. The party tried not to alienate nearly a million African-American voters, even as it tried to avoid a white backlash upon which Democrats could feed. African-American leaders tried to stimulate the party's zeal. They could threaten. But they could threaten only so far, for politically they had nowhere else to go. Nothing in the policies or spirit of the Democratic Party promised any welcome.

---

91 Washington *National Republican*, January 21, 1874.

92 Atlanta *Constitution*, January 27, 1874.

93 Students Carter and Smith, named summarily in the *Constitution's* account, can be identified, listed among alumni in the Catalogue of Atlanta University of 1878. Carter then was working as a teacher in Sparta, Georgia, Smith as a pastor in Raleigh, North Carolina.

94 Chattanooga *Times*, February 11, 13, 1874.

95 Cincinnati *Commercial*, February 12, 1874.

The National Civil Rights Council applied pressure. Opponents held a counterweight. If the school clause remained they would add a clause to it – a mandate for separate-but-equal schools. The amendment was already proposed. A Republican, Lloyd Lowndes of Maryland, had offered it on the third day of debate. By the end of January the Judiciary Committee began to consider the proviso.

Merely the possibility panicked the National Civil Rights Council. To be sure, separate-but-equal was practiced everywhere. But it was not yet established in the law of the nation. If Congress attached this proviso it would enshrine that concept, officially and irrevocably. Black people would become citizens apart, quarantined by law. Downing delivered the appeal in person. He, John Mercer Langston, John F. Cook, Milton M. Holland and Charles Purvis appeared before the Judiciary Committee. They carried a petition, "on behalf of the colored citizens of the United States." Anything, they protested, was better than legalizing separate-but-equal. Better no school clause at all.

> Our Constitution and our laws ... recognize and tolerate no measurement of individual rights predicated upon complexion. The word "white" is not to be found in our Constitution. The fathers, after due deliberation, refused to put it there. By what authority can Congress legislate as if it were there? ... We feel deeply on this subject. This consideration of justice has great weight with us. It seems to be better to have no mention made of schools in your proposed civil rights bill than to have this proviso made law.[96]

For the moment George Downing's intervention had an effect. Talk of separate-but-equal died down. The Judiciary Committee kept the school clause alive. But it kept the bill from the House floor. In the Judiciary Committee, as in the nation, restlessness reigned. Eleven frustrated legislators squirmed. They heard calls for mixed schools and calls for war if mixed schools remained. The gentlemen of the committee argued discreetly, behind closed doors. Reporters caught a few gleanings. Historians are more fortunate. We possess a chink through which to peer past the closed committee-room door. It was not a pretty sight. Left behind among papers scattered in its files the committee preserved evidence of its dilemma. Drafts of the members' thoughts survive. Hastily scrawled, revised, erased, rewritten, they display futile attempts at amending the bill. Along with its drafts the committee abandoned the detritus

96 Washington *National Republican*, January 27, 1874.

of its deliberations: newspaper clippings, letters, editorials pro and con. They tell the tale of eleven baffled congressmen.[97]

Telegrams accumulated in the committee's mail. Dr. John H. Henry cabled from Alabama: "Colored men must have civil rights. The South will not give it. The life of the Republican Party depends on it." From Jefferson City, Missouri, wrote M. Henry Smith, principal of the Lincoln Institute Normal School for Colored Children: "This [mixed schools] I consider the most important part of the bill. I hope it will not be changed."

On the other side, someone clipped a column from *The National Teacher,* organ of the National Educational Association. It will have perplexed the perplexed. Mixed schools were right. They were just. But they were justly dangerous. They should exist. But they should not. "Race prejudices are too strong for such a measure." That left segregated schools. And yet, the national educators warned, segregated schools were bad. Inevitably they became second-class schools: "They must be made EQUAL." That would cost taxpayers a heavy load. "Prejudices are, at best, an expensive luxury," concluded the *National Teacher*, "and if white people will cherish them, let them pay the cost." That conclusion must have given the committeemen a good laugh. Evidently it cost the *National Teacher* nothing to suggest that politicians suggest to taxpayers a rise in taxes.

One committee member clipped a different message. The Washington *National Republican* reprinted a long editorial written by Thomas Conway, Louisiana's former Superintendent of Education. Conway had actually presided over a system of mixed public schools, an experiment enshrined in Louisiana's Reconstruction constitution. The experiment, the superintendent insisted, had succeeded beyond all hope. The unknown committeeman took up his pencil. He underlined Conway's exuberant passages, picturing the joyful camaraderie of white children and black at the opening of New Orleans schools: "Before I reached my office that day the children of both races, who, on the school question seemed like deadly enemies, were, many of them, joined in a circle, playing on the green, under the shade of the wide-spreading live-oak."

Conway's idyll impressed some committeemen. Others fretted over the *National Teacher's* concerns. An expert arrived, the nation's preeminent educator, Rev. Dr. Barnas Sears, Director of the Peabody Education Fund. Rev. Dr. Sears ordered them to disregard every lyrical word Superintendent Conway had written. Ring-around-the-rosy under spreading oaks: nonsense! Integration would

---

97 Unsorted papers, National Archives, Judiciary Committee File, Forty-third Congress.

destroy the public schools. Drop it, or else the Peabody Fund would drop its support of education in the South.[98]

Amendments. Perhaps the committee could split the baby. Leave in mixed schools, but make them palatable. Two artifacts of aborted legislative surgery remain, handwritten drafts composed in different hands. Both were rejected evidently, then scrapped in frustration. They lay derelict on the committee-room table, whence someone swept them up into the disused files.

One draft remains anonymous. Its author left his work unfinished, disjointed. Let the clause remain, but allow states to opt out. If they opted out they must demonstrate a genuine commitment to adequately-funded separate schools. Ah, but how did one define adequacy? What criteria should satisfy the law? What deadline should the law impose for compliance? The draftsman threw down his pen.[99] That draft fell by the wayside. No one wished to impose undefinable mandates, calculate pro rata expenditures for colored schools.

Another draft originated outside the committee. Its inspiration, however, came from inside. Its author was a celebrated social activist, best known for his work in prison reform, Enoch Cobb Wines of New York. He submitted his thoughts for the members' consideration. His thoughts came from the mind, if not the pen, of Benjamin Butler. "Dear General," Wines endorsed the back of the paper, "I have drafted a short act agreeably to your suggestions. Can you come to the Speaker's room & glance over it?" Not adequacy, said Wines and Butler. They must ensure absolute equality. If not, the law would intervene. Students denied equal facilities could transfer – and sue.[100]

Problems abounded. Who was to define the state of equality (underlined twice)? What constituted equivalency "in accommodations and instruction?"

98 On Dr. Sears' intervention, see below, 502–503.

99 Provided: that the provisions of this act as far as the laws apply to common schools shall not take effect in any state in which ~~separate~~ provision is made by law for separate schools ~~and~~ for colored children, and a prorata of the public school fund, applied to the support of such separate schools ~~shall not take effect in such states~~ until after the ~~adjournment~~ ^ close of session of the legislature of such state next after the passage of this act.

100 Amendment to the Civil Rights Bill. Provided, that when separate public schools are established and sustained in any school district or community for the youth of different races, such separate schools shall provide equal educational advantages, in length of session, accommodations, and ~~in~~ instruction; and Provided further that whenever separate public schools ~~thus~~ established and sustained in any school district or community for youth of different races do not furnish said youth with equal educational advantages, the youth thus unjustly denied school privileges equal to those enjoyed by others, shall have the right to enter and attend the ^ public schools which ~~are~~ ^ may be superior to those provided for them, and their exclusion from such ^ superior schools by school officers, teachers, or other persons shall be a misdemeanor punishable as hereinafter provided by this act.

How was one to judge schoolrooms which "may be superior" or models that might be, relatively speaking, inferior? "A youth," claiming to be denied equal privileges, could demand transfer. His claim would have to be weighed. The matter would have to be adjudicated in court, a federal court, as the rest of the Civil Rights Bill required. States might find separate schools a headache not worth the cost to bear. Then they might surrender to a regime of mixed schools. But what if states de-funded their schools entirely, ending the pursuit of public education? Draft two planted a minefield of troubles.

Amendments failed. The committee's Radicals, Ward, Wilson, Cessna and Frye, accepted no compromise. Republican conservative Alexander White preferred separate-but-equal. Moderates Luke Poland and Lyman Tremain struggled to find some middle ground. No help will have come from the Democrats, Eldredge, Potter and Jewett. They wanted no amendments, no bill at all.

Butler's quandary continued. He needed an excuse for delay. He found it in the illness of Lyman Tremain. He wanted Tremain's agreement, the Chairman said, before any decision. In point of fact Butler had made a decision. He decided not to decide. He passed the baton to the Senate. Let Sumner's bill go first. Then the House could act on it. The Senate was slow. Tremain recovered. Butler waited. His postponement stretched on for five months. George Downing's campaign to generate public enthusiasm faded. At the end of March Frederick Barbadoes, secretary of the National Civil Rights Council, wrote disconsolately: "We are constantly at work doing all we can, but without that support from the people which the importance of the occasion demands."[101] Downing became the butt of jokes.[102] Until the Senate moved, civil rights stuck fast.

H.R.796 was recommitted. Butler nevertheless marked the event with a splendid farewell. He had reserved for himself the final hour of debate. He intended to use that hour even in the anticlimax of retreat. His valedictory brought down the House. "Equality!" he thundered. "We do not propose to legislate any equality!"[103]

---

101 San Francisco *Elevator*, March 28, 1874.

102 An amusing dialogue circulated in the press, playful banter, at George Downing's expense. Two "colored gentlemen" meet upon a street corner, the joke began: (First gentleman): "De reckonition ob our rights hab giben rise to some curus questions ob etiquette.... The fust is, wich ought to call fust de families ob de white members ob Congress on de families ob de culled members or wisy wersy?" (Second gentleman): "Well, Mr. Johnsing, I'se in favor of wisy wersy.... As for Mr. Downing, he's on bofe sides and bodders us mor'n enuff, fur it's my private opinion dat dat man Downing jist talks to hear hisself talk. He's been so long hollerin down a hole, 'eysters for two,' dat he can't stop. But for dat question. Some ob us tink dat de families ob de culled members ought to call fust, for you see de families ob de white members is prejdiced an we ain't." Chicago, *Gem of the West and Soldier's Friend*, March 1874: 108.

103 Speech of Benjamin Butler: *Cong. Record*, 43rd Congress, 1st Session: 455–458.

> Equality – and I will embody it in a single phrase, as the touch-stone of civil liberty – is not that all men are equal, but that every man has the right to be the equal of every other man if he can.... Every man has the inalienable, God-given right to be the equal of every other man if he can. And all constitutions, all laws, all enactments, all prejudices, all caste, all custom in contravention of that right is unjust, wicked, impolitic, and unchristian, and surely will be brought to naught.[104]

Previous speakers had threatened to destroy the public schools. Butler spurned the threat.

> We are told that if we do pass this bill we shall break up the common-school system of the South. I assume this is intended as a threat. If so, to that I answer, as Napoleon did, "France never negotiates under a threat." ... Break up the common-school system of the South? Why, sir, until we sent the carpet-baggers down there you had not in fact a common-school system in the South.

Previous speakers had praised prejudice. Butler damned it.

> We were told yesterday that we must respect, in this regard, the prejudices of the South. Pardon me; we must lament the prejudices of men in the South. We cannot respect them; we lament them, and we pity them .... You talk of your prejudices against social equality! ... Who is the highest in the social scale, a slave or a freeman? You once associated with the slave in every relation of life. He has now become a freeman, and now you cannot associate with him; he has got up in the scale, and now you cannot stomach him. Why is this? ... It is because the laws of your land, the Constitution of your country, gave all men equal rights in accordance with the fiat of God Almighty which has made some of them your equal in all things, and therefore he is no longer to be associated with or tolerated!

Butler improvised imperturbably. Strange, he noted, few northern Democrats had risen to speak against the bill. Were they ashamed? New York's David DeWitt called out: "I, for one, repudiate the inference which the gentleman

104 Butler cherished his phrase. His children, Blanche and Paul, placed the words upon his grave: "The true touchstone of civil liberty is not that all men are created equal but that every man has the right to be the equal of every other man if he can."

chooses to draw from my silence in this debate." Butler peered at him mildly. "Who is next?" No one answered. Laughter rippled across the galleries.

Finally Butler offered a personal explanation. In antebellum days he had been a Democrat, as everyone knew. At the Democratic Convention in Charleston in 1860 he cast 56 ballots for Jefferson Davis. What had occasioned his conversion? How had the scales so fallen from his eyes? War had delivered him of his blindness. In the days of his first command at Fortress Monroe he had seen close up the absurdity of the prejudice that reigned over the south. As military governor of New Orleans he had seen the loyalty of black men who stepped up to fight for their nation. And in his command of the Army of the James in Virginia he had seen those men fulfill the promise.[105] He closed with a story. It was a tale he had told before many times, but not as now, to Congress assembled, the nation at attention. When he finished, the House was on its feet. The nation took notice. He recited the Charge at New Market Heights.

The facts were simple. On the 29th of September, 1864, war raged. A desperate charge was required against an entrenched and desperate enemy. Glory or death! He gave the order to a division of black soldiers, three thousand men at the foot of New Market Heights, Virginia. Take the position at the point of the bayonet: "No shot must be fired.... Your cry, when you charge, will be 'Remember Fort Pillow!'" And so, Butler recalled, they marched, onward, up the slope, across a swampy brook. Enemy fire came upon them: "They broke a little as they forded the brook, and the column wavered." Now an abatis loomed, a barrier of piled logs. Axmen rushed forward. "O, it was a moment of intensest anxiety!" Bullets cut them down. New men took up the axes. They broke through. Butler switched to the vivid present tense:

> The head of the column seems literally to melt away under the rain of shot and shell; the flags of the leading regiments go down, but a brave black hand seizes the colors; they are up again ... the column rushes forward, and with a shout which now rings in my ear, goes over that redoubt like a flash, and the enemy never stop running for four miles.

"It became my painful duty, sir, to follow in the track of that charging column." Every foot of ground they had gained could be counted by counting the bodies of the dead. Upon that battlefield, Butler concluded, he had sworn an oath: "May my right hand forget its cunning and my tongue cleave to the roof of my mouth if I ever fail to defend the rights of these men who have given their blood for me and my country this day and for their race forever." He fixed his

105 See Trefousse, *The South Called him Beast!*, 213.

gaze upon the House: "God helping me, I will keep that oath." From the heights of New Market Ben Butler descended deftly to earth.

> Now, Mr. Speaker, these men have fought for their country; one of their representatives has spoken, as few can speak on this floor, for his race; they have shown themselves our equals in battle; as citizens they are kind, quiet, temperate, laborious; they have shown that they know how to exercise the right of suffrage which we have given to them, for they always vote right; they vote the Republican ticket, and all the powers of death and hell cannot persuade them to do otherwise. [Laughter] ... They have all the good qualities of citizens, they have bravery, they have culture, they have power, they have eloquence. And who shall say that they shall not have what the Constitution gives them – equal rights? [Continued applause]

Reaction to Butler's oration followed predictable political lines. Democrats greeted it with silence, or disdain. "He was more than usually insolent toward the South," sniffed the Goldsboro *Messenger*, "and he grew very pathetic over the bravery of the colored troops."[106] Republicans flooded their districts with copies of the speech. Butler received requests for reams of off-prints: a hundred for Rep. Samuel Dobbins of New Jersey, to be distributed to his constituents; a hundred for Alexander McDill of Wisconsin; yet another hundred sent to the Customs House at New Orleans.[107]

Butler's martial anecdote was more than just a slab of extravagant oratory. The charge of the black troops assumed an importance beyond the narrative of a simple wartime incident. It hovered over the civil rights debate. It framed the civil rights movement. It embodied the Civil Rights Bill's supporters' strongest argument. Equality could be justified on the grounds of liberty, on the grounds of humanity. But in the plainest terms it was justified on the grounds

---

106 Goldsboro *Carolina Messenger*, January 12, 1874.

107 Samuel Dobbins to Benjamin Butler, April 3; Alexander McDill to Butler, February 17; John M.G. Parker, New Orleans Customs House, to Butler, November 12, 1874. Butler Papers, Library of Congress. Parker requested another 100 copies. The speech had been read aloud to an audience of "old veterans." Their cheers would have given the general "reason to be prouder even than he is to-day of that heroic effort." Butler heard from men who made the charge. Gen. Giles W. Shurtleff, now a professor at Oberlin College, wrote his former commander: "I was severely wounded in that engagement & you promoted me from Lt. Col. to the [command] of my regiment, the 5th U.S.C.T. I am glad you remember so well the incidents of that terrible charge & that you could use them in the House of Representatives with such telling effect." Parker to Butler, November 29; Shurtleff to Butler, February 2, 1874.

of bravery. If the black man, as a soldier, was good enough to die with whites, how could he not, as a citizen, live with them in possession of common public rights? "I will never," General Philip Sheridan had said, "look at the color of a man's face who stands pointing with his battered bayonet to his title deeds of citizenship."[108] Republican speakers found every occasion to allude to the valor of the black troops. Democrats found every occasion to deride that valor.[109] Butler's story drove home to a hostile or indifferent public the case for civil rights.[110]

The saga of New Market Heights, its stirring recapitulation amid echoing applause, ended the first round of debate. Ben Butler's battalions had stormed the storied entrenchments. But the war went on. Robert Elliott, Alonzo Ransier, Joseph Rainey, Josiah Walls had stormed the congressional battlements. Victory eluded them. The Civil Rights Bill was recommitted. The siege in the House continued. The campaign turned to a second front, the action of the Senate.

---

108 Washington, *New National Era*, December 3, 1869.

109 Critics ridiculed Butler's story. North Carolina Congressman ex-Confederate Major William Robbins professed first-hand knowledge. Butler's ballad of the blacks, Robbins joked, had as much reality as the Falstaffian battle of Gads Hill, Butler as much veracity as Sir John in his cups. Butler indeed embroidered, but he preserved the essence of the event, as the war's Official Records confirm. Two brigades of black soldiers under Colonels Samuel Duncan and Alonzo Draper made the assault, at a staggering loss of 885 casualties out of some 2,000 men engaged, 134 killed. The definitive account remains Richard J. Sommers, *Richmond Redeemed: The Siege of Petersburg* (Garden City: 1981). Also James S. Price, *The Battle of New Market Heights: Freedom Will Be Theirs By The Sword* (Charleston: 2011). In addition we note the unpublished letter of Capt. Paul Brodie to Benjamin Butler, January 11, 1874, eyewitness account in support of Butler's description of the battle. Butler Papers, Library of Congress.

110 "The people will remember," said Frederick Frelinghuysen in 1875. "The same blanket covered a lamented son and the colored soldier on the morass; they shared their waning canteens together … they bivouacked in death." *Cong. Record,* 43rd Congress, 2nd Session: 489. Ninety years later war again made the case for equal rights. "The war [World War II] uncorked many things in the thinking of our people," said Wyoming Senator Gale McGee in 1964. "They discovered that the blood of a colored man was as red as the blood of a white man." Ohio's Senator Frank Lausche all but reproduced Frelinghuysen's words – another time another war: "When the Negro boy fell on the battlefield the white boy did not question whether he should go to help him on account of the color of the lad who was lying in agony, bleeding for his Nation. When he begged for water, it was given to him. When he begged for strength, it was provided for him." Speeches of Senators McGee and Lausche, *Cong. Record* 88th Congress, 2nd Session: 7,795, 14,503. "War," George Orwell wrote, "is the greatest of all agents of change. It speeds up all processes, wipes out minor distinctions, brings realities to the surface." So it was with the reality of civil rights.

CHAPTER 4

Purblind Child of Darkness: Sumner's Civil Rights Bill Passes the Senate

May 22, 1874. Night settled over the capitol. House members took their hats from the cloak room and retired to rest. Gas-lights flared in the Senate chamber. Outside, a rainstorm broke against the dome. Inside, senators huddled in the eighth hour of debate. They sat to decide one issue: S.1, the Civil Rights Bill. On the floor, Missouri's Lewis Bogy evoked the darkness.

> Mr. President ... if [this bill] is to be consummated at all, night and darkness, storms and hurricanes, would be fitting concomitants of the act. It seems to me peculiarly appropriate that a child like this, begotten of fanaticism and conceived in the spirit of fraternal hate, should come purblind into the world, during the hours of natural darkness, adapted as it is not to abate but to increase, the sectional animosities and race antagonisms which have so marred our peace and prosperity in the past, and now threaten the very integrity of the nation. I am not one of the doctors on this occasion ... but I would not perform surgical Caesarism on the poor mother to save the life of so foul a monster. I can only hope that if this bad fruit of political miscegenation should ever come to be christened, its god-father will give to the piebald thing the honest name, not of "Civil Rights," but of Uncivil Wrongs.[1]

The senator's timetable was off. Twelve hours of debate remained. Morning midwifed the "piebald monster" into being. But his conclusion was correct. Republicans were determined to see the baby born. The House had acted swiftly on civil rights then stopped. The Senate hesitated long then acted with decision.

The earliest news appeared on March 5. The Judiciary Committee had perfected its review of S.1. It prepared to report the bill favorably.[2] Charles Sumner would see his hopes fulfilled. Others, meanwhile, hoped in him. In January the National Women's Suffrage Association arrived for its annual convention. It called for expansion of the Civil Rights Bill. "Can you not amend and let your

1 *Cong. Record*, 43rd Congress, 1st Session, Appendix: 319.

2 New York *Tribune*, March 5, 1874.

bill read 'race, color, sex, or previous condition, etc.,'" Belva Lockwood wrote. "That one little word of three letters will call down upon your head many a blessing." Sumner was not encouraging: "I have to say," he replied, "that the pending civil rights bill is supplementary to the existing law on that subject, and concerns only the denial of rights on account of race."[3]

On January 14 Susan B. Anthony opened the Women's Suffrage Convention in Washington. Black men, she declared, had gained their rights. Women asked for equal consideration. She read letters of support, including one from Benjamin Butler.[4] She expressed exasperation at Sumner's attitude. She led a delegation to the House Judiciary Committee to present it with a formal petition.[5] The women left disappointed. The House deferred to the Senate. The Senate bill remained genderless.

On March 11 Charles Sumner, who had waited so long to see his legacy live, died. Frelinghuysen, the New York *Times* reported, had assured him only days before that the bill would come to the floor. It had the committee's approval.[6] Sumner's coronary complications cheated him of the chance to see that day. His death at that moment came unexpectedly, though given the fragile state of his health it was not unexpected. He left the Senate for the final time on March 10. In the last moments he sat on a sofa at the rear of the chamber and talked with Connecticut's Senator Orris Ferry, also a dying man. Then he took his hat and coat and walked out. That evening in his big new house on F Street he collapsed. Servants laid him in bed. Friends called to bid adieu: Speaker Blaine, Senators Windom of Minnesota, Morrill of Vermont, Frederick Douglass, Montgomery Blair. Carl Schurz, George Downing and Ebenezer Hoar stayed until the end.[7]

The grim vigil, the senator's slow decline through the night and morning allowed for the report of touching scenes and the remembrance of tender thoughts. Sumner lingered, passing in and out of consciousness. Unfinished business, a task undone, weighed on the senator's mind. Those who sat by his bedside heard his whispered injunction. He bequeathed a final demand. He spoke most insistently, it seemed, to Ebenezer Rockwood Hoar. Hoar recorded it in a letter that same evening to Ralph Waldo Emerson: "During the morning

3 Baltimore *Sun*, January 10, 1874.

4 New York *Tribune*, January 16, 1874.

5 Boston *Commonwealth*, January 24, 1874.

6 New York *Times*, March 18, 1874.

7 On Sumner's demise, see David Donald, *Charles Sumner and the Rights of Man* (New York: 1970), 585–587. *Scribner's Monthly* magazine published an eyewitness account, "Recollections of Charles Sumner," September, 1874, pp. 475–490; also Edward L. Pierce, *Memoir and Letters of Charles Sumner* (Boston: 1893), vol. 4, 596–599.

he had repeated to several persons, to me among the rest, 'You must take care of the Civil Rights Bill.' That was his last public thought."[8]

Friends wept privately. Publicly the ritual that followed was friendless, a cold, official protocol of death. The nation, as required, offered Sumner a formal farewell. Ulysses Grant ordered the capital draped in black. In fact he had already ordered this tribute, not for Sumner but to mark the death two days earlier of former President Millard Fillmore. It could honor Sumner as well.

Sumner's body was delivered to the capitol. There in the rotunda it gazed out of a glass-lidded coffin. From the rotunda it moved to the Senate. At twenty minutes past noon on March 13, the House entered in solemn procession. President Grant, the Cabinet, the justices of the Supreme Court followed and took places at the front. Reporters noticed Senator Ferry. He looked pale and unsteady.[9] Vice-President Wilson was ill. Ferry's Connecticut colleague, Senator Buckingham, also with less than a year to live, took the chair. Kansas' John Ingalls witnessed a depressing scene.

> The day is dreadful – cold, cloudy – with a gusty tempest from the north bearing a storm of dust and gravel that blinds, wearies, and disgusts.... A dense surge of humanity moved endlessly through the corridors, aimlessly, curiously, black and white, ragged, unkempt, chilled with the cold blasts and filing past the cold, livid, discolored face that lay beneath the transparent glass like a drowned man under the ice. There were no tears. The scene was heartless. Loud talk, vain babbling, and senseless laughter.

In the Chamber all was somber: galleries packed, "tier above tier, a solid mass of faces, relieved against the dark drapery behind." The president sat near the head of the casket, "expressionless as stone, sometimes drumming his hat upon his knee." That evening Ingalls mailed off the missive to his wife. He enclosed a clump of violets plucked from the enshrouded coffin, "flowers that exhaled their fragrance in the dim chamber that shall know him no more forever."[10] Chaplain of the Senate Rev. Byron Sunderland spoke the prayer. A political speech, some thought, disguised as a sermon. "When enormous evils had to be encountered, when the order of things had to be overcome, when the new conditions for the new energies of the human race had to be created, Thou hast

8 Hoar to Emerson, March 11, 1874. Ebenezer R. Hoar Papers, Harvard University, Houghton Library.

9 Baltimore *Sun*, March 14, 1874.

10 John J. Ingalls, *A Collection of the Writings of John James Ingalls. Essays, Addresses, and Orations*, William E. Connelly ed., (Kansas City: 1902), 524.

planted Thy workmen at every point.... White men and black men, all men of every race throughout the world, shall this day be touched with the grief of this sudden stroke of Thy providence."[11] "When he finally reached a conclusion," wrote the reporter of the Baltimore *Sun,* "everyone felt exceedingly relieved."[12]

Reaction to Sumner's obsequies split along party lines. For the Atlanta *Constitution* his demise was God's judgment upon him for the sin of the civil rights bill: "Let the fanatics who still think it right to curse the country with such madness take Sumner's sudden death in the heat of his most cherished fanaticism as the Providential condemnation of the unnatural scheme."[13] The Columbia, South Carolina, *Phoenix* noted the rapid discoloration of the body: "What a strange thing it is that the fanatical negro-worshipper should have turned black at last."[14]

Black people took Sumner's death as the watchword of future action. Downing's National Civil Rights Council ordered homes and churches draped.[15] At Savannah houses appeared wreathed in crepe, in their windows engraved portraits of the late senator.[16] The New York Civil Rights Association hosted a meeting in the hall of the Cooper Institute. Banners proclaimed Sumner's epitaph: "Do Not Let the Civil Rights Bill Fail."[17] At Washington, Frederick Douglass, Pinchback, Congressmen Rapier and Cain addressed crowds in the auditorium of the Sumner School at 17th and M streets. Signs covered the building outside: "No Compromise With Human Rights;" "Don't Let Them Crush the Civil Rights Bill;" "Equal Rights To All;" "Senate Bill No.1."[18]

Historians have frequently attributed the Senate's passage of S.1 ten weeks later to Sumner's fortuitous death. The Civil Rights Bill was merely a feeble

11 *Cong. Record,* 43rd Congress, 1st Session: 2143.

12 Baltimore *Sun,* March 14, 1874. The reverend's ornate effusions exasperated his critics. "A first-class charlatan and a professional hypocrite," said Washington's *Sunday Chronicle* (March 22). A spinner of "stump speeches in the guise of prayers to Almighty God," wrote the New York *Tribune* (March 4). "Parson Sunderland is paid out of the Treasury to do a certain amount of praying in the Senate," the Cincinnati *Commercial* snickered (March 13), "[though] that body seems to be past praying for."

13 Atlanta *Constitution,* March 12, 1874.

14 Quoted in Dayton *Journal,* March 26, 1874. The unsightly darkening of Sumner's corpse suggested a need for better preservation. One enterprising mortician telegraphed Frisbie Hoar: "If permitted I will keep the remains of Senator Sumner thirty days in the best condition without embalming or freezing it & the body can be exposed to the public if not satisfactory free of charge." S.H. Crump to George Hoar, March 13, 1874. George F. Hoar Papers, Massachusetts Historical Society. Hoar's reply is not known.

15 New York *Times,* March 12, 1874.

16 Savannah *News,* March 19, 1874.

17 New York *Tribune,* March 31, 1874.

18 Washington *National Republican,* March 17, 1874.

farewell, a sappy *hommage* to a dead associate, a "pietistic" gesture by politicians temporarily overcome with sentimentality – an impulse they soon came to regret.[19] "The Senate momentarily succumbed to a contrite sentimentalism," one authority concluded.[20] "The civil rights bill," according to another, "would probably never have passed the Senate had it not been for the sudden death of Charles Sumner."[21] Being simply sentimental slosh, the bill amounted to no more than "a memorial to the Massachusetts idealist."[22] Even recent contributions repeat the canard: "A memorial to the Massachusetts idealist…. It is hard to imagine another explanation other than Sumner's death for the sudden reemergence of Sumner's bill…. If Sumner had not died … the bill would have died in committee."[23]

Nothing could be more mistaken. Sumner's Civil Rights Bill did not "suddenly reemerge." The Judiciary Committee had no intention of killing it. Both the New York *Tribune* on March 5 and the *Times* on March 18, as we have noted, reported that fact. Frelinghuysen had already announced the committee's decision. Sumner's death was not required. Politics, not sentiment, guided the senators' course. Hard-headed operators – Conkling, Edmunds, Cameron, Morton, Chandler – did not permit emotion to overthrow reason. To effect critical, and politically dangerous, legislation in an access of maudlin sentimentality at the death of an irascible colleague would have struck them as the height of absurdity. Carl Schurz, perhaps the most sentimental of senators, was also Sumner's closest senatorial friend. Publicly Schurz wept bitter tears. He voted against the bill. The Senate, through its Judiciary Committee, had perfected S.1 before Sumner's death. Republicans moved it forward with dry eyes, focused on policy not bedewed with sloppy sentiment or blinded by love.

Sumner's Senate seat, his chair and desk, went to Thomas Ferry of Michigan. His place, that is, his replacement, went nowhere. The Massachusetts legislature found itself hopelessly entangled. Two aspirants split the mass of votes almost evenly: Henry Dawes and Ebenezer Hoar. Ballot after ballot failed to break the impasse. Factions entrenched. Butler threw his support to Dawes. Butler-haters rushed to his opponent. On an emotional level Hoar seemed to have the advantage. Few people had been closer to the dearly departed.

---

19 S.G.F. Spackman, "American Federalism and the Civil Rights Act of 1875," *Journal of American Studies*, 10 (1976): 314.

20 Bertram Wyatt-Brown, "The Civil Rights Act of 1875," *Western Political Quarterly*, 18 (1965): 770. Cf. Donald, *Charles Sumner and the Rights of Man*, 586–587.

21 Heather Cox Richardson, *The Death of Reconstruction: Race, Labor, and Politics in the Post-Civil War North, 1865–1901* (Cambridge: 2001), 141.

22 Kelly, "Congressional Controversy over School Segregation," 554.

23 Brandwein, *Rethinking the Judicial Settlement of Reconstruction:* 67, 69.

Hoar, moreover, being the recipient of his dying request to "take care of the Civil Rights Bill," could plausibly claim the late senator's endorsement.[24] Those deathbed words, however, came back to haunt and not to help his candidacy. Civil rights emerged as a litmus test for those who aspired to succeed the sainted Sumner. Rockwood Hoar flunked the test. He did not accept the constitutionality of the Civil Rights Bill.

Sumner had known of his friend's misgivings. To the moment of his death he pleaded with him to reconsider. Those portentous dying words now appeared in a new light, not the commissioning of a loyal lieutenant but an exhortation to a mutinous ally. Wendell Phillips stated it plainly. Sumner had told him he had tried and failed to convince Rockwood Hoar to support the bill. He tried again with almost his last breath. Sadly, Phillips concluded: "I should have preferred Mr. Hoar to Mr. Dawes, had he given that morning the pledge for which the dying Senator vainly asked."[25]

The New York *Tribune's* reporter witnessed Sumner's deathbed drama. He noted the insistence with which the senator repeated to Hoar "with much feeling and pathos" his plea to save the Civil Rights Bill. "He seemed to want a promise or a word." He did not get it. "Overcome with feeling, Mr. Hoar stooped and kissed the hand he held within his own." No word or promise passed.[26] Sumner, journalist James Redpath observed, had urged his dying wish on all who stood by his bed. But he urged it on Hoar most of all. "Why did he do this, if he was sure of him? ... When Senator Sumner asked him on his death-bed to take care of his civil rights bill, did Judge Hoar forget the lawyer in the man and promise to do so? No; he held his tongue, as he does now."[27]

Henry Dawes also faced questions. Black State Representative Joshua Smith wired the congressman: "Is the Civil Rights Bill constitutional? Will you support

---

24 Sumner's dying declaration became at last a joke, a mischievously misplaced comma not entirely respectful to Hon. Ebenezer Hoar. Small boy to parent: "'Father, do you think Bill Hoar will get Mr. Sumner's place in the Senate?' 'My son,' replied the father, 'there is no such person as Bill Hoar, and, if there was that is not the proper way for you to speak of him.' 'Why father,' said the boy, 'that's the way Mr. Sumner spoke of him himself.... I read it in the papers. When Mr. Sumner was dying he said to Mr. Hoar, 'Take care of my civil rights, Bill.'" Knoxville *Press and Herald*, March 29, 1874.

25 Springfield, Massachusetts, *Republican*, April 7, 1874.

26 New York *Tribune*, March 12, 1874. Edward Pierce, Sumner's biographer (also a friend of Ebenezer Hoar), allowed Hoar a more ambiguous answer: "To Judge Hoar he said three times, varying the words somewhat, in the tone of earnest entreaty, 'You must take care of the civil-rights bill, – my bill, the civil-rights bill, – don't let it fail!' and the judge assured him that all that was possible should be done to carry out his desire." Pierce, *Memoir and Letters of Charles Sumner*, 598.

27 Springfield *Republican*, April 4, 1874.

it if elected to the Senate?" Redpath cabled: "It is asserted that you evade a direct answer to this question – are you in favor of Sumner's Civil Rights Bill – will you please answer?"[28] The contest went on. On the 33rd ballot, on April 17, after a month of deadlock, Massachusetts legislators deserted both Dawes and Hoar. William Washburn, the sitting governor, took the seat to serve Sumner's unexpired term. He announced at once that he gave the Civil Rights Bill his warm support: "He regarded it as it was regarded by Charles Sumner."[29]

Meanwhile events began to move. For some weeks illness caused delay. George Edmunds' health failed. On his doctors' advice he took a prolonged stay in Florida. Now the Chairman returned to Washington. On April 14th Frederick Frelinghuysen brought the Civil Rights Bill out of committee. Sumner's vision remained intact. In the first section, public accommodations, the committee tightened Sumner's legal prose, putting the injunction in positive terms ("all citizens shall be entitled") rather than negative ("no citizen shall be excluded"). It directed the law toward institutions ("the full and equal enjoyment of the accommodations and privileges of inns, public conveyances, theaters, common schools") rather than operators of those institutions ("privileges furnished by innkeepers, licensed managers or lessees of theaters"). It added coverage of agricultural colleges. The committee reduced some of the fines Sumner had proposed. It removed the redundant final section banning discriminatory use of the word "white."[30]

In one vital aspect Edmunds and his colleagues strengthened Charles Sumner's original. In Section 3 they placed civil rights cases under direct jurisdiction of the federal courts, a point Sumner had left implied only by reference to the Civil Rights Act of 1866. "The district and circuit courts of the United States shall have, exclusively of the courts of the several States, cognizance of all crimes and offenses against, and violations of the provisions of this act."[31] Finally, the senators refused to succumb to the House's anxiety. The school clause remained.

The committee took another significant decision. It retained the framework of the Fourteenth Amendment. Despite evident concern – replacing language citing individuals with language citing institutions, drawing a positive injunction, "all citizens shall be entitled," to fortify the argument of

28 Joshua B. Smith to Dawes, telegram March 22, 1874; James Redpath to Dawes, telegram April 7, 1874. Henry Dawes Papers, Library of Congress.

29 Indianapolis *Journal*, April 22, 1874.

30 For complete texts see Appendix B.

31 See J. David Hoeveler, "Reconstruction and the Federal Courts: The Civil Rights Act of 1875," *Historian*, 31 (1969): 610.

state neglect – Conkling, Edmunds, Frelinghuysen and Wright stuck with the Amendment.[32] Constitutional critics lay in wait.

Two weeks passed, as the Senate cleared away pending business. On April 29, 1874, S.1 commenced its run for passage. Frederick Frelinghuysen stood to take up civil rights. That same day in the House of Representatives Joseph Rainey sat to take the Speaker's chair. Rainey's hold on the gavel was brief. Yet, as the hammer passed from presiding officer Isaac Parker's hand to Rainey's, a new era opened. "It will make the history of the session memorable in American annals," wrote the New York *Herald*.[33] Free at last, the Chicago *Times* mused: "The African is free – free of soap, free of decent garments, of education, decency, progress, value to human kind ... and the glorious labor of getting Rainey thither ... has reduced all white men to a worse slavery than that from which the African has just been rescued."[34]

As the House marked its memorable moment, Frelinghuysen spoke. "I invoke for this bill a calm, impartial, and unpartisan consideration, and ask its adoption only as it commends itself as consistent with the permanent interests of the nation."[35] He examined first the constitutional objections. The Slaughter-House decision posed no obstacle. The Fourteenth Amendment conferred on all people United States citizenship. It lay within the nation's power to safeguard the rights of the nation's citizens. He assumed a broad definition of those rights.[36]

He dealt with the mixed school clause. Let a senator imagine it for himself. "What would be the objection in his mind to his children being excluded from the public schools on account of their supposed inferiority of race?" Having touched on schooling, Frelinghuysen went on to make a crucial distinction.

---

32 The bill might have rested on the interstate commerce clause, Article I, Sec. 8, Subsection 3. When civil rights returned to the United States Congress ninety years later, the legislation indeed hung on that hook. Discrimination impeded the conduct of interstate commerce. Hence it fell under the regulatory power of Congress. In their 1883 decision, eight Supreme Court justices declared the Fourteenth Amendment insufficient. But they asked "whether Congress, in the exercise of its power to regulate commerce amongst the several States might or might not pass a law regulating rights in public conveyances." They did not answer because Congress had not appealed to it for justification: "a question which is not now before us, as the sections in question are not conceived in any such view." The committee, Matthew Carpenter later noted, had considered the commerce clause, but found it weaker than the Amendment. See below, Chapter 15.

33 New York *Herald*, April 30, 1874.

34 Quoted in Richmond *Dispatch*, May 6, 1874.

35 Speech of Frederick Frelinghuysen: *Cong. Record*, 43rd Congress, 1st Session: 3450–3455.

36 Frelinghuysen repeated his position in a letter to Supreme Court Justice Joseph Bradley in July. See Robert J. Kaczorowski, *The Nationalization of Civil Rights: Constitutional Theory and Practice in a Racist Society, 1866–1883* (New York: 1987), 300.

The mixed-school clause, he said, did not mandate mixed schools. It required mixed schools if no other alternative existed. If the people of a given community preferred to establish separate schools, nothing in the Civil Rights Bill prohibited it. Let segregation be. But, if segregation obstructed or denied education, *then* did the law demand mixed schools. Frelinghuysen's definition shaped debate thereafter. From that moment, discussion of schools ceased to concern mixed schools. It concerned access to education. That shift in focus, so Republicans hoped, just might persuade a hostile public to accept an idea it found abhorrent.

Frelinghuysen returned to the Constitution. This time he invoked the Thirteenth Amendment. That amendment, offspring of civil war, abolished slavery. "Slavery caused the war. The war in fact destroyed slavery." Discrimination was a residue of slavery. Its residue must also be erased. "We are authorized to pass all laws appropriate to efface the existence of any consequences or residuum of slavery."[37]

> Sir, if we did not intend to make the colored race full citizens, if we purpose to place them under the ban of any legalized disability or inferiority, and there to hold them, we should have left them slaves.... It may be said that in the morbid imagination of the proud someone may fear that the result of this measure will be to place alongside of him in inn or theater someone in every respect his peer except that he differs in complexion. And he may feel that such an event would be an indignity and humiliation. Be it so, sir. The dissatisfaction of a vain pride does not have the weight of the dust in the balance in the eye of reason or in the sight of Him who made of one blood all nations of men.

Allen Thurman spoke for the Judiciary Committee's minority. He began with the penalty clause. The committee had given parties the right to sue in federal court for violation of their civil rights. For Democrats that spelled disaster. Civil rights laws might come and go. As long as local courts and juries presided they

---

37 Justice John Marshall Harlan in his dissent from the Civil Rights Cases decision in 1883 repeated the argument: "Discrimination practiced by corporations and individuals ... is a badge of servitude which Congress may prevent under its power by appropriate legislation, to enforce the 13th amendment." The idea remained alive a century later. "The paramount purpose of article XIII was to abolish slavery and to secure for men those rights which slavery denied," argued Vermont Senator Winston Prouty in 1964. "Among those rights which slavery denied the Negro was the right to buy a meal, a loaf of bread, or even a hoe in the accommodation of his choice." *Cong. Record*, 88th Congress, 2nd Session: 17,442.

could be nullified. Civil rights under state jurisdiction would be a toothless tiger; federal justice was far more dangerous. Thurman struck at the danger. Did not federal jurisdiction, he demanded, "oust the jurisdiction of the State courts, occupying the whole ground?" Several states had passed civil rights laws. They would find their efforts superseded by a redundant federal statute. "If this bill is passed, will not that State law become a nullity?"[38]

Roscoe Conkling rose to respond, as Thurman knew he would – as he must have in the committee. A person denied accommodations in a hotel by reason of race could seek justice for his personal injuries, in which case he could proceed under the statutes of his state. Or he could prefer federal jurisdiction and sue "not for the physical wrong done to him," but for the denial of his civil rights. The law did not annul a state's jurisdiction. It reinforced it. Thurman was ready for Conkling. In that case, he replied, it was monstrous, double punishment for a single offense.

Conkling was ready for Thurman. He held out a paper, an extract from a Supreme Court opinion. Frelinghuysen, he said, had noted it for him. An offense, said the Court, might be judged an offense both against a state and against the United States. The Court saw no difficulty with "double punishment." Thurman thought he knew the matter, a counterfeiting case; the Court had already reversed its ruling. No, Conkling rejoined. The matter was slavery, and the ruling was not reversed.[39] Democrats had not objected then. They had no qualms about punishments designed to rivet the bonds of slavery. Why did they object now to punishments designed to remove slavery's last residuum?[40]

---

38 Speech of Allen Thurman: *Cong. Record*, 43rd Congress, 1st Session: 3455–3456;

39 *Moore v Illinois*, 55 U.S. 13 (1852). Plaintiff in error Richard Ealls had been convicted in 1842 of harboring fugitive slaves, in contravention of Illinois law, and fined $400. Because of pre-existing federal law, the Fugitive Slave Law of 1793, his counsel argued, Ealls had been exposed to a "double punishment." The Court, Judge Stephen A. Douglas presiding, disagreed, the decision written by Mr. Justice Grier (Justice McLean dissenting): "An offense, in its legal signification, means the transgression of a law. A man may be compelled to make reparation in damages to the injured party and be liable also to punishment for a breach of the public peace in consequence of the same act, and may be said in common parlance to be twice punished for the same act."

40 Remarks of Roscoe Conkling and colloquy: *Cong. Record*, 43rd Congress, 1st Session: 3456–3457. Republicans made no secret that fugitive slave laws served as models for their theory of federal enforcement. Lyman Trumbull himself employed the Fugitive Slave Act of 1850 as a blueprint for the enforcement provisions of his Civil Rights Act of 1866. See Schwartz, *Statutory History of the United States: Civil Rights, Part I*, 113; Robert J. Kaczorowski, "To Begin the Nation Anew: Congress, Citizenship, and Civil Rights after the Civil War," *American Historical Review*, 92 (1987): 59; Brandwein, *Rethinking the Judicial Settlement of Reconstruction*, 36–37.

> This bill lays hold of a studious, deliberate, intentional act, for which no commiseration and charity can be invoked.... It punishes only the man who indulges in assault, in opprobrium, in injury of his fellow-man, merely because he cherishes a lawless prejudice, merely because he carries in his heart a base and paltry hate insulting to the spirit and civilization of the age, a hate which has been trampled out on this continent in blood, it is to be hoped forever. A man who sins thus deliberately, who in cold blood selects as the object of his vengeance and injustice the most inoffensive, the most friendless, the most unarmed member of society, puts himself beyond the pale of that extenuation.

Conkling's flourish concluded the first round of debate. When senators met next they heard a different voice. Georgia's junior senator, Thomas Norwood, hitherto had made little impression. He was, the Atlanta *Constitution* explained, like a patient pearl diver. "He did not come to the surface for a while; he was diving for the pearl of distinction."[41] The Springfield *Republican* disagreed. "Norwood of Georgia, although a Senator, seems to be a good deal of an ass."[42] Norwood laid his oyster before the Senate on April 30. His speech left more bad feeling than any comparable effort. Mocking, ironic, full of merry but unkind jests, he bowed first to Frelinghuysen.

> Nothing sustains me but the ambition to share with the Senator from New Jersey the imperishable honor of bringing about the happy consummation foreshadowed by him on yesterday, when the white man and black, the mulatto and quadroon, the coolie and Digger Indian, shall be gathered together, a united family, in one unbroken circle, around one common soup-bowl and using the same spoon, while shielded by the Stars and Stripes and regaled by the martial measure and inspiring strain of "John Brown's soul is marching on." [Laughter][43]

Laughter receded. Norwood plunged gaily ahead.

---

41 Atlanta *Constitution*, December 31, 1874. See William H. Bragg, "The Junius of Georgia Redemption: Thomas M. Norwood and the 'Nemesis' Letters," *Georgia Historical Quarterly*, 77 (1993): 91–92. Norwood, even in his context, stood out, "a racism extreme even for his time and place." See also George L. Jones, "William H. Felton and the Independent Democratic Movement in Georgia, 1870–1890," Diss. University of Georgia, 1971, 165. When Norwood ran in 1880 as an independent candidate for governor of Georgia, black people frantically voted for a Bourbon Democrat rather than see him preside over their fate.

42 Springfield, Massachusetts, *Republican*, May 4, 1874.

43 Speech of Thomas Norwood: *Cong. Record*, 43rd Congress, 1st Session, Appendix: 233–240.

> When the "morning stars sang together for joy" it might have been worth some dollars to the American people and the balance of mankind, if there be any, had the Republican party been present.... For when the Almighty said, "Let us make man," this Senate would have given its advice, and with much certainty would never have consented to man's creation except in accordance with the Declaration of Independence. The party would have caucused on the question.

More laughter. The audience warmed up, he mocked next at the battle of New Market Heights. Black soldiers, heroism; an oxymoron, a joke.

> I refer, as you know, to that Balaklava charge made by the colored troops, at the witching hour of dawn, on empty stomachs – bayonets fixed, nipples uncovered – under command of a general of renown ... wholly uncertain whether the charge would be feebly to the front or with frantic heroism to the rear. [Laughter]

He laughed at the soldiers. He laughed at their general, Benjamin Butler.

> He rode, with arms akimbo ... over that hecatomb of his companions, to the farther end ... and administered to himself a solemn, corporal, and general oath that so long as his surviving colored companions would vote to make him governor of Massachusetts or a Representative in Congress, he would spasmodically devote the idle moments of the remainder of his political and official life in a feeble effort to secure to them the great constitutional right to attend ... every theater, circus, and menagerie in the United States of America and the Territories thereof. [Laughter and applause in the galleries]

Now Norwood's words took a serious turn. He nurtured a serious hurt, more deeply even than race hatred: the resentment of class struggle. This pitted the poor against the rich. It pitted the South against the North – the North, land of capitalists and their heartless crew. Greed was their obsession, inhumanity their creed. A handful grew rich. Millions sank into poverty. "He who laid the foundations of His footstool did not place Avarice at its cornerstone."[44] Avarice and oppression, civil rights and capitalism: twin pillars of evil.

---

44 Thomas Norwood, *A True Vindication of the South in a Review of American Political History* (Savannah, 1917): vii-viii. Norwood indulged literary ambitions. In 1888 he produced his "socio-political novel" *Plutocracy, or, American White Slavery*: capitalist villains, virginal

> We, the millionaires – we who are paid out of your pockets, will take your money and will send our children to select schools, to foreign lands, where no negroes are; but you shall send your ragged, hungry urchins to the common schools on such terms as we dictate, or keep them away ... to wander on the streets and learn to syllable the alphabet of vice and crime.... You tell [your child] not to make companions of negroes – not to marry one – but you tie him side by side in the tenderest age of life with negroes. And thus you tell him the negro is as good as he.

When the inaugural ball came off last year, he demanded, how many Republicans invited black companions to share the festivities? "Which Senator here, with blandest suavity, or even by act perfunctory, solicited the pleasure and honor of the company of his friend Scipio Africanus, or of his sister, Miss Cleopatra Congo, or even of his distant relative, Miss Angelina Octoroon?" Hypocrisy! No one danced with Miss Angelina. "The whole objective aim of this Republican statesmanship," Norwood concluded, was to make sure that blacks ate good food. Congress delegated itself to stand behind them at the feast:

> A sub-committee adorned with white aprons ... armed with stomach-pumps ... and whenever Java coffee and loaf sugar, linen napkins, ivory-handled knives and silver forks, boned turkey, and hams, with champagne sauce, be given to whites, this vigilant committee must see to it that bean coffee and brown sugar, cotton napkins, buck-handled knives and two-tine forks, bacon and greens, rancid butter and ancient eggs are not given to the blacks. [Great laughter on the floor and in the galleries, with indications of applause]

Norwood's words boosted civil rights again onto the front pages. The Savannah *News* printed the entire text. It was "unanswerable. His satire is equal to Swift ... no man but a master mind, a towering intellect, could make such a speech as this."[45] For the New Orleans *Abeille* it signaled the doom of the Republican Party. Once he would have been censored by a ruthless majority. Now they

victims, merged with the muck of racial defilement. As the novel opens plutocrat-in-chief Galusha Smiling gazes from his Wall Street lair. A snowstorm blankets the pavement below. Snowflakes, tender, white, feminine beings, speak to him. "We are falling, Mr. Smiling! We are sinking! ... We are pure – see how white we are.... We shall be shoveled ... shoveled into the gutter – mixed with mud and all uncleanness." Smiling hears them not. His stock-market manipulations drive more pure, white, working girls into the gutters, unemployment, degradation.

45 Savannah *News*, May 15, 18, 1874.

could only gnash their teeth while his satire flayed them. "He pierced the Radical party like an iron shaft. They could only sit by to suffer, while he filled them with shame."[46] Others found it less piercing. Reporters interviewed Alexander Stephens recuperating at his Georgia home, "Liberty Hall." Norwood's effusion, he thought, was regrettable. "He feared it would irritate the Northern members, when conciliation ought to have been his aim."[47]

Norwood's diatribe lit the fire. Yet once more with victory in sight the Civil Rights Bill faltered. Prospects for a vote receded. Once again mixed schools loomed up. The Judiciary Committee had left them in; others wished them out. Senate Republicans caucused. Civil rights was only part of their problem. Five months into the session they had achieved none of their legislative goals. No one could agree on how to fix the Louisiana elections muddle. The Currency Bill had gone down in flames, killed by a presidential veto. Now the Civil Rights Bill left them paralyzed. Even the weather weighed them down. The thermometer stuck in the 90s, though it was only May. "Senators and Representatives will begin to mop their noble brows and think of going home," suggested the New York *Tribune*.[48]

The caucus met on Friday, May 8. Some members worried about Thurman's argument. The "double penalty" was unjust. Others agreed with Matthew Carpenter. The bill would fail a constitutional test. They feared the mixed-schools clause. And they feared the prospect of a filibuster. That would stop everything in its tracks. Reports filtered out. The Civil Rights Bill, as designed by the Judiciary Committee, was dead. Even its "best friends" conceded that fact.[49] The mixed school clause would go. At the very least separate-but-equal would be added to the text, and perhaps added to the public accommodations clauses as well.

Those who hoped to dilute the bill underestimated George Edmunds, George Wright, Roscoe Conkling and Frederick Frelinghuysen. The caucus adjourned to meet again on Monday, May 11. For more than two hours the senators argued. When they emerged the bill stood as the committee had framed it. It remained only to decide when to call it to the floor. There was still the danger of a filibuster. Frelinghuysen agreed to suspend the civil rights debate. The Geneva Awards should come first. They would deal next with the modified Currency Bill, then the more important appropriations bills. When these

46 New Orleans *Abeille*, May 2, 1874.

47 Atlanta *Constitution*, May 14, 1874.

48 New York *Tribune*, May 11, 1874.

49 New York *World*, May 11; Washington *National Republican*, May 11; Washington *Sunday Chronicle*, May 11, 1874.

had been cleared away, the opposition could filibuster S.1 at will. The purblind child would walk forth.[50] The caucus retained the mixed school clause. Despite intense pressure Senate Republicans determined to pass it. Credit for that decision lay with the stalwarts of the Judiciary Committee. They preserved the bill as Sumner had conceived it.

Mixed schools, more than any other feature, generated a fevered reaction, among the people of the North as of the South. Even black leaders feared it was too much, too fast. Justice and morality might demand integration. Common sense and political reality called for circumspection. The issue often is perceived as an all-or-nothing proposition: desegregated education or racial separation. Rather, it was, as one historian has put it, "the connection between nonexclusion and integration."[51] Public opinion, the senators understood, needed persuasion. It needed to be guided not bullied.

The Judiciary Committee carefully considered Sumner's draft. From the outset uncertainty settled over the meaning of the words: "All citizens and other persons within the jurisdiction of the United States shall be entitled to the full and equal enjoyment of the accommodations, advantages, facilities, and privileges of ... common schools and public institutions of learning." Democrats demanded to know what those words meant. Did they mean that all public schools must be integrated? Or did they not? They found Frelinghuysen's answer unconvincing. He said they did not. Nothing in that clause mandated mixed schools. It mandated only that no child of a United States citizen, or of a non-citizen, could be denied the facilities of education. If separate institutions provided such facilities they could exist, so he insisted.

Democrats insisted it was a trick, a sly piece of political prestidigitation crafted to hoodwink an unwary public. The committee kept the clause unchanged so as to give it a false interpretation. They claimed mixed schools would not result. Meanwhile a regime of mixed schools would settle itself into law. Democrats were correct. Edmunds, Frelinghuysen, Wright and Conkling hoped to ensure a future of desegregated education. But the future was not now. For the present they could not hope to pass a blatant mandate. The House had faced it and flinched. Better to unlock the door, but wait. In another time, when accommodation had worn down prejudice, then the door might open. They could, however, leave it ajar. Mixed schools magically would vanish now,

---

50 Baltimore *Sun*, May 12; New York *World*, May 12; New York *Times*, May 12, 1874.

51 J. Morgan Kousser, "Before Plessy, Before Brown: The Development of the Law of Racial Integration in Louisiana and Kansas," in Paul Finkelman and Stephen C. Gottlieb, eds., *Toward a Usable Past: Liberty Under State Governments* (Athens, Ga., 1991), 225.

disappear from the debate, only to reappear when the civil rights regime became reality.

Frelinghuysen performed the sleight of hand. He professed no concern about separate schools. His worry indeed was not that separate schools existed but that separate schools did not exist. Black children were barred from white schools. Yet they had none of their own. Even Democrats did not deny the problem. Evidence mounted from north and south. Communities were poor, populations scattered. It was impracticable if not impossible to maintain double facilities, even if the will existed. For that reason, Frederick Frelinghuysen declared, the Civil Rights Bill existed.[52]

Illinois provided a practical example. The Chicago *Inter Ocean* reported. "Democrats declare that they are perfectly willing he [the Negro] should be educated, but he must be educated in black schools." There were, the *Inter Ocean* observed, any number of counties in Illinois containing only a marginal black population. Crawford County possessed exactly three black residents. Brown County had one.[53] "In that event we shall behold a school house and teacher devoted to the training of the one little 'nigger' of Brown County.... What would the tax-payers say to that?" Tax-payers, of course, said no, and denied education to the lonely orphan of Brown County, to her sisters in Crawford County, and to huddled handfuls in counties uncounted.[54] This, as Frelinghuysen explained, was the problem the "mixed schools" clause addressed. If districts did not sustain double schools, the Civil Rights Act would act. A single school-house door would open for all.

The constitution of Illinois guaranteed public education to all citizens without distinction. It levied fines on school boards or school directors who violated that mandate. Yet discrimination abounded. The Illinois Senate wrestled with the issue. In February Republican George Henry moved to instruct the Committee on Education to investigate officials who "ignored or disregarded altogether" the constitution of the State of Illinois.[55] Henry's fellow lawmakers objected. Senator Thomas Casey insisted, "as long as time should last," better the exclusion of some than the mixture of all. Senator Beatty Burke "dwelt at length on the unpleasantness of the odor of the [Negro] race, which was a conclusive objection to the co-education of the races." Some Democrats, Chicago's Miles Kehoe, Francis Youngblood of Shawneetown, Charles Voris of Shelby, supported the call. Negroes should be educated, said Voris, "so they could read

52 See J. Morgan Kousser, *Dead End: The Development of Nineteenth-Century Litigation on Racial Discrimination in Schools* (Oxford: 1986), 16.

53 According to the 1870 census Crawford County had 4 Negro residents, Brown County had 26.

54 Chicago *Inter Ocean*, July 21, 1874.

55 Chicago *Tribune*, February 3, 1874.

the newspapers and convince themselves of the corruption and rottenness of the Republican party." Voris' colleagues preferred to keep them illiterate. Senator William Archer: "He would rather eighteen negroes would go uneducated in a given district than put them as a firebrand into a school for white children." The Illinois legislature handed the question of obeying its constitution to a committee for further study.

In Indiana the state's constitution required universal public education. But the state's statutes outlawed mixed schools. The result, the Indianapolis *Journal* reported: "They make it impossible to educate any black children except in the large cities." Of the state's 92 counties, 52 possessed 100 or fewer black persons. Eleven counties had no more than 200. School districts in such counties ignored these irksome clusters. In the South "they whip and expel teachers of the Negro," the *Journal* concluded. "In Indiana they do it with a sneaking law that hides under a lying, impracticable policy."[56]

Even as the *Journal* wrote, a case was proceeding in the Indiana Supreme Court to challenge that very point. A black man residing in a rural locality found his children and grandchildren banned from the one public school. The district provided no separate facility. He sued for admission. The decision in this, the Corey-Carter case, did not come until November. When it came it gave spectacular confirmation to the argument Frederick Frelinghuysen advanced.[57]

The town of Bethany, West Virginia, lay in Brooke County at the northernmost end of the northern panhandle. School directors were perplexed. Twenty-five Negro children encumbered the district. They could not, of course, share a school with the whites. But the budget could not bear the charge of a separate facility. The board hit upon an expedient. Within the white school building there was a large, empty room. Into this spare space the black scholars could go. The board promised to take every precaution. A separate entrance would lead directly into the separate classroom. A fence would transect the schoolyard to prevent a meeting of the twain. White parents remained adamant. "It seems," commented the Wheeling *Intelligencer*, "that there are people sending their children to this school who object to the same roof covering the heads of children of different races." In that case, the board responded, it would have to cut salaries by a third. Teachers would quit. "Upon the whole there is a right smart chance of war … of having no school either for whites or blacks."[58]

---

56 Indianapolis *Journal*, July 30, 1874. See Emma Lou Thornbrough, *The Negro in Indiana before 1900: A Study of a Minority* (Bloomington: 1993), 317–325.

57 On the circumstances of the Corey-Carter ruling, see 504–506.

58 Wheeling *Intelligencer*, September 1, 1874.

Republicans in Kentucky tried and failed to pass an appropriation for the upkeep of colored schools. One frustrated legislator wrote to Ben Butler: "Unless you pass your bill the negroes in Kentucky will get no aid, in this generation, from the State School Fund."[59] Some weeks later the legislature did approve aid. Kentucky's white taxpayers paid nothing; black taxpayers paid for black schools. The appropriation drew on an income tax of 20¢ per $100 on all such said black persons, supplemented by a capitation tax of $1 on colored male persons, also the proceeds of dog licensing fees, such dogs to be owned exclusively by non-white persons. State School Superintendent H.A.M Henderson counted up the results. If those measures produced the expected revenue, black pupils would receive the educational benefit of 46¢ each. This compared with $2 for each white student.[60]

North Carolina apportioned its taxes on a more equitable basis. It dedicated 75% of all capitation revenue to education, also a tax of 8⅓% on property, taxes on the licensing of auctioneers and vendors of spirituous liquors. State Superintendent of Public Instruction Alexander McIver advised county school directors that these funds ought to suffice to keep schools open two or three months of the year, but only if communities contributed half the cost of building and maintenance. Teachers should receive salaries on a scale of $20 to $40 a month, if their schools contained a minimum of 20 students. Teachers of smaller schools could expect $1, $1.50 or $2, depending on their certification status, per student enrolled. In case of shortfall, school boards must rely on local assistance, any additional taxes being "submitted to the vote of the electors of the county."[61] Odds were extremely slim that electors would submit to tax themselves additionally to open additional schools for disregarded black children.

California faced the problem resolutely. Zealots, including Governor Newton Booth, pressed for mandatory desegregation. San Francisco Assemblyman Jabez Cowdery cited the figures.[62] Precisely 944 black children inhabited California. There were 139,596 white children. How could communities sustain separate schools for an almost invisible minority? It could be done in San Francisco, where a quarter of the state's residents lived. San Jose, the state's second largest city, possessed 22 black pupils. It had consolidated them into a single school. A teacher, Mr. George W. Hamilton, saw to their enlightenment.[63] All

59 W.M. Brown to Butler, January 6, 1874. Butler Papers, Library of Congress.

60 Louisville *Courier-journal,* March 2, 1874.

61 Elizabeth City *North Carolinian,* March 11, 18, 1874.

62 San Jose *Mercury,* February 12, 1874.

63 San Jose *Mercury,* June 3, 1875.

other towns were smaller. It was impossible. Cowdery called for desegregation. The Assembly voted his proposition down. California's senate also tried. There the instigator was a man of mystical mind, Selden Finney of Pescadero.[64] Democrats conceded the point. Exclusion was unfair. Schools should open their doors to all. But they added a proviso. Local consultation must come first.

> When there shall be in any district any number of children other than white children whose education can be provided for in no other way, the Trustees may by a majority vote and with the consent of a majority of the parents of the children attending such school, in writing, and filed with the Trustees of the district, permit such children to attend the schools for white children.[65]

That generous provision, of course, gutted the entire measure, barring the unlikely event that white parents welcomed black children, in writing, to sit beside their tender offspring. It left most of the state's black population, and other "other than white" persons without the means of education.[66] Then the senate voted down the whole thing.[67]

Journalist Horace Redfield, southern correspondent of the Cincinnati *Commercial,* summed it up: "The hardship is the absence of schools for colored

64 Selden J. Finney, spiritualist, Abolitionist, advocate of women's rights, a founder of the Religio-Philosophical Society, ended his pilgrim life purposely some months later. He walked from his home in Pescadero, taking along a rifle. Searchers recovered the body. The bullet had entered the jaw and exited the temple. San Jose *Mercury*, August 12, 1875.

65 Santa Clara *Argus*, March 2, 1872.

66 This verbal construction, "other than white," did not include persons of Mexican/Spanish ancestry, "native Californians," whose presence predated United States annexation. The first of their number, Romualdo Pacheco, soon ascended to the governorship and then to a seat in Congress. Native Californians of Native American ancestry, whose presence predated that of native Mexican Californians, did qualify for "other than white" status, along with non-native Californians of Chinese ancestry.

67 Santa Clara *Argus*, March 16, 1872. Finally the California Supreme Court stepped in. Fourteen year old Mary Frances Ward, a black child, sued for admission to the all-white Broadway Grammar School in San Francisco. The court, in *Ward v. Flood*, turned her down. It upheld separate schools. But, it noted, those schools must actually exist. If not, common schools would have to open their doors to all. Chief Justice William T. Wallace wrote for the majority: "The exclusion of colored children from schools where white children attend as pupils cannot be supported except under the conditions appearing in the present case; that is except where separate schools are actually maintained for the education of colored children." Charles A. Tuttle, *Reports of Cases Determined in the Supreme Court of the State of California at the January, April, July & October Terms, 1874*, vol. 48 (San Francisco: 1875), 56–57.

children in the more thinly populated rural districts. In a district where there are, say, half a dozen negro children, they are without a school. This is unfortunate, but there is no remedy."[68] The remedy, Frelinghuysen repeated, was the Civil Rights Bill. It did not mandate mixed education. It mandated education. Democrats remained unconvinced. Senator John Stockton, Frelinghuysen's New Jersey colleague, demanded that Republicans explain:

> Be candid, be truthful to the American people. I ask again of my colleague … do you mean or do you not mean that you propose by a compulsory system to educate the young people of different colors together, with the wish that all prejudices shall be eradicated and that they shall be one? Do you mean miscegenation or not? Do you mean to degrade the white race of this country, to prostitute the power you have to degrade the white people of this country? Do you mean that, or do you not mean it?[69]

Frelinghuysen refused to be trapped. "Not exactly recognizing the right of the Senator from New Jersey to catechize me in that style," he huffed, "I will answer him in the negative." Another committee member answered more forthrightly. A fellow Republican tripped him up. California's Aaron Sargent, the Senate's champion of women's rights, also favored civil rights. But he feared the consequences of mixed schools. Public education itself might come to ruin. He had a solution. Let the clause remain, but amend it. Put the word "system" after "school." School systems would have to accommodate all children. Schools would not. Facilities could remain separate. But no school district could deny any child access to facilities. The clause would state unambiguously what the committee said it meant to state. George Edmunds rose. The political prestidigitator revealed his hand. He admitted the trick. Sargent's separate school loophole, he declared, was unacceptable. There must be equality; as with railroad coaches and hotels, so should it be in the schools.[70] If Democrats beheld in the Judiciary Committee's school clause a Trojan horse, they had good reason.

---

68 Cincinnati *Commercial*, June 14, 1874. Statistics gathered by United States Education Commissioner John Eaton in 1875 underscored the problem. Tennessee funded 923 colored schools, presided over by 921 colored teachers. These establishments accommodated 23,446 colored pupils, from a colored school-age population of 103,856, leaving 78% of that population uneducated. Virginia did somewhat better, finding school benches for 52,086 colored children out of 177,317. John Mercer Langston, *Freedom and Citizenship. Selected Lectures and Addresses of Hon. John Mercer Langston* (Washington: 1883), 281–282.

69 *Cong. Record*, 43rd Congress, 1st Session: 4169.

70 *Cong. Record*, 43rd Congress, 1st Session: 4171–4172; see Earl M. Maltz, "The Civil Rights Act and the Civil Rights Cases: Congress, the Courts and Constitution," *Florida Law Review*, 44 (1992): 617.

On one point both sides agreed. Neither public opinion nor political will would tolerate a mandate for mixed schools. It struck a nerve too acute to be thrust thus nakedly upon the nation. The people, Horace Redfield wrote, "have as much antipathy to mixed schools as a mad dog to water. They would rather see their children grow up as ignorant as the heathens in Asia."[71] Both sides agreed, too, that on the solution of the mixed school question depended the fate of the Civil Rights Bill.

There were indications that the public, even the southern public, just might tolerate the bill's provisions – except for mixed schools. The Democratic Charleston *News and Courier* spoke from a state that already lived under a civil rights regime anchored in its constitution. As the prospect of a federal law approached, the *News* was unconcerned. "All the provisions of the Civil Rights Bill have been in operation in South Carolina for years." Those provisions were not so bad.

> It was expected that there would be social revolution; that no whites could possibly ride again in the street cars or in the railroad coaches, or go to the theaters, or take luncheon at Branchville.... We did not like the Civil Rights law ... but we have found our scare-crow to be nothing more dangerous than an armful of old clothes stuck on a broom-stick, and we cannot get up any fresh alarm or uneasiness about it.[72]

That calm opinion, however, embraced only the public accommodations clauses. Luncheons at Branchville were one thing. Mixed schools were another. On that topic the *News and Courier* invoked the French Revolution. *Ça Ira,* its editorial proclaimed. Never would white people allow their little ones to sit on school benches with Negroes.[73]

Henry Ward Beecher's *Christian Union* noted the state of opinion in Virginia. Correspondent Orra Langhorn reported. Virginians could accommodate themselves to Negro civil rights. But they would not suffer mixed schools. "Two hours will suffice to repeal all the laws in regard to Free Schools in the State."[74]

In some places the two-hour clock had begun to tick. Maryland Governor James Groome notified his legislature to prepare for an extra session, "to break up root and branch the public schools of the State, in the event of the passage of the civil rights bill."[75] School Board Trustees in Clarke County Virginia voted

71 Cincinnati *Commercial,* November 23, 1874.
72 Charleston *News and Courier,* February 11, 1875.
73 Charleston *News and Courier,* May 28, 1874.
74 *Christian Union,* July 29, 1874, 64–65.
75 Annapolis, Maryland, *Gazette,* October 6, 1874.

to suspend appropriations until it was clear the bill would not pass.[76] Both houses of the Georgia legislature agreed to rescind appropriations if mixed schools became law.[77] At Macon, Bibb County commissioners authorized a school tax of $25,000 but, "if the Civil Rights Bill passes Congress," authorization was annulled.[78] In Tennessee, Maury County cut its school tax on May 11. Hamblen County de-funded its schools on the 13th. Wilson County repealed its tax on the 15th.[79] Nashville Alderman Hugh McGavock proposed that the city suspend construction of school buildings; there would soon be no need of school buildings.[80]

One warning note rose above the rest. On May 27, Col. John M. Fleming, Tennessee Superintendent of Public Instruction, sent a directive to all district supervisors. Mixed schools conflicted with the laws of Tennessee and also the state constitution. Fleming's solution: shut down the schools in Tennessee.

> I deem it the part of prudence to suggest for the present, and until further advised, no new contracts with teachers, for either white or colored schools, be entered into by school directors. Should the civil rights bill … become a law in its present shape, then further instructions from this office will become necessary, and will be promptly given.[81]

The New York *Times* reported Fleming's directive on the 27th, the very day the school boards of Tennessee received it. The New York *World* ran the story on the 29th. That same day it appeared in papers across the nation. The Indianapolis *Journal* denounced it on the front page. The Baltimore *Sun* and Charleston *News and Courier* praised it. Superintendent Fleming acknowledged the dilemma. In some places segregation worked to the disadvantage of whites: "There are colored schools in some localities where white children are not sufficiently numerous to constitute a school, and yet the law would not permit such white children to attend the colored schools."[82]

Behind the threats came the voices of expert opinion. Those experts were of one opinion. They pronounced mixed schools folly. Most expert of all, Dr. Barnas Sears of the Peabody Education Fund spoke plainly. It would be the

76 Richmond *Dispatch*, January 5, 1874.
77 New York *Tribune*, January 23, 1874.
78 Memphis *Appeal*, June 5, 1874.
79 Knoxville *Press and Herald*, May 12, 13, 16, 1874.
80 Nashville *Union and American*, May 27, 1874.
81 Memphis *Appeal*, May 29; Knoxville *Press and Herald*, May 30, 1874.
82 Nashville *Union and American*, May 1, 1874.

end of education. Public schools, all public schools, teetered on the brink. Critics were legion. Common schools, they cried, bred Communism. Creeping totalitarianism, children torn from the parental hearth, indoctrinated, molded into creatures of the State.[83] Mixed schools, said Dr. Sears, would make matters worse, embolden the critics' outcry, hasten the disaster.

Rev. Dr. Robert Dabney of the Virginia Union Theological Seminary was one such critic. Public schools, he proclaimed, poisoned the public. The South had fought to preserve Christian civilization. Who had defeated it? Not men but the mob, a horde of hirelings hurled from the North, the underclass, the glut of the world's gutters. Where had that gutter-spawned rabble learned its audacity? Common schools! Education empowered the proletariat. It unfit the servile classes for service. It must be stopped.

> The theory that the children of the Commonwealth are the charge of the Commonwealth is a pagan one, derived from heathen Sparta and Plato's heathen republic, connected by regular, logical sequence with legalized prostitution and the dissolution of the conjugal tie.... It was this system which prepared the way for the "International Society," and the horrors of the Paris Commune.[84]

Public schools were the breeding-ground of degeneracy. Parents plunged their precious progeny into this cesspool at their own risk. They exposed their little ones to contact with the riff-raff. "All the moral lepers among the children of a given district must be thrust into the society of our children at school. They must daily be brought into contact with the cutaneous and other diseases, the vermin (Yes, dear reader, it is disgusting!) ... the obscenity, the profanity, the groveling sentiments, the violence of the *gamins*, with which our boasted material civilization teems."[85] Worse than cutaneous disease was the inevitability of sexual congress.

---

83 *Proceedings of the Trustees of the Peabody Education Fund*, vol. 2 (Boston: 1881), 24, 30.

84 Robert Dabney, *Discussions by Robert L. Dabney, D.D., LL.D.* (Mexico, Mo., 1897), vol. 4, 194, 205–208.

85 The blackboard jungle, a fear that retains its resonance; e.g., home-school advocate Dr. Greg Sherman: "Bullies physically harm smaller, weaker kids in the reality of schools ... children are regularly abused emotionally by their peers. Deadly concealed weapons are a reality in school. And an accelerated sense of sexuality and dating are a reality in school. I understand that these are realities outside school, and my children will someday claim membership in this reality. But not today." "Ten Good Reasons to Homeschool," *Home Educator's Family Times*, homeeducator.com/familytimes (2010).

> The satanic artificers of our subjugation well knew the work which they designed to perpetrate; it is to mingle the blood which flowed in the veins of our Washingtons, Lees, and Stonewall Jacksons, and which consecrated the battle fields of the Confederacy, with this sordid, alien taint.[86]

Dr. Dabney perhaps was an extreme outlier. But sober sages joined the chorus. The most elaborate critique came from the pen of Rev. Dr. William H. Ruffner, Superintendent of Schools of Virginia. Dr. Ruffner, unlike Dr. Dabney, enjoyed the reputation of a man of liberal views. He professed sympathetic regard for the Negro. His attitude indeed infuriated conservatives. He spent too much public money on Negro schools. "He hugged the nigger; he made no difference in the schools for colored children and those for the whites."[87] He had even been seen at an official function shaking hands with Gen. Oliver O. Howard. (Ruffner apologized for that mishap. The loathsome general had "advanced upon him so swiftly with his hand outstretched that he could not avoid the courtesy.")[88] Dr. Ruffner's thoughts appeared in *Scribner's Monthly*, the May issue, "The Co-education of the White and Colored Races," just in time to provide senators and congressmen interesting reading as they voted on civil rights. In double-columned pages Ruffner argued his point: mixed schools could not exist in the world as it stood.

> An act of Congress requiring the south poles of all magnets to attract each other would not be a whit more absurd than one requiring education to be conducted on a race-mixture in the late slave states. Will politicians never learn that social laws are laws of nature, and hence invariable and inflexible?[89]

From classical sources, on the authority of Plutarch and Xenophon, Plato and Horace, it was evident. Once-enslaved people could never integrate into society. Emancipation did not efface the rot of servile origin. Even to the present day, a hundred generations on, the offspring of such peoples inflicted misery.

---

86 Dabney, *Discussions*, 185–186.

87 *Christian Union*, July 29, 1874, p. 65.

88 Richmond *Dispatch*, June 27, 1874. Opponents were not appeased. "While such dogs as he [Howard] are on the platform our people should be conspicuous for their absence from it." Petersburg, Virginia, *Index and Appeal*, June 16, 1874.

89 "Co-education of the White and Colored Races," *Scribner's Monthly*, May 1874, pp. 86–90.

Descendants of ancient Roman slaves polluted the Old World. They were "the founders of the detested proletariat, whose filthy stream has defiled and burdened European society … with the forms of pauperism, crime, and communistic rebellions." In the New World race deepened the divide.

> What then would be the practical result, as respects education, of the so-called Civil Rights Bill, as originally introduced into Congress by Gen. Butler? Would it secure the co-education of the races? Impossible! Would education be facilitated in any way? It would inevitably be destroyed!

Personally Ruffner wished the best for black people. Perhaps, in the far future, humanity would heal its heart. Negroes might reach a status equal to that of the most advanced peoples. The only hope now was not to destroy hope.[90]

Ruffner's article circulated. Congressmen read it. Senators quoted it.[91] Finally the master spoke: Rev. Dr. Barnas Sears. Seven years Secretary of the Massachusetts Board of Education, twelve years President of Brown University, for eight years General Agent of the Peabody Education Fund, he was the voice of authority. He appointed himself to the task of warning the country.[92] In January Dr. Sears went to Washington. He imparted his wisdom to the House, then to the Senate. He finished at the presidential mansion.

> My first aim was to see its [the Civil Rights Bill's] friends and to induce them to omit the clause altogether, or to require only equal privileges of education without mixing the two races in the schools. I think I convinced them all that the bill would overthrow the State systems of free schools and leave both the blacks and the poor whites, who are now provided for by the rich chiefly, destitute of schools … that if Congress itself should for a shadowy abstraction entail popular ignorance upon the

90 Dr. Ruffner was not hopeful: "[Negroes] are without moral stamina. Hence they live very immoral lives, and particularly in respect to that class of vices which are characteristic of the prognathous races … brutal indulgence such as is nowhere else to be found within the limits of civilization." New York *Times*, November 23, 1874.

91 Wisconsin's Timothy Howe read Ruffner's item to the Senate. He denounced it. In the House Virginia's John T. Harris praised it: "There is no power on earth, moral or physical, which can mix the children of the white and colored races in the same schools." *Cong. Record*, 43rd Congress, 1st Session: 377, 4151.

92 See William P. Vaughn, "Partners in Segregation: Barnas Sears and the Peabody Fund," *Civil War History*, 10 (1964): 266–274.

> South, after giving universal suffrage and after all the States had established a free school law, somebody would have a terrible responsibility, which the Southern people of all parties would be slow to forget. Butler himself said the bill should be re-committed, and that he was willing to make a reasonable compromise. In the next place I saw leading Senators – not Sumner nor his trained negroes, but Morton, Buckingham, and others, who will see that the objectionable clause is left out or changed, or that the bill is defeated in the Senate. Lastly, I saw the President, who viewed the subject as you and I do.[93]

Just to be safe Dr. Sears called for help. United States Commissioner of Education John Eaton joined him in making the circuit of politicians. Writing in his memoirs, Eaton expressed himself more sympathetically. He omitted the observation in regard to Sumner and his "trained negroes." He admired Sumner. Sumner meant well. "Good men," he wrote, "saw in the separation of the white and black races in the schools of the Nation a dangerous tendency toward the creation of class distinctions in our American life." But good men followed a foolhardy dream. "It was the expression of a theory of equality right in itself, but which it would have been fatal at that moment to enforce."[94] Butler, Eaton recalled, listened closely. Then he rose to declare: "This has settled one of the most serious problems of my life!" President Grant cried out: "I have made up my mind that if it comes to me I shall veto it."

Eaton and Sears were disappointed. Butler retained the mixed-school clause. Senators Morton and Buckingham voted to keep it in the Senate bill. The nation's representatives remained maddeningly obtuse. God took up the call. Henry Ward Beecher spoke for Him: "Popular education is the supreme need of the South," his *Christian Union* declared, "and that the Civil Rights Bill would go far to overthrow it seems to me the weightiest possible reason against its passage."[95] Only a feeble few, as Louisiana's Thomas Conway, voiced a lonely objection: "All that is wanted in this matter is to let the foes of the measure simply understand that we mean it," he pleaded. "Do this, and as in the case

---

93 Letter of Barnas Sears to Robert Winthrop. Jabez L.M. Curry, *A Brief Sketch of George Peabody and A History of the Peabody Education Fund Through Thirty Years* (Cambridge: 1898), 64–65.

94 John Eaton, *Grant, Lincoln and the Freedman: Reminiscences of the Civil War with Special Reference to the Work for the Contrabands and Freedmen of the Mississippi Valley* (New York: 1969), 262–264.

95 *Christian Union*, September 23, 1874, p. 230.

of the enemies of free schools in Louisiana, they will be quiet."[96] Respectable educators mocked him. Conway was a kook.[97]

All this weighed on one side of the balance. On the other side lay a light, feathery object, the intangible vision of racial harmony. The school clause, and the school clause alone, its advocates insisted, had the power to end prejudice. That miracle overrode all disadvantages. Sumner's Massachusetts colleague George Boutwell recited his dream to the Senate on May 21.

> The only way by which ideas [of equality] can be made universal is to bring together in public schools, during the forming period of life, the children of all classes, and educate them together. The public school is an epitome of life, and in it children are taught so that they understand those relations and conditions of life which, if not acquired in childhood and youth, are not likely afterward to be gained.... In the public school, where children of all classes and conditions are brought together, this doctrine of equality can be taught, and it is the chief means of securing the perpetuity of republican institutions.[98]

Boutwell's opponents also dreamed. Equality could be taught. Prejudice could be unlearned. That was the nightmare. Maryland's Congressman Ephraim Wilson spoke to the House on June 4.

> Who does not see that if the white and black children can be brought together in the same school-room, and there be made to pass the long years from early childhood through youth to early manhood upon terms of perfect equality such as you propose, sitting upon the same bench, joined in the same class, studying out of the same book, reciting the same lessons – possibly to a negro school-master – engaged in the same sports, enjoying the same amusements, all in the fullness of sympathy and freedom from restraint characterizing their tender years, and this system should go on

---

96 Conway's idyll exaggerated Louisiana's educational utopia. His vision nevertheless possessed more substance than his critics, Dr. Sears and others, cared to admit. Perhaps a third of New Orleans' schools had achieved some degree of integration. See Louis R. Harlan, "Desegregation in New Orleans Public Schools during Reconstruction," *American Historical Review*, 67 (1962): 664–667.

97 "Conway is a dog ... a miserable apology for a white man." Richmond *Dispatch*, June 2, 1874.

98 Remarks of George Boutwell, *Cong. Record*, 43rd Congress, 1st Session: 4116.

> from generation to generation, then social equality would not be a horrid eventuality to be feared, but a dread actuality realized.[99]

For both sides school-rooms were the battleground: social equality or degradation, life or death of education. Democrats pondered Republican intransigence. Republicans, they surmised, feared mixed schools. But they feared to drop the school clause because they feared to lose the support of their black adherents. Historians have agreed. "The demand from Negro voters for mixed school legislation was powerful and insistent." Pressure from black people forced them to uphold mixed schools.[100]

This theory, convenient as it may be, does not meet the facts. There was pressure, but it was far from insistent. Black people too wavered. Great leaders, to be sure, demanded integration. Out in the districts doubt set in. In states living under threat of a shut-down of the schools, in localities where barely any schools existed, a mandate certain to infuriate whites who held the purse-strings seemed a dangerous provocation.

In Tennessee, land of Col. Fleming's circular, black people met at Somerville in the west and at Rogersville in the east. They declared support for the Civil Rights Bill. But they preferred to abandon the mixed school clause. "Earnestly desiring the elevation of our race morally, socially, religiously, and deeming the education of our children essential to the attainments of these ends," read the Rogersville resolution, "we favor the present liberal provisions made for the education of our children."[101]

In Alabama black leaders argued bitterly over mixed schools. Some declared them essential. But a majority disagreed. They accepted the state party's platform: civil rights without mixed schools.[102] North Carolina's black assemblyman Edward Dudley submitted a civil rights bill for his state. He carefully omitted all reference to schools.

---

99 Speech of Ephraim Wilson, *Cong. Record*, 43rd Congress, 1st Session, Appendix: 419. Congressman Wilson was prophetic. He foresaw what would be, a hundred years later, the fight over forced busing: "You may even go a step further and vote to compel the whites to send their children to your seminaries of social equality. You will then see of what strength is the pride of race, color and mastership. The world has never seen such unflinching endurance, such heroic resolution, such sublime self-sacrifice as will then mark the white men and women of the South in their attempt to escape what they believe to be the degradation of their children and the ultimate contamination of their race."

100 Kelly, "Congressional Controversy over School Segregation," 539.

101 Savannah *News*, May 15, 1874; see also Daniel W. Crofts, "The Black Response to the Blair Education Bill," *Journal of Southern History*, 37 (1971): 51–55.

102 On the Alabama controversy, see below, 337–341.

Even the high command hesitated. Congressmen Elliott and Lynch advised the House Judiciary Committee. According to some reports they insisted on a mixed school clause. According to other accounts they urged Butler to strike it out.[103] Lynch and Elliott almost certainly suggested the course they later adopted publicly: support mixed schools, but not if they jeopardized everything else. If it came to a choice between a civil rights bill and mixed schools, yield the schools. Save the bill.

Rumors spread that the black congressmen had agreed to just such a concession. Those rumors reached Charles Sumner. Richard T. Greener, the black lawyer from South Carolina, tried to reassure the senator. "I sat in that very chair [in Sumner's study]," he told the Boston *Commonwealth*. "I saw his flaming indignation at the rumor that the colored representatives were about to desert him on the field of battle – such were his words – being willing to surrender the school clause in the civil-rights bill. With what conscious pride I bade him not be alarmed, for every representative from South Carolina would do his duty."[104] Greener was wrong. By the time he delivered his proud assertion the black representatives, led precisely by a South Carolinian, had deserted. On June 1 Richard Cain wrote directly to Ben Butler. He underlined his words for emphasis:

> The great interest which the colored people feel in the passage of the Civil Rights Bill at this time would demand that it should be passed either <u>with or without</u> the school clause.... We regard the jury and travel clause as essential to the whole people of the country, and rather than lose all, we believe that we would lose less by having the Bill pass without the school clause, believing that in the future that question will adjust itself in time. Many friends will vote for the bill without that <u>clause</u>, and will it not be better to have it now with that clause <u>out</u>? We confide in your wisdom and better judgment. If you can pass it today without that clause – for the people's sake let us have it.[105]

Every indication augured an early burial of the mixed school clause. Yet Republicans resisted. They stared down public opinion. They shrugged off Col. Fleming's threats. They ignored the learned advice of Dr. Sears, Dr. Ruffner and Commissioner Eaton. They declined Richard Cain's invitation, on behalf of the

103 Indianapolis *Journal*, January 31, 1874.
104 Boston *Commonwealth*, July 18, 1874.
105 Richard Cain to Benjamin Butler, June 1, 1874. Butler Papers, Library of Congress.

black people, to let the matter go. The school clause survived in the House. Stalwarts on Butler's Judiciary Committee refused to compromise.

It survived in the Senate. Frelinghuysen, Edmunds, Wright and Conkling advertised it as a measure of non-exclusion. Mixed schools did not survive in the end. But the demise of that clause came only after a monumental struggle. That Republicans dropped it is no surprise. It is remarkable they sustained it as long as they did. They conceded the fact finally: there was only one chance the nation might accept a civil rights law; it must be relieved of the impossible burden that dragged all else down.[106]

For the moment, in May, 1874, as the Senate prepared to act, the school clause lived. Republicans caucused again on the afternoon of the 18th. Some reports emerged that they considered coupling civil rights with an amnesty measure, so as to "sugar coat" it.[107] Nothing came of that. They agreed that the debate would commence on Wednesday, May 20. "The session should continue until the bill passed."[108]

No one doubted it would pass. Democrats might filibuster. Republicans now had the leisure to wait them out. Democrats complained that S.1 was a party measure; no Republican would oppose it in defiance of his leadership. Party solidarity, in fact, lay with the Democrats. No Democrat cared, or dared, to vote for the Civil Rights Bill. On the Republican side there were dissenters. Five Republicans defied the caucus; they voted their opposition. Two dissidents dwelt in the South. One lived on the border. The fourth came from New England. Matthew Carpenter of Wisconsin was the fifth. The southerners were William Brownlow of Tennessee and John Francis Lewis of Virginia. Brownlow's opposition was unyielding. Palsy prevented him from speaking on the Senate floor. He broadcast his views nonetheless to a national audience, dictating messages painfully through the pages of the press. He warned black people. Do not oppress the white race.[109]

Lewis of Virginia, facing reelection, had no hope of returning to the Senate from a state that had turned decisively Democratic. Instead, he withdrew in November to his home base, the Shenandoah Valley, to run for the House. That district currently belonged to the stalwart enemy of civil rights, Congressman John T. Harris. Harris had taken the popular position against the bill. It did not behoove his competitor to disagree. Lewis explained to his black constituents

106 In 1964 Congress' task was easier. The Supreme Court had done it a gigantic service, thanks to its decision in *Brown v. Board of Education* ten years earlier. It removed school desegregation from the table. One wonders how 1964 would have fared with that monster rattling in its cage.

107 Mobile *Register*, May 21, 1874.

108 Baltimore *Sun*, May 19; New York *World*, May 19, 1874.

109 On Brownlow's campaign of open letters, see below, 203–205.

why he could not, in good conscience, support their measure. Civil rights agitation would prove a disaster to the Republican Party. That would "be a calamity, and your race would be the greatest sufferers." It would ruin public education. Finally, said Lewis, he failed to see that black people suffered under the present state of things. They had their own schools, churches, their own vehicles of public conveyance. "What rights have my race that are not enjoyed by yours?"[110]

The recalcitrant border-state senator was Arthur Boreman of West Virginia. He made no speech to explain his misgivings. He waffled back and forth. He voted "no" when called upon in May. When the final civil rights bill came before the Senate in February, 1875, he switched and gave it his support.

The fourth dissent came from Lot Morrill of Maine. He did not speak in the forthcoming debate. But he had expressed his views during discussion of Sumner's earlier amnesty bill effort. He agreed with Matthew Carpenter. He could not reconcile the bill with the Constitution of the United States. It could not rest on the Thirteenth Amendment, which was "a mere negation of slavery." It could not rest on the Fourteenth Amendment, which was "in essence and effect a prohibition to the States." He sympathized with Sumner's dream, "to make freedmen freemen." He hoped to see the day when all would be treated equally. God alone could soften the hearts of the people. "I hope these things will be. But that is not a question for the Congress of the United States. That lies in a province outside of ours."[111]

Those five renegades apart, Republicans united behind the Civil Rights Bill. Democrats united against it. One additional bloc of senators, the six Liberal Republicans, remained. They could not swing the result one way or the other. If they could be persuaded to look kindly on the bill their support might soften some of its partisan edge. Ultimately none – Missouri's Carl Schurz, Thomas Tipton of Nebraska, Morgan Hamilton of Texas, New York's Reuben Fenton, Orris Ferry of Connecticut, William Sprague of Rhode Island – voted for the bill. Ferry, as he told Sumner, sympathized with civil rights. But he honored the Constitution.

> If it means all that he [Sumner] says, God help us; the foundations of civil liberty are stricken away from under us.... I would protect and buttress human rights in this land by the salvation of those local institutions which have made those rights so sacred to us, and which have made them now at last dominant over the continent. It is because this amendment is an insidious entering-wedge to overthrow those bulwarks, and because ...

110 Norfolk *Virginian*, June 18; Fredericksburg *Ledger*, June 19, 1874.

111 *Cong. Globe*, 42nd Congress, 2nd Session, Appendix: 1–4.

> if it be received as the law of this country we may bid farewell to our hopes of American liberty for the generations to come, that I oppose it.[112]

The Liberals' position nonetheless remained embarrassing. They proclaimed their love for the emancipated people. They professed to want equal rights. They rejected measures meant to secure those rights. "Juggles and tricks," Roscoe Conkling called it. They talked of principles but practiced deception, "these sinister men who have left us after many betrayals, to deceive the country as to the attitude of parties and individuals touching amnesty and Civil Rights."[113]

The Liberal viewpoint was hard to pin down. Journalist Samuel Bowles admitted Sumner's measure was flawed: "We do not shut our eyes to the fact that the pending bill is open to grave objections." But Bowles supported it. "It is the right and just thing." Indeed, Bowles asserted, had Liberal Republicans gained power in 1872, they would have upheld the promise of civil rights. There would have been no backsliding in a Horace Greeley administration, "with such men as Sumner, Schurz and Lyman Trumbull in its councils."[114] Most Liberals backslid frantically. Carl Schurz professed undying love for Sumner, none for his bill. Lyman Trumbull had written the Civil Rights Act of 1866. He opposed the measure intended to supplement it. Yet Bowles was not the only civil rights bill advocate in the Liberal camp. Nathaniel Banks prepared to run again for Congress in Massachusetts' 5th District. If elected, he said, he would vote for the bill.[115]

Liberal Republicans delivered a muddled message. Their most eloquent spokesman, Carl Schurz, squirmed under the weight of the Civil Rights Bill. He sat by Sumner's death-bed. He heard the senator's dying injunction: save my civil rights bill. He eulogized his departed friend to tearful audiences. He declined to honor the sacred legacy. The Senate debated. Schurz was mute. The Senate voted. Schurz was absent.[116]

"Where was Schurz?" demanded the Chicago *Inter Ocean.* "Where was this champion and friend of Mr. Sumner, who announced only a few days ago that he assumed the fallen mantle.... Whatever of honor he has merited and

---

112 *Cong. Globe*, 42nd Congress, 2nd Session: 894.

113 Roscoe Conkling to Gerrit Smith, May 17, 1872. Gerrit Smith Papers, Syracuse University.

114 Springfield, Massachusetts, *Republican*, June 16, 1874. On Bowles see Richard Allan Gerber, "Liberal Republicanism, Reconstruction, and Social Order: Samuel Bowles as a Test Case," *New England Quarterly* (1972): 393–407.

115 Springfield *Republican*, October 23, 1874.

116 On Schurz see Richard Allan Gerber, "Carl Schurz's Journey from Radical to Liberal Republican: A Problem in Ideological Consistency," *Mid-America*, 82 (2000): 71–99. Cf. Hans L. Trefouuse, *Carl Schurz A Biography* (New York: 1998).

received is wrecked by this craven act."[117] Schurz's desertion, said the Boston *Commonwealth,* proved the hollowness of the Liberal Republican movement.[118] Schurz's home state press was hardly more forgiving. The St. Louis *Globe* laughed at him, "the spotless and useless Senator from Missouri."[119] At the moment of the civil rights vote, it was true, illness had immobilized him.[120] Still he could have paired off with a colleague, and thus stood by his opinions. "But Mr. Schurz has a way of 'pairing off' with himself." "Where was Schurz?" echoed the Springfield, Missouri, *Patriot.* "He is playing it very fine; but no half way grounds will do any more."[121] "The great German Senator forgot to vote," noted the Gallatin *Democrat.* "Will he 'rise and explain' why 'these things are thus?'"[122] Even his German compatriots criticized him. "True, he has been ill," conceded the *Anzeiger des Westens.* "But he might at least have written a line or two to let his constituents know how he would have voted on the bill, and what position he intends to occupy hereafter."[123]

Carl Schurz could not remain silent. On September 24 he stood before an overflow crowd at the Temple Hall in St. Louis. For five hours he held forth: the state of the nation. The present political system, power revolving endlessly between two parties, was crumbling. "The old dingdong of party cant begins to fall stale upon the ear." Democracy was in danger. "By a sort of dry-rot our institutions may gradually lose their vitality.... Government will become the football of rapacious and despotic factions." The South was in disarray. Race hatred raged. He came at last to the Civil Rights Bill.

> That measure was brought forward and pressed by the dearest friend I ever had among the public men of America.... Nobody knows better than I do that it sprung from the purest motives.... But it was based upon a theory of Constitutional power and upon views of policy upon which my friend and I had for years agreed to disagree.

The Civil Rights Bill, Schurz insisted, was not a solution but part of the problem. It trapped black people. It beguiled them into allegiance to one party. Lured by the Republicans' shimmering promises, they entered the tar pit

117 Chicago *Inter Ocean,* May 26, June 1, 1874.
118 Boston *Commonwealth,* May 30, 1874.
119 Quoted in Washington *National Republican,* June 6; Galveston *News,* June 6, 1874.
120 Reports confirmed Schurz in late May "severely ill," confined to bed, unable to return to the Senate until June 8. Paterson *Press,* June 9, 1874.
121 Springfield, Missouri, *Patriot,* May 28, 1874.
122 Gallatin, Missouri, *Democrat,* May 28, 1874.
123 Quoted in Mobile *Register,* June 14, 1874.

and were sucked down. They alienated whites, who might otherwise be their friends. They deepened dependence on false friends, who exploited them for political gain.

Schurz had a remedy. Abandon civil rights legislation. Would that not perpetuate discrimination? Quite the opposite. Let the freedmen trust in the better instincts of human nature. Surely those instincts would prevail. If they waited in quiet, industrious patience, assimilation would do its work. Schurz propounded a paradox: "Not in union is their safety, but in division." United, black people marginalized themselves on the side of a fading Republican Party. Divided, they could wield a powerful force. They must demand equality not from Republicans but from Democrats, as the price of their votes.

> Here, I think, is the way to solve the most difficult part of the problem. They cannot too soon give up the delusion that they will be safe only as long as they remain together in the same political organization.... As soon as every one of them casts his vote on this side or the other, as his opinions or inclinations may dictate, each party will make their protection a special object in order to attract a majority of those votes.... When the colored voters become an important element, not only in one, but in both parties, under an impulse of self-interest each party will rival in affording them the fullest measure of protection.[124]

The flaw in Schurz's thesis, of course, a flowering of social justice born of politicians' self-interested grasping for votes, resided in the near impossibility of conceiving any reason why a black person, "as his inclinations may dictate," would ever feel inclined to cast a vote on the Democratic side. That did not worry the Liberals. Whites, they were convinced, would come around to the blacks, if only the latter gave them a chance.[125]

Nathaniel Banks advanced the same proposition: "All differences would be righted swiftly, for there were no enmities so great between men that could not be softened in politics. No Southerner had so great a hatred toward the negro that he would not ask of him and accept his vote." Banks imagined the scene: white men recover power in the South; fine; soon the victors divide into

124 Carl Schurz, *Speeches Correspondence and Political Papers of Carl Schurz*, ed. Frederic Bancroft, (New York, 1913), vol. 2, 90–95.

125 Republicans commented caustically: "Senator Schurz thinks that the blacks would avoid all persecution if they would only divide their votes between the two parties.... There could be no difficulty if they did not insist on voting against the party that encourages the persecution and massacre of their race.... If another Know-Nothing movement arose ... would he advise the men of his own nationality and other foreigners to divide their votes between their friends and their enemies?" Terre Haute *Express*, September 26, 1874.

factions; those in the minority appeal to black voters; black people acquire by their own strength what they could not otherwise.

> They [dissident Democrats] would go to the negro and say, "Come and we will oust these men." The negro would inquire: "Will you allow us to go into the same hotel with you, to ride in the same car or steamboat with you, to go to the opera, the theater, or ball with you?" If they were answered "No," then they would say, "We will not vote for you." But they would receive no such answer. They would, in fact, hold the balance of power, and could secure for themselves whatever was right.[126]

Nebraska's Liberal Republican Thomas Tipton addressed the Senate on January 13, 1875. He repeated the mantra. Divide and ye shall receive your rights.

> Call home your Army.... The first result might be power in the hands of the conservatives; and what would be the next result? The colored man would go to his rice-field; he would go to his sugar-plantation; he would work, work, work, prepare to educate his children, prepare himself to discharge the duties of political life. He would not be left long in that attitude. O, no; an independent democratic conservative candidate would come up ... and what would he do? Go right to the colored element, conciliate it – gentlemen, you know how that is done – get all that vote for himself. They would not be assassinated, for then they would be voting for a conservative ... and everybody would be singing paeans to the glory of the colored voters and how bravely the colored troops had fought.[127]

In fact, the Liberals' scenario had already failed. The fall elections exploded it. Cracks did appear in the Democrats' solid southern phalanx. Independent candidates vied for the vote. By exploiting those cracks black people, such was the theory, ought to have received some of their desires. They received none. Georgia's 7th District provided a perfect test. A bolting, independent conservative, just as Tipton imagined him, Dr. William Felton, challenged the Democratic establishment. Black voters voted for him, as Carl Schurz recommended.[128] Felton won. But he made no attempt to "conciliate." He denounced civil rights bills, during the campaign and after.[129]

---

126 New York *Tribune*, December 9; Chicago *Tribune*, December 9, 1874.

127 Remarks of Thomas Tipton, *Cong. Record* 43rd Congress, 2nd Session: 487.

128 Jones, "William H. Felton and the Independent Movement," 53; Rebecca Latimer Felton, *My Memories of Georgia Politics* (Atlanta, 1911), 156.

129 Jones, "Felton," 41.

In the Alabama 6th District another test came and went. Democrats declined to re-nominate their incumbent, Joseph Sloss. He too ran as an independent. Black people voted for him. Sloss repaid them by voting against the Civil Rights Bill.

Liberals dreamed. Republicans let them dream. They prepared to produce the purblind child. Before that moment, one last prenatal event occurred. On May 4 California's Aaron Sargent introduced Senate Bill 774. He called for desegregation of the army: "A bill to repeal so much of the laws relating to the organization of the Army of the United States as establish distinctions to the prejudice of one class of American citizens." S.774 revoked provisions of the Army Act of 1866 which restricted the service of black soldiers to certain designated regiments. Henceforth all formations were to be open and mixed in all branches of the military service. Sargent's bill instructed the Secretary of War to effect the end of discrimination by the transfer and reassignment of black troops into existing units. Recruitment of black soldiers must also reflect the proportion of black people in the population of the country. The bill was read twice by title and referred to the Committee on Military Affairs.[130] There it died. It was left to President Truman to enact Sargent's proposition.

Meanwhile Sumner's civil rights bill took to the floor. Debate recommenced on May 20, as the caucus had ordained. Norwood's taunts still rankled. The rejoinder came in the avuncular guise and homespun cadences of James Flanagan of Texas. Norwood had mocked Frelinghuysen. He had laughed – he who, though of age and fit, had sat out the war – laughed at the dead soldiers of New Market Heights. Flanagan laughed at Norwood. "Show me a man who was not in the army," he drawled, "I will show you a man that is ready to fight like the man who fought the Indians at Tippecanoe."

> There was a soldier who had early in the action found a secure place and gotten into it, and he lay there quietly until the battle was all over.... At length his head emerged like a turtle and out he came. He looked around and saw no eye upon him. He saw a musket hard by with a bayonet, lying by a dead man. He ran to it and took hold of it and ran it through the first dead Indian he came across, saying, "I will let you know, Mr. Indian, that I'm some pumpkins, too." Now these gentlemen who were never in the war first or last are some pumpkins.[131]

130 San Francisco *Elevator*, May 9; Nashville *Union and American*, May 10, 1874.

131 Speech of James Flanagan, *Cong. Record*, 43rd Congress, 1st Session, Appendix: 371–377.

Civil rights, Norwood said, meant amalgamation – Miss Angelina Octoroon and her kin. Amalgamation, Flanagan mused. Gentleman need not fear amalgamation. They had been amalgamating for generations.

> I come down to the simple, plain fact and illustrate it thus: In the happy South the cotton-planter plants his seed, or he who grows corn puts the corn in the ground, or he who cultivates his rye and his wheat and all cereals plants the seed; and now I ask, without pursuing that idea further, are the mulattoes, quadroons, and everything else he invoked so beautifully, indigenous? ... There must have been some planting, yes, and by Democrats principally.[132]

"Moonshine!" Norwood called out from his seat, chipper as ever.

"My friend says it is moonshine," Flanagan returned. "Yes, moonshine. I take it for granted he understands that exactly. When the moon is shining the eyes of the world are not upon A, B, and C. The races get along very well then ... behind the haystack."

Flanagan rummaged in his waistcoat pockets. He pulled forth a fragment of paper, a clipping torn from that day's edition of the Washington *Daily Chronicle*: "a little matter that meets my observation this morning." Passengers on the Chesapeake and Ohio Railroad leaving West Virginia were startled to see a couple board the train, a black man and a white woman. They were bound for the north to get married. "The man was of gingerbread color," Flanagan read, "about twenty years of age, and the woman was a good-looking young girl, recently from England, and about thirty years of age."

> Now I have this to say on that matter. The English woman, mind you, was thirty, the boy was only twenty. She had crossed the Atlantic; she had seen much of the world. The boy had seen but little. If there was any running off between the two, which ran off with the other, the white woman with the black boy, or the black boy with the old white woman? [Laughter] Social equality! It is hard to say whether it preponderates upon the side of the woman or the man, the gingerbread man or the white woman.

---

132 "Preech agin amalgamashen," the satirical Nasby echoed Flanagan's advice to Democrats. "Preech agin amalgamshen at least four Sundays per month. A man uv straw that yoo set up yerself is the easiest knockt down, partikelerly if yoo set him up with a view uv knockin uv him down.... Learn to spell and pronounce Missenegenegenashen. It's a good word." David Ross Locke, *The Struggles ... of Petroleum V. Nasby*: 117.

> If I could guess, I should say that the gingerbread boy got the worst of that bargain. [Laughter]

Flanagan concluded.

> Mr. President, let my expressions go for what they are worth, and that may be very little. I will not undertake to put an estimate upon them; but one thing I well know: Sleeping or waking, standing or lying, living or dying, I stand forth in defense of five millions of people who have recently been emancipated, and I will ever stand by them, so far as my vote or influence can go, for perpetual and eternal freedom.

Flanagan's performance contrasted with the other major speech of the day. Allen Thurman delivered another legal objection. He raised the Democrats' fundamental point. The Civil Rights Bill could not rest on the Fourteenth Amendment.

> It is not aimed at any law of a State. It is aimed against the acts of individuals; it is aimed against keepers of theaters, keepers of circuses, keepers of hotels, managers of railroads, stage-coaches, and the like.... We, the Federal power, will seize the man ... we will treat the keeper of a theater as the State; we will treat the hotel keeper as the State; we will treat the stage-driver as the State.... That is what this bill is; and no sophistry can make it anything else.... If this is not monstrous, if this is not inhuman, if it is not a violation of the first principles of right ... if it is not legislation utterly disgraceful to a civilized people, then I confess, Mr. President, that I am not able to see correctly what is the scope or purpose of this legislation, or what are the principles of right and justice that should prevail under a civilized government.[133]

Thurman turned to the Judiciary Committee's distorted interpretation of the mixed-school clause. The deception was obvious. The simplest grasp of grammar proved it.

> They say this bill does not require mixed schools.... Yet that [same clause] means mixed audiences, does it not [at a theater]? It means mixed guests at a hotel, does it not? It means mixed travelers on a railway or in a stage-coach, does it not? If not, it does not mean anything.... Mixture is meant

133 Speech of Allen Thurman: *Cong. Record*, 43rd Congress, 1st Session: 4083–4090.

> in inns, in public conveyances on land or water, in theaters, in other places of public amusement, and then it goes right on, "and" – there is the copulative conjunction, and as if to make that more emphatic the word "also" is added – "and also in common schools and public institutions of learning."... There is no getting rid of it.

Thurman's oration ended the session of May 20. On the 21st debate resumed briefly. George Boutwell also expressed dismay at Frelinghuysen's interpretation of the mixed school clause. He recited his dream. Prejudice would end when schoolhouses opened to all. "Narrow-minded, bigoted, and withal a coward, a charlatan, a hypocrite, and a fraud," commented the Richmond *Dispatch*. "It is a good thing such a man cannot live always.... Not even his theories will survive him."[134]

Republicans had vowed to sit it out, to debate until the bill passed. But after Boutwell's plea they adjourned again. They took time for a pleasant interlude, a White House wedding, presidential daughter Nellie Grant and her dashing English beau Algernon Sartoris. The choice required little reflection: a wedding feast or a sleepless night of civil rights speeches. Black people's aspirations could wait one more day.

Friday, May 22. The wedding came off splendidly, though the marriage did not. Republicans determined to uphold their caucus pledge. The session would not end until S.1 passed. Timothy Howe of Wisconsin began the festivities. Democrats were not fond of the Wisconsin statesman, his cool mannerisms and didactic speeches. Tall, angular, his face "innocent of hair," he posed like an exasperating old schoolteacher.[135] "I find it is not easy to frame an argument in defense of this bill," Howe observed. "No truth is so hard to demonstrate by reasoning as that which is self-evident; and to me the simple justice of the provisions of this bill is self-evident." He contended first with Thurman's constitutional questions. The Constitution was not as the senator from Ohio conceived. The senator's reading was out of date.

> I admit that when your Constitution was framed originally, there was committed to the Government of the United States no power to do the things we propose to do in this bill. I admit when that Constitution was

134 Richmond *Dispatch*, June 4, 1874.

135 "He approaches his seat in a painfully nonchalant manner," wrote the Greeneville Tennessee *Democrat* (June 4, 1878). "When he rises to speak he will carelessly shift a book on the desk with an air of absent-mindedness, thrust his left hand into his breeches pocket, pull up his right pants leg, lift his right foot into a chair, place his right elbow on his knee and begin to shake his forefinger in a most impressive manner."

> framed its makers committed the status and condition of individual citizens to the control of the States within which they lived.... There was a malign power reserved to the government of every State to deprive any ... of its citizens of every one of the commonest rights of the commonest man, and they did it. The time was when every State did it. The time is, thank God, when no State can do it.... The Constitution has been changed, you may have heard, sir. Some prerogatives have been withdrawn from the States; some new faculties or powers have been given to the Government of the United States. Three whole chapters have been added to the organic law. One of them ... was made on purpose to transfer the control of citizens to the Government of the United States.[136]

The Fourteenth Amendment, Thurman had argued, applied only to the acts of states. No state, by legal act, had abridged its citizens' privileges; the national government could not intervene. Howe disagreed. The government could intervene. It had intervened, even before the Fourteenth Amendment. Fugitive slave laws provided the precedent.

> You passed an act in 1850. It was not directed to any State; it was directed to all the citizens of all the States. It did not merely tell them in the language of the Constitution let the master take his escaped servant back; give him up; it did not tell them that; but the law told all the citizens of all the States to "*catch him, take him back,*" and they did it.[137]

Still gentlemen insisted that only state action could trigger the Fourteenth Amendment. That prerequisite too had been met. "Sir, if we must wait until we find a State which does not decree what this bill does, I am sorry to say we have waited long enough. I will introduce you to the State. You will find it in the State of Georgia." He lifted a heavy tome: *The Civil Code of Georgia*, revised edition, 1873. "Georgia is discriminating," Howe thumbed the text, "acutely so. Georgia makes rather minute divisions of persons."

> "Natural persons are distinguished" – says the Code – "according to their rights and status into: first, citizens; second, residents not citizens; third, aliens; fourth, *persons of color.*" – Pretty accurate that! – Says

136 Speech of Timothy Howe: *Cong. Record*, 43rd Congress, 1st Session: 4147–4152.

137 John Marshall Harlan repeated the argument in 1883: "The right of the master to have his slave, thus escaping, delivered up on claim being guaranteed by the Constitution, the fair implication was that the national government was clothed with appropriate authority and functions to enforce it."

> Georgia: "Among the rights of *citizens* are the enjoyment of personal security" – very necessary – "of personal liberty" – a convenient thing to have – "private property and the disposition thereof, the elective franchise, the right to hold office ... to appeal to the courts, to testify as a witness, to perform civil function, and to keep and bear arms." It is a good thing to be a citizen in Georgia, provided Georgia recognizes you as a citizen. It is of no account to be a citizen of Georgia if you are a colored person.

Dr. Ruffner's dissertation sat badly, in Howe's opinion. He quoted the expert's words.

> "Will politicians never learn that social laws are laws of nature?" ... No, Mr. President, they will never learn that; never, never. It is not true.... There is not in Washington a white child, until politics gets possession of the unfortunate to some extent, that makes the slightest discrimination between the white and black race; not one. Politicians teach that prejudice. It is not a law of nature; it is one of the worst and most degrading lessons we learn, and one of the most mischievous.

Timothy Howe, who professed he could not find words to defend a self-evident proposition, found words.

> The bill imposes no burdens upon any one. It simply commands that we get off from the freedman; not partly off, but altogether off, not off his neck alone, but off his skirts as well. You are not required to lift him to his feet, but to let him get on to his feet if he can; not to lead him on his way, only not to trip him as he staggers on his way.... The Republican party only requires that you stand back and let the oppressed of centuries stagger to their feet if they can.... We are told that a pebble dropped into the middle of the Atlantic will cause its multitudinous waters to pulsate on either shore. Is there an American who does not yearn for that happy day when the hand of insult wantonly laid upon any citizen shall awaken a throb of indignation in every home throughout the Republic?

James Lusk Alcorn of Mississippi took the floor. Of all the southern Republicans civil rights seemed to cause him agonies of indecision. He had opposed Sumner's project and voted against it in 1872. Now he supported it. Yet before the end of his life he opposed it. He helped write into law the disfranchisement of those same black people whose rights he defended. For the moment at least, he defended them.

> Are we of the South prejudiced against the negro? In my childhood the negro was my playmate; in my early manhood he was my confidant; in my mature years he was my friend; as my slave he was my friend.... Ah, Mr. President, I was transferred to the arms of a colored nurse.... Do you tell me, I repeat, that we feel a prejudice against the colored people? It is unnatural. It is not possible.

Mississippi, Alcorn declared, needed no Civil Rights Bill. "We have a civil-rights bill of our own more stringent than any you will pass in this Congress, its penalties more severe, its workings more in detail – complete in itself for the protection of the colored people." As it was in Mississippi, so it could be everywhere.[138]

Alcorn won new friends. Frederick Douglass discovered a renewed esteem for the senator. Alcorn thanked him: "The course I have pursued is but the response of my heart."[139] His warmhearted response, concluded the Memphis *Appeal,* reflected his coldhearted desire to keep black people's votes.[140]

Lewis Bogy took the floor. Night had arrived, inspiring his evocation of the dark. After that Gothic opening, centralization was his theme. The federal government, ravenous, insatiable, drew everything into its maw: steamboats, inns, theaters, schools, and everyone connected with them.[141] The civil rights bill was one more facet in a crown of despotism riveted upon the republic. Other bills even now were being considered: a bill to establish a national university; a bill to establish a federal commission on alcoholic beverages; a bill to fund national institutes for the advancement of science and industry; a bill to establish a national board of health. "If we possess the power to do these things it would save a vast deal of expense, and a vast deal of trouble, many useless elections, to do away with the entire State governments and let us have one grand imperial Prussian government here, because it will be so in fact."

Ten hours into the debate Republicans had spoken their piece. They fell silent. The Senate chamber emptied. Republicans made themselves scarce. They commenced to rest in shifts. Democrats labored to keep the session going. Eli

138 Speech of James Alcorn, *Cong. Record,* 43rd Congress, 1st Session: App., 302–307.

139 Washington *New National Era,* June 4, 1874. In his biographer's opinion there was "a basic consistency" in Alcorn's behavior. During Reconstruction he "trimmed his sails to the prevalent political winds," but he viewed black people at best with paternalistic forbearance. He respected their rights paternally, until the political winds changed again. Lillian A. Pereyra, *James Lusk Alcorn: Persistent Whig* (Baton Rouge: 1966), 195–197.

140 Memphis *Appeal,* May 26, 1874.

141 Speech of Lewis Bogy: *Cong. Record,* 43rd Congress, 1st Session: App., 318–323.

Saulsbury of Delaware watched the Republicans go, filing into the cloakrooms to smoke and sleep. Let them go. They slept the sleep of the damned.

> So far as I am concerned, I say to them sleep on; take your rest now; there is coming a day when the American people will hold you and your party to a strict responsibility for present indifference to their wishes, and for the great wrong you propose by this bill to inflict upon them.[142]

For those still awake Saulsbury had a word: Prejudice.

> We have been told that all this is prejudice. The Senator from New York the other day ... spoke of the feeling to which I have referred as a paltry hate, as a prejudice which had been trampled out in blood. Suppose it is prejudice; suppose it is nothing but prejudice? Why, sir, all history attests that men will die for their prejudices.... Call it prejudice if you please; it exists, and I hope and trust it may forever exist.

Three types of Americans, said Saulsbury, only three, willingly endured contact with Negroes. First there were the fools: "a class of misguided, fanatical gentlemen who suppose that by association with colored people they may better their condition." Then there were the depraved: "that class of mankind who have lost their own self-respect by indulgence in vice, or by the commission of crime ... conscious in their own bosoms of their own self-degradation." Finally there were the Republicans: "corrupt politicians, who for partisan purposes alone, for the purpose of securing the vote of the colored man, may be willing to associate with him." Folly, depravity, and corruption; from that foul mixture the Civil Rights Bill was confected. Saulsbury closed hopefully. "If the Party to which I belong shall come to be in the ascendant in this Chamber and at the other end of the Capitol, it will be one of the proudest acts of my life, if I am permitted to be here, to move the repeal of the statute which you now propose to pass."

Twelve hours of debate had passed. Sleep overspread the chamber. "Four-fifths of the Senators are in the cloak rooms, either smoking or asleep," the New York *Times* reporter wrote, "and the other fifth asleep on the floor." Republicans snored. Democrats too tried to rest. But the paucity of their numbers told in the exhaustion of their speakers. "Shades of evening began to wrap the Capitol in gloom," the Charleston *News and Courier* described the scene. "The electric

142 Speech of Eli Saulsbury: *Cong. Record*, 43rd Congress, 1st Session: 4157–4162.

flash put life into the myriads of gas burners which encircle the glass roof of the Senate chamber." Unequal combat continued.

> On one side ... nothing but vacant seats were to be seen while most of those to whom they belonged were stretching themselves in careless abandon on the luxurious sofas in the rear, or gathering in groups in the retiring rooms, puffing their Havanas.... On the other side the feeble band fighting for the rights of all the people ... fighting in vain, no one to listen to their pleadings... Such was the scene as the hours wore on.[143]

Other observers took a merrier view.

> Time: half past one o'clock. Mr. Howe of Wisconsin has the floor. Senators Hager and Mitchell are industriously writing letters to loved ones at home; Senator Chandler is reading his correspondence; Senator Pease is enjoying the peaceful slumber of the just; Senators Carpenter and Frelinghuysen are attempting to pay attention to the speaker's words; Senator Conkling is writing; Senator Hamlin, when not squirting tobacco juice on the carpet, is reading a Maine newspaper; Senator Flanagan sleeps sweetly, but snores occasionally.... Senator Bogy is reading an account of the Grant-Sartoris wedding, and wondering why the reporter forgot to describe the gorgeous appearance of the Missouri statesman. Half past two o'clock. Mr. Howe is still speaking, but a change has occurred in the attendance. The first relief has arrived.... Flanagan's head has fallen back over the back of his chair, and there is great danger that he will break the spinal column; Cooper reads a Memphis paper.... All other Senators have gone out to see a man – or woman.[144]

Vice-President Wilson was long gone. Presiding officers – Carpenter, Stewart, Spencer, Wright, Ingalls – rotated in the chair. One senator maintained his vigil: Roscoe Conkling. Frelinghuysen came and went. Edmunds made his presence felt at the end. Conkling was there, always to be seen and heard through the night. He questioned Senator Kelly, who spoke at nine o'clock. He perturbed Senator Merrimon at 11. At 3:00 he traded jokes with Hamilton of Maryland. The conductor of an orchestra, he sat at the front of the hall, occupying a place

---

143 Charleston *News and Courier*, May 28, 1874.

144 Boston *Post*, quoted in Wilmington, North Carolina *Journal*, June 11, 1874. The reporter's observation was slightly inaccurate. Senator Hamilton, not Senator Howe, spoke from 1:30 to 4 a.m.

at the clerk's desk.[145] He was still there when the Civil Rights Bill, S.1, passed the Senate at 7 o'clock on the morning of May 23, 1874.

The floor fell to Augustus Merrimon. North Carolina's junior senator was 43, beginning his first and only term. Earnest, clean-shaven, with a round, benevolent face, he was eager to join the debates. Though a Democrat, he owed his unexpected election victory over ex-governor Zebulon Vance to Republican support in the legislature. "As a Senator, by the blessing of Providence," he announced to North Carolinians, "it is my unalterable purpose to do my utmost to benefit and bless the whole people.... I shall insist upon right for all. I will not willingly tolerate wrong or oppression to any."[146]

Merrimon opened his mouth. As if on cue, the chamber emptied. He stopped. The exodus accelerated. Merrimon's frustration grew. He suggested the absence of a quorum. He yielded for that purpose to his fellow North Carolinian, Matt Ransom. Ransom for some reason, perhaps befuddled by sleepiness, called not for a quorum but to adjourn. Senators stumbled back to the chamber. The motion was voted down. Roscoe Conkling jumped up: "Question on the bill." Ransom was stunned. His motion had cost Democrats the floor. The clerk called Alcorn's name, first on the roll. He responded: Aye.

Merrimon, alarmed: "I think I had the floor."

Old Hannibal Hamlin answered, no doubt with mischief in his eye: "If my friend will allow me, there is a parliamentary rule which declares that a man shall sit down when he gets done speaking. [Laughter]"

"That is the very point," returned Merrimon. "I am not done speaking by a great deal, but I do not want to speak to empty seats."

Hamlin: "I do not think you will get much else to speak to to-night."

Conkling: "I would suggest, if the Senator from North Carolina wishes to speak to the Senator from Maine, as that Senator is spending the night in the cloak-room, he would be compelled to go there in order to have a conversation with him. [Laughter]"

Merrimon: "I am equally anxious to speak to the honorable Senator from New York."

Conkling: "I have been remaining here all the time for the pleasure of hearing the Senator." Republicans had no real intention of spoiling the Democrats' filibuster. They returned the floor to a flustered Merrimon. He continued his speech to an ever more somnolent audience. He posed a series of conundrums:

145 New York *World*, Washington *National Republican*, Wheeling *Intelligencer*, May 23, 1874.

146 Maud L. Merrimon, *A Memoir: Augustus Summerfield Merrimon* (Raleigh: 1894), 75.

> Why did God make our skins white? Why did He make the negro's skin black? Why did He make the other races of different colors? Why did He make these different races materially different, physically and mentally? Why did He make the mountains? Why did He make the seas? Why did He make the sun, moon, and stars in their orbits? Why did He make us with life? Why did He make us with souls? If you will answer one of these questions, I will answer the others. But these natural facts exist, and who shall dare to change, or attempt to change the course and harmony of nature? And who shall dare to blot out the distinctions of race?[147]

No one answered. No one woke up. Merrimon warned nonetheless. "I tell the negroes that they owe it to themselves.... Keep the white race away from them; and I say on the other hand, that the white race owe it to themselves in like manner to keep the negro away from them.... The Almighty for all-wise purposes has made this distinction ... and when we shall strike down His law, so sure as we do it, He will curse us."

At 1:20 Merrimon sat down. His relief emerged from the cloak-room. William Hamilton made the night's final speech. One can only regret the circumstances that compelled him to deliver his words to an empty, echoing chamber. The Marylander provided one of the most cogent discussions on the opposition side. He argued not for prejudice, nor the worship of God's design. He argued for free enterprise and private property in a country worshipful of free enterprise and private property.

> If there is a right that is natural and that belongs to me because I am a citizen and entitled to the protection of the laws, it is to transact my own private business in my own way without the interference of government, so that I do no injury to others. Have you not a right, Mr. President, has not every person a right, to carry on his own occupation, to secure the fruits of his own industry, and appropriate them as best suits himself? ... A man has an equal right to keep an inn; and when you undertake to say that because inns are licensed establishments they derive their existence from government, and that therefore they are an institution under the regulation and control of government, it is to me thoroughly absurd.... This idea that because a theater is licensed, because a hotel or a saloon or an oyster-house or a store of any kind is licensed, therefore the business is

147 Speech of Augustus Merrimon, *Cong. Record*, 43rd Congress, 1st Session: App., 307–318.

> of such a nature that it cannot be carried on without the direct and written authority of government, with a license to do so, is a great mistake.[148]

Licenses, licensing; that was the majority's excuse. For that they intruded into the affairs of private enterprise. For that they told a man whom he must respect, whose society he must endure, whom he must accept as a customer. Licenses did not exist so the State could dictate to free people. They were devices established for taxation. They were that and nothing more. They gave the State no power to control the proprietor.[149] A tradesman might treat the public as he inclined. He could decide to whom he would deliver, or refuse to deliver, services he rendered. Provision of a license gave government no license to interfere. Freedom otherwise became a formality.[150]

Furthermore, said Hamilton, the bill limited itself to licensed establishments. Yet an entire world of unlicensed entities existed. Why not add them on to the bill?

> Why limit this bill to inns? ... Why not apply it to eating-houses? ... You have eating-houses everywhere. He [the Negro] cannot go into an eating-house under this bill unless it comes under the generic words "other places of public amusement." They are not allowed to go into grocery stores, where they can get bacon, and flour, and lard, and whisky – that is in the days of whisky – and tobacco, and sugar, and molasses – why

148 Speech of William Hamilton: *Cong. Record*, 43rd Congress, 1st Session: App., 361–368.

149 Licensing was vital to civil rights' proponents in 1874. It remained so in 1964. "Restaurants, hotels and motels generally operate under license from municipalities, which in turn are creatures of the State. Therefore they are in a sense State agents," Senator Paul Douglas declared. "The 14th amendment protects individuals against acts of the States, and therefore the 14th amendment can protect individuals against acts of the licensees of the State." *Cong. Record*, 88th Congress, 2nd Session: 13,923.

150 Hamilton's argument, death of freedom, pointed to another idea: civil rights regulations reinstituted slavery, as the Thirteenth Amendment phrased it, involuntary servitude. That line of thought did not appear in 1874, but it became a favorite theme in 1964. "Discrimination is but another word for free choice," wrote constitutional scholar Alfred Avins. "In dealings between men, both cannot be free unless each acts *voluntarily*; otherwise one is subjected to the other's will.... When a white woman [employed as a masseuse] is compelled to give a Negress a Swedish massage, that is involuntary servitude." (Alfred Avins, "Freedom of Choice in Personal Service Occupations: Thirteenth Amendment Limitations on Antidiscrimination Legislation," *Cornell Law Quarterly*, 49 (1964): 228–256) Avins' article, reprinted in newsmagazines, replete with legal citations, provided fodder for the filibuster of his day. Senators Thurmond, Smathers, Sparkman, Hill and Ervin all read it repeatedly into the Record. *Cong. Record*, 88th Congress, 2nd Session: 6,429, 7,917, 8,505, 8,633, 9,622, 13,474.

> not include grocery stores? ... A colored man may go to a store, and the store-keeper can say "I will not sell to you. To your race and color I object, and you must leave my store." Why is this? The store-keeper is not embraced in the provisions of the bill.... Then your shoemakers. Negroes want shoes; the shoemaker may decline to sell them shoes, and the tailor may decline to make clothes for them.... Why not make your bill coextensive with the needs of the existence of the colored man, commencing with the shoemaker or butcher if you please, and going up to the inn?

Hamilton's prescience suggested another problem faced a century later: fair housing.

> The colored man has a right to live in a house, that is, if he can get one. One may refuse to rent him a house because he is a colored man. Why not make that an offense? Though the house is taxed, yet it may be refused. A colored man may call on you, Mr. President, to rent him your house; it is known to be for rent; it may be advertised in the paper for rent; and you may tell that colored man, "You cannot have my house because you are a colored man," and the fourteenth amendment leaves him helpless against you, that is, so far as this bill is concerned, for it does not deign to notice this kind of injury.

Hamilton concluded. The bill was an absurdity. It imposed government control on private enterprise, where it was not warranted. It left discrimination untouched where it was rampant. He drew out his pocket-watch. "This is the bill, Mr. President. It is now near three o'clock in the morning."

Conkling, keen as ever: "Is that in the bill?"

Hamilton, unperturbed: "That is not in the bill, but it should be, so as to have it appear that at three o'clock in the morning or thereabout a bill was passed ... to enforce, among equally strange things, upon proprietors and citizens in the States the obligation of admitting people of color into their own theaters, their own private property.... I shall take up this bill and look over it with them [my constituents], and I know I can talk to my African fellow-citizens as well as to my white brethren upon some details of this bill."

Conkling: "You will have to do that, because that will be a place of amusement when you come to do that. [Laughter]"

At 4 o'clock Hamilton finished. Daybreak approached. Democrats surrendered. They could speak no more. The Civil Rights Bill commenced its passage through the Senate.[151] Amendments came first. Aaron Sargent called for a vote

---

151 Votes and passage, *Cong. Record*, 43rd Congress, 1st Session: 4166–4176.

on his proposal to add separate-but-equal to the school clause. It failed by a slim margin: 21 to 26.

Boutwell called for the question on his opposite amendment, to clarify the school clause; all schools must be integrated. Fellow Republicans confronted him. Stewart of Nevada: drop it "for the sake of education." Conservatives needed only an excuse to wipe out the public schools. Then truly, said Stewart, the South will have won the war. Ignorance would reign. Ignorance was the foundation of slavery.[152] Boutwell was unmoved. Mixed schools alone could eradicate prejudice. Senators voted. It was not close: 42 against; 5 in favor. Robertson of South Carolina, Spencer of Alabama, West of Louisiana, and the enigmatic James Alcorn, supported George Boutwell's utopian dream.

Sargent proposed his second amendment, to add the word "system" after "school." The majority put its weight on the other side. The separate-school loophole failed, 16 in favor, 28 opposed. No amendments remained. William Hamilton called for the vote, on passage of the bill.

The count reversed the result on the final amendment: 29 voted for S.1, 16 against. Fourteen senators paired: Oliver Morton in favor, John Stevenson against; Simon Cameron in favor and Allen Thurman opposed; Zachariah Chandler for and Thomas Bayard against; Ferry of Michigan for, George Dennis of Maryland against; John Sherman in favor and George Goldthwaite opposed. Two Nebraskans, Phineas Hitchcock and Thomas Tipton, paired: Hitchcock for and Tipton against. Generals Logan and Gordon joined up again on opposite sides. Gordon was absent. Logan paired his yea with the Georgian's nay. Arkansas' Powell Clayton, feeling ill, had gone home during the night. He left a statement for the record: had he been present, he would have voted yea.

The roll-call ended. Simon Conover rushed into the chamber. The rakishly handsome senator from Florida, having sat up all night for this moment, had missed it while taking breakfast in the capitol restaurant. He hurried upstairs only to find the vote closed. He too entered a personal statement. Had he been present he intended to vote aye. Sixty-one senators expressed an opinion. Counting votes paired and the statements of Clayton and Conover, 38 approved the Civil Rights Bill, 23 opposed its passage.

152 Stewart was sincere. He had already proposed a 16th Amendment to the Constitution, making public education mandatory for all citizens. New Hampshire's Henry Blair in the 44th Congress, also a champion of public schools, begged the House. If education failed, slavery would triumph. "I do not mean that they will seek to restore the *form* of slavery, certainly not for many years, but its substance they may and mean to seize by preserving the intellectual degradation and consequent subjection of the ignorant masses below them.... Knowledge will destroy their supremacy and therefore they must destroy knowledge." Speech of Henry Blair, *Free Schools – Are They in Danger? If So, from What Sources?* (Washington, 1876): 6.

The sun rose. Gas-lamps were extinguished. The hands of the clock stood at ten minutes past seven on the morning of May 23, 1874. Roscoe Conkling, fittingly, said the final word: "Now I move that the Senate adjourn." Senators went home to bed. One month exactly remained in the first session of the Forty-third Congress. The Civil Rights Bill completed one half its journey into law.

CHAPTER 5

The Deadest Corpse: No Exit in the House

The Senate's purblind child romped through the rotunda to the House of Representatives. It landed, along with other senatorial measures, on the Speaker's table. There it stuck. From that moment S.1, "the Senate Bill," lay like a dead weight upon the neck of Congress. It lay immobile as other bills disappeared around it. It lay still as the first session of Congress ended. It remained as the second session began half a year later.

This persistent immobility did not result from a lack of effort by Ben Butler. In March the Chairman had been at the height of his influence. His cordial alliance with the president made his services a thing greatly to be desired.[1] "His office is besieged every evening by a numerous crowd of persons of both sexes who are anxious to obtain his influence," reported the New York *Tribune*. "It requires the services of two clerks to help attend to this mass of business."[2] By May, when the Senate bill arrived, Benjamin Butler had fallen into a quagmire. Charges of corruption weighed upon him. It required his utmost efforts merely to defend his position in the House.[3] Then his usually robust health failed. For weeks he lay at home. Reporters joked they would have to scour their files to find some upright act he had done, in order to compose a respectful obituary.[4] He returned on May 21, a shadow of himself. On the 22nd he called together his Judiciary Committee. At that very moment the Senate commenced its final debate. The committee must decide now on the most contentious problem. The members had hesitated since January. They came to a resolution. If the Senate retained the school clause they would accept its decision.[5]

More than enough votes existed in the House, as Butler knew, to pass the Senate bill, if he could wrest it from the Speaker's table. In that detail lay the devil. For a small but critical bloc of Republicans, S.1 went too far. Under a quirk of House procedure they held the balance of power. A motion to take a bill from the Speaker's table required a suspension of the rules. Suspension of

1 See William D. Mallam, "The Grant-Butler Relationship," *Mississippi Valley Historical Review*, 41 (1954): 268–276. "The physical bond that united Chang and Eng," wrote the Omaha *Herald* (referring to the lately-deceased Siamese twins), "was not stronger than the political bond which unites Grant and Butler." Quoted in New York *Tribune*, March 23, 1874.

2 New York *Tribune*, March 3, 1874.

3 See Trefousse, *The South Called Him Beast!*, 228–229.

4 Harrisburg *Patriot*, May 11, 1874.

5 Harrisburg *Patriot*, May 23, 1874.

the rules required the vote of a two-thirds majority. That vote, like a recurrent nightmare, frustrated advocates of the Civil Rights Bill for the rest of the session and beyond.

On paper Republicans possessed a two-thirds majority, but only if they mustered every vote. Democrats, with all votes in place, fell six short of the threshold. Three of the House's four Liberal Republicans, Alabama's Frederick Bromberg, Henry Banning of Ohio and New Yorker John Whitehouse, pledged to vote against a civil rights bill. The gap narrowed to a whisker. Democrats understood. Success or failure depended upon strict command and use of parliamentary skill. They turned to the party's unrivaled parliamentarian, Samuel Jackson Randall of Pennsylvania, and his lieutenant, the Judiciary Committee's Charles Eldredge. By their efforts, aided by Republican disunity, civil rights remained rooted to the Speaker's table.

On May 25 Ben Butler made his first attempt to raise S.1 from its resting place. He moved to take up the Senate bill, without objection, and refer it to the Committee on the Judiciary.[6] Then, as chairman, he might report it at any time. He asked for unanimous consent. Democrats objected. He called for suspension of the rules. Butler's move surprised even those on his own side. He took the floor from a colleague, Chairman of the Appropriations Committee James Garfield. Garfield was annoyed. Randall was nonplussed. Monday, May 25, a slow day in the routine of the House, the Senate bill had barely arrived. No one imagined it would be launched on its way so quickly. Fifty-one members had left the hall. No one could count heads fast enough to tell whether the remainder could block a two-thirds vote.

"Have not the Committee on the Judiciary the right to make reports on Wednesday next," Randall sputtered?

Yes, Butler replied. Taking in the Senate bill now would let him report it then, Wednesday if the gentleman preferred. Randall could only wait for the yeas and nays.

Two hundred thirty-seven congressmen spoke at the call of their names. Thirty-eight Republicans were missing or silent. Democrats needed 80 nays to stop the motion. Only 77 rose on their side. But 8 Republicans crossed party lines. Their defection was decisive. By a margin of five votes the motion failed. Progress of the Civil Rights Bill stopped. For almost a year thereafter Republicans butted their heads against a two-thirds barrier that refused to crack.

That band of Republican renegades who voted no on May 25 became the core of a group whose opposition shackled civil rights. Their number never rose much above a dozen. It was enough. All but one, for the moment, were southerners: Tennesseans Roderick Butler and Jacob Thornburgh; Virginians

6 *Cong. Record*, 43rd Congress, 1st Session: 4242–4243.

James Sener, Christopher Thomas and John Ambler Smith; William A. Smith of North Carolina; Lloyd Lowndes of Maryland. Horace Strait, representing the 2nd District of Minnesota, alone among northern Republicans, voted no. Ben Butler's assault on the Speaker's table failed. But it had come close. Vigilance, pleaded the Atlanta *Constitution*: "Every Democratic member should be in his place until the monstrosity is worried to death."[7]

General Butler, as the *Constitution* feared, had only performed a strategic retreat. He struck again on June 1.[8] Congress' first session approached its close. The House plodded through a mass of backlogged bills. It expected to recess, then continue into the evening for the purpose of expediting measures referred to the Committee on the Judiciary. Butler took occasion to announce that the Committee did not intend to bring up the civil rights bill at that time. Democrats received the reassurance. Vigilance relaxed. He had set them up. The afternoon drew on. Members' thoughts turned to the recess – dinner, perhaps a drop of fortifying liquor. Butler rose suddenly. He would not indeed bring up civil rights in the evening session. He brought it up now. Suspend the rules. Refer the Senate bill to his committee. He added an inducement. He would allow, extraordinarily, a motion to amend, to reconsider the mixed-schools clause.

Randall: "Will you agree to strike it out?"

Butler: "No, sir. But we will allow a motion to strike out or amend."

Democrats rejected the temptation. But the general's maneuver still threatened to outflank them. Their ranks were thinned. Seventy-six members had left the hall. Butler's timing, however, had to be perfect. He waited long enough for members to drift away. He waited just a trifle too long. The recess, scheduled for 4:30 p.m., had already been ordered. If Democrats could delay until then, Butler's vote would not occur. Randall paced the floor: "It will be a great relief when that hour [4:30] comes."

Democrats had one chance. They took it. By parliamentary rules, one motion could preempt Butler's. A motion to adjourn carried the highest privilege. James Beck rose. Let the House adjourn. Beck's motion was meaningless, but time-consuming. The clock stood past three. The process of ordering the tellers, dividing the House, seconding the motion, calling the roll, might occupy the time Democrats required. The last vote was recorded. The House rejected Beck's call to adjourn. It no longer mattered. The time was up, Speaker Blaine announced. The hour of half past four had arrived. "Pursuant to order," the House recessed until 7 p.m. Sam Randall exhaled.

---

7 Atlanta *Constitution*, June 4, 1874.

8 *Cong. Record*, 43rd Congress, 1st Session: 4439.

By now newspapers began to observe that the Civil Rights Bill might fail. Yet one other mechanism for achieving passage remained available – one that did not depend on the elusive two-thirds vote. It was not absolutely necessary to remove S.1 from the Speaker's table. Chairman Butler could ignore that bill and return to his Judiciary Committee. There he could amend his own bill, H.R.796, substituting the text of the Senate's version. Then the committee could report the House bill, which would be in effect the Senate bill. It could report that measure at any time. It required only a simple majority to pass. Observers watched and waited. The substitution did not occur.

Why did Butler not seize upon this seemingly simple solution? The answer to that question lay behind the closed doors of the Judiciary Committee room. The Radical faction refused to accept a substitution. If the Senate bill were brought to the floor as a House bill it laid itself open to amendment, to as many amendments as the opposition cared to devise. Democrats feared the majority would reject their attempts to amend. Radicals feared the opposite. Given the opportunity, members from moderate or doubtful districts might embrace a chance to dilute the Civil Rights Bill. They might particularly be tempted to remove the school clause. Butler had toyed with that notion on June 1. It must not be allowed to happen again. The only way to be sure of an undefiled civil rights bill was to take the Senate bill – take it up in its own name – and pass it. The vote would be straight up, amendments not in order. Such a strategy, of course, risked prolonged stalemate against the obstacle of the two-thirds vote. True believers preferred that risk to passage of an amended bill. When Chairman Butler reconvened his Judiciary Committee on June 3 he faced open revolt.

The committee had long since given up hope of crafting its own mixed-schools compromise. The unhappy drafts of its provisional provisos lay scattered on the committee-room floor. Four uncompromising committeemen refused to countenance any change: Jasper Ward, John Cessna, Jeremiah Wilson and William Frye, determined that the Senate bill would not become the House bill. They proposed to block their own bill inside the committee. Then only the Senate bill could advance.[9] If it failed they were content to carry on into the second session of Congress. The motion came from Jasper Ward: to reconsider the reporting of H.R.796. Never, he told his hometown Chicago *Tribune*, would he consent to half-measures, to a bill "which should open the theatre to the colored man, and close the school upon him." Better no bill at all.[10] By a strong majority the committee supported Ward's motion. He

9 Paterson *Press*, June 4, 1874.

10 Chicago *Tribune*, June 5, 1874.

counted on his allies, Cessna, Wilson and Frye. The committee's three Democrats gladly joined the radical four. Anything that obstructed the Civil Rights Bill made their task easier. Stalemate suited them perfectly. From both sides Butler found his options cut. The committee left him one route. He must lift S.1 from the Speaker's table.

Butler's maneuvers on May 25 and June 1 had not breached the Democrats' defenses. He ordered the charge on June 8. Randall was ready. The vote was not close: 138 for, 88 against. There would be no suspension of the rules. Democrats cheered. "Sain et Sauf!" the Memphis *Appeal* proclaimed: safe and sound.[11] The Nashville *Banner* took the news hot off the wires: Civil Rights Bill blocked in the House. It ran up a bulletin outside its offices at 18 Deaderick Street. Crowds gathered on the curb. Whites appeared "jubilant;" black people "went away with a rather depressed state of spirits."[12]

Even worse, defections increased. Several Republicans whose silence set them in the record officially as absent actually sat quietly in their seats, but declined to vote.[13] The crew of openly mutinous Republicans grew larger. Six new members joined the original eight. Not all lived in the South. The company now included New Jersey's William Walter Phelps, reneging on his promise to the National Civil Rights Convention, William Ray of Illinois, James Lofland of Delaware and Sherman Houghton of California. Tennessee's Horace Harrison and Edwin Stanard of Missouri also voted no.[14] Worst of all, five yeas turned to nays. Lofland, Harrison, Ray, Houghton and Stanard had voted in favor at the end of May. Two weeks later their convictions had changed. They were, no doubt, reading the newspapers.

Passage of the Senate bill and the swift series of votes that followed awakened the slumbering columns of the press. Democratic papers, of course, were remorseless. "Unrestricted meddling by Congress," screamed the New York *Sun*. "If this is a sample of what we are to expect from our lawgivers, it were better at once to have a czar or sultan."[15] The Baltimore *Gazette* castigated the Senate:

11 Memphis *Appeal*, June 10, 1874.

12 Nashville *Banner*, June 9, 1874.

13 Baltimore *Sun*, May 26, 1874.

14 Ray's central Illinois district harbored a Liberal Republican streak. Lofland struggled to survive in a solidly Democratic state. California's vast 4th District, from Monterey to Mexico, swung unsteadily between Republican and Democratic control. Congressman Houghton swung accordingly. Phelps offered no excuse. He paid a heavy price for his renegade stand.

15 "Grave and reverend seniors of Congress," the *Sun's* editorialist concluded, with a wink at Othello and a truly ecumenical disdain for ethnic diversity, "do not compel us to invite to our annual feast of turkey and pumpkin pie on Thanksgiving Day King Quashee of

"The chief of the hunt, Mr. Frelinghuysen, and his whippers-in, Mr. Sumner's enemies in life, raise this pernicious funeral pyre on his fresh grave."[16] The Montgomery *Advertiser* blamed the dictionary: "Language is powerless to portray the infinite cruelty and vile injustice of the measure. It is the most tyrannical and arbitrary abuse of power known to the history of the whole world."[17] The Gallatin, Tennessee, *Tennesseean* had an idea. Deny Negroes employment. Starvation would pinch their civil rights ardor. No, no, the Nashville *Union and American* chuckled. It was inhumane. "Better hang a man than starve him."[18]

Democratic vitriol one might expect. Republican voices also pronounced civil rights unwelcome. The preeminent Republican sheet, the New York *Times,* had decried the prejudice of Harris and Beck. Now it decried the concept of a civil rights bill.

> Nobody would think for a moment of making such a law as the one now proposed for the benefit of the Irish or German immigrants, and it is not singular that the popular sense of justice, which is always in advance of that of legislators, should be already asking why the negro should be thus especially favored.... If it is accepted as a Republican measure, the party is sure to suffer from it.[19]

After the vote of June 8, the *Times* concluded, it was best to bury it forever:

> Public opinion has been plainly arrayed against the measure. There is a general feeling that enough has been done for the negroes to enable them to take care of themselves.... We cannot regret the failure of this bill to become a law.[20]

The staunchly Republican Cincinnati *Gazette* voiced sentiments that Democratic papers gladly repeated:

> The so-called civil rights bill makes so great a stretch of governmental interference into social customs and business affairs which have hitherto been outside the province of litigation; it sets up a surveillance and

---

Senegambia, Roaring Bull of the Nez Perces, or Ki Fun of the Mongolian Empire." Quoted in Santa Clara *Argus,* June 13, 1874.

16 Quoted in New York *Herald,* June 1, 1874.

17 Montgomery *Advertiser,* May 27, 1874.

18 Gallatin *Tennesseean* quoted in Nashville *Union and American,* June 2, 1874.

19 New York *Times,* May 27, 1874.

20 New York *Times,* June 9, 1874.

> espionage hitherto so foreign to the spirit of our government; it makes so large a transfer of affairs from the State to the national tribunals ... that reflecting people may well inquire whether this is not the sacrifice instead of the protection of civil rights.[21]

Horace White's Chicago *Tribune* adopted a ponderous tone of sarcasm:

> The country would sneer at the proposal of a bill which should read: "Be it enacted, etc., that every white man in the South shall love every negro."... The present bill needs several important amendments. Let it be enacted, then, that when a negro runs for office no votes shall be cast against him by Caucasians.... Let it be enacted that at every social entertainment equal numbers of whites and blacks shall be invited ... that "colored gentlemen" shall be the only phrase used in referring to our fellow-citizens of African descent. Let "aunty" and "uncle" and "contraband" and "nigger" and "freedman" be banned forever. The old colored woman who replied to the greeting: "How d'ye do, aunty?" "I ain't your aunty, I ain't your uncle, I'se your ekal," was but foreshadowing the future social millennium.[22]

Some journalistic voices professed to see a measure of virtue in civil rights. The New York *Tribune* nodded sympathetically, but doubted that any good would come from it.[23] The Chicago *Inter Ocean* and the Indianapolis *Journal,* organs respectively of Senators Logan and Morton, urged action.[24] *Harper's Weekly* exhorted passage of the bill.[25] The Jersey City *Journal* stood out, one of the few who did not waver. The *Journal,* however, pointed an accusing finger not at Democrats but at its fellow Republicans:

> Prejudice, and especially a prejudice which is unjust, irrational, indefensible, and cruel, has no business to override justice, and if it will not yield

21 Quoted in Memphis *Appeal,* June 2, 1874.

22 Chicago *Tribune,* May 31, 1874.

23 New York *Tribune,* May 25, 1874.

24 Indianapolis *Journal,* May 28; Chicago *Inter Ocean,* June 16, 1874.

25 *Harper's Weekly,* May 23, 1874, 430–431. Out on the prairie, the Kansas City *Journal of Commerce* chided its neighbor the Kansas City *Times*: "We have inquired of several colored men as to their purposes should the bill become a law, and have the assurance of every one without exception that they do not intend to associate with the *Times* or invite it to their social parties or to take tea with them ... or even to marry any of their daughters, or *vice versa,* as the case may be." Kansas City *Journal of Commerce,* May 28, 1874.

> to the persuasion of common sense and justice, it must be compelled to succumb to law.... We have been, no – not surprised at, as we were on the point of saying, but ashamed of the cowardice of a large portion of the Republican press in their treatment of this subject.[26]

Murat Halstead's Cincinnati *Commercial* endorsed the bill. It warned Congress nevertheless to proceed with caution: "Mistakes in legislation, in matters so grave as this, are difficult of correction; and before we proceed to the full trial of so formidable an experiment ... we should be very sure we are right, both as to the end and as to the means."[27] The most striking editorial stance appeared in the New York *Herald*. In January James Gordon Bennett, Jr.'s paper commented benignly.

> Whether a people or a class can be legislated into social equality is a question fairly open to controversy ... [but] in so far as the Civil Rights bill seeks to protect the colored people in the free use of public conveyances and hotels we think it will meet the approval of a majority of the nation.[28]

The *Herald* kept a kindly disposition in May, even accepting mixed schools.

> The common schools are for the children of every citizen, regardless of color, and to talk about taxing the whites for the education of the negroes is talking very far behind the age. To afford separate schools for the two races where it is practicable may be well enough, but it is, after all, the mere gratification of a prejudice which must not be allowed to deprive any child of the right to an education.[29]

On that very day the Senate passed S.1. In a twinkling the *Herald's* sympathy vanished. It recalled suddenly that it despised the bill. It was unconstitutional.

26 Jersey City *Journal*, May 25, 1874. The *Journal* renewed its exhortation on June 10: "The Republican party can survive mismanagement; it can endure ring rule; it can even live with the burden of the corruption of bad men upon it; but the Republican party cannot live when it must stand before the world convicted of moral cowardice, of not daring to maintain and carry to their legitimate and righteous conclusions its own long cherished and much vaunted principles of freedom and of equal rights for all citizens."

27 Cincinnati *Commercial*, May 23, 1874.

28 New York *Herald*, January 7, 1874.

29 New York *Herald*, May 23, 1874.

It was a crude trap to catch Negro votes, unenforceable, an infringement on human rights.

> The Senate simply fulminates a bull against a comet. It has no more authority over the subjects which it pretends to regulate than the Shah of Persia or the Emperor of China or any other magnificent potentate, upon whose intellect his lunar relationships have had a bad effect.... It enforces conflict by causing the law to give an equality which the Creator has denied.... If law and human nature are in conflict it is human nature that prevails.[30]

Why did the *Herald's* stance swing so suddenly? Its columns offer no explanation or excuse. Was it, as southern papers sneered, typical Yankee two-facedness? More likely the *Herald's* editorialists were reading their mail. Their turnabout reflected the somersault of public opinion as civil rights moved from abstraction to reality. Henry Ward Beecher, voice of enlightened morality, spoke through the pages of his journal, *The Christian Union.* A civil rights measure was unwise, undoubtedly unconstitutional, certain to produce unfortunate results.[31] In Chicago a grand gathering of old abolitionists met on June 10. Even here, amidst the Antislavery Reunion, the Civil Rights Bill received a frosty welcome. A delegate, Rev. Sinclair, proposed resolutions endorsing Sumner's bill. Uproar greeted him. "Having done my duty to God," he declared, "if gentlemen are disposed to judge them [the resolutions] and give them the 'go-by,' let the responsibility rest on their heads." Gentlemen gave them the go-by. They settled for a recommendation: "It should be held the Christian duty of

30 New York *Herald,* May 24, 1874. Countermeasures, the *Herald* declared, were in order: "Persons skilled in the art of expressing contempt would have no difficulty in surrounding disagreeable people with such an atmosphere of contumely as would be inexpressibly wounding to the pride or vanity of the few negroes who could bear the expense of asserting their equality.... If, in consequence of full tables, he [a Negro] should sometimes chance to be seated in unwelcome proximity to white people, they would have no difficulty in making their disgust so unpleasantly manifest without incurring legal penalties as to poison all the satisfaction the intruder might feel in eating his meals with persons who despised him.... If negro children are sent to schools where their presence is distasteful they will be so humiliated by the insults of the white children as to make their attendance intolerable." New York *Herald,* May 28, 1874.

31 *Christian Union,* July 15, 22, 1874. That position accorded with the reverend's consistently conservative reconstruction views, which placed conciliation of southern whites above social justice for blacks. See Edward J. Blum, *Reforging the White Republic: Race, Religion, and American Nationalism, 1865–1889* (Baton Rouge: 2005), 90.

the people to conquer the prejudice by which the freedmen are still subject."[32] Civil rights perturbed pious abolitionists. It unnerved complacent congressmen. The Baltimore *Sun* reported:

> The unexpected opposition which has developed toward the civil rights bill has been a matter of some surprise to such of the Republican Senators and Representatives as take the trouble to make themselves acquainted with the views of the press and the people. A Republican Senator remarked to-night that in perusing a large number of Republican journals he had found but a small proportion which indorsed the action of the Senate in passing the bill.[33]

"The opposition to it throughout the country has been so emphatic," reported the Evansville *Journal*, "that no serious effort will be made to give it the finishing touches."[34] The Chicago *Tribune* put it bluntly: "The House responded to public opinion that manifestly swung against the measure ... a sensibility fresh from the people who were reconciled to negro-citizenship, but not to negro-companionship."[35] "Since its passage through the Senate an exhibition of public feeling has come to the surface, especially in the South, that is not calculated to popularize it in the House," noted the Wheeling *Intelligencer*. "Elections are coming on this fall and the members have loads enough to carry in the canvass without adding the Civil Rights bill to their embarrassments."[36] Southern papers chuckled with knowing satisfaction at the sudden reversal of the New York *Herald's* opinion: "The great weather-cock has snuffed a coming storm in the air," clucked the Nashville *Union and American*, "and does not hesitate a moment to range itself promptly on the opposite side of the question."[37]

Members of the House of Representatives also snuffed the stormy air. "Congress, having displayed the wretched bantling to the gaze of the public, has heard the universal cry of disgust uttered through the press, and now hesitates to consummate what it began," wrote the Chattanooga *Times*. "The press and the people have frightened them from their purpose. They stopped to count the cost and that was fatal."[38]

32 Chicago *Inter Ocean*, June 12, 13; see Larry Gara, "A Glorious Time: The 1874 Abolitionist Reunion in Chicago," *Journal of the Illinois State Historical Society*, 65 (1972): 290–291.

33 Baltimore *Sun*, May 28, 1874.

34 Evansville *Journal*, June 8, 1874.

35 Chicago *Tribune*, June 25, 1874.

36 Wheeling *Intelligencer*, June 6, 1874.

37 Nashville *Union and American*, May 29, 1874.

38 Chattanooga *Times*, June 2, 9, 17, 1874.

Newspapers alarmed politicians. Public opinion, as the *Herald's* frantic *volte face* witnessed, alarmed the newspapers. The reporter for the New York *World* passed through the hills of western Maryland, the district of Republican Lloyd Lowndes. He found party leaders in despair. It was "all up." The elections would be a disaster. Poor whites, small farmers, people who had stayed with the Union through years of war and with the Republican Party thereafter, now were thoroughly alienated. They could tolerate many things, but not the insult of civil rights:

> Don't you see this Civil Rights bill gives Southern "white trash" (as the niggers elegantly call them) much harder measure than they ever got from the "aristocrats" in the prime and culmination of their pride? No Southern gentleman, no matter how much he might have despised the ignorant "cracker," his neighbor, ever went so far as to treat the nigger as his equal, set him at the same table, or feed him with the same food.... They are not in the least deceived by the tinsel tattle of Radical orators, by appeals to the Declaration of Independence, and all that muckmammocky rot about liberty and equality and "philosophy of first principles" in which the Senators indulged. They would like to show their opinion of Mr. Boutwell – they would do it in a coat of tar and feathers, laid on *con amore.*[39]

Proceeding to Baltimore, the *World's* reporter talked with railroad workers:

> Poor fellows! They had a black prospect before them – they were part of 850 just discharged for want of work in the machine-shops at the Mount Clare depot of the Baltimore and Ohio Railroad. They did not however talk of the dearth of work, but of the Civil Rights bill and the prospects of its becoming a law.

Medical students joked facetiously. They would reap a harvest in the supply of cadavers for their anatomy lessons. They would "resurrect every nigger that gets himself buried in any of our cemeteries. And they'll do it, too. Is there anything particular in the Civil Rights bill against Ku-Kluxing dead darkies?" In North Carolina one aspiring candidate for coroner placed his campaign notice in a local paper. Should the Civil Rights Bill become law the public would need a capable person to deal with death's debris:

---

39 New York *World*, June 13, 1874.

> We are authorized to announce the name of Poovy Ramsoure for Coroner of Iredell County. He has lived in the county for a long time ... [he is] willing to serve his county, whenever and in whatever capacity his services may be needed. If the Civil Rights Bill passes the next Congress, the duties will be grave and important, hence it behooves the people to select some one possessing all the qualifications requisite to the prompt discharge of the duties of the office.[40]

Events, as Poovy predicted, turned violent. First came Memphis. The city already had witnessed one of the South's bloodiest race riots. It wavered on the verge of another. Mayor John Loague, a Republican, moved to integrate the city's largely Irish fire department. The firemen rebelled. The city council backed them. The mayor persisted. Tensions ran high. Then on May 30, Decoration Day, crowds gathered at the national cemetery. Black citizens, organized into their benevolent societies – the Pole-Bearers, the Sumner Guards, the Sons of Ham and Union Star Society – marched under the Pole Bearers' president Thomas Swan. At the gates they found a swarm of merchants and vendors hawking refreshments. They drove them away and overturned the stands.

Edward Shaw, Memphis wharf-master and leader of the black community, addressed the people.[41] The Civil Rights Bill was coming. It would be "the last crowning glory to befall them." White folks fear we will come into their parlors once that bill is passed: "From the looks of this congregation it seems that the white people have been in our parlors oftener than we have been in their parlors. They say, 'Oh you want to marry our daughters.' From the looks of this congregation it seems that one could hardly marry any other than their daughter." The procession returned to town. A nearby grocery store was trashed, its proprietors terrorized, its cashbox emptied.

Angry firemen, vandalizing mobs, civil rights speeches – the situation spiraled toward disaster. Authorities charged Tom Swan for the destruction at the cemetery. Then a white man, Thomas Farrell, and a black man, Henry Porter, argued in the street over the Civil Rights Bill. Porter produced a razor and

---

40 Cincinnati *Commercial*, August 5, 1874. The Savannah *News* printed another forthright statement, orthography unchanged. Mr. William Smoot, of Pike County, Georgia, asked friends and neighbors not to obstruct his election to a job that promised financial rewards: "I hereby announce myself as a candidate for Kurrener of your county. I do this because I believe the Sivil rites bill will pass Congress and the offis will be worth something. People always laffed at it herebefore, but as it is going to be worth something this time I hope everybody won't be pitchin' in agin me for it." Savannah *News*, October 17, 1874.

41 On Ed Shaw see David Tucker, "Black Politics in Memphis, 1865–1875," *West Tennessee Historical Society Papers*, 26 (1972): 14–16.

ripped Farrell's abdomen. Farrell's friends rushed to support him. Among them were already-disgruntled firemen. Only barely were they restrained from riot. (A fortuitous cry of "Fire!" distracted their attention.)[42] Rumors spread. The Pole Bearers had secured rifles; they were drilling for the extermination of the whites. Local papers, the *Register* and the *Ledger,* fanned the flames. Ed Shaw and Tom Swan convoked a meeting. Swan commanded his men to refrain from drilling while the Civil Rights Bill remained unsettled in Congress.[43] Both sides stepped back. Memphis had avoided another bloody massacre, by inches.

Next came Virginia. Civil rights terror descended along the Chesapeake Bay. The passenger steamer *N.P. Banks,* bound on the morning of June 9 from Norfolk to Fortress Monroe, fell under attack. A party of seven, the steward informed the captain, including General Oliver Otis Howard, wished to reserve a table for breakfast. Captain McCarrick consented. The one-armed general, "of negro worshipping fame," might be unsavory. But he was the correct color. Two of his companions, it turned out, were not. Breakfasting was forbidden. "He was the Captain of that boat," McCarrick declared, "and until the Civil Rights bill was passed, and he was compelled to admit them, no negro should ever sit at the table in his cabin." The steamer touched land. Howard and his party descended the gangway in great haste. McCarrick dashed a warning. Too late. They raced to the Hygeia Hotel, "forced their way into the dining room and obtained their breakfast."[44]

Just days after the assault on the *N.P. Banks* the steamer *Hampton* sailed for the city of Norfolk. Three Negroes appeared on board. They had tried to purchase cabin-class tickets at the dock and were repulsed. Through the agency of renegade white persons, they procured the tickets. Now they emerged, to the consternation of all, in the first class saloon. The mate required them to retire to the lower deck reserved for their race. Captain Schermerhorn arrived. "Seeing that moral suasion was of no use," he struck one of the recalcitrant party and kicked them bodily down the stairs. There the invaders regrouped. Reinforced, they encompassed Capt. Schermerhorn. Only the arrival of the ship's engineer armed with a menacing monkey wrench prevented a tragic denouement. "There is some rascality at the bottom of these frequent attempts at forcing social equality," warned the Norfolk *Virginian.* "Railroad and steamboat officials and hotel keepers cannot be too much on the alert."[45] The enemy left steamboats. It attacked through the church.

42 New York *World,* June 2; Springfield, Massachusetts, *Republican,* June 6, 1874.

43 Memphis *Appeal,* June 7, 9; New York *World,* June 6, 1874.

44 Headline: "An Anticipation of the Civil Rights Bill," Norfolk *Virginian,* June 12, 1874.

45 Norfolk *Virginian,* June 16, 1874.

Sunday, June 14, the Baptist church at Hampton. Several young black men walked casually down the aisle and seated themselves among the worshippers. The sexton hurried up. He requested they remove their presence to the gallery allotted to persons of African descent. They sat still. An unseemly quarrel ensued. The young men left, "giving vent audibly to their disgust at their treatment." Once again the sinister hand of General Howard hovered. The intruders were identified, his "protégés," students at the Normal School, where whites and blacks mixed shamelessly. All this, the *Virginian* warned, was just a taste of evils that awaited passage of the Civil Rights Bill.

Another incident, far to the north, in the very cradle of abolitionism, seemed to validate the *Virginian's* point. Talk of civil rights was hypocrisy. Northerners preached a pretty line. When confronted with reality they acted no differently than southerners. The Connecticut Literary Institute dispensed its boarding-school enlightenment in the town of Suffield, on the border of Massachusetts. Its current class included two black students. They had come up from the south, freed from slavery, seeking education and a better life. The school defrayed their expenses through a work-study program. To cover tuition, room and board they worked as janitors in the facility. Isaac Harris and J.A. Montgomery enjoyed equality in the classroom. They perceived slights elsewhere, particularly in the dining room. Six white boys approached the school's steward, E.J. Avery. They declared they would quit the institution. The blacks, they said, persisted in sitting with them at meals. Mr. Avery informed Harris and Montgomery. They in turn repaired to the editorial offices of the Springfield, Massachusetts, *Republican* and unleashed an open letter.

"We were born as slaves in the South," they declared. "After our liberation by the war, we came North with the determination of securing an education. Being destitute of means, we have been obliged to pursue our studies where we could pay our expenses by our labor." At first all went well. "We had discharged this duty for nearly a year and a half.... We had recited regularly in the classes, had taken our meals at the common table, and had mingled without restraint with the students as classmates and friends." Hence it came as a shock when the steward requested they sit apart. "Have we no rights to be respected? Is the civil rights law necessary in northern Connecticut? There were but two alternatives left us, one to remain at the school in tolerated disgrace, and the other to respect our own manhood and depart. We have elected the latter."[46]

The Connecticut Literary Institute hastened to tell a different version. According to the steward and the principal, the eminent philologist Professor

---

46 Springfield, Massachusetts, *Republican*, June 2, 1874.

Joseph Shores, no one had infringed upon the rights of the black students. No one forced them to dine at a segregated table. Seven tables were available. They could sit at any they wished with any classmates who chose to join them. But they should not impose themselves on a table occupied by those who, for whatever reason, did not want their company. Dr. Shores offered alternatives. If they preferred, the institute would pay them a weekly stipend that they could use to board and dine in town. Mr. Avery welcomed them to share meals with his own family in his private quarters.[47]

White students of the Connecticut Literary Institute also protested. One wrote to the Waterbury *American.* It was not they who acted with a bigoted superiority, but Harris and Montgomery who adopted an attitude of superior privilege.

> For a year and a half they have been treated kindly by both teachers and students. We have often neglected our own lessons to assist them when it was not asked as a favor but demanded as a right. We admire their spunk in pursuit of education, but all things considered, do not think they should be treated any better than white people under the same circumstances.[48]

It was hardly the stuff of great moment. Yet in an atmosphere of civil-rights-bill-induced effervescence the Connecticut Literary Institute became a national story. Papers reported it across the country. Civil rights mania, the New York *Tribune* declared:

> We have had something too much of this. The idea of appealing to the public and propounding startling conundrums about equality and civil rights because half a dozen boarding-school boys refuse to sit at table with two colored janitors is carrying the special politics of the past twenty years almost to the point of absurdity.[49]

The story made popular reading in the South. It was precisely as they had warned. The Civil Rights Bill legislated privilege. It bred arrogance. It fostered

47 Springfield *Republican,* June 4; Hartford *Courant,* June 9, 1874.

48 Quoted in Hartford *Courant,* June 12, 1874. Subsequently Isaac Harris repented his decision and returned to school. Of dining arrangements we have no word. Springfield *Republican,* September 21, 1874.

49 New York *Tribune,* June 15, 1874.

an undue sense of entitlement. "It works badly for the colored people even in New England."[50]

Boarding-school tiffs, steamboat scuffles, such one might discount. More official warnings followed. Governor Preston Leslie wrote from Kentucky. He feared rebellion. Race war was imminent.[51] In Nashville civil rights bill fear set the town in an uproar.

> It matters little where you find yourself, it is all that is talked about.... If you go to the railroad depots it is remarked upon and strongly denounced; if you happen to drop into a hotel you hear one topic elaborately discussed; if you chance to stray in upon the school children at recess, they have read of it.... It is believed here that should the bill pass into a law all the hotels in the State will close.... Many predict that the passage of the bill will be the production of a war of races.[52]

Nashville's congressman, Republican Horace Harrison, heard the message. Harrison had voted for civil rights on May 25. When the second vote arrived he wisely changed his mind. On May 27 the Richmond *Whig* printed a letter to the editor. Its plaintive cry seemed to sum up the feeling on one side.

> Dear Sir: Please request the praying people of the South to pray earnestly to Almighty God to avert from us such a calamity as the passage of the civil rights bill. All things are possible to Him. If we pray earnestly He will hear us. We cannot – Oh! Mr. Editor – we cannot submit to the civil rights bill. I would rather that our whole race was exterminated. Appeal to the people to pray to God to spare us from such degradation; please do sir, and greatly oblige. – A Virginia Woman.[53]

On the other side black people fretted. Why could not the Republican Party pass a measure that embodied the very principles on which it had been founded? Public opinion swayed some legislators. They "stopped to count the cost." But

50 Memphis *Appeal*, June 15, 1874. Other reports in the Richmond *Dispatch* of June 5, the Nashville *Banner*, the *Union and American* and Knoxville *Press and Herald* on June 6, the Shreveport *Times* on June 16; finally the story reached the continental limit, Santa Clara, California, *Argus*, June 27, 1874.

51 New York *World*, June 1, 1874.

52 Nashville *Banner*, May 26, 1874.

53 Quoted in Knoxville *Press and Herald*, June 2, 1874.

a majority still professed support. Democrats had a simple answer. The Civil Rights Bill was a ruse, a seduction dangled in front of black men to attract their votes. "This bill is merely a trap to catch colored votes," asserted the Atlanta *Constitution*. "It was hoped the desired object might be attained without the passage of the measure.... The Radical monkey wants to use the black cat's paws to rake the chestnuts of official station out of the fire of coming elections – that's all."[54] A shell-game, concluded the *Abeille de la Nouvelle Orléans* (the New Orleans *Bee*). The Senate passed a bill. The House failed. Then the House could pass one and the Senate refuse: "*un tour de passe-passe*."[55]

Cats, chestnuts, deceptions: variations appeared. Ben Butler, one story went, coveted Charles Sumner's senate seat, once the short term of Senator Washburn expired. He needed to cut out his rival, Rockwood Hoar, to whom of course Sumner had commanded "don't let the civil rights bill fail." Butler, intending precisely to let the bill fail, feigned his mightiest efforts to save it. Sumner's legacy and Senate seat would fall to him. Civil rights would fall by the wayside.[56]

Alexander Stephens had a different theory. The mastermind was not Butler but Speaker Blaine. He had sabotaged his own party's efforts to take the bill from his own table by warning Democrats to be ready for procedural votes.[57] Considering the Democrats' disarray on May 25, when Randall himself stood unprepared for a snap vote, and June 1, when only a desperate call for adjournment saved them from disaster, either the Speaker's secret signals were disregarded or reports of the Speaker's treason lacked reality. That did not stop the rumors.

The most persuasive explanation for the Republicans' confused behavior was that they feared a presidential veto. Ulysses Grant twice had called for a civil rights bill. But now, as the bill approached, word emerged that presidential support was rescinded. "It is reported by persons who have had conversation with the President in regard to this bill that he has some doubt about signing it," noted the Harrisburg *Patriot*, "but there is nothing reliable or definite in the report."[58] Soon more definite reports arrived. Grant hoped the bill would fail. If it did not he planned to kill it. The habitually taciturn president did nothing to dispel these rumors, nor did he confirm them.

54 Atlanta *Constitution*, June 9, 1874.

55 New Orleans *Abeille*, May 27, 1874.

56 Charleston *News and Courier*, June 5, 1874.

57 William Gillette, *Retreat From Reconstruction, 1869–1879* (Baton Rouge, 1979): 207.

58 Harrisburg *Patriot*, May 25, 1874.

Was there any truth to reports of presidential duplicity?[59] If there were any one issue Ulysses Grant seemed certain to sustain, that issue was civil rights legislation. He had endorsed it in his second inaugural speech and again in his Annual Message to Congress. Black delegates called upon him during the National Civil Rights Convention. They came away convinced of his blessing. Yet barely three weeks later the rumors commenced. "The President having shown his hand," declared the Mobile *Register*, "it becomes proper to say that he sometime ago assured certain of the Conservative friends that he should veto the Civil Rights bill when it came to him, unless the clause in it enforcing educational miscegenation should be stricken out."[60] Mixed schools, the New York *Herald* reported, were only part of the problem. The *Herald* elaborated a list of eight concrete reasons why the president would block the Civil Rights Bill. He opposed the mixed-school clause, to be sure. He also disliked the enforcement of "social equality." He preferred to let time effect social change. He considered the bill sectional legislation. He feared it would antagonize the South. It would oppress white people. It would be a political disaster to the Republicans. Finally, if it passed, credit would go to Charles Sumner, whom he detested.[61]

In May the rumors grew. On the 27th the Atlanta *Constitution* declared the Civil Rights Bill dead: "the influence of the President is supposed to be against the bill." On June 2 the Charleston *News and Courier* reported "on good authority" that President Grant would veto the bill unless the school clause were stricken out. The New York *World* informed its readers on June 6, on the word of unnamed congressmen, the president had decided to veto the measure no matter what its final form might be. Butler had withdrawn the bill, the New York *Tribune* declared, because he knew he faced a veto.[62] Civil rights' friends were irate. Presidential intimidation of Congress! sputtered the Pittsburgh *Commercial*. "It is as disgraceful as it is unparalleled! No other President has ever dealt in vetoes in advance.... This is Caesarism pure and simple."[63]

---

59 Historians have been as confused as the president's contemporaries: "To be sure, in 1873 Grant had twice recommended that Congress pass some sort of civil rights legislation, but his qualified commendation sounded pro forma, and to many it lacked conviction and resolution, for he publicly opposed legislating social equality and privately made unenthusiastic remarks about it.... All that was rumor, however, so that whether he would have vetoed the bill had it been enacted remains an open question." Gillette, *Retreat From Reconstruction*, 208.

60 Mobile *Register*, January 17, 1874.

61 New York *Herald*, January 7, 1874.

62 New York *Tribune*, June 9, 12, 1874.

63 Quoted in Harrisburg *Patriot*, June 5, 1874.

No sooner had these assurances spread than doubts set in. The *World* on June 6 had been certain of a veto. It changed its mind a week later. Veto rumors were a mirage. They were, the *World* now revealed, part of a plot. Dissembling Republicans pretended to support a civil rights bill. But they did not. Other Republicans, actual supporters, pretended to fear a veto. They did not. The pretending proponents attempted to deceive the dissembling dissidents. "Sundry Radical Congressmen are at heart opposed to the Civil Rights bill." They hope it will fail, yet "are fishing around it in a perilous way in the hope to capture some political capital; they wish to run with the hare and hunt with the hounds." They would vote for a bill only if they felt assured it could not really become a law. Thus the bill's sincere supporters concocted rumors, entirely false, of a presidential veto, hoping to fool their faithless colleagues. In his grave Machiavelli smiled.

> It is to act upon the minds of these selfish and timid, temporizing "statesmen" that the shrewd Radical "managers" have lately circulated the rumor that the President was determinedly hostile to civil rights, and that it would be good policy to pass the bill in order to expose Grant to the odium of rejecting it.

Truly, as the *World* now believed, the president would sign the Civil Rights Bill.

> Grant is a matter-of-fact sort of person, not given to *double-entendre*.... He is bound to sign a civil rights bill – even one originated by Sumner – because in his last message, December 1, 1873, he told Congress that he suggested for their consideration "the enactment of a law to better secure the civil rights which freedom should secure, but has not effectually secured, to the enfranchised slave." Under the circumstances nothing can be more conclusive than this as to President Grant's probable action.[64]

The Cincinnati *Commercial* was unconvinced. Grant did plan to veto the Civil Rights Bill. In this way he hoped to make himself a hero to the South. But Blaine, his rival for the next presidential nomination, refused to give him the chance. Hence the Speaker himself acted through clandestine maneuvers to insure that the bill failed.[65] Others insisted the plot was all on behalf of Grant's political aspirations. The more uncertainty he created, or allowed to be created, the harder it was for his party to act decisively. The *World* might conclude

---

64 New York *World*, June 12, 1874.

65 Cincinnati *Commercial*, June 8, 1874.

that the matter-of-fact president would not renege on a public promise or veto a measure his party approved. Members of Congress could not be so sure. Indeed, they had before their eyes a blatant instance of just such presidential behavior. That cautionary example was S.617, the Currency Bill.

For a nation still suffering the effects of a severe recession, S.617, far more than S.1, constituted the paramount piece of legislation of the 43rd Congress. After months of debate, both Senate and House agreed on April 6 to expand the nation's money supply, to allow for the application of a soft money policy. That decision, to be sure, split members of the Republican Party; it split both parties. But powerful Republican senators, Morton, Logan, Carpenter, Cameron, Ferry of Michigan, backed it. Its sponsor in the Senate was John Sherman. In the House it had the support of Benjamin Butler. Those supporters pointed to presidential assurances. In his Annual Message in December Grant had endorsed both civil rights (as the *World* recalled) and monetary expansion. On the day the Currency Bill passed, the New York *Herald* reported: "It can be stated authoritatively that such an act will be promptly signed by the President."[66]

Soon, however, conflicting rumors materialized – just such rumors as now surrounded the Civil Rights Bill. On March 24 the New Orleans *Abeille* assured its readers that veto reports were unfounded. The president, the Memphis *Appeal* reported, had denied any suggestion of a veto: "If he were himself a member of congress he should regard an intimation of a veto in advance of legislation as an unbecoming threat by the executive and should resent it."[67] Then, on April 22 he unloaded his veto. Supporters of the Currency Bill felt betrayed. "When he was last in Philadelphia," the Philadelphia *Inquirer* cried foul, "he most positively declared that if the measure passed the House he would regard it as a demand of the people for its consummation.... The veto message is a rebuke to Congress for carrying out the Presidential recommendation."[68]

Attorney-General George Williams recalled the moment triumphantly. The president, in the midst of wild speculation, had stood firm, "unshaken, like a rock in the midst of the waves of the ocean."[69] Others recalled a rockier situation. According to Education Commissioner John Eaton, he actually sat down intending to sign the bill then changed his mind and wrote a veto message

66 New York *Herald*, April 6, 1874.

67 Memphis *Appeal*, March 23, 1874.

68 Philadelphia *Inquirer*, April 29, 1874. James Blaine recalled the shock of the Currency Bill's supporters: "At the beginning of the session of Congress, President Grant had clearly intimated that he had come to the same conclusion ... [but] he now vetoed the bill, which did not seem so radical in its provisions as his own recommendation had been." James Blaine, *Twenty Years of Congress: From Lincoln to Garfield* (Norwich, 1884–6), vol. 2, 562.

69 George H. Williams, *Occasional Addresses* (Portland, 1895), 18.

instead.[70] On the contrary, Frisbie Hoar claimed, Grant had misled the inflationists all along. He wanted to veto their measure. "If you send it up to me," he told the Massachusetts congressman, "make it just as bad as you can."[71] Among the misled was Ben Butler. Reporters questioned him. "Well," he spat, "if the President will deny his own acts, let him do it."[72] Congress imbibed a lesson. What Grant could do with the Currency Bill he could do with the Civil Rights Bill.

Civil rights, moreover, had become mixed up with another issue, the complex question of a third term in the White House. Would the general, undoubtedly the strongest figure in his party, attempt another presidential mandate? The Constitution allowed it. But precedent was against it; no president had asked the voters to sanction it. The issue raised emotional currents that played into the hands of Democrats: the cry of dictatorship, "Caesarism." Since the war, through their constitutional amendments, enforcement acts and Ku Klux acts supported by federal troops, Republicans had injected the power of the United States ever deeper into affairs once left to local authorities. Centralization of government, Democrats never failed to warn, grew alarmingly. Caesar had turned Rome's republic into imperial rule. Now an American Caesar inaugurated an imperial presidency. The next step to *imperium* was a third consecutive term.

A simple statement renouncing undue ambition might have defused the issue. Silence fed another busy mill of rumors. Pennsylvania Republicans repudiated the third term idea. Their state convention endorsed its own sitting governor, John F. Hartranft, for the next presidential nomination. New York Republicans, including Governor Dix, also denounced a third term. Third-term fever took on a life of its own. The North was unfriendly third-term territory. Therefore, political observers concluded, Grant needed the South.[73] In the

---

70 John Eaton, *Grant, Lincoln and the Freedman: Reminiscences of the Civil War, with Special Reference to the Work for the Contrabands and Freedmen of the Mississippi Valley* (New York, 1969), 278–279.

71 George F. Hoar, *Autobiography*, vol. 1, 206–207.

72 New York *Herald*, April 25, 1874. See also William D. Foulke, *Life of Oliver P. Morton, Including his Important Speeches* (Indianapolis, 1899), vol. 2, 333–334.

73 To some extent the specter of third-term Caesarism rose from the imaginings of an overstimulated press; see Mark Wahlgren Summers, *The Press Gang: Newspapers and Politics, 1865–1878* (Chapel Hill, 1994), 266–275. The substance of Ulysses Grant's aspirations remained, however, and also substantial evidence of his courtship of the South; see Michael Perman, *The Road to Redemption: Southern Politics, 1869–1879* (Chapel Hill, 1984), 160–164. Also note William S. McFeely, *Grant: A Biography* (New York, 2002); Joan Waugh, *U.S. Grant American Hero, American Myth* (Chapel Hill, N.C. 2009); H.W. Brands, *The Man Who Saved the Union, Ulysses Grant in War and Peace* (New York, 2012).

South no point carried more weight than civil rights. Two rumors entwined: President Grant's apparent desire for a third term, coupled with a veto of the Civil Rights Bill – the fate of one entangled with the progress of the other.

The idea was not unreasonable. Only two years before, Democrats had gone along with a candidate from another party, Horace Greeley, adopted from the ranks of the Liberal Republicans. Why should they not consider doing the same with a stronger candidate, if he promised to respond to their grievances? Ulysses Grant did not lack supporters in the South. Southern politicians let it be known that they might countenance an alliance, provided he convinced them he opposed the excesses of Radical rule. "After taking Horace Greeley as the embodiment of their party and principles in 1872, why should there be any difficulty with the democrats in adopting General Grant in 1876?" queried the New York *Herald*. "They swallowed Greeley. After such an act of deglutition no mouthful could be too bitter and nauseous for the Democratic stomach." According to the *Herald*, southern politicians welcomed Ulysses Grant. But they required a sign of bona fides: a veto of the Civil Rights Bill. "With the proviso that he will not sign the Civil Rights Bill, they all say, we would only be glad to trust him with another term."[74]

Among those trusting politicians was Alexander Stephens. The rapprochement between the general and the ex-Confederate vice-president began almost as soon as the latter returned to Congress. Stephens called at the White House. He met a warm reception. The wheelchair-bound visitor could not ascend to the presidential office. The president descended to him. Stephens acknowledged the courtesy. As to the next presidential election, he anticipated the rise of another third-party movement. "The time will raise up the man – it always does. I have no idea who it will be; but whether it is Grant, or Hancock, or Kemper, he will have my support if I live."[75]

Georgia's Senator John B. Gordon also flirted openly with the idea. Grant, he opined, wanted a third term. If Republicans denied him, he would run as an independent, "as a candidate of a Grant party – if you please." His willingness to provoke radicals like Morton and Butler on the Currency Bill signaled a move away from his present political affiliation. "A man cannot be with Grant any length of time before he catches his kindly drift in favor of the Southern people."[76] "Like some other well-known southern democrats of Confederate antecedents," noted the Springfield *Republican*, Gordon "has latterly struck up a famous friendship with the republican president and runs over to the

74 New York *Herald*, August 5, 13, 1874.
75 Richmond *Dispatch*, April 25, 1874.
76 Baltimore *Sun*, July 11, 1874.

White House at all hours."[77] Gordon protested; he opposed a third term for anyone, even "a Democratic President whom I regard as pure as Cato." But, he insisted, he found Ulysses Grant "cordial and considerate towards Southern gentlemen."[78]

Georgia's Governor James Smith did not deny it. He welcomed a third term for Grant, or a fourth, "if he should save us from the calamities of the civil rights bill."[79] In Atlanta Judge Osborne Lochrane pronounced the third term the rock on which the Civil Rights Bill would break. Ulysses Grant, rising "above the reach of fanatical excitement or sectional influence," would destroy it before it destroyed the South.[80] From Tennessee Gideon Pillow wrote the president: "Your acts in the past 12 months have produced upon the public mind in this section of the country a most favorable impression.... If you could only get a chance to veto the Civil rights bill for its mixed feature, it would make you the strongest man, with the southern people, there is in the nation."[81]

Perhaps the most unlikely voice in Grant's chorus of southern sympathizers belonged to Robert Toombs. That flamboyantly unreconstructed rebel began to see virtues in the commander whose forces had crushed his freedom. In May he too paid the White House a visit. He too received a "strikingly cordial" reception and emerged with a glowing report of its occupant.[82] Toombs repeated his disdain for the Republican Party: "I shall never acquiesce in the fourteenth and fifteenth amendments, and I never shall tolerate the damnable doctrine that there can be good government where negroes participate." But he repealed his disdain for the Republican president: "We are willing to give Grant any number of terms to make him our ally.... Grant will help us, I believe, and with that understanding I am heartily for him."[83]

In Louisiana, "third-termism" received the approval of former governor Paul Hébert. In Virginia, R.M.T. Hunter joined the choir: "Who shall cry shame upon her [the South] if she should be willing to sell something of her liberties to escape the pollution of miscegenation? Not I."[84] Alabama Democrats offered Grant a coronation for the price of a veto. If he were willing "to put his foot on this invention of ultra Radicalism in the interest of ultra Hottentotism, we are

77 Springfield, Massachusetts, *Republican*, July 8, 1874.

78 Norfolk, *Virginian*, July 11; Petersburg, Virginia, *Index and Appeal*, July 30, 1874.

79 Savannah *News*, July 30, 1874.

80 Atlanta *Constitution*, July 12, 1874.

81 Gideon Pillow to Grant, June 19, 1874. John Y. Simon, ed., *The Papers of Ulysses S. Grant* (Carbondale: 2003), vol. 25, 404.

82 Louisville *Courier-Journal*, May 11; New York *Herald*, May 17, 1874.

83 New York *Herald*, August 26, 1874.

84 New York *Herald*, September 3, 1874.

willing to forget the wrongs and evils he has countenanced in the past, and to rally to his support."[85] The Richmond *Dispatch* printed the view of one subscriber. He signed himself "Ku Klux." "As between the civil rights monstrosity and Grant," wrote Ku Klux, "score one for Grant."[86]

Not all southerners agreed. "The third term would be a perpetuation of power in the hands of a man who is by nature a despot, by education a soldier – a man of ambition, unscrupulous, without fear and without conscience," warned the Raleigh *Crescent.*[87] "True white men of the South," said the Savannah *News,* "are not prepared to offer General Grant a third term of the Presidency as a bid for his veto of the civil rights bill, which owes its existence to-day as much to his recommendation ... as it does to the malignity of the dead Sumner."[88] Many, however, prepared to make the offer. The Vicksburg *Vicksburger* urged its readers to accept the lesser evil.

> If it comes to be a question of more nigger or more Grant, the South will jump at the latter. All the dangers of imperialism, Caesarism, etc., shrink into insignificance.... We'll risk Grant another time if he will give us a rest from the eternal, irrepressible nigger.[89]

Would a coincidence of interest unite Ulysses Grant and the South with hands joined over the corpse of the Civil Rights Bill? In Mississippi Ben Butler's son-in-law, Governor Adelbert Ames, kept a lonely Republican vigil. He wrote his wife, the former Blanche Butler, who remained with her father in Massachusetts: "Grant has made friends with the Southern Democracy.... They are disposed to support him for anything." Ames was not hopeful. "Next year I shall be busy keeping the peace and giving protection to the helpless."[90] Whatever the president actually intended, politicians perceived a threat. It can only have dampened their civil rights ardor as the critical moment approached.

Rumors suggesting a "Southern strategy" brewed at the White House also identified the brewer, another of the president's strange bedfellows, Colonel

85 Montgomery *Advertiser*, January 13, 1874.
86 Richmond *Dispatch*, August 20, 1874.
87 Quoted in New York *Herald*, July 5, 1874.
88 Savannah *News*, July 9, 1874.
89 Quoted in New York *Tribune*, September 11, 1874. Likewise the Lynchburg, Virginia, *News:* "If such an election were the only alternative to save the South from civil-rights rule, or if an empire only could save us, we would go for either in preference to that abomination ... we would rather have an empire out and out than the Civil Rights bill."
90 Blanche Butler Ames, *Chronicles from the Nineteenth Century: Family Letters of Blanche Butler and Adelbert Ames* (Clinton, Mass., 1957), vol. 1, 698–699.

John S. Mosby. The Confederacy's ex-guerilla chief enjoyed an undoubted post-war friendship with the president whose armies he had harassed. "Gen. Grant finds in his former troublesome foe a kindred spirit and valuable supporter," wrote the Baltimore *Sun*.[91] Mosby urged the quid pro quo. Grant wanted a third term. The people of the South wanted to escape Radical rule. They despaired of electing a Democrat. Grant would rise above party. As a "people's candidate" he would free the South from its nightmare. It required only the sign of good faith: a veto of the Civil Rights Bill. The idea was not original. But in Col. Mosby it found a determined advocate. Early in February Mosby spoke to the press. White men, the colonel believed, must rule. Their fraternal embrace, North and South, would restore good government. On this, he said, he had the president's agreement.[92] The result was to be achieved by uniting the forces of conservatism and Grant. They would begin with an erasure of the Civil Rights Bill.[93]

Mosby sought allies. He recruited newly-elected Democratic Governor of his own state of Virginia Gen. James L. Kemper. Politician, soldier, a hero of the Lost Cause, Kemper was yet a man of reputedly moderate views.[94] Kemper saluted Mosby's idea:

> Better to elect Grant for the third and the seventh term.... Surely Grant and all Northern gentlemen know that our white men, including over fifty thousand ex-Confederate braves in Virginia, are the real, model, intellectual and political power of the State, if not of the whole South, are implicitly to be relied upon and are invaluable as friends. It cannot be that he will spurn a proffer of reconciliation.[95]

Mosby handed the governor an invitation to visit the president for an intimate interview.[96] "We are all for Grant in Virginia. Governor Kemper has come into my schemes.... I have but one object, and that is to have the white men of the

91 Baltimore *Sun*, April 4, 1874.

92 Baltimore *Sun*, February 9; New York *Tribune*, February 9, 1874.

93 Savannah *News*, May 28, 1874.

94 Kemper did demonstrate restraint. Conservatives assailed his veto of the Petersburg charter revisions. Moderation remained nonetheless a matter of degree, compared with the extremism manifested elsewhere. See Robert R. Jones, "James L. Kemper and the Virginia Redeemers Face the Race Question: A Reconsideration," *Journal of Southern History*, 38 (1972): 393–414.

95 Baltimore *Sun*, July 1; Norfolk *Virginian*, July 2, 1874.

96 Baltimore *Sun*, January 12, 1874.

South and the white men of the North co-operate for the general government of the country."[97]

Kemper's carriage stopped at the White House on February 12. Both parties emerged smiling twenty minutes later. Grant, true to his custom, said nothing. The governor was more talkative. Reporters found him at the Willard Hotel. His visit, he said, had been a courtesy call, not arranged for any purpose of Col. Mosby's. He had been favorably impressed, the President receiving him in a spirit of "marked friendship." Kemper explained that he stood for a solid conservative agenda; he was prepared to co-operate with anyone so inclined.[98] Other reports took his words further. Grant had informed Kemper: henceforth he would not "lend his influence to any but liberal measures towards the southern country."[99] Those measures, the New York *Tribune* reported, portended no good for civil rights. Kemper was a nonentity, "a man of limited intelligence and unlimited personal vanity." His alliance with Grant meant a veto of the Civil Rights Bill.[100] Ben Butler read an anxious letter from black Virginians: "It is thought that Gen. Kemper will visit Washington in regard to the Civial Question as he is advised by Col. J.S. Mosby to do so.... That is Kemper's whole object there."[101]

Kemper's trip to the White House proved to be the high point of Mosby's operation and also the beginning of its dissolution. In the Virginia senate Mosby's supporters proposed a resolution: "his Excellency U.S. Grant is the choice of the [Democratic] party for next President of the United States." Angry legislators ordered it stricken from the record.[102] Governor Kemper got the message. The longer he pondered the implications of his White House visit the more he regretted it. In June Democratic operative George C. Wedderburn published a scathing exposé. Kemper had sold out the party.[103] Kemper responded with an open letter. Written "in the bold and manly style for which General Kemper is noted," it accomplished a bold and manly retreat that put the general safely back in his own political lines, leaving bags, baggage and Colonel Mosby behind. He denied having been tempted by the third-term siren: "We are going to have either popular self-government or central imperialism. I intend to stand for the liberty side as long as a fragment of it remains." Nonetheless, he

97 Baltimore *Sun*, February 9, 1874.
98 Chattanooga *Times*, February 13, 1874.
99 Baltimore *Sun*, February 16, 1874.
100 New York *Tribune*, July 3, 1874.
101 R.A.S. to Benjamin Butler, January 12, 1874. Butler Papers, Library of Congress.
102 Richmond *Dispatch*, February 13, 1874.
103 Norfolk *Virginian*, June 21, 1874. See Jack Maddex, Jr., *Virginia Conservatives, 1867–1879: A Study of Reconstruction Politics* (Chapel Hill: 1970), 136–137.

admitted, veto of the Civil Rights Bill was indeed in the wind. "I went [to the White House] when the fate of our social system was trembling in a doubtful balance, when my going might add, and did add, some weight, however slight ... against the passage of a national civil-rights bill ... against civil-rights fanaticism and barbarism."[104]

Ulysses Grant's true intentions remained impenetrable. Some were convinced. He would veto the bill and win the South to a third term. "He will veto it and be President again, and 'that's what's the matter with Dinah,'" crowed the Memphis *Appeal*. "Grant is agin Dinah now."[105] Some maintained quite as stoutly he would sign it, as he had pledged to do. Others scratched their heads. "Will he veto the Civil Rights Bill?" the Galveston *News* pondered. "Is he willing to undertake the work of purging from the South the ghastly and putrid death-in-life of reconstruction ... to purge civilization from an Ethiopian cataclysm?"[106] Ulysses Grant coolly left town.[107]

On June 13 he departed for an excursion to the sea-shore at Cape May, New Jersey. A congenial group of companions included Attorney-General Williams, Secretary of the Treasury Bristow, his private secretary Orville Babcock, Senator Hamlin and Governor Edward McCook of the Colorado Territory. No political rumors emerged from that expedition.[108]

A week later Congress completed its failure to pass the Civil Rights Bill. He left again, this time for West Virginia. Officially the object was to visit an elderly aunt, Mrs. Rachel Thompkins, who dwelt in the Kanawha Valley. It soon became evident that the objective was not fortuitous. Politics merged with family ties. He stopped first at the resort of White Sulphur Springs. The town was a meeting place of the southern elite. Grant exchanged a cordial greeting with influential gentlemen, including ex-Confederate General McCausland, whose most celebrated wartime exploit had been the burning of the town of Chambersburg, Pennsylvania. But that was not all. A buzz of political rumors began. "The subject of politics is pretty thoroughly eschewed at White Sulphur during the season," travel writer Edward King shrewdly noted, "except when the President goes there to hear what the Southern politicians have to say."[109] "There was something more than mere idle political rumor in the third-term

104 Norfolk *Virginian*, July 2, 1874.
105 Memphis *Appeal*, June 21, 1874.
106 Galveston *News*, June 2, 1874.
107 "Grant's simplicity," Henry Adams said later, "was more disconcerting than the complexity of a Talleyrand." Henry Adams, *The Education of Henry Adams* (New York, 1931): 276.
108 New York *Herald*, June 14, 1874.
109 Edward King, *The Great South* (Baton Rouge, 1972), 677.

suggestion which emanated from a bevy of Southern politicians at the Virginia Springs during the visit there of the President and his family."[110]

Grant proceeded to Charleston. He arrived on June 29 by the 2:30 train. Crowds cheered. Brass bands blared. Cannons boomed. The president repaired to the stately home of his dear aunt's son-in-law Col. Thomas B. Swann. The next day, Sunday, he attended church services. Then he received the visits of all and sundry in the colonel's parlor. Night fell. Before he had settled himself to sleep a singular incident occurred. A tardy visitor appeared at the door. It was past 11 o'clock, but the man was so insistent that Col. Swann let him in. The president, in dressing gown and slippers, descended. He found himself in the presence of a humble black person. Reporters recorded, or imagined, his heartwarming salutation, adorned with appropriately dialectical utterances.

> As soon as he gave him a hearty handshake our colored hero made the following earnest speech. "Dis is de President. Well God bless you. I'se glad to see you, Massa Grant. I followed you all de way down into Louisiana. I fit with you all through de war. I'se been a mighty faithful servant, Massa President, and is glad to live to see you dis day. I knows you'se a good man from de look of your eye, and dat you're gwine whar good men go. I rejoice in your prosperity and knows you deserve it all. God bless you, Massa President."[111]

Whatever the "colored hero's" actual words, Ulysses Grant heard something. In one weekend trip he heard both sides: southern gentry at White Sulphur; a plain black citizen at Charleston. The nocturnal visitor left, having delivered his soliloquy. One man remained alone with the general: Tom Swann. He and his famous relative, Swann recalled, sat in the late evening quiet and sipped a glass of soda water. The president unburdened himself.[112] Later Swann shared those insights. He spoke to the congressional nominating convention for the West Virginia 3rd District at Charleston on August 25:

> He [Grant] will prove equal to the trials of the present as he was equal to the trials of the past, and he will be equal to the future. A man just to all.

110 Altoona, Pennsylvania, *Morning Tribune*, August 8, 1874. Sources speculated Grant would return in August, "when the season is at its height." He might consult with Toombs and Gordon, Ben Hill and Henry Wise, perhaps generals Johnston and Beauregard. New York *Herald*, July 9, 1874.

111 Wheeling *Intelligencer*, July 3, 1874.

112 Wheeling *Intelligencer*, September 5, 1874.

> He will save to the East her bonds, and to the South her schools and her civilization, and to the freedman his equal rights.[113]

If Col. Swann were indeed made privy to the president's thoughts, Grant envisioned a compromise. He was willing to accept monetary expansion, but the provisions Congress fashioned went too far. His veto of the Currency Bill forced it to find a more moderate substitute. Thus had he saved to the East her bonds. He wanted to sign a civil rights bill. The one that emerged from the Senate went too far. It must assume a more moderate form. He would save to the South her schools (hence her civilization). But he would give the freedman equality.[114] He very much planned, that is, to sign a civil rights bill. It must be rid of the impenetrable impediment, the mixed-school disaster.

In September the New York *Herald* recorded an interview with another informant, whom it identified only as "a leading Republican of West Virginia." He had been present at White Sulphur Springs, he said. He heard Col. Swann speak at Charleston. The *Herald's* informant emerged convinced. Grant would sign the bill. Third-term vetoes, quid pro quo deals, angling for southern votes, were an illusion. In fact, among all the conflicting sources, the imaginings of rumor mills, the punditry of political prognosticators, this anonymous West Virginian produced the only completely accurate prediction of events to come.

> The bill will pass in February or March beyond question, and ought to pass, and I do not believe the President will veto it. He recommended it in his Message of December 1873, and he is not given to changing front. It is part of the price we paid for the federal Union; the keeping of a promise made to the negro, sealed with his blood when we called him to aid in putting down the rebellion – no less sacred than the national debt. It is the inevitable logical consequence of the fourteenth amendment.[115]

Ulysses Grant's murky position was not the only obstacle. No matter how the House acted, whether the president vetoed it or signed it, with or without the school clause, the Civil Rights Bill was a losing proposition for the Republican Party. If it passed, it unleashed a backlash of resentment among white voters. If it failed – if it failed, it had already unleashed that backlash. The ardently

113 Wheeling *Intelligencer*, August 29, 1874.

114 Thus Brooks D. Simpson, "Ulysses S. Grant and the Failure of Reconstruction," *Illinois Historical Journal*, 81 (1988), 269–271: "Grant's deceptively simple 'Let us have peace' statement summarized his vision of Reconstruction: peace not only between blacks and whites, but between North and South. Indeed, he saw the two as inseparable."

115 New York *Herald*, September 4, 1874.

Democratic Harrisburg *Patriot* surveyed the scene: "The Civil Rights Bill, with its invasion of social distinctions and its invocation to civil conflict, sits like a nightmare on the Republican party."[116] The Baltimore *Sun* predicted it as early as May. Merely the agitation of the bill would cost Republicans control of the House.[117] The New York *Times* regretted the whole senseless, suicidal civil rights adventure. The thing was a godsend for Democrats. The *Times* reported on the situation in North Carolina:

> Having no principles calculated to attract the support of intelligent people, the Democrats are trying to make capital by insisting that every Republican shall define his position on the question of civil rights. If they endorse the bill now before Congress the Democrats call upon the white men of the western counties to vote down such candidates; if they do not endorse the bill, the Democrats cry out to the colored element in the east that the Republicans have deserted them. So it is expected that this play upon the question of civil rights will be of immense advantage to the Democrats, in the west by driving off the white men from the Republican party, and in the east by making the colored men lukewarm to such an extent that they will not vote. This is the chief plank in the Democratic platform, and upon which they mainly rely.[118]

The Civil Rights Bill, so it seemed, placed Republicans between two fires. No one questioned the danger on one side. There would be an exodus of white voters. It had already begun. Lemmings fled over the horizon. The attitude of black voters, despite the *Times'* apprehensions, appeared less certain. Would they desert the party of emancipation if it disappointed them on this issue? Frederick Douglass hurled a furious threat:

> By the treachery of Republican members of Congress, elected in large part by colored votes, the negro is continued an outlaw. Fortunately the negro has the ballot.... Our people are not the cowards to kiss the hand that smites them. They must not be led into the support of pretended friends by sophistry nor by intimidation. Defeat every pretended Republican who voted against the Civil Rights Bill.[119]

116 Quoted in Newark *Journal*, August 27, 1874.
117 Baltimore *Sun*, May 25, 1874.
118 New York *Times*, June 1, 1874.
119 New York *World*, June 26, 1874.

Douglass' true grit seemed crumbly. Many doubted whether the threat would, or could, be carried out. As congressional elections soon proved, the doubters were right. Frederick Douglass himself, faced with reality, retracted his threat. Once the campaigns got underway he commanded his people to support every Republican, even those who voted against the Civil Rights Bill.[120] Failure to pass the bill, the New York *World* concluded, would cost Republicans nothing. No civil rights disappointment could pry black voters loose from their party.[121] The Mobile *Register* agreed. "If the Radical Senate had set out to shape a bill to weaken its party and to unite white men against it, it could not have succeeded better.... As for the negroes, the party was sure of them before."[122] Even foreign correspondents saw the obvious. "A bribe is wasted on a faithful adherent," noted the London *Saturday Review*."[123] White votes would be lost. Black votes were safe anyway. Why would Republicans pass the Civil Rights Bill?

Republicans caucused. Members of both House and Senate assembled on the night of June 8. Venerable Hannibal Hamlin took the chair.[124] Richard Parsons of Ohio and John Roy Lynch of Mississippi acted as secretaries. Following a discussion of finance, the Currency Bill being vetoed, Lynch rose to address the matter of civil rights. Lynch resented his colleagues' inability or unwillingness to pass a bill they held in their hands. But he concluded with reassurance. No matter how deep their deception, black people would not forsake the party: "He assured the caucus of the strict fidelity of the colored people. There was to be no reconciliation between them and their old masters.... The party had been true to them in the past, and they put their trust in it for the future."[125]

Lynch's words calmed some jittery nerves. They also gave party leaders even less incentive to pass the bill. Nor did they quiet the cacophony of voices that offered advice from all sides. Benjamin Butler heard those voices. His correspondence yields a kaleidoscopic confusion of contradictory counsel, each explaining the wisdom – or the folly – of passing civil rights legislation.

Georgia's black ex-congressman Jefferson Long telegraphed on January 7. He repudiated the "representations" of Alexander Stephens and others who claimed that his people were content without a civil rights bill. They were not content. Another black politician, Peter K. Jones, of the Virginia House of Delegates, also telegraphed. He was furious with the Virginia House of Delegates, which had issued an anti-civil rights bill resolution: "It is useless to say that we

120 See below, 435.
121 New York *World*, May 26, 1874.
122 Mobile *Register*, May 30–31, 1874.
123 Quoted in Mobile *Register*, July 17, 1874.
124 New York *World*, June 9, 1874.
125 New York *Times*, June 9, 1874.

will go into their parlors, and churches and etc. That is all bosh, Nothing!" Pass the bill at once.[126]

Nor did opinions sort themselves by race. W.M. Brown, white, member of the Kentucky legislature, wrote on January 6. Pass the bill. Keep the school clause. Without it there could be no hope of education for the freedmen.[127] Isaac Myers, black, president of the Colored National Labor Union, wrote on the 8th. Do *not* pass the bill. It would only anger whites and make things worse: "We stand in danger of losing much that we have gained, without hope of recovery."[128] That same day's post brought the letter of another black leader, Thomas Malcom of the Philadelphia African Aid Union. Pass the bill. But remove the school clause. "As the great Apostle Paul said, 'All things are lawful but all things are not expedient.'"[129] On January 9 Butler received the letter of yet another black man, J.S. Tyler of Columbus, Ohio. It was entirely expedient. Keep the school clause. "Suffer no emasculated substitute to take the place of a comprehensive bill."[130]

The deluge of communications continued. Judge Elias Keils, a leading white Republican of Alabama, wrote from Eufaula. Pass the bill at once. "Enforce it to the letter."[131] Bishop Gilbert Haven wrote from Atlanta. "Don't let the Civil Rights Bill fail. Now that Mr. Sumner is gone, the oppressed men of color look to you."[132] On April 1 Butler read the simple yet eloquent appeal of Robert Holyer, a citizen of Boston:

> I hope you will carried this Bill safe across the red sea.... I read your speech on the 9 of Jan. and it lift me up in my mind it done me so much good that I have to keep it to read to my colored friends when they call on me I tell them what good work you is doing for me and my race ... for a race you know that can't give you nothing but good will but I hope you will receive your reward in heaven.[133]

The decisive vote drew nearer. Butler's correspondence grew more political, its tone more insistent, the advice more scattered than ever. He preserved the letters of two prominent African Americans from Athens, Georgia. Styles Linton

126 Telegrams, National Archives, House Judiciary Committee File, 43rd Congress
127 W.M. Brown to Butler, January 6, 1874. Butler Papers, Library of Congress.
128 Isaac Myers to Butler, January 8, 1874. Butler Papers, Library of Congress.
129 Thomas S. Malcom to Butler, January 8, 1874. Butler Papers, Library of Congress.
130 J.S. Tyler to Butler, January 9, 1874. Butler Papers, Library of Congress.
131 Elias M. Keils to Butler, January 19, 1874. Butler Papers, Library of Congress.
132 Gilbert Haven to Butler, March 18, 1874. Butler Papers, Library of Congress.
133 Robert Holyer to Butler, April 1, 1874. Butler Papers, Library of Congress.

Hutchins threatened: "Believe me, dear sir, painfully persuaded that, unless a civil rights Bill be passed by the 43 Congress it will never pass, and that in the case of the 43 Congress' failure to do so, it will set the colored citizens at variance with the Government and the republican party."[134] Eugene Brydige cajoled: "General, we feel proud that we have such a friend in this great time of need, for if you fail to get Civil Rights we are gone.... You will not only confer an honor on our departed hero Charles Sumner ... but upon yourself and will ever find a place in the affections of the colored race until time itself shall end."[135]

Others urged the opposite opinion. They stared into the abyss of political disaster. Eugene Drake, Republican editor of the Statesville, North Carolina, *American,* pleaded. Stop the bill. At least delay it until after the elections.

> The Democrats are endeavoring to use the passage of the Bill through the Senate to our damage already, and if it pass the House their clamor will increase to an extent that will know no bounds, magnified by misrepresentation, falsehood and other appliances which they so well understand how to use.[136]

David H. Graves, "one of your old soldiers of the 10 Army Corps," also wrote from North Carolina. Graves, a transplanted New Yorker, felt hostility close in on all sides: "We Republicans in No. Carolina feel confident that if the bill passes and becomes a law our party is doomed."[137] Contrarily, Thomas Conway, as ever the dreamy Louisiana schoolmaster, begged Butler not to run scared: "My friend, Gen. George A. Sheridan of La., tells me you have agreed to drop the Free School feature of the Civil Rights Bill. If you have it is the only cowardly thing I ever knew of you. Please, General, deal the finishing blow to this monster of inequality of civil rights, this remnant of slavery and rebellion. Do not back down on the bill as it is."[138]

Finally Butler heard from the ultimate authority: Charles Sumner, deceased. His communication crossed the awful gulf through the medium of a séance. More directly, it came in the terrestrial mail, on monogrammed stationery, from Mrs. Elizabeth Kennedy of Buffalo, New York. "I send you by request of Mr. Charles Sumner a message received by me through planchette from him." The Senator, incorporeal, remained inflexible:

134 Styles Linton Hutchins to Butler, March 10, 1874. Butler Papers, Library of Congress.
135 Eugene Brydige to Butler, March 25, 1874. Butler Papers, Library of Congress.
136 Eugene B. Drake to Butler, June 2, 1874. Butler Papers, Library of Congress.
137 D.H. Graves to Butler, June 12, 1874. Butler Papers, Library of Congress.
138 Thomas W. Conway to Butler, June 4, 1874. Butler Papers, Library of Congress.

> I wish to say to my countrymen that having passed into real things I confirm all I ever said or did in the cause of humanity and I charge you all as you value your immortal happiness to carry into action my last request do not let the civil rights bill fail.[139]

During the months following recommitment of H.R.796 Republicans struggled to find their footing. The formal debate had ended on January 7. The Civil Rights Bill languished on the Speaker's table. But meanwhile members of the House spoke out. Those who had not risen before found occasion to make their views known. On January 10 Democrat Robert Vance of North Carolina took the floor. Six times elected to the House, he yet resided in the shadow of his elder brother Zebulon Vance, once governor and future senator. War honored Robert Vance with a general's rank, yet war had not been kind. He watched from a prison camp as his nation fell. Now his beard grew grey. A deeply religious man, he dreamed of peace, of the beloved woods, valleys and mountains of his Asheville home. A little book of poems that he left to posterity, dedicated "to the good people of the dear old eighth congressional district," evoked those hills and vales. There, he wrote, in verses sweetly rhymed, there dwelt the southern heart, the southern faith: gospel camp-meetings "in the saffron woods;" nostalgia for the "wearin' of the gray."[140] Civil rights do not appear in Vance's poems. Gospel fountains and camp-meetings appeared in his civil rights speech.

The South had fought to sustain slavery. Vance admitted it. Now it delighted in the freedom of its slaves. "I have yet to meet the southern man (and I thank God for it) who does not in his heart rejoice that the colored man is free." Why then did southerners oppose the Civil Rights Bill? Sex. Civil rights incubated promiscuity. Why were freedmen not content with what they already had, equal rights but separate? Why did they clamor for "social equality?" Why else but to mingle and interbreed? If such was their intention – the poet's voice grew stern – they would come to regret it.

> I ask, what race has ever been able to stand before the Caucasian? Look at the history of the world. Where is the Indian? Why, sir, less than two centuries ago on this spot the Indian reared his wigwam and stood upon

139 Elizabeth W. Kennedy to Butler, April 2, 1874. Butler Papers, Library of Congress. Butler endorsed it on the back with malicious humor: "Respectfully submitted to the Hon. E.R. Hoar for his information. I suspect there must be some mistake in the direction of this note." Apparently he thought better of the cruel joke. The letter stayed in his files.

140 Robert B. Vance, *Heart-Throbs from the Mountains* (Nashville, 1887).

> these hills and looked upon the broad, beautiful Potomac, or his eye swept over the hunting grounds of the West, and he had the title to this magnificent country. Where is he now? He has gone back, step by step, before the advancing march of the white man. No race, sir, in the world has been able to stand before the pure Caucasian. An antagonism of races will not be good for the colored man.[141]

Vance deployed the boot-strap argument. If black people possessed any character, let them show it. If they thought they could rise to the level of the whites let them do it: "If I belonged to the colored race I would come up by my own merit ... I would not stand here as a beggar asking for these social rights." He finished with a joke. A gospel meeting in the saffron hills, the Holy Spirit descended on an old black man who commenced to shout. The preacher encouraged him: "'Shout on, brother, shout on, if you feel like it; we shall all be white in heaven.' The old fellow replied: 'Bless the Lord, I feel the white coming now.'"

Laughter rippled through the galleries. Joseph Rainey was not amused. The gentleman thought it funny. He called it unseemly for black people to beg for their rights. How did he feel about southerners who came begging to Congress for restoration of their political rights, rights they had forfeited in lawless rebellion? Vance was unfazed. The South never begged. Its people fought and died for a cause. And that cause, truly, was the cause of humanity: "No southern man is ashamed, thank God, to stand here and say that he did what he thought was right.... The bones of my kindred and my countrymen lie in their narrow graves, wrapped in their bloody blankets, because of what they conceived and believed to be the best interests of human rights in this country of ours."

Richard Cain joined the discussion. The gentleman had no business preaching to the House about human rights from the position of one who had denied them to a whole race. The gentleman asserted that black people already enjoyed equality. "Now, it may not have come under his observation but it has under mine, that such is not really the case; and the reason why I know and feel it more than he does is because my face is painted black and his is painted white." A few days ago, said Cain, traveling to attend this very Congress and passing through the "Old North State," he and his colleague Robert Elliott could not eat when they were hungry. They entered the restaurants. No table tolerated their presence. Nor could they eat inside the railroad cars. "They refused us in the restaurant, and then did not desire that we should eat our meals in the cars, although we paid for them. Yet this was in the noble State of North Carolina."

141 Speech of Robert Vance: *Cong. Record*, 43rd Congress, 1st Session, 554–557 and following colloquia.

> We do not come here begging for our rights. We come here clothed in the garb of American citizenship. We come demanding our rights in the name of justice ... in the name of justice, equity, and law, in the name of our children, in the name of our country, petitioning for our rights.... In the name of the dead soldiers of our race ... in the name of the confederate soldiers who fell upon the same fields, I conjure you let this righteous act be done. I appeal to you in the name of God and humanity to give us our rights, for we ask nothing more.[142]

New York's David Mellish spoke. Of all the white Republicans perhaps who rose for civil rights Mellish was the most sincere. His seat, the New York 9th, a Democratic district in a Democratic city, hung by a thread. Civil rights speeches could only hurt him. He told a story. During the war years in New York City a black woman had stepped into a "whites only" car as it passed the Astor House hotel. A policeman dragged her off. Police Commissioner Thomas Acton suspended the patrolman. He decreed the same for any officer who acted in like manner. That sufficed. Street-car operators removed restrictions. Apocalypse did not arrive. Sexual promiscuity did not run rampant. "I venture to predict that this bill will produce none of the terrible results that have been conjured up by the affrighted imaginations of the opposition." David Mellish's words were his last; before civil rights came to a vote he was dead.[143]

On January 24 another North Carolinian joined the rhetorical fray. Ex-Confederate Major William Robbins, as Gen. Vance, knew the face of war: four years' service in the 4th Alabama regiment, four times wounded. Five brothers had entered the conflict with him. One survived. Robbins did not subscribe to the notion that the South had fallen to an unworthy foe, as Dr. Dabney declared, beaten "not by manly force" but by a foreign rabble.[144] Robbins respected his former enemies, Americans all.[145] At their hands he could endure

---

142 Remarks of Richard Cain, *Cong. Record*, 43rd Congress, 1st Session: 565–566.

143 Remarks of David Mellish, *Cong. Record*, 43rd Congress, 1st Session: 567.

144 Dr. Dabney's vision, soothing to the southern ego, took root widely, a source of solace in defeat. "Defeat created a dark night of the soul, so troubling that it took all his human will to calm his doubts, the religious fears of southerners who had lost a holy war." Charles Wilson, "Robert Lewis Dabney: Religion and the Southern Holocaust," *Virginia Magazine of History and Biography* (1981): 79.

145 The Senate's Thomas Norwood disagreed. The South's destroyers were *not* Americans but an alien, polyglot, multi-ethnic horde. Their linguistic diversity alone was the stuff of nightmares. "Think of the horrifying effect," wrote Norwood, "when bawled, screeched, screamed, howled, roared by an army of three millions of negroes and whites, brothers in arms, and in sixty odd different languages and nearly all nationalities except the Simian and Gorilla, among which were Russian, Greek, German, Norwegian, Swedish, Lapland,

defeat. He could not endure defeat at the hands of an inferior race. Particularly he could not endure the saga of New Market Heights. Negro valor was an oxymoron. White men had not retreated before Negroes. Negroes, whatever else they might be, could not be soldiers.

> The negro is different from the white man. In some things he excels the white man. He has much music in his soul. He can outsing, outdance, outlaugh, and outfrolic the white man. He is more docile, more self-satisfied, more imitative, more affectionate, more passionate, and perhaps more naturally eloquent than the white man. He is the world's "merry-andrew." He is the world's star actor on the comic stage.... But when you come to the grand tragic and heroic parts in the drama of humanity, where all will, force, courage, forethought, the sense of masterdom, and the instinct of dominion are required to shine, the negro fails. Despite all that we have heard on that subject, the negro is no fighter.... Yes; infuriated with whiskey, he was brought to the scratch a few times, only to be sacrificed without result.[146]

A voice called out: Josiah Walls, veteran of the 3rd Regiment, United States Colored Troops. "Did you ever meet the negro on the battle-field?" Robbins, unlike the prickly Virginian Harris, replied calmly to a question from the floor. "Yes, sometimes; and whipped him easily too." He injected a little civil rights humor. "It was my business for four years on the battle-field to meet all comers without regard to 'race, color, or previous condition of servitude.'"[147]

Robbins dismissed Thomas Jefferson's idea: all men are created equal. "That sentence contains more error and untruth than has ever been embodied, perhaps, in the same number of English words." Inequality, not equality, was God's decree. "He made the oak to battle with storms, and the daisy to shelter

Hungarian, Polish, Turkish, Syrian, Spanish, French, Austrian, Egyptian, Chinese, Goth, Hessian, Belgian, Dutch, Swiss, African, Italian, Sicilian, Corsican, Portuguese, Barbarian, Yiddish, Milesian, some Celt, English, a little Scotch and less American. With these tongues, guttural, sputteral, hissing, sizzing, roaring, the thunderous Babel was enough to scare a thousand Devils. The wonder is that the 'poor white trash' of the South, who always easily won every battle when the odds against them was not more than two to one, did not use their heels for flight instead of their guns to fight." Thomas Norwood, *A True Vindication of the South*, 423.

146 Speech of William Robbins: *Cong. Record*, 43rd Congress, 1st Session: 897–900.

147 Robbins was disingenuous. It is unlikely the 4th Alabama ever faced black troops. None were employed in its early battles through Gettysburg and Chickamauga. At Petersburg the 4th did not join in the Battle of the Crater, where the Army of the Potomac engaged its only division of United States Colored Troops.

underneath; the eagle to soar above the clouds, and the mocking-bird to sing in the thicket." Black people were mocking-birds. Or rather, they were crows. Take down the soaring eagle as the nation's emblem. Replace it with a crow, black, thieving, and inferior. Having made what might seem an invidious comparison, Robbins protested he meant no disrespect, to man or bird.

> In speaking of the characteristics of the negro, I do not mean any disrespect to him.... I believe in these things, because such seems the plain teaching of that Book which southern men generally rely upon as the embodiment of perfect truth.... The negro is a clinging parasite. He looks up to others as his superiors. He is an inveterate servant. Free him how you will, enfranchise him as you may, he still waits for guidance and submits to command.[148]

The true victims were the southern whites, ruined in war, oppressed in peace. "We have been sorely tried, sorely humiliated. Try us no further; trample on us no more; sport with our miseries no longer. Else you will break the spirit of a generous race."

Richard Cain rose once more. William Robbins' *cri de coeur* failed to move him. The gentleman from North Carolina reprehended black people for lack of cultural accomplishment, apart from "outsinging or outfrolicking." Why did those people lack refinement? "The gentleman upbraids us with our ignorance and stupidity." He would do better to upbraid himself.

> You robbed us for two hundred years. During all that time we toiled for you ... without pay, without the means of education, and hardly of subsistence. And yet you upbraid us for being ignorant; call us a horde of barbarians! Why, sir, it is ill-becoming in the gentleman to tell us of our barbarism, after he and his have been educating us for two hundred years. It ill-becomes them to taunt us now with our barbarism and ignorance.... Mr. Speaker, if I had that gentleman upon the floor, with my foot upon his neck, and holding a lash over him, with his hands tied, with him bound hand and foot, would you expect that I should boast over him?

148 Ninety years later Florida's Senator George Smathers echoed Robbins' lament: "If anyone is generally discriminated against it is the people of the South. It is unfortunate, but it is true. All we have to do is to look around the country to see who is the victim of the most discrimination. Who is taken to the woodshed regularly? It is the South. What does the Senator think it is? It is prejudice. That is the cause of it. I have been in places where I heard it said, 'He is a southerner.' I know a little about these things." *Cong. Record*, 88th Congress, 2nd Session: 7,799.

> … And yet such was the condition in which he had my race. Why, sir, the whipping-post, the thumb-screw, and the lash, were the great means of education in the South. These were the school-houses, these were the academies, these were the great instruments of education, of which the gentleman boasts, for the purpose of bringing these barbarians into civilization.… How long would it have taken us to get ready under their kind of teaching? How long, O Lord, how long![149]

Robbins had mentioned Jefferson. "The gentleman states that this idea of all men being created equal is a fallacy, announced some years ago by Thomas Jefferson, that old fool-hardy man.… If he was a foolish man, I would to God that North Carolina had been baptized in that foolishness about two hundred years ago."[150]

On January 13 Sunset Cox offered his only official remarks, a speech delivered in Cox's customary precious style, impeccable timing and clever punchlines. He too took time to deride Butler's New Market Heights oration. The general, said Cox, had painted a masterpiece – a masterpiece of fiction.

> Time has a relentless tooth.… What may not be said of the distinguished gentleman from Massachusetts when the 4th of July 1900 shall be celebrated? … Where then this battle of the blacks? A dactyl, a spondee – the hexameter verse of some New Zealand Virgil, or some Alaskan Longfellow – singing of a suppositious general on an imperceptible horse upon an imaginary battle-field, with an army of impalpable blacks cutting away a fictitious abatis with intangible axes, to capture an airy redoubt, held by a ghostly enemy, who did not fly incontinently over any number of miles, with nobody in pursuit! Such is the fickleness of fame and the unreliance of history.[151]

---

149 Speech of Richard Cain, *Cong. Record*, 43rd Congress, 1st Session: 901–903.

150 Democrats struggled with the embarrassment of Jefferson. He was, on one hand, their party's founder, but also the author of a most infelicitous phrase. Republicans threw Jefferson in their faces. None did it better than satirist David Ross Locke. "We are all descended from grandfathers," he declared in a celebrated piece. "Nearly a century ago the grandfathers of some of us, in convention assembled, uttered as doctrine, which they believed could not be gainsaid, these words: 'We hold these truths to be self-evident, that all men are created equal.' … Thomas Jefferson was the particular grandfather who wrote these high-sounding words, and, as a consequence, he has been ever since hailed as the father of the only political party which never believed in them." David Ross Locke, "Cussed be Canaan," in *The Struggles (Social, Financial, and Political) of Petroleum V. Nasby* (Boston: 1873), 629.

151 Speech of Samuel Cox: *Cong. Record*, 43rd Congress, 1st Session: 614–619.

The occasion of Cox's effort was not precisely the discussion of the Civil Rights Bill. He chose to speak upon another measure, brought forward separately but whose fate seemed to walk together with H.R.796. This was the Education Fund Bill, H.R.477. That proposal belonged to George Frisbie Hoar. It envisioned the establishment of federal aid to education paid for through subsidies to the states. Those subsidies were to be derived from a portion of the revenues of sales of public land. One-half of all proceeds, invested in United States bonds bearing 5% interest, would serve to create a perpetual fund in the Treasury. From that deposit the Commissioner of Education, as directed by the Secretary of the Interior, would allocate funds to each state for the education of its citizens in proportion to its population between the ages of four and twenty-one. The whole concept was anathema to Democrats. Federal aid to education! It meant, of course, dictatorship. Government would seize control of education, thus to control the minds of the people.

Radicals, they insisted, had designed their measures with devilish symmetry. The Civil Rights Bill would destroy the public school system. As white students fled, states would withdraw funding for the black remnant. Therefore had the friends of the Negroes prepared the Education Fund Bill. The government would educate blacks, while it consigned poor whites to ignorance. The Education Bill and the Civil Rights Bill conjoined, said Democrat Charles Milliken of Kentucky, somewhat indelicately, they resembled the lately-deceased Siamese twins: "Like Chang and Eng, they travel together, they are at home together, they lie down together and get up together, they sleep together and wake together, and I hope will soon die together."[152]

Cox deployed his multilingual eloquence: *Hic niger est, hunc tu, Romane, caveto*; "this too is black, O Roman, beware!" It was a sign that Republicans, though they hesitated, had not abandoned mixed schools. Recommitted the Civil Rights Bill might be. It could not return without that clause. "You may give them the freedom of the inn, the railroad, and the theater; you may bury them side by side with the white in the cemetery ... but the broad-voweled African tongue will talk, and the elegant education of the successor of John C. Calhoun [Robert Elliott] will still make its music of agitation."[153]

Saturday, February 28, brought the House an unpleasant interlude. John Young Brown, Democrat of Kentucky, rose to speak. Young Brown, as the press called him (to distinguish him from a famous person of similar name), was one of the House's most volatile members. Three times elected to Congress, he had

152 Remarks of Charles Milliken, *Cong. Record*, 43rd Congress, 1st Session: Appendix, 70–74.

153 The Latin quote, as Cox well knew, from Horace, had nothing to do with race or color of skin, but to blackness, that is turpitude, of morals and character.

yet to complete one full term. His first term, to which he had been elected in 1858, was postponed because, at 24, he had not yet attained the statutory age. Elected again in 1860, he was promptly expelled for advocating secession. He spent the war years inveighing against Yankee aggression, though he refrained personally from shouldering a musket to repel the aggressors. He returned in 1873 unrepentant, his intemperate rhetoric undiminished. When he spoke Republicans made a show of not paying attention, so as to demonstrate their disregard. Actually they listened carefully, hoping to catch tactless sallies or censurable words. On this occasion Young Brown did not disappoint them.

Republican leaders, said Brown, "have not put their feet in the 'tracks of our forefathers.' Their policies are like the tampering of pygmies with the finished work of giants.... With criminal folly [new constitutional amendments] they have undone in a day that which cost the brain-sweat and heart-sweat of wisdom years to perfect." The masses cry for bread. Republicans give them "civil rights."

> Toil on ye sun-bronzed sons of labor. Wipe the sweat from your aching brows, and stifle if you can the despair filling your hearts, for you must bear your burdens patiently, though the wolf come to your doors. It is not for you the American Congress will first legislate. Your interests are suspended and subordinated to those which concern the darling ward of the Government – the negro; to him the first labors of this body are dedicated. He must be given "civil rights."[154]

Brown launched into one of his patented tributes to the rebel cause. Republicans had expected some such obnoxious material. A black man, Joseph Rainey, and a white man, Connecticut's Henry Starkweather, rose together. Rainey passed a document to the reading clerk: a letter to the editor of the Louisville *Courier,* dated April 1861. If President Lincoln called for troops from the State of Kentucky, wrote John Young Brown, no Kentuckian must respond. Volunteers ought to be shot down dead. Let such sentiments, Rainey declared, inform the House of the spirit that animated the gentleman.

Brown waited for his revenge. He took it on April 23. He lashed out at Starkweather, Rainey being beneath his notice. Here he displayed one of his more unsettling qualities: a penchant for personal abuse. He drew on Shakespeare and Dickens. "I do not know which excels most in him [Starkweather]," he announced, "the insolence of the Dogberry or the canting morality of the

154 Remarks of John Y. Brown, *Cong. Record,* 43rd Congress, 1st Session: 1864–1867.

Pecksniff."[155] Brown's words ought to have been subject to a point of order. They violated the House's honored rule of decorum, which forbade casting personal insult to members upon the floor. Starkweather remained silent. The injurious words passed without rebuke. Now Young Brown went too far. All honor to an American hero, John C. Breckinridge! Republicans rose in an uproar. Cries rang out. Parker of Missouri, Rice of Illinois, Garfield of Ohio: point of order. Burrows of Michigan jumped up: "I do not propose to sit here and listen to such eulogies pronounced upon such men." Crooke of New York: "If everybody but myself should say go on, I would not sit here to listen to this disgusting thing." Speaker Blaine ruled the objections out of order. The gentleman had a right to praise whomever he chose. Brown disdained to continue. Let them muzzle him, as they muzzled the voices of patriots. The incident seemed over. But it was remembered. When the final civil rights debate began, Republicans lay in wait for John Young Brown.

On June 4 the House's other Butler, Roderick R. Butler, rose. From Tennessee's 1st District, the state's far east, he had held his seat for four terms. He was a Republican. But he could not support his party's civil rights measure. Let no one think, however, that he wished ill to black people. He opposed the bill for humane reasons. He asked the party simply to refrain from the disastrous pursuit of an unattainable goal.

> I certainly can have no prejudice or feeling against the colored race. I would not do one act knowingly that would injure them in the least particular. I was born and reared in their midst and have been identified with the institution of slavery, and I arrogate to myself that I know as much about the colored race as any living man. I was his friend and advocate in the war for the suppression of the rebellion. I voted to make him a free man, advocated and sustained all the amendments to the State and Federal constitutions for his advancement and protection.[156]

The task of war had been to secure freedom. The task of peace was to elevate the freed people. Elevation of one race must not entail humiliation of the other.

> Let us forget the past. It has no pleasant memories to either side. Lost friends, ruined fortunes, and blasted hopes, emaciated forms ... all tell of a fruitless effort to perpetuate human slavery in an age when the civilized world revolted at the idea. O let us forget the past ... let us not pass laws to divide and distract our people; let the colored people live in the land

155 *Cong. Record*, 43rd Congress, 1st Session: 3311.

156 Speech of Roderick R. Butler: *Cong. Record*, 43rd Congress, 1st Session: 4592–4594.

> of their fathers; let them enjoy their rights as citizens; but let us also remember we have the two races; that we must legislate for both, that our legislation must be with a view to harmony, peace, fraternal feeling, and good will to all.

On that same day the House heard the magnificent rhetoric of Maryland's Ephraim Wilson. The slight, clean-shaven Democrat, more eloquently than any speaker, pronounced an encomium of prejudice. Prejudice, not justice, propelled the course of history. Prejudice, not reason, provided the lever and fulcrum that moved the world. Prejudice had motivated the grandest moments of human achievement. It served as the means God himself employed to bring salvation to humanity.

> Sir, if anything I have ever heard in this Capitol has astonished me, it has been to hear wise men assume as a postulate that the deep, hoary, pervading prejudices of nine millions of people are not an element to be taken into consideration.... Human prejudice has been one of the mightiest levers that has moved the world. How many millions of voters in this land take their sides from cool reason, and how many, think you, from the results of prejudice acquired in early life or from locality of birth? How many millions of religionists in this land and other lands have adopted their creeds from conviction, and how many from the prejudices instilled in childhood days? It rankled in the hearts and gave expression to the tongues of those who cried out "Crucify him, crucify him!" and thus became the ministering spirit that crowned the tragedy out of which arose the salvation of man.... It has arrayed one-half of the world against the other, walling in millions as could no walls of stone from all contact with their fellow-men.... It now lives in all its energy, and will ever flourish as long as human nature remains unchanged.[157]

No people preserved a prouder prejudice than the Southern people. Their warm, gifted nature had absorbed its cultural conditioning for two centuries. What mad doctor dared to purge it with the physic of a sickening law? Sanctimonious northerners shared those prejudices. Let them live as men lived in the South, surrounded by Negroes. They would feel differently. "Sir, southern parents see the repulsive companionship into which you seek to thrust their children.... Pray do not mock us, gentleman. As well might the physician deny that his emetic will tend to produce nausea.... You seek to force to the lips of others a cup you would be the first to put from you."

157 Speech of Ephraim Wilson: *Cong. Record*, 43rd Congress, 1st Session: Appendix, 417–421.

On June 9 the last but one of the African-American representatives placed his statement on the record. James Rapier put before the House an enigma, "the anomalous, and I may add the supremely ridiculous" position in which he stood. "Just think that the law recognizes my right upon this floor as a lawmaker, but that there is no law to secure to me any accommodations whatever while traveling here to discharge my duties.... Here I am the peer of the proudest, but on a steamboat or a car I am not equal to the most degraded." He looked to the visitors' gallery.[158]

> I feel ashamed for my country, if there be any foreigners present, who have been lured to our shores by the popular but untruthful declaration that this land is the asylum of the oppressed.... Here a foreigner can learn what he cannot learn in any other country, that it is possible for a man to be half free and half slave.... Here he will see a man legislating for a free people, while his own chains of civil slavery hang about him.... I affirm without the fear of contradiction, that any white ex-convict (I care not what may have been his crime nor whether the hair on the shaven side of his head has had time to grow out or not) may start with me to-day to Montgomery, that all the way down he will be treated as a gentleman, while I will be treated as the convict ... forced into a dirty, rough box with the drunkards, apple-sellers, railroad hands, and next to any dead that may be in transit, regardless of how far decomposition may have progressed.... Tender, pure, intelligent young ladies are forced to travel in this way if they are guilty of the crime of color, the only unpardonable sin known in our Christian and Bible lands. Sir, did you ever reflect that this is the only Christian country where poor, finite man is held responsible for the crimes of the infinite God, whom you profess to worship? But it is; I am held to answer for the crime of color, when I was not consulted in the matter. Had I been consulted ... I think I should have objected to being born in this gospel land.

Rapier arraigned the words of Wilson and Stephens. Alexander Stephens had returned to the nation's councils with all the wisdom accumulated by Rip Van Winkle while he slept: "I sympathize with him in his inability to understand this great change. When he left here the negro was a chattel, exposed for sale in the market places within a stone's throw of the Capitol; so near that the shadow of the Goddess of Liberty reflected by the rising sun would fall within the slave-pen." As for Wilson's paean to prejudice, it was a peculiar prejudice.

158 Speech of James Rapier: *Cong. Record*, 43rd Congress, 1st Session: 4782–4786.

White men felt revulsion in the presence of black men instinctually. Why did they take pleasure, instinctively, in the presence of black women?

> Now, sir, no one respects reasonable and intelligent prejudices more than I. I respect religious prejudices, for example; these I can comprehend. But how can I have respect for the prejudices that prompt a man to turn up his nose at the males of a certain race, while at the same time he has a fondness for the females of the same race to the extent of cohabitation? Out of four poor unfortunate colored women who from poverty were forced to go to the lying-in branch of the Freedman's Hospital here in the District last year three gave birth to children whose fathers were white men, and I venture to say that if they were members of this body, would vote against the civil-rights bill. Do you, can you wonder at my want of respect for this kind of prejudice?

Finally, Rapier observed, he had traveled abroad. He found freedom on foreign shores.

> In order that I might know something of the feelings of a freeman, a privilege denied me in the land of my birth, I left home last year and traveled six months in foreign lands, and the moment I put my foot upon the deck of a ship that unfurled a foreign flag from its mast-head, distinctions on account of my color ceased.... It was in other countries than my own that I was not a stranger.[159]

Speeches continued in a desultory fashion. Meanwhile the mountain of bills gathering on the Speaker's table assumed alarming proportions. Nothing could move without a two-thirds vote, least of all the mournfully marooned Civil Rights Bill. Iowa's John Kasson made an innocent suggestion. When they finally did come to consider that mass of legislation, members should be allowed five minutes to speak on any measure they opposed. Speaker Blaine replied. They would have to sit for three solid weeks to get through it in that fashion.[160]

159 Rapier's European sojourn took him to the capitals of western civilization. In Vienna he stopped at the Archduke Karl Hotel. He dined in elegant restaurants, sampled the cafés and strolled on the boulevards unmolested. Then he came home. Schweninger, *James T. Rapier and Reconstruction*, 117–118. Mark Twain noted the same incongruity. He described his tour guide in Venice, a black American expatriate, cultured and respected: "Negroes are deemed as good as white people in Venice, and so this man feels no desire to go back to his native land. His judgment is correct." (*The Innocents Abroad*, Chapter 23).

160 *Cong. Record*, 43rd Congress, 1st Session: 5203.

They did not have three weeks. Congress' first session would end on June 22. It would not reconvene until December. They must find some expedient to break the logjam, and some maneuver to deal with the Civil Rights Bill.

On June 11, eleven days from the end, Henry Dawes had an idea. They might consider those measures, but only those measures, upon which they could agree with unanimous consent. Some portion of the backlog could be removed. The House commenced to wade through the stack of bills – S.272, for the relief of Bishop & Co., bankers, of Honolulu, Hawaiian Islands (referred to the Committee on Claims); S.529, promotion of Major Absalom Baird to the rank of lieutenant-colonel (passed); S.793, to change the name of the schooner *Jenny Speer* to *Santa Rosa* (passed); S.218, to authorize a settlement with the Pottawatomie Indians (returned to the Speaker's table); S.1, supplementary to an act entitled "An act to protect all citizens of the United States in their civil rights." James Garfield rose. "I hope gentlemen will not object to that bill being considered as read three times and passed." Randall objected. "The gentleman is very anxious about it," said Eldredge. "He will have to wait a little."[161]

On the 16th Dawes had another idea. Let the House take up bills from the Speaker's table without suspension of the rules. Pass them or refer them by majority vote. There would be one exception. Leave the Civil Rights Bill aside. Now Garfield objected. Julius Burrows joined him. Garfield demanded a vote then and there. No one was prepared for that. The proceeding with exception was not ordered.[162]

James Garfield still showed fight. Others conceded defeat. Ben Butler was among them. On the 18th he asked the House again, by unanimous consent, to refer the Senate bill to his Judiciary Committee. Eldredge objected. S.1 stayed on the Speaker's table.[163]

Finally, on June 19, three days from adjournment, Henry Starkweather proposed the only way remaining. "We have tried, and could not go to the Speaker's table, making any exception, to dispose of bills by a majority vote. I now move that we go to the Speaker's table unconditionally, and that a two-thirds vote be required to pass any bill."[164] The decisive moment had arrived, not an abstract motion to suspend the rules but a straight-out test of strength on the Senate bill. Members must take a stand. Two-thirds of those present were wanted to fulfill the promise of civil rights.

The test came on the night of Saturday, June 20. At 8 p.m., after a long, arduous day, with a daunting pile of bills yet to be disposed of, the House convened

161 *Cong. Record*, 43rd Congress, 1st Session: 4873.
162 *Cong. Record*, 43rd Congress, 1st Session: 5045.
163 *Cong. Record*, 43rd Congress, 1st Session: 5162–5163.
164 *Cong. Record*, 43rd Congress, 1st Session: 5201–5203.

for an evening session. James Blaine sat in the chair. The litany of legislation began. Fourteen bills came and went. It was again the turn of S.218, settlement with the Pottawatomie Indians, this time referred to the Committee on Indian Affairs. S.1 rested atop the pile. Its chances were slight. Democrats worried nonetheless. Eldredge moved that the House adjourn. The majority declined. Luke Poland called for the vote. The final voice spoke. Civil rights died in the first session of the 43rd Congress.[165]

The bill failed by a comfortable margin: yeas 139, nays 91. No Democrat voted aye. The record now was clear on the Republican side. Fourteen members refused to accept the party's measure. Two of the earlier dissenters, Smith of North Carolina and Lofland of Delaware, were absent. Houghton of California, who had voted in favor of suspension of the rules on May 25 and against it on June 8, oscillated again. He voted for the bill. But opponents maintained their ranks by the addition of three new Republicans: William Crutchfield of Tennessee; Ira Hyde of Missouri; Charles St. John of New York. Crutchfield and Hyde had voted aye previously on both occasions. St. John, representing a precarious Republican district in Orange County, had voted aye on May 25; he was recorded as absent on June 8.

Why had the Civil Rights Bill failed? Some damned the crew of recalcitrant Republicans. Others set it down to the mysteriously menacing attitude of President Grant. Some charged Butler with incompetence. Democrats insisted the result was precisely as Republicans had intended, their only purpose having been to offer a sop to black voters. Historians have agreed with the Democrats. Retreat from Reconstruction was underway. The Republicans' treatment of the Civil Rights Bill confirmed their withdrawal, their cowardice, their duplicity. It foreshadowed their surrender.

None of this is correct. The Civil Rights Bill failed not through the action of its enemies. It failed not through the inaction of false friends. Its troubles marked not a retreat from Reconstruction but an obstinate refusal to retreat. Its failure came through the act of its true friends. They let it fail because they wanted it to succeed.

If any one man put a face to that inspirational failure, that man was Illinois' Jasper Delos Ward. He and his unyielding companions, John Cessna, Jeremiah Wilson and William Frye, wanted more than a civil rights bill. They held out for *the* civil rights bill, the bill designed by Charles Sumner, including above all its mixed-schools provision. They feared – and their fears in the end proved justified – that public opinion in its relentless barrage would sway the House to strike out that feature. To save the bill they had to stop the bill. Ward's motion in the Judiciary Committee blocked the amendable House bill from reaching

165 *Cong. Record*, 43rd Congress, 1st Session: 5329.

the floor. It forced the continuation of two-thirds votes. It ended all chance of passage in the first session. There was more than a little irony in this. Four white members demanded what their black colleagues were willing to forego. Richard Cain urged Butler to disengage from mixed schools. Jasper Ward refused to let him.

For the moment, it was finished: S.1 glued to the Speaker's table, H.R.796 frozen in the Judiciary Committee. To Democrats it seemed the bill had received its death blow on the night of June 20. Republicans surely would not renew a struggle that had caused such distress, discord and embarrassment. Eldredge permitted himself to pronounce the obituary: "It is buried any way; it has been buried half a dozen times beyond the power of resurrection. It is the deadest corpse you ever saw; and you are all glad of it."[166]

Eldredge was mistaken. The Civil Rights Bill was not a corpse. It refused to stay buried. The resurrectionists were men of Eldredge's own party. Dead the Civil Rights Bill served Democrats no purpose. Alive it was their fondest friend and helpmate. Elections were coming on. Democrats lit up the Civil Rights Bill. It became the bogeyman to awaken midnight terrors in the white masses. All through the summer of 1874, as the nation prepared for mid-term elections, civil rights played upon the public mind. The people's representatives had spoken. Now the people they represented would speak. The civil rights issue – on this observers agreed – could only hurt Republicans. How deep the hurt remained to be seen.

Congressmen dispersed to the bosoms of their districts. Sunset Cox's moths zippered up their cocoons, hoping the whirlwind of elections would not shake them out. Thomas Nast watched the final gavel fall. He drew a dismal picture of the end. His sketch appeared in *Harper's* July 4 edition: its scene the House chamber, deserted, desolate; in the foreground Lady Liberty weeping over the Speaker's vacant chair and fallen fasces; congressmen in top hats departing through the exits; in the gallery a dispirited observer, head bowed, a laborer with hammer and square cap and a farmer angrily shaking his broad slouch hat; on the Speaker's table a pile of forsaken bills, each labeled with unfinished business; atop the pile prominently "The Civil Rights Bill (Tabled) Afraid to Pass It or Kill It."[167] (see Illustration 5)

The exodus of legislators began. "Trains heavily filled," reported the Baltimore *Sun*, "the city will settle down to its summer dullness."[168] For Republicans nothing would be dull. Civil rights had been referred to the voters. Their verdict would determine the fate of many political careers.

166 *Cong. Record*, 43rd Congress, 1st Session: 5329.
167 *Harper's Weekly*, July 4, 1874, pp. 560–561.
168 Baltimore *Sun*, June 25, 1874.

ILLUSTRATION 5 Adjournment of the 43rd Congress, First Session
SOURCE: THOS. NAST, *HARPER'S WEEKLY*, JULY 4, 1874

CHAPTER 6

Horace Redfield's Journey: The Long Hot Summer of 1874

Horace V. Redfield – HVR, as he signed his newspaper dispatches – was an uncommon journalist. His widowed mother left New York and settled in Tennessee soon after Horace's birth in 1845. He spent his youth surrounded by the culture of the South. Until his last years, when he became a Washington correspondent, Redfield remained rooted at Chattanooga, making his residence in nearby Jasper. He found his vocation in the employ of the Cincinnati *Commercial* under its editor, Murat Halstead. Halstead assigned him a unique journalistic beat. It covered the South. Traveling across the southern states he described in his columns the life and the troubles of the people. In the summer of 1874 the trouble that most concerned those people was the looming of the Civil Rights Bill. To Horace Redfield, the inquiring reporter, they confided their fears.

Redfield's reports reflected his experience. He abjured prejudice. He regretted the oppression of black people. But he understood the whites. Shortly before his death in 1881, at the age of thirty-six, he published his magnum opus, a study of violence comparing the South against the North. He titled it *Homicide, North and South.*[1] He based his analysis on a compilation of criminal records, supplemented by his years of travel and observation. There existed, he said, in the South a spirit of violence, an acceptance of lawlessness not found elsewhere. It was not, as others had proposed, a byproduct of the old slave system.[2] It was a phenomenon of the culture. The rule of law had never properly flourished. Personal retaliation took its place. What southern orators called "the temper of a spirited race,"[3] Redfield regarded as a demoralizing effect bred

1 Horace Redfield, *Homicide, North and South, Being a Comparative View of Crime Against the Person in Several Parts of the United States* (Columbus: 2000), introduction by Douglas Eckberg, xii–xvi.

2 See Bertram Wyatt-Brown, *Southern Honor: Ethics and Behavior in the Old South* (New York: 1982), 152–153, 366–371.

3 "Veracity and honor in man, chastity and fidelity in women, intelligence, culture, chivalry," such was the code in the words of Gen. Bradley T. Johnson. See Howard Dorgan, "Rhetoric of the United Confederate Veterans: A Lost Cause Mythology in the Making," in Waldo W. Braden, ed., *Oratory in the New South* (Baton Rouge: 1979), 153. "Strictly," Henry Adams

into each generation. He lamented the excesses of the southern temper. But he understood them.

However one may evaluate Horace Redfield's sociological insights, his views colored his coverage of the Civil Rights Bill's advent. It was an insult. It was a firebrand. It could only have been thrown into southern society, into the midst of the "spirited race," by men acutely insensitive to every feature of that spiritedness. Its authors did not grasp the precarious temper of violence he tried desperately to describe in his columns and later in his book. In the summer of 1874 the civil rights debate went forth among the people. In the South the debate reached a bloody climax. Redfield's columns, reprinted in many papers, brought that climax home.

HVR's odyssey began with a frantic dispatch dated from his home base, Chattanooga, on June 1, 1874. The Senate had barely passed its measure. No one knew whether it would get through the House. Already signs of reaction had appeared.

> The Senate has never passed a measure causing as much anxiety, alarm and excitement in this section as the Civil Rights Bill. It is the all-absorbing topic in all circles ... followed, as it certainly will [be], by a train of dire calamities. The bare discussion of the miserable subject, and the excitement raised in consequence, has awakened a feeling of hatred and ill-will between the races that will require years to cool down, even should the bill fail to become a law.[4]

The Republican Party in Tennessee, he reported, was shaken to its core. It held presently seven of ten congressional seats. It would be lucky to hold three after the voters next had spoken. (In fact it held only one.) The mixed school question, of course, excited the most violent passions. "As for the education of the races together in this latitude, it is not worth while to talk about it. Four hundred Congresses sitting in continuous session four hundred years, and doing nothing but pass civil rights bills, can not bring the people to it." Why could not northern politicians understand the outrage they created among the southern people? The spirited race would unleash its spirit.

> The Civil Rights Bill they regard as the crowning infamy – the greatest effort yet put forth to degrade and humiliate them ... not for the good of

---

concluded, "the Southerner had no mind; he had temperament." *The Education of Henry Adams* (New York: 1931), 57.

4 Cincinnati *Commercial*, June 4, 1874.

> the negro but that Southern whites may be humiliated to the last degree and their proud spirits crushed and broken. You may laugh at this, but it is a serious matter.... I don't believe the Republican Senators realize how badly they have complicated matters here.[5]

"It makes my heart sad," he sighed on June 20. Victims had begun to fall.

> The exasperated whites, not being able to reach the men who passed the law, take their vengeance out on the miserable creatures that the law is supposed (Oh, how erroneously!) to benefit.... I am convinced, should the bill become a law, a dire train of calamities will follow. I would not for an instant apologize for the foolish prejudice against the negro, but I know that the prejudice exists, that it is bone of the bone and flesh of the flesh, and to attempt to ignore it is as foolish as the prejudice itself.[6]

In July Redfield rested. In August he journeyed to North Carolina. Elections were in full swing. On every stump he heard the same questions: "Whar does yer stand on Civil Rights!" "How is yer on Civil Rights!" "Are yer agin Civil Rights?" "How 'bout mixed schools?" Such interrogations "make the average North Carolina white Republican orator squirm like a skinned eel." He questioned Senator Augustus Merrimon. His party would reap a harvest of votes. Whether the Republicans passed the Civil Rights Bill mattered little. They had proposed it. That alone would destroy them: "If we can keep it off until the new Congress meets we are safe, for the November election is going to knock down the Republican majority, if not entirely annihilate it."[7] To Redfield we owe the ominous campaign announcement of Poovy Ramsoure, aspiring coroner of Iredell County. Redfield's quick eye plucked that item from the pages of the Statesville *Landmark*.

> Sadly I say it, but it is true. If the Civil Rights Bill becomes a law in its present shape the duties of Coroners in Southern States will increase fourfold.... Poor blacks will fall one by one like the leaves of the forest.... My heart goes out in sympathy for the unfortunate negroes. I have the same feeling for them that I would for a lot of little children in a pen with a herd

5 Cincinnati *Commercial*, June 16, 1874.
6 Cincinnati Commercial, June 20, 1874.
7 Cincinnati *Commercial*, August 4, 1874.

> of mad bulls, and the "friends" of the children upon the outside throwing red rags and sharp spikes over the inclosure.[8]

Redfield moved on to Virginia. He interviewed Governor Kemper:

> If that [civil rights bill] becomes a law I shall immediately call the Legislature together, and we will wipe out every free school in the State from the mountains to the sea. Not one shall be left for either color. We prefer that our children should grow up in the blackness of ignorance; yea, we prefer death itself rather than submit to this degradation. There will never be mixed schools in Virginia, never, never![9]

By the middle of August Redfield was in despair. He headed his column "Notes of a Southern Tour – A Doomed Race." He predicted nothing less than the extinction of black people. They could not compete on terms of equality with white men. Yet this precisely the Civil Rights Bill compelled them to do, even as it generated the enmity of their white competitors. He confessed shame for his own race. Its brutal conduct knew no excuse. But no other result was possible. Untold numbers of black people already had been exterminated. Survivors flocked to the cities. They perished "in want, degradation, and wretchedness." Such was the misguided consequence of the Senate's humanitarian impulse. "Especially are New England Congressmen ignorant on this subject, or they would not insist upon forcing the unfortunate blacks into the jaws of death by the enactment of the civil rights bill.... Either the law will be a dead letter or the negroes will be dead negroes."[10]

Newspaper readers across the country read Redfield's reflections. Civil rights would trigger a holocaust. Negroes would die. Virginia's Rev. Dabney looked on the bright side. "Christian men," he suggested, "find a grain of private consolation in the *hope* [italics original] that a race of human beings among us are advancing to the miseries of extermination. I do not find fault with the hope; it is natural."[11] Another reader wrote to Redfield's *Commercial*. He identified himself only as a Tennessean:

> The old slave owner has no fear of the negro ... neither hates nor fears the negro, [but] we have a large class in our country who appear to have

8 Cincinnati *Commercial*, August 5, 1874.

9 Cincinnati *Commercial*, August 7, 1874.

10 Cincinnati *Commercial*, August 17, 1874.

11 Robert Dabney, *Discussions by Robert L. Dabney, D.D., LL.D* (Mexico, Mo., 1897), vol. 4, 182.

> a natural antipathy for them. Your readers will remember during the late war one-half the Southern army was composed of men who never owned a slave. Yet this war was waged for the perpetuation of slavery.... We have today the same population. They have no negroes hired; they have but little to do with them, and hate and fear them alike.... If the Civil Rights Bill passes, thousands upon thousands of good men will submit to its provisions, but the reckless (and there are many) and desperate will not, and the poor negro, who was born a slave, freed without any effort on his part, ignorant and poor, will be the greatest sufferer. Is it humanity to pass it?[12]

Charles Nordhoff, the New York *Herald's* roving correspondent, recognized the potential of this toxic mix. Poor whites "are ignorant, easily prejudiced, and they have, since the war, lived in a dread of having social equality with the negro imposed upon them. This fear has ... found expression in brutal acts to which, I believe, in the majority of cases, they were instigated by bad men of a class above them."[13] "Spirited people" primed by prejudice: incidents arose irrepressibly, occasioned merely by the innocent insolence of emancipation.[14] Add the intentional impudence of equality, the cup overflowed. David Ross Locke, the nation's satirist, parodied the southerners' chagrin:

> Now, bein the nigger hez rights, he is our ekal.... They hev become sassy and impudent, and say, "Go to; are we not men?" I bade one git off the sidewalk, and he bade me be damned.... I chastised wun who gave me lip; and he sood me, a Caucashun, for assault and battery, and got a judgment. We killed Linkin in vain.[15]

Cruel mimicry, but prophetic. Equality roused resentment; resentment provoked violence; violence fed fear. A Great Fear haunted the white southern masses: genocidal plots, conspiracies, phantom armies lurking in the darkness. Massacres commenced. Victims were black. Killers were white: terrorists propelled by their own terror.

---

12 Cincinnati *Commercial*, letter to the editor, September 1, 1874.

13 Charles Nordhoff, *The Cotton States in the Spring and Summer of 1875* (New York: 1876), 17–18.

14 On the problem of "Negro insolence," and resulting episodes, see Jane Dailey, "Deference and Violence in the Postbellum Urban South: Manners and Massacres in Danville, Virginia," *Journal of Southern History*, 63 (1997), especially her discussion on 559–563.

15 David Ross Locke, *The Struggles (Social, Financial, and Political) of Petroleum V. Nasby* (Boston: 1873), 273, letter 103, "A Wail of Anguish. – The Passage of the Civil Rights Bill over the Veto."

Southern violence, to be sure, seemed to peak on schedule, coinciding with each election season.[16] The worst slaughter of all, at Colfax, Louisiana – 100 black men shot down or burned to death – came in the off-year of 1873.[17] But the election season of 1874 brought with it a new feature. Civil rights fear fed panic. Even as Redfield's Cassandra-like columns filled the newspaper pages, reports began to trickle out.

The storm built slowly. Civil rights and southern unrest did not at once coalesce to dominate the summer news. Foreign affairs were quiet, apart from insurrection in Cuba and civil war in Spain. Through July the lurid Beecher-Tilton trial provided titillation: adultery in the highest pulpit, hypocrisy among the clerical elite. Music lovers continued to regret the loss of the diva Parepa-Rosa. Crime watchers enjoyed chronicles of Jesse Pomeroy, child murderer of children. On July 1 the abduction of little Charlie Ross hit the press. Snatched by mysterious men into a black carriage in front of his Philadelphia home, Charlie's body was never recovered. Sightings continued.[18]

More apocalyptic terror could be found in Coggia's Comet. Mark Twain proposed hitching up the celestial visitor for a trip across the solar system. He offered selected politicians, Ben Butler for one, complimentary tickets to outer space. He invited missionaries aboard, "to shed the true light upon all the celestial orbs which, physically aglow, are yet morally in darkness."[19] Scientists speculated on cataclysmic consequences as the comet neared its closest approach on July 22. In New York City reporters pestered Mayor William Havemeyer about the city's comet-related catastrophe preparedness. "Do you think it would strike us?" the exasperated mayor shot back. "I wish it would. I think it is high time it did."[20] Pennsylvanians read alarming reports. A phosphorescent rain of iron particles would fall, attracted to the state's magnetite-bearing

16 See George C. Rable, *But There Was No Peace: The Role of Violence in the Politics of Reconstruction* (Athens, Ga., 1984), 71–72.

17 Political contentions set off the massacre. But even here a pervading fear contributed to the tragedy, as one white defendant recalled: "threats of the Negroes to kill every man, woman and child in the parish." Charles Lane, *The Day Freedom Died: The Colfax Massacre, the Supreme Court, and the Betrayal of Reconstruction* (New York: 2008), 154.

18 Scarifying editorials appeared. "There are villainous influences awaiting around every doorstep.... Let parents be on the watch. Keep the children more around the home fireside and less in the alleys, the by-ways, and streets, where scoundrels can get hold of them." Xenia, Ohio, *Torchlight*, December 2, 1874.

19 New York *Herald*, July 6, 1874.

20 New York *Sun*, quoted in Raleigh *Crescent*, July 10, 1874.

mountains, "hurled at the swoop of the comet's tail upon Pittsburgh, Erie and Weehawken."[21]

Pittsburgh escaped. The South did not. The drumbeat of reports built gradually, pushing comets and adulterers from the headlines. By August press coverage was heavy. "Certainly the South as viewed through the medium of the newspapers is not a very inviting section of the country just now," a worried Blanche Butler wrote her husband in Mississippi.[22] Both parties understood the stakes. The impression southern violence made upon the voting public, violence linked to the issue of civil rights, might turn the elections to one side or the other. On the elections turned the fate of the Civil Rights Bill.

The Great Fear crept up almost imperceptibly. Perhaps its first shadow appeared in Georgia. White residents of Columbia County noticed a disturbing trend. Negroes had commenced to appear together. Whispers spread. The blacks intended to massacre all the whites in Columbia County, a war of races. Ringleaders were identified: three brothers, Sake, Delaney and Elliott Doggett, and their father Fountain Doggett. Delaney had threatened a white planter: "The Ku-Klux had killed the negroes in 1870 and they were going to have blood for blood." Deputy Sheriff Wright and his posse set out. They seized the culprits and marched them toward Appling Court House. They failed to reach that destination. Coming upon an isolated spot, for reasons unexplained, the deputy halted the march. For reasons unexplained he loosed the prisoners' bonds. Delaney Doggett chose that moment to grow insolent. He was shot. The others took to their heels. The posse shot them too, trying to escape.[23]

Fear struck next in Tennessee. Sinister events, "civil rights deviltry," multiplied in Carroll County. They drove local people into a panic. First a black man stepped casually up to the house of Dr. Newsome at McLemoresville. He helped himself to a dipper of water from the well. He remarked that the weather was warm. Near Clarksburg black men attempted to enter a white person's house. They asked for food. They were chased into the woods but escaped. This left the whole community in a state of "intense excitement." Next a black man approached a white girl. He declared his desire to kidnap her. He was hanged. At Huntingdon another scoundrel broke into the home of a sleeping white family.

---

21 Altoona *Morning Tribune*, August 8, 1874. Citizens of Dayton, Ohio, were reassured. Astral catastrophe "would in no way affect the price of goods at the shop of Mr. B.N. Davis, No. 29 South Jefferson Street. Mr. Davis always keeps in stock a great variety of boots, shoes, gaiters, &c., for men, boys, ladies, and misses wear." Dayton *Journal*, July 11, 1874.

22 Blanche Butler Ames, *Chronicles from the Nineteenth Century: Family Letters of Blanche Butler and Adelbert Ames* (Clinton, Mass., 1957), vol. 2, 12–13.

23 Louisville *Courier-Journal*, July 15, 1874.

He fled and could not be found.[24] "A reign of terror," the Huntingdon *People's Paper* announced. Behind the devilish doings lurked civil rights, "schemes of social equality." The *People's Paper* warned. Terror would be met with terror, "if need be, by the extermination of the negro."[25]

Tension mounted in Hart County, Kentucky. Black persons had been seen. Whites organized to patrol the woods and fields.[26] Then a sinister discovery made reports across the country. They were mute but eloquent: three black corpses lashed together on a raft, drifting on the Mississippi. Pinned to one was found a note: "They have a ticket for New Orleans, please let them pass."[27]

On August 12 the battle of Austin blazed across the headlines. Fear had been rising at the northern Mississippi town since June. Then a white man, Dr. Guy V. Smith, found himself disturbed by the presence of a Negro. He aimed his pistol and fired. The bullet missed its mark and killed a little black girl standing nearby.[28] With that, war commenced. Black armies appeared, as if from nowhere. White men prepared defenses. Frantic news reports. Black forces were on the rampage, "murdering women and children on the surrounding plantations." White militiamen commanded by ex-Confederate Gen. James Chalmers arrived on the scene. Chalmers, coming down-river, landed his forces below the town, marching to cut off the enemy hordes.[29] Chalmers' men entered Austin. They found no enemy. They found no war. Then a new alarm: a hundred blacks, having eluded Chalmers, descended upon Byhalia, Mississippi. White Rangers under Colonel Manning rushed to meet the threat.[30] A sheriff's posse arrived first at the site of the rebellion on Ball's Farm. No one was there.[31]

Such sundry alarms – phantom wars, shadowy plots, abortive massacres, floating corpses – set the tone. As yet they failed to generate a sense of shock. The public required a human face on which to focus. It found it in the murder of Julia Hayden. The facts indeed told a sickening story.[32] She was eighteen.[33] If her portrait is to be believed, she was beautiful. (see Illustration 6) The scene was Trousdale County, Tennessee, the stage a rough cabin occupied by a black

24 Nashville *Banner*, July 22, 1874.
25 Nashville *Banner*, August 1, 1874.
26 Louisville *Courier-Journal*, August 26, 1874.
27 Nashville *Banner*, August 29; New York *Herald*, September 1; Washington *New National Era*, September 10, 1874.
28 Washington *New National Era*, August 20, 1874.
29 Harrisburg *Patriot*, August 14, 1874.
30 Louisville *Courier-Journal*, August 14, 1874.
31 Mobile *Register*, August 19, 1874.
32 Nashville *Banner*, September 9–10, 13, 1874.
33 According to her father Henry Hayden she was only 16. Knoxville *Press and Herald*, September 4, 1874.

MISS JULIA HAYDEN, THE MURDERED SCHOOL-TEACHER.—[FROM A PHOTOGRAPH.]

ILLUSTRATION 6 Julia Hayden
SOURCE: *HARPER'S WEEKLY*, DECEMBER 5, 1874

man, Henry Lowe, and his family. Lowe, known to his friends as Uncle Hembry, ran the ferry a mile off at Hart's Crossing on the Cumberland River.

In the midnight hours of August 22 a banging roused the occupants of Uncle Hembry's cabin, seven people huddled in two bare rooms connected vertically by a ladder. Julia had come a month before from her home at Spring Hill to open a school for black children. She slept in the upper room with Hembry and his wife, Easter. Pale light came in through a window. Darkness below; all was boarded against the night.

The old man called through the bolted door. Voices replied: "We want the girl that's in there." Julia and Easter Lowe crouched on the downstairs bed. Hembry rushed to the upper window. He saw two men. They wore long coats. One had a white hat. From their inflection he identified them as white men. One turned, cocked a pistol and fired. A single shot pierced the cabin. Julia's head fell on Easter's shoulder. Someone lit a match. Light reflected on sightless eyes. She was dead.

Headlines spread across the nation. Local authorities realized they had to act. Tennessee Governor John C. Brown offered $500 reward for information. With that incentive came the arrest of two white men, Bowen Saunders and Pat Lyons. Their motive: to drive off the teacher of the black school. Saunders and Lyons pointed the finger at a black man, John Jackson, who lived two miles from the ferry. Alternatively they hinted the crime had been the work of outsiders. Masked men had been seen abroad. They had long coats, such as Uncle Hembry had described. Some wore white hats. They covered their faces. They swore they were bent on "getting niggers."

The prosecution countered with its witness, Andrew Seagraves. He appeared in the courthouse at the town of Lebanon under escort, guarded for his life. Bowen Saunders, he said, had confessed to the deed. On the morning after the murder Saunders showed him a pistol, a five-shooter with a five inch barrel. One of the chambers had recently been fired. Finally, said Seagraves, Saunders admitted the whole affair. He insisted only that the murder was an accident. He had not imagined his blind shot would strike home. The fact that it had killed Julia did not distress him overly much: "I asked him if he felt bad, and he said he minded it no more than killing a hog."

Julia Hayden became the poster child of southern violence. In San Francisco, the *Elevator* offered her engraved portrait for sale to its readers at 10 cents a copy, unlimited supply.[34] *Harper's Weekly* printed Julia's picture across its pages. It called to account not only the murderers but the politicians who hid behind them and incited their deeds.

> It is the followers of Toombs and [Jefferson] Davis who have brought upon us the shame of assassinations and midnight murders, who shoot down Republican voters in the open day, and murder young lady schoolteachers in the excess of their insanity. The aim of these Thugs of the South is the total extermination of the colored race.... Their Democratic

34 San Francisco *Elevator*, October 7, 1874.

> allies of the North encourage them (it may be hoped unconsciously) in their policy of blood.[35]

Papers everywhere expressed revulsion. When details remained elusive journalists supplied their own detail. Even the usually staid New York *Times* lapsed into lurid prose. According to Easter Lowe's testimony, Julia exited the world quietly. She expressed only a whispered reflection, "Lord, mamma," as she expired. The *Times* offered a more melodramatic recital: "The cruel bullet did its fatal work, red blood streaming out over the sheets.... A piercing death shriek from Julia followed the report of the gun."[36]

Southern violence, stoked by civil rights agitation, filled the front pages. Newsboys cried shrill headlines. Cries reached to the President himself. One came up from the black people of Lebanon, Tennessee:

> The Col people of the adjoining county are coming in to our Town for they cant Stay there for the night Riders are troubling them too great to Stay there at their homes – the person that was killed was a Leady we want to know What to do tell us what to do.... If you will not help us send us arms and Say that you will help us.[37]

Horace Redfield thought he had plumbed the depths of his despair. He found deeper depths to plumb.

> Is there a God of Justice in heaven? Is there a hell deep enough and black enough for the murderers of this poor girl? ... These murderers shall not go unpunished – these murderers, if not punished in this world, can not escape in the next. The mask and the darkness of night can not hide them there.... "Vengeance is mine, I will repay," saith the Lord. There is solid consolation in this.[38]

The Hayden murder was only the beginning. Just three days later the Gibson County massacre awoke the nation. Tennessee, once again, brewed the perfect storm. Civil rights horror hung over the events. "We will drive Sambo to the

35 *Harper's Weekly*, October 3, 1874, p. 813.

36 New York *Times*, September 7, 1874.

37 M.C. Manson et al. to Ulysses S. Grant, August 22, 1874. *Papers of Ulysses S. Grant*, vol. 25, 230.

38 Cincinnati *Commercial*, August 31, 1874.

wall," exulted the Memphis *Appeal*.[39] Never would white people permit the pollution of their sanctuary:

> The white people of the south have submitted to oppression, humiliation and shame ... but they have sworn in their hearts that they will never submit to mixed schools and social equality; to see their lovely children with pure Caucasian blood throbbing through their pure white veins, jumbled and intermixed with dirty, lousy pickaninnies ... to see their beautiful daughters sandwiched at the theater, in a public conveyance, or at the dinner-table between the stench of two musty Africans, whose hideous blackness only reflects the whiteness and beauty of the lovely object they would defile by unnatural and loathsome contact.[40]

Politicians exploited the theme with merciless insistency. General William Bate, advertising himself for the U.S. Senate seat of the retiring William Brownlow, called for a muster of the old Confederate host to destroy the greatest of Yankee iniquities, the Civil Rights Bill, "the fruit of the brain of Charles Sumner."[41] Bate's comrade General William Quarles hoped for a seat in the state senate: "Let the white people bury this civil rights question right now and here."[42] Governor John Calvin Brown, yet another ex-general of Confederate vintage, pushed the hottest button of all, the primal fear of miscegenation. "Let this legislation obtain and the next step will be to annex penalties against the refusal of a white woman to marry a negro because of his race and color."[43]

Ex-governor Neill S. Brown, brother of the incumbent, called for war: "If appeals of reason will not satisfy the friends of this measure – if nothing will do but a conflict of races, let it come."[44] Relentless demagoguery had its effect. Even the Democratic Chattanooga *Times* foresaw, as it were, unforeseeable consequences.[45] The Republican Knoxville *Chronicle* warned Democrats.

> Not since the close of the war have our Southern exchanges been so filled with reports of trouble between whites and blacks. It is but the legitimate outgrowth of the outrageous misrepresentations of the Civil Rights

39 Memphis *Appeal*, July 17, 1874.
40 Memphis *Appeal*, September 22, 1874.
41 Nashville *Banner*, July 26, 31, 1874.
42 Nashville *Union and American*, August 4, 6; Nashville *Banner*, August 6, 1874.
43 Nashville *Union and American*, July 28, 1874.
44 Nashville *Union and American*, July 26, 1874.
45 Chattanooga *Times*, August 2, 1874.

> Bill put forth by Democratic papers for the purpose of influencing the elections.[46]

Quite the contrary, Democrats replied. For consequences Negroes had themselves to blame. They first had used the rhetoric of excess. By this they referred to the great convention of black people that had met at Nashville in April. The Nashville Convention of Colored People had indeed been a signal event. The call went out on February 16:

> [We meet] to exact of the State of Tennessee expurgation of all laws and parts of the constitution of the State of every vestige of discrimination which they now contain, of proscription against us as a race, on account of color and race. We ask the first rights due to us as citizens of a common country – "civil rights" without freedom, such as we have, will prove a farce.[47]

The convention met on April 28.[48] Nashville's Abram Smith addressed the assembly: "We know and acknowledge that a partial recognition of our manhood is only a fact, that our freedom is a delusion and mockery.... No government can prosper that withholds equal rights from a portion of its citizens." W.F. Yardley of Knoxville spoke words that haunted white men's deepest fears: "Should a colored man be punished simply because he happens to marry a white woman ... or a colored woman a white man?" If the Civil Rights Bill did not bring that about, "he would spurn it from him." ("Everywhere," cried the Knoxville *Press and Herald,* "the eye is greeted with the glaring headline, 'A White Wife for Every Negro.'"[49]) "The colored people demand to ride in first-class cars, to stop at hotels, the Maxwell House, for instance," another speaker declared. "The time would come that he would take a white woman on his arm and go around Nashville with her." The convention composed its resolutions. It insisted on the Civil Rights Bill. It demanded mixed schools. It promised ruin to equivocating politicians.

> We consider the omission of the Republican party to enact this measure a base surrender of the rights of humanity to our insidious foe that has

---

46 Quoted in Knoxville *Press and Herald,* August 15, 1874.

47 Memphis *Appeal,* February 16, 1874.

48 Accounts in Nashville *Banner,* April 28–30; Nashville *Union and American,* April 29, 30; Knoxville *Press and Herald,* May 1, 2, 1874.

49 Knoxville *Press and Herald,* August 15, 1874.

> contested upon the avenues of civil life every right we enjoy, as they did every right of freedom on the field of battle. And we will use our utmost to stamp upon every demagogue who seeks to betray the privileges of our children the brand of the traitor Judas, as deserving politically a traitor's doom, with whom we will never, never, join hands nor support, but will regard as our public and private enemy.[50]

Next the convention took up the cause of David Galloway, a black man currently languishing in prison. Galloway had married "the wife of his choice," a white woman. "For his marriage in conformity with his privilege as an American citizen in the land of his birth, with his heart loyal to the flag of his country he [was] deprived of his liberty and divested of his manhood." Mixed marriages, mixed schools, mixed sex – Democrats could ask for no better propaganda than the convention handed them on its own.[51]

Worse followed. From the ranks of Republicans themselves an incendiary appeared, Senator William Brownlow, heedless of consequences, hurling explosives into the fire. He defined the Civil Rights Bill: "The Sum of All Villainies; The Quintessence of Abominations." His words went out to the country. "I have never seen among the masses of people anywhere in the South such violent manifestations of pride of race," the correspondent of the Memphis *Appeal* reported.

> Brownlow's letters have been reprinted everywhere and circulated as pamphlets, until every cottage in Eastern Tennessee, western North Carolina, Virginia, and northern Georgia has a copy. They have been

50 Nashville *Banner*, April 30; Nashville *Union and American*, April 30; Knoxville *Press and Herald*, May 2, 1874.

51 The Galloway affair, as even the *Union and American* admitted, was a case of true love. David, a.k.a. Daniel Galloway and Malvina Brandon, a.k.a. Malvina Vines, were convicted on October 20, 1872 for violating the law against "intermarriage of white persons with negroes." The court sentenced Galloway to two years and his illegal wife to one year in the state penitentiary. The couple had hoped to slip under the radar, passing off Malvina as a lightly-colored colored person. The black Rev. Armstead Shelby performed the marriage. He recalled that the room arranged for the ceremony was dimly lit: "I saw the woman was a yaller woman – but then she mout a bin a white woman.... You know there's some mighty white colored people in Nashville." Evidence established Malvina, despite a soupçon of yaller-ness, to be officially white. Eminent lawyers assisted Galloway. Among them was ex-senator and governor of Mississippi Henry S. Foote, who threatened to appeal his conviction to the United States Supreme Court. Ultimately David Galloway served 21 months. He was released, only to be caught again in the arms of his beloved Malvina; wherefore the couple returned to jail. Nashville *Union and American*, May 1, October 15, 1874.

> absolutely read from pulpits by itinerant preachers and made the subject of laudatory sermons. The Senator said to me that he was amazed by the degree of excitement begotten among the mountaineers and the most humble people of the State. They write to him till he can no longer listen.[52]

Brownlow began his crusade on February 10. He wrote to his hometown paper, the Knoxville *Chronicle*. Black people must not press for civil rights: "Be careful upon insisting upon that which can do no good." William B. Scott, black editor of the Maryville *Republican*, replied. The senator had betrayed the Negro voters who put him in office. Brownlow shot back. Let black people consider. Should the Civil Rights Bill become law it would be "a pretext for a general kukluxing of those of the colored race."[53] Scott returned fire: "According to the hypothesis advanced by the Senator, it is better to withhold justice and pander to prejudices of exceedingly ancient date, which the Republican party deny that they possess."[54]

Had it ended there, things might have settled down. But Brownlow exploded against his critics, who now included everyone at the Nashville Colored Convention. He was preeminently the Judas whose hand black people would "never, never clasp again." Brownlow spurned to clasp hands. Blacks, not whites, had betrayed their friends, they "who seem to have reversed Taney's decision and proclaimed in substance that a white man has no rights which a negro is bound to respect." He ended with words soon to be celebrated: Never would white people of Tennessee submit to "this sum of all villainies and quintessence of abominations."[55]

New champions entered the fight. Prof. P. Mason Bartlett, President of Maryville College, an outpost of integrated education in the South, damned "Parson" Brownlow. His outpourings proved he was "not worthy of the position" he occupied, spouting "nothing but humbug and the merest demagogueism, unchristian, unworthy of a man who once pretended to preach the Gospel."[56] Brownlow spared no part of Professor Bartlett.

> I do not believe that the personal freedom of all the white people of the South, and all their rights of self-government, should be sacrificed to accommodate a few thousand insolent negroes, or to gratify the caprices of

52 Memphis *Appeal*, June 11, 1874.
53 Chattanooga *Times*, April 15, 1874.
54 Nashville *Banner*, April 19, 1874.
55 Knoxville *Press and Herald*, May 14, 1874.
56 Knoxville *Press and Herald*, May 26, 1874.

> negro-worshipping white men and selfish politicians.... Yes! Mr. Bartlett, you can rally the miscegenation brigade and the white dodging politicians who agree with you that the poor white people have no rights, and I will meet you with the honest laborers and poor men whose rights are outraged and trampled upon by this abomination.[57]

Brownlow found himself exalted. The Associated Press relayed his words over its wires. Democrats all but made him an honorary member of their party. "The people of the South will heartily thank Senator Brownlow," declared the Knoxville *Press and Herald,* "for the noble appeals he is making for his race."[58] Neill Brown sent congratulations: "I regard this [civil rights] measure with horror. In fact it is the meanest proposition I ever saw. I would leave any party or act with any party to defeat it. I hope it is dead-dead-dead."[59]

The controversy attracted national attention. Retired Senator Truman Smith of Connecticut addressed himself to the "Parson" in an open letter in the New York *Tribune.*[60] Smith, a one-time Whig who had migrated to the Republicans, feared disaster. The Civil Rights Bill provoked reactionary forces. They would eviscerate the constitutional amendments and return the country to antebellum evils. Smith thanked Brownlow. Brownlow thanked Smith.[61] Events rushed to tragedy.

August 25, Gibson County, Tennessee, the familiar pattern played itself out: a formless fear; a sudden alarm; a reflexive reaction; a massacre. The correspondent of the Memphis *Appeal,* closest to the epicenter, telegraphed a staccato series of dispatches:

> Humboldt, Tenn. – The greatest excitement prevails here ... five hundred armed negroes are marching; they have already killed two white women.
>
> Great excitement ... women and children have moved to Humboldt for safety – Later developments expected hourly.
>
> Alarming reports of murder by negros reach here. Can't tell anything definite. Reported skirmishing at Gibson. There is no interruption of trains.

---

57 Knoxville *Press and Herald,* June 3; Memphis *Appeal,* June 4, 1874.

58 Knoxville *Press and Herald,* May 14, 1874.

59 Neill Brown to Brownlow, June 30, 1874. William Brownlow Papers, University of Tennessee. Black people longed to see Brownlow dead-dead-dead. "He deserves only contempt. God has already afflicted him in such a manner that he can scarcely talk or walk, and in a few weeks, or months at most we hope to be spared further insult from that quarter." Letter to the editor, Cincinnati *Commercial,* August 11, 1874.

60 New York *Tribune,* July 11, 1874.

61 New York *Tribune,* September 5, 1874.

> 6:30 PM. Negroes at Humboldt excited beyond all reason ... Six wagon loads of women and children from the neighborhood of Pickettsville came in to escape feared murder by negroes.
> 8:30 PM. Up to this hour no negroes have been discovered, but are thought to be near Trenton, and will, it is thought make attacks on that and surrounding towns to-night.[62]

At daybreak things became clearer. No white women had been slain. But sixteen black corpses (later information reduced the number to six) rested in the woods. Terror had begun on the night of Saturday, August 22, the very moment of the murder at Uncle Hembry's cabin. Two white men, James Warren and Morgan Monroe, staggered into the town of Gibson. Ambush, they gasped, Negroes, thirty or more, armed. Only a zigzag run to the cover of nearby woods had saved them. A posse set out. It found no black battalion. But it captured one black man, Ben Ballard by name, discovered walking in the night. His captors urged him to speak: "The prisoner, being led a short distance, was asked to make a full confession of the shooting that night, the reason of the organization among the negroes, its purposes and aims. This he did."[63]

With the posse's encouragement, Ballard revealed a stupendous plot, nothing less than the wholesale slaughter of the white population of Gibson County, or the majority of it at least. He named a co-conspirator, Nelson McGhee. The posse took him, "surprised in his bed," shortly after midnight. It escorted him into the woods and informed him of what he too should confess: "It was no use to deny his complicity in or knowledge of the attempted assassination and the intended outbreak among the negroes." The party returned to Gibson. They found the place seething with excitement. While the posse looked in one direction, the enemy had massed in another, an army of Negroes, advancing. No one had seen it exactly. But it was there, somewhere, waiting to strike. It might be among them already, a fifth column in their midst. Preemptive arrests ensued. Fourteen black men who could be found were bundled into jail along with Ballard and McGhee.[64] Interrogations followed. One suspect, Jarrett Burrows, cracked. Three hundred whites gathered around the prisoner as he told his tale.

---

62 Memphis Appeal, August 25, 1874.

63 Account in Nashville *Banner*, August 18, 1874.

64 Reports named ten: George Green, Steve Bryant, Dan Williams, Bob Love, Dick Shaw, Douglas "Dug" Jamison, Hays Peebles, Jarrett Burrows, Alfred Williams, Nick Ivey. Nashville *Banner*, August 18, 1874.

Black people, Burrows explained, wanted to own property. They believed President Grant would help them. Accordingly they had determined "to extirpate the whites, so as to own the 'lands, tenements and hereditaments,' and cultivate their own land. They wanted to make it a negroes' country, to do which it was necessary to kill at least the majority of white people." Why had they shot at Warren and Monroe? It was a practice run, "an experiment, to see if they could kill a white man with impunity."[65]

At dawn town marshal J.A. Dungan led the conspirators north to Trenton, the county seat. He lodged the suspects in jail. Meanwhile at Gibson shadows lengthened. Fear crept out again. The black army undoubtedly was lurking, ready for revenge. Night closed in. Terror spiked. Isolated gunshots cut the darkness. Morning sunlight melted the shadows. "With it came an end to the fearful belief that the town would be overrun by a mob of infuriated negroes." People of Gibson breathed. Prisoners in Trenton did not.

There an eyewitness described the scene. He was a traveler, stopping to rest. He became an onlooker to death. Sounds of voices and horses' hooves woke him in his room at the Hicks House hotel in the court-house square. It was two o'clock on the moonlit night of August 25.

> Springing from my bed, I saw through the window a band of about eighty mounted men galloping in from the southeast corner of the square.... I saw now that the men were masked, and understood their mission. They were after the sixteen negroes.... The full moon lit up the indescribable scene, obscured by occasional clouds, and horses, mules, men and most of the grotesque costumes were distinctly visible.... A few on the fence kept up a running banter with some of the masked party ... "Look at the old gal" (referring to one with a black gown on), "Hey, Bob Lee, thought you was killed at Shiloh." "Yes, I was killed at Shiloh, but I'm here." ... Darkness and quiet seemed to be in the jail.... About three o'clock there was a rush at the door of the jail – a whistle sounded – the order "Mount" given, and we saw a dark looking group being pushed ahead of the column. "We've got them," was whispered along the court-house fence – but not a cry – not a groan from the doomed men.[66]

Masked riders disappeared in the night. Townsmen waited: the echo of gunshots.

65 Nashville *Banner*, August 18, 1874.

66 Nashville *Union and American*, August 28, 1874.

> A few of us started off.... About half a mile away, just beyond a bridge over a small stream ... we found six bodies lying in various positions apart, but all within three or four yards square. Four were dead, but the pulse of two still beat. Matches were lit, and by the flitting light we examined them, called to them, but no answer.... Water was called for and brought in a hat, and the wounded men placed in as comfortable a position as possible and a physician sent for. I went back.

Back at Trenton, daylight came but not calm. At 10 o'clock a furious rider dashed into town. The black army, ubiquitous yet ever elusive, again had materialized. It was coming to avenge the murder of its leaders. Consternation, "a momentary paralysis," seized the townspeople. They contemplated what forms the vengeance of "infuriated, bloodthirsty negroes" might take. "There were blanched faces.... Men rushed to and fro as if in painful uncertainty." Guns were grabbed. A line of defense formed. The wily adversary once more outwitted them. The Trentonians waited for a terror that never arrived. Inquiries at last traced the source of the panic to Mrs. Gleason. She was the wife of a farmer, living some five miles out of town. Some black people had appeared at the farm and asked to speak to Mr. Gleason. From this Mrs. Gleason deduced that an attack was imminent, "at once became terrified, blew her horn and alarmed her neighbors. She told them her fears which grew at once to all manner of frightful rumors."

For sixteen prisoners it was no rumor. Their captors bound their hands. They marched down the road to the point at which the bodies were found. A survivor, Dug Jamison, related details. The massacre, though not unintended, was impromptu. This accounted for its inefficiency, leaving a majority of victims alive. The procession crossed the creek and its bridge. Jarrett Burrows fainted. He failed to rise on command. One of his guards shot him through the head. The prisoners ran for their lives. Jamison himself, having loosened his bonds, hid in a cornfield. Behind him he listened to sounds of gunfire; "and then I thought about dead niggers."[67]

Another eyewitness supported Dug Jamison's account. One of the masked avengers, taken by authorities, turned state's evidence. Ben Davis was only seventeen. Fear, he said, was the motivator. "The people in his neighborhood fully believed that the negroes, who had maintained a threatening attitude, had intended to war upon the whites." On the fatal night they met, 68 riders in all, at a point on the Lexington road some four miles from Trenton. A number of participants had borrowed female attire. Assorted masks covered their faces.

---

67 Nashville *Union and American*, September 15, 1874.

Having selected a Captain, they proceeded to business. Until the last moment, Davis protested, when he saw men carrying rope, he assumed the business was benign. They would "rescue" the Negroes from jail, whip them some, extract information relating to the incipient war of racial extermination.[68]

Rebel yells punctuated phases of the operation. Speak no names, on pain of death, the captain commanded. Only one prisoner spoke: Nick Ivey, pleading for his life. "He was told by one of the crowd, with an oath, to shut his mouth or he, the disguised man, would kill him." Ben Davis did not recall the execution of Jarrett Burrows. As the party reached the bridge he heard someone holler "Go!" The prisoners scattered. The guards, mounted on their horses, or perhaps encumbered by their dresses, did not pursue. But some targets did not "go" fast enough. They constituted the evening's fatalities.

> The shooting was indiscriminate. Every object which seemed to have the appearance of a negro was shot at.... The disguised men shot four or five negroes in the head after lying there, supposed to be dead. Some one said that they had better go round and shoot every damn one in the head. They were thus shot with pocket pistols. Three of the negroes were lying there groaning, and that is why they shot them. If they had made no noise they would not again have been shot. One of the men said, "Let's go down and kill those damn devils that are groaning." The boys were in a mighty big hurry, and left the place mighty fast.

Reaction to the Trenton massacre, on the heels of the Hayden murder, was intense. Horace Redfield exhausted his supply of adjectives. "I drop my pen and pace the floor in agony of spirit that there should be those of my own race in my adopted State to justify this cruel, barbarous, inhuman, savage, cold-blooded, beastly, brutal butchery."[69] Headlines crossed the nation. Sweet Julia's sad face merged with the image of bound men in a dark wood shot down in cold blood. Even unpartisan sheets blamed the Democrats. "They worked up the masses to a state of frenzy," wrote the San Jose *Mercury*.[70] Democrats sensed a public relations disaster. The Knoxville *Press and Herald* had done its part to work up the frenzy. Now it censured the frenzied people, "murdering maskers ... spirits of the damned called forth to a festival of death."[71] Republicans rushed to make

68 Ben Davis' account, Greeneville, Tennessee, *Intelligencer*, October 2, 1874.

69 Cincinnati *Commercial*, September 1, 1874.

70 San Jose *Mercury*, September 3, 1874.

71 Knoxville *Press and Herald*, August 29, 1874.

the atrocities "southern outrages," a unifying theme. Democrats scrambled to contain the damage.

That unenviable task fell most immediately to the Governor of Tennessee, John Calvin Brown. He offered $500 reward for information leading to the detection of the Trenton killers. He added another $500 for Julia Hayden's murderers. He sent an order to the Gibson County attorney-general. At all costs keep the national authorities out of it: "This is a test of the power and efficiency of the civil law to protect society. If we fail in this it will afford the most plausible pretext of bringing the military power of the Federal Government into requisition, of which God knows we have had enough."[72]

Gov. Brown followed that with a telegram to President Grant. Don't meddle in Tennessee. Let local authorities handle it; they would spare no effort "until the majesty of the law is fully vindicated."[73] The president persisted. Attorney-General George Williams issued federal indictments. Ultimately it all worked out. The United States District Court for Western Tennessee returned the case to state jurisdiction.[74] In state court killers rested easy. Democrats did not rest easy. The New York *Herald* warned: "If the white men in the South imagine that acts like these will be tolerated by the nation they are sadly mistaken."[75] Henry Watterson's Louisville *Courier-Journal* despaired:

> We give it up. There was a chance that the next House of Representatives would not be Radical. That chance has gone.... There is no use writing, talking, speaking, argufying, contradicting, proving, so long as the bloody sum-total, recorded within the last fortnight, goes out to the world unchallenged by adequate redress ... and it is hardly likely that anyone is going to be hung.... As surely as the South begins to get on its feet do its madmen proceed to kick the fat in the fire. The Radicals only want pretexts. The South supplies them.[76]

72 Nashville *Union and American*, September 2; New York *Times*, August 30, 1874.

73 John C. Brown to Ulysses Grant, September 18, 1874. *Papers of Ulysses Grant*, vol. 25, 229.

74 Judge Halmer Emmons, presiding at Memphis, cited the Supreme Court's Colfax decision and anticipated its Cruikshank ruling. Federal intervention was unconstitutional. "Shameless murderers shed innocent blood, not only confessed but boasted of their crimes ... [and are] acquitted by juries, their coadjutors in crime, amid the acclamations of their co-conspirators." There was no remedy, said Judge Emmons, sorrowfully, no remedy in law.

75 New York *Herald*, August 27, 1874.

76 Louisville *Courier-Journal*, August 31, 1874.

The Knoxville *Press and Herald* pleaded: "Tennesseeans are not monsters of cowardly cruelty, but brave and generous men.... Let white men continue their earnest opposition to the Civil Rights Bill and try to save the negroes from themselves, but let us, as intelligent and good citizens, set an example of forbearance and peace-loving."[77] The Nashville *Banner* sermonized:

> These social excrescences, these worthless spend their beautiful lives in whittling chips from horse-blocks or dry goods boxes, wearing out the patches which more industrious wives or mothers have charitably applied to their nether garments to conceal their nakedness. They may vary the monotony by drinking mean whisky ... or breaking jails to murder disarmed prisoners of the State.[78]

The most infuriating commentary flowed from the pen of Nasby – the pen, that is, of the nation's preeminent satirist, David Ross Locke. To skewer his targets Locke created a fictional world. His protagonist: Petroleum V. Nasby a bigoted, semi-literate, rusticated racist, political panderer and Democrat; he was everything Locke was not. Initially Nasby dwelt in Ohio, then in New Jersey. Finally Locke settled his creation in the suitably southern locality of Confederate Crossroads, "wich iz in the State uv Kentucky." He surrounded Nasby with a classical cast of characters: Bascom, keeper of the general store and its all-important supply of whisky; Issaker Gavitt, "Deekin" Pogram, and others. Nasby's nemeses, Joe Bigler, an embittered ex-Confederate soldier, and Pollock, a transplanted northerner, added dramatic tension.[79]

Each week Nasby produced a "letter to the public," printed in Locke's own paper, the Toledo *Blade*. On August 27, 1874, Nasby's letter recounted thrilling events. The war of races had reached Confedrit Xroads.[80] "The white race hed suffered enuff from bein ground into the yearth by the yoosurpers, and his

77 Knoxville *Press and Herald*, August 29, 1874.

78 Nashville *Banner*, August 29, 1874.

79 See John M. Harrison, *The Man Who Made Nasby, David Ross Locke* (Chapel Hill: 1969). Mark Twain recalled Locke: "a great burly figure, uncouthly and provincially clothed.... His letters were copied everywhere, from the Atlantic to the Pacific, and read and laughed over by everybody – at least everybody except particularly dull and prejudiced Democrats and copperheads." Mark Twain, *The Autobiography of Mark Twain*, (Berkeley: 2010), vol. 1, 146–147. Locke remained, until his last years when he embraced temperance, a dedicated drinker. "I took a very strong liking to this fellow," Twain concluded, "who has some very noble qualities." For the 1873 edition of Nasby's "collected letters," Charles Sumner wrote the Introduction. Abraham Lincoln was an admirer. "For the genius to write these things," he declared (according to Sumner), "I would gladly give up my office."

80 Text in Chicago *Inter Ocean*, September 19, 1874.

blood biled when he thot of it. Shood niggers – an inferior race – lord it over the proud Caucashen? Shood their heels be forever on our neck?" White men gathered. They fortified their courage with an ample round of libations at Bascom's bar. They loaded their guns. They waited, as had their brethren at Gibson and Trenton, "for the comin uv the black hosts." Those hosts, as at Gibson and Trenton, failed to come. They sallied forth to carry the war to Africa.

> The first nigger we saw was a blood-thirsty wretch who wuz a hoein corn. He looked at us a glared defiance, leanin in an offensive manner on his hoe. One look of hizzen was suffishent to inflame Captain McPelter with rage. "That double-dyed villin voted the clean Republican ticket last fall – ef he lives he will do it agin this fall." And putting his faithful gun to his shoulder he giv one look at the hidjus bein and shoutin "Death to our persecooters!" drawd the trigger. There wuz one fiendish persecooter less, for the top uv that nigger's head wuz blowd into a adjoinin field. Fortunately there happened ten or a dozen niggers conspiring agin us in ez many fields in the vicinity, and when they heerd the report uv McPelter's gun they cum runnin to the spot. Seein the lifeless body uv their fellow invader a lyin there, and notisin that McPelter wuz calmly reloadin the empty barl uv his shot gun, they defiantly fled in every direkshun. This wuz enuff.... Away thro the corn, over the stubble, down the gulches and over the hills we chased the infooriated demons. The re-assurin note uv the revolver, the swisly explosion uv the shot gun, the clear sharp ring uv the deadly rifle was heerd in all direckshuns, proclaimin each in its own sweet voice that the proud Caucashin wood never, never rest with the heel uv an inferior race onto his neck.

Only one white casualty occurred. Deekin Pogram fired at an invader who ducked. The enemy turned on the Deekin and knocked him down with his hoe ("wich weepin he had doubtless kept with him for the purpose"). Luckily, Gavitt arrived in time to shoot "the feend who had thus slaked his thirst for blood and wuz runnin away in the most insultin manner." The war ended when Bigler appeared leading a company of black men armed with guns rather than hoes. In a subsequent letter Nasby related that the governor himself came down to negotiate a truce. This he did by insinuating to Bascom that he might increase his profits if he let Negroes into his store.

Nasby's taunts joined the thunder of Republican orators. "Darkness has as much fellowship with light, and Belial with Christ, as the South has with the North," William Lloyd Garrison channeled St. Paul. "All her sufferings are by her own infliction, and she is her own implacable enemy – besotted, desperate, insane." "These deeds show a diabolism scarcely excelled by wild Indians," screamed the Annapolis *Gazette*.[81] James Blaine took the stump. "I beg you, my friends ... I tell you the strength of government protection to citizenship is not that which goes out to the wealthy and the influential, to the strong and the mighty, but it is that which protects and upholds the lowly, the poor and the weak."[82]

Democrats fretted. "Every 'outrage' reported from the South gives me a chill to the very marrow," wrote former Senator Eugene Casserly. "It gives new life to Radicalism and all its atrocities."[83] Party leaders realized they had to stop the bleeding – the political bleeding, the public relations hemorrhage.[84] They called for an Indignation Meeting. An open demonstration, something between a mea culpa and a whitewash, might serve to reassure the public. The party would express official Indignation and clear itself before the nation, particularly the northern part of the nation. It would denounce evildoers and disassociate itself from their doings. Then those doings would do no harm, politically.

The Indignation Meeting met at Memphis on August 28. Governor Brown did not attend. General Nathan Bedford Forrest did. Joining him were ex-governor Isham Harris and, the star of the occasion, Jefferson Davis. Davis resided in Memphis, keeping a low profile. He mounted again the public stage, namely the hall of the Memphis Exposition Building. To emphasize reconciliation, organizers invited blacks and Republicans. All awaited Davis' speech. It did not altogether suit the occasion's needs. The ex-president at first summoned up a proper dose of indignation, suitably directed.

> Friends and countrymen, you have assembled here to-night ... for what you owe to the living and what you owe to the gallant dead who fell for the sacred cause of Southern independence. [Apparently he had forgotten the invitation to blacks and Republicans.] You come to appeal to the

81 Annapolis *Gazette*, August 18, September 15, 1874.

82 James G. Blaine, *Political Discussions, Legislative, Diplomatic, and Popular, 1856–1886* (Norwich: 1887), 146–147.

83 Eugene Casserly to Thomas Bayard, September 10, 1874. Thomas Bayard Papers, Library of Congress.

84 A century later Southern Outrages again flooded the media: lynchings, Klan burnings, police brutality. In 1963 the Birmingham church bombing lit up television screens. New Jersey Congressman Joseph Minish echoed the old prose of *Harper's Weekly*: "The blame [lies] not solely on the murderers themselves but on the officials and the society which created that nerve-taut atmosphere in which the seed of hate could quickly germinate and bear its deadly fruit." *Cong. Record*, 88th Congress, 1st Session: 19,807.

> moral sense of the world. Your words are to go abroad to mankind; let it understand that you are not a race of assassins; that you are not the men who mask but stand in the dignity of your manhood, and the likeness of your Creator ... and to the end of your lives will go forward with honor which never seeks concealment, wears no mask, and never blackens its face.[85]

As Davis warmed to his message he drifted into less felicitous notions. He drew a nostalgic picture of past times, halcyon days, before Yankees had sundered the proper, the "useful" and divinely-ordained relationship of the races.

> The negroes were not our enemies; why should they become so? We are their friends. Yes, and the Southern men are the only friends they have to-day in any part of the world.... Every Southern man in his memory runs back to the negro woman who nursed him, to the boy who hunted and fished with him, to the man who first taught him to ride and to swim ... and while he has such memories clustering around him he cannot be the enemy of that useful race which was the main strength of our country when we stood in this relation which I believe God intended us to occupy.

Having delivered this wistful evocation of slavery, Davis forgot the proposed target of his "indignation," the masked riders. He vented his wrath upon the masked riders' victims.

> The only feeling of indignation I have is against the white men who have disturbed this relation between us, who have fomented discord, who have led the imaginative negro into evils; against them, I say, I hurl the thunderbolt of your vengeance.

Bedford Forrest followed. He at least stayed on message.

> I am here to-night as an humble citizen, to enter my protest against the atrocities that have been committed in Gibson County. I stand here as a citizen ready to start to-morrow ... and hunt those men up. I am ready to protect the black man as much and as quick as the white man.... They [masked riders] should be stopped; they must be stopped ... They will be stopped.[86]

---

85 Text of Davis' speech, Baltimore *Sun*, September 2, 1874.
86 Chicago *Tribune*, September 1, 1874.

The target audience of the Indignation Meeting was northern public opinion. The Associated Press telegraphed its speeches across the country. Democratic sheets applauded. Republicans remarked on the incongruity, if not hypocrisy, of exhibiting such men as Bedford Forrest and Jefferson Davis as spokesmen for racial harmony. "The act of the kuklux assassins of Gibson County was merciful in comparison with the deed which gave General Forrest notoriety," wrote the Philadelphia *Bulletin*. "He is not precisely the man to assume position as the champion of the persecuted race."[87] Davis' retrograde remembrance of slave days provoked acid comment:

> Mr. Davis indulged in a lachrymose effort at sentiment in regard to the former relations between whites and blacks at the South.... This was followed, of course, by the assertion that God had intended the negro nurse to remain a slave, and the negro boy to remain a slave to the end of time, that both might minister to the white baby and the white boy forever.... All of which shows conclusively ... that he is as cowardly a rebel at heart to-day as he was on the day when in a disgraceful disguise he was captured and became the prisoner of the nation.[88]

People of Gibson County also protested. An interracial reconciliation conference met at Pickettsville, pledging to work for peaceful coexistence. Participants denounced the heavy-handed rhetoric of the Memphis meeting which seemed to lump them all together as thuggish masked marauders. Their spokesman, Col. Sharpe, lashed out at the "unjust and ungenerous speeches" of President Davis, Gov. Harris and Gen. Forrest, "the father of the Ku-Klux."[89]

Democrats certified indignation. Indignation failed to deter violence. A fresh corpse landed near Memphis on the very night following the indignation meeting.[90] Another fell in Smith County, an old black farmer named Dick McKinney. He had unwisely allowed himself to be quoted: "He intended to die at home, rather than be run off by the Ku-klux or anybody else in disguise." Disguised visitors promptly appeared at Mr. McKinney's cabin near the town of Carthage. The old man defended himself with an ax. One assailant seized the implement and smashed in his head. A second shot him in the stomach. Another shot him in the back. Authorities arrested seven suspects on the confession

87 Memphis *Appeal*, September 10, 1874; Forrest's "deed" a reference to the Fort Pillow massacre of 1864.

88 Chicago *Inter Ocean*, September 8, 1874.

89 Nashville *Union and American*, September 4, 1874.

90 Nashville *Banner*, September 1, 1874.

of an eighth. Masked riders liberated their comrades from jail and murdered the informer. The people of Smith County held an Indignation Meeting.[91]

Those murders formed an undercurrent of unease. Two deaths rose to headlines as violence metastasized into Alabama: the killings of Thomas Ivey and Walter Billings. Ivey was black. Billings was white.

Tom Ivey fell on August 29. He had long been a marked man. He was educated. His father, also his owner, had sent him for schooling in Philadelphia. After emancipation he threw himself into politics, recruiting and organizing black voters. Congressman Charles Hays secured Ivey's appointment as mail agent on the Alabama and Chattanooga Railroad. He rode the trains across Sumter County until, at 3 p.m. on that late August day, he came to a spot about six miles beyond the town of Livingston, four miles from York. A man stood upon the track. Engineer Charlie Briggs stopped. Four men leaped from the bushes. Ivey stepped from the mail car. Bullets riddled his body.[92]

Ivey had received death threats. He had asked to be relieved of his route.[93] Off duty he employed an armed bodyguard. But he refused to stop his political activities. "A dangerous man," said the Meridian *Mercury*. "He made speeches ever more violent, dwelling much on the civil rights bill, in every way to enkindle the minds of the simple blacks against the whites." Ivey's friend Bob Reid, a black member of the Alabama legislature, confirmed it: "He dared advocate the passage of the Civil Rights Bill."[94] According to Congressman Hays, his murderers cut out his tongue. His tongue, Democrats insisted, remained attached. With or without, Thomas Ivey became, on August 29, 1874, the nation's first civil rights martyr, the first person verifiably killed as a result of advocating a civil rights act.[95]

The train deposited Ivey's body at York station. Authorities set it on the platform to await the coroner's inspection. The coroner came and went. The corpse lay still. After two days exposed to midsummer sun and flies, it was deemed advisable to remove it. His wife buried what remained of Tom Ivey at

91 Knoxville *Press and Herald*, August 30, September 9, 13, 1874.

92 Accounts in Hartford *Courant*, September 15; Mobile *Register*, September 2, 1874, both including quotes from Meridian *Mercury* and Selma *Times*.

93 Chattanooga *Times*, September 1, 1874.

94 Jackson *Mississippi Pilot*, February 20, 1875.

95 Ivey's enemies made no secret of their motivation. Bob Reid narrowly missed being martyr number two. In a rally at the town of Coatopa, he recalled, Ivey demanded the Civil Rights Bill. Reid, when his turn came to speak, avoided the topic. Watching was High Sheriff William Williamson. "I will protect you," said he afterward to Reid, "but we will not stand the way Ivey spoke." Other white men, the brothers Zack and Jimmie Tutt, muttered the same message: "Ivey could not go on in that way, talking as he did." Three weeks later Ivey was dead. Bob Reid's testimony, 43rd Congress, House Report 262: 16–24.

Livingston.[96] "The assassination," the *Mercury* noted, "seems to have had a narcotic effect upon the blacks."[97] Even better, the Selma *Times* reported, "some fifty or more negroes organized a Democratic club, which is daily increasing in number."[98] Alabama's Senator Spencer and Congressman Hays called upon Postmaster-General Marshall Jewell to appoint a special agent to investigate the murder. Jewell was not sympathetic: "If Ivey had been attending to his official duties instead of distributing incendiary and inflammatory speech among the negroes he would probably never have been molested." "If some gentlemen had not gone around the country making speeches," Spencer retorted, "they would not be in the cabinet."[99] The senator's reply was clever, but the postmaster-general was correct.

The Billings murder was more mysterious. Walter Billings was 35. He was a northerner, transplanted from Brooklyn, New York. He engaged in political organizing and served as chairman of the Republican Executive Committee of Sumter County. His killers ambushed him as he rode from a political meeting to his home near Ramsey's Station on the evening of August 1. Republicans seized upon the affair: blatant political assassination. Congressman Hays rushed to the scene "in a towering rage." He conferred with Governor David P. Lewis at Meridian. Then he rode off to Mobile to expedite a federal police investigation.[100] Democrats pooh-poohed. "It was a horrible thing," the Meridian *Mercury* admitted, "to shoot a man down, but we fail to see how the shooting of a mischief-making carpet-bagger demands such a hulla-baloo."[101]

Details came out in the trial of three men arrested under the Enforcement Act and brought before United States Commissioner James Gillette in October.[102] According to the government's prosecution, the assassins had clumsily

96 One reporter visited the spot some months later. Ivey's moldering body had gone. But a dismal scene remained: "A populace which creeps out in broken-down fences, broken windows, wagons with only three wheels.... The men are idlers, gambling and drinking at the saloons with Colt's revolvers at their belts and knives in their boots; the negroes are lying around in the sun, ragged and squalid, and everything seems to have the trade-mark of Satan stamped plainly upon it." Chicago *Inter Ocean*, October 7, 1874.

97 Mobile *Register*, September 3, 1874.

98 Quoted in Hartford *Courant*, September 15, 1874.

99 Harrisburg *Patriot*, October 10, 1874. The gentlemanly Postmaster-General, formerly Governor of Connecticut, annoyed some fellow Republicans. "A majolica statesman in pumps and ruffles with a porcelain smile," snapped Senator Ingalls. *Writings of John James Ingalls*, 425. Spencer had more success with Secretary of the Treasury Bristow. Treasury detectives Hester and Beach, sent to investigate the Billings murder, also looked into Ivey's case.

100 Details in Mobile *Register*, August 6, 8, 12, 16, 1874.

101 Mobile *Register*, August 8, 1874.

102 Mobile *Register*, October 8, 1874.

committed their deed in the presence of eyewitnesses, and then permitted the eyewitnesses to walk away. Two black men testified: Richard Wright, sixteen years old, a field hand on a farm near Livingston, and Nelson Doyle, an itinerant carpenter. Coming up the road, Wright related, they saw Billings approach on horseback. It was "between sunset and dusk." A white man, Stephen Renfro, stepped from the shadows. He called out: "Halt! God d – n you!" Twenty men, concealed in the darkening woods, "riz up and fired." The shooters left the body on the road, where the victim's family located it the next day. They handed Wright $20 in paper currency, advising him to keep his mouth shut. Nelson Doyle too was warned. Some days later masked visitors reinforced the message. They removed him from his cabin and beat him with wooden implements. Bob Reid described the result.

> They beat him so bad that he did not come to his right senses for two or three days. I went to see him; pulled off his shirt, and took my finger and squashed the blood out of his back the same as if it was a rotten pumpkin, and pulled splinters fully an inch long out of his back. From his hips to his shoulders it was puffed up as if something had been stuffed. It was a long time before I could get him to tell who did it.[103]

Three suspects, Renfro, Charles Bullock, and Philip A. "Billy" Hillman, were taken in charge for the Billings murder. Panic swept the community of night-riders. "The swamp was full of white men," Bob Reid recalled, "expecting to be arrested." Swamps emptied once the heat was off, but resentment boiled. One white acquaintance informed Reid: "If Bullock gets out of these things I will be damned if these woods and rivers don't stink with [dead] negroes."[104]

The Billings murder confronted Democrats with another public relations mess, the victim not a sinister black but a prominent white man. They hunted for alternative theories of the crime. Billings, the *Mercury* discovered, was a professional provocateur, "a special emissary from [Gov.] Lewis to stir up the Negroes of Sumter and prepare them for the fall election." At a rally just before his death Billings had displayed $10,000 in greenbacks with which he intended to carry the elections. After waving the cash about, he announced to the assembled Negroes that he could be found riding home alone on a dark road. No money was present on his corpse. The matter was evident "Probably some of

103 House Reports 262: 23.
104 House Reports 262: 21, 24.

the very negroes to whose cupidity he had catered preferred getting their share of the booty immediately."[105]

That theory seemed possible, but not positive. Perhaps the murderers were Richard Wright and Nelson Doyle. What was really in that heavy box of carpentry tools Doyle carried on that night? Wright had $20 in his pocket. Where had he hidden the other $9,980? Even better, the deceased's business partner, Henry J. Greatta, fit the bill. He was an underhanded carpetbagger. Hence he lusted after the money. A family friend, he lusted after the victim's wife. One could not discount collusion between lady and lover.[106] At last the Mobile *Register* hit upon the answer. The Civil Rights Bill had done Walter Billings in. In the course of his "stirrings up," he had urged black people not to insist upon that measure. Its agitation could only hurt the Party. Thus his murder was arranged by pro-civil-rights-bill Negroes – who also helped themselves to the cash, why not?[107]

Fallout from the Billings affair presented Democrats another headache. Details reached the desk of Ulysses Grant, enclosed in a letter from Senator Daniel Pratt. The senator urged the commander-in-chief to take military action.

> Since the assassination of Mr. Billings not one single Republican meeting has been held in this county – And this is what the Democrats are fighting for – Unless Martial law is declared hundreds of the poor negroes will be killed – even now they do not sleep in their houses & are hunted down like wild beasts by the Democracy because they will not vote their ticket.[108]

Fear meanwhile moved on to Louisiana. On August 7 chilling dispatches flashed across the wires. "A dreadful plot of the negroes has just been discovered," the Mobile *Register* gasped, "to kill the inhabitants and to set fire to the residences and plantations in the parish of St. Martin." Killing was to commence at the Lastrapes place, and continue as far as St. Martinville. "The negroes were to keep for themselves the most beautiful women." Someone informed. Their design uncovered, the plotters fled.[109] St. Martinville escaped. The explosion

105 Eutaw *Whig*, quoted in Mobile *Register*, August 16, 1874.

106 Montgomery *Advertiser*, August 16, 1874.

107 Mobile *Register*, October 19, 1874. The existence of the disappearing $10,000 was never confirmed.

108 Daniel Pratt to Ulysses Grant, August 24, 1874. Simon, *The Papers of Ulysses Grant*, vol. 25, 195.

109 Mobile *Register*, August 11, 1874. One ringleader was caught, a black man named Louis Michel. "He was arrested by a party of vigilants, and taken to the woods and hung." Forty-third Congress, Second Session, House Reports 261, Part 2: 785–786.

came three weeks later, westward along the Red River at Coushatta. It followed the inevitable pattern – fear, panic, murder – but offered some variations. An odor of politics pervaded the affair, as it took place against the backdrop of a heated campaign in the Fourth Congressional District. The spark was fear, as usual. But the slaughter afterward was calculated. All the victims were political officers. All the victims were white.[110]

Politics in the Shreveport district had been reduced to a single issue: race. Even old-line Democrats subordinated themselves to a new organization, the White People's Party. White Leagues, paramilitary auxiliaries, powered the movement. The victims saw disaster coming. "We are on the verge of a Civil War," wrote Frank Edgerton, Sheriff of Red River Parish. "An accident, a drunken man, or a crazy fanatic is liable to start it at any moment."[111] The accident came on August 28.

Initial dispatches bore a suspicious similarity to those from Gibson and Trenton: the spectral black army, its ranks swollen, a brigade force 800 strong, moving from the direction of Cotton Point toward the defenseless town of Coushatta. Its mission: "the extermination of the whites." Reinforcements mobilized. From Shreveport 75 mounted men set out, followed by a hundred white infantry and supplies aboard the steamer *Clifford.* The enemy advanced. They were spotted at Brownsville. Two blacks and one white man had fallen. More auxiliaries rushed toward the scene: 25 from Mansfield, with 150 more to follow; 40 from Cotton Point; 100 from Board's Landing.[112] Panic spread to Texas. Only a miracle, said the Galveston *News,* could avert a bloodbath.[113]

Then it was over. The will-o-the-wisp black army yet again evaporated. But prisoners remained, the ringleaders of the genocidal campaign. They were the white Republican officials of the parish: Sheriff Frank Edgerton; Tax Collector and Postmaster Homer Twitchell; the Register Clark Holland; William H. Howell, Parish Attorney; Monroe C. Willis, Justice of the Peace; Robert Dewees, Collector of De Soto Parish.[114]

---

110 On the Coushatta Massacre, see the work of Ted Tunnell, *Crucible of Reconstruction: War, Radicalism and Race in Louisiana, 1862–1877* (Baton Rouge: 1984), 195–201; *Edge of the Sword: The Ordeal of Carpetbagger Marshall H. Twitchell in the Civil War and Reconstruction* (Baton Rouge: 2001), 188–192.

111 Tunnell, *Edge of the Sword*: 195.

112 Shreveport *Times*, August 30, 1874.

113 Galveston *News*, August 30, 1874.

114 Tunnell, *Edge of the Sword,* 95, 197–210; Oscar H. Lestage, "The White League in Louisiana and its Participation in Reconstruction Riots," *Louisiana Historical Quarterly*, 18 (1935): 657–682.

Tunnell, *Edge of the Sword,* 95.

Gradually facts emerged. Once again a small incident precipitated panic. Late on the night of August 25, White Leaguers, sporting masks de rigueur, called upon a black farmer near Brownsville. He defended himself more successfully than Dick McKinney. The visitors fled, leaving one dead. White Rangers retaliated, removed another black man from his cabin and applied a shotgun to his head. That sufficed to call up, *de profundis*, the hellish apparition, the great black army, "swearing vengeance against the white race, and declaring they would not leave a white man, woman or child, alive in the parish."

Had it stopped there, Coushatta would have been a minor affair. Circumstances, however, inspired a political cleansing. Republicans dominated the county offices, relying on their black majority. The quickest way to reverse that situation was to cut off the head that controlled the body. In exchange for their lives the prisoners wrote out their resignations from public office. They agreed to leave the parish and the state, never to return. They set out for the border under guard. They did not make it. As they crossed the Red River they paused at Robinson's plantation. There, so it was related, a party of fifty Texans overtook them. The Texans had come for the war but found it over. Unwilling to leave without some accomplishment, they liquidated the prisoners. Edgerton, Twitchell and Dewees were shot directly, Holland, Howell and Willis allowed a few moments to pray. Local citizens buried them, eventually.

This time things had gone too far, a butchery of whites instead of blacks, undisguised political assassinations. Screaming headlines greeted the northern public: "Reign of Hate – A Saturnalia of Crime – The Revelry of the Bullet – White League Barbarians – Civilized Union Men the Victims – A Deed of Unparalleled Atrocity."[115] Even the truculent Shreveport *Times* ran scared. Slander, it protested, fake news.

> We have been subjected to a despotism of ignorance and rascality, and every conceivable outrage has been heaped upon us. So long as we submit quietly ... allow ourselves to be robbed, our homes to be burned, and our people to be murdered, all the North is lavish in its sympathy ... we are a "most loyal people."... But the moment we make a manly effort to protect ourselves; the moment we strike down the oppressor, the thief and murderer; the moment we rise up to assert our dignity as men, and our rights as American citizens, we are pronounced guilty of being rebels, cut-throats, assassins, ku-klux.[116]

115 Terre Haute *Express*, September 3, 1874.
116 Shreveport *Times*, September 10, 1874.

The *Times'* anguished cry at first seemed unpersuasive. Sixteen blacks at Trenton, six whites at Coushatta, a bloody toll for one week's work (not counting Tom Ivey and Julia Hayden). The government truly might intervene. Citizens of Shreveport telegraphed the White House. They began contritely: "We shall not attempt to justify to your Excellency the killing of six white men." They ended defiantly: "Knowing as we do the deep and bitter wrongs our people have endured ... we cannot participate in what of indignation their violent death may have stirred within your heart."[117] Before the president could consult the stirrings within his heart, in the nick of time, justification arrived. Two black men, Paul Williams and Louis Johnson, supplied the information.[118] They, along with other black persons, had been rounded up by the White League. Their captors urged them to reveal any and all genocidal plots. Before being lynched, they complied.

The late Republican officers, it now came out, were not the innocent victims they appeared to be. The black army, later mysteriously to disperse, was a diversion. Edgerton, Twitchell and Dewees prepared a holocaust at Coushatta. They deployed a second black brigade, hidden outside town. They chose the night of the 27th, the moment of a town dance. "The time had come," Twitchell told his minions, "for them to strike for their rights."[119] He "packed" the Negroes into a cornfield behind his house, waiting to slaughter the revelers at the hoedown. Dewees, however, left the cornfield to spy on the dancers. Too many people, he reported. The massacre was postponed.

These astounding facts of course were not known at the time; they could not logically have motivated the murderers of the Republican officials. They turned out to be false. Cornfields behind Twitchell's house showed no sign of damage. The marauding Texans who had done the killings in impetuous Texas style turned out to be a gang of local Louisianans under one Richard Coleman, known as "Captain Jack," an unsavory associate of the White League.[120] Corrections appeared later in small print. One had the comforting knowledge, in retrospect, that the villains deserved their end.

Republicans insisted all this was hogwash. The true motivation was and had always been to decapitate the leadership of their party. White League forces, operating under the innocuous banner of the Citizen's Tax-Reform Association, had performed a similar coup in Natchitoches Parish. There they forced

117 S.J. Wood et al. to Ulysses Grant, September 4, 1874. Simon, *Papers of Ulysses S. Grant*, vol. 25, 217.

118 Shreveport *Times*, September 5, 9, 1874.

119 Nashville *Union and American*, September 4, 1874.

120 Tunnell, *Edge of the Sword*, 203–207.

the Republican officials to resign, though they refrained from killing them.[121] State Senator Marshall H. Twitchell, brother of the late Homer, denounced "a reign of terror." Two years later a costumed assassin shot him. He survived the amputation of both arms.[122] The Mobile *Register* stated the case: "The carpet-baggers and scalawags are our hostages.... If the darkey fights he must go it on his 'own hook' without his white leaders."[123]

Some northern papers called for action. "Had there been more hemp and fewer pardons distributed among the Ku-Klux," the Burlington, Iowa, *Hawkeye* snarled, "there would be fewer White League murders to-day."[124] White people, others reasoned, had acted nobly.[125] For Carl Schurz's St. Louis *Westliche Post* the problem was Civil Rights.

> While we are here advocating the so-called Civil Rights Bill with so much unanimity, how can we blame the unhappy white people of Louisiana as they make an effort to throw off the yoke of slavery? ... If they should succeed in driving the Northern carpet-baggers out of the State, every honest man would rejoice, and even if some of them should be deprived of life and limb, you could not find twelve honest men who would not render a verdict of "Not Guilty – done in self-defense." ... We would not only excuse, but rather advise violent measures.[126]

No one was punished for the Coushatta killings.[127] Two months later Lieutenant William Gerlach of the U.S. Army's 3rd Infantry led a detachment into the

121 Lestage, "The White League in Louisiana," 649–657. Lives were spared in Natchitoches, but they were disrupted. Judge Henry C. Myers, one of the fugitive officials, described various posted notices that convinced him to run: "KKK – Your fate is sealed;" "Nothing but your blood will appease us." He left behind his family, an infant son deathly ill. The little child died, Mrs. Myers recalled. She found no one who dared erect a headstone to mark her baby's grave. House Report 261, Part 2: 280–281, 302–303.

122 Tunnell, *Edge of the Sword*, 242–247.

123 Mobile *Register*, September 2, 1874.

124 Quoted in New York *Tribune*, September 1, 1874.

125 Harrisburg *Patriot*, September 4, 1874.

126 Quoted in Shreveport *Times*, September 3, 1874.

127 The murders did produce a burst of political rhetoric. Nothing came of that either, though it inspired a dialogue of revealing incomprehension. On January 13, Black Jack Logan rose in the Senate. How, he asked, could such crimes remain unpunished? Gordon of Georgia answered: That was the government's job. "Where was the United States court at that time? Where was the enforcement act? Where was the Army of the United States?" "I will inform the Senator where they were," Logan replied. "The district attorney was in his grave, put there by your political friends. The judge had been murdered a year before. The one appointed in his place had to resign to save his life. The United States court was in

area. He spoke to George Frisbie Hoar's congressional investigative committee, sent to examine reports of irregularity in the Louisiana elections. He crossed a land swept clean by fear, roads and fields eerily deserted. At the sight of federal uniforms black people emerged. "They had been lying out in the woods for night after night; they were afraid to come in ... afraid of being taken and whipped and suffer all kinds of abuse." One frightened little boy described the bodies of Holland, Willis and Howell, days unburied, bullet-shredded, decaying in the dust. Black persons "were pretty well cowed; they appeared to have lost faith in everybody," Lt. Gerlach concluded.[128] (see Illustration 7)

One final outburst of violence marked the violent summer of 1874: the Penn Rebellion in New Orleans. In a sense Ulysses Grant paved the way for this outbreak. His policy of reconciliation led some to misread his motives. He had dangled a veto of the Civil Rights Bill. He had declined to intervene on behalf of Republican Governor Edmund Davis of Texas who disputed the results of his election defeat. He allowed Democrats to force him out. He declined to intervene when Arkansas descended into civil war between rival governors. He allowed Democrats to seat their man. In Louisiana a disputed election had left Republican Governor William Pitt Kellogg and Lieutenant-Governor C.C. Antoine in possession of the State House. It left their Democratic and Liberal Republican rivals, John McEnery and Davidson Penn, in possession of a grudge, and in possession of the White League. The *Abeille* of New Orleans concluded as early as July that Grant, having abandoned the "Negroid platform," having failed to save his party in Arkansas, would not save Kellogg should the people of Louisiana remove him.[129]

On Monday, September 14, they removed him.[130] At four o'clock White League forces marched, 3,000 strong, under the orders of their portly general, Fred Ogden. Federal troops garrisoning New Orleans stood aside to watch. Five hundred Metropolitan Police, of black companies and white, deployed against

---

New Orleans. And he asks where was the United States Army? Great God! Do you want the Army? I thought you had been railing against its use." Gordon seemed taken aback: "I confess to the Senator now that I am entirely overwhelmed. When he comes at me with that argument I am utterly undone." But he rallied. "It is always easier to attack the defeated; it is always easier for power to triumph than for truth; but truth will prevail in the end." *Cong. Record*, 43rd Congress, 2nd Session: 424.

128 House Report 261, Part 2: 148–149. Captain Arthur Allyn of the 16th Infantry, stationed in Grant Parish, also testified. The committee's William Frye asked: could he, Congressman Frye, have ventured into rural Louisiana without military protection? The captain's reply: "I don't think you would have lived 24 hours." House Report 261, Part 2: 158.

129 New Orleans *Abeille*, July 22, 1874.

130 See Stuart Omer Landry, *The Battle of Liberty Place: The Overthrow of Carpet-Bag Rule in New Orleans, September 14, 1874* (New Orleans: 1955).

SOUTHERN REBEL. "Come on, boys! Old Grant's bluster about our killing Republicans is only a Military Scarecrow, after all."

ILLUSTRATION 7 Southern Outrages
SOURCE: *HARPER'S WEEKLY*, SEPTEMBER 26, 1874

the League. At their head was City Police Commissioner Gen. Algernon Badger. With him rode James Longstreet, once a Confederate hero but now reviled by former friends. The police advanced up Poydras Street. White League volleys repulsed them. They retreated to an exposed position on the levee. Converging fire swept down from alleyways and buildings. Gatling guns responded. General Badger fell, his mangled leg requiring amputation. Longstreet survived his last battle.[131] Thirty-five policemen did not.[132]

The battle briefly put the White League in possession of Louisiana. This time, however, Ulysses Grant intervened. Federal forces under Col. William

---

131 "Longstreet retreated like a cur," the New Orleans *Bulletin* gushed. "It was only by a miracle that he escaped with his life." House Report 261, Part 2: 809.

132 Landry, *The Battle of Liberty Place*: 205–206.

Emory moved. White Leaguers still hoped. Racial solidarity: American soldiers, surely, would "affiliate with the whites."[133] Emory's soldiers obeyed their orders. On the 19th the Montgomery *Advertiser* reported sadly: "Our latest dispatches indicate the final surrender of the people of Louisiana to the Government of the United States."[134]

In terms of propaganda, the Penn Rebellion was an uncertain affair. Republicans denounced armed rebellion reborn in the South. Democrats decried federal interference, the act of a dictator in support of a usurper.[135] Black citizens wired the president. Put the city under martial law. "Send us General Benjamin F. Butler here for only Six months and if he dont Cure them of there deseased We be Willing to be reinstated [re-enslaved] as We were before butler Came to town."[136]

The Penn Rebellion put the final punctuation to a pre-election summer of fear and violence. Politicians prepared to exploit that violence. From Democrats the message was clear. Remember the fate of the Coushatta six, of Walter Billings and Thomas Ivey. Republicans saw themselves in the crosshairs: "Who will be the next victim? How long will democrats continue to justify or wink at such murders? How much longer are republicans expected to submit?"[137] Party leaders replied: no longer. Rather than submit they counterattacked. Public opinion hung in the balance. It was time for an Outrage Meeting to counteract the Indignation Meeting. A bold political demonstration might persuade voters to join the Republican side. Thus came about the Southern Republican Convention, known to Democrats derisively as the "Outrage Convention," or, in mockery of its mixed composition, the "Mongrel Convention." The inspiration came from the fertile mind of Arkansas' Senator Powell Clayton.[138] Indiana's Oliver Morton gave it his blessing.[139] In September the call went out:

---

133 Mobile *Register*, August 29, 1874.

134 Montgomery *Advertiser*, August 19, 1874.

135 Mobile *Register*, September 17, 1874.

136 We the Colored People of New Orleans to Ulysses Grant, September 25, 1874. *Papers of Ulysses S. Grant*, vol. 25, 235.

137 Talladega, Alabama, *Our Mountain Home*, August 12, 1874.

138 Memphis *Appeal*, September 23, 1874: "the rear basements of the vicious brains of Clayton and [Senator Stephen W.] Dorsey."

139 Little Rock *Gazette*, August 15, 29, 1874. In August Democrats observed a suspicious gathering, Oliver Morton, Clayton and Dorsey, Congressmen Hodges and Hynes at the spa of Hot Springs: "infamous and soulless plotters," engaged in a "satanic conference." From that conclave, "the cry that started at Hot Springs with O.P. Morton," there rose the Southern Republican Convention. Hilary A. Herbert, *Why the Solid South? or, Reconstruction and its Results* (Baltimore: 1890), 319.

> All Republicans ... who will earnestly seek to maintain the principles on which the Union was defended, and to inaugurate which, in the South, reconstruction was begun, and who feel an interest in the preservation of law, order and the rights of citizenship, are invited to attend this convention. All should come possessed of the facts as to the true condition in their respective localities, so that an authoritative statement may be made to the country.... Those who doubt as to the purposes or capacity of Southern Republicans, or who believe the oppressions under which we are laboring have been magnified, let them come and see and hear for themselves.[140]

At first the convention considered meeting in Atlanta. Chattanooga, however, offered a more hospitable Republican environment, and a closer connection to scenes of notable outrages. The Chattanooga *Times* welcomed delegates to "the most cosmopolitan city in the South."[141] Michigan's Zachariah Chandler, chairman of the Republican National Committee, endorsed the gathering.[142] Ulysses Grant received an invitation, but declined to visit the South.

The Southern Republican Convention opened on October 13. Even before delegates arrived the civil rights issue made its presence felt. The incident at Sixty-two Mile Siding set the tone. Located, as advertised, 62 miles north of Canton, Mississippi, on the New Orleans, St. Louis and Chicago Railroad, this little way station featured a restaurant offering refreshment as trains pulled off for a stop. On the morning of October 12 the northbound train stopped. On board were politicians headed to Chattanooga, black delegates John Roy Lynch, P.B.S. Pinchback, Mississippi Secretary of State James Hill, Isaac Shadd, Speaker of the Mississippi House, and white delegates, among them Senator Henry Pease. The travelers, except for Pinchback who carefully remained on the train, entered the "eating stand." Major Raphael, the owner, rushed up. They must go elsewhere. They refused. "We will eat it on this line or fight it, just as you please." The major ordered his waiters not to serve them. The breakfasters ate anyway, appropriating left-over items already set out. They put down full price, as a matter of honor. They announced they would repeat the triumph at dinner. Word raced ahead of them. As the train came into Holly Springs that

140 Vicksburg *Times*, September 16, 1874.

141 Chattanooga *Times*, September 12, 20, 1874.

142 New York *Tribune*, September 7, 1874.

evening a menacing crowd waited on the platform. A foray into the station restaurant wisely was canceled.[143]

The convention gathered in James Hall, Chattanooga. Flags festooned the stage. Upright placards marked the seating of state delegations.[144] Two hundred delegates represented all the southern states except South Carolina and Kentucky.[145] Powell Clayton called the session to order. Delegates heard a communiqué from the Republican National Executive Committee, signed by its Secretary, James M. Edmunds. He urged them to record all evidence of disorder, lawlessness and oppression. Set it before the American people. Great results might then be expected. Alabama's ex-Governor Lewis Parsons gave the keynote speech. "The tree of liberty" had been planted in the South. "The Republican party had planted it and watered it, and had a right to suppose that it would become a beacon light to the world." Murder and oppression blighted that hope. The ruling caste of southern society had never reconciled itself to the new state of things. "Their minds were not prepared for anything more than that slavery must be abolished, but they still expected to make use of the colored population for their own ends, and in some way get under control their labor.... This is why murderers cannot be punished." Two solutions were possible: change the culture of the South (a doubtful enterprise), or bring on the use of force (far more effective), "until these terrible evils are eradicated."[146]

The convention organized its committees. The most important carried the title Committee on Facts and Statistics, the "Outrage Committee," tasked with compiling and documenting all incidents, persecution, murder or violence. Louisiana's Judge Henry Myers, recently exiled from home, wife and children by White League terror, chaired the panel. Among the members sat Elias Keils of Alabama, destined soon to become a fact and statistic himself, the victim of an outrage worthy of setting before the public.

---

143 Louisville *Courier-Journal* and Memphis *Appeal*, October 13; Nashville *Banner*, October 16, 1874.

144 Accounts in Chattanooga *Times*, Savannah *News*, New York *Times*, October 14–15; New York *Tribune*, Louisville *Courier-Journal*, October 14, 1874.

145 New York *Times*, October 14, 1874. Attendees included Senators Clayton and Dorsey, West of Louisiana, Spencer of Alabama, Pease of Mississippi, ex-Governors Davis of Texas, Brooks of Arkansas and Parsons of Alabama. Among black delegates were Pinchback, Lynch, Georgia's Jefferson Long, George Price of North Carolina, James Napier of Tennessee. Media coverage was all one could have wished. Major sheets sent reporters. The New York *Times'* man, Edward Crapsey, stood out. Supremely supercilious, celebrated as chronicler of the urban scene, he made clear his resentment of an enforced purgatory in backwoods Chattanooga.

146 Chattanooga *Times*, New York *Tribune*, October 14, 1874.

Two dispossessed Republican governors, Joe Brooks of Arkansas and Edmund Davis of Texas, now read fiery speeches. Davis particularly captivated the assembly with accounts of murder and mayhem in his state. Democrats had determined to cement the South into one-party rule. They employed "the decisive argument of the knife and the cord." Homicide in Texas was as common as in a savage tribe "where the streets are daily decorated with a score or so of freshly decapitated bodies." Northern papers claimed that six hundred political murders had occurred in Texas since the beginning of the year. Not true. The number was much higher. Only federal force could stop the violence.[147]

On the second day the convention heard from its Committee on Facts and Statistics. The committee reported itself overwhelmed. Not if it sat for weeks could it compile a true picture of the outrages. Delegates allowed it additional time. Then they turned to civil rights. Pinchback offered a resolution: "Nor can there be perfect peace in the land until every citizen enjoys equal privileges with other citizens in all the public relations of life.... The Republican party must not stop now until all these rights are not only conceded in principle but secured in justice."[148]

Pinchback's resolution brought dismay. Clayton, Parsons and Brooks: civil rights were essential, but now was not the time to mention it. Northern public opinion was the target. They must focus on outrages. Even black delegates agreed. The object, Jefferson Long concluded, "is to secure the mighty arm of the nation to hold up those who have been imposed upon.... [We] need protection at the ballot box more than anything else." The resolution was dropped.

The convention bequeathed the nation an Address. Its opening lines summed up the message. "In this country the law is sustained by public opinion. Public opinion is stronger than the law."

> Our fathers, in the foundation of our system of government, never realized that the day would come when the lives of American citizens could be taken unlawfully and in great numbers, and no witness to such deeds could be found to prefer a complaint, no sheriff to execute a warrant and no sentiment in the community sufficiently strong to secure the condemnation of the offense, or the punishment of the offender.... We lay before the country unmistakable evidences ... we leave it to the sublime sense

---

147 Galveston *News*, October 11, 13, 1874. "There has lately been a pretty liberal killing of Mexicans in our southwestern counties," Davis noted. "They stand killing better than any other race we have yet come in contact with. This, and the custom of our country, may be considered as sufficient reasons why we kill them."

148 Nashville *Union and American*, October 15, 16, 1874.

of right and justice that characterizes the American people to judge us aright.[149]

The Chattanooga Convention disbanded. Some observers feared it had gone too far. Others deplored its weakness. Mississippi Governor Adelbert Ames had chosen not to attend. He debriefed the state's representatives when they arrived home. "Our delegates" he wrote his beloved Blanche Butler, "are loud in denouncing the cowardice of the convention. It failed to endorse the civil rights bill! Instead of building up respect for Southern Republicanism they have drawn down upon it ... the contempt people ever bestow on a pusillanimity."[150] Ames had a point. But Clayton was right. Public opinion must be the battleground. "Public opinion is stronger than the law." The laws they hoped to pass, including the civil rights law, needed the public's backing. Their mistake lay in entrusting that hope to the public's virtue. "The sublime sense of right and justice that characterizes the American people" proved a feeble friend. It wept for the southern white man, and overlooked his trespasses.[151]

Initially at least the Chattanooga Convention caused cold terror in Democratic officialdom. Perhaps they should hold a gathering of their own, a counter-outrage convention, "a convention of the white people of the South," to demonstrate their equal commitment to peace and justice. "The good results of an address to the people of the United States by such a Convention cannot be questioned," suggested the Mobile *Register*.[152] The proposal came from the hard-pressed Governor of Tennessee, John C. Brown, and his colleague Preston Leslie of Kentucky. It was endorsed by the editor of the Louisville *Courier-Journal*, Henry Watterson. First they conceived of a convention featuring all the Democratic governors of the South. Those statesmen would issue a preemptive proclamation, "resisting the anticipated incendiary pronunciamento of that partisan cabal [the Chattanooga convention]."[153]

Watterson and Leslie met Governor Brown at Nashville on October 3. By then, however, they had consulted with colleagues. They found some, notably Coke of Texas and Kemper of Virginia, unenthusiastic. Such a conference might be counterproductive, serving only to dignify the Republicans' conclave. Brown

149 New Orleans *Republican*, October 20, 1874.

150 Blanche Butler Ames, *Chronicles from the Nineteenth Century: Family Letters of Blanche Butler and Adelbert Ames* (Clinton, Mass., 1957), vol. 2, 29–30.

151 "The great putty-hearted public," Mark Twain called it, "that always turns around and weeps for an odious murderer, and prays for him." Mark Twain and Charles Dudley Warner, *The Gilded Age: A Tale of To-Day* (Hartford: 1899), vol. 2: 133.

152 Mobile *Register*, October 2, 1874.

153 Louisville *Courier-Journal*, October 4, 1874.

and Leslie suggested enlarging their convention to include all Democratic governors, North and South. Then they considered a national convention, uniting all governors of all states of the United States. They could neutralize the Chattanooga "mongrels" with "a calm, earnest and patriotic discussion of the broader questions of conflict between the State and Federal jurisdiction."[154] None of these plans came to pass. Nobody, except the beleaguered governors of Tennessee and Kentucky, in the heat of an election season, was in the mood for a national reconciliation conference.

They need not have worried. The Chattanooga convention's "pronunciamento" fizzled. Press coverage slanted toward the Democrats. An editor for the Associated Press massaged his copy before sending it out to ridicule the Republicans' appeals.[155] Few newspapers championed the Chattanooga call, or cared even to admit the justice of its protests. In the South it was simply dismissed as a convention of liars. Democrats commenced to laugh. Republicans pronouncing upon persecuted southerners was like Jesse James sitting on a coroner's jury to deliberate over the corpses of his victims.[156] The Democratic Brooklyn *Eagle* defied the public to believe one word that came from the mouth of such men as Powell Clayton and his carpetbagger friends.

> Their scurviness, thievery, poltroonery, mendacity, and utter infamy are well apprehended by both parties. They are known as the inciters of the late slaves to indolence, rapine and communism. They are known as the robbers of States, as the burglars of governments.... An emetic thrown into the deepest hell would bring up their superiors.[157]

The Republicans' convention, said Henry Ward Beecher's *Christian Union,* was a stew of rotten elements, "the carpet-bagger and the fluent negro." The best policy was the pursuit of benign neglect. Let the murders play out. Eventually the murderers would stop. "Let there be no useless exasperation of the whites, and no blow at the public school system by passage of the Civil Rights Bill."[158]

On the fringe ridicule went further. The New York *Day-Book,* published by the incurably racist Dr. John H. Van Evrie, announced a scoop. The "outrages" were a government conspiracy, a disinformation campaign. Federal agents in

---

154 Louisville *Courier-Journal,* October 4; Nashville *Banner,* October 4; Chicago *Tribune,* October 5, 1874.

155 Mark Wahlgren Summers, *The Press Gang: Newspapers and Politics, 1865–1878* (Chapel Hill: 1994), 220–221.

156 Little Rock *Gazette,* October 18, 1874.

157 Quoted in Knoxville *Press and Herald,* October 20, 1874.

158 *Christian Union,* October 14, 1874, p. 290; October 21, p. 315.

the Attorney-General's office fabricated fanciful stories of massacred blacks and Republicans, "dressed up in the strongest colors and sent out to the country." The Justice Department operated the scheme with the help of the Treasury Department, to which it had lent a slush fund of $100,000. The Treasury Department in return unleashed the Secret Service. Clandestine agents prowled about the south, ostensibly to infiltrate Ku-Klux cells but actually to organize them, "to inveigle wild young men into them," and to instigate outrages. Government created terrorists, then hunted down its own creations.[159]

The New York *Tribune* delivered the final blow. It decided to investigate the matter of southern violence. By the time the *Tribune's* investigator was done no compilation from the Committee on Facts and Statistics could redeem the Southern Republicans' cause. The occasion of the *Tribune's* work actually occurred a month before the Chattanooga meeting. This was the publication of the Hays-Hawley Letter. Alabama's Congressman Charles Hays proposed to write, and fellow Republican Congressman Joseph Hawley of Connecticut, owner of the Hartford *Courant*, agreed to publish an open letter, a true account of terrorism in the South. The result emerged, splashed on the front pages of the *Courant* on September 15. The Chattanooga Convention struggled to get out its word. The Hays-Hawley letter spread like wildfire.[160]

Hawley ran Hays' missive under dramatic headlines: "The Temper of the South – Political Murders – The Negroes in a Condition Worse than that of Slavery – Death to Republicans, White and Black." Hays' urgent prose matched the headlines' promise. "To-day riots, murders, assassinations and torturings for the purpose of terrorizing the true friends of the government are more common than they have been at any hour since Lee surrendered to Grant." Hays listed a litany of outrages, lurid, circumstantial accounts.

> We see our comrades swept away like chaff before the wind. Every midnight breeze brings to us the dying groans of some man who has fallen in the cause of right and liberty.... The faithful old slaves who fell upon their knees at New Years' dawn 1863 ... are now begging and imploring to be put back into slavery to protect themselves and their little ones from murder and destruction. Many, many of my old slaves have come to me

159 Quitman, Georgia, *Independent*, September 12, 1874. On Dr. Van Evrie and his diligently distorted journal, the *Day Book*, see Forrest G. Wood, *Black Scare: The Racist Response to Emancipation and Reconstruction* (Berkeley: 1968), 35–36.

160 William W. Rogers, "Reconstruction Journalism: The Hays-Hawley Letter, A Sensational Letter to the *Hartford Courant* Ignites a National Controversy," *American Journalism*, 7 (1989): 235–244; *Black-Belt Scalawag: Charles Hays and Southern Republicans During Reconstruction* (Athens, Ga., 1993), 105–115.

> and begged me to take them back and save them from the reign of the drunken desperado and the midnight marauder. I am powerless to help them, but as long as life lasts let me appeal to my northern friends to stand by and protect these sable sons of the south.... Shall I not bear to my persecuted people of all races and colors the glad tidings that a better day is dawning?[161]

Newspapers printed the Hays-Hawley letter and reprinted it. Republican papers hailed it as proof of persecution. The New York *Times* gave it credence. Finally, it seemed, Republicans had reached the reluctant heart of the northern public. Then doubts set in. Fact checkers set to work. Parts of Hays' narrative appeared questionable. Some incidents he had exaggerated, others misrepresented. One murder victim popped up to pronounce himself alive and well. Horace Redfield expressed reservations: "I conceive that the truth is about midway between what the Democrats declare to be the truth and what is contained in Hays' statement. This makes the condition of affairs bad enough in all conscience. Let us make it no worse."[162]

The *Tribune* announced it would get to the bottom of the story. It dispatched its ace reporter, Washington correspondent Zebulon L. White, on a mission to the South. White's first article, sent from Alabama, set the tone – headline: "A Slandered State." Hays' so-called outrages were nonsense, a calculated distraction, lies created to keep Republicans in power. There was no bloodbath of blacks. Hays himself and others of his ilk perpetuated bloodshed. They incited the Negroes: "Always the raw head and bloody bones; always this sort of appeal to the passion, the hate, the rancor, and the bitterness of the war that ended more than nine years ago. Is it always to go on? Never to cease?"[163]

Meanwhile the Chattanooga Convention had met and pursued its endeavors to document the terror. Zeb White calmly poured cold water on it all. On October 17 he headed his column "Alabama at Peace." Only two of the pretended outrages, the Billings and Ivey murders, were real. Those were isolated incidents. The profoundest peace prevailed. Blacks were "contented and unmolested." Hays had cited the reports of Captain William Mills of the 2nd Infantry stationed at Livingston. In dispatches to Secretary of War William Belknap, Mills drew a picture of roving, uncontrolled bands of white marauders bearing terror to the countryside, defying the efforts of his small command to suppress their activities. White, the reporter, questioned Mills. His conclusion: the

161 Rogers, "Hays-Hawley Letter," 241–243; *Black-Belt Scalawag*, 111–113.

162 Cincinnati *Commercial*, October 1, 1874.

163 New York *Tribune*, October 9, 1874.

captain was a coward. His dispatches amounted to no more than alarmist communiqués concocted by a cringing officer fearful of a non-existent enemy.

White proceeded further into Alabama. He interviewed Treasury Department detectives Hester and Beach, sent to hunt for the killers of Billings and Ivey. He dismissed their evidence along with that of Capt. Mills. He discounted facts he himself had counted. Billings, a Republican politician, just happened to be murdered while returning from a political meeting. No robbery had occurred. White found those facts irrelevant. Outlaws often killed for obscure reasons, for no reasons at all, or just for sport.

Tom Ivey's death? Unconnected to terror. It was only a bit of drunken mischief. Racist sentiment regrettably existed. When it mixed with whiskey it led to regrettable acts. "Ivey was killed because he was a nigger." His outspoken opinion, his call for the Civil Rights Bill and consequent death threats, were merely coincidental.[164]

Even Julia Hayden died for innocent reasons. If she had not insisted on being so pretty she could have avoided her fate. Black women, Zeb White was informed, were known for promiscuity; they were "wanting in chastity." Julia's assailants, white men yet again in an excusable state of inebriation, assumed she would gratify them if they called upon her in the night. One of the boys, fogged by liquor, indulged in a casual parting shot. "It was a reckless, fiendish thing to do and the men engaged in it ought to be punished as they probably will be." But no harm intended.[165]

Finally the reporter came full circle. Terrorism existed in the South: Republican terrorism. Blacks lived serenely; whites cowered in fear.[166] Based on White's reportage the *Tribune* called for a congressional investigation. The public must demand a halt to crimes committed against unoffending white people, "the lies of Charles Hays, the vaporings of the Department of Justice,

164 New York *Tribune*, October 22, 1874.

165 New York *Tribune*, October 27, 1874. The perpetrators' actual aims remain uncertain, since they failed to gain access to Julia. On the organized and ritualized use of rape by the southern night-riding fraternity, its social and political motivations, see Hannah Rosen, *Terror in the Heart of Freedom: Citizenship, Sexual Violence, and the Meaning of Race in the Postemancipation South* (Chapel Hill: 2009), 202–221.

166 Later it came to light that the intrepid reporter had helped the cowering whites. While chatting with Capt. Mills and others he gathered information on army movements. This he passed along to white militia. Summers, *Press Gang*, 201–205: "White's letters made convincing propaganda for the other side, and undoubtedly that was how he designed them. For propaganda they were, from the by-line to the headline."

the feigned terror."[167] Republicans seethed. They had been outplayed. Roscoe Conkling vented his frustration in a letter to Gerrit Smith:

> Was there ever since Satan began to sin a case of more perverse and wretched outlandishness than this conduct of the southern men? ... And then if you or I speak the truth about it even to suggest remedies, as a physician must consider the nature of the disorder to be cured, we are reviving the war, and the gospel of hate.... I sometimes wonder if right and wrong may not sometime come to be regarded as wholly conventional.[168]

Zebulon White returned to Washington. On the train he met an affable gentleman who seemed eager to chat. They parted at the Potomac station. As the reporter turned away, his companion called out: Are you, by the way, the author of those articles in the *Tribune*? He had time to answer, yes. His hands encumbered by valises, he had no time to obstruct the gentleman's fist. Shortly afterwards one dazed newsman collected himself from the platform. One impenitent congressman, Charles Hays, left the scene in police custody.[169] By then the elections were over. The country turned a deaf ear to the Republicans' tales of woe. The press wars left them beaten.[170] A few months later Charles Nordhoff of the *Herald* visited Louisiana. In the land of Colfax and Coushatta

---

167 New York *Tribune*, October 31, 1874. The New York *Times* also unleashed its bloodhounds. Its special correspondent, the young, consummately cultured Howard Carroll, relished his first independent assignment. He reported from Montgomery. None of "Mr. Reign-of-Terror Hays'" tales were true. "The people of this State are being denounced as a set of blood-thirsty cut-throats, whose chief delight is to shoot white Republicans, and who have less regard for negroes than most men have for stray dogs. No one who will come to Alabama and travel among the people can fail to discover that these statements are untrue in every respect.... There is absolutely no excitement and no fear." He recorded a jailhouse interview with Stephen Renfro, accused assassin of Walter Billings. Renfro, he found, was a kindly, God-fearing man, a family man, tearfully languishing, unable even to assist his wife who had just given birth to their first son. Finally the reporter quoted "an old negro." Asked his opinion of the outrages, he cogitated. "Looking up from the ground upon which he was working, he said: 'I don't know noffen 'bout 'rages ... the pork ain't no ways so fat as it used to be, that's the only trouble wid this 'ere nigger.'" Paucity of pork; such was Howard Carroll's conclusion. New York *Times*, October 24, 1874.

168 Roscoe Conkling to Gerrit Smith, October 6, 1874. Gerrit Smith Papers, Syracuse University.

169 Harrisburg *Patriot*, November 21; Mobile *Register*, November 28, 1874.

170 New Hampshire Congressman Henry Blair summed up the Democrats' winning public relations strategy: "A pestiferous demagoguery, a false pretense to personal and political virtue and capacity, and deafening shouts for 'peace,' 'peace,' at the South, when there is no peace but in the grave." Henry W. Blair, *Free Schools – Are They in Danger? If So, From What Source? Speech of Hon. Henry W. Blair of New Hampshire in the House of Representatives, Saturday, July 29, 1876* (Washington: 1876), 18.

he found an oasis of repose. No terrorism existed, or had existed. "No one pretends that murder is practiced for political purposes."[171]

The summer of 1874 left an atmosphere charged with bitter feeling. Charles Sumner's poisoned legacy contributed to a witch's brew of fear and violence. Horace Redfield had warned of it. The Civil Rights Bill "has produced its legitimate fruits."[172] In October General Irvin McDowell, commanding the Department of the South, sent his annual report from headquarters in Louisville. Since the passage of the Senate's Civil Rights Bill, he concluded, violence had spread decisively. He called for more troops.[173]

Ulysses Grant too felt the storm rising. Letters filled the White House mail. One arrived from black citizens of LaGrange, Georgia. Inside the sealed envelope was a second communication, a clandestine letter. It came from their brethren at Tipton: "We don't sign No Names because the White men Mighty Catch up with us. We says to you the White men is fixing for war evry day & tells us to Lookout for ourselves for they Exspects to kill us all out." They named no names. But they named their fear. "We knows whats the matter with them this Civil right Bill is the cause of it."[174]

Two weeks later Grant heard from a white correspondent. Theodore Nunn of Autaugaville, Alabama, signed his name. He had fought for the Confederacy, he informed the President. He was now, "after subjugation, very Reluctantley, a faithful citizen." But beware. Faithfulness had limits. Civil rights tested those limits.

> Sir… I want peace and I want no rupture in this government and I intend to do all I can to have peace. But allow me to say that I fear the actions of the Administration, the 14 & 15 amendments, and worse than all the Civil Rights Bill … which in my opinion will never be until after some of the worst Tragedies that has ever been Performed will be and let me beg of you as our Ruler to stop and reflect before it is too late.[175]

On September 19, *Harper's Weekly* ran another of its double-page illustrations. Thomas Nast gave his work a dramatic caption: "The Same Old Pirate Afloat

171 Charles Nordhoff, *The Cotton States in the Spring and Summer of 1875*: 68. Also Summers, *Press Gang*, 192: "On the special correspondents would lie a heavy responsibility for the loss of faith in the Reconstruction experiment in general and in the Negro voter in particular."

172 Toledo *Daily Blade*, September 21, 1874.

173 New York *Herald*, October 31, 1874.

174 A. Feeny et al. to Ulysses Grant, September 2, 1874. *Papers of Ulysses S. Grant*, vol. 25, 189.

175 Theodore Nunn to Ulysses Grant, September 20, 1874. *Papers*, vol. 25, 196.

ILLUSTRATION 8 The "New Alabama"
SOURCE: THOS. NAST, *HARPER'S WEEKLY*, SEPTEMBER 19, 1874

Again." (see Illustration 8) In the foreground he sketched the pirate ship, its bowsprit rushing outward upon the viewer. It flew the black flag; its motto: "This is a White Man's Government." On deck, one sailor aimed a cannon. Another trampled the American flag. On the ship's side its name: "New Alabama," the old Confederate commerce raider reborn, emblazoned beneath the emblem of a phoenix rising from its ashes. Written on the ashes was the word "Slavery." Off at the horizon another ship emerged, flying the national flag, wreathed in smoke, guns firing. A great black shell crossed the sky, headed for the New Alabama. On the projectile's cylinder a penciled greeting: "Equal Rights to All."[176] In Thomas Nast's vision battle lines were set. When the smoke of battle cleared, when the long hot summer was over – when the elections of 1874 concluded – the Republicans' ship had sunk. Had the Civil Rights Bill sunk with it?

---

176 *Harper's Weekly*, September 19, 1874, 776–777.

CHAPTER 7

The Shirt of Nessus: Elections in Georgia, North Carolina, Virginia

"The Civil Rights Bill," declared David M. Nelson, beleaguered Republican candidate in the Third District of Tennessee, "hangs on the party like the Shirt of Nessus."[1] Col. Nelson did not go to Congress. His campaign was soon forgotten. Yet in one cutting remark he encapsulated the maddening civil rights dilemma of Republicans everywhere. The Shirt of Sumner consumed their flesh, a poisoned garment incinerating all who wore it. Nor could it be removed.[2] It clung to the party, as to Hercules, no matter how a candidate might tear it off.

No one doubted it; 1874 was bound to be a losing year for Republicans. Midterm elections seldom express gratitude to the incumbent party. This year the public seemed especially ungrateful. The New York *Herald* foretold a sad slide into "an exhausted and sleepy sunset."[3] The *World* predicted extinction.

> The unhonored carcass of Radicalism now lies out in the fields, putrid, swollen, poisonous, fit food for the beaks of the vultures that swarm around it and the jackals that gather to the banquet. Men will long hold their noses and cry "Pah!" … A party that has outlived itself and survived only to plunder and destroy shall shrink into nothingness and be forgotten.[4]

Party managers expected a heavy toll. They prepared for a loss of sixty seats in the House.[5] They hoped only to retain some majority. Even this sober assessment under-estimated the disaster.

1 Chattanooga *Times*, October 31, 1874. The *Times'* text reads as printed, "hangs on the Democratic party like the shirt of Nessus," undoubtedly a copy error.

2 The haberdashery in question, fashioned, according to the lore of ancient Greece, by Nessus the centaur, and being impregnated with the corrosive poison of the Hydra's blood, possessed the peculiarity of dissolving the body of its wearers. Once worn it was impossible to remove without also removing the flesh beneath. Thus had it destroyed the mighty Hercules after his wife Deianira unwittingly slipped it on him.

3 New York *Herald*, January 1, 1874.

4 New York *World*, May 15, 1874.

5 Cincinnati *Commercial*, August 31, 1874.

Various ingredients contributed to the recipe of Republican distress: the nation's seemingly incurable economic woes; third-term unpleasantness; above all the persistent perception that corruption had crept into the fiber of government haunted the campaigns of the venal and upright alike. The ship of state, worm-eaten within, was crumbling.[6] A sour mood lay heavy on incumbents of all stripes.

Another irritant fed the public's sour mood: the "Salary-Grab." That legislative disaster was the final iniquity of the 42nd Congress. On March 4, 1873, with one foot out the door, congressmen voted themselves an increase in compensation. Their take-home pay rose from $5,000 to $7,500 annually and, unconscionably, that remuneration was retroactive; departing members "grabbed" an immediate gift of $2,500. A pay raise in the midst of an economic recession, one correspondent wrote to George Frisbie Hoar, "the behavior of Congress certainly shows that there are a number of gentlemen who cannot see many feet beyond their own desks."[7] Too late the 43rd Congress voted a hasty repeal, hoping to put the matter out of mind. The public did not forget. "This year is likely to be memorable for the 'slaughter of the innocents,'" growled the Portland, Maine, *Argus*, "those innocent light-fingered salary-grabbers who coolly put their hands into the people's treasury and took out more than a million of dollars."[8]

A stagnant economy, salary-grabs, sour anti-incumbency, all figured in the recipe for Republican defeat. Furthermore, thanks to the 1872 election, Republicans were bloated. They occupied more seats in Congress than their voter strength entitled them to occupy. For that unwarranted proliferation Horace Greeley could be blamed. Nominated by the Liberal Republicans, Greeley received the reluctant co-endorsement of the Democratic Party. Democratic voters did not surge to the polls to vote for him. Republicans woke on post-election

6 "The storm that makes the waves boil and the masts crack has less danger in it than the borer gnawing unnoticed in the dark, or the dry rot creeping silently and stealthily from plank to plank … the subtle corruption that eats out the heart of popular institutions." Gallatin, Missouri, *Democrat*, May 14, 1874.

7 Charles H. Doe to Hoar, January 4, 1874. George F. Hoar Papers, Massachusetts Historical Society.

8 Quoted in Chicago *Tribune*, August 15, 1874. Politicians protested. "I certainly do not claim to have been free from error," Alfred Waddell of North Carolina placed a card in the press. "If you can find a representative who will never make a mistake, you ought by all means to get him, but a search-warrant in the hands of every Constable in the District would fail, I think, to discover such a candidate." Wilmington *Journal*, April 9, 1874. Humorist Josh Billings quipped, "wealth won't make a man virtuous, but there ain't anybody who wants to be poor just for the purpose of being good."

morning, after an epic landslide, to find themselves with a host of accidental congressmen. They could return only with difficulty.[9]

Harbingers came early. In certain states local elections preceded the summer and fall canvasses.[10] On January 2, citizens of Memphis elected a Republican mayor, John Loague. A few weeks later Philadelphians re-elected Mayor William S. Stokely over Liberal Republican Alexander McClure. The New York *Herald* conceded Republicans "a crumb of comfort."[11] The crumb crumbled. In March New Hampshire voters reversed a Republican majority to elect Democrat James A. Weston governor. He was only the second Democratic win there since 1856; he was the last until 1912. On April 6, Connecticut voters re-elected Democratic governor Charles R. Ingersoll and swept both houses of the legislature. They assured themselves the Senate seat of the retiring William Buckingham. Handwriting appeared on the wall.

Amid all the variables of this lengthy, unpromising election season, Republicans faced the civil rights dilemma. Sumner laid the Shirt of Nessus on the party's back. The Senate had put one arm through. Would the party pin the corrosive cloth onto its candidates? Or would it ignore, avoid, dismiss that poisonous object? Two events signaled the start of campaign season. On civil rights they sent conflicting messages.

On July 16 the Republican National Congressional Committee broadcast its platform "To the People of the United States." That manifesto represented the fruit of the joint House-Senate Republican caucus that had met on June 8. On that occasion, it may be recalled, John Roy Lynch had urged the party to move forward on civil rights. Also on that occasion the members agreed, on a motion of Henry Starkweather, to put before the people a unified statement. A Platform Committee of forty members set to work.[12] The document's principal author was Wisconsin's Senator Timothy Howe.

9 Richard Allan Gerber, *The Liberal Republicans of 1872*, Ph.D. Diss., University of Michigan, 1967. See also Lawrence Grossman, *The Democratic Party and the Negro: Northern and National Politics, 1868–1892* (Urbana: 1976), 34–35, 43.

10 Elections for Congress spread over a lengthy period. The first canvass commenced in Oregon on June 1. North Carolina held its election on August 6. Ohio and Indiana, along with Iowa and Nebraska, voted on October 13. Most of those remaining voted on the 3rd of November. New Hampshire, Connecticut, Rhode Island, California and Mississippi did not vote until 1875.

11 New York *Herald*, January 3, 1874.

12 Among them were senators Logan, Chandler and Cameron, Clayton, Stewart, West, Spencer, Conover and Flanagan. Its House contingent included friends of the Civil Rights Bill – Eugene Hale of Maine, Richard Whiteley of Georgia, George McKee of Mississippi, John Coburn of Indiana – and adversaries, Jacob Thornburgh of Tennessee, James Lofland of

The final product appeared in papers across the country. The New York *Times* printed it, six dense columns of type, on the front pages. In those columns it covered all points of public interest. It laid out the Republican program on issues economic, social, and political. It looked back to attack the Democratic record of forty years. It looked ahead to describe the party's goals. Its position on the Civil Rights Bill required careful reading – in the sixth column of six, under a brief heading, "Our Mission Not Ended:"

> The Fourteenth Amendment to the Constitution is not yet enforced by "appropriate legislation." Millions of American citizens are denied even the common law rights of locomotion because they are black. If such wrongs are to be redressed the Republican party alone can do it.[13]

That was it. The words undeniably endorsed the Civil Rights Bill. On the other hand the party hardly proclaimed that pledge from the rooftops. The Republicans' wise men thought to rest the Shirt of Nessus lightly upon their candidates. Democrats were not fooled. They zeroed in on the three fatal sentences. "The Republican Party Pledged to Civil Rights!" screamed the headline of the Goldsboro, North Carolina, *Messenger*: "'Millions of American citizens are denied their rights because they are black! The Republican party alone can redress those wrongs.' Aye, very true, it's the Republican party alone will ever redress these fancied wrongs by bending the necks of the white men of the South and inaugurating a reign of Negroism in our midst."[14]

Two weeks later, on July 31, Indiana Senator Oliver P. Morton issued his campaign declaration. He did not soft-peddle civil rights. The RNCC whispered. Oliver Morton shouted. The senator appeared before an overflow crowd at the Terre Haute Opera House. He abandoned his crutches and sat to read from a chair in the middle of the stage. For an hour and a half Morton held forth. He reserved a great blast for opponents of the Civil Rights Bill. The Terre Haute *Express* headlined: "A Noble Plea For Civil Rights."[15] The Democratic Party, Morton declared, had "gone down upon its knees to the prejudices against color and the hatred of the negro." In his own name and that of his colleague Senator Pratt he denounced those prejudices. Social equality was a "bugbear" that Democrats used to frighten babies. Morton defended even mixed schools.

Delaware, Horace Strait of Minnesota. There were civil rights waverers, California's Sherman Houghton and Clinton Cobb of North Carolina.

13 New York *Times*, July 16, 1874.

14 Goldsboro, *Carolina Messenger*, July 20, 1874.

15 Terre Haute *Express*, August 1, 1874; see William D. Foulke, *Life of Oliver P. Morton, Including his Important Speeches* (Indianapolis: 1899), vol. 2, 344–348.

> What harm would these colored children do in the public school? They would interrupt nobody, though in many places they would be the victims of insult and oppression. The man who would say that under such circumstances these colored children must grow up without education, to be poor, ignorant, helpless and perhaps vicious throughout their lives, simply because it would be offensive to have them go into the same school house with white children, himself needs some education in the principles of our common humanity.[16]

Morton's speech resonated beyond Indiana and into the nation. Other senators – Logan in Illinois, Frelinghuysen in New Jersey, Sherman in Ohio – followed Morton's lead. State parties constructed their platforms. Those platforms revealed the judgment of Republican leaders, the benefits, or dangers, they perceived in the Civil Rights Bill.

Massachusetts gave the measure its heartiest welcome. The Republican convention met at Worcester on October 7. Henry Dawes spoke: Massachusetts had a sacred legacy to the civil rights bill, which she could not barter away nor entrust to any unfriendly keeping.[17] Elsewhere in New England the issue was moot. Few black persons existed. Neither party bothered to mention it in their platforms.

New York presented a less clear-cut situation. For the moment Republicans held the legislature and boasted a sitting governor. The coming election overturned their control and handed the statehouse by a landslide to Democrat Samuel J. Tilden. Republicans met at Utica on September 23. Ex-governor Edwin D. Morgan took the chair. Governor Dix and Lieutenant-Governor Robinson received re-nomination. On civil rights the convention adopted a disinterested posture. It contented itself with denouncing southern violence. It called for federal protection of all rights under the law.[18]

Democrats had a harder time. New York was not Tennessee. They could not condemn civil rights outright. New York was not Massachusetts. They could not praise it openly. Their convention met at Syracuse on September 16. The Platform Committee, guided by ex-governor Horatio Seymour and journalist Manton Marble, dodged the problem neatly. Resolution 6 called for "equal and exact justice to all men; no partial legislation." The second half of the

---

16 Terre Haute *Express*, August 1, 1874.

17 Springfield, Massachusetts, *Republican*, October 8, 1874. Even Democrats gave civil rights a friendly nod in Massachusetts. They could not in good conscience endorse the bill. But they endorsed the idea. Their resolution called for "equal political rights for all races, colors and conditions of men."

18 New York *Tribune*, September 24, 1874.

statement cancelled out the first half – a sly locution designed to shoot down the Civil Rights Bill without mentioning its name. The problem with that bill was its partiality. It favored one race at the expense of the other. Equal justice, yes. Partial legislation, no. No Civil Rights Bill. In the delicately-balanced world of New York politics Democrats wriggled around the issue.

New Jersey appeared more problematic. Senator Frelinghuysen embraced the bill. Fellow Republicans hesitated. They met at Trenton on August 27. The platform dodged all controversies. Republicans of the State of New Jersey confined themselves to state issues. For all else they referred voters to the party address: "We deem it unnecessary to advert to national questions, further than to declare that we approve and will continue to uphold the principles upon which the Republican party was founded."[19]

New Jersey Democrats advertised their opposition. They met on September 15. Judge Joseph Bedle took the nomination for governor. Ex-governor Theodore Randolph wrote the platform. The fifth resolution made it clear. "Born of vindictive partisanship, intended for humiliation, the passage and enforcement of the Civil Rights bill would foment the worst passions of both races, give pretext for constant Federal interference, and indefinitely delay the return of peace and prosperity."[20]

In Pennsylvania both sides staked out firm positions. Democrats delighted in an issue that would help their cause. Republicans met them boldly. The Democrats convened at Pittsburgh on August 26, with State Senator William A. Wallace at their head. Resolution 6 disposed of the Civil Rights Bill: "a gross invasion of the right of the States to control their domestic concerns in their own way."[21] Republicans met at Harrisburg on August 19. State Chairman Russell Errett and Philadelphia District Attorney William B. Mann defied the opposition: "Equality of civil rights having been guaranteed by the fourteenth amendment, it is the imperative duty of Congress to see that such guarantee is enforced by appropriate statutes."[22] Pennsylvanians faced a clear choice.

Likewise in Ohio the issue was fairly joined. Democrats gathered at Columbus on August 26. Resolution 10 stated the case. "While we admit the equality of all persons before the law, we protest against the attempts of the Radicals in Congress to enforce social equality by unconstitutional pains and penalties."[23] Republicans refused to back down. Ex-governor Edward Noyes spoke: "The colored people are degraded and oppressed from generation to generation.... The colored man should be permitted to eat and sleep and travel whithersoever

19 Paterson *Press*, August 28, 1874.
20 Paterson *Press*, September 16, 1874.
21 Harrisburg *Patriot*, August 28, 1874.
22 Harrisburg *Patriot*, August 20, 1874.
23 Chicago *Tribune*, August 27, 1874.

he will, entitled to the same privileges as others, and protected by the same law that is over us all."[24]

In Indiana Democrats threw down the gauntlet. Oliver Morton picked it up and flung it back. Morton's fellow Republicans ran scared. Their convention at Indianapolis on June 17 featured a keynote speech by future president Benjamin Harrison. He made no mention of the Civil Rights Bill. Nor did the platform bring it up.[25]

Republicans in Illinois, Iowa, Michigan, Minnesota and Nebraska endorsed the bill. Democrats opposed it. Minnesota Democrats adopted the New York formula, copying the phrase down to its slippery semi-colon. In states of the far west few black people resided. One percent of California's population was black. Mixed schools caused some unrest. But racial tension there, as in Oregon and Nevada, focused on the Chinese.

The civil rights battlefield covered the nation. In some sectors, New England, the far west, skirmishing was desultory. War blazed in the South. One fact was constant. Wherever the contaminated garment appeared Republicans marched to their fate. Democrats rejoiced. No one perhaps said it better than the satirical Nasby:

> On nigger we [Democrats] air invulnerable. Why? yoo ask. Becoz he has no frends.... O, bless the Lord for the nigger! He is our tower of strength.[26]

1 Georgia[27]

"Redemption" reached Georgia in 1872.[28] In 1874 some Republicans survived. In August voters reduced them to insignificance in both houses of the state

24 Dayton *Journal*, September 3; Chicago *Tribune*, September 3, 1874.

25 Indianapolis *Journal*, June 18, 1874.

26 David Ross Locke, *The Struggles ... of Petroleum V. Nasby* (Boston, 1873): 97.

27 We cannot in what follows analyze or describe the contests in 290 congressional districts across the nation, not only an unmanageable but an unwarranted task. The question to which we aim is, how did those elections, the campaigns experienced by the candidates, affect their subsequent votes on the civil rights issue? We focus therefore on Republican districts, particularly those held by sitting members, members who would return to reconsider a vote on the Civil Rights Bill. In some states the question was muted. In others an unbalanced political situation allowed the issue little play. Absence or inadequacy of sources prevents consideration of some districts. Mississippi and California voted in 1875; the civil rights contest was past. We present a cross-section, albeit, we hope, a comprehensive cross-section, of the relevant and observable districts to judge the elections' impact on the act for civil rights.

28 See Alan Conway, *The Reconstruction of* Georgia (Minneapolis: 1966); C. Mildred Thompson, *Reconstruction In Georgia: Economic, Social, Political 1865–1872* (New York: 1915);

legislature. The November elections eliminated their remaining congressmen. Republicans themselves reacted with resignation. "The Savannah papers are rejoicing because the Dutch have taken Holland," sighed the Jacksonville *Union*.[29] Violence and intimidation assisted the redemption. A poll tax also helped. This $1 charge, traveling correspondent Charles Nordhoff estimated, effectively disenfranchised two-thirds of Georgia's black voters.[30] Fraud disposed of much of the rest. Some citizens saved up the money, took their precious dollar to the registrars, only to have the payment rejected. Others penetrated that obstacle but found no polls available. Still others made it to the polls, but found access blocked by menacing election monitors.[31] Then there was civil rights. In Atlanta Robert Toombs spoke. The time for submission was over:

> What is that [civil rights]? To put your niggers in your theaters, in these halls, into your churches – stick the nigger even into your own bedchamber.... Fellow-citizens, you have nature. There is a time when free men shall say, "Thus far shalt thou come, and no further!" The time comes when freemen must seize their arms, and live free or not live at all.[32]

Republicans held three districts in the 43rd Congress. (see Map 1, below) No Republican from Georgia entered the 44th Congress. No Georgia Republican entered Congress for a century thereafter.

Judson C. Ward Jr., "Georgia under the Bourbon Democrats, 1872–1890," Diss., Univ. of North Carolina, 1947; Charles E. Wynes, "The Politics of Reconstruction, Redemption, and Bourbonism," in Kenneth Coleman, ed., *A History of Georgia* (Athens: 1991).

29 Jacksonville *Florida Union*, September 10, 1874.

30 Charles Nordhoff, *The Cotton States in the Spring and Summer of 1875* (New York: 1876), 110. Nordhoff was unsympathetic: "This is, I think, perfectly just. Poll and road tax is all that the greater part of them pay toward the support of the Government; and if they evade this, they do not deserve to vote."

31 Black citizens of LaGrange, Georgia, wrote to President Grant. They explained the futility of voting, or attempting to vote, in their locality. "The Democrats, to show that they was not going to give a fair Election, put a large Goods box in the Court house door & nail a rope out on top it turn the hollow side in the Court house shut all the Doors of the court house but the one that the Box was in & put all Democratic managers in side & one on Top the Box to receive Tickets and hand them to them that was in side. Therefore we saw that they was going to rascal us out of the Election. We concluded not to cast a vote. To this end we all left the Polls and never voted at all.... Further more there was several hundred persons tried to pay their Tax So as they could get a chance to vote but could not find the man to pay Tax to and when they did find him he refuse to own his names or take the money for I fail my self to pay my Tax at the proper time and was requested to pay Two Dollars & never got a chance to pay it.... The devil ment that is carried on here I am unable to state. Shall such election as this pass? I ask your honor is you going to suffer to see such pass as a fair Election?" A. Feeny et al. to Ulysses Grant, September 2, 1874. John Y. Simon, *The Papers of Ulysses S. Grant* (Carbondale: 2003), vol. 25, 190.

32 *Harper's Weekly*, February 14, 1874, p. 147.

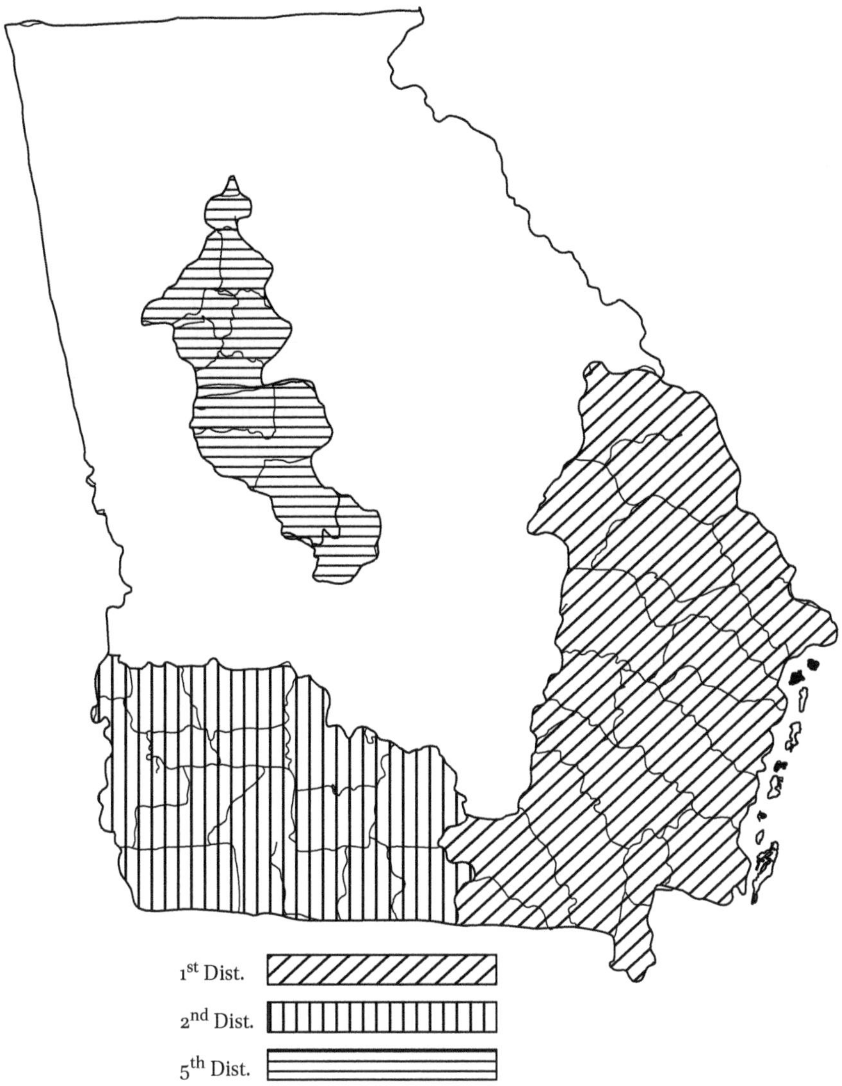

MAP 1 Congressional Districts, Georgia
SOURCE: AUTHORS OF *WELCOMING RUIN*.

Georgia, Fifth District
Joseph G.W. Mills (R), Milton A. Candler (D)
Population: 51% white

The Fifth Georgia District, shaped like an inverted comma, cut across the middle of the state from Fulton County, with the new capital city of Atlanta, south to Houston and Crawford Counties. It included DeKalb County, with the town of Decatur, Clayton County with Jonesboro, and Spalding with its seat at Griffin. The district's population, according to the census of 1870, was 147,257, divided almost evenly between white and black; 71,282 black persons coexisted with 75,975 whites.[33] Fulton County held roughly 15,000 black and 18,000 white residents. Whites dominated most of the remaining areas. Two centers of black population compensated in Houston and Monroe counties.

The privilege of representing this uneasily mixed district belonged to Hon. James C. Freeman. The congressman was 54, bearded, significantly bald, a native Georgian, a native of his district, making his home at Griffin. He was a Republican of moderate inclination. He had in antebellum days exploited the labor of more than a hundred slaves, but he had opposed secession and war. Freeman's margin of victory in 1872, a good year for Republicans, was 279 votes.

Civil rights left James Freeman in a shaky spot, with 49% of his constituency black and 51% white. His inclination was to support the black half of his electors, hoping to supplement it with a sufficient number of white Republicans. But he was wary. In three House calls on civil rights he spoke "Aye" only once. The first procedural vote, on May 25, marked him absent. He responded affirmatively on June 8. On June 20 he absconded again, leaving behind a timid aye paired with a naysayer's nay.

Republicans began their campaign early. The nominating convention met on June 16 at the court house in Griffin, the congressman's home town. James Freeman received the delegates' endorsement on the first ballot, whereupon the result was made unanimous. Harmony and a smooth campaign seemed in order.[34] All did not go smoothly.

On the eve of his nomination, Freeman gave a dinner for supporters at his home. Shocking scenes unfolded. Black men and white men – townspeople

---

33 For all demographic purposes, this study refers to the Census of 1870. This reference requires qualification. To begin, those figures are four years out of date. Comparison with the 1880 count yields no more than an approximation. The censuses themselves, moreover, are inaccurate to differing degrees. That of 1870 remains notorious for perpetrating a severe undercount, especially in the South. Regarding the whites alone, census-takers missed perhaps 10% of the population. Regarding the black population one can only speculate. Counters in 1880 appear to have operated much more rigorously. See J. David Hacker, "A Census-Based Count of the Civil War Dead," *Civil War History*, 57 (2011): 324–325. In addition, the beginnings of black emigration from areas of the South had already begun. Yet the census of 1880 does not record a significant decline in the black population. In noting therefore that 13,708 "colored persons" inhabited Pulaski County, Arkansas, or that only 27 black persons lived in Gilmer County, West Virginia, along with precisely 4,311 whites, the reader should not take it as an infallible enumeration but rather as a general indicator of the demographic, and consequently political, situation in those localities.

34 Bainbridge, Georgia, *Weekly Sun*, July 2, 1874.

saw it clearly through the lit windows – sat and ate together. Word spread. The Griffin *News* ran the story. Two nights later it happened again. Black persons were seen in Freeman's parlor. Some even emerged, lounging on his front porch. The Atlanta *Constitution* broadcast the news. "If he has come home to practice social equality the people want to know it, and we intend they shall know it."[35]

Democrats dove in enthusiastically. They made civil rights the entire focus of the campaign. "We have no choice," the *Constitution* declared. "Our opponents unflinchingly appeal to their constituents in bold advocacy of the sum of all villainies." Freeman's timid civil rights votes made no difference. Democrats pinned on the Shirt of Nessus.

> Our sole hope of crushing this essence of Radical hate and tyranny lies in an overwhelming expression by the people at the polls this fall in favor of the purity and supremacy of the white race. If the autumn elections result in a Democratic House of Representatives, the hands of partizan conspirators will be stayed in their wicked work.... The men or act of men who stand in the way of such a protest should be marked for public scorn, and for political burial that will know no resurrection.[36]

James Freeman got the message. On August 29 he quit the race. He could not endure it, the *Constitution* reported. He could not bear "to swallow the whole hog of civil rights," though he tried. He could not "reconcile himself to its legitimate consequences. The impossibility of dodging the issue ... finally induced his withdrawal in disgust."[37]

Republicans disintegrated. Their convention met again on September 15. Radicals opposed moderates. Blacks quarreled with whites. A new nominee emerged. Joseph George Washington Mills was white, but he pledged support for the Civil Rights Bill. Black delegates applauded. White delegates bolted. An Independent candidate, John L. Conley, appeared. Conley did not support the Civil Rights Bill. Democrats exulted. "When the election day comes," the *Constitution* chirped, "he [Mills] will not muster a respectable corporal's guard.... [Conley] is youthful and aspiring, and it really makes us sad to think how completely he, as well as Mills, will be extinguished."[38]

35 Atlanta *Constitution*, June 23, 1874.
36 Atlanta *Constitution*, August 5, 1874.
37 Atlanta *Constitution*, August 30; Savannah *News*, August 31, 1874.
38 Atlanta *Constitution*, September 18, 1874.

Democrats looked for a candidate. They looked first to Robert Toombs. "General Toombs," the Atlanta *Herald* cried, "could get the nomination in the fifth at any time he wants it, by simply stretching out his hands and taking it." Toombs' hands, however, were ineligible. He had been stripped of his American citizenship. He refused to petition for its restoration. Nor did he want to go to Congress. "If every man, woman, and child in this district was to rise and press it upon me, I would not take it. I hate the Government of the United States."[39]

Democrats looked again. Milton A. Candler accepted the honor. He was 37, during the war a member of the Confederate Congress. He had served after the war as a state senator from Decatur. In 1868 he achieved celebrity with his call for the expulsion from that body of all his non-white colleagues. That did not happen. But the comment raised Candler's profile and his party's enthusiasm for his further political advancement.[40] Candidate Candler kicked off his campaign with a splendid barbecue. A crowd of more than 2,000 assembled in the fields before the railroad depot at Decatur. "Many fair women" appeared, "to do honor to Milt Candler, whom they all love." For that female contingent Milt had a message. He wove a singular word into his discourse: degradation.

> They [Republicans] emancipated the slaves, gave them the franchise, and now seek to degrade the whites to their level.... They seek the passage of the so-called civil rights bill or more truly a social rights bill.... Their hatred extends to old and young; they have no respect for sex or age; they aim not to elevate the negro but to degrade the whites ... degrading the high to the lowest debasement.[41]

Sordid contact with black persons; no escape permitted, enforced by law.

> You are to meet with them in every public place, hotels, railroads, public schools, churches, social gatherings, in fact entitling them to full and equal privilege of every other citizen, no matter what his race or standing.... You shall be *together* in contact. You shall not be able to say to a negro when he takes a seat by your wife or daughter that you object.... Omnipotent congress declares it to be a crime for you to say to a man, "I don't want you in my house."

39 Forty-Third Congress, 2nd Session, House Report 262: 226.
40 Alan Conway, *The Reconstruction of Georgia* (Minneapolis: 1966), 165–166.
41 Atlanta *Constitution*, September 10, 1874.

"There are but two sides to this question," he reached a simple conclusion. "You must be either for us or against us. No white man will be found against us."

John Conley dropped out. It didn't matter. Milton Candler's victory in a district divided almost evenly between blacks and whites came in at a landslide of 6,177 votes. Not a single county recorded a Republican majority. Fulton, where the black vote should have roughly equaled the white, handed Democrats a 2,000 vote edge. Houston County, 75% black, returned a white majority of 400 votes. In Monroe County, two-thirds black, Candler enjoyed a 537 vote advantage. Terrorism held down Republican numbers.[42] The poll tax siphoned off votes. But those expedients were already standard procedure. Freeman had overcome them in 1872. The destruction wrought by the Civil Rights Bill tore apart the Republican campaign. It provided Milton Candler a splendid success.

Georgia, First District
John E. Bryant (R), Julian Hartridge (D), Jesse Wimberly (I)
Population: 53% black

Georgia's 1st District presented Republicans a problem. Black voters comprised a majority of 53%. That was too little, given the Democrats' expertise in voter suppression. But it was too much to neglect the question of Civil Rights.

The 1st District sprawled across the state's southeast, from Burke and Screven Counties through the city of Savannah, to Camden, Clinch and Echols on the Florida border. Eight of its eighteen counties held a black majority. Burke County possessed 18,000 inhabitants, three-quarters of them black. Camden, Bryan, McIntosh and Chatham Counties sheltered large populations of emancipated persons. And yet, in every election since the war the 1st had returned a solid white Democratic majority. The election of 1872 was no exception. But this time the fraud was too blatant.[43] Republicans contested the official count. The House Committee on Elections overturned the results. Republican Andrew Sloan took the oath of office on March 24, 1874, four months into the session.

42 Man-eating catfish, the Galveston *News* explained. "Georgia KuKlux report the frequent mysterious disappearance of colored men. The catfish in the Chattahoochee this season are so large and voracious that they run away with hook, line, darky and all." Galveston *News*, June 6, 1875.

43 Certified returns accorded Democrat Morgan Rawls the usual majority. Among other expedients the State Board of Canvassers had coolly discounted three precincts in Chatham County where Republicans polled 1,239 votes and Democrats 2. See Chester H. Rowell, *A Historical and Legal Digest of All the Contested Election Cases in the House of Representatives of the United States from the First to the Fifty-Sixth Congress, 1789–1901* (Washington, D.C., House Document 510, Fifty-sixth Congress, Second Session, 1902), 288–290.

Congressman Sloan was 29, possessed of a modest record of public service as assistant collector of customs and United States District Attorney in Savannah. His civil rights opinions also left a slim trail. He could not ignore the 53% of his constituents of African ancestry. But he could be sure that their votes would diminish at election time. Nor could he assume that the Democrats' fraud would be as maladroit in 1874 as in 1872. He could afford nothing tending to antagonize the white minority that delivered a majority of counted votes. His own votes on the Civil Rights Bill evidenced his perplexity. The first procedural call, on May 25, marked him absent. On June 8 he voted "aye." On June 20 the record marked him absent.

Andrew Sloan returned to Savannah still hopeful. Democrats thought he had a chance at re-nomination, but not re-election. If he got that far civil rights would drag him down. "The social equality incubus," wrote the Savannah *News*, "sits too heavily on his youthful shoulders."[44] A pounding civil rights headache afflicted Congressman Sloan all through July. In August the Republican convention soothed his migraine. It denied him re-nomination. Freed in Congress' second session to vote his conscience, he voted "No."

Republicans faced further problems. African Americans dominated the party rolls. They believed the time had come to take the congressional seat. When the convention opened at Savannah on August 20 a black delegate sat as president, but a white faction took control. It backed a white candidate. John Emory Bryant, transplanted to Georgia from Maine, was a sincere man sincerely interested in the welfare of the emancipated people.[45] But he knew the dangers of the civil rights issue.

As for the convention, a gag rule limited speeches to five minutes, effectively cutting off debate. Bryant's supporters pushed through his nomination. Andrew Sloan held out briefly. One other name appeared against Bryant's, that of black politician Jesse Wimberly. Bryant's forces asked the convention to make his nomination unanimous. Dissidents from Burke and McIntosh Counties refused. They adjourned to a nearby saloon and organized a counter-convention. Delegates from Ware, Chatham, Liberty, and Emanuel Counties joined them. They demanded a black man, Jesse Wimberly.

The Bryant faction took the nomination. But it could not dictate the platform. Black delegates insisted on approval of civil rights. Congressman Sloan fought against it. Whether the convention endorsed him did not matter. He

44 Savannah *News*, July 22, 1874.

45 See Ruth Currie-McDaniel, *Carpetbagger of Conscience: A Biography of John Emory Bryant* (Athens, Ga., 1987).

"could not swallow" a civil rights plank.[46] Bryant kept silent. The civil rights resolution passed. Wimberly would not be appeased. He held both Bryant and Sloan responsible for the attempt to reject it from the platform. He rejected the ticket and the convention. He accepted the independent challenge. He made civil rights the heart of his campaign.

Democrats, meanwhile, nominated their candidate. Julian Hartridge, Savannah lawyer and former Confederate congressman, was a strange, quiet man. He accepted the nomination at the urging of friends. Then he withdrew. Friends dragged him out again. He withdrew the withdrawal.[47] He campaigned intermittently, leaving election crowds searching for a candidate who hid elsewhere. At the final rally in Savannah an eager audience awaited his appearance, only to discover that Hartridge had left the building.[48]

Julian Hartridge was a man of diffidence. "Gentle and unobtrusive," said his friend Congressman Philip Cook, "so shy sometimes that those who knew him little mistook for hauteur what was really a modest reserve." Sunset Cox remembered him from college days: "a dainty and refined sensibility;" his favorite pastime was to stand in the Botanical Gardens to watch the orchids.[49] On race relations, however, the gentle man displayed a steely resolve. As a student at Brown University he refused to recite his lessons in moral philosophy because College President Francis Wayland criticized the institution of slavery.[50] In Congress he seldom spoke. He would rise, recalled Illinois' Carter Harrison, who sat next to him, as if to ask for the floor, then sit down quickly before he could be recognized.[51] He took the floor resolutely on one occasion, to speak in defense of South Carolina's white militiamen after their slaughter of black people in the Hamburgh Massacre of 1876.

Democrats nominated their reluctant candidate at Blackshear on September 2. Promptly the candidate disappeared. He arranged no rallies, gave no speeches. "A little enthusiasm," pleaded the Savannah *News*. "We have had a

46 Atlanta *Constitution*, August 29, 1874.

47 *Memorial Addresses on the Life and Character of Julian Hartridge, (A Representative from Georgia) Delivered in the House of Representatives and in the Senate, Forty-fifth Congress, Third Session* (Washington: 1879), 14 (eulogy of Congressman Philip Cook).

48 "Mr. Hartridge was vociferously called for, and after several minutes waiting for his appearance, it was announced that he was not present." Savannah *News*, November 3, 1874.

49 *Memorial Addresses*, 16, 30, 32–36. Those who penetrated his reserve found friendship. Congressional eulogies in 1879 expressed genuine sorrow. In public affairs, said William Frye, they agreed on little. He loved the Georgian still for his "beautiful" nature. He was also the revered forbear and namesake of French novelist Julien Green, inspiration perhaps of his romance set on a Georgia plantation, *Les pays lointains*.

50 *Memorial Addresses:* 28–29.

51 *Memorial Addresses*, 39.

good quiet nap – now let us make it lively for those who want social equality forced on the people."[52] On October 12 Hartridge spoke for the first time, facing supporters at Savannah. He regretted that defeat made it necessary to send a representative to Washington ("we can't get out of this if we would"). Therefore he was willing to take the job. He denounced carpetbaggers. He ended with the Civil Rights Bill, the "damnable doctrine of social equality." It could be stopped if voters sent Congress a message. The audience, lulled into somnolence, woke up – "vociferously cheered, an evidence of the temper of the people."[53]

The Democratic campaign sputtered along. The dainty candidate failed to exploit the civil rights issue as he might have. Civil rights dismembered Republicans anyway. Bryant supported the measure officially, but timidly. His independent rival, Wimberly, blasted him. On September 14 Wimberly, the "people's Republican candidate," as he styled himself, published his campaign manifesto. The people's Republican appealed to the "working Republicans," as opposed to parasitic white office-holders beholden to Bryant. He insisted on the Civil Rights Bill. "I favor and shall, if elected, vote for the civil rights bill now pending before Congress, and will do everything in my power to have such legislation effected." Bryant was no better than Sloan. Black people beware. "They will call you 'Mr. Jones' now; after the election they will call you Old Tom or Old Ike – or, ten to one, they will not call you at all."[54]

Bryant denied Wimberly's charges. He did support civil rights. Civil rights meant separate-but-equal. "The civil rights bill as it now stands amended, simply means 'equal rights,' but not 'mixed rights.'" He was, the *News* reported, "rather embarrassed on that subject."[55] On October 12, he came to Darien in McIntosh County. Wimberlyites rushed the platform. They overthrew the stand. Bryant brought legal action. The *News* rejoiced. "He has sealed the disaffection in the Radical ranks."

Bryant turned to face his Democratic opponent. Hartridge proved difficult to corner. Bryant tracked him to Homerville in Clinch County, where the Democrat had scheduled a speech. He challenged his adversary to debate. Hartridge contemplated him vacantly. Then he turned and walked away, leaving Bryant openmouthed on the stage. "The idea of a respectable white man arguing with such a creature," the *News* expectorated. "Bah! Pass around the carbolic acid. Faugh!"[56]

52 Savannah *News*, October 13, 1874.
53 Savannah *News*, October 13, 1874.
54 Savannah *News*, September 22, 1874.
55 Savannah *News*, September 26, 1874.
56 Savannah *News*, October 17, 19, 1874.

Results came in as expected. Black votes disappeared. Polls somehow failed to open in areas where those votes resided. Burke County, with an overwhelming black majority, recorded nearly as many tallies for Hartridge as for Bryant and Wimberly combined. Columns of black men marched to Savannah, hoping to find a place to vote. Julian Hartridge went to Congress, almost despite himself, with a majority of 4,432. (The *News* oddly proposed the stage-shy freshman for Speaker of the House.)[57] Jesse Wimberly polled only 974 votes. Despite his waffling, despite his civil rights dodges, despite Wimberly's civil rights appeals, Bryant retained black support. It did not suffice. Wimberly's partisans called him a civil rights traitor. Hartridge's Democrats called him a civil rights fanatic. The Quitman *Independent* called him a loser. It drew an editorial cartoon: a winged devil standing under an ominous sky; beside him a downcast figure of John E. Bryant; in the caption Satan upbraided his luckless candidate.

> You have caused me to lose the First District. It will now be represented by an honest man, whose name and character is too pure for your father's Satanic lips to utter. The Civil Rights Bill is the best bill for my purposes, if it could have passed, that ever originated in hell, and my oldest son, Sumner, who is now a distinguished member of my Cabinet, is marshaling the entire forces of my Dominion to have it passed, and if it fails, my political power is forever gone, both North and South, and the Government of the United States will again be purified.[58]

Georgia, Second District
Richard H. Whiteley (R), William E. Smith (D)
Population: 54% black

Southwest Georgia comprised the state's 2nd District. It ran from Quitman County at its northern end south to Berrien and Lowndes Counties. Its principal towns included Albany, Bainbridge, Thomasville and Valdosta. Black majorities resided in 11 of 17 counties, most heavily in Baker County with 5,000 black persons to fewer than 2,000 whites, and Dougherty County where 2,000 whites lived among 10,000 blacks.

That majority had sustained incumbent Congressman Richard Henry Whiteley for three terms.[59] But the base was rickety. Violence took a toll. The

57 Savannah *News*, November 17, 1874.

58 Quitman, Georgia, *Independent*, October 31, 1874.

59 See Richard A. Gerber and Alan Friedlander, "The Civil Rights Act of 1875 A Reexamination," *Transactions of the Connecticut Academy of Arts and Sciences*, 60 (2008): 1–50.

poll tax eliminated other potential voters. The congressman's margins were precarious; in 1872 he was returned by precisely 86 votes. Whiteley, as Sloan and Freeman, could afford nothing – civil rights bills, for instance – that would alienate the small but indispensable element of white support he enjoyed.

The congressman understood the calculation. In Georgia's 2nd the indispensable element consisted of small farmers, "poor white people; white men from the country," who were willing to vote Republican as long as Republicans did not unduly ruffle their prejudices.[60] Whiteley referred to himself as the "poor man's candidate," the friend of the country man.[61] Unfortunately, those same poor white men, situated just one tick above the bottom of the social hierarchy, were precisely the element most sensitive to the civil rights issue. Richard Whiteley struggled to retain his vital quotient of white support while not betraying his black constituents' aspirations. In 1874 he failed.

The congressman was a southerner by adoption, a boyhood immigrant from County Kildare, Ireland. The war found him in Bainbridge, a lawyer and cotton-mill owner.[62] He opposed secession, but fought for the South, establishing an impressive wartime record. Rising from the ranks to major, he took his men, the Second Georgia Sharpshooters, through bloody fields, Chickamauga and Chattanooga. He led a tattered remnant to the surrender of the Confederacy's last army. Outwardly he seemed an unpromising warrior, short and slender: "a little white tom-tit looking head poking out of a stove-pipe hat," the *Constitution's* Washington correspondent Tommy Hauck described him.[63] An oversize mustache struggled to compensate for his undersize features.

Major Whiteley returned from war a Republican. Republicans welcomed him, a Confederate hero, to their ranks. Frederick Douglass congratulated the congressman on his reelection: "He is not of that class that fail to remember after arriving here that they leave a constituency behind them that is denied the exercise of the rights and privileges of American citizens."[64] Democrats despised him, a collaborator with the enemy.

For three terms Richard Whiteley clung to his seat, evading all efforts to dislodge him. Opponents honored him with a distinctive sobriquet: "Slippery Dick." On the question of the Civil Rights Bill Slippery Dick's convictions showed no sign of lubricity. Alone among the Georgia Republicans he voted for it consistently. He was present for all three House calls. On all three occasions

60 Savannah *News*, August 22, 27, 1874.

61 Savannah News, August 31, 1874.

62 See William W. Rogers, *A Scalawag in Georgia: Richard Whiteley and the Politics of Reconstruction* (Urbana: 2007).

63 Atlanta *Constitution*, December 23, 1874.

64 Washington, *New National Era*, April 10, 1873.

he voted Aye. He voted Aye on final passage in 1875. "I am glad to see that my little countryman R.H. Whiteley did not dodge," a Georgia correspondent wrote to Ben Butler, "but faced the question like a man, while Sloan, who was elected by negro votes voted against it and old man Freeman could not be found."[65] Whiteley presented Democrats an easy target. From the outset they made it plain. The campaign would run on one rail: the Civil Rights Bill. On that rail they planned to run Slippery Dick out of Congress.

Dick Whiteley had sustained such attacks before, and survived. In 1874 the contest promised to be more acute, his chances more doubtful. A real civil rights bill was closer to passage, the public temper darker and more menacing. The congressman spoke through his own journalistic organ, the Bainbridge *Weekly Sun.* In its columns he answered the Democrats' charges. The *Weekly Sun* mocked the absurdity of prejudice: "You meet your neighbor on the sidewalk, give him a good caning, he gets up, shakes the dust off his clothing, and says to you, 'I did not know you had anything against me.' To which you respond, 'No, I have not. I am only opposed to your walking on the sidewalk.'"[66] In January he printed Butler's New Market Heights speech on his front pages. Democrats drew the noose tighter. The Thomasville *Times* fumed.

> Every white man who votes for him votes for the bill too. The country will look upon all such white men as traitors to their race, ready and willing to sell, not only their own worthless souls, but their innocent wives and children to endless infamy. The man who votes for it must expect that even another generation will cast it in the face of his children, and it will be a worse stigma to them than was the name of "tory" in the days of our fathers.[67]

The Valdosta *Times* exhorted.

> Whiteley and other leaders have swallowed the social rights pill and are taking the negroes into their loving embrace.... Where will you stand? ... If you are not lost to honesty, to pride of State, pride of race, pride of honor, you will not tarry upon the fence, nor fall on the "black vomit" side. The die is cast, and the contest can be waged under no other guise.[68]

65 James Fitzpatrick to Benjamin Butler, February 8, 1875. Butler Papers, Library of Congress.
66 Bainbridge *Weekly Sun*, October 22, 1873.
67 Thomasville *Times*, August 29, 1874.
68 Quoted in Savannah *News*, July 21, 1874.

The Quitman *Independent* warned.

> Left to his own volition the negro necessarily returns to his own original Africanism, while the white man marches forward to indefinite perfection, and therefore, sooner or later, they must, of necessity, exterminate each other. What a fearful sin, therefore, for the man of the North to thus force this awful doom on his brother of the South – a doom that compels him to massacre the poor negro to save himself![69]

The message was set. It needed only a candidate to deliver it on the stump. On August 21, meeting at Albany, Democrats chose their champion. Captain William E. Smith, a lawyer from Dougherty County, had seen much hardship. War had cost him one of his legs. He left it, the Thomasville *Times* related, on a lonely Virginia battlefield. The *Times* was unworried. "Whiteley has got such a heavy load to carry in that Civil Rights Bill, which he voted for every time, that a man who had lost both his legs in the Confederate army could outrun him."[70]

Capt. Smith laid out his platform. The federal government had no right to protect the rights of individuals. All laws devised for such purpose were invalid. They were the road to dictatorship. The South had lost its independence. It hoped for a magnanimous peace, "to manage its domestic matters in its own way." Instead came the Civil Rights Bill, its aim, "ruthlessly to crush out the free spirit of the people."[71]

Georgia Democrats concentrated their fire upon Richard Whiteley. Senator Gordon, Governor Smith, Benjamin Hill all stumped the district. Their cavalcade reached Thomasville on September 30. Gordon chose as his theme Oliver Morton's Terre Haute speech, with its large dose of civil rights. He read it out and denounced it point by point. They went on to Bainbridge. Gen. Gordon greeted his veterans. "Old soldiers flocked around him to grasp his hand … he had a kind word for each and all."[72] In the face of this monumental campaign Whiteley's editorials at first remained steadfast.

> Instead of shunning the negro and blocking his efforts to raise himself to their level of manhood; instead of treating him as an enemy and a conspirator, it is time that they [white people] began the relationship of mutual co-operation. Such a relationship does not obliterate social

69 Quitman *Independent*, August 8, 1874.
70 Thomasville *Times*, August 22, 1874.
71 Bainbridge *Weekly Sun*, September 10, 1874.
72 Savannah *News*, October 2; Thomasville *Times*, October 3, 1874.

> distinctions. It does not interfere with personal dignity.... The white man cannot refuse it on any ground which finds justification in laws human or laws divine.[73]

He followed the well-rehearsed Republican line, throwing Horace Greeley in the Democrats' faces. Greeley had supported Sumner's measures; Democrats had supported Greeley. Republicans were honest. "What we said in 1872 we say in 1874.... Equality for all men before the law we promised and asserted in 1872 was the right of every freeman. True then, it is true now."[74]

True, perhaps. But as the campaign progressed he sensed that this time he stood on civil rights quicksand. On August 27 a delegation of white supporters called at the congressman's offices in Bainbridge. They were precisely those on whose loyalty he relied. They hurled the Civil Rights Bill at him. "Slippery Dick, with good clothes on, stepped out and attempted to whip them in with the old party lash. It was no go. They told him they had minds of their own, could read the civil rights bill for themselves, and wanted none of his bosh about it."[75]

Whiteley took his campaign into Berrien County. He stopped at a gentleman's house to ask for dinner. "Major Whiteley," his host replied, "I understand you voted for the civil rights bill, hence you believe in social equality. I shall be glad for you to partake of my hospitality, and knowing your preference for colored society, I have made arrangements to accommodate you accordingly. You will find your dinner in the kitchen, Major."[76] Real or invented? The story provided Democrats a priceless anecdote.

At Valdosta Whiteley found his steps dogged by a gang of mischievous youngsters. Everywhere the congressman went the little boys went too. They saluted him with a "tin pan serenade," a clanging concert performed on "tin pans, clevises, cow-horns, etc."[77] Elisha the prophet, similarly harassed, struck down the naughty boys of Bethel with the curse of God. Whiteley settled for U.S. Commissioner Edward C. Wade. Ten tiny urchins marched solemnly off to jail, charged with violation of the Federal Enforcement Act. Commissioner Wade left town to attend the Chattanooga Convention. The Savannah *News* chuckled: "The little children in Quitman and Valdosta can go out to play now without fear of being arrested."[78]

---

73 Bainbridge *Weekly Sun*, August 6, 1874.
74 Bainbridge *Weekly Sun*, August 13, 1874.
75 Savannah *News*, August 27, 1874.
76 Atlanta *Constitution*, October 31; Petersburg *Index and Appeal*, August 31, 1874.
77 Quitman *Independent*, October 3; Savannah *News*, October 5, 1874.
78 Savannah *News*, October 16, 1874.

Worse followed. The black Rev. Jack Carter, candidate for the state legislature, spoke at Duncanville. "This reverend apostle of Civil Rights and disciple of Dick Whiteley," the Thomasville *Southern Enterprise* reported, "with the malignity of a fiend and with tone and gesture of savage defiance, announced his creed:"

> The negro is better than the poor white man now.... We mean to go into the biggest hotels and the best railroad cars with the white men and women; we mean to fix the law that a black man can take any white woman for a wife when he loves her and wants her; we mean that the law shall say there must be no separate schools for white and black men's children, and it won't be long before they will not know there ever was any difference between white and black. It will make you mighty sick at first, just as emancipation made you sick, but you'll come in mighty pretty when you find you can't help yourselves.[79]

Rev. Carter's words spread. The Savannah *News* ran them. The Thomasville *Times* put them under its masthead in every issue through the election. "We can pass no higher encomium on the law-abiding spirit of our citizens," it declared, "than to announce that this scoundrel still lives unmolested."[80]

The disintegrating situation at last forced the congressman to dodge. The Civil Rights Bill, he now explained, did not mandate integration. It did not require mixed schools. It did not require mixed accommodation in railroad cars or theaters or hotels. Separate-but-equal would do: "Equal comforts and equal facilities furnished by proprietors will be a sufficient compliance with the spirit of the act." He put out a circular: "The civil rights bill as it passed the Senate and I voted on it in the House as your Representative does not require either mixed schools or a mixture of the races in the cars."[81] He would see to it personally: "If any hot-headed men seek to injure the cause of education by attempting to treat the law as requiring mixed schools, I shall move to strike out this portion of the bill."[82] Dodging only invited ridicule. "He did not hint at any such thing a few weeks ago," noted the Thomasville *Times*.

> The school clause was all right then. But a little cloud began to gather soon after, about the size of a man's hand, and Mr. Whiteley has since

79 Quoted in Thomasville *Times*, September 12, 1874.
80 Thomasville *Times*, September 19, 1874.
81 Thomasville *Times*, October 17, 1874.
82 Bainbridge *Weekly Sun*, September 10, 1874.

> found out that the school clause is wrong. What will your black adherents say to that Mr. Whiteley? It won't do to try and hoodwink the white men of the district with a promise to vote to strike out this obnoxious clause of the bill. *The whole thing is obnoxious.* There is no part of it which the white people of this district will endorse."[83]

The Quitman *Independent* supplemented its purple prose with black-and-white cartoons. One artistic offering presented a portrait of Slippery Dick. He was endowed with two heads, turned in opposite directions: "Janus-Faced Whiteley." Each face addressed a different figure, a black man on one side, on the other a white. To the former, the talking head promised equality: "Without the Civil Rights Bill you are not free men, and when that bill passes your children will be educated in the same school ... all will be socially equal." The backwards head swore the opposite: "The Civil Rights Bill doesn't affect the social relations of the races; it doesn't create mixed schools; it don't put white and black in the same car or in the same steam-boat or hotel."[84] A campaign song commenced to enliven Democratic rallies: "Farewell, Richard," sung to the wistful tune of "Just Before the Battle, Mother:"

> And you need not hope, oh Richard,
> E'er again to lift your head
> To the white man's level, Richard,
> For such hope will soon be dead.
> Oh! Thou "civil righteous" Richard
> Dark and gloomy is your fate;
> Loathed, despised by all true white men,
> With the negro you must mate.
> (Refrain)
> Farewell, Richard, may you never
> Go to Congress any more,
> But we'll not forget you, Richard,
> For your actions there before.[85]

On September 20 fire destroyed the offices of the Bainbridge *Weekly Sun*. It was a fitting end to the end of a congressional career. Before his paper died in the flames Richard Whiteley wrote his political obituary:

83 Thomasville *Times*, September 19, 1874.
84 Quitman *Independent*, October 3, 1874.
85 Thomasville *Times*, October 17, 1874.

> [This campaign] began by appeals to the passion and prejudice of people ... paraded before the people by unscrupulous demagogues who seek to arouse the races to madness.... It was passion that placed the South in the chains of a despotic intolerance that is a disgrace to any age or country.... With reason uppermost, our sense of justice will not be deadened, our sympathy for right not destroyed, our duty as a common citizenship not forgotten, our humanity as a civilized people not disgraced, our respect for law and order not disregarded. But with reason gone and passion in its stead, we are on a limitless sea without chart, compass, or rudder, without even a solitary star from which to hope.[86]

Smith's majority came in at 2,309. Only Decatur, Dougherty, Randolph and Calhoun Counties gave Whiteley a significant margin. In Berrien County the congressman received 11 votes, against 800 for his opponent. Various factors facilitated the Democrats' victory. Economic violence supplemented physical violence. The Thomasville *Times* placed a notice: "Read This, Colored Laborer:" Employers can do without your labor; northern workers would be glad to come down for generous wages offered in the district. "We do not allude to this as a threat."[87] An illustrated flier supplied the threat: a black man surrounded by knives and pistols, all pointed in his general direction.[88] Yet the Democrats' campaign song had it right. Slippery Dick marched to his farewell every step to the tune of a civil rights lament.[89] The same applied throughout Georgia. Charles Nordhoff visited a few months later. "The Civil Rights Bill killed the Republican party in this State," a Republican official confided. "It put us back to 1867."[90]

2 North Carolina

In North Carolina, as in Georgia, Republicans held three congressional seats. All three lay in the eastern half of the state, most heavily adapted to the uses of slavery and so provided with black people. Except in the decisively black Second District, the party's base was fragile. Civil rights would play the devil with the Republicans' fragile chances.

North Carolina Democrats had raised civil rights storms before. Republicans had ridden them out. Now a whirlwind threatened to sweep them away. The

86 Bainbridge *Weekly Sun*, September 10, 1874.
87 Thomasville *Times*, October 31, 1874.
88 Quitman *Independent*, October 24, 1874.
89 Rogers, *Scalawag in Georgia*: 150.
90 Nordhoff, *The Cotton States in 1875*: 110.

difference in mood was striking. Back in 1872, having Charles Sumner's early civil rights proposals as a target, Democrats in Raleigh had armed an explosive campaign newspaper, *Blasting Powder for Democrats and Conservatives.* As implied, *Blasting Powder* supplied Conservatives combustible material with which to blow up Republican candidates. Civil rights furnished a prime ingredient:

> To your tents, O Israel! and preserve the difference which God has made and which man has recognized as existing between the two races. Beat down this party which advocates putting negro children and white children together at schools – which makes it a $500 crime for any teacher to refuse to take a negro scholar. The next step will be to make it a crime for any white woman to refuse to marry a negro man! ... White men of North Carolina, are you willing to accept such abominable legislation? Are you prepared to receive into your parlors as guests the lying, thieving, lousy, depraved negro? ... Vote down radicalism and prevent the perpetration of the greatest social outrages that the world has yet seen.[91]

Blasting Powder named the culprits of the moment, the Republican candidates for governor and lieutenant-governor, Tod Caldwell and Curtis Brogden. Republicans in 1872 shrugged off the assault. Caldwell and Brogden won. Republican William A. Smith carried the 4th District. 1st District incumbent Clinton Cobb pledged to support Sumner's civil rights amendments.[92] They went further. They initiated a Civil Rights Association. Curtis Brogden composed the call in his patented "spread-eagle" rhetoric.

> We will second his [Sumner's] noble efforts, by every lawful means in our power, to obtain for us the full measure of our rights, wherever we may be, whether at home or abroad, upon the private or public highway, among the rock-ribbed mountains of the North, whose summits are clothed with perpetual snow and ice, or the sunny plains and tepid waters of the South, where the balmy breeze is wafted almost into a zephyr's sigh, whether upon land or sea, so that wherever the American flag floats over an American citizen he shall be entitled to equal civil and political rights.[93]

91 Raleigh, N.C., *Blasting Powder for Democrats and Conservatives*, June 26, 1872.

92 Raleigh, *Daily Republican*, July 3, 1874.

93 Goldsboro *Carolina Messenger*, July 23; Raleigh *Sentinel*, July 24, 1874. "Brogden, with his pointless, foamy rhetoric, his contracted, stubborn intellect, his agrarian, leveling principles, and his bombastic, egotistical, self-sufficient ignorance," cried the New Bern *Newbernian*, "the very man to make us pass under the rod." Quoted in Raleigh *Republican*, July 16, 1874.

This was 1872. Two years later all had changed. Republicans ran panic-stricken at the mere mention of civil rights. Congressman Cobb trembled at the thought of campaigning for a civil rights bill. Congressman Smith denounced Sumner's folly. All factors pointed to a much closer election. Republicans could not count on a Greeley drag to keep angry white men at home. The new Civil Rights Bill roused those angry men to sally forth and vote. Travel writer Edward King found tensions dangerously taut, white people "more inclined to bitterness and less reconciled to the results of the war than anywhere else in the South."[94] Declared Stephen D. Pool, Democratic candidate for State School Superintendent, "I consider no man mean, low, white trash, unless he supports the Civil Rights Bill."[95] After the elections ex-governor William W. Holden telegraphed the White House. North Carolinians, he assured Ulysses Grant, did not hate his party. They hated the Civil Rights Bill.[96] The *National Republican* agreed.

> Everywhere the civil rights issue was forced upon public attention, even in the election of constables, and war against the blacks became the recognized battle-cry of the Conservatives in the bar-rooms, in the highways and byways, on the hustings, in their churches, in their camp-meetings, and in the privacies of social life.... To this we attribute the loss of North Carolina.[97] (see Map 2, below)

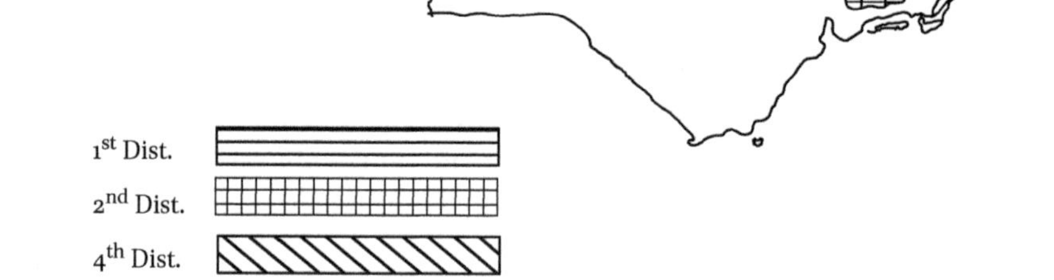

MAP 2 Congressional Districts, North Carolina
SOURCE: AUTHORS OF *WELCOMING RUIN*.

94 Edward King, *The Great South: A Record of Journeys in Louisiana, Texas...* (Baton Rouge: 1972), 468.
95 Wilmington, North Carolina, *Journal*, June 11; Goldsboro *Messenger*, June 15, 1874.
96 William W. Holden to Ulysses Grant, August 11, 1874. *Papers of Ulysses S. Grant*, vol. 25, 419.
97 Washington, *National Republican*, August 7, 1874.

North Carolina, First District
Clinton L. Cobb (R), Jesse J. Yeates (D), Edward Ransom (I)
Population: 55% white

"If I go for the Civil Rights bill I am beaten; and if I don't go for it I am beaten; and what in the h – l am I to do?" Newspapers across the country reported the anguished words of Republican Congressman Clinton L. Cobb. The Baltimore *Sun* deleted the expletive; the Chicago *Tribune* more tactfully deleted the middle letters.[98] Either way, for Clinton Cobb the expletive-laden civil rights noose tightened quickly.

North Carolina scheduled its elections early, August 6, first in the nation other than faraway Oregon. It was the country's weathercock, whose feathers would show how the political winds were blowing. That August date, moreover, required congressmen to begin a campaign before Congress had adjourned. North Carolina's representatives had to fidget, stuck behind their desks in Washington while competitors criticized them freely at home. They had to consider contentious issues, civil rights bills for instance, in the midst of an active canvass. Congressman Cobb alone among North Carolina's sitting Republican representatives won re-nomination. He alone contemplated a civil rights vote while his opponent thundered against it on the stump. He sent his desperate query to the Republican Executive Committee in Raleigh in May. The Executive Committee's response is not recorded.[99] A fortuitous attack of diphtheria prostrated the congressman. He kept to his bed, excused from all votes on civil rights. When his fever broke he found Civil Rights Bill fever raging across his district.

Clinton Levering Cobb – "Lev" to his friends – was 32, in his third congressional term. Supporters complimented his appearance, natty and clean-shaven: "a young gentleman of pleasing address, affability of manners, and fine intellectual powers."[100] Opponents mocked him: "a pigmy in brains and stature."[101] The New York *Herald* dismissed him: "a mongrel sort of diminutive Jew of no ability."[102] The religious aspersion was unjust; the congressman remained resolutely Episcopalian. He was well connected, descended from a family noted among the earliest settlers of the Albemarle region. In 1873 he married Pattie Gaskins Pool, niece of John Pool, outgoing United States Senator, and sister of

98 Baltimore *Sun*, July 31, 1874; Chicago *Tribune*, July 11, 1874.

99 Goldsboro *Carolina Messenger*, June 11, 1874. Republican sources denied the whole story, but, the *Messenger's* correspondent insisted, he had seen ex-governor Holden himself with the letter in his hand.

100 Asheville *Pioneer*, quoted in Elizabeth City *North Carolinian*, March 5, 1873.

101 Raleigh *Sentinel*, July 13, 1874.

102 New York *Herald*, July 21, 1874.

Walter F. Pool, later congressman-elect. Alliance with the Pools, the elite of Pasquotank gentry, gave Lev Cobb a solid base.

The 1st District covered the northeast quadrant of North Carolina. Sixteen counties ran from Currituck on the coast west along the Albemarle Sound, southwest to Pitt County, then back along the Pamlico Sound to the southern Albemarle counties of Dare, Tyrell and Washington. Elizabeth City and Greenville in Pitt County were its principal towns. The 1870 census recorded some 73,000 black persons and 80,000 whites. Their distribution was remarkably homogenous. Only in Currituck and Dare Counties did white residents strongly outnumber blacks. Elsewhere the figures balanced almost evenly.

Lev might have rested easier if his civil rights record had matched the balance of his district. It did not. He became a civil rights congressman. The *New National Era* quoted him in 1872: "I am not able to say whether Mr. Sumner's Civil Rights Bill will pass the Senate in its present shape or not, but let me assure you that if it does, I shall work earnestly for its passage through the House." The *Era* wished him long life. "May his hair grow grey in Congress."[103] Civil rights put grey in Congressman Cobb's hair.

A bitter struggle preceded the Republican nomination. Republicans in Camden County met on May 7. They wished the incumbent well in his retirement "and all his future works," so long as he retired.[104] Cobb's supporters were led by Dr. Palemon John, editor of the district's leading Republican sheet, the Elizabeth City *North Carolinian*. Experience, said Dr. John, was the incumbent's strength. He had won the district new post roads, post offices, lighthouses, life-guard stations along the coast. He "put his work 'where it will do the most good.'" Rivals swarmed nonetheless. Chowan County gave its support to Judge Augustus M. Moore. Camden and Perquimans preferred Col. Daniel McD. Lindsey. Tyrell and Hyde Counties brought out Dr. Edward Ransom. Of these aspirants Col. Lindsey was the most radical. Dr. Ransom was the most determined.[105]

The convention met on May 21 at the town of Plymouth. After three days of wrangling Cobb's partisans (the congressman remaining ill in Washington) emerged victorious. Lindsey withdrew. Ransom rejected reconciliation. He declared an independent candidacy. Augustus Moore joined him.[106] A splintered

103 Washington *New National Era*, February 29, 1872.

104 Elizabeth City *North Carolinian*, May 13, 1874.

105 Elizabeth City *North Carolinian*, April 8, 15, 22, 29.

106 Elizabeth City *North Carolinian*, May 27, 1874.

Republican Party stumbled into the campaign, with civil rights hanging over its head.

Democrats experienced no such difficulties. Major Jesse J. Yeates of Hertford County took the nomination on May 28. The *North Carolinian* affected unconcern. Yeates was inoffensive, a "corpulent, genial, social gentleman."[107] His views were moderate; he had even worked with Republican administrations. The newspaper was soon disabused. On June 6 candidate Yeates made his appearance at Elizabeth City. "His speech was full of bitterness," the *North Carolinian* cried, "full of wormwood, full of gall.... He virtually declared himself an apostle of hate, a missionary to array race against race."[108] Yeates launched his assault on the Civil Rights Bill. The *North Carolinian* tried to parry the attack. It printed the full text of the Senate bill. The thing was harmless:

> We publish on our front page the Civil Rights Bill as it passed the Senate. Read it, scan it, analyze it and tell us frankly, men of judgment and fairness, what is there in it to alarm or horrify any good citizen? It does not favor any color or any class, but maintains the equality of all citizens before the law.... They are only making an attempt to frighten the timid. But they'll find the people won't scare worth a ____.[109]

Yeates knew better. Opposition to civil rights was a scarifying, and a winning, tactic. Clinton Cobb, for his part, was nowhere to be seen. Barely three weeks remained to campaign before he could get to his feet, leave Washington and return home. Democrat Yeates and Independent Ransom meanwhile stumped the district. At Greenville on the 4th of July they debated. Col. Lindsey stood in for the absent Cobb. Yeates ignored him and struck at the absentee. "It were better for him that a negro were hanged about his neck and he basking in the sweetness of Sumner's Civil Rights bill by the side of his dear friend Butler." Dr. Ransom, though officially independent, also reserved his fire for the Republican. The confrontation of Lindsey and Ransom "is death to the rats but fun to the boys," the Raleigh *Sentinel* clucked. "Yeates, with his irrefragable logic and burning eloquence is consolidating the white people into one irresistible mass."[110]

107 Elizabeth City *North Carolinian*, July 29, 1874.
108 Elizabeth City *North Carolinian*, June 10, 1874.
109 Elizabeth City *North Carolinian*, June 17, 1874.
110 Raleigh *Sentinel*, July 13, 1874.

The *North Carolinian* struggled to respond. Dr. John fell ill. The congressman's brother-in-law Walter Pool took over the editorial page. Step by step he retreated. First his columns renounced social equality: "Talk about social equality is all moonshine. Is any man fool enough to believe that he cannot regulate his own social associations, go where he may? Is any man so lost to his own self respect?" Next he renounced mixed schools: "The Republican party of North Carolina are not in favor of mixed schools. The white Republicans have never advocated it, the colored have never asked for it.… The Civil Rights Bill, as we understand it, does not mean forced mixed schools." Then he renounced the Civil Rights Bill: "The Fourteenth Amendment to the Constitution guarantees perfect equality before the law, and that is all the Republicans of North Carolina demand. They neither ask for nor desire an action upon the 'Civil Rights' question."[111] Finally, in a flurry of clipped editorials, he tossed the hand-grenade back to the other side. Democrats in 1872 had endorsed Horace Greeley. Greeley had endorsed civil rights. Democrats, not Republicans, desired a civil rights bill.[112]

Clinton Cobb returned home. In advance he sent his constituents an open letter. He hoped they would recall the benefits he had secured, post-roads, lifeguard stations etc. He defended the Civil Rights Bill. He refused to adopt his brother-in-law's stance, to renounce his past acts. "The Civil Rights Bill is not yet perfected in details," he assured his readers. "When it is perfected, I believe there will be no division of sentiment in regard to the propriety of the law on the part of either white or colored persons."[113]

The congressman confronted his antagonists finally at Greenville on July 15. The Civil Rights Bill, he insisted, would pass. It should pass. His opponents played upon the people's fears "to foment discord, trouble, and possibly war between the two races." White voters must see past the deception. He called

111 Elizabeth City *North Carolinian*, June 24, July 1, 1874.

112 "HORACE GREELEY WAS IN FAVOR OF MIXED SCHOOLS AND MIXED CHURCHES. MAJOR YEATES VOTED FOR HIM. Let all who are opposed to the doctrine vote for C.L. Cobb – Major Yeates cast a ballot in 1872 exactly similar to that cast by Chas. Sumner, the author of the Civil Rights Bill – The Democrats vociferate that they are opposed to social equality of the races; yet they are the only set of people on the face of the earth that ever voted for a man that endorsed it – … Yeates voted for a man who was in favor of forcing the two races to MIX TOGETHER against the wishes of both." Elizabeth City *North Carolinian*, July 8, 1874.

113 Elizabeth City *North Carolinian*, July 22, 1874.

out to black people in the crowd. Did they want social equality? "They replied with an unanimous 'No!'"[114]

That spontaneous "no" reflected a growing fear. Black people too began to feel the incendiary effects of Major Yeates' agitation. Their candidate tried to hold the line. They retreated in disarray. At Greenville they gathered to frame a resolution: "We, the colored portion of the Republican party, assure the white people that they need have no fears of social equality.... We are opposed to the so-called Civil Rights Bill."[115]

The election reversed the results of 1872. From a majority of 1,429 Clinton Cobb sank to a deficit of 1,481. He won Pasquotank, Bertie, Chowan, Hertford and Martin Counties, all by reduced margins. Gates, Beaufort and Currituck gave Yeates his strongest support. At the precinct of Lee's Mills in Washington County turnout was 100%. "One year ago this box gave nearly 150 Radical majority," the Norfolk *Virginian* reported. "Yesterday Yeates received 10 majority."[116] The Richmond *Dispatch* cheered: "A fearful death-blow has been given to civil rights in the First North Carolina congressional district. Victory has perched upon the banner of the white man's party."[117]

North Carolina, Fourth District
James Headon (R), Joseph J. Davis (D)
Population: 57% white

North Carolina's 4th District carved out a portion of the state's north center. It included Wake County with the capital city, Raleigh, Johnston County to the south, Chatham and Orange to the west, Franklin and Nash to the east and Granville County on the Virginia border. The electorate was white. Only Granville and Franklin held a small black majority. Wake County sheltered a black population of some 16,000, along with 20,000 whites. The incumbent was a Republican, William Alexander Smith, "Billy" Smith, as he was known (or, in the more unfriendly Democratic press, "Blow-Your-Horn-Billy"). He was a railroad man.

114 Elizabeth City *North Carolinian*, July 15, 1874.
115 Elizabeth City *North Carolinian*, July 15, 1874.
116 Norfolk *Virginian*, August 15, 1874.
117 Richmond *Dispatch*, August 10, 1874.

Congressman Smith approached reelection with diverse liabilities. He represented a white district. His electoral edge was slim. Multifarious business interests, revolving around railroad combinations, burdened him with an aura of doubtful integrity.[118] He had entered office with a margin of 729 votes. The Raleigh *Sentinel* counted registered voters. It found a decidedly Democratic majority.[119] Republican victory in 1872 had resulted from a Greeley drag and a measure of white support. Greeley's deadening hand had departed. The Civil Rights Bill had arrived to sap the support of white voters. Republicans would need a unanimous rally of all their partisans. Instead conflicts divided blacks from whites, and sometimes whites from whites.

In Wake County, the heart of the district, rivalries beset Republicans, one faction led by county sheriff Timothy F. Lee, another by Raleigh mayor Joe Holden. In May each side held its own convention. Each refused to recognize the other. Black delegates led by State Senator James H. Harris sided first with Holden then switched to Sheriff Lee. Finally Harris held his own convention to protest both sides' unfair distribution of patronage to colored people.[120]

Civil rights further fractured the party's forces. Congressman Smith had opposed the bill from the start. He became one of the original dissidents, one of the eight Republicans whose renegade votes halted the bill in the crucial House test of May 25. He voted against it again on June 8. Democrats approved: "Radical though Major Smith is, he has not lost all the independence of a white man. By that vote alone he has atoned for a multitude of his political sins."[121] Black Republicans accounted Billy Smith a sinner.

The Republican convention met at Franklinton on June 12. William Smith failed to last long enough to see his name put in nomination.[122] A delegate from Chatham County rose. The incumbent had betrayed his constituents. He

118 Smith held the presidency of the North Carolina Railroad. A consolidation approved by the legislature allowed the N.C.R.R. to purchase the Eastern North Carolina road and also to merge with the Atlantic and North Carolina Railroad. In February he added the Western North Carolina Railroad. This line was incomplete, and also bankrupt. A new act joined it to the N.C.R.R. with Billy Smith as receiver, authorized to issue bonds for completion of the track. Advocates hailed the benefits of a continuous line of transport from the mountains to the sea. Detractors denounced a "Railroad Ring," with William A. Smith at its center. Goldsboro *Carolina Messenger*, January 19; Raleigh *Sentinel*, April 20, 1874. See Cecil K. Brown, *A State Movement in Railroad Development: The Story of North Carolina's First Effort to Establish an East and West Trunk Line Railroad* (Chapel Hill: 1928), 62–163, 214–221.

119 Raleigh *Sentinel*, May 8, 1874.

120 Raleigh *Sentinel*, April 4, May 12, 16, 30, 1874.

121 Goldsboro *Carolina Messenger*, June 11, 1874.

122 Account of Republican convention, Raleigh *Sentinel*, June 13, 1874.

had voted against the Civil Rights Bill. This remark "was received with tremendous applause from the negroes." Smith had come down from Washington. He defied his critics. He had indeed voted against the bill, he declared, and would do so again: "It would afford me pleasure to repeat that vote." This retort was greeted with tremendous silence. Nominations began. No one nominated Billy Smith.

The ultimate nominee, James M. Headon, was an unexpected choice. A recent convert to the party, he had previously sided with the Democrats. As a member of the State Secession Convention in 1861 he had voted for the ordinance of secession. He claimed really to have favored the Union. As proof, he observed, he had evaded service in the Confederate army.[123] Having witnessed the convention punish his predecessor for opposing civil rights, candidate Headon might have preferred to favor it. He did not. Before nomination he remained silent. Afterwards he prudently renounced it.

The candidate opened his campaign on June 22 at the court house in Raleigh. The *Sentinel* ridiculed his oratorical effort, "an inoffensive speech – it could neither strengthen a Republican nor weaken a Democrat."

> He opposed the civil rights bill and called it "raw head and bloody bones," introduced in Congress by the fanatic Sumner, not because he approved it, but because Brooks had caned him and he hated the South.... Gentlemen who knew Sumner knew he was not for social equality, for he was a cold, haughty aristocrat who would not take much notice of ordinary men, or put himself on a footing with them.[124]

Black Republicans, having dismembered Billy Smith, ought, one would think, to have objected. They did not object. Senator James Harris followed Headon to the platform. He voiced no criticism of the candidate's preceding remarks. He criticized the Civil Rights Bill. It was unnecessary. He could do without it. Let it go. Democrats jeered. "Jeemes Harris," the *Sentinel* proclaimed, "is not a true representative of his race. The negro who says he is opposed to civil rights is a hypocrite, and in our opinion is guilty of falsehood."[125] But Harris was not alone. Wake County's black State Representative Stewart Ellison had loudly demanded passage of a pro-civil rights bill resolution in January. Now he reassured voters. He too questioned the propriety of the bill.[126]

---

123 Wilmington, North Carolina, *Journal*, June 27, 1874.
124 Raleigh *Sentinel*, June 22, 1874.
125 Raleigh *Sentinel*, June 18, 1874.
126 Raleigh *Sentinel*, July 20, 1874.

Republicans' civil rights flight infuriated Democrats. "Give no encouragement to radicals who swear loftily that they are against civil rights," the Raleigh *Crescent* snarled. "A vote in favor of the Republican Party is a vote in favor of the passage of this Bill."[127] Democrats chose a candidate: Joseph J. Davis of Franklin County. His stump speech, the Goldsboro *Messenger* reported, was a lacrimal occasion: "On the Civil Rights question the speaker expressed himself so feelingly that many eyes unused to weep shed tears."[128]

The 4th District rivals agreed to debate. The *Sentinel* recorded one confrontation, at Hillsborough in Orange County. It did not go well for the Republican. Davis featured a "forcible" denunciation of the Civil Rights Bill. Headon raised no objection. "He was quick to say that he was as much opposed to the Civil Rights Bill as Mr. Davis or any gentleman in the house. The negroes themselves were opposed to it." That assertion agreed with the back-peddling pronouncements of Harris and Ellison. But it unsettled the crowd. Murmurs rose. The murmurs unsettled James Headon. He commenced to declaim: "We colored people intend!" Laughter. He stopped. He started again: "Oh! well, if you laugh, I say *we colored people.*" Guffaws. "This brought down the house, and at no part of his speech was there such applause."[129]

Capt. Davis laughed to victory. He erased the 729 vote deficit of 1872 and added 1,612 to it. James Harris lost his senate seat. Democrats celebrated. At Raleigh the parade formed on Fayetteville Street. Banners proclaimed the good news: "'Take Care of My Civil Rights Bill' – Sumner, We've Done It!"[130]

North Carolina, Second District
John A. Hyman (R), George W. Blount (D), Garland H. White (I)
Population: 58% black

North Carolina's 2nd District, the "Black Second," presented Democrats an impossible challenge. Ten counties stretched from north, Warren, Halifax and Northampton, to south, Lenoir and Jones, with a finger pointing east to the sea, Craven County. Two large towns, Goldsboro and New Bern, lay within its limits. Enormous black majorities in Halifax, Edgecombe, Craven and Warren Counties held it firmly in the Republican fold. Democrats themselves had crafted the gerrymandered monster with the aim of marginalizing African-American

127 Raleigh *Crescent*, July 10, 1874.
128 Goldsboro *Carolina Messenger*, July 13, 1874.
129 Raleigh *Sentinel*, June 24, 1874.
130 Raleigh *Sentinel*, August 11, 1874.

votes confined to one district.[131] This suited the party but caused no lack of chagrin to the local white people, caged with a black beast they could not control. Disheartened Democrats declined even to nominate a candidate. Republicans, confident of victory, ran a black man. A civil rights bill should cause little anxiety in the 2nd District. It caused anxiety.

The incumbent Republican was white. Charles R. Thomas had held the seat for two terms. Thomas was a native North Carolinian, a lawyer and former judge and secretary of the state.[132] He had not voted against Sumner's bill. But he displayed little enthusiasm. On May 25 Thomas voted Aye. The next two calls listed him as missing. He was frankly apathetic. So he informed his black constituents. If the people of his district really wanted the bill, he allowed, he would vote for it. Judge Thomas was as good as his word. When the final call came he was a lame duck. Those black constituents had denied him re-nomination. He owed them nothing. He voted to pass the Civil Rights Act.

Congressman Thomas possessed a rare commodity, a safe Republican seat in the South. Rivals coveted the prize. Powerful white politicians, State Senator Richard W. King of Lenoir County and present Lieutenant-Governor Curtis Brogden, eyed the seat. Black people also considered the Second District a reasonable reward for their loyalty. Leading them was a young, energetic future congressman, James O'Hara. State Senator John Hyman had challenged the incumbent in 1872. Assemblyman Edward R. Dudley, author of the proposed state civil rights statute, also aspired to the post.

On March 21 Wayne County Republicans opened their delegate convention at Goldsboro. The bulk of the assembly was black, but a select committee of white men called for the endorsement of a white man, Curtis Brogden. James O'Hara rose. The nomination, he declared, must go to a black man. He himself would accept the honor. A revolt against the white office-holders appeared underway. "They [black people] know that they do the voting and deem themselves entitled to some consideration."[133]

The Wayne County movement began the push for a black candidate. By the end of the month many within the Republican organization conceded the point. In that case they preferred Dudley or Hyman. O'Hara displayed too much independence of spirit.[134] Wayne County delegates met again on April 11. "The negro element evidently means to cut loose from these unscrupulous wire-workers," the *Messenger* reported.[135] O'Hara took the stage. "He proceeded to

131 See Eric Anderson, *Race and Politics in North Carolina, 1872–1901* (Baton Rouge: 1981), 3–33.
132 Anderson, *Race and Politics*, 35–40.
133 Goldsboro *Messenger*, March 23, 1874.
134 Goldsboro *Messenger*, March 30, 1874.
135 Goldsboro *Messenger*, April 13, 1874.

'skin the coon,' showing no mercy … greatly to the delight of the larger portion of his race present." The white chairman, finding his gavel insufficient, pounded his chair against the table. The meeting dissolved in chaos.

On the 18th one more try. Congressman Thomas came down from Washington. A black delegate called out: where did he stand on the Civil Rights Bill? "My colored friends," he began, "you have nothing to gain." Cries drowned him out. When he could be heard, Thomas replied. "He preferred not to fight on either side; he would vote however for the bill in Congress if the majority of his constituents desired it."[136]

The congressional nominating convention assembled finally at the Goldsboro Court House on May 14. Fifteen delegates represented the district's ten counties. Thomas held the votes of four, from Wayne and Craven Counties. O'Hara had the endorsement of two, from his base in Halifax County. Hyman held two from Warren County. Two pledged to King. The rest scattered. James O'Hara made a lively speech. Let North Carolina follow South Carolina, Mississippi and Florida; send a black man to Congress.

Balloting commenced. None of the black contenders united forces. Nor did whites rally behind a single candidate. On the 22nd vote one of O'Hara's delegates came over to Hyman. On the 29th the other followed. On the 30th ballot it was a white contender, King, who threw his support to a black man, Hyman. That decided it. "A roaring applause," the *Messenger* reported, broke out "on the part of the colored men present."[137]

Delegates finished on a note of reconciliation, making the nomination unanimous. But would white Republican voters reconcile themselves to a black nominee? Democrats saw a ray of hope, a weakening of the Republican machine. "We shall confess to some surprise if the white wing of the Radical party cheerfully and honestly support Hyman," wrote the Wilmington *Journal*.[138] History inspired the Goldsboro *Messenger*. It evoked glorious battles that had presaged the downfall of tyranny, the end of Napoleon I: "This is only the Leipzig which is to be followed by Waterloo. It is the opening of brighter skies for the Conservative banner!"[139]

The nominee, John Adams Hyman, was 33. He had been born enslaved in Warren County. During the war sold south to new owners in Alabama, he returned to North Carolina a free man. In 1868 he entered the state senate.[140] His

136 Goldsboro *Messenger*, April 20, 1874.
137 Account in Goldsboro *Messenger*, May 18, 1874; see Anderson, *Race and Politics*, 40–42.
138 Wilmington *Journal*, May 20, 1874.
139 Goldsboro *Messenger*, May 18, 1874.
140 See George W. Reid, "Four in Black: North Carolina's Black Congressmen, 1874–1901," *Journal of Negro History*, 64 (1979): 229–231.

success story, from rags to respectability, did not impress Democrats. He was not one of the good blacks. "Not even a creditable specimen of his race," huffed the New York *Tribune,* "for it is freely charged that he is a hypocrite, a swindler, a bribe-taker and a railroad jobber, having earned these complimentary titles while a member of the notoriously purchasable Legislature of 1867–8."[141] Venal or not, Hyman was a shrewd politician. Turmoil had surrounded his nomination. He needed no alienation of white voters. He carefully backed away from the Civil Rights Bill. He began with silence. He ended with denial.

His silence galled the Democrats. Nothing would have pleased them better than to report the black candidate a civil rights bill fanatic. They found nothing to report. They poured over Hyman's utterances, trying to distill some essence of fanaticism. Civil rights, the *Messenger* insisted, was "in the air." Hyman and O'Hara spoke together at Goldsboro. Democrats listened expectantly. Not even a sound bite of civil rights rhetoric emerged. O'Hara held his tongue. Hyman confined himself to a pious sentiment: "He hoped there was not a white man … who would deprive the negro of his political and social rights." He urged white and black "to stand shoulder to shoulder."[142] At the end of July the *Messenger* was still looking for a smoking gun. It could only argue a logical association. Hyman was a black man. He *had* to support the Civil Rights Bill, even if he refused to admit it. Republicans "are just as culpable as Hyman, for they elect him to vote for the bill of abominations."[143]

Hyman's silence became suspect. He commenced to speak against the Civil Rights Bill. Democratic frustration exploded. "He is against it for the sole purpose of getting the votes of white Republicans," railed the Raleigh *Sentinel.* Radicals, the paper declared, were "incensed at Hyman for opposing and denouncing the Civil Rights measures."[144] Hyman fled from the Civil Rights Bill. Democrats chased after him, waving it frantically. The *Messenger,* still obsessed with Napoleonic imagery, broadcast an epic appeal. Forget Leipzig; Waterloo was upon them. On that field, with the fate of empires in the balance, one man failed his cause. Marshal Grouchy did not appear when his divisions might have won the day. "The imperial guard was beaten back. Napoleon died a prisoner at St. Helena because one of his Marshals was behind time."

> White men of North Carolina – especially ye white men of Wayne County – will you be behind time on the 6th day of August? On that day

141 New York *Tribune,* July 28, 1874.
142 Goldsboro *Messenger,* July 13, 1874.
143 Goldsboro *Messenger,* July 27, 1874.
144 Raleigh *Sentinel,* July 20, 23, 1874.

> a great battle must and will be fought. On the ridge of every hill in North Carolina the enemy is posting his columns and daring you to the combat. The commanders of the enemy are hovering over you with an army of undisciplined, ignorant negroes.... Your institutions, your laws, your customs, are threatened with destruction. As if poverty were a crime, the children of the poor white man are to be confined on the same bench, in the same school room with the children of the negro, that they may learn to associate on terms of perfect equality, be taught by a negro and finally intermarry. In all places of public resort – in your churches, your railroad cars, your hotels and in your very graves, you are to be degraded.... This is Civil Rights. Your blood polluted, your language corrupted, your laws abolished, your customs overthrown, and, to speak plainly but candidly, to see your daughters wedded to negroes is only a part of the abominations meditated against you by the infamous advocates of Civil Rights.... Every white man to the front, and may God defend the right.[145]

Democrats fled the battlefield. Party leaders held a belated convention at Goldsboro on July 8. The meeting was short: "It being the sense of the convention that it would be inexpedient to nominate a candidate, and no further business appearing ... the convention adjourned *sine die*."[146] Ultimately a candidate did arrive. He was no Marshal Grouchy. George W. Blount, a country lawyer, announced his candidacy a week before the election. He received 11,144 votes. A Republican bolter, the black Rev. Garland White, took 1,091 votes.[147] Hyman buried them both with 18,176. The Black Second held. Even so, civil rights did the party no good. John Hyman, a black candidate, running in a safe, black district, saw the oncoming Shirt of Nessus. He ran from it, as if the devil was chasing from behind.

3 Virginia

After being buffeted by waves of Reconstruction, Virginians had redeemed their state. The election of 1873 put Democrat/Conservative James L. Kemper in the State House, along with a Democratic legislature. Republicans still held five congressional seats. The elections of 1874 swiftly reduced that number to one. Those results were perhaps inevitable once the state's white majority

---

145 Goldsboro *Messenger*, July 27, 1874.
146 Goldsboro *Messenger*, July 9, 1874.
147 Anderson, *Race and Politics*, 44.

resumed its political dominance. The advent of the Civil Rights Bill nonetheless terrified Virginia Republicans. Three of the party's five congressmen and its lone senator, John F. Lewis, opposed it. Democrats determined to deploy the civil rights issue anyway, against any and all Republicans.

Virginians eschewed the vulgar style of political intimidation fashionable in more southerly locales. They preferred a gentlemanly, paternalistic pursuit of white supremacy. "Remember the darkie as I have, kindly;" one recommended, "for it is his misfortune & not his fault that he is cursed with freedom."[148] Yet, when circumstances required, Virginians, too, could use fear to inflame the passions. Civil rights provided one such circumstance. It overrode kindliness and paternalism.

For the moment Virginia's Republicans held the 1st District (Fredericksburg), the 2nd (Norfolk), the 3rd (Richmond), and the 4th (at Petersburg). (see Map 3, below) They also held the 5th District. This ran along the North Carolina border, including the town of Danville, the counties of Pittsylvania and Halifax, west to Carroll and Grayson Counties. The election in the 5th District, lacking sources, we cannot observe in detail. It was in any case an unlikely district for Republicans. The incumbent, Christopher Y. Thomas, had won the

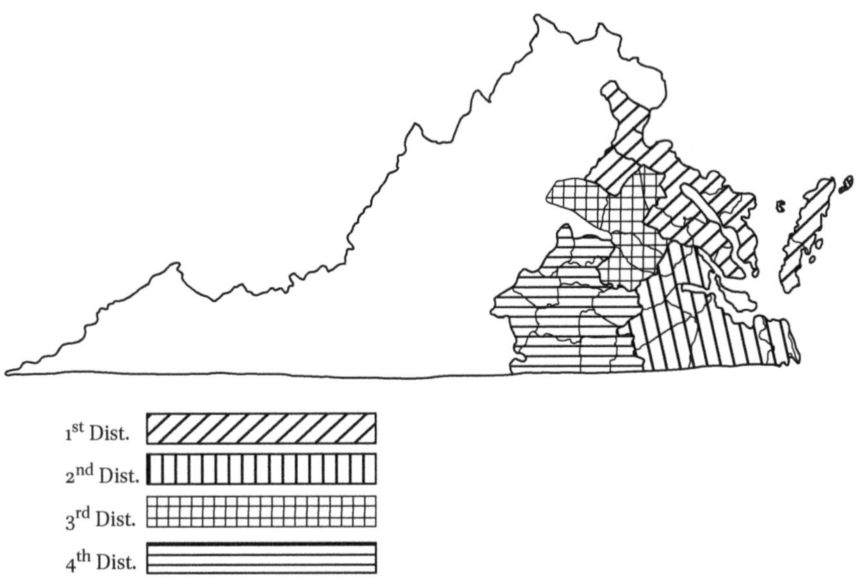

MAP 3 Congressional Districts, Virginia
SOURCE: AUTHORS OF *WELCOMING RUIN*.

148 Jack Maddex, Jr., *Virginia Conservatives, 1867–1879: A Study of Reconstruction Politics* (Chapel Hill: 1970), 197.

seat by a scant margin of 122 votes in 1872, and only then after contesting the initial results. Thomas prudently voted against civil rights on every occasion. He achieved a respectable defeat in 1874.

Virginia, First District
James B. Sener (R), Beverly B. Douglas (D)
Population: 53% white

Congressman James Sener of the 1st Virginia District entered the 1874 election a maverick. He exited a lame duck with a badly broken wing. Sener saw himself rising above parties. He discovered that no party cared for a partisan who was unpartisan.

"Jimmy Sener," one reporter recalled him, "is a plump little man, with a smile upon his face," his "nearly-closed eyes" perpetually squinting to compensate for bad vision.[149] During the war he acted as a correspondent for the Southern Associated Press accompanying Lee's Army of Northern Virginia. He witnessed the great battle fought over his home town, Fredericksburg. He ended the war a Republican and now, at 37, editor and proprietor of his own paper, the Fredericksburg *Ledger*.

Jimmy Sener won election to Congress in 1872 by 373 votes out of 21,000 cast. In his estimate 3,000 white Republicans existed in his district. The other 70% of his electors were black.[150] He feared to upset his black constituency. Even less could he afford to alienate the white vote that provided his margin of success. He presented himself as a unifier, a conduit of bipartisan moderation. He could represent black people but also the whites. He could bridge the gap between Yankee and Rebel. He cherished a hope that both Republicans and Democrats would endorse his reelection as the "People's Candidate."[151] People forced him into a nasty partisan campaign.

Sener's situation, and his conscience, led him to oppose the Civil Rights Bill. In all House votes he stood with the Republican dissidents. He voted No on May 25. He voted No on June 8 and on June 20. He voted No for a fourth time in 1875. It was folly for northerners to force utopian schemes upon the South.

149 Chicago *Tribune*, November 27, 1874.

150 Fredericksburg *Ledger*, July 10, 28, 1874.

151 Fredericksburg *Ledger*, May 15, 1874. While in Congress he tried to act the role he had cast for himself. He did his best to show good will to all. He felt aggrieved when all did not reciprocate. One ungrateful constituent was Gen. Fitzhugh Lee. For the famous general's benefit he introduced a bill to remove political disabilities. Lee repaid his gesture by introducing his Democratic opponent and calling on white men to elect someone who was "with us" in the war. Fredericksburg *Ledger*, September 8, 1874.

"We can conceive of nothing that would be as injurious to the colored race," his *Ledger* editorialized, "as the passage of the civil rights bill."[152]

No one scolded James Headon when he ran against the bill, or noticed John Hyman when he renounced it. But James Sener resided too close to the nerve center of the black elite, the Washington headquarters of such men as George Downing and Frederick Douglass, not to be noticed and scolded. The district, with its 3,000 uncertain white Republican votes and 7,000 black, began in the northern counties of Prince William and Stafford. It ran along the east of the state to the Chesapeake Bay, including the peninsular counties of Accomack and Northampton. Black people constituted a majority in eight of the sixteen counties, most notably in Essex. They nearly equaled the whites in three others. From the start Congressman Sener found his actions put under the microscope. Frederick Douglass' *New National Era* discovered traitors in Virginia.

> The colored people of two districts of Virginia can do the cause of their race much service by refusing to vote to return to Congress two gentlemen [Sener and J. Ambler Smith of Richmond] who claim to be Republicans yet perpetuate tyranny over colored men. These men must be defeated by colored votes. No colored man with a grain of self-respect will support traitors to the cause of humanity.[153]

This time there would be a true test of black voter loyalty, or so it seemed. Jimmy Sener's black constituents gathered to arrange for his retirement. Delegates from Lancaster and Richmond joined others from Northumberland County. Under their leader, Alexander Day, they met at Heathsville. Their communiqué reached the press on July 4.

> Whereas our Representative in Congress, J.B. Sener, has opposed and steadily voted against the Civil Rights Bill, and by other acts exhibited a want of sympathy and interest in Republican measures and principles, Resolved, that we repudiate Mr. Sener as a representative of our sentiments and principles, and cannot and will not under any circumstances vote for or support his re-election.[154]

Through the columns of the *Ledger*, Sener struck back.

---

152 Fredericksburg *Ledger*, May 24, 1874.

153 Washington *New National Era*, June 25, 1874.

154 Washington *New National Era*, July 9, 1874.

> A word to the colored voters of Virginia.... I do not say this as a threat, but it is not too much to imagine that one day Virginia will have a proscription ballot, and the only way to avoid it is to stand united with the white Republicans and you are safe; but sever your party relations and you are eventually done, because the Democrats are down on you and your race numbers one to seven; therefore it is unwise and rash to sever your connection with us or to make unreasonable demands upon us.[155]

The congressman's object was to avoid the turbulent forum of a district nominating convention. Let the District Executive Committee choose a candidate. Executive committeemen duly met on July 28 at Tappahannock Court House. Democrats awaited a black revolt. No revolt occurred. Jimmy Sener found a wealth of black supporters. They did not object to his objection to the Civil Rights Bill. Armistead S. Nickens, member of the House of Delegates from Lancaster, and James H. Johnston of Fredericksburg on behalf of all black people endorsed his candidacy. With them stood Alexander Day, the same who only three weeks before had repudiated the congressman. Now he "pledged the entire support of the colored people of Northumberland County."[156]

Sober reality had come home to black politicians of the Virginia 1st, as it had to their confreres in Goldsboro, Raleigh and Savannah, as it would to black politicians in Knoxville and Nashville, in Mobile and Montgomery. A defiant stand on civil rights was well and good. But if it cost them Congress they suffered more than they gained. Even the *New National Era* paused to reconsider. It published an appeal by the Virginia Republican chairman, John Wolz:

> It is well known to you that I am an earnest advocate of the Civil Rights Bill. It is true, Mr. Sener did not vote as I would have him when the civil rights bill was before Congress ... but at this time there are more important questions to be considered.... Let us not take any risk by failing to elect men, if possible, who will stand by us.[157]

George Downing too saw wisdom in those words. The National Civil Rights Council sent an emissary. Rozier D. Beckley brought startling news: James Sener had *not* voted against the Civil Rights Bill. This assertion conflicted with the plain words of the *Congressional Record*. That could be explained. His votes were cast against the adoption of procedural matters, not against the bill itself.

155 Fredericksburg *Ledger*, July 17, 1874.
156 Fredericksburg *Ledger*, July 31, 1874.
157 Washington *New National Era*, September 24, 1874.

All was forgiven.[158] Jimmy Sener secured his left flank. He faced the Democrats' mounting threat on his right.

Those Democrats convened at Tappahannock on August 5: a festival of Virginia nobility. General William Taliaferro presided. General Fitzhugh Lee appeared. General Richard L.T. Beale, ex-congressman John Critcher and lieutenant-governor Robert Montague attended. For a time the convention deadlocked. Then it broke by acclamation for a proud contender. Major Beverly Browne Douglas was a plumed knight, Confederate cavalryman, member of an exclusive society, the First Families of Virginia (FFV). His acceptance speech reflected his combative character. He disdained bipartisanship. He ridiculed his opponent's professed moderation, his pathetic attempt to pose as a unifier. Sener represented the "plunderers and traitors" of Virginia. "He did not know what part of the traitor Sener he would cut off but he would bury his carcass so deep that the hand of resurrection would never reach him." Having dismembered his opponent, he drew the color line around his remains: "This is, must and shall be a white man's government."[159]

Sener's civil rights stand meant nothing to Major Douglas. "Even if he should cast a direct vote against that abominable thing intended to degrade the white people, even then if you look at his past record you can never forgive him."[160] The Richmond *Dispatch* anointed Sener officially "the civil rights candidate." His supposed opposition was a decoy, the Tidewater *Index* declared, an "assumed hostility."[161] The Gloucester *Herald*, defying all evidence, insisted he had voted *for* the bill; reports to the contrary were "simply false."[162] The Fredericksburg *Virginia Herald* conceded he had voted against the Civil Rights Bill. But it was a trick. The *Herald* unearthed shocking information: a secret Republican memorandum, a sworn attestation countersigned by Rozier Beckley. The congressman certified to black people that his hostility was only an election dodge. Sumner's measure had his "hearty approval." Beckley protested. The document was a fraud.[163] The damage was done.

Class warfare sharpened the asperity of the campaign. The First Families made clear their disdain for an inferior. Sener's supporters in return praised his modest roots, planted among the common folk. The *New National Era*, having repented of its quarrel, painted a heroic portrait: the people's congressman, "of humble origin, and with the disadvantage of being raised in one of the most

158 Fredericksburg *Ledger*, July 28; Petersburg *Index and Appeal*, October 1, 1874.
159 Fredericksburg *Ledger*, August 11, 1874.
160 Fredericksburg *Ledger*, August 25, 1874.
161 Fredericksburg *Ledger*, September 22, 1874.
162 Fredericksburg *Ledger*, September 25, October 9, 1874.
163 Fredericksburg *Ledger*, October 20, 1874.

aristocratic communities of our aristocratic State … risen from the poor and friendless boy."[164] By contrast there was the aristocratic Douglas, raised on his plantation, surrounded by haughty Taliaferros and godlike Lees. Overlords, Sener's *Ledger* declared, they exploited the poor people. Fifteen years ago they had manipulated fear and prejudice to lead them into a hopeless rebellion. Now they invoked civil rights fear to maintain their power.[165]

The candidates agreed to a series of joint discussions. Placing the dynamic Douglas and the sensitive Sener on the same platform promised an unpleasant ending. It ended unpleasantly. The adversaries met first at King George Court House on September 4. Sener enumerated his votes against the Civil Rights Bill. Douglas declared those votes irrelevant, inspired by political cowardice not "fixed principle."[166] They met on September 9 at Fredericksburg. Sener once more reviewed his course in regard to civil rights. He urged whites to put aside hard feelings: "The fathers of many of his audience knew him well…. He felt that he could talk to the people as one of them. The prejudices, hate and intolerance of the past cannot make a great people." Let whites not resurrect hatreds. Let blacks not revive hatreds with civil rights bills.[167]

The debate reached King and Queen Court House on the 20th. Sener suggested irregularities. His opponent had bought his nomination with bribes. Douglas all but called for a duel: "Sir, I pronounce you a base calumniator and slanderer." After a tense moment the candidates stepped aside. Sener agreed to retract his statement. Douglas fumed: "I recall my remark for the present, but with the certainty of doom. If ever you repeat the offense I will repeat my remark and more besides."[168]

On October 26 at King William Court House doom arrived. The candidates mounted to the high porch of Powell's tavern. An unruly crowd gathered below. Sener mentioned the salary grab, noting Democrats' culpability therein. He cited Kentucky's Congressman James Beck. Douglas exploded. Sener had slandered him. Now he insulted a friend, a fine Kentucky gentleman. Douglas reached for a weapon. His hand seized upon a heavy glass tumbler. Sener grabbed a matching missile: "If you throw that glass, I'll throw this one." They threw. The crowd surged forward. Douglas' supporters swarmed over the congressman. Pummeled, punched and pushed, Sener fell backwards through the railing and off the porch. He landed on his back. There he was stomped upon.

---

164 Washington *New National Era*, September 24, 1874.
165 Fredericksburg *Ledger*, August 28, September 8, 1874.
166 Fredericksburg *Ledger*, September 4, 1874.
167 Fredericksburg *Ledger*, September 11, 1874.
168 Norfolk *Virginian*, October 21, 1874.

Jimmy Sener regained consciousness in his hotel room. Doctors tended to a badly bruised body, a disfigured face, a broken nose, and a left arm shattered in two places. Major Douglas, seeing his opponent projected over the porch rail, walked off to catch the next train. Sener's campaign ended.

James Sener, despite his civil rights apostasy, won all eight black counties. He lost all eight white counties. He lost his seat in Congress. Jimmy Sener passed from the political scene unlamented. His conciliatory course had not won him the gratitude of Democrats. It cost him the sympathy of his own party. "For his good name and fair fortune," snarled the *National Republican,* "it would have been better if the rowdy gang had broken his neck instead of his very weak arm."[169]

Virginia, Third District
Rush Burgess (R), Gilbert C. Walker (D), Robert Paul (I)
Population: 50.1% black

Richmond's John A. Smith was the nation's youngest representative. He took his seat from the Virginia 3rd District two months past his 26th birthday. The press dubbed him promptly "the boy congressman," an appearance his whiskerless face and weak chin did nothing to conceal. He did affect to part his name in the middle. He referred to himself, and thus was referred to, as Hon. J. Ambler Smith. He was a young man of property. His interests inclined to land speculation, from which large sums passed into his private fortune.[170] He was also a son-in-law of United States Senator John F. Lewis. When in Washington he shared his father-in-law's townhouse at 1007 K St. NW.[171] Along with his colleague Sener, Smith took a rebel position on civil rights.

Ambler Smith's civil rights dilemma sprang in large part from the nature of the district. At its heart sat the city of Richmond, then the counties of Henrico, Louisa and Hanover in line, with Caroline County as an appendage to the north and Chesterfield County to the south. Outlined on a map, or visualized from an aerial perspective, it resembled a bird with outstretched wings. It was a winged nightmare. No district in the nation balanced more delicately between white and black than did the Virginia 3rd. The census of 1870 recorded a difference of

---

169 Washington *National Republican,* February 2, 1875.

170 His most recent transactions included the sale of 160,000 acres in Wyoming County, West Virginia. They netted the congressman profits of $110,000. Fredericksburg *Ledger,* May 12, 1874.

171 Fredericksburg *Ledger,* December 16, 1873.

precisely 310: 66,427 black persons and 66,117 whites dwelt in uneasy proximity. Blacks predominated slightly in Caroline County and Hanover, and by a larger majority in Louisa County. Whites held their greatest advantage in Richmond. Congressman Smith's margin of victory in 1872 measured 468 votes.

Smith approached his dilemma forthrightly. He rejected the Civil Rights Bill. He voted No on May 25. He missed the call on June 8. He returned on June 20 to vote No. When the final vote was taken on February 5, 1875, he had become a lame duck. He voted No again. He voted his convictions. His conviction was not rooted in racism. In other respects he displayed an enlightened attitude. After Robert Elliott delivered his great speech, Ambler Smith was among those who rose to shake his hand.[172] Civil rights, he believed, were good; civil rights bills were bad. "For five years," he explained to black constituents, "I have labored to secure to your people their legal rights, but I am not willing to vote for that bill. It will bring about strife between the white and black races. It will destroy the present school system of our State.... The vanity of a few colored men will be gratified at a cost of ninety-nine out of the hundred."[173]

Such sincerity put him in the crosshairs. Congress adjourned. Ambler Smith came home to find a district in disorder. He calmly turned and walked away. He left for Europe on July 1. Money beckoned. Politics would have to wait. He held in his portfolio the deeds to "several million acres of Virginia mineral and agricultural lands" available at reasonable prices. He made his pitch in London, Glasgow and Belfast, then moved on to Alsace and Lorraine, those "dissatisfied districts lately annexed to Prussia" where emigrants might consider transplanting themselves to good Virginia soil.[174] If sales were plentiful, he hinted, he might not seek re-nomination. Virginians, on good Virginia soil, were unconvinced. He seemed rather to have made an escape, expecting the party to smooth things over in his absence. When he returned in September his political fortunes had taken a decided downturn.

While Smith pursued mammon across the water a rival pursued politics at home. Rush Burgess was a well-known figure. He had come south in 1850, at age 12, from Herkimer, New York. His family settled at Hatcher's Run in Dinwiddie County. He had established solid Republican credentials. He achieved postwar prominence as Mayor of Petersburg, appointed by military authority in 1868. In that shattered city he labored for the welfare of destitute freedmen. The Petersburg Relief Association and the Impartial Relief Association distributed largesse. He organized the city's first public school system. That success came at the expense of increased taxes and municipal debt. It exasperated

172 Richmond *Dispatch*, January 8, 1874.

173 Richmond *Dispatch*, January 7, 1874.

174 Richmond *Dispatch*, June 6, 1874.

Petersburg's whites as it endeared the mayor to his black constituents. Now, he told black people, he would uphold them again, on civil rights, if they upheld him for Congress.[175]

The rivalry between Smith and Burgess tore 3rd District Republicans apart. The Civil Rights Bill became the sword of their dismemberment. The battle began in earnest on August 20. The Republican District Committee met to set a date for the nominating convention. It proposed September 16. Smith's ship was still out at sea. His proxies suggested that the District Committee make the nomination. That suggestion failed. They requested a postponement until October. The committee agreed on October 7. Now Burgess' adherents protested. They turned to black delegates, only to find that most maintained allegiance to the congressman. "If Mr. Smith receives the nomination," they assured the *Dispatch*, "all of the negroes in the district will give him their support."[176]

Third District Republicans disintegrated. Andrew Washburn, chairman of the district committee, switched to Burgess. He overruled his own committee; a convention must meet on September 16. The committee overruled Chairman Washburn; delegates must abide by October 7. Smith reached dry land. A "peace conference" met on September 8, under the auspices of the Republican State Committee.[177] It achieved nothing. On the 9th Ambler Smith announced he would seek re-nomination. His forces rallied at the Court House in Richmond. A considerable contingent of black men came out. They cheerfully endorsed the anti-civil-rights candidate. They roundly rejected the pro-civil-rights candidate. They denounced the Civil Rights Bill: "a dangerous subject for national legislation."[178]

Burgess held his convention a week later, on September 16, at Assembly Hall in Richmond. Black State Delegate William P. Lucas presided. He demanded a civil rights bill. Civil rights became Burgess' rallying cry: "Public privilege and accommodations shall be accorded to all men alike."[179] Smith rallied on the 23rd. Black men rallied alongside. Rev. William B. Derrick of Richmond's Third Street African Methodist Church stood by the congressman. The congressman rejected the Civil Rights Bill.[180]

On the 27th Smith and Burgess debated, facing each other on the steps of the Louisa Court House. Burgess, Smith declared, "had as much chance of going to Congress as a cur dog." From then on Burgess' partisans dogged the

---

175 See William D. Henderson, *The Unredeemed City: Reconstruction in Petersburg, Virginia, 1865–1874* (Washington: 1977), 177–178, 234–235.

176 Richmond *Dispatch*, September 1, 1874.

177 Richmond *Dispatch*, September 9, 1874.

178 Richmond *Dispatch*, September 15; Washington *New National Era*, September 24, 1874.

179 Richmond *Dispatch*, September 17, 1874.

180 Richmond *Dispatch*, September 24, 1874.

congressman. Canine cries, "bow-wow-wow," rose from the crowd wherever Smith tried to speak.[181]

Republican leaders noticed that matters had gotten out of hand. Warnings reached President Grant. Railroad magnate Williams Wickham wrote urgently. The White House must intervene to stop the feud "which will lose us this district."[182] Peacemakers proposed a compromise. Both candidates should withdraw in favor of a third man acceptable to all. For that role they proposed Henry A. Wise.[183] The erstwhile Democratic Governor of Virginia had signed for the execution of John Brown. He had accepted a general's commission in the Confederate Army. But he had since drifted steadily toward the Republicans. ("The old general has always been a little peculiar in his political views," the Democratic Petersburg *Index and Appeal* observed.[184]) Henry Wise declined. The Smith-Burgess battle resumed.

On October 10 the Republican Executive Committee tried again. "I have the honor to suggest," Chairman James Edmunds suggested, "the voluntary withdrawal of both [candidates] and the selection of some other prominent and able man upon whom all the Republicans of the district can cordially unite."[185] Another peace conference. Smith came prepared to accept a mutual withdrawal. It became apparent that the party wanted Burgess. It had stacked the conference with "neutral delegates," really Burgess' partisans. Declaring it a "put-up job," Smith's men withdrew in a huff. The rump endorsed Rush Burgess.[186] Smith lashed out at Burgess and at the Civil Rights Bill. "I am opposed to the whole of that infernal machine and everything connected with it." Governor Kemper had guaranteed the Negroes in Virginia all the rights they required. A black supporter sang out: "three cheers for Kemper."[187] Democrats looked on gleefully. "It is hard enough to defeat one man," the *Dispatch* chuckled, "let alone two such puissant gentlemen as now thunder forth their threats."[188]

---

181 Richmond *Dispatch*, October 6, 1874.

182 Williams C. Wickham to Ulysses Grant, September 1, 1874. *Grant Papers*, vol. 25, 139.

183 Richmond *Dispatch*, September 16; Petersburg *Index and Appeal*, September 29; Martinsburg *Independent*, September 19, 1874.

184 Petersburg *Index and Appeal*, September 29, 1874. On Henry Wise's postwar mellowing, see Craig M. Simpson, *A Good Southerner: The Life of Henry A. Wise of Virginia* (Chapel Hill: 1995), 285–313.

185 Richmond *Dispatch*, October 11, 1874.

186 Richmond *Dispatch*, October 20, 1874.

187 Richmond *Dispatch*, October 22, 1874.

188 Richmond *Dispatch*, October 21, 1874.

Finally Ulysses Grant stepped in. On October 27 Mr. Smith went to Washington. On the 28th he withdrew.[189] The *New National Era* endorsed Burgess, "a true Republican [who] deserves the support of all good men who favor equal political and civil rights."[190] Smith's black adherents refused to yield, not to Burgess' blandishments, not for the sake of civil rights bills, nor even to the word of Frederick Douglass. They nominated their own candidate as an independent Republican. Robert A. Paul, an aspiring associate of Rev. Derrick, took up the banner of "our honored friend John A. Smith."[191]

Democrats nominated a candidate. Gilbert C. Walker was a carpet-bagger from Chicago. He had arrived, fabric-covered valise in hand, to seek his fortune after the war. He rose to be Virginia's provisional governor in 1869 and its elected governor in 1870. He swiftly brought civil rights to the voters' attention: "Let this bill once become a law, and the doors of your hotels, your theaters and places of public amusement, your railroad cars and public conveyances … your common schools, will be thrown open to the colored people."[192] On September 10 Walker's forces rallied at the Richmond Theater. Governor Kemper lent his services. His alliteratively-labeled political organization, the Kemper Kampaign Klub (commonly referred to, without further allusion, by its first initials) arranged the festivities, providing music and refreshments. The candidate spoke: "Stamp this infamous [civil rights] bill and send it to perdition – bury it in its own swaddling clothes, and its infamous author along with it."[193]

Walker's majority over Burgess came in at 2,615. Exactly 58 persons cast a ballot for Robert Paul. Civil rights again shattered Republicans. Vote for civil rights, Rush Burgess begged. White voters fled. Black voters failed to rally to the candidate who promised them their presumably most cherished desire.

189 Smith bowed out gracefully. His notice "To the Voters of the Third District" thanked loyal Republicans: "I respectfully withdraw my name from the congressional canvass. In doing this I cannot fail to express my warmest thanks to the people of the district for their cordial support in the past. I sincerely believe that my steadfast and whole-souled Republican friends who may be disappointed at my retiring will in the future be satisfied of its wisdom and its justice to them." Petersburg *Index and Appeal*, October 31, 1874.

190 Washington *New National Era*, October 22, 1874.

191 Daniel B. Williams, *A Sketch of the Life and Times of Capt. Robert A. Paul* (Richmond: 1885), 11–12.

192 Richmond *Dispatch*, August 27, 1874.

193 Richmond *Dispatch*, September 11, 1874. Ben Butler, presumably, since Sumner was already buried.

Virginia, Second District
James Platt (R), John Goode (D), Robert Norton (I)
Population: 53% black

James Sener opposed the Civil Rights Bill. He got no relief. Rush Burgess supported it. He got no reward. The embattled incumbent of the 2nd District, James Platt, supported the bill. Its supporters opposed him. Its opponents denounced him. He defended his seat against a double envelopment.

The 2nd District centered on the city of Norfolk. It possessed a black majority of some 9,000. It also possessed a navy yard, source of patronage supreme, filled with happy workers, all federally employed, grateful to the politician who sustained their employment. Sunset Cox, in his "moth" speech, congratulated the Virginia congressman on the abundance of such rich food on which to feed. Congressman Platt was well fed, at 37, a portly gentleman, sartorially correct. Democrats insinuated that his citizenship was questionable.[194] It was not. Dr. James Henry Platt, Jr. had entered the world at St. John's, Newfoundland. His parents were American citizens. They raised him in Burlington, Vermont. Platt received his medical degree from the University of Vermont in 1859. When war came he volunteered in the 4th Vermont infantry. Cited for gallantry at the battle of Fredericksburg, he rose to lieutenant-colonel. Captured at Cold Harbor, he survived Libby Prison. After the war he remained in Petersburg, a detested carpetbagger. Thus the Norfolk *Virginian:*

> As hyenas with stealthy step slink by the ghost that guards the grave to glut their greed with the dead body it contains; as vultures who swoop upon the stricken hind when the life blood has scarcely ceased to ebb from his breast; as wolves dart to despoil and devour the helpless dying men – Platt, Jr. and his dastard battalion came into Virginia and the South to hack and hew and insult and oppress a chivalrous though prostrate people.[195]

Platt began his congressional career in the Petersburg district, the old Virginia 2nd. He occupied that seat for two terms, then moved on to run in the newly redrawn 2nd at Norfolk. He won in 1872 in a landslide of 5,200 votes over Democrat Baker P. Lee. That margin was misleading, magnified by a Greeley drag. One year later Republican gubernatorial candidate Robert Hughes carried the

194 Norfolk *Virginian*, June 17, 1874.
195 Norfolk *Virginian*, August 15, 1874.

district by fewer than 2,000 votes. Platt professed no worry. "Lightning would not strike him."[196]

Platt's 2nd District occupied the south-east corner of the state, from New Kent and Charles City southward to Nansemond, Southampton and Norfolk. Its jewel was Norfolk's Gosport Navy Yard. Black persons held a majority in all but three of the district's fourteen counties. They dominated in Sussex, Prince George, York and Elizabeth City. Whites held their greatest edge in Norfolk city.

Congressman Platt's black constituents required him to support civil rights. He did. He endorsed it on the House floor. When the votes came, he spoke aye on May 25. He spoke it again on June 8. Then he flinched. On June 20 he was silent. It was a slight deviation, and politically understandable. His hiccup gave opponents just enough to unleash civil rights misery on James H. Platt, Jr.

The congressman approached re-election calmly. "Politically everything is quiet here," he wrote in July. "The campaign will not open until Sept." But attacks had already begun. The *Virginian's* editorial appeared on June 11:

> Our Platt was the only Congressman from Virginia who voted to take up the Civil Rights bill.... Our Platt has played upon one string so long that he knows no other, having made his dirty fortune by the pretence of championing the negro ... [but] our Platt's career draws near to a close. Next fall this district will dismiss him from the place he got into by means of reconstruction. A few short months and he will be numbered with the host of his forerunners and companions in sudden rise and fatal downfall.

On the 17th the *Virginian* struck at the incumbent's most vital point. It addressed the laboring men, the navy yard workers on whose votes their patron relied.

> By that bill Congress tries to force every laboring man's children down to the level of the negro.... Your boys and girls must have his to sit by them. Your children must breathe the same air as his ... and all for what? In order that a New Hampshire adventurer may draw the pay of a Virginia Congressman.... Let laboring men of this District consider these things and determine with one consent to pluck down from his place next November this renegade to his race, this enemy of the poor man, this vile drift weed floated to us on the waters of a civil war.[197]

---

196 Mary Hinsdale, *Garfield-Hinsdale Letters: Correspondence between James Abram Garfield and Burke Aaron Hinsdale* (Ann Arbor: 1945), 232.

197 James Platt to John P. Foley, July 20, 1874. Benjamin Butler Papers, Library of Congress.

This volley struck home. Three days later Congressman Platt chose to avoid the last civil rights vote. Meanwhile another danger took shape. Black people, as at Savannah and Goldsboro, considered the time had come to elect a black congressman. Reports circulated that John Mercer Langston intended to seek the Norfolk nomination.[198] Langston declined. State Delegate Robert Norton of York County stepped in.

The Nortons, Robert and his brothers Frederick and Daniel, were a determined clan. Born enslaved, risen against the odds,[199] their strength lay in Yorktown. There black people felt aggrieved. Congressman Platt lavished patronage on his Norfolk workers. He neglected those on the Peninsula, all the while demanding their votes. Norton toured the district, discharging vitriolic verbiage upon the incumbent's head. Even his diction displayed his distaste. "Whenever he had occasion to mention him [Platt] he would send the name forth through his clenched teeth with a hiss."[200] On the 4th of July at Yorktown Robert Norton's sibilance resounded. "The time had come," he declared.

> The black man in Virginia should demand from the Republican party the right of representation in the offices. The Conservative party would not grant the right to the negro to hold office, but our so-called white Radicals granted the right, but took good care that no one but themselves enjoyed the office.[201]

Norton focused on the Civil Rights Bill. Democrats accused James Platt of championing it. Norton accused him of betraying it. The congressman had left himself vulnerable: the missed call on June 20. Norton railed against carpetbaggers, "kept in office while the best of the colored men are kept out in the cold." Platt was one of the worst, "this man who is opposed to the Civil Rights Bill."[202] Such rhetoric delighted Democrats. The *Virginian* happily broadcast the manifesto of the Norton Campaign Club:

> Republicans! While we have been fighting and abusing each other, the carpet-bagger has been fattening, growing rich, and enjoying ease and luxury, all at our expense.... Rally to the standard of true Republicanism and vote for a colored man to go to Congress to help pass the Civil Rights

---

198 Louisville *Courier-Journal*, February 13, 1874.

199 Robert and Daniel before the war had escaped to freedom. Daniel returned from New York City with a medical degree. Frederick and Robert entered the House of Delegates. Daniel served in the state senate.

200 Richmond *Dispatch*, November 3, 1874.

201 Norfolk *Virginian*, July 11, 1874.

202 Norfolk *Virginian*, August 1, 1874.

> bill. Colored men, we beseech you not to vote for this man [Platt]; he is *opposed to the Civil Rights bill*.... Everything that concerns the colored man most he opposes.[203]

White enemies insisted James Platt supported civil rights. Black rivals insisted he did not. For the *Virginian* it made no difference. "Either way, J.H. Platt convicts himself as unworthy the confidence of the race he lives on, cheats, and laughs at, and on the white men of this district he has long made it impossible he should have any claim."[204]

The Republican convention assembled at Hampton on July 14. "In the various bar-rooms whites and blacks hob-nobbed very sociably," the *Virginian* reported, "practical equality being the order of the day." Some black delegates, nevertheless, murmured of a stacked convention. The convention endorsed Platt. Platt officially endorsed the Civil Rights Bill. Norton called him officially a liar.[205]

Democrats met at Suffolk. Former Confederate congressman John Goode, Jr. took the nomination on the first ballot. Delegates paraded to the tune of "Dixie." Banners proclaimed: "We nominated a GOODE candidate." Goode, modestly, recalled in his memoirs that he accepted the nomination "as a forlorn hope;" thus was his victory all the more outstanding.[206] He might also have recalled that his forlorn hope benefited from two far-from-forlorn assets. He had the Civil Rights Bill, and he had Robert Norton. He played on civil rights fear. And he played Robert Norton against James Platt. He treated his black competitor with the utmost respect, a deference usually reserved for whites. He treated his white competitor with all the contempt gentlemen usually reserved for blacks:

> There are two candidates besides myself before the people: the Hon. Robert Norton and James H. Platt, Jr. Mr. Norton comes from Yorktown, a place made famous by the surrender of Cornwallis; Mr. Platt comes from Vermont, or Canada, or somewhere else in the direction of the North Pole, nobody knows where.... [Mr. Norton] is an American citizen of African descent, a man of marked ability and ambition, and it was the most natural thing in the world that he should seek to represent his race.[207]

203 Norfolk *Virginian*, August 23, 1874.
204 Norfolk *Virginian*, August 26, 1874.
205 Norfolk *Virginian*, August 11, 1874.
206 John Goode, Jr., *Recollections of a Lifetime* (New York: 1906), 107.
207 Norfolk *Virginian*, September 2, 1874.

As for the Civil Rights Bill, Goode insisted, Platt definitely supported it – "I charge Platt with being the champion of civil rights, that odious measure that would open up our hotels, theaters, churches, common schools and universities to the mixture of blacks." Thus he was a traitor to the white people. But Platt did *not* support it – "On the 25th of May and on the 8th of June he voted for the measure. Why then did he not vote for it on the 22nd [sic]?" Therefore he was a fraud upon the black people.[208]

Goode and Norton became inseparable comrades. Platt challenged Goode to debate. Goode declined, unless Norton stood upon the stage to share equal time with the white men. Platt refused. He tried to debate his Democratic opponent, but he would not legitimize the campaign of his Independent rival. Norton lay in wait to bushwhack Platt. Goode assisted the bushwhackers at every opportunity.

The allies set their first trap on September 14. Goode offered Platt the joint discussion he so eagerly desired. They would meet at Suffolk. The congressman arrived unsuspecting. Suddenly Nortonites emerged. Platt scampered away, leaving surrogates to plead his cause. Goode and Norton ambushed their quarry again at Williamsburg on the 24th. Platt had scheduled himself to speak, alone. Goode cut short a rally at Surry Court House. He rushed to the James River, commandeered the ferry: now on land, miles to go, no transport. Afoot, a long dusty road, he descended upon a dumbfounded congressman. Before Platt could react Norton emerged, with fifes and drums, marching from the opposite road. Trapped. Platt accepted Goode's challenge. He refused to recognize Norton. Mark the insult, Norton called to black people in the audience. He departed.

At 7 p.m. the debate commenced. Goode fired civil rights at Platt. "He charged him on his support of the Civil Rights Bill, and his advocacy of mixed schools, and with such burning language and honest indignation as to bring forth a spontaneous outburst of applause that caused Mr. Platt to rise and deny the charge." He denied it, yet he could not deny it. He did favor the bill, he admitted, but he did not favor the mixed school part. Ah, Goode inquired: why then had he voted twice for the bill and the school clause was distinctly included? The *Virginian* exulted: "James H. Platt, Jr. will never forget, should he live to the years of Methuselah, the forced march and flank movement of John Goode."[209] Nor, the paper might have added, the flank movement of Robert Norton.

On October 12 the allies struck again. Platt had scheduled a speech at Suffolk in Nansemond County. Accordingly he stepped into Norfolk's early morning

208 Norfolk *Virginian*, September 15, 1874.
209 Norfolk *Virginian*, September 25, 1874.

mail coach on the Atlantic, Mississippi and Ohio Railroad. He closed the carriage door and opened a newspaper. John Goode slipped unseen into the ladies' coach. Robert Norton, followed by his brothers, jumped onto the smoking car, mingling with nondescript black travelers. They came all together upon the platform at Suffolk. The congressman looked up to see his rivals athwart his path; he "smole a sickly smile." This time Norton refused to be disregarded. Platt did the best he could. He spoke first and got out fast. He avoided all mention of the Civil Rights Bill, whether he had voted for it or neglected to vote, with mixed schools or without. He vanished down the road. Norton and Goode waved him on his way. The ex-Confederate ushered the emancipated gentleman up to share the platform. Together they apostrophized the departed congressman in the most unflattering terms.[210]

Goode took to sharing his stump with Norton on a regular basis. They joined forces next at Jerusalem in Southampton County. Norton was far from his friendly peninsular base. Black supporters of Platt appeared in the crowd. A riot was narrowly averted.[211] Undeterred, the allies marched on. Goode took a detour to New Kent County to receive the benediction of a Lee, General William Henry Fitzhugh Lee, at Tunstall's Station. Lee blessed Goode's candidacy. Virginians must stand now, he declared, as they did in 1861, to defend "the dearest right of the white race." Goode hurried to a rally at Burnt Ordinary. Frederick S. Norton took his brother's place for the occasion.[212]

The Goode-and-Norton caravan reached New Kent Court House on the 22nd. A crowd of mixed race awaited. A white man called out: "Platt is agin mixed schools, and he's right." Goode replied: "Yes, he tells *you* he is opposed to mixed schools because that would destroy your means of educating your children; but when he is in Congress he votes exactly opposite to his lies, and votes for the Civil Rights bill with mixed schools, hotel features and all." Norton raised no protest.[213] A barbecue followed the speaking. There, reporters noted, the social code remained in force. "After the white people had been amply supplied, the colored ones partook of what was left."[214]

Platt had been ambushed repeatedly. Now he sprang an ambush of his own.[215] His rivals had arranged a rally at Yorktown on October 30. A U.S. government tug, the *Miles Standish,* crossed the estuary, carrying two hundred

---

210 Norfolk *Virginian*, October 13, 1874.
211 Norfolk *Virginian*, October 20, 1874.
212 Norfolk *Virginian*, October 22–23, 1874.
213 Norfolk *Virginian*, October 24, 1874.
214 Norfolk *Virginian*, October 27, 1874.
215 Account in Richmond *Dispatch*, November 3, 1874, including an interview with Norton. Also Norfolk *Virginian*, October 31, November 1, 3; Petersburg *Index and Appeal*, November 2, 1874.

Platt supporters pulled from the Navy Yard and the Norfolk docks. They came armed with knives, cudgels and pistols. Goode took up his post near Dawson's Hotel closest to the waterfront. Norton set up across from the store where he and his brothers sold general goods. Platt addressed his people in an open lot near the Nelson House hotel. Each speaker retired to his stand and commenced an oration. Then a party of Platt's dockworkers broke away. They assaulted the Norton platform. Norton's men retreated to the store and grabbed firearms. Reports spoke of four dead. Witnesses counted three bodies laid out on the wharf. Norton circulated a card.

> Colored men for expressing their opinion shot down in the streets; Platt's hirelings armed with cannon, pistols, knives and clubs. Shall black men submit any longer? Rise, freemen, and throw off the yoke of political slavery. For years we have borne the whip and lash our political task-masters have used on us. Before the war it was the whip of servitude we suffered from. Then we were by law slaves, and we had no recognized right or chance to resist. Now, by the law of the land, we are freemen. Yet in what way are we treated by those who claim to be our saviors? Are we not used to help them in their base purposes? used to put them in office? used to lift them up in the high places of the land? And if we dare to express dissent, if we dare to aspire to place, if we dare to be free, not only is the political whip used on us, but the knife and the pistol, and the club.... Remember Yorktown, colored freemen, vote for your rights and liberties.[216]

Results came in slowly. The *Virginian* reported Goode ahead by 700 votes on November 5. On the 6th returns put Platt in the lead by 200. Norton's vote was small. Black people, once again, remained loyal to the party organization. Norfolk city recorded the suffrages of 1,619 black persons; 1,587 voted for Platt, 20 preferred Goode, 12 cast a ballot for Robert Norton. Some 2,343 white Norfolkers voted; 2,151 chose Goode. Platt had the support of 192. Norton had none.[217] Goode carried York County, along with Princess Anne, Nansemond, Isle of Wight and Southampton. Platt won Norfolk County, Elizabeth City, Prince George, Surry, Charles City and Sussex.

Days passed. The result was not confirmed. Platt confined himself to his house. He asked the mayor to provide police protection. The *Virginian's* reporter knocked at his residence on York Street. Platt himself opened the front door. He was entirely at peace. Come what may, he said, this would be his last campaign. At the garden gate he paused to pluck a flower. He begged the

216 Petersburg *Index and Appeal*, November 3, 1874.
217 Norfolk *Virginian*, November 4, 1874.

reporter "to grant him the favor of pinning it on the lapel of his coat as a covenant of good feeling.... I do not expect long to remain in your midst, and I wish to leave your beautiful city with its broad and capacious harbor ... as a monument to my humble efforts. I do not desire to have the ill will of any one."[218]

The congressman's complaisance may have come from the feeling that he had won. He still had the weight of his navy yard workers.[219] Final returns gave Platt the victory by 324 votes, 14,377 against 14,053 for Goode, with 444 for Norton. Democrats refused to let the 2nd District slip away. Goode contested the returns from James City, Southampton, York, Sussex and Prince George Counties. His challenge came before the State Board of Canvassers. Its five members all were Democrats: Governor Kemper, Attorney-General Raleigh Daniel, Secretary of the Commonwealth James McDonald, Auditor William F. Taylor and Treasurer R.M.T. Hunter. After due deliberation, the canvassers overruled the voters. The board did not interfere in all the contested counties. It sufficed to disqualify one. All ballots from Prince George County were thrown out. The county clerk, it was said, had improperly sealed the returns. Platt's majority in Prince George was 455. Simple subtraction sent Goode to Congress by 131 votes.[220]

This procedure, discounting an entire county on a technicality, seemed highly suspect – particularly since the negligent clerk and county election officials were Democrats. Platt protested. Virginia courts rejected him. He took his case to the 44th Congress. Henry Wise, still pursuing good deeds for Republicans, represented him. So flagrant was the Board of Canvassers' manipulation that the House Elections Committee, even one now controlled by Democrats, decided in Platt's favor. A very close vote on the House floor reversed the committee's recommendation. John Goode held his seat.[221]

Virginia, Fourth District
William H.H. Stowell (R), William Hodges Mann (D), Charles Porter (I)
Population: 65% black

---

218 Norfolk *Virginian*, November 8, 1874.

219 Platt's agents posted a sliding scale of campaign "contributions" required of all workmen: "Mark opposite each man's name paid, or why." Contributions considered each worker's pay grade: $20 required of a foreman; $3.26 from a first-class machinist; $1.26 from a laborer; $1.02 – not $1, opponents snickered, but one dollar and two pennies – from the water-boys. Anticipating Platt's defeat, Democrats composed a mischievous musical jingle: "Water Boys Rejoice." Petersburg *Index and Appeal*, October 14, 1874.

220 Richmond *Dispatch*, November 23–24, 1874.

221 Goode, *Recollections of a Lifetime*, 108–109; Rowell, *Digest of Contested Election Cases*, 318–320; Simpson, *A Good Southerner*, 312.

The 4th District began in Powhatan and Cumberland Counties. It ranged south to Mecklenburg, Brunswick and Greensville bordering on North Carolina. The area was mostly rural but possessed one urban center, the city of Petersburg. Black persons held the majority in all eleven counties. In most they dominated by a ratio of more than two to one, overall by nearly two-thirds. Democrats despaired. The Petersburg *Index and Appeal* declared hope of redemption "forlorn." White people, trapped in a black fiefdom, referred to their district as "Hayti."[222] A congressional campaign seemed pointless.

A white man represented Virginia's black republic. William Henry Harrison Stowell was a Yankee from Vermont. He had not, as Platt, fought his way south but rather arrived in Virginia as an official of the Freedman's Bureau.[223] He took the post of Collector of Internal Revenue at Petersburg in 1869, and was elected to Congress from the old 4th District at Norfolk the next year. In 1872, after redistricting, he switched places with Platt to take the new 4th District at Petersburg, while the latter moved over to Norfolk. Stowell had demonstrated good will to black people through his work in the Freedman's Bureau. He continued to show it with unwavering support of the Civil Rights Bill. Every House vote found him present. In every vote he voted Aye.

Black people, nonetheless, eyed Stowell's position. Aspirants included a seasoned politician, State Senator George W. Graham, and a novice, Mr. Mark R. De Mortie. The latter posed the greater challenge. He was a cultivated gentleman and, most significantly, Cordelia's husband, Cordelia, daughter of George T. Downing. Through her he enjoyed entrée into Washington's black society. He envisioned himself, and Cordelia, dining at his father-in-law's congressional restaurant. "Mr. Downing takes a very great interest in the election," the New York *Times* related, "and there is no doubt if Mr. De Mortie succeeds, his wife, who is quite fond of fashionable life, will make something of a sensation in social circles, as Mr. Downing has hitherto exercised all his civil rights."[224] De Mortie moved from Norfolk to Burkeville Junction in Nottoway County. "Ostensibly," it was said, "he engages in the humble business of running a sassafras mill."[225] He ran for election in the 4th District.

There seemed, however, no reason, other than race, to dismiss the incumbent. Stowell had shown little legislative zeal during his stay in Congress.[226]

222 Petersburg *Index and Appeal*, September 5, 1874.

223 William H. Barnes, *The American Government: History of the Forty-third Congress* (Washington: 1875), vol. 2, 245.

224 New York *Times*, July 15, 1874.

225 Louisville *Courier-Journal*, February 13, 1874.

226 The New York *Tribune* found his entire existence uninspiring: "With no great vices, he is deficient in virtues. In fact, he is as near a nonentity as is consistent with sanity. How it

But he displayed exemplary zeal on behalf of civil rights. The *New National Era* called upon its people to desist from a challenge. "We have found him [Stowell] true to his trust. He has advocated strongly for the Civil Rights Bill in all its respects.... Our friend Mr. De Mortie is doing well in the sassafras business. Why not continue?"[227]

De Mortie was not alone. A white contender also emerged. Former congressman Charles Porter had served two terms from the Richmond district before retiring in 1872. Now he mounted a comeback. The Republican hopefuls engaged in a primary debate at Petersburg on July 15. Stowell repeated his support of the Civil Rights Bill. De Mortie acknowledged Stowell's position but added that, "colored men could be better trusted as to the civil rights bill than any white man." Porter hedged. "He did not exactly define himself as to civil rights, but seemed to favor that abominable doctrine."[228]

Shortly after this event De Mortie withdrew. The *New National Era* applauded his self-sacrifice: "It would be a sin of ingratitude" to abandon a faithful incumbent.[229] The Republican convention met at Farmville on September 16. Stowell won re-nomination. Speechifying was emphatic: "a bitter appeal to race pride and prejudice in support of the Civil Rights bill.... In this district the colored men have the majority and the powers of hell shall not deprive them of victory."[230] De Mortie departed. Porter did not. Now he defined himself on the Civil Rights Bill. He opposed it. He urged white voters to take refuge under the banner of an independent campaign, the "Anti-Ring Republicans."[231] Still Democrats nominated no one. "Stir up the district committee," the *Index* pleaded. "The slough of despond is a dirty mud-hole." No one stirred.

Rain fell heavily in Virginia's late summer. But election day dawned clear, with bright prospects for W.H.H. Stowell. The *Index* resigned itself to defeat: "It would have been gratifying to follow the standard of some eloquent champion of the party, who would have filled this district with the same blaze of enthusiasm that Goode has excited in the Second and Walker in the Third District."[232] The lament was premature. Democrats had not surrendered. They had prepared a trick, hoping to take Republicans off guard. They launched a "sprung contest," a stealth candidate contrived to pop up jack-in-the-box-like

ever occurred to anybody to send him to Congress no one knows." New York *Tribune*, July 4, 1874.

227 Washington *New National Era*, June 11, July 16, 1874.

228 Petersburg *Index and Appeal*, July 16, 1874.

229 Washington *New National Era*, September 10, 1874.

230 Petersburg *Index and Appeal*, September 18, 1874.

231 Petersburg *Index and Appeal*, September 29, October 1, 1874.

232 Petersburg *Index and Appeal*, August 10, 14, 1874.

when least expected. Fourth District voters awoke on November 3 to find there was a Democratic candidate. Thousands of ballots, "tissue ballots," had been prepared in his name. Candidate and ballots emerged as the sun reached its zenith.

Morning belonged to the Republicans. "The henchmen of Stowell poured in with a continuous stream," the *Index* reported. So matters stood until noon. Suddenly white voters appeared on the streets. Each carried something in his hand, "a very diminutive ballot" containing the name of a new contender. William Hodges Mann of Nottoway County revealed himself. Little ballots, like snowflake flurries, began to fall into the boxes. Stowell's forces, perhaps, lulled into complacency, would be caught napping. The sprung contest might surge to victory.[233]

Nor was surprise the Democrats' only ploy. The tissue ballots, "delicate and fairy-like tickets," also had a role to play. Marked in tiny letters, each measured 1 ⅞" long and barely ¾" wide. Stowell's normal-sized tickets, 4 ½" × 2 ½" with the candidate's name printed boldly beneath the emblem of a soaring eagle, dwarfed their petite companions in the boxes. But quantity counted, not size: tiny tickets so unobtrusive that any number might be intruded unseen into an average ballot box. Every box in Petersburg, Republicans complained, contained from 50 to 200 more ballots than there were voters.

The tissue ballots were insidious even when detected. Virginia's election code instructed officials to check the number of ballots cast against the number of voters named on the rolls. In case of an "over-vote" procedure required officials to replace the ballots and reshuffle. One election judge then donned a blindfold. He inserted a hand into the box and drew out at random a number of ballots sufficient to correct the imbalance. Randomness depended on touch; touch defied randomness when ballots differed in size and texture. Political proclivities compromised the evenhandedness of the blindfolded judge. "He put his hand in the box, and whether he drew the big ballot or the little one was a matter of taste and convenience to himself."[234]

Even this "Petersburg Method" – so it came to be called – did not overcome the Republicans' advantage. Whether by instinct or suspicion, Stowell had mobilized his supporters. He won by 6,388 votes. Democrats, fraud having failed, charged fraud. Many a dead "nigger," they insisted, rose from the grave "to renew his life [and vote] in the person of his friends."[235] Charles Porter amassed

233 Petersburg *Index and Appeal*, November 4, 1874.

234 John Tyler Morgan, *Radical Political Morality. Tissue Ballots in Virginia. The Bourbon Democracy* (Washington: 1881): 26–29; speech in *Cong. Record*, 47th Congress, Senate Special Session: 295–296.

235 Edward King, *The Great South*, 581.

36 votes. (He might have had 37, had he not forgotten to vote for himself.) He protested. He had been ill used, "badly served and deceived," by the Democrats. "Politics is not child's play," retorted the *Index*.[236] Democrats also expressed dissatisfaction. Too few tissue ballots arrived in the countryside properly to stuff the boxes, the Farmville *Mercury* grumbled.[237] The *Index* advised that future elections make it a "square fight." It praised the sprung candidate, Judge Mann, who did go on to become Governor of Virginia in 1910. But deception did not accomplish noble deeds.[238]

Democrats hoped for a Republican split. De Mortie refused to play Robert Norton's role. They encouraged Porter's campaign. His "anti-ring" message fizzled. They sprang the sprung contest. Very few politicians possessed Stowell's antidote to civil rights poison, a 65% majority of black voters and a campaign free from violence.

236 Petersburg *Index and Appeal*, November 11, 12, 1874.
237 Petersburg *Index and Appeal*, November 13, 1874.
238 Petersburg *Index and Appeal*, November 5, 1874.

CHAPTER 8

Quintessence of Abominations: Elections in Tennessee and Alabama

1 Tennessee

Nowhere in the South did black people advocate more strongly for the Civil Rights Bill than in Tennessee. The Nashville Colored Convention set the agenda, even to the right of mixed-connubiality. Martyrs lay in Tennessee soil – Julia Hayden, Jarrett Burrows. White people expressed Indignation. Senator Brownlow's public colloquy calling out the "sum of all villainies, quintessence of abominations" lit the fire. Local elections in August refined the tensions in the crucible of political propaganda. Nowhere did the Civil Rights Bill carve the racial divide more starkly than in Tennessee.[1] Governor John C. Brown notified Tennesseans. Vote for your race. "Let every white man who loves his race and retains his self-respect rally to the white man's ticket."[2]

For Democrats prospects could not have been pleasanter. Only two irritants might threaten their triumph: apathy and disunity. Those factors had hurt them in 1872. Greeley had gone. The Civil Rights Bill arrived. Apathy would not infect the white masses. Disunity was another matter. Independent candidacies must not arise. Party leaders in Memphis took the lead. On February 14 they organized a conference at the town of Bartlett in Shelby County. Luminaries included Gen. Bedford Forrest, Col. Andrew Kellar, editor of the Memphis *Avalanche,* and former Congressman Henry Emerson Etheridge. They drew the blueprint of success. "All anti-Radical citizens" come together! "The united co-operation of the Liberal, Conservative and Democratic voters, shoulder to shoulder and march upon the common enemy."[3]

---

1 The state was white: 1,258,520 Tennesseans responded to the census of 1870; 322,331 counted as "colored." Their numbers were greater in the west than in the east. In only one congressional district, the 10th at Memphis, did they hold a slim majority.

2 Memphis *Appeal,* July 26; Knoxville *Press and Herald,* Nashville *Union and American,* July 28, 1874.

3 Nashville *Union and American,* February 17, 1874. Split tickets in 1872 had cost Democrats three winnable contests – the 6th District including Nashville, the 8th north of Memphis, and the at-large seat won by Horace Maynard when Andrew Johnson challenged the party's nominee Gen. Benjamin Cheatham.

A gubernatorial election stirred the political brew. Democrats had redeemed that office in 1870. They seemed certain to retain it. But the need to consider the governorship compelled both parties to convene state conventions. Democrats held theirs at Nashville on August 19. Gustavus Henry of Montgomery County presided. The nomination went to James D. Porter. Chairman Henry made it clear:

> The long reign of despotism, corruption, and anarchy in the Southern States has been unbroken by a single mitigation of charity or humanity to the fallen.... Yet they must humiliate the whole South still further and for that purpose they have passed in the Senate the Civil Rights bill ... more properly called a Pandora's Box.... [But] after every evil that can afflict mankind has flown out of it, hope is *not* found at the bottom.[4]

Democrats gleefully predicted that civil rights would shatter their opponents and sink them. That prediction was correct.

Republicans assembled at James Hall in Chattanooga on September 16. Congressman Horace Harrison presided.[5] Two practical considerations confronted delegates. Should they attempt a nomination for governor? Should they endorse the Civil Rights Bill? Black delegates and white recognized the civil rights measure for the political minefield it was. The two considerations merged. Only one Republican, Horace Maynard, had the stature to undertake a run for governor. Maynard stood as an advocate of the Civil Rights Bill. He stressed his opposition to the mixed school clause, but he did not disavow the rest. A nomination that set Maynard at the top of the ticket raised civil rights along with it. If he made a square campaign he would inject the Civil Rights Bill into every congressional race. Therefore, many concluded, concede the governorship. Make no contest at all, rather than permit Horace Maynard to drag civil rights across the length and breadth of Tennessee. As the convention opened, white delegates resolved to oppose any gubernatorial nomination. Black delegates insisted on Horace Maynard.

A white man, ex-congressman Lewis Tillman, threw the first punch. Democrats were driving the civil rights stake into the party's heart. They used it "with such effect that it would be useless to have a standard-bearer in the coming

4 Nashville *Union and American*, August 20, 1874; also accounts in Knoxville *Press and Herald*, August 21; Chattanooga *Times*, August 22, 1874.

5 Fullest account, Knoxville *Press and Herald*, September 18, 1874; also Nashville *Banner*, September 17, 18; Nashville *Union and American*, September 18, 19; Memphis *Appeal*, September 22, 1874.

election." Better no nomination than compel candidates "to face the music of the Civil Rights Bill endorsed by Horace Maynard." A black delegate, Knoxville's W.H. Porter, replied: cowards never conquer. "Suppose we did get beat last August. If I am whipped, is that any reason I dare not go out of my home again?" Another black delegate, William Butler of Nashville, invoked the reviled name of Brownlow. Republicans who agreed with him might go with him to the devil:

> God says every man shall have equal rights, and what man is that who expects to go to Heaven and dares to say they shall not have them? ... I say to those men, go back to the Democratic party where you belong, and go now.... Great God! Have we not courage? Let us nominate a standard-bearer for Governor, and standing by Republican doctrines go onward.

The governorship remained undecided. Discussion turned to the platform. The Committee on Resolutions had been sent out to compose the text. No one had seen it since. One member reported that he had passed the committee-room door. It was locked. "From the stormy character of the proceedings within, he judged there was trouble." Finally the Resolutions Committee emerged. It laid before the convention a platform of nine articles. Number three took up the Civil Rights Bill. It was a masterpiece of evasion.

> We are in favor of the full and equal enjoyment of accommodations, advantages, rights, and privileges by all citizens and other persons within the jurisdiction of the United States, without regard to race, creed or color.... At the same time we deem it unnecessary and unwise to attempt, by Congressional legislation, or otherwise, to compel as between such races, creeds or colors, the joint exercise of such accommodations, advantages, rights or privileges.[6]

Lewis Tillman moved the text be passed forthwith. Former congressman Samuel Arnell moved it be stricken forthwith. Another voice moved the whole convention adjourn forthwith. A black delegate, William J. Smith of Shelby County, took the floor. How could it be? The Civil Rights Bill's principles were correct; its existence was not.

> It says that the Civil Rights bill is "inexpedient and unwise." Inexpedient and unwise to do what? To recognize the rights of the colored men! You

6 Knoxville *Press and Herald*, September 18, 1874.

> stand up before Congress and the people of Tennessee and declare it is inexpedient and unwise.... The Republican party demands equal rights. That is why I am a Republican. That is why I stand under the Republican flag.[7]

Voices cried out: adjourn! Others: vote! Amid the hubbub Resolution 3 passed. Attention turned to the governorship. Black delegates moved the nomination of Horace Maynard. Whites objected. Jeers drowned them out. Maynard closed the convention with rousing oratory. He stood for the Civil Rights Bill, he said, with the one exception of mixed schools. Civil rights was a bogeyman Republicans need not fear. "We have lived too long in the woods to get scared at such an owl as the Civil Rights question."[8]

Reporters interviewed departing delegates. Whites seemed "sullen and melancholy," blacks jubilant. "The Civil Rights plank in the platform was understood to be all right, and Maynard's nomination a triumph of Civil Rights," so one black delegate informed the *Union and American*. "Maybe the white delegates got the platform, but de niggers got de Governor."[9] Democrats got all they could have hoped for.

The race began. Republicans realized their worst fears. Horace Maynard and James Porter pursued a campaign in the grand political tradition. They agreed to engage in a series of "joint discussions:" 28 debates in 33 days, they crossed the state from mountaintops to river bottoms. From Jonesboro and Greeneville they descended through Knoxville and Nashville, Maryville, Paris, Athens, Tullahoma, Clarksville, Union City, Brownsville. They ended at Memphis on the Mississippi. Republican candidates cringed as the gubernatorial sideshow approached their districts. Journalist Edward King reported. The "colored people are clamorous for the [civil rights] bill." Congressman Maynard, "their present candidate for Governor, is helping them in their crusade."[10]

Maynard crusaded enthusiastically. The "Narragansett" appeared at Chattanooga. He spoke, the Chattanooga *Times* related, "with the pedagogical

7 Knoxville *Press and Herald*, September 18, 1874.

8 Nashville *Union and American*, September 18, 1874.

9 Nashville *Union and American*, September 18, 1874.

10 Edward King, *The Great South*, 731. Maynard's campaign was unwinnable, "political suicide" said the New York *Tribune* (September 24). Perhaps, some speculated, he aimed to advertise himself for the next vice-presidential nomination (Atlanta *Constitution*, September 20; Chicago *Tribune*, September 24; Nashville *Banner*, September 26; Knoxville *Press and Herald*, September 22). Or he hoped to earn the party's thanks in a comfortable ambassadorship (Nashville *Banner*, May 1, September 26; Knoxville *Press and Herald*, April 29). That reward he did acquire: Minister to Turkey, a villa on the Bosphorus among the European diplomats and expatriates, a collaboration with the discoveries of Heinrich Schliemann.

singsong of his peculiar delivery.... To the low-crowned felt hat and long straight hair and swarthy visage beneath it, there was needed but the crowning feature of a rooster's feather to present the perfect picture of Spotted Tail or Red Cloud over a council fire."[11]

Maynard's aboriginal eccentricities could not overcome the issues against him. Horace Redfield sympathized: "Maynard is a more able man than Porter, and you may expect to see the latter gentleman pretty well used up before the campaign closes. But he will be elected by a large majority, which will no doubt compensate for the pains of being driven into a corner by Horace Maynard on the question of the rights of men."[12] Redfield had it backwards. Rather the rights of men drove Maynard into a corner. His civil rights views would crush him, the Knoxville *Press and Herald* declared.[13] "Horace Maynard. Who is he?" demanded Col. John F. House, Democratic candidate in the 6th District. "A man that said a rebel had two rights, one to die and the other to be damned, a man who voted for the civil rights bill."[14]

Maynard labored most under the weight of the Thorn Grove Speech, as it came to be called. On July 29, as the local elections approached, he had stopped to address the people at that rural locality in Knox County. Civil rights fever was in the air. At first, he told the crowd, he preferred not to dwell on that issue. But since no amount of common sense could stop the agitation, he would set the record straight. He was tall, he said. He stood up for civil rights. "He thanked God that he had the manhood to come up and meet the issue squarely and defend the action of the Republican party." The war had set free the slaves. Government must protect their rights. The present hysteria was but the same nonsense manufactured every time to hinder every advance of social justice.

> When each of the amendments had been proposed, a great hue and cry was raised on the "nigger" question. The most terrible things were going to happen. They were going to ravish our women and murder our men, and "big buck niggers" were going to marry our daughters.... Well, he had children of both sexes, but he had never been uneasy about their marrying; he expected his sons to marry respectable ladies, and his daughters not to marry "big bucks" of any kind but to marry young gentlemen.... He would not have his colored neighbor's boy hampered, but would give him an equal start in life with his own boy, and if he outran him, let him run.[15]

11 Chattanooga *Times*, October 20, 1874.
12 Cincinnati *Commercial*, September 21, 1874.
13 Knoxville *Press and Herald*, June 26, 1874.
14 Nashville *Banner*, August 20, 1874.
15 Accounts of the Thorn Grove Speech, Knoxville *Press and Herald*, July 30; Chattanooga *Times*, July 31; Nashville *Banner*, August 1; Nashville *Union and American*, August 1, 1874.

The Thorn Grove Speech defined Maynard's position. He repeated that message a day later in a speech at Harbison's Crossroads. He took the same ground at the nominating convention. He stated it again in a speech at Knoxville on September 24. "Assassination, murder and violence are the weapons of the Democratic party to defeat legislation that does not suit them. They do not like the Civil Rights bill, so they have some of their emissaries go and shoot a poor colored girl teaching a school of her own race. They don't like the Civil Rights bill, so they take sixteen colored prisoners from the jail of one of our counties, and without a trial kill them." Even the mixed-schools clause need not frighten white people. The bill, as Senator Frelinghuysen had explained, did not mandate mixed schools.[16] He maintained his stand throughout the campaign.

That grand exercise in democracy began its parade in the hills at Jonesboro on September 29.[17] The gladiators came up on the same train from Chattanooga. Andrew Johnson greeted them at the station. He walked on with Porter to the stand, where he introduced the candidates. Jonesboroans enjoyed five hours of fine political debate.

Porter spoke first. He defended his party. He disavowed the bloody incidents that had coincided disturbingly with agitation of civil rights fear. White men did not hate black people. They did not want to kill them. Negroes knew this. During the war they had not risen, even against an undefended homeland. "Thus they demonstrated that their eight million of masters were not merciless despots, and that contrary to all outside views a kindly feeling did exist between the two races." Why the current violence? Northerners. They had unleashed their monstrosity, the Civil Rights Bill, to forge hatred where none existed. No matter what Maynard might say that measure *did* include a mandate for mixed schools. He quoted George Boutwell's plea to the Senate: prejudice would be unlearned; the school-house was to become the laboratory of social change. He paused to reach for a glass of water. A voice called out: "Don't you want a drink of whisky?"

Maynard hushed the crowd. Show respect to his opponent. It was all hypocrisy anyway. Had not Democrats accepted civil rights when they accepted Horace Greeley? They used it as a smokescreen to divert attention from real problems. They had run the state finances into the ground. When anyone criticized them, "what's the answer? nigger equality, mixed schools. Julia Hayden is shot down in cold blood. What is the reason? Why, it is said that the Civil Rights bill did it all."

16 Nashville *Union and American*, September 26, 1874.

17 Account of the Jonesboro debate, Nashville *Union and American*, September 30, October 1, 2; Nashville *Banner*, September 30, October 2, 1874.

The debaters met next at Greeneville. Maynard delivered an indictment of Gov. Brown's administration; "a few minutes he devoted to the Civil Rights Bill, and denied that it enforced co-education of the races." Porter "arraigned his opponent on the Civil Rights Bill and very happily devoted about an hour to its discussion.... A few minutes was occupied in discussion of State matters."[18]

They met at Cleveland in Bradley County. Maynard stood firm: "I am a Civil Rights man." He opposed only mixed schools.[19] They met at Murfreesboro on the 13th. By now Maynard's passage had left a trail of wrecked Republican candidates in its wake.[20] Black people remained enthusiastic. Porter called to them to come around and "vote for their friends." They hooted him down.[21]

The final discussion came at Memphis. Maynard appealed to voters' discernment: "They are trying to delude the white people by a false fear of civil rights to get their votes, but that will fail if the voters use any intelligence."[22] Intelligent voters chose to follow their fears. Maynard lost by 47,000.[23] Against those undercurrents Tennessee's races progressed. Redistricting had eliminated the at-large seat. Republicans held six of the ten reorganized districts. They held one after votes were counted.

Sources allow us to observe all except the 9th District, previously the old 8th in the northwest. That district had witnessed some of the country's worst scenes of racial unrest. Gibson County lay within its borders. Republican incumbent David A. Nunn had voted in favor of the Civil Rights Bill. Democrats despised him. "He represents no single living white man in the south," screamed the Memphis *Appeal*. "He sank into the filthy groove down which he glided two years ago into African bosoms, and poor Nunn is down there yet – still sloshing around filthily."[24] Across the district fear ran high. "Those who live at a distance may easily indulge in criticism because they rest in perfect security and their homes and dear ones are not exposed to the fury of demons and savages," one white constituent wrote. "Let them imagine themselves placed

---

18 Greeneville *Intelligencer*, October 2, 1874.

19 Nashville *Union and American*, October 9, 1874.

20 Chattanooga *Times*, October 21, 1874.

21 Nashville *Banner*, October 14, 1874.

22 Memphis *Appeal*, November 1, 1874.

23 Andrew Johnson added to the excitement, as he pursued a speaking tour designed to raise his profile for the legislature's election to succeed the retiring Senator Brownlow. He was, he reminded audiences, the only man to have vetoed a civil rights bill – the original civil rights act of 1866. At Murfreesboro Johnson's banter took an amusing turn. Some persons, he observed, advocated the extermination of black people. That was a bad idea, counterproductive. Better let them live. Otherwise white men might have to work: "He preferred negroes as laborers rather than the Chinese. They must have labor in the country, as a great many had been spoiled." Nashville *Banner*, October 8, 1874.

24 Memphis *Appeal*, May 29, 1874.

upon a volcano, where they can feel the rumbling beneath their feet, hear its roaring thunders and see the black sulphurous smoke emitted from the deep chasm before them."[25]

The volcanic district did not erupt. But it buried David Nunn. Democrat William P. Caldwell won by 7,000 votes. Few black people ventured to the polls. Haywood County contained 18,000 black residents to fewer than 8,000 whites. It gave Republicans a scant majority of 72 votes. In Lake County 691 black persons lived. No living person emerged to vote for David A. Nunn. (see Map 4, below)

Tennessee, Tenth District
Barbour Lewis (R), Hiram Casey Young (D)
Population: 50.2% black

Barbour Lewis, David Nunn's neighbor to the south, presided over a more hopeful district. It contained three counties: Fayette, Hardeman, and Shelby with the city of Memphis. Redistricting had detached a fourth county, Tipton, a change that removed a slight white surplus. Shelby County, the most populated, possessed 39,000 white and 36,000 black inhabitants. Whites held a majority in Hardeman County. Blacks predominated in Fayette. Fewer than 400 souls made the difference.

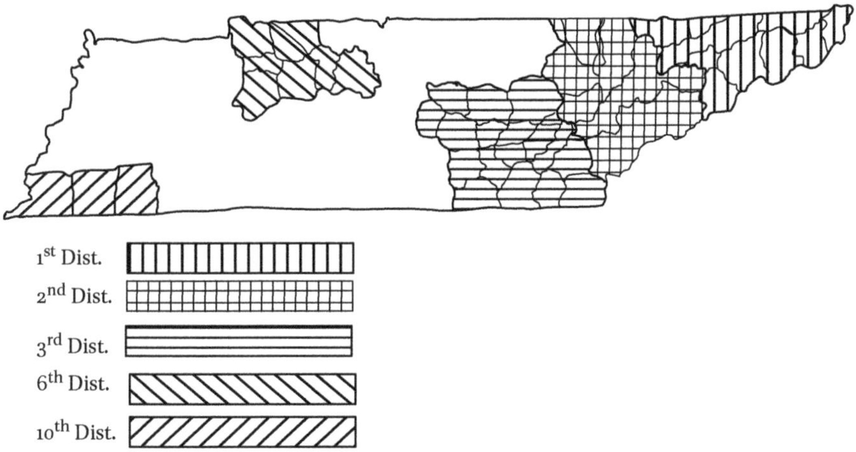

MAP 4 Congressional Districts, Tennessee
SOURCE: AUTHORS OF *WELCOMING RUIN*.

25 Memphis *Appeal*, September 4, 1874.

The incumbent was by all accounts a pleasant man and plump, "in his personal and physical shape very like an uncompressed cotton bale."[26] Lewis haled originally from Vermont. He spent his youth in Illinois, recalling a pre-presidential friendship with Abraham Lincoln. He developed a penchant for Abolitionism. After early wartime service in the cavalry, commended for gallantry at the battle of Pea Ridge, Capt. Lewis arrived in Memphis as military judge of the occupied city.[27] Whites spurned him. The *Appeal* mocked his portly carriage: "The capitol of the nation trembled in pride of its new accession, like a mountain convulsed by an earthquake, when the rotund person of Judge Lewis grandly strode through the happy rotunda."[28] The Chattanooga *Times* simply dismissed him: "a vile caricature of human nature, an advocate of the Civil Rights Bill."[29]

Ethnic politics in Memphis divided the district. Disparate blocs of voters – white, black, German, Irish, Jewish – caused the partisan balance to sway. Republicans relied for the moment on an uneasy coalition, Irish and black. Only eight years earlier Irish policemen and black citizens had engaged in one of the South's bloodiest race riots, a massacre that left 56 dead, 54 of them black. That terror in 1866 had coincided with the passage of the first Civil Rights Act.[30] Another civil rights act approached. Republicans hoped ancient enemies would reconcile. That electoral combination had given Republican John Loague the mayoralty in January. Mayor Loague's own Irish ancestry, his rise from poverty-stricken Londonderry youth to prosperous Memphis merchant, helped win the Celtic vote. His embrace of civil rights endeared him to the blacks.

Democrats found consolation in the conduct of other immigrant groups. The *Appeal* praised the German and Jewish citizens. They had voted "as Americans" against the mongrel coalition.[31] Abraham Frankland, leader of the Jewish community, received special praise. Already a Confederate hero, he helped to save the city from yellow fever in 1873. Now he helped rally Memphis' Jewish

---

26 New York *World*, June 13, 1874.

27 See Walter J. Fraser, "Barbour Lewis: A Carpetbagger Reconsidered," *Tennessee Historical Quarterly*, 32 (1973): 148–153.

28 Memphis *Appeal*, April 15, 1874.

29 Chattanooga *Times*, September 12, 1874.

30 The two white fatalities were self-inflicted. Further damage included 75 black men wounded, numerous women raped, 91 homes burned. See James G. Ryan, "The Memphis Riots of 1866: Terror in a Black Community during Reconstruction," *Journal of Negro History*, 62 (1977): 243–257; Barrington Walker, "This is a White Man's Day: The Irish, White Racial Identity, and the 1866 Memphis Riots," *Left History*, 5 (1997): 31–55; Hannah Rosen, *Terror in the Heart of Freedom*, 61–66.

31 Memphis *Appeal*, January 12, 1874.

voters to the Democratic side. They awarded him a prized place on their ticket, candidate for tax assessor of Shelby County.

For Republicans, Jews and Germans were a lost cause. And now Mayor Loague proceeded to alienate his Irish base. Trouble swirled around the fire department, the preserve of the Irish. The mayor moved to integrate it. He had already begun to integrate the police force. Within days of taking office he discharged a number of veteran white officers and placed black patrolmen on the rolls. In April he proposed the addition of twenty more black officers.[32] The city council objected. The mayor ignored it. He hired ten Negro firemen. He ordered Fire Chief Mike McFadden to place a hose-carriage in the black neighborhood of the ninth ward and man it with a mixed crew. Chief McFadden refused. The mayor insisted. There would be black firemen in Memphis.[33]

Meanwhile the city seethed in the aftermath of the Decoration Day disturbances that had come close to igniting race war. Civil rights came to a vote in Congress. Supporters telegraphed Barbour Lewis. Vote against the bill. He had already voted for it on May 25. On June 8 he was silent. By the 20th Lewis had steadied his nerve. He voted Aye. Democrats were delighted.

Battle raged over the uncertain swing of the Irish. General James Chalmers rode up from Mississippi: "Do you desire your daughters, the progeny of fair-skinned Celtic blood, compelled by law to the social level of the African?" Republicans reminded Irishmen that prejudice had made them its victims. Not long ago Know-Nothings called Irishmen inferior. They discriminated against Irish children, just as Democrats now discriminated against black children.[34]

The first test came in the county elections of August 6. Democrats carried the offices by a 3,500 vote majority. Thanks went to the Germans and the Jews. The Irish vote remained obstinate, but weakened. Civil rights was doing its work. In that troubled atmosphere Republicans assembled their convention on September 8. They could afford no internal dissension. Ed Shaw, leader of the black community, proposed Barbour Lewis' re-nomination, which was carried directly. He also endorsed the platform, which directly made no mention of civil rights. Shaw himself mentioned mixed schools. He renounced them distinctly.[35]

---

32 See Dennis C. Rousey, "Yellow Fever and Black Policemen in Memphis: A Post-Reconstruction Anomaly," *Journal of Southern History*, 51 (1985): 364–366. Gerald M. Capers, "Yellow Fever in Memphis in the 1870's," *Mississippi Valley Historical Review*, 24 (1938): 486–491.

33 Memphis *Appeal*, May 21, 23, 25–26, 28, June 4, July 2, 1874.

34 Memphis, *Appeal*, August 2, 1874.

35 Memphis *Appeal*, September 9, 1874.

Democrats convened at Bolivar in Hardeman County. The choice fell on Col. H. Casey Young. The colonel, with square jaw and clipped mustache, displayed a military bearing. His nomination, however, was a moderate coup. He had served the Confederacy, but opposed secession. He urged his party to recognize the changes war had wrought. He had no love for civil rights bills. But he cultivated a gentlemanly tone. He offered his hand to Republicans. He expressed sympathy for black people.

Candidates Lewis and Young arranged a series of joint discussions. Those debates assumed the usual form. Young accused, Lewis defended, until he choked under the weight of the Civil Rights Bill. The first engagement came at Bolivar on October 5. Young began. There was room in Tennessee for white and black, for native and immigrant. Even the carpetbagger was welcome, provided he behaved as an honest man. The war had changed the South's social relations. The clock could not wind backward. Black people had emerged from slavery "helpless, dependent." White people must help them, "not only as a Christian duty but as a political policy based upon the soundest wisdom." Help, however, did not include a civil rights bill. It did not include social equality, mixed accommodations in theaters, hotels, trains, or schools. Lewis, for his part, adhered to a standard line: civil rights, yes; mixed schools, no. Black people did not want mixed schools. Ed Shaw did not. There was no need to fear civil rights.[36]

The debates traveled on to Grand Junction, Somerville and other points. They ended at Memphis. Blacks and whites sat together in the Greenlaw Opera House, decently separated yet in precarious proximity. Discussion turned to civil rights. A restless wave moved through the crowd. The strain wore on Congressman Lewis. His opponent, he declared, offered nothing but fear of the Civil Rights Bill. "If he would take civil rights out of the canvass he had as well go home." Young retorted: "Unless he [Lewis] did take it out he would go home from Congress." Black people could not assimilate into white society. "You can't make a hen swim." Lewis fumed. Young "thought of nothing but a seat in Congress and howling about civil rights. He drank civil rights, fed on it, dreamed of it, and had the civil rights nightmare."[37]

To keep the peace, federal troops patrolled Memphis. No need, the *Avalanche* complained: "Massachusetts does not contain a county freer from political disturbances than Shelby County."[38] Undisturbed, Casey Young completed the Democratic sweep. He won, in a barely white district, by 4,700 votes.

---

36 Memphis *Appeal*, October 6; Nashville *Banner*, October 8, 1874.

37 Nashville *Union and American*, October 27, 1874.

38 Quoted in Nashville *Union and American*, October 27, 1874.

Tennessee, Sixth District
Horace H. Harrison (R), John F. House (D)
Population: 65% white

For Republicans the 6th District was the least promising. Redistricting had altered it. Its heart remained Davidson County with the capital, Nashville. It still included neighboring Cheatham County. Gone were Robertson, Sumner, Wilson, Trousdale and De Kalb Counties. Added were Dickson, Humphries, Stewart, Houston and Montgomery. In its old configuration the district had been 67% white, in its new form 65%. The new district was an alien landscape to the Republican incumbent. The Democrat, chosen from one of the newly-added counties, knew the territory. Democrats looked confidently at their chances in the 6th.

The incumbent of euphonious name, Horace Harrison Harrison, resided in the capital city. Nashville had sustained Republican Mayor Thomas Kercheval for two terms. An active and vocal black population provided support. But Nashville could not outweigh Democratic advantages elsewhere. Harrison held his seat by a thread. He had won in 1872 with a plurality. Independent William G. Brien took 5,600 votes from Democrat Edward I. Golladay. Now civil rights added to Congressman Harrison's woes.

Stocky, mustachioed, Harrison had opposed secession. He fled at the start of the war. He returned to hold important offices in the succeeding Republican administrations: judge of the Supreme Court, chairman of the State Central Committee.[39] Black constituents considered him a faithful ally. Their organ, the Nashville *True Republican,* proposed Harrison for governor, standing on the platform of the Nashville Colored Convention.[40] That endorsement occurred prior to Congress' civil rights votes. When those tests arrived, Horace Harrison Harrison flinched. At first the congressman kept the faith. On the 25th of May he voted Aye. Then political reality struck. Democrats vowed they would tear him away from civil rights, or tear him down. He tore himself away.

The Democrats inaugurated their campaign on July 25. A grand political barbecue assembled at Bosley Springs outside Nashville. William H. Morrow, Chairman of the State Central Committee, promoted it: a release from fear, a rebirth of political freedom. Ex-governor Neill Brown waxed nostalgic: "I always wished to attend one more barbecue, as I have not seen one in fifteen years."[41] Trains and carriages rolled in from Nashville. Captain Gibson's Rock

39 William H. Barnes, *The American Government,* vol. 3, 93.

40 Knoxville *Press and Herald,* May 20, 1874.

41 Nashville *Union and American,* July 26; Nashville *Banner,* July 26, 1874.

City Band greeted arrivals with the lively beat of the Grenada Quickstep. The speakers' stand rose on a gentle knoll. Vendors of ginger-pop plied the crowd. Smoke from the barbecue drifted overhead, carrying a foretaste of savors to come. A taste of civil rights rhetoric spiced the pre-prandial proceedings.

Davidson County Attorney-General Andrew Jackson Caldwell began the speaking, a tribute to barbecues past. "It was a custom among us in the golden days of the republic to frequently meet under the umbrageous shade of these trees for friendly intercourse upon subjects of great importance." Civil rights now was of most importance.

> The passage of the Civil Rights bill woke everybody up, and the sentiment of every party – even the decent negroes in the country – was to demand that the Parthian arrow of hate should be broken. And it is broken and is now lying upon the Speaker's table. The people will break it again, and not only break it but will bury it deep beyond all hope of political resurrection.

Neill Brown mounted the platform. If the Parthians shot an arrow, let it be war.

> In the name of both races I protest against the firebrand lately thrown into the national councils and called the Civil Rights Bill.... If nothing will do but a conflict of races, let it come. If you force me to take sides upon this question, of course I will be for the race from which I spring.

Gen. William Bate strode to the stand: for God and southern womanhood.

> When grave personal and social rights are at stake – when the dominance and status of the white race is involved ... he who will not stand up for his race would be false, not only to his country, but to his God.... Those who are most involved in this infamous bill for social equality are the delicate and sensitive women of the country, hence our gallantry, if not pride of race, should inspire our hate to its sentiments and our contempt for its advocates. Let us gird on our armor and fight with locked shields.[42]

After three hours of oratory the people adjourned to feed. They returned sated in body but with minds still hungry for political nourishment. Col. John F. House of Clarksville provided sustenance.

---

42 Speeches of A.J. Caldwell, Neill Brown, William Bate, Nashville *Union and American*, July 26, 1874.

> Republicans have well nigh ruined our country; they have made slaves of the most chivalrous, the most honorable men and women God ever permitted sun to shine upon. This Civil Rights Bill will bring about a contest which every good man must deprecate; a contest which every man who desires the welfare of his race and that of the colored race must desire to avoid. If it comes to the worst, the contest will be short, sharp and decisive, and it will not stop until every drop of Anglo-Saxon blood in the South boils with indignation.

On June 8 the Civil Rights Bill came up for its second vote in the House. Horace Harrison voted No. On June 20 it arrived at its decisive vote. Horace Harrison voted No. Nashville's Colored Convention demanded civil rights. Nashville's congressman discarded civil rights. Black voters, nonetheless, could not afford to discard Harrison. In Nashville, as at Goldsboro, Savannah, Fredericksburg, Raleigh, Knoxville, they followed their anti-civil-rights-bill candidate to the polls.

The Republican convention met on September 30. The elite of Nashville's black citizenry, Abram Smith, James Napier, William Butler, Alfred Menefee and Nelson Walker sat among the delegates. The Colored Convention's high resolves dissolved. Civil rights bills and political success were incompatible items. Smith and Butler put Horace Harrison's name before the assembly. The assembly acclaimed him.[43]

Democrats met at Clarksville. Col. House, he whose words had buoyed Bosley Springs barbecuers, took the nomination. The colonel knew that the pulse of the district beat Democratic. The seat was his for the taking, unless unmanageable ugliness upset his plans – massacres of unarmed blacks, innocent schoolmarms shot down; bad publicity all around. Therefore he advised white people to cool their sanguinary circulation, at least until after the election. "The man who breaks open jails and hangs negroes does infinitely more damage to his country and party than one million Radical votes." Still, Col. House did not turn all swords into ploughshares:

> The Northern people had been our enemies in war, and they were our enemies in peace. We asked of them bread, and they gave us a stone.... He prayed that God would speed the day when the South would take control of the Government and give laurels to her country; when a party would rise who would not convert an African field hand into a Daniel Webster.[44]

43 Nashville *Banner*; Nashville *Union and American*, October 1, 1874.

44 Nashville *Banner*, September 3, 1874.

The candidates debated in the true Tennessee tradition. They began at Clarksville on October 19. They passed through cities, towns and villages. Newspapers recorded one encounter, on October 27th at the town of Edgefield.[45] House rejected every aspect of Reconstruction. The South, which once had "rejoiced and blossomed as a rose was now a wilderness." Recently he had walked the battlefield of Fort Donelson. All those northern dead, in victory they had died. They died in vain. They fought to unite the people. Republicans drove the people apart. He denounced the Fourteenth Amendment: "By this act every colored man in the United States was made a citizen of the United States. He thought that was bad policy." Citizenship led to civil rights, "a measure which, in scope and design, would revolutionize the whole social system of the South."

Harrison too rejected the Civil Rights Bill. But he struggled with his vote of May 25. That motion, he said, would have prepared the bill for amendment. So he voted for it. It was not amended. So he voted against it. House replied. Why bother about amending it? Vote it down altogether. It was not dead. It only slept. Make its slumbers eternal. "Defeat my honorable competitor by as overwhelming a majority as he can stand."

Democrats appealed to Nashville's proletariat. "Workingmen, do you favor mixed workshops?" the *Union and American* inquired. "No workingman who opposes Civil Rights in theory or in practice can vote for either Harrison or Maynard."[46] Workingmen agreed. White plasterers formed a union. Their first demand to employers: discharge their black co-workers. Some bosses resisted. Mr. W.T. Cooper, employing nine white and two black plasterers, defied the threat. His white employees quit. Another contractor, Mr. A.C. Lea, wisely yielded to the union's demands. He fired his black plasterers.[47]

The results inspired no surprise. Harrison tumbled to defeat by 4,765 votes. He carried none of the seven counties. He drew 56 votes in Houston County, out of nearly 600 cast, 179 out of 1,171 in Stewart County. Horace Redfield passed through the area after the election. He found white people exhilarated. "I breathe freer," one old farmer confided. "I know now that the Civil Rights Bill can't be passed and we be degraded to the level of the negro." What did the election mean, Redfield inquired? "It means that a nigger must keep a nigger's place," one informant replied. "The Southern people are the best friends the negroes have, but to keep our good will they must not puff themselves up with the thought that they are as good as we are."[48]

45 Edgefield debate, Nashville *Union and American*, October 28, 1874.
46 Nashville *Union and American*, November 1, 1874.
47 Nashville *Union and American*, October 29, 1874.
48 Cincinnati *Commercial*, November 19, 1874.

Tennessee, Third District
David Nelson (R), George Dibrell (D), William Stokes (I)
Population: 86% white

The 3rd District featured the candidacy of David Nelson, he who had evoked the Shirt of Nessus. Nelson did not, as Maynard, advocate civil rights minus mixed schools. He was not, like Harrison, a politician betrayed by an errant vote, or, like Jacob Thornburgh of the 2nd District, by a wayward signature on a party document. He was as innocent as a Republican could be. Yet civil rights stuck to him.

The district centered on the city of Chattanooga. In racial terms it was practically monotone. Hamilton County possessed a white majority of two to one. That was the closest ratio in the district. Census takers in 1870 noted 56 nonwhite persons among 2,500 residents of Sequatchie County. They discovered 186 scattered among 2,700 people in Van Buren County, 344 among 7,000 inhabitants of Polk County. The 3rd, nonetheless, as other east Tennessee districts, was hopeful territory for Republicans. Union sentiment remained rooted in the state's east. Chattanooga lay on the western edge of the eastern zone. It had sent Republicans to Congress.

The present Republican, William Crutchfield, was one of Congress' undoubted characters. "Uncle William," as admirers called him, roamed the House in "stogy" boots and farmer's jacket. Arriving on Congress' opening day, he found the doorkeeper unwilling to admit a shabby fellow with disheveled hair and battered hat, until a colleague vouched for his credentials. "He cannot be tempted to join the congressional Temperance society," wrote the Memphis *Appeal*. "Uncle William is a man of large means and of a very independent turn of mind, and it is not likely he cares very much whether he is in Congress or not."[49] As long as he was there, he expressed his opinions, and he voted as he pleased.[50]

---

49 Memphis *Appeal*, March 10, 1874.

50 Once already his opinions, or antics, had almost curved the course of national events. In January 1861, Senator Jefferson Davis, preparing to resign from office, made his way back to Mississippi. He stopped at the Crutchfield House, Chattanooga's foremost hotel. The future Confederacy's future president treated hotel guests to an impromptu speech calling for secession. Crutchfield leaped upon a table to denounce the senator. Davis bristled. Pistols were cocked. Davis, so it was said, challenged Crutchfield to a duel, an event whose outcome might have produced curious effects on the history of a nascent southern nation. Friends hustled Crutchfield away, avoiding a fateful rencontre. See Oliver and Mary Temple, *Notable Men of Tennessee: From 1833 to 1875, their Times and their Contemporaries* (New York: 1912), 109–112; also Barnes, *American Government*, vol. 3, 83–84.

Dishevelment did not mean destitution. Crutchfield possessed large properties. In bygone days he had held numerous slaves. During the war he chose the Union. He joined no army, yet marched in several. He stood at Grant's side during the battle of Chattanooga. He volunteered on the staff of General James Steedman, who commanded a full division of African-American troops at the battle of Nashville. Black people expected good things of William Crutchfield. The *New National Era* hailed him: "He is ugly – all great men are – yet few, indeed, have so much good quick common sense; and, as to personal courage, Julius Caesar never had more."[51] Congressman Crutchfield dashed the *Era's* hopes – as always in a bewilderingly eccentric way. He voted for the Civil Rights Bill on May 25. He did it again on June 8. Then on June 20 he turned against it. And yet, even before his meandering votes, he had become an anti-civil rights bill hero. He rose on January 7 to propose the Crutchfield Amendment:

> Sec. 3: Provided, That any white female who shall, by reason of the race, color, or previous condition of servitude of any negro who shall make to her any proposal of marriage, refuse such proposal, shall, on conviction thereof, be fined not less than $1,000 and not more than $5,000 for each such offense.[52]

Crutchfield's proviso was meant to mock. Democrats smiled. Republicans raged. Ben Butler reserved for Uncle William a volley of his choicest verbiage.[53] Crutchfield explained: it was a *reductio ad absurdum*.[54] The compulsory marriage proviso did not pass. The *Appeal* nevertheless framed it and mounted it in its front office.

The congressman's sally did not amuse black people. Republican competitors rose. Former congressman William B. Stokes raised one challenge. Another rival, General John T. Wilder, threw in his hat. Wilder was a transplanted New Yorker, he, too, a Union hero of Chattanooga. As commander of the XIV Corps mounted infantry brigade he spearheaded the advance of Gen. Rosecrans' army in 1863, then settled in the city he had helped capture. In 1871 Wilder became Chattanooga's mayor. A tireless promoter of industrial development, he brought the city a burst of entrepreneurial spirit. Democrats considered

---

51 Washington *New National Era*, March 6, 1873.

52 *Cong. Record*, 43rd Congress, 1st Session: 452.

53 *Cong. Record*, 43rd Congress, 1st Session: 455.

54 If the amendment passed, Crutchfield declared, he would put the absurdity to the test. "He would have twenty of the finest black beaux each session at Washington, selected from the comeliest on his plantation, and give each congressman with marriageable daughters the choicest benefactions of social equality." Memphis *Appeal*, July 8, 1874.

him their strongest potential opponent. A third aspirant, Mr. Henry Snyder of Chattanooga, was an honest burgher, a banker and a former alderman. He had support in the city and in Hamilton County. He also took the endorsement of Bledsoe County.

Then there was Nelson. Young David came from a distinguished family, the mercurial son of a formidable father, Thomas A.R. Nelson. Persecuted in wartime for pro-Union views, he joined the federal forces, earning the rank of lieutenant-colonel. He also earned a reputation as an unpredictable, impetuous character, particularly when under the influence of drink. Yet he retained a disarming geniality. "His misfortunes," wrote the Chattanooga *Times*, "came not through badness of heart, but when he was some other fellow, and not the genial, bright fellow nature has made him."[55] His most spectacular misfortune, to which the *Times* alluded, was the murder of ex-Confederate General James Clanton at Knoxville on the afternoon of September 27, 1871. Fortunately, an insult had preceded the gunplay. An affair of honor, the jury took five minutes to acquit David Nelson. This freed him to pursue congressional ambitions.[56]

At the Republican convention on September 3 the battle came down to Nelson and Snyder. Nelson prevailed. Republican unity crumbled. Parliamentary tricks, Snyder's supporters complained. They refused to endorse the convention's choice. Wilder withdrew in good grace. But Stokes declared an independent candidacy. As for civil rights, Dave Nelson renounced it, quite sensibly, as the incumbent sensibly had done.[57]

Democrats meanwhile selected another Confederate warrior. George G. Dibrell, with long flowing white beard, rose from humble beginnings in the town of Sparta in White County. He enlisted as a private soldier at age 40. He finished the war a brigadier. Gen. Dibrell accepted his party's nomination at McMinnville on August 27. The candidate faced an enthusiastic assembly: "He is your man, he is the people's man. He is the Moses of the white man and not

55 Chattanooga *Times*, October 7, 1874.

56 Clanton, chairman of the Alabama Democratic Party, was on a visit to Knoxville. He possessed evidently a prickly personality, given to perceiving slights in what might otherwise appear indifferent circumstances. Friends introduced Gen. Clanton to Col. Nelson upon the street. The latter offered to show the former some interesting parts of town, "if you are not afraid." The former deduced an imputation upon the sufficiency of his courage. "If you think I am afraid, try me," he suggested. Nelson tried him. The general had time to draw his pistol and fire one ineffectual shot before meeting an untimely end. See Allen J. Going, "A Shooting Affray in Knoxville with Interstate Repercussions: The Killing of James H. Clanton by David M. Nelson, 1871," *Publications of the East Tennessee Historical Society*, 27 (1955): 39–48.

57 Knoxville *Press and Herald*, September 5–6, 1874.

of the negro."[58] Those who wanted social equality, said Dibrell, were welcome to it. Let them vote Republican. Then let them consort with Negroes, if such was their desire; let them do it at home as well as in public.

> Remember when you come to vote in November next, that if you vote the Republican ticket you vote our social and political liberties away. You say by your vote that you are willing to send your children to school with negro children. You say that you are willing that your wife and daughters shall occupy the same seats at church or on the cars, and that they shall eat at the same hotel table with the colored men and women. And if you favor social equality thus publicly, why not throw open your parlors and invite them to a full and free family circle? Go the whole hog or none.[59]

The candidates arranged a schedule of debates. These proved to be extraordinary occasions. Voters in Virginia witnessed the deadly hatred of Sener and Douglas and the false fraternizing of Norton and Goode. Here friendship truly prevailed. The gentlemanly Dibrell avoided intemperate rhetoric. Dave Nelson spoke with a puckish insouciance that disarmed even hardened opponents. The contestants met at McMinnville on October 17. The civil rights issue, Nelson proclaimed, was a gigantic humbug, Dibrell's "go the whole hog," his imaginings, Negroes lounging in one's parlor, a ludicrous invention. His opponent had worked it up to scare the voters. Indeed, he had scared himself: "The general was with child, eight months gone, and would give birth to a colored child about the third of November." Dibrell replied good-humoredly:

> Colonel Nelson tells you that he, too, is opposed to the civil rights bill, but I tell you, if you send him there [to Congress], old Ben Butler would get him by the ear, lead him up to the altar, bring the lash across his back, while Hoar would twist his tail, and the first thing my young friend would know, he would come out a thorough civil rights man.... If I am with child, when the period of accouchement arrives, the child would be called Dave Nelson.[60]

General and colonel continued their banter across the district. On the 22nd Dibrell scheduled a rally at his home town of Sparta. He invited his opponent to

---

58 Chattanooga *Times*, August 29, 1874.

59 Chattanooga *Times*, October 13, 1874.

60 Nashville *Banner*, October 20, 1874.

come along. Democrats enjoyed another "umbrageous barbecue." Dave Nelson munched contentedly. Orators denounced Republicans. They denounced the Civil Rights Bill. Dave Nelson listened calmly. Thunder rolled in over the hills. Proceedings adjourned to the court house hall. His hosts gave their Republican guest the last word. "He made the best speech he has made in the canvass," the Chattanooga *Times* reported, "paid high compliments to Gen. Dibrell. He had never met a man for whom he entertained a higher regard. Though a Union man and a Federal soldier he felt no bitterness toward the Confederate. He could drop a sympathetic tear over the grave of a Confederate as well as over a Federal soldier." He offered three cheers for the Republican Party. The *Times'* reporter failed to note a cheering response.[61]

The final debate in this most congenial of campaigns came at Chattanooga. The contestants met at James Hall, lately the scene of the Republicans' Outrage Convention. Nelson recalled a local event. Just recently, the mayor, a Democrat, had hosted the board of aldermen at a dinner to honor the city's fire brigade. One alderman, Robert Marsh, was black. Yet he partook of the town's liberality – and its supply of liquor – swilling side by side with tipsy white colleagues.

> Here in Chattanooga, some of our leading Democratic politicians sat around the jovial board with Bob Marsh, who is as black as a patent leather saddle. There was Tomlinson Fort and Mayor Sims, and there was A.M. Johnson, and Summerfield Key, with his collar unbuttoned and about a pint under his belt; and these distinguished citizens, some of them ex-Confederates, sat around the board and passed wine and tipped glasses with Bob Marsh, who is one of the members of your city government. If that isn't civil rights and social equality, in God's name what is it? (Laughter and applause)

Nelson concluded with another dig at Dibrell's nightmare.

> He said he supposed when Dibrell died he would go to heaven and have a pair of wings and become an angel. And when the poor old decrepit negro shuffled off this mortal coil he too would get a pair of wings and become an angel. Then wouldn't Brig. Gen. Dibrell of the Confederate States army look nice a bull-batting it through heaven with a nigger angel! (Laughter).[62]

61 Chattanooga *Times*, October 25, 1874.
62 Chattanooga *Times*, October 31, 1874.

Dave Nelson pulled within 2 votes in James County, 47 in Hamilton. He lost Bradley County by 6. Elsewhere he was swamped. Dibrell's margin was 4,692. Black voters, despite his civil rights denial, stuck by the Republican candidate. One explained it to the Chattanooga *Times:* "If you elect a Republican who falters in extending such right as we ought to have as citizens, at least they do not try to take any rights away." White voters, despite his civil rights denial, fled the Republican candidate. They dealt a death blow to the Civil Rights Bill, the *Times* declared: "The spirit that begat it was rebuked."[63]

Tennessee, Second District
Jacob M. Thornburgh (R), George W. Mabry (D)
Population: 89% white

In the roughhewn realm of east Tennessee politics, Colonel Jacob Montgomery Thornburgh presented the picture of tailored elegance. "The colonel showed the evidence of good living," the Knoxville *Press and Herald* described him at one of his campaign rallies, "a black frock coat, white vest, light pantaloons, gold shirt buttons, his whiskers neatly trimmed, hair well brushed, and showed loud gold sleeve-buttons."[64] His father, Judge Montgomery Thornburgh, died in 1862 in a Confederate prison camp. The son, as had Dave Nelson, fled to the federal army. He commanded the Fourth Tennessee (Union) Cavalry. Hence his honorable military title. Despite the gilt wardrobe and neat manner, or perhaps because of it, something suspect hovered about the elegant colonel. Even as he mounted his campaign he fended off a politician's worst nightmare, a sex scandal: two innocent, fatherless girls, 13 and 16 years old, lured to the Knoxville fleshpots, secluded in a bagnio, forced to satisfy degenerate desires. The charges were dubious. The "victims," it turned out, and their mother, had more likely lured the congressman than he them, for purposes of a shakedown. A shadow, nonetheless, followed the dandy candidate as his campaign progressed.[65]

Jacob Thornburgh had inherited the 2nd District from Horace Maynard in 1872 when Maynard ran for the at-large seat in Congress. The district sent Thornburgh to Washington with a majority of nearly 7,000 votes. Redistricting had altered it, depriving it of its "battering-ram" configuration.[66] But it remained a Republican bastion, perhaps the party's strongest stronghold in

63 Chattanooga *Times*, November 3, 1874.
64 Knoxville *Press and Herald*, August 23, 1874.
65 "His character has been known for a long time," hinted the Nashville *Banner* (April 14, 1874).
66 See Thomas B. Alexander, *Political Reconstruction in Tennessee* (New York, 1968): 237.

the South. Not until 1895 did the Knoxville district send a Democrat to Congress. Nine in ten inhabitants were white. Unionist sentiment, forged in war, sustained their political loyalty. The district had lost its western arm, Cumberland, Fentress, Overton, Clay, Jackson, White and Putnam Counties. It acquired a more compact shape, gaining Blount, Monroe, Loudon and Roane Counties to the south and Union County on the north. Its heart remained Knoxville, its political leanings unchanged. For July 4th festivities Knoxville's Union veterans invited their liberator, General Ambrose Burnside, to return. He did, saluted by a thunderous welcome. A parade filled the streets with cheering crowds.[67]

Those cheery Republican sentiments, however, did not extend to the party's civil rights bill. Congressman Thornburgh's white constituents made their misgivings plain. At Knoxville's Decoration Day ceremonies 15,000 Union veterans gathered at the cemetery. "But not one negro," reporters noted "was suffered to enter the portals. The common assertion everywhere is: 'We fought for the Union, not for the negro. We will not be forced downward that the negro may be uplifted, and our children shall not be imbued with the idea that they are no better than those of slaves.'"[68] Democrats customarily despaired of the 2nd District. In 1874 they sensed an opportunity.

The attitude of Thornburgh's black constituents complicated the congressman's condition. William F. "Squire" Yardley, Knoxville Justice of the Peace, led them. On his word black voters voted. He it was at the Nashville Colored Convention who had called for vengeance, "the brand of Judas, a traitor's doom," on Republicans whose zeal was found wanting. But Thornburgh could count. Ninety percent of his constituents were white. They disliked civil rights bills. Ten percent would have to endure disappointment. If they imposed a brand of Judas, so be it. The congressman voted no on May 25. He voted no on June 8. He voted no on June 20. Reality came home to Knoxville's black citizens, as it had to their fellows in Chattanooga, in Raleigh, in Goldsboro and Savannah. Even Squire Yardley backed down. As the election approached, he forgot his Nashville ultimatum. He insisted on no civil rights litmus test. In fact, he no longer insisted on a civil rights bill.[69]

Jacob Thornburgh seemed safe. He was not. A nomination battle engulfed Republicans in civil war. Civil rights emerged as a central front in that war. Thornburgh faced rivals. Chief among them was a persistent competitor, Judge Leonidas C. Houk. The judge was a determined character. He had lived a Lincolnesque life. Born in backwoods poverty, fatherless from the age of 3, "a humble

67 Knoxville *Press and Herald*, July 7, 1874.
68 Memphis *Appeal*, June 11, 1874.
69 Knoxville *Press and Herald*, July 18, 1874.

ploughboy in homespun breeches," eulogists pictured him, "seated upon a low bench in the chimney corner of a log cabin, drawing his knowledge from books conned by the light of flaming pine knots."[70] He studied the law. He rose to the dignity of the bench. But he kept a common touch. His speeches echoed rustic remembrances, "quaint figures drawn from the life of his people."[71] He yearned to sit in Congress. He challenged Maynard in 1865 and 1868. He challenged Thornburgh in 1872.[72] He tried again in 1874.[73]

This time Judge Houk perceived an opening: civil rights. The congressman thought his votes had inoculated him. But he left a tiny chink in his armor. It sufficed to let his enemies in. Col. Thornburgh had accepted a party honor. He sat as a member of the Republican National Congressional Committee. That body had produced the party's campaign platform. The platform, as noted, alluded to the need for legislation in support of equality, "a task still undone." A fleeting mention; it gave Jacob Thornburgh's rivals the crack they needed. The civil rights reference was brief. The congressman had not written it. He may not even have read it. He allowed his name to appear. It was enough. In July, with the smoking gun of the platform document in hand, Houk launched his assault. Thornburgh, he proclaimed, had called for civil rights.[74]

Thornburgh hoped the storm might subside. It did not. Then the sex scandal, buried a year before, resurfaced. The *Press and Herald* gallantly declared the charges unproven, all the while reminding readers of the details. Where there was smoke there was fire, the Maryville *Republican* hinted.[75] Thornburgh faced his problems head on. He agreed to meet Houk in open debate. Let the chips fall.

70 *Memorial Addresses on the Life and Character of Leonidas Campbell Houk, (A Representative from Tennessee) Delivered in the House of Representatives and in the Senate, January 30th and February 9th 1892, Fifty-Second Congress, First Session* (Washington: 1892), 24, 41, eulogies of Joseph Washington of Tennessee, Amos Cummings of New York.

71 *Memorial Addresses*, 59, eulogy of Jonathan Dolliver of Iowa.

72 See Gordon McKinney, "The Rise of the Houk Machine in East Tennessee," *East Tennessee Historical Society Publications*, 45 (1973): 61–69.

73 Houk fulfilled his ambition finally in 1879, taking a seat in the 46th Congress. He held that place until his death, under peculiar circumstances, twelve years later. On a mild May evening in 1891, having returned to Knoxville during a break, he walked out to buy cigars at the local druggist. Some gentlemen entered the shop. Pausing to chat. he felt thirsty. A glass of water lay invitingly unattended on the counter. Suspended in the liquid lurked a lethal dose of arsenic. Doctors induced vomiting. The congressman died at dawn.

74 Knoxville *Press and Herald*, August 11, 1874.

75 Quoted in Knoxville *Press and Herald*, April 3; Nashville *Banner*, April 14, 1874.

As those debates opened, it became evident that Thornburgh suffered from yet another malaise: an attack of conscience. As a congressman he had cast his votes against the Civil Rights Bill. As a man he could not cast away his convictions. He defended the very thing he had voted against. The rivals met at Kingston. Thornburgh trimmed.

> He defined the Civil Rights bill to be a corollary of those rights already guaranteed by the 13th 14th and 15th Amendments, with the exception of the penalties imposed. He was for the principle, but he was opposed to the penalty. And [neither] Congress nor any other assembly could enforce social equality.[76]

"He accepts the three theorems and deduces the corollary," the *Union and American* snickered, "but hesitates at the penalty, and then proceeds to deny the corollary." The debates moved on to Maryville. Houk struck again. True, his opponent had voted against the Civil Rights Bill. But he had signed the RNCC platform. "His name is there as large as life." The signature was a mistake, Thornburgh sputtered. He had not read the text. He repudiated whatever such statement it contained.[77]

They met at Knoxville on August 22. It was 1 o'clock, mid-day in midsummer, the courthouse jammed, waves of suffocating heat. Thornburgh sweltered in his nattiest attire. Houk perspired without collar or tie. Thornburgh recalled his role as one of the stalwarts whose votes had prevented the Senate civil rights bill from reaching the House floor. "Before I would vote for it I would resign and come home." So far so good. Then his bothersome conscience returned. Charles Sumner's law was foolish. But Sumner's ideals were noble. *Something* must be done. *Some* measure must ensure equality. He recalled black people's oppression, emancipation, citizenship. "I am almost afraid to say civil rights," he sighed, "for fear some mean puppy will misrepresent me, as the cowardly, lying little fellows have been doing about me." Houk waved the RNCC document. "Why does he not explain the language of the Congressional Address, instead of calling people who read it for themselves 'low down puppies?'"[78]

They debated at Rockwood in Roane County on September 11. By now the events had aroused interest across the district. George Mabry and William A. Henderson, candidates for the Democratic nomination, asked to join the

76 Nashville *Union and American*, August 15, 1874.
77 Knoxville *Press and Herald*, August 19, 1874.
78 Knoxville *Press and Herald*, August 23, 1874.

discussion. Houk and Thornburgh agreed. Four men, two Democrats and two Republicans, debated the issues – extraordinarily, before the conventions, before the nominations, before the election campaign. Four men, but the battle came down to three against one, Congressman Jacob Thornburgh. Mabry posed stolidly, a son of the soil, "erect, courteous and horny-handed." Houk radiated energy, "active, affable, determined." Henderson, known as a local wit, "abounded in good humor." The congressman looked humorless, "gloomy, reserved and dictatorial." The crowd was white. A few Negroes approached, "hanging on the outskirts – not by their necks, however" (the *Press and Herald's* reporter couldn't resist a playful aside) "as might be supposed in the light of recent events." Each speaker spoke for an hour. Each took ten minutes to rebut. After five hours the people retired, having relished a rare event.[79]

George Mabry spoke first. He came straight to the point: the Civil Rights Bill. That evil belonged to all Republicans. Thornburgh's signature on the party document gave the lie to his pretended opposition. Mabry appealed to the country folk.

> It is in the country that its operation will be harsh. In the city where there are numerous private schools, the children can be sent to them, but in the country districts, generally, it will be either mixed schools or none.... What are the teachers of the State to do? They will say to Johnnie and Bettie, "Johnnie, you can't go to school any more. You'll have to stay home and work on the farm." And Bettie will be told she will have to stay at home and work about the house. Then the Northern Republicans will say ... we will pass Hoar's Compulsory Education Bill, and make the white children and the black children go to the same school and sit on the same bench.

Houk took up the chase. Thornburgh as much as signed the Civil Rights Bill when he signed the RNCC platform. Senator Brownlow opposed it. Thornburgh had criticized Brownlow, the people's hero. He, Houk, stood with Brownlow.

> Thornburgh says he voted against the bill. But he did not. The Congressional Address, which Thornburgh signed, calls for "appropriate legislation" to enforce the amendments. What does that mean? ... It means to take up Sumner's Civil Rights Bill and pass it.

79 Account of the debate and speeches, Knoxville *Press and Herald*, September 12, 1874. See also following paragraphs.

William Henderson stepped up, a Tennessee Twain, folksy storyteller and humorist. He mocked both Republicans. "Here stand two professed representatives of the party vociferating about the Civil Rights policy of the National Republican Party: 'You're for it and I ain't!' and 'No I ain't for it, but you are!'" Brownlow aside, the only honest Tennessee Republican was Maynard. Maynard supported civil rights and said so. "Fellow-citizens, 'Civil Rights' is emblazoned on every true banner of the Republican party, and the day is near when upon all its standards shall 'Ichabod!' be written."

> I imagine Morton with the bit, and Blaine with the whip, and Butler twisting his tail behind. If the young mule from Tennessee should kick up his heels the whip would crack, the leaders pull, and it wouldn't be long before the mule would pull all right to the Civil Rights wagon. He turned to Thornburgh: "Of course you would vote for it. (Sensation) A Baptist might as well say he was opposed to water. A Catholic might, with as much reason, say he was opposed to the Pope." It is a party measure, and Thornburgh says so in his Address.... It won't do for Thornburgh to say he didn't do it, and for Houk to say he didn't do it, thus passing it from hand to hand like a hot potato. It is their hot potato. They have got to take it. It is theirs. It was not made in our shop.[80]

Three hours into the debate, Thornburgh rose. His exasperation fairly exploded. Brownlow! "You can quote me as well as Brownlow.... Rather than vote for that bill I would resign my seat." Then Thornburgh's annoying conscience popped up. "What does 'civil rights' mean?" he demanded. "The rights of American citizenship. Civil Rights is the right of every citizen, white and black to the rights of life, liberty and the pursuit of happiness." His voice rose: "'Negro equality! Negro equality!! Negro equality!!!' For years this same cry has met the Republican party at every forward step." Negroes had earned equality. The constitutional amendments had given them equality. Civil rights laws enforced equality. One way or another equality would come: "Now I tell you such appropriate legislation as is necessary to secure the amendments will be enacted.... And I tell you this: If Ku Klux assassinations continue and the civil authorities do not exert themselves, I *will* vote for such laws as will mete out merited punishment."

---

80 Henderson's most popular lecture told the tales of Tennessee pioneer John Sevier, on whose life he had accumulated a treasury of anecdotes. These he shared for the public's entertainment – "The Adventures of Nolichucky Jack" – 25¢ a ticket. Knoxville *Press and Herald*, October 27, 1874.

The foursome "danced a final quadrille" at Madisonville on September 15. Henderson was in fine form. Let the people reward the Republicans as they deserved: "If you like Houk personally, give him a clean paper collar. If you like Thornburgh, show your appreciation of him by giving him – what? Well, give him a gold sleeve button.... But if you cast a vote for either one of them for Congress, in doing so you endorse the policy of their party – Civil Rights."[81]

Events moved swiftly. The first round went to Thornburgh. He still had the power of incumbency and the inducements of patronage. Houk took the endorsement of Blount and Loudon Counties. The colonel roped in delegates from Knoxville. Houk made a fatal mistake. He brought Brownlow into the game. He announced he would withdraw if a third party whom he respected entered the contest: for instance, the senator.[82] This ploy doomed Houk's chances. On September 23rd Republicans convened at the Opera House in Knoxville. Houk, sensing defeat, spurned the proceedings. Thornburgh took the nomination. Houk defied him. He declared an independent candidacy. Democrats cheered. The vote was split. The 2nd District was theirs.

Just as night seemed darkest, daylight shone for the incumbent. Brownlow made his move. The Parson had been biding his time. In one of his June diatribes he had declared his intention never again to seek public office.[83] But things had changed since June. In August, as the Thornburgh-Houk war raged, disgruntled Republicans called on him to reconsider.[84] On September 30, a week after the convention, he notified voters of the 2nd District: "I take this occasion to say that I am a candidate to represent them in the next or Forty-fourth Congress of the United States."[85] Democrats cheered louder. Three battling Republicans were even better than two. "The old man shoved his hat back on his ear, rolled up his sleeves, expectorated on his hands and sailed in," clucked the Memphis *Avalanche*. "He'll teach the boys what four story adjectives were made for."[86]

Brownlow, however, had sailed in with a very precise plan. He hoped that his entry would clear the field. Quarreling Republicans would bow to the party's great man. Democrats would slink away in fear. Civil rights could not harm him. He would accept the people's homage.[87] On the other hand, he had no

81 Knoxville *Press and Herald*, September 17, 1874.
82 Knoxville *Press and Herald*, September 20, 1874.
83 Knoxville *Press and Herald*, June 10, 1874.
84 Nashville *Banner*, August 16, 1874.
85 Knoxville *Press and Herald*, October 1, 1874.
86 Quoted in Chattanooga *Times*, October 6, 1874.
87 Brownlow's appeal had potential. On the 7th the *Press and Herald* printed the thoughts of one reader. He signed himself "Democrat." Democrats, "Democrat" declared, should

intention of fighting, either for the nomination or for the election. If his plan failed he planned to sail out.

The most immediate reaction came from Squire Yardley and his black followers. They had restrained their disappointment as Houk and Thornburgh vied for the privilege of opposing the Civil Rights Bill. Thornburgh at least spoke for the principle. Brownlow, arch-villain of the hour, he who had labeled their hopes "the quintessence of abominations," was a pill they could not swallow. A petition signed by 116 black citizens of Knoxville called upon one of their own, Rev. George W. Levere, pastor of the Shiloh Presbyterian Church, to become a candidate.[88]

Levere's entry put four Republicans in the race alongside two Democrats. That number decreased rapidly. Brownlow's housecleaning plan took effect. The very day after Levere's move, on October 7, two candidates surrendered. Houk had no choice. He published his withdrawal in a lengthy card. Civil rights, he insisted, was the key. All else was secondary. Brownlow alone had the force to stop it. Henderson also gave up. The great ship's wash had swamped two of the small struggling boats. But two others refused to go down. Thornburgh held fast. And on the 8th Mabry published a defiant card: "The report that I would withdraw from the Congressional race before the election having been extensively circulated, I take this method of informing my friends that I shall certainly see the race through." Brownlow's play had failed. On that same day he scuttled his ship. He would not divide a Republican vote against continued Democratic opposition. "Therefore it is that I withdraw from the contest.... I shall continue to fight the abominable Civil Rights bill, and all such sectional legislation, but I shall do it inside the Republican party."[89] For Jacob Thornburgh the Brownlow whirlwind wrought a miracle. Houk was blown away. Rev. Levere had entered only in hatred of Brownlow. He too departed. One Democrat, George Mabry, remained.

Mabry, known to his people as Farmer George, was indeed a Knox County farmer. When not mentioning civil rights, he promoted himself as the candidate of the country folk. The citified Thornburgh, with glinting cuff-links and perfect hair, was clueless on the needs of farmers. The congressman, he

defer: "If Henderson and Mabry could rise to the importance of the occasion and assist, by that declension in his favor, in the election of Senator Brownlow, would it not greatly strengthen him in his efforts with the President? ... Personal preferences and personal ambition should be sunk and ignored, and only one thing considered, to wit: the most effective plan and most effective man to defeat this great calamity [the Civil Rights Bill]."

88 Knoxville *Press and Herald*, October 6, 1874.

89 Knoxville *Press and Herald*, October 9; Knoxville *Union and American*, October 11, 1874.

sneered, had mailed sacks of seeds as pre-election presents. What more idiotic sign of incomprehension could he offer?[90]

Three weeks remained to conduct the campaign: sixteen more debates in sixteen days. They began on October 15 at Strawberry Plains. They passed through picturesque places: New Market, Mansfield's Gap, Pigeon Forge, Ellejoy, Brick Mill, then on to Beaver Gap, Coal Creek, Careyville, Fincastle. They finished at Loy's Crossroads in Union County. At each stop Mabry called out his opponent as a secret supporter of the Civil Rights Bill. Thornburgh protested his innocence. The congressman urged black voters to remember their loyalty. Brownlow had gone. Return to the fold. They did. Mabry distributed a circular. If Thornburgh were so opposed to civil rights, why did Yardley and Levere support him? Surely they would not back a candidate who betrayed them on that issue. "My friends … I am a plain man. But no man ever heard me say I was for Civil Rights."[91]

Jacob Thornburgh survived, barely. His majority in 1872 provided him a cushion of 6,752 votes. He squandered almost 6,000. A mere 830 votes separated him from Farmer Mabry. He lost Knox and Monroe Counties. Wide Republican margins were shredded: 184 votes in Roane County, 50 in Anderson, 12 in Morgan County. Thornburgh's signature on the RNCC platform was a mistake, but it was his conscience that confounded him. He spoke too many kind words to black people. He repudiated the Civil Rights Bill. He failed to repudiate civil rights.

Tennessee, First District
Roderick R. Butler (R), William McFarland (D)
Population: 91% white

In the mountains of easternmost Tennessee lay the den of the Red Fox. So his constituents saluted the four-term Republican incumbent of the 1st District Roderick R. Butler, in honor of his rusty hair and sly politics. Civil rights should not have ruffled the tranquility of the vulpine politician. He sniffed out civil rights danger and avoided it with the acuity of a furry forest creature. Black persons, moreover, were a scarce species in the 1st District. Only Hawkins and

90 Knoxville *Press and Herald*, September 12, 1874. The practice of pre-election seed distribution in fact was not uncommon. Sunset Cox recalled his early days, running in central Ohio. He sent sacks of seed, guaranteed "weevil-proof," to Muskingum County farmers. Opponents accused him of dealing out an adulterated mix. The grain proved wholesome. Weevils went away. Cox won the seed wars and election to Congress. Samuel S. Cox, *Why We Laugh* (New York: 1969), 353–362.

91 Knoxville *Press and Herald*, October 28, 1874.

Greene Counties contained an appreciable population, some 4,000 among 40,000 residents. Johnson County possessed 470, along with 7,300 whites; in Carter County census takers unearthed 628 among 10,000 white inhabitants.

Despite this demographic, civil rights worries rose in the hills. At first the Nashville *Banner's* local correspondent, signing his dispatches with the *nom de plume* Xela, reported all quiet among the mountain folk. "The Civil Rights question has not elicited much discussion," he wrote on February 18. "If there be oppression let that be removed at once. If not, let every man prove his equality to every other man by his worth in a community. We are not frightened at the scare-crow, 'social equality.'" By June, Xela had changed his mind. Candidates, he reported now, were "foaming" at the evil of the Civil Rights Bill.[92] By August news of panic emerged from far-east Tennessee.[93]

Only gradually did February's complacency rise to August's fury. The turning point came in April, the manifesto of the Nashville Colored Convention. Those strident demands – mixed schools, mixed marriages – stampeded public opinion. "The excitement occasioned throughout East Tennessee by the demand of the State colored convention," the Knoxville *Press and Herald* reported, "is as great as that which followed the firing on Fort Sumter."[94] Brownlow's diatribes put the finishing touches to hysteria.

Word reached Washington. The Red Fox caught the scent. When the time came he joined Jacob Thornburgh and voted No on the Civil Rights Bill. But Roderick Butler too suffered from a touch of Thornburgh's malaise, an uneasy conscience. On June 4 he rose in the House to excuse his vote. "I certainly can have no prejudice or feeling against the colored race. I would not do one act knowingly that would injure them." He opposed the bill in the interest of peace.[95] It seemed a superfluous gesture. Most observers, Xela included, considered the foxy incumbent secure, even in the teeth of a civil rights typhoon. He was, after all, Roderick Randum Butler.

Perpetually smiling, always affable, he lived, unlike his literary near-namesake, far from the sea. He came from the hills. He had been once, like Andrew Johnson, a poor tailor's apprentice in Mountain City. He knew his people, how to associate himself with their concerns. He practiced the politics of retail salesmanship. Riding the rutted roads of the 1st District, he reached out to

---

92 Nashville *Banner*, June 13, 1874.

93 Chattanooga *Times*, August 9, 1874.

94 Knoxville *Press and Herald*, May 15, 1874.

95 See above, Chapter 5. On the hesitant but, for a time, beneficial relationship between white Republicans and black persons in the highlands, see Gordon B. McKinney, *Southern Mountain Republicans, 1865–1900: Politics and the Appalachian Community* (Chapel Hill: 1978), 30–32, 124–141.

embrace the masses. "The secret of his strength is that he has a kind word for everybody," wrote the Memphis *Appeal*. "He will dismount from his horse and wade through a rod of mud to shake hands with an old woman and ask her about her children, her calves, her hens and chickens, old sows and pigs.... I do not hear that the Democrats are going into the fray with much spirit. They cannot successfully fight so many smiles, so many square drinks, often with sugar in them ... so you may as well consider Butler good for a fifth term."[96] "Modesty is not one of his gifts or graces," added the Greeneville *Union and American*. "He is a man of infinite brass."[97]

He was also infinitely corrupt. He could steal a horse each day, he joked, and still win his elections hands down.[98] A trail of malfeasance followed the kindly, smiling congressman. Bribe taking, pension fraud, influence peddling, cadetship peddling, he had survived them all. In 1871, for lack of proof, the government dropped its prosecution in the "Pension Ring" case, a shady affair involving submission of claims for non-existent veterans' widows, who, though imaginary, had signed over to R.R. Butler their power of attorney to receive the government's largesse.[99] As to the matter of selling a West Point cadetship to the highest bidder ($900 cash), Butler pleaded no contest. The House censured him but could not quite muster the two-thirds required to expel him. That was in 1870. He won re-election anyway. He won again in 1872.[100]

Roderick Butler nonetheless faced challengers. Andrew Johnson, rumors said, contemplated a run. The ex-president opted for Tennessee's open Senate seat. But one nettlesome Republican rival, a former friend and ally, entered the contest. Judge Edward E. Gillenwaters of Rogersville felt betrayed. When Butler resigned from the First District Circuit Court to enter Congress in 1867

---

96 Memphis *Appeal*, September 10, 1874. Oliver Temple knew R.R. Butler and remembered him: "simple, affable, approachable, and exceedingly kindly in manner and disposition." Temple, *Notable Men*, 77–78.

97 Greeneville *Union and American*, April 6, 1876.

98 Verton M. Queener, "The Origins of the Republican Party in East Tennessee," *Publications of the East Tennessee Historical Society*, 13 (1941): 80; Temple, *Notable Men*, 77–78; Alexander, *Political Reconstruction in Tennessee*, 22–23.

99 Greeneville *New Era*, January 12, 1871.

100 Most recently came a new scandal, the Sugg Fort affair. Mr. Sugg Fort of Fort's Station in Robertson County asserted that the United States owed him the exact sum of $23,723.50 as payment for 2,791 barrels of flour appropriated by the federal army and removed from his mill in 1862. The congressional Committee on Claims rejected the suit. Fort's congressman, Horace Harrison, refused to help. He turned to Butler. Butler applied some monetary grease to lubricate the bureaucratic wheels. Abruptly the Treasury Department settled matters in favor of the claimant. Congress opened another investigation of R.R. Butler. New York *Tribune*, November 3; Nashville *Union and American*, November 6, 1874.

Gillenwaters took the judicial job. He thought he had an assurance that in due course Butler would retire and he would inherit the congressional job. "The bargain of 1867" remained unfulfilled four terms later. Now Butler sought a fifth term. Gillenwaters' patience expired.[101]

As early as January, papers reported a Gillenwaters-for-Congress movement. Republicans in Hawkins and Sullivan Counties petitioned the judge to enter the race. The Jonesboro *Herald and Tribune* endorsed him. The Morristown *Spy* began publication as a campaign organ of the insurgency.[102] Judge Gillenwaters produced a platform. He favored the common man. He opposed "a financial system which drains the rural and agricultural districts of currency and concentrates it in the hands of capitalists for speculation in stocks and other paper.... We must not take bread from the mouth of labor and give it to capital." He mentioned, rather conspicuously, that he would not mention matters of corruption, should there be any such matters to mention in any candidate's résumé.[103]

The contest began with a solicitation of the district's black voters. Those voters met at Bull's Gap in Hawkins County on May 1. Gillenwaters hoped for a sympathetic hearing. He found most delegates committed to Butler. He walked out.[104] Bull's Gap ought to have been the opening of a nomination struggle. There was no nomination. Republicans did without that formality. Neither contender agreed to a convention of the other's designing. Two candidates asserted their right to wear the party label.

Butler went on the offensive. He appeared at Elizabethton in Carter County. He emphasized his opposition to the Civil Rights Bill.[105] The Red Fox snapped next at Gillenwaters. He showed up suddenly outside the court house at Taylorsville, where the judge was holding session. Butler invited spectators to hear him speak. A large part of the courthouse crowd followed him. Before the next day's trials began, Gillenwaters treated the public to a political speech delivered from the bench.[106]

101 Though he failed in 1874, the judge seemed likely to be the Republicans' candidate in 1876. An unexpected death on March 27 of that year frustrated his plans. The Greeneville *Union and American* printed a respectful obituary. He was "a Christian gentleman," a minister of the Methodist Episcopal Church. He was honest, a quality that Butler lacked. But he lacked Butler's folksy ways, the smiling common touch. Even his polite obituary recalled a chronically dyspeptic character. He commanded respect, "but he could not make warm personal friends." Greeneville *Union and American*, April 6, 1876.

102 Knoxville *Press and Herald*, January 17, 1874.

103 Knoxville *Press and Herald*, January 14, 1874.

104 Knoxville *Press and Herald*, May 2, 1874.

105 Knoxville *Press and Herald*, July 16; Nashville Banner, July 17, 1874.

106 Knoxville *Press and Herald*, July 25, 1874.

Soon civil rights began to plague the incumbent's efforts. He spoke at Jonesboro He repeated his unalterable opposition to the Civil Rights Bill. He had not voted for it. He would not vote for it. "Appealing to the negroes he said if that bill ever passed and became a law it would be the darkest day the colored people ever saw."[107] Gillenwaters called it a lie. He produced a circular showing that Butler was "soft" on civil rights: "Of course he favors it. The dodging politicians all do." Pro-Gillenwaters sheets, the Jonesboro *Herald* and Morristown *Spy,* spread the word, "satisfactorily proving that Roderick Butler was in favor of the Civil Rights Bill."[108]

Light dawned on the Democrats. They had been inclined to stand aside while the Red Fox glided to another victory. Now they perceived benefits in holding a convention, even in nominating a candidate. They met at Greeneville on October 1. Chairman William B. Carter expressed optimism: "He believed that we could at last redeem this district from radical ruin which is the rule of ruin."[109] Candidates stepped up. At first Gen. George R. McClellan of Sullivan County and Col. William Green of Hawkins County held the lead. On the 15th ballot the name of Andrew Johnson, Jr. was put in nomination. He received four votes. He withdrew. On the 29th ballot the convention chose Judge William McFarland of Hamblen County. The platform proposed only four resolutions. The first objected to corruption: "We are opposed to cadet peddling and cadet peddlers, to salary grabbing and salary grabbers." The second warned of centralization of power. The third rejected a presidential third term. The fourth stated: "We are unconditionally opposed to the supplementary Civil Rights Bill."[110]

Judge McFarland claimed humble roots. He had started life as a tanner, selling leather goods from a small store. He boasted wartime loyalty to the federal cause ("I was a Union man and opposed to the war"). He professed kindly feelings for the freedmen ("no party desires to take from them a single right secured to them; I am sure I do not").[111] But he opposed Civil Rights. His competitor, he said, had nowhere to hide.

> Civil Rights and Republicanism mean the same – the degradation of every noble impulse and every generous aspiration in the white race in the South. Every vote given, every speech made in favor of the Republican party without Civil Rights assists in riveting the chains upon us.... Beware

107 Knoxville *Press and Herald,* August 5, 1874.
108 Knoxville *Press and Herald,* August 23, September 6, 1874.
109 Greeneville *Intelligencer,* October 2, 1874.
110 Greeneville *Intelligencer,* October 2, 1874.
111 Greeneville *Union and American,* October 26, 1874.

> of men who claim to oppose Civil Rights and yet champion the cause of the Republican party.[112]

On October 16 the Greeneville *Intelligencer*, edited by Andrew Johnson, Jr., printed McFarland's manifesto, "An Address to the Voters of the First Congressional District of Tennessee:" 5,000 words covered the front pages, nearly two-thirds devoted to a denunciation of the Civil Rights Bill. That, he proclaimed, "is the only vital question on which the great parties of our country are now directly at issue," a matter of life or death, "involving, as I believe, the extermination of one or the other of the races."[113]

The judge's Address produced evidence that his opponent, notwithstanding his votes, actually favored the villainous sum and quintessential abomination. The proof was on the record, the congressional record. Until recently, when the instinct for political self-preservation kicked in, Butler had been a friend of civil rights legislation. He had voted for it. He had spoken for it. He even admitted it in his speech to the House on June 4: "If my colored friends desert me, they desert a man who has stood by them in many hard-fought contests for the rights and privileges they enjoy." McFarland laid out the paper trail. From the pages of the *Congressional Globe* Roderick R. Butler emerged, a civil rights supporter. On February 19, 1872, a civil rights bill appeared for the first time before the House. Butler endorsed it. On May 28, 1872, Horace Maynard moved to take that bill from the Speaker's table. Butler spoke aye. On June 7, 1872, Luke Poland moved to suspend the rules and pass the bill. Butler of Tennessee voted yes. On December 9, Charles Eldredge moved to table the bill. Butler voted no. On March 11, 1872, West Virginia's Frank Hereford introduced a resolution condemning civil rights bills. Roderick Butler voted no. Now he pretended to feel a holy horror of civil rights bills.

McFarland added further evidence. On April 10 of this year Butler himself had placed a letter in the Jonesboro *Echo*. Enemies, he said, accused him of opposition to the bill. He denied it: "I was not opposed to the bill.... I have stood by them [the colored people] on all occasions when their rights were in jeopardy. I have been denounced as the 'nigger candidate' since 1867." McFarland agreed. His opponent was then, in 1867, and was still, in 1874, the "nigger candidate."

Following the civil rights section of his Address, the judge remembered some other points. He turned to the salary grab: "He had the money. He kept it; he has it yet." He recalled the cadetship-peddling scandal. He paused a moment

112 Morristown *Gazette* quoted in Greeneville *Intelligencer*, October 2, 1874.

113 Greeneville *Intelligencer*, special "Campaign Supplement," October 16, 1874.

over government centralization and the tyrannical Third Term. He dismissed Gillenwaters. Whatever applied to Butler applied to him: "they stand side by side." McFarland offered voters a one-course meal: the Civil Rights Bill, served up with a garnish of salary-grab and a twist of cadetship-peddling. Andrew Johnson, Jr. wrapped up his Campaign Supplement: "McFarland was nominated by the white men at Greeneville on the 1st of October. Butler and Gillenwaters were both nominated by the darkeys at Bull's Gap on the 1st of May last. Who [sic] will you vote for?"

In the last weeks the candidates debated: 11 meetings over 17 days. From Rogersville Junction they traveled to Tazewell, Elizabethton, Taylorsville, Fish Springs, Blountville, Turley's Mill. McFarland stuck to his script, "saddling" the incumbent with civil rights. Gillenwaters joined the chorus. The Red Fox clawed at his tormentors. Republicans could stand no more. On October 15 Gillenwaters exited. "The Radicals of Greene County called in a body on Gillenwaters and asked him to 'step down and out.' The judge wilted, and has gone back to the bench."[114]

It was not enough. McFarland raced to victory. Some Republicans blamed Gillenwaters. They called for the judge's impeachment.[115] Gillenwaters hurt, but he was not the essential problem. Corruption weakened Roderick Butler. He had overcome such trifles before. Horace Redfield surveyed the scene. The Red Fox had slid out of many traps, he wrote, but Sumner's snare trapped him. "His record as a peddler of cadet appointments he survived. He also seemed in a fair way to survive the back-pay grab." He did not survive the Civil Rights Bill.[116]

2 Alabama

Population accorded Alabama eight congressional seats. Six corresponded to geographic districts. Two were awarded at large. Republicans held five places, including the at-large seats occupied by Alexander White and Charles Sheats. In the 4th District an unassailable black majority sustained Charles Hays. Republicans held the 2nd District, covering the area from Montgomery to the state's southeast. For the moment they held the 3rd District, in the east-center. But their margin was slim, 562 votes having separated the candidates in 1872. Democrats enjoyed strength in the north, the 5th District and the 6th, currently

114 Knoxville *Press and Herald*, October 15, 1874.
115 Knoxville *Press and Herald*, December 3, 1874.
116 Cincinnati *Commercial*, November 23, 1874.

occupied by the chivalric Col. Joseph Sloss. The 1st District, Mobile and the southwest, contained a large black majority. It had accidentally fallen to a Liberal Republican through Republican disunity.

As in Tennessee, Arkansas and Missouri, Alabama's congressional elections coincided with a gubernatorial contest. Democrats were hopeful. A vigorous campaign led by a strong candidate for the governorship ought to awaken the white masses. That would redeem the at-large seats. There was every probability of retaking the 3rd District. The southern districts appeared more problematic. Demography obstructed redemption. But an energetic outbreak of terrorism might correct that disadvantage.

Civil rights handed Democrats another weapon. Fear already haunted white Alabamians. The proposed state civil rights statute of 1873 would have enacted the integration of public accommodations, public transportation, public amusements, and cemeteries. It would have mandated a regime of mixed schools, imposed fines of up to $1,000 and imprisonment for a year on violators, and fines of up to $1,000 on officials guilty of lax enforcement. A mere handful of votes had defeated this horror. Now Republicans prepared to do by federal fiat what they had failed to do by state statute. The Montgomery *Advertiser* quoted black leader Greene Shadrach Washington Lewis:

> We are done begging and pleading for our rights. Hereafter we intend to demand them and to press them on every occasion; and the day is not far distant when you will find on the bench of the Supreme Court of the State a man as black as I am, and North Alabama may help herself if she can.[117]

As Sumner's civil rights bill progressed through Congress Alabama Democrats rejoiced. "It will unite the white race as one man against Radicalism," the *Advertiser* declared, "and enable us to redeem Alabama from misrule and corruption."[118] The paper recalled George Boutwell's speech to the Senate. Mixed schools would enlighten little children; they would end the instinct of prejudice. To emphasize the enormity of that wicked sentiment the *Advertiser* printed Boutwell's words entirely in bold capitals.

Other Democratic sheets joined in. The Tuskegee *News* questioned. "Are you in favor of maintaining the purity of the Anglo-Saxon blood and the consequent respectability of our wives and children? Or are you for miscegenating and mixing with the filthy blacks?" The Fayette *Watchman* barked. "It is the

117 Montgomery *Advertiser*, March 28, 1874.
118 Montgomery *Advertiser*, May 26, June 3, 1874.

blackest among the many infamous doings of modern times. Negroes are admitted to the full enjoyment of all the rights and privileges granted white men." The St. Clair *Aegis* mused. "It more than ever forces the great question upon us: 'How to get rid of the Negro.'"[119]

Horace Redfield passed through north Alabama. He found white Republicans fleeing their party. "They have been swallowing nigger, nigger, nigger, for the past seven years, but this last dose is a little too much. They're all a'throwin' up."[120] The white Republican vote in Alabama, the Louisville *Courier-Journal* reported, "will be scattered like chaff before the wind."[121] Death threats descended. Congressman Charles Pelham reported from the 3rd District. His vote on the Civil Rights Bill "had so incensed the whites of the country that if he stayed the night they would kill him before morning." In the 4th District Charles Hays carried pistols wherever he went.[122] Corpses piled up: Walter Billings, Tom Ivey, others scattered over the landscape.

The corpses (Billings' apart) were black. That did not reassure white Alabamians. Fear infected the masses. Shadowy plots, murmured mysteries, armies lurking in the dark, reports popped up across the state. "When these howling and sneaking hypocrites cry out against supposed violence of the white men," the Mobile *Register* hissed, "we put this thought for their consideration, to wit: That white violence will keep active pace with black violence; that for one blow they shall have two."[123]

Preemptive violence in Choctaw County terminated one presumed rebel, Jack Turner, before he actually rebelled.[124] He was quoted: "D – d if he didn't have his civil rights or die."[125] He was lynched. Phantoms lurked in Madison County. Armed Negroes in the hills, the Huntsville *Democrat* reported: "Be prepared for any emergency."[126] Black battalions were sighted around Selma. They were massing in Greene County, awaiting shipments of government arms. They were seen in Winston County, raising "considerable apprehension."[127] On September 17 the Democratic State Executive Committee sent out a circular

---

119 Tuskegee *News*, Fayette *Watchman*, St. Clair *Aegis*, quoted in Montgomery *Advertiser*, June 6, 1874.

120 Cincinnati *Commercial*, September 28, 1874.

121 Louisville *Courier-Journal*, October 5, 1874.

122 New York *Times*, September 1, 1874.

123 Mobile *Register*, August 18, 30, 1874.

124 See William W. Rogers and Robert D. Ward, *August Reckoning: Jack Turner and Racism in Post-Civil War Alabama* (Baton Rouge: 1973).

125 Mobile *Register*, August 18, 1874.

126 Quoted in Mobile *Register*, August 9, 1874.

127 Mobile *Register*, September 3–4, 1874.

warning of insurrection.[128] No insurrection happened. Still, at the town of Forkland various "insurgents" had to be killed before the election.[129] At Eufaula dozens more were shot down during the election, along with a further pruning at Spring Hill. Black citizens of Greene County wrote to Ulysses Grant:

> They are killing and Ku-Kluxing us both day and night; killing harmless women, running our wives and children through the woods, run your school-teacher off, and whipping some to death. We have for the last nine years been cheated out of everything we have made. President Grant, who stands at the head of the republican party, look on our struggling condition.... For heaven's sake do something for us, for we have to have better living than we are living.[130]

In the midst of all this, Republicans realized, they had to decide on civil rights. Should they stand up for principle? Or should they duck and hide? White politicians waited anxiously. How would their black counterparts handle the powder keg? At Nashville the Colored Convention had boldly lit the fuse. In Montgomery a convention gathered. It fumbled with fearful, jittery fingers. The Alabama Equal Rights Association, the cream of Alabama's black political leadership, met on June 25 in Montgomery's Hall of Representatives.[131] Congressman Rapier, detained in Washington, did not attend. State Senator Jeremiah Haralson played the critical part. White Republicans – among them

128 Montgomery *Advertiser*, September 17, 1874.

129 Mobile *Register*, September 18, 20, 1874.

130 "Republican Citizen" to Ulysses Grant, October 3, 1874. *Papers of Ulysses S. Grant*, vol. 25, 197. Attorney-General George Williams ordered an intervention. Troops were posted. Arrests came in the Billings case. Democrats reaped a propaganda windfall: three helpless white men cruelly shackled, paraded across the state, exposed to the jeers of Negroes. "Even the bloody Duke of Alva did not chain and handcuff innocent men ... a new mode of convincing men that the Civil Rights Bill should be endorsed by Alabama." Montgomery *Advertiser*, October 7, 11, 1874.

131 Alabama's parvenu black politicians exasperated Democrats. The *Register* characterized some of them. J.T. Harris of Perry County it found "the most intelligent mulatto in the House ... ungainly in person but dignified in manner." Willis Merriwether of Wilcox County, it agreed, was "the noisiest negro in the House ... impudent as well as ignorant." Greene Lewis was certainly "the most vindictive ... but above the common negroes in information and intelligence." Mobile *Register*, November 24, 1874. Some white men saw humor in the situation: "A letter writer in the South says you cannot go into a cotton plantation in Alabama now without hearing the commands; 'Senator, start right smart to your cotton picking;' 'Judge, you go and bring my horse around;' or, 'Colonel, you have a shoe put on that mule right along.' Undoubtedly things are considerably changed in Alabama." Newark *Journal*, October 17, 1874.

Henry Greatta, partner of the soon-to-be-deceased Walter Billings – paced the lobby, eavesdropping intently.[132] Haralson introduced a resolution. The Equal Rights Association must endorse the Civil Rights Bill, but with qualifications. First Haralson qualified away mixed schools.

> Resolved, that in declaring ourselves in favor of the passage of the Civil Rights Act we do not therefore wish to be understood as favoring mixed schools, nor do we believe said bill requires the same. All we ask in this respect is that our children shall enjoy equal educational privileges established by the public school laws of the State and of the United States, and prefer that the white and colored schools shall be kept separate and distinct.[133]

Then he qualified the need for social equality: "Those who pretend that said bill has any such purpose willfully misrepresent the facts." Haralson's interpretations provoked chaos. Delegates rushed to deconstruct the constructions. Black politicians argued. White politicians listened aghast. For Democrats every word was golden, a gift to their store of campaign fodder. "Don't destroy this copy," the *Advertiser* urged its readers: "Save it to read to your neighbors."

Delegates in the hall knew they were feeding ammunition to the enemy. In principle civil rights remained non-negotiable. In practice it dragged the party to defeat and thus defeated itself. Some insisted on principle. An equal rights convention, Thomas Walker of Dallas County declared, cannot approve segregation. Alexander Curtis of Perry County replied. No one advocated segregation. But they had to consider political survival. Walker retorted. "Colored people would lose nothing by demanding all their rights. Whenever they went out on an equality platform they won, but when they took a milk and water course, as they did in 1870, they were defeated."

Robert Whittaker of Montgomery supported Walker. "He would be less than a man not to vote that his children had equal rights and privileges in the public schools." Curtis protested: "I am in favor of the Civil Rights bill, and am man enough to stand up to my opinions; but I do not wish to do anything which may endanger the success of my party in the State." John Jones of Lowndes County agreed: "I believe that a large majority of my race in that county would vote against mixed schools because it would drive out the white members of the party and give the Democrats the advantage over us. The idea is to hang

---

132 Accounts in Montgomery *Advertiser*, June 26–30; Mobile *Register*, July 1–2, October 30, 1874.

133 Montgomery *Advertiser*, June 30, 1874; also account and quotes of the debate following.

on to what we have got and get all we can." Henry St. Clair of Macon County upheld Jones: "We must work for the success of our party and not take up a club to break our own heads." William Turner of Elmore "besought his fellows to pause, and not to drive the white Republicans from their ranks.... The rights to be gained by the passage of the bill would be conferred in time, if nothing happened to defeat the Republican Party."

William H. Councill of Madison County took the floor. The convention turned expectantly. The shrewd, bespectacled politician, acknowledged leader in north Alabama, did not equivocate. Expediency was just another word for cowardice. "It was impossible to make a man half free, and for himself he wanted no half freedom." Robert Carver of Jackson County nevertheless put in a plea for expediency, or cowardice: "Once upon a time I sold whiskey. Some men with strong stomachs would call for their whiskey or brandy straight; others, with weaker stomachs, required much water in it. So it is with the members of our party.... We must wait until their stomachs grow stronger and must do nothing that will drive them off."

The convention voted. Qualifications were stricken out. They took their whisky straight. Out in the lobby news reached eavesdropping white politicians. "By this time," the *Advertiser* noted, "all the scalawags and carpet baggers in the city were in a cold, clammy perspiration." The lobby sent in a note, a final request before the hammer fell. The convention agreed to add a disclaimer: "Whereas we did not meet as Republicans, but as colored men ... therefore, resolved, that this is not a political convention, and no political party is responsible in the least for the individual or collective views, opinions or expressions of the members of this convention."

The curtain rang down on the Equal Rights Convention. But Republicans still must hold their state convention. No disclaimers would apply. They would meet as Republicans. That ordeal was two months away. Intransigent black spokesmen meanwhile did not make it easier. Philip Joseph, Alabama's foremost black journalist, editor of the Mobile *Watchman*, warned: "We will no longer tolerate the hypocritical cant of policy, which means defeat. While we may not be able, at the worst, to build up, we are sufficiently strong to hold on, and powerful enough to tear down."[134]

Republicans gathered at last at Montgomery on August 20. The weather was hot. Debate was hotter. The convention opened in the Hall of Representatives.[135] At first all went smoothly. Delegates attended to their state ticket. Governor David Lewis received re-nomination. Then they selected their Platform

134 Montgomery *Advertiser*, July 22, 1874.

135 Accounts in Montgomery *Advertiser*, August 22–23; Mobile *Register*, August 21–25, 1874.

Committee. Its white contingent included federal district court judge Richard Busteed, Congressmen Hays and White, ex-congressman Robert Heflin and ex-governor Lewis Parsons. Jeremiah Haralson and Henry J. Europe of Mobile led the black committeemen.

Delegates retired to dinner. They returned to face their fate. Busteed demanded that the convention exact a pledge. Every candidate placed in nomination must declare support for the Civil Rights Bill. Henry Europe objected. Setting candidates a litmus test was sheer demagoguery. There was no need to mention civil rights. Busteed: he had fought the war "for the liberation of the race to which Europe belongs." Civil rights was the party's great measure. If Alabama Republicans denied it they denied their party.

William Councill rose, he who had demanded unqualified endorsement of the Civil Rights Bill at the Equal Rights Convention. Cowardice then, he said, was treason. Now, he said, Busteed's proposal was treason. "It put sticks in the hands of the Democratic party with which to beat the Republican Party.… If the Republican party went down the negroes went down with it."[136] The convention digested Councill's astounding flip-flop. Philip Joseph jumped up. He renewed Busteed's motion. Candidates must answer the question: "Are you in favor of equal Civil and Political rights for all men?" Cries cascaded from the galleries. Joseph shouted over the din: "There was no use dodging this question. Every black man on the floor was in favor of the Civil Rights bill, and they had told him as much." Busteed's motion was tabled. Charles Sheats and Alexander White accepted re-nomination. They took no pledge. Republicans went to bed.

In the morning delegates took time to direct some outrage at the Democrats and their campaign of terror. In the afternoon they again ventilated civil rights. The Platform Committee presented its work: a preamble and resolutions. The preamble walked a fine line: civil rights, good; social equality, bad. "The Republican party of Alabama declares its unshakable confidence in and its unalterable devotion to the great principles of human liberty which called it into existence, viz., the civil and political equality of all men without distinction of race or color.… But we have neither claimed nor desired the social equality of different races or of individuals of the same race, neither do we claim or desire it now." Objections? None. Then the reading reached resolution no. 5:

> We neither desire nor seek the invasion of the rights of the white people by the colored. We only ask equal advantages in matters of public and common right – this we conceive to be all that is embraced in what is

136 Montgomery *Advertiser*, August 22.

> known as the Civil Rights Bill. And in order that we may be understood and no false charges made against us, we hereby declare that the Republican party does not desire or seek mixed schools or mixed accommodations for the colored people with the white people, but they ask that all of these advantages shall be equal.[137]

Separate-but-equal, straight out! The convention exploded. Allen Alexander of Mobile jumped up. He accepted the statement against mixed schools, but not the rest. Separate (except for schools), no matter how equal, was intolerable. "He wanted to go to any hotel that he desired to, and no innkeeper or restaurant keeper should have the right to discriminate against colored people."

Philip Joseph: "If it is a degradation for a colored man and a white man to ride in the same car together, it is a degradation for white men and black men to sit together on these floors."

Alexander White: "I want the gentleman to tell us what caused the Democrats to carry Tennessee and North Carolina in the last elections."

Joseph: "I ask the gentleman if he is prepared to ask me to sacrifice principle for his election."

Henry Europe defended the platform: "The 5th resolution was all that colored people wanted as it demanded equal and impartial justice before the law.... He wanted to be prudent until the Republican party in Alabama can get the power into their hands." William Councill rose once more. In June he had called for principle. Yesterday he called principle treason. Today he called for survival. "They must do nothing to injure the Party. The Civil Rights Bill would inevitably become a law. Then every right would be secure to them. Meanwhile let not the Party in Alabama fall."

The platform resolutions passed. The convention adjourned *sine die*. "The animals have quieted down," joked the *Advertiser*. "They will be beaten so badly in November that the people of Alabama will never see such a menagerie in session again."[138] Alabama Republicans met the issue squarely. Pragmatism preempted principle.

Pinchback's New Orleans *Louisianian* was livid: "It is such a travesty upon the principles and objects of the National Republican party that we are pleased to know the prospect is excellent for the defeat of the tricksters who framed it and endorsed it."[139] Other observers conceded that the convention had done what it had to do. The Vicksburg *Times* (Republican) found the resolutions

137 Mobile *Register*, August 25, 1874.

138 Montgomery *Advertiser*, August 23, 1874.

139 New Orleans *Louisianian*, September 5, 1874.

brilliant: "Alabama Democrats insist on a race issue and have insisted on it for the last eight years, but the Republicans have completely outflanked them.... Now what are the Democrats going to fight?"[140] The Mobile *Register*, under its relentless editor John Forsyth, found plenty to fight. "The artificers of this piece of joinery had a job before them.... Its object was to fool both the white people and the black on the Civil Rights bill." Col. Forsyth was not worried. "The net result is that they have succeeded in fooling neither, but have simply made fools of themselves."[141]

Democrats convened at Montgomery on July 29.[142] George S. Houston took the nomination for governor, Burwell Lewis and William Forney for congressmen at-large. James L. Pugh, later distinguished United States Senator, spoke the address. Waves of hideous blackness broke against the sun-bright shores of white supremacy.

> We hear the roar of the black wave that had its formation in the overflowing bounty of the federal government ... to drive its mad surges against the mountain barriers erected by nature; but the glorious white cliffs of Caucasian supremacy, illuminated by eternal sunshine, will roll back this black sea and sink it forever from the face of this lovely land it threatens to desolate and destroy.[143]

The convention reported a platform of eight articles. Resolution 1 drew the race line: "The Republican party in this State persistently ... have inflamed the passions and prejudices of the negroes as a race against the white people and have thereby made it necessary for the white people to unite and act together in self-defense and for the preservation of white civilization." Resolutions 2, 3 and 4 all condemned the Civil Rights Bill. No. 5 invited white people "from every clime" to come to their brethren in Alabama to substitute their labor for that of Negroes, who would then, presumably, flee.

A ratification rally filled the nighttime streets of Montgomery. Chinese lanterns and luminous transparencies glowed in the dark. One displayed "a locomotive with a negro's head for smoke stack running down and crushing [white] women and children." Another pictured a civil rights school-house, white children and Negroes sitting on the same bench. Brass bands, sky-rockets,

140 Vicksburg *Times*, August 26, 1874.
141 Mobile *Register*, August 26, 1874.
142 Accounts in Montgomery *Advertiser*, July 30–31; Mobile *Register*, July 31, August 1–2, 1874.
143 Mobile *Register*, July 31, 1874.

"shouts of enthusiastic men; the scene was grandly inspiring," so the *Advertiser* thought.[144] The Opelika *Times* too was inspired.

> There are white men enough in Alabama, if they will so determine, to make treason to race odious. A united, expressed hate, in word and action, is a scorpion scourge.... The vote is for color and blood, and intelligence and property and law and *white supremacy.* I am with men, my brothers.[145]

The elections redeemed Alabama for the next century. It became a white man's country. Republicans saved a few scraps. The 4th District's massive black majority gave Charles Hays another term. Jeremiah Haralson recovered the 1st District. Everywhere else Republicans met disaster. George Houston raced to the governorship. Both at-large seats became Democratic. In the 6th District Democrats refused to re-nominate their incumbent, Joseph Sloss. Col. Sloss had fraternized with the enemy. He had voted for the Centennial Bill, a measure that expended Alabama taxpayers' money to celebrate the birth of the United States of America. Worse, he befriended his black colleague James Rapier. "While I differ from Mr. Rapier in politics," he said, "I respect him as a man."[146] Joseph Sloss ran as an Independent, and lost. Democrats held the 5th District. They redeemed the 2nd. They won back the 3rd.

Many factors contributed. Economic coercion played its part. The Montgomery and Mobile Railroad discharged all Negro foremen on the line "and substituted strong, intelligent white men in their places; this is just as it should be."[147] Violence did its job. Years later one white trooper recalled those heady times: youthful days of derring-do; midnight rides on moonlit roads; the wearing of gaudy masks; terrorizing a meddlesome Connecticut carpetbagger who had organized Negro voters in Hale County; stuffing ballot boxes when the Negroes got "rolicky;" "regulating" the town of Carrollton; shooting various people for various reasons. "The effect of the Ku Klux Klan was the salvation of our country."[148] In almost its first act, the newly-Democratic legislature repealed the state's Ku-Klux statute. No longer need authorities fear prosecution should they fail to protect citizens from the night riders' salvation. (see Map 5, below)

144 Montgomery *Advertiser*, July 31, 1874.

145 Quoted in Mobile *Register*, May 13, 1874.

146 San Francisco *Elevator*, November 30, 1872.

147 Mobile *Register*, August 11, 1874.

148 John Hunnicutt, *Reconstruction in West Alabama: The Memoirs of John L. Hunnicutt*, ed. William S. Hoole (Tuscaloosa: 1959), 51–104.

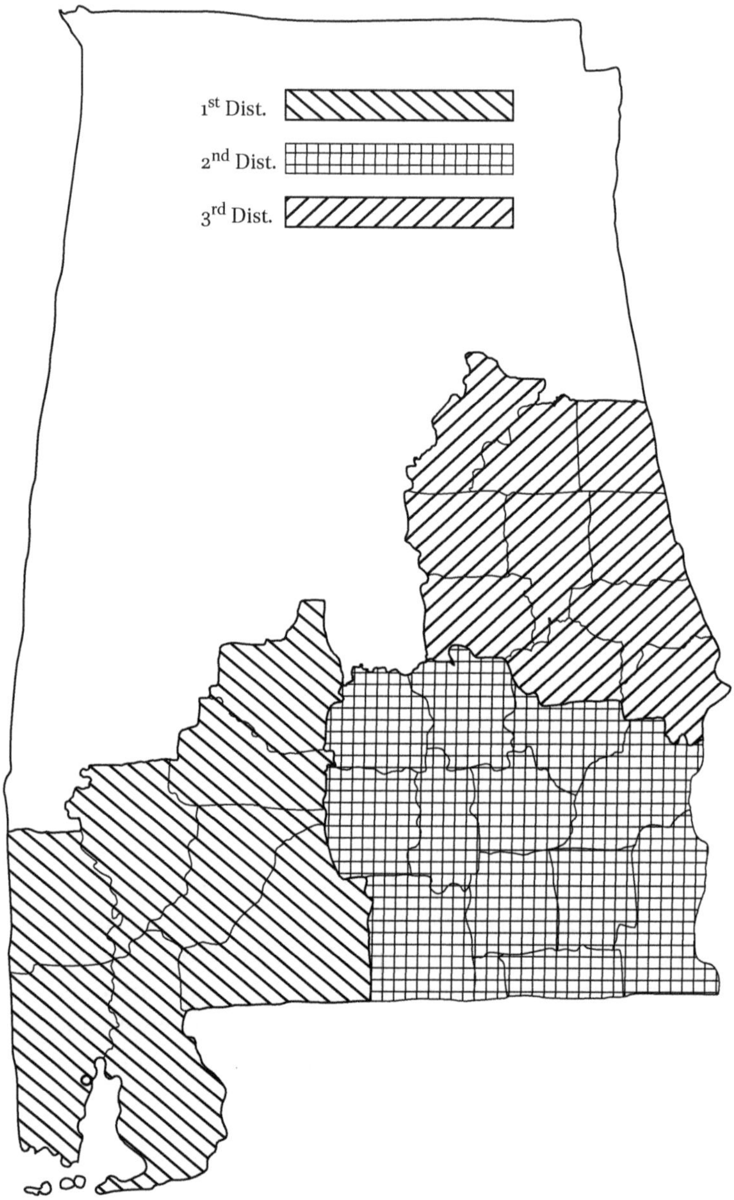

MAP 5 Congressional Districts, Alabama
SOURCE: AUTHORS OF *WELCOMING RUIN*.

Alabama, Third District
William H. Betts (R), Taul Bradford (D)
Population: 54% white

The 3rd District occupied the east-center of the state, from Randolph, Chambers, Lee and Russell Counties along the Georgia border to Talladega, Coosa and Elmore. Talladega and Opelika were the principal towns. Black persons held solid majorities only in Macon and Russell Counties. Republican Charles Pelham sat precariously on a cushion of 562 votes.

Capt. Pelham was a southerner, born in North Carolina. He resided at Talladega. In war he had served the Confederacy. In peace he served the Republicans. On civil rights he did not flinch. Each procedural vote in the House saw Congressman Pelham rise and vote Aye. The Republican Talladega *Our Mountain Home,* edited by George Parsons, extolled his virtues: "a tower of strength in the mountain counties."[149] The Republican convention met at Opelika on September 16. The tower of strength faltered. Two days and 113 ballots, exhausted delegates threw the nomination to a dark horse. William H. Betts had served as customs inspector at Mobile. Currently he was employed as government agent for distribution of flood relief at Opelika. Few of Alabama's recently-flooded rivers flowed past Opelika. The government's "flood bacon" remained in a warehouse, undistributed. The result, the *Advertiser* concluded, was "about the weakest nomination that could have been made."[150] Betts had one asset. He was a genuine Confederate hero, colonel of the 13th Alabama, one of the South's fighting regiments from the Peninsula to Appomattox. Republicans considered Colonel Betts a prize acquisition. Democrats considered him a scalawag supreme.

Democrats had no difficulty. Col. Taul Bradford of Talladega, lawyer and former state representative, proclaimed that his campaign would rest on opposition to civil rights. "Better find our home in the deep than that our grandchildren should dandle their mongrel offspring in a hovel!"[151] Colonel Bradford avoided debates. He avoided Colonel Betts. He toured the district: from Wedowee to Wetumpka, 35 appearances in 40 days. "Remember that your wife and children demand your protection, and you can never again do them the favor that you now have the opportunity of doing.... Vote, and vote right."[152]

Democrats took up the message. "We, white men of Lee County," resolved the white men of Lee County, "turning from the horrid picture of racial intermixture, social depravity, and moral corruption, as insolently presented to us in the civil-rights bill ... do boldly and unflinchingly accept the issue of

149 Talladega *Our Mountain Home,* April 8, 1874.
150 Montgomery *Advertiser,* September 18, 1874.
151 Talladega *Our Mountain Home,* August 19, 1874.
152 Montgomery *Advertiser,* October 25, 1874.

white or black supremacy in Alabama."[153] The Opelika *Times* printed the unflinching thoughts of one reader:

> The ashen lip and fixed eye of Alabama interpret a purpose.... The negro and his ally hath not known and cannot feel the pent-up wrath that burns like a seven-fold furnace in the bosom of the people.... Victory or Death! one or the other. This is the pulsation of the Southern heart – the old and young – men, women, and children.[154]

Democrats reinforced that appeal with various expedients. Ostracism worked well. White men unwilling to vote the white people's ticket became nonpersons among white persons. The Tuscaloosa *Butcher Knife* printed a list of socially-erasable individuals. Lee County Democrats marked down for ostracism "all who are in the least sympathy with the so-called civil-rights bill."[155] Fraud helped. Canvassers in Opelika arranged to discount one of two ballot boxes available (the one containing Republican votes), thereby discarding 1,243 unfavorable tallies. Special trains arrived from Georgia, loaded with favorable Democratic voters. They voted repeatedly.[156]

Violence at least was minimal. Three black churches served as meeting places in the Wacoochee Valley. They burned. But no one died. Lt. Frank Taylor, stationed with the 18th Infantry in Russell County, recalled minor incidents in his vicinity.[157] At Opelika black people from the countryside, fearful of approaching the polls in their precincts, flocked to vote in the relative safety of town. For better security they arrived en masse. White citizens also massed, blocking access to the poll. Sheriff John R. Hubbard feared a calamity. He appealed to the army, Capt. Edgar Kellogg, commanding a company of U.S. soldiers stationed in town. The captain held standing orders. Observe but do not interfere. The mob grew. Kellogg disobeyed orders. He deployed a detachment. They formed a cordon, allowing black voters to pass. For that effort Capt. Kellogg drew a sharp rebuke from headquarters. Bloodshed, nevertheless, was averted.[158]

---

153 Forty Third Congress, Second Session, House Report no. 262 ("Affairs in Alabama,"), 100.

154 House Report 262, 100.

155 House Report 262, 100; Mobile *Register*, July 2, 1874.

156 House Report 262, 30–38, 46, 170–175.

157 House Report 262, 28.

158 House Report 262, 78–83. The army's General Order 75, issued in 1871, prohibited officers from intervening in matters of civil disturbance, except in response to a direct appeal from a federal marshal or to assist the work of a posse comitatus. This made the monitoring of polls effectively pointless. At Eufaula and Spring Hill army detachments watched while white militias shot down a hundred black citizens. Capt. Kellogg's disobedience

Economic incentives also persuaded voters to vote correctly. At the Cherecla Lime-Works factory outside Opelika workers who voted Republican lost their jobs directly after they voted. Uncooperative tenant farmers saw their tenancies terminated. Lt. Taylor spoke to the congressional investigative committee of 1875. Black sharecroppers, he explained, ate very little. If they voted their convictions they ate less.

> They are poor beyond anything of which you have any experience. I doubt if any case of such abject poverty as I have seen in that county has ever come before any member of this committee.... The system on which the negroes now cultivate the ground leaves them scarcely anything at the end of the year. I venture to say that nine-tenths of them are now living on cow-peas boiled in water without even meat to cook them with.[159]

Democrats were magnanimous. They offered to release white Republicans from ostracism. *Our Mountain Home* replied with just a hint of sarcasm.

> Republicans are conscious that they have committed a heinous crime in voting for the principle of equal rights and exact justice to all men, conscious that they have been declared social pariahs for having the manliness to act as free men in a free country; [they are] preparing applications for pardons in due and regular form, and will present them to the democratic leaders for formal endorsement and approval, hoping thereby to reinstate themselves in the good opinion of this most Christian and enlightened community.[160]

Alabama, First District
Jeremiah Haralson (R), Frederick Bromberg (D)
Population: 58% black

Republicans ought to have owned the 1st District, blessed with a huge black majority. In 1872 a factious rivalry between two black candidates, Philip Joseph and incumbent Benjamin Turner, had divided the Republican vote. Democrats

---

may have saved a hundred more. The captain at least did not suffer from his reprimand; he retired in 1899 with the rank of brigadier general.

159 House Report 262, 28. Not everyone ate cow-peas. Bob Reid, Tom Ivey's friend, in Sumter County was, at age 51, a substantial share-cropper, 600 acres leased. He supported a wife and three children, apparently well fed. House Report 262, 16.

160 Talladega *Our Mountain Home*, November 18, 1874.

took advantage to elect Liberal Republican Frederick Bromberg. They hoped to reelect him in 1874 as a regularly-anointed Democrat. Against a reunified Republican candidacy anti-civil rights rhetoric would not avail. Ostracism would not suffice. Fraud was possible, but it would have to be uncomfortably massive. They must rely on terror.

The 1st's ten counties stretched from Mobile Bay north to Selma and east to Conecuh and Covington Counties. Its great black majority concentrated in the northern salient. Dallas County held 40,000 citizens, 32,000 of them black. Wilcox County had 21,000 blacks and 6,000 whites. Black voters predominated in Clarke, Conecuh and Monroe Counties. Mobile County, with roughly 50,000 inhabitants, possessed 28,000 white residents. Over its entire extent the district produced some 36,000 votes. All factors being equal, 20,000 belonged to the Republicans.[161]

The beneficiary of those votes in 1874 was a black man, State Senator Jeremiah Haralson of Dallas County. He was young. He was energetic, outspoken. Born a slave in Georgia, he had risen by force of will and determination. Democrats did not take him lightly: "Jere, black as the ace of spades and with the brogue of the cornfield, shrewd and fully aware of the strength of his people, insolent to his opponents ... uncompromising, irritating, and bold," so the *Register* described him.[162] On the Civil Rights Bill, Jeremiah Haralson showed shrewdness. But he was hardly bold. On June 17 he announced his candidacy to an enthusiastic audience at Mobile.

> I am for the Civil Rights bill, and my people are all for the Civil Rights bill. The XIV Amendment is worth nothing until a bill is passed to put it into effect, and I am for that bill. I am a candidate for Congress on that bill. It is just and right.... The party will not have done us justice until it becomes a law.[163]

The Mobile *Register* congratulated the candidate on his forthright sentiment. "[We thank] Mr. Jere Haralson, with his race issue founded on the sine qua non of a civil rights and social equality law ... for drawing a line on only one side of which even the white scalawag will find tolerable and tenable standing ground."[164] One week later Haralson stood at the Alabama Equal Rights

161 In 1872 Philip Joseph and Benjamin Turner shared a combined total of 20,198 votes. That same year Republican gubernatorial candidate David Lewis polled 20,542 across the district. Two years later, despite the Democrats' best efforts, Jeremiah Haralson took 19,500.

162 Mobile *Register*, June 18, 1874.

163 Mobile *Register*, June 18, 1874.

164 Mobile *Register*, June 26, 1874.

Association. With qualifying amendments he tried to pull back the throttle on civil rights. The debris from that disaster still lay scattered on the tracks. In August as a member of the Republican State Convention platform committee he jammed on the brakes, bringing the endorsement of civil rights to a screeching halt. His reasoning was irreproachable. Nomination rhetoric secured nominations. Election oratory won elections. Civil rights must go underground, at least until the votes were counted. Even in a district freighted with black voters, Haralson perceived the Civil Rights Bill as an obstacle on the rails.

His road to the nomination still did not go smoothly. Alabama's fratricidal Republicans had thrown away the election in 1872. They seemed bent on throwing it away again. The convention opened at Selma on August 10. Three aspirants took the field. Two were black: Haralson and Allen Alexander. One was white: State Representative John Bruce. Four days later, with hundreds of ballots cast, the convention remained deadlocked. At the first day's end, with two-thirds needed to nominate, the delegate count stood at 32 for Alexander, 28 for Haralson, 24 for Bruce. By the second day 96 ballots had come and gone. The count stood at 32 for Alexander, 28 for Haralson, 24 for Bruce. After the third day 180 ballots had passed into history. The count remained unchanged. On the fourth day, after the 224th ballot, the reporter for the Selma *Times* remarked that the convention resembled "a menagerie and its members animals." Indignant delegates expelled him. On the 239th ballot the deadlock broke. Bruce stood to announce he would withdraw in favor of Haralson. The floor erupted in cheers. Delegates hailed Jeremiah Haralson.[165] Civil rights remained as the state platform had left it.

Civil rights did not let Republicans escape so easily. As the delegates departed, Judge Richard Busteed, champion of a pure civil rights bill, headed back to Mobile. He entered the "Ladies' Car" of his train on the Western Railroad. He was not alone. With him was his valet, Samuel A. Johnson, a black man. All would have been well had Mr. Johnson remained a slave. But, he was free. A white passenger, J.S. Williamson, took exception to his presence. Conductor Dibble tried to separate Johnson from his seat. Johnson clung to it. Williamson directed a blow to Johnson's jaw. Busteed drew a pistol. He ran to the smoking car and returned with an escort of armed Negroes. Lady passengers adopted an attitude of hysteria. Dibble struggled to calm them, simultaneously trying to save Williamson from destruction. Only barely was disaster avoided. Busteed holstered his pistol. Johnson withdrew to the smoking car. Later he sued the Western Railroad for $20,000.[166] Democratic papers spread the story. The

165 Accounts in Mobile *Register*, August 12–14; Montgomery *Advertiser*, August 12–14, 1874.

166 Montgomery *Advertiser*, August 18, October 27, 1874.

whole sorry debacle proved the Republicans' culpability: "No man but a fool or a traitor can deny that the Radical party in Alabama endorses the whole of the Civil Rights Bill."[167]

Democrats bestowed the nomination on the incumbent. Frederick G. Bromberg was a cultured gentleman. Born in New York City, raised in Alabama, he held degrees in chemistry and mathematics from Harvard University. He had served the state's military government in a civilian capacity, and then its peacetime Republican administration. He broke from the Republicans in 1872 and led Alabama's Liberal Republican movement. He was, as his biographer has described him, an oddity, "a Republican representing Democrats, a Liberal from conservative Mobile, a Unionist serving Southerners ... a paradox to most people of his era."[168] Before his political conversion Democrats placed the paradoxical politician on their roll of dishonor, a list of "black dupes and white renegades."[169] After his conversion Bromberg made amends. He threw civil rights at the Republicans: "This South, with its glorious traditions, shall [it] become a mere mulatto dependency ... or be inhabited, developed and governed by men who will stand some chance at least of being recognized by their ancestors in the day of general judgment?"[170]

In a district 58% black, Jere Haralson ought not to have feared the civil rights issue. He feared white terror. Terror was the Democrats' only option. Night-riders, organized and affiliated terrorists, needed no special inspiration to make them saddle up. But most white men did not ride by night. Fear might inspire them – civil rights fear. Democratic organs poured it on. Civil rights was coming! the *Register* shouted its Paul Revere-like warning, "to make our State a howling wilderness, the whites the mudsills of the social fabric, a St. Domingo with a negro king ... chuckling over the time (*never to come*) when they can put their ponderous black hoofs on white necks."[171] Bromberg produced an address. Beware "the odious Civil Rights Bill with its Pandora box of ills ... wrongs and ignominies that pen or pencil cannot adequately portray."

> Men of Mobile, the issues are before you. As you regard the proud distinction conferred upon the Caucasian race by the Almighty Father; as you would preserve inviolate your domestic hearths ... by the graves of your honored dead; by your devotion to your wives and children; by your

---

167 Montgomery *Advertiser*, August 15, 1874.

168 Margaret D. Sizemore, "Frederick G. Bromberg of Mobile: An Illustrious Character, 1837–1928," *Alabama Review*, 29 (1976): 104.

169 Sizemore, "Bromberg," 111.

170 Mobile *Register*, September 24, 1874.

171 Mobile *Register*, June 21, 1874.

> hatred of mongrelism in all its forms ... we entreat you to give of your means, your energies, and your votes for the success of the Democratic and Conservative ticket.[172]

In almost daily reports the *Register* relayed fearful news: Negro uprisings, plots and conspiracies, the rising of the great black army. "Gather arms and munitions.... End that moderation which so far meets these savages with embassies of peace and conciliation."[173] William H. Curran, a black man, keeper of Mobile's city dog pound, seemed an unlikely mass murderer. Yet he had sworn he would massacre a million whites before the election day. So the *Register* solemnly reported.[174]

Night-riders fell short. Haralson gathered most of the votes he expected, 19,551. He won by 5,000 in Dallas County, 2,000 in Wilcox. He won by 3,000 overall. Bromberg contested the results. Voter intimidation, he protested. White people were terrorized.[175] Jere Haralson survived. Yet even he feared civil rights and kept it at arm's length.

> Alabama, Second District
> James Rapier (R), Jeremiah Williams (D)
> Population: 54% black

The 2nd District's wedge of counties pointed to the state's southeast corner. It extended to the capital city of Montgomery. The 2nd presently was the bailiwick of Alabama's black congressman James T. Rapier. Rapier's civil rights views were on the record. He had spoken for the bill. He had voted for it. He shared nonetheless Jere Haralson's worries. Civil rights inspired white terror. Terror would be his undoing.

The New York *Times* covered the election. It reported an ominous situation. It printed the account of a traveler. In September the *Times'* informant, a Marylander passing through, had stopped at the town of Union Springs in Bullock County. Seated on his hotel porch, he watched a rally fill the court house square. Speakers held forth. Fragments of their words, harsh and disconcerting, drifted

---

172 Mobile *Register*, October 23, 25, 1874.

173 Mobile Register, September 23, 1874.

174 Mobile *Register*, August 28, 1874.

175 See Chester H. Rowell, *A Historical and Legal Digest of All the Contested Election Cases in the House of Representatives of the United States from the First to the Fifty-Sixth Congress, 1789–1901* (Washington: 1901), 303–304; Richard Bailey, *Neither Carpetbaggers Nor Scalawags: Black Officeholders During the Reconstruction of Alabama, 1867–1878* (Montgomery: 1991), 286–290.

across. The Civil Rights Bill was coming, coming "to establish socialism." It was coming "to force the negro into their families." It meant war. "The time had come to protect their firesides, their wives and daughters.... Exterminate the negroes and their supporters." The visitor turned to a local idler lounging nearby. Of course, he was informed, the speaker was quite correct. The Negroes must die. "We have come to the conclusion that they, like the Indians, must be exterminated." But, the Marylander inquired, "what would they do for labor to till their lands?" "Why," said he, "we want white labor – immigration is what we want." I asked if their persistent hostility was caused by fear of the Civil Rights bill. He said "yes."[176]

The Montgomery *News* watched events in Butler County. "The Civil Rights bill and social equality are the topics wherever you go.... A chord has been touched that will vibrate within the innermost chambers of the most secluded home of this noble old county."[177] The Montgomery *Advertiser* covered a rally at Robinson's Crossroads. Speakers hammered the Civil Rights Bill, "its hideous deformity and hell-born corruptions." Many fair ladies attended, "to cheer us (God bless them) with their approving smiles, and add their silent and gentle influence to the great cause." The reporter ogled the fair ladies. "At the horrors of the abominable Civil Rights Bill I could see the warm blood of resentment rush to their cheeks."[178]

Democrats chose a candidate. Major Jeremiah Williams, late of the 1st Alabama Infantry, was "spotless, a man of elevated moral worth."[179] He struck a martial tone.

> Shoulder to shoulder, white men! Beat back the mongrel foe! Your wives, your children, your country call upon you. Forward in solid column. He is both a traitor and fool who plays false in this hour of extreme need and terrible peril. Ring out the charging cheer all along the Caucasian line.[180]

The New York *Times* continued to follow the campaign. It dispatched a special correspondent. Howard Carroll, barely twenty years old, fabulously wealthy but unwilling to indulge a life of indolence in his castle on the Hudson, set out on a journalistic adventure. He conferred with Horace Redfield

176 New York *Times*, September 12, 1874.

177 Quoted in Mobile *Register*, June 5, 1874.

178 Montgomery *Advertiser*, September 12, 1874. On the 2nd District campaign, its accompaniment of terror, see Loren Schweninger, *James T. Rapier and Reconstruction* (Chicago: 1978), 133–147.

179 Montgomery *Advertiser*, August 8, 1874.

180 Montgomery *Advertiser*, October 31, 1874.

at Chattanooga. He reached Montgomery. Dissatisfied with the usual sources, he went to see for himself. A nocturnal expedition, an armed convoy carrying Republican politicians headed into the 2nd District's heartland. Darkness descended as they reached their destination, a secluded crossroads near Snowdoun. One general store and a blacksmith's shop marked the place. There they witnessed a gathering. From the fields black people emerged, tattered men and bedraggled women, "some wearing ingeniously contrived garments of rags ... a torn flannel shirt and calico pants, many of them covered with freshly picked cotton."

Tins of sardines provided the feast. There was dancing. Then came speeches. In the fire-lit circle politicians spoke of freedom and its obligations. A black man rose from his place on the bandwagon. Asa Barber reminded them of their dignity; he too had been a slave. "You are the bone and sinew of this county, this state, this entire southern country. You have rights that were given to you by the heavenly hosts. You are your own masters, and don't need to take no impertinence from no man." A white speaker, former congressman Charles Buckley, Rapier's predecessor, reminded them of the Civil Rights Bill. "All their wrongs would be righted if they voted the Republican ticket." In the early morning hours men drew out double-barreled shotguns. Why was there need for such armament? Carroll asked. Response: "it was none of his business."[181]

The business was plain enough. No one precisely counted the dead. At the town of Eufaula alone casualties exceeded Coushatta and Trenton many times over. Other victims died in lonely anonymity. Events fulfilled the Marylander's premonition. Eufaula, on the Georgia border, provided the textbook example. Barbour County was a hotbed of Republicanism, a black majority which had to be suppressed. It sheltered a white scalawag of unusual persistence, who had to be removed: Elias Keils, judge of the municipal court. Recently Judge Keils had attended the Chattanooga Convention. He joined its Committee on Facts and Statistics. He became a statistic himself.

Keils knew he was a marked man. In January he had fled the town. He returned. Eufaulans organized a committee of public safety. They published a litany of the judge's misdeeds. Elias Keils had taken it into his head that freedmen were oppressed, and also systematically cheated by the farmers for whom they toiled. That situation he set out to remedy. He stacked his grand jury with black men. He positioned menacing-looking Negroes to stand about as court officers. From the bench he railed against the landowners. Their organization,

181 New York *Times*, November 4, 1874. Carroll was not pleased. The dancing was indecent, he wrote. Worst of all, while everyone went home to sleep, the cotton remained unpicked on the plantations.

the Patrons of Husbandry, was "nothing less than a second Ku Klux." They starved their field hands. Starving people turned to stealing. Then they herded them into prison to be used as forced labor. It was slavery under another name. "Gentlemen," Keils instructed his grand jurors, "you ought to examine and find out whether such persons had been paid by their employers and if they had not been – why then you ought to find bills against the employers also." He released without bail all manner of undesirables: "fugitives, vagrants, thieves, perjurers, burglars ... the gallows have gone out of fashion here; the penitentiary is but little used – the chain-gang has become a sort of myth."[182]

In February municipal elections arrived. Black people insisted on voting. White citizens called out the Eufaula Rifles. This veteran company of ex-Confederate soldiers, celebrated in war, had maintained its organization in peace. To keep the peace it surrounded the polls. Only one black man, Bill Flagg, was shot down on this occasion. Better shooting came in November.[183]

Events on November 3 followed the standard format. Black voters, fearing obstruction, approached Eufaula in a solid column.[184] As they entered town, a white policeman rode up. He consulted a pocket-watch. "In about an hour's time," he remarked, "we will have a frolic."[185] Frolic began on schedule. White militia swung into action. They formed ranks, flank marched, poured volley fire from both sides into the enemy. General Alpheus Baker, late of the Confederate States Army, commanded the action. A separate detachment, posted in the armory building, fired from above. Smoke cleared. A hundred bodies littered the street. Eight blacks lay dead. Eighty lay wounded. Six white casualties resulted from friendly fire. Voting of black persons at Eufaula ceased.

The massacre missed Elias Keils. The judge had gone to the town of Spring Hill to serve as election supervisor. As the poll closed, Keils locked himself, his son Willie, two counting clerks and the ballot box, into a storeroom. Night fell. White men gathered. Tom Swanson, the Democratic clerk, unbarred the door. Shotgun fire raked the room. Someone kicked over the oil lamp. Keils ducked behind a counter. He survived, but bullets riddled young Willie crouching at his side. He died a few weeks before his seventeenth birthday. The ballot box lay overturned, its contents burned.[186]

182 Montgomery *Advertiser*, April 14, 1874.

183 Montgomery *Advertiser*, February 24, 26, March 4, 1874.

184 See Melinda M. Hennessey, "Reconstruction Politics and the Military: The Eufaula Riot of 1874," *Alabama Historical Quarterly*, 38 (1976): 117–123.

185 House Report 262, 214–215.

186 House Report 262, 3–6; Hennessey, "Reconstruction Politics and the Military," 121–124.

Democrats disclaimed responsibility. The fault lay with Judge Keils. He had organized black voters and encouraged them to vote. He had requested federal troops, in order to terrorize white men. Those troops, following General Order 75, watched the killings from a distance.[187] Gen. Baker had already warned President Grant not to let the army intervene.[188] The Eufaula *News* summed it up:

> We hope the negroes will learn a lesson from this and understand that they cannot run "ruffshod" over white men and go unpunished. Every drop of blood shed on Tuesday was the natural, the inevitable result of the murderous midnight teachings of that archfiend of darkness E.M. Keils.... In the name of God and justice is there no way to reach the conscience of this fiend in human shape? Will not the ghastly dead faces of these wretched negroes fill his soul with bitter remorse when he well knows that they met their fate solely on account of his bad advice? ... Let this sad lesson sink deep in his soul, if he has one.[189]

Keils fled the state. Newly-elected Governor George Houston appointed Alpheus Baker to succeed him as judge. Congressman Rapier tumbled to defeat. From a 3,000 vote majority in 1872 he fell to a 1,000 vote deficit in 1874. He protested: incineration of ballot boxes, slaughter of black voters. His protests led nowhere.[190] Economic intimidation assisted the Democrats' efforts. "Pledge-meetings" occurred across the district. Employees pledged to vote the Democratic ticket; employers pledged not to fire them.[191] In the countryside starvation stalked. Bob Reid explained. "The people are poor, and they say to them, 'If you vote the Republican ticket you have got to leave.' If they go and vote, as soon as the election is over they go and strip them right naked.... They go to a man's crib, take all his corn and every mouthful of meat, and leave him helpless without a thing to eat or to wear."[192]

187 General Order 75 presented commanders a distressing dilemma: sit by and watch death unfold, or act and suffer reprimand. Some tried to find a way out. At Greensborough in Sumter County Lieut. Thomas McDougall led a detachment of the 7th Cavalry. He obeyed the rule. He kept his troopers in camp a half mile from the court-house poll. But he personally appeared in town, an officer in uniform, to make his presence known. By that means, he reported, he averted catastrophe: "If I had not been there, the crack of a whip would have brought on a serious difficulty." House Report 262, 211–212.

188 Alpheus Baker to Ulysses Grant, telegram, October 30, 1874. *Papers of Ulysses Grant*, 197.

189 Quoted in Montgomery *Advertiser*, November 7, 1874.

190 Schweninger, *James T. Rapier*: 145–147.

191 House Report 262, 213.

192 House Report 262, 21.

A jollification filled the streets of Montgomery. Banners proclaimed the good news: "Civil Rights Bill – Requiescat in Pace;" "Exit Ye Rapier – They are Going to Open a Mixed School in Africa." Above Adolph Munter's dry-goods store on Commerce Street hung an enormous sheet. It pictured a row of coffins neatly labeled: "Radicalism; Caesarism; Butlerism; Civil Rights Bills."[193] The Mobile *Register* gave credit where it was due. "We verily believe, had it not been for the madness of the Republican party in listening to the call of the Civil Rights bill this State could not successfully have overridden the lawless forces which were marshaled to suppress the true voice of the majority."[194]

193 Montgomery *Advertiser*, November 11, 1874.
194 Mobile *Register*, December 29, 1874.

CHAPTER 9

Carry the News to Hiram: Elections in Florida and Louisiana

1 Florida

The Democratic blizzard blanketed the nation; 94 Republicans resigned themselves to return as lame ducks. The Democratic presence would leap from 88 to 182. In New Jersey Democrats held one seat out of seven in the 43rd Congress; in the 44th they held five. Seven seats in New York turned Democratic. Governor Dix lost in a landslide to Democrat Samuel J. Tilden. Even Massachusetts inaugurated a Democratic governor and cast aside four Republican congressmen. Among the victims was Benjamin Butler, defeated in the 6th District by Democrat Charles P. Thompson. Connecticut Republicans held three of four seats. The election reversed that situation. Joseph Hawley lost in Hartford and Stephen Kellogg in New Haven. Only Henry Starkweather in the New London district survived. In California, a continent away, Republicans held three of four seats. Democrats reversed that situation. San Francisco's Charles Clayton fell. Sherman Houghton in the great southern district – from Monterrey to Mexico – went down to defeat. Horace Page survived alone in Sacramento.

Voters sent a message addressed to the President. His policies were found wanting. The Goldsboro *North Carolina Messenger* drew an editorial cartoon: a swift side-wheel steamer pounding the waves; above it a caption, "Carry the News to Hiram"; beneath it a picture of the President, Hiram Ulysses Grant, cigar falling from his mouth, jolted headfirst from a bucking mule.[1]

As to civil rights, even where the Shirt of Nessus did not roast Republican candidates it toasted them crisply. Local circumstances mitigated the effect in some places. In South Carolina the overpowering superiority of black voters remained intact. The Democratic/Conservative State Convention met belatedly in October. It endorsed an Independent Republican ticket for state offices. The opposite situation prevailed in Texas, a Democratic majority so entrenched that Republicans could mount no serious challenge. Kentucky, home of James Beck, offered few civil rights fireworks. In only two of ten districts were Republicans competitive. In only one did their candidate dare to speak kindly of the Civil Rights Bill. He lost. In Florida, Louisiana and Arkansas state civil rights

1 Goldsboro *Carolina Messenger*, August 10, 1874.

statutes already operated. Federal legislation held less terror for white voters accustomed to sidestepping inconveniences. Still, the news was bad.

Florida, 1st District
William Purman (R), John A. Henderson (D)
Population: 54% white

Florida for the first time prepared to send the House two members from geographically-defined districts. The 1870 census had doubled the state's representation. Two Republicans spoke for Florida in the 43rd Congress, incumbent Josiah Walls and freshman William J. Purman. Both had won their places as general ticket candidates representing the state at large. Now they stood for reelection in circumscribed districts. Legislators drew district lines with party considerations in mind. They divided the state roughly in half the long way. The 1st District, slightly larger, went to Purman, whose residence was in Jackson County. It encompassed the western side, panhandle to the Keys. The eastern half, with the cities of Jacksonville and Gainesville, formed the 2nd District. (see Map 6, below)

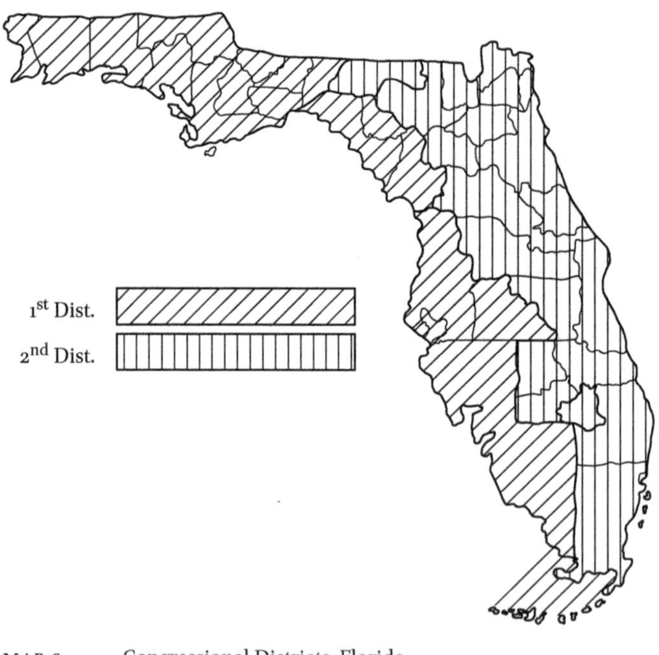

MAP 6 Congressional Districts, Florida
SOURCE: AUTHORS OF *WELCOMING RUIN*.

Democrats complained that Republicans had designed both districts to secure their party a majority. The Tallahassee *Floridian* mocked the gerrymandered 1st, "the Corkscrew District, as crooked as a ram's horn." It held 97,000 people. The 2nd District included 90,000. The assorted counties of the 1st District had given Republicans a 650 vote cushion in the elections of 1872. Those coalesced into the 2nd District had recorded a margin of 882. In neither district did Republicans command a robust majority. A vigorous effort in the conservative southern counties of Hernando, Polk, Hillsborough, Sumter and Manatee could overcome Democratic disadvantages in the 1st District. In the 2nd a recent wave of white immigration might spoil the Republicans' calculations.[2]

In the 1st District the 1870 census found 45,000 black people and 52,000 whites. Republicans would have to appeal to some of that white majority, or hope that many whites did not vote. In 1873 Republican gubernatorial candidate Ossian Hart won only five of the district's twenty-two counties. They were, however, the five most populous – Leon, Jefferson, Gadsden, Jackson and Escambia – with 56,000 of the district's 97,000 residents, a majority of whom were black. In Gadsden the black majority held at nearly two to one. Republicans accumulated a margin of 450. In Jefferson County, with a black majority of three to one, Republicans won by 1,600 and in Leon by 1,500 votes. In Jackson County a recent campaign of white terror – more than a hundred black persons murdered – reduced the Republican vote.[3] The remaining seventeen counties were white. They returned Democratic majorities. Turnout was the key.

Florida's 1st District presented Democrats the perfect stage to produce a civil rights melodrama. Republicans depended on an insufficient black population. Democrats needed to stimulate lethargic white voters. The Republican incumbent openly supported Sumner's project. An injection of civil rights bill fear seemed made to order. The Democrats' problem lay in civil rights ennui. Florida was a civil rights state. White people had lived with their civil rights law for more than a year. They found the consequences far from apocalyptic. Hordes of black intruders did not overrun first-class establishments or jostle genteel white persons from places of public resort. None had yet been caught invading the gracious parlors of white households. Schools were not integrated. Floridians relaxed. The civil rights debate in the House raised barely a ripple in the press. S.1 passed the Senate. The *Floridian* paused only to say that the president would probably veto it.[4] No one asserted that white Floridians liked civil rights acts, but neither did they view them with fear and trembling. J. Willis Menard,

---

2 Tallahassee *Floridian*, February 17, 1874.

3 See Daniel R. Weinfeld, "More Courage than Discretion: Charles M. Hamilton in Reconstruction Florida," *Florida Historical Quarterly*, 84 (2006): 501–502.

4 Tallahassee *Floridian*, June 2, 1874.

Jacksonville's black politician, wrote the New York *Tribune.* The state law had not brought the "Negro's millennium."[5]

Still, the campaign in the 1st District did not go easily for the incumbent. William Purman was an arrival from Pennsylvania. He began his post-war career in Jackson County, assisting his friend Charles M. Hamilton as agent of the Freedman's Bureau. Hamilton moved on to the federal Congress. Purman entered the state senate. He made enemies among some black Floridians, notably the ambitious Secretary of State Jonathan C. Gibbs,[6] but others recalled him positively.[7] White conservatives conceived conspicuous contempt for the carpetbagging interloper. In 1869 he narrowly escaped assassination, ambushed and shot through the neck. That incident sparked the campaign of terror in Jackson County.

The Republican nominating convention opened on August 11.[8] It ended in a bolt, a riot, a counter-convention and finally two nominations. First Purman's partisans seized control of the convention as it opened at 1 o'clock on a sultry afternoon in Tallahassee's Representative Hall. Purman's rivals fumed, and sweated: oppressive heat, a too-large crowd crammed into a too-small small space with too little ventilation. Governor Marcellus Stearns, a portly gentleman, collapsed, overcome with heat and excitement. He begged for someone to fan him. At 6 o'clock Purman's supporters retired to dinner. The opposition locked the doors and nominated a rival, black State Senator Robert Meacham.[9]

Purmanites returned to find the enemy in their camp. They battered down the doors. With broken chairs, clubs and pistols Purman's men fought their way inside. Opponents hurled them out. The sheriff arrived to restore order. Miraculously, no deaths occurred. Both parties spilled into the street. Purman mounted an overturned dry-goods box. He called upon his forces to rally. They met the next morning to nominate the incumbent. The regular convention saluted Robert Meacham.

Purman invaded his rival's territory, Jefferson and Gadsden Counties. He spoke at Monticello on the 19th, then at Coon's Bottom and St. John's Church.

5 New York *Tribune*, February 1, 1875.

6 On Purman's rise and position, see David L. Hume, "Membership of the Florida Constitutional Convention of 1868: A Case Study of Republican Factionalism in the Reconstruction South," *Florida Historical Quarterly*, 51 (1972): 3–9.

7 T. Thomas Fortune recalled him as a "superior" type of white man, one who had tried genuinely to help the freedmen. Weinfeld, "More Courage than Discretion," 493.

8 Accounts in Tallahassee *Floridian*, August 18; Jacksonville *Florida Union*, August 18; Savannah *News*, August 13, 1874. See also Canter Brown, Jr., "'Where Are the Hopes I Cherished?' – The Life and Times of Robert Meacham," *Florida Historical Quarterly*, 69 (1990): 1–36.

9 Canter Brown, "Where Are the Hopes?" 20–21.

Meacham denounced him, "a crawling slimy snake, a firebrand and disorganizer who would sink the party to perdition to secure his own advancement."[10] Purman appeared at Chattahoochee on the 24th. The crowd grew restless. A burst of gunfire rang out. The congressman beat a hasty retreat.[11] Republican disunity, it seemed, would doom yet another congressional district.

Cooler heads prevailed. On September 4 Tallahassee residents beheld Congressman Purman and Governor Stearns together, strolling on the streets of the capital. They met again at Purman's headquarters and reconciled. Meacham's campaign disintegrated. Democratic exhilaration faded. "Where all was smooth sailing before," wrote the *Floridian*, "it will now require the hardest efforts."[12]

To make those efforts Democrats assembled on August 18 in Representative Hall, recently vacated by battling Republicans. John A. Henderson, a lawyer and state senator from Tampa, took the nomination on the first ballot. Henderson announced a full schedule of speaking appointments. He hoped for a strong vote in the southern counties and to reduce Republican margins in the north. The key, the *Floridian* repeated, was voter turnout. In 1873 Republicans had "polled every vote they could muster, dead or alive." Democrats failed to vote.[13] "Rally to the Front." cried the *Floridian*. "Stand by the colors that wave o'er the land! ... Shall adventurers that sweep down with Northern blast upon us scoop us up and soar away in mocking triumph? Ah, no! ... Rally to the Front!"

The Democrats' rally did include an anti-civil rights plank. Their fifth resolution denounced the bill, "a firebrand intended to be thrown amidst the two races now for the most part harmoniously co-operating."[14] Then the topic dropped out of sight, an afterthought in campaign rhetoric. No text of Henderson's stump speech survives. He may have raised the civil rights issue. Journalistic organs now lost may have pursued it. His prime supporter, at any rate, the *Floridian,* saw little value in playing upon the theme. Late, on October 20, it occurred to the *Floridian* to print the text of the Senate bill for its readers' information. But it attached no desperate cry, degradation and mongrelization to come.

Congressman Purman showed no fear. "Pass this [Civil Rights] Bill," he rose on the House floor. "The tyranny of prejudice, violence, and error will disappear like the miasma of night before the morning sun." He evoked the blessings

---

10 Jacksonville *Florida Union*, August 25, 1874.

11 Canter Brown, "Where Are the Hopes?" 23–26; Jacksonville *Florida Union*, August 25, 1874.

12 Tallahassee *Floridian*, September 8, 1874.

13 Tallahassee *Floridian*, July 21, 1874.

14 Tallahassee *Floridian*, August 18, 1874.

of Florida's civil rights statute: "It has been a panacea for many of the ills in our State. When kindness and common courtesy fail the law intervenes.... One particle of dust in the human eye obstructs the free vision. Is the eye of liberty less sensitive?"[15]

As the *Floridian* had predicted, the election became a close-run affair. Democratic strength in the south balanced Purman's in the panhandle. In the campaign's final days Democrats realized they had made a mistake. They had neglected a crucial constituency. The election of 1874 in the 1st Florida District, foreshadowing many a future contest, came down to the vote of the Cubans. Their communities clustered in the far south. They sheltered many revolutionaries, exiled or driven abroad in the struggle against Spanish colonial rule. Politicians courted them. Free Cuba planks appeared in both parties' platforms. Governor Stearns sent a telegram to the president to pledge his state's support for a war against Spain, should the Administration consider that idea favorably. Generally the Cuban vote leaned Republican. But that support had wavered. In 1873 Democrats carried Monroe County by 352 votes. They counted on doing it again.[16] Purman conceded nothing. On June 19, he rose again in the House, to plead the cause of Cuba Libre:

> Mr. Speaker, the first cry of freedom in Cuba, though in a different language from ours, sobbing across the narrow Gulf Stream, received a ready response and re-echo in the chivalric hearts of Florida.... The blood of a historical consanguinity yet courses through the veins and memory of our people.... Were I, from any possibility, to remain silent upon this floor upon this stirring question of a people who are our neighbors by geography, political aspirations, and reciprocal interests, fighting and dying for liberty and independence, I would be recreant to my own convictions.[17]

Purman made sure his words were read where needed, in Cuban circles. The Key West *Dispatch* printed a full Spanish translation.[18] His rhetoric moreover joined a free Cuba and civil rights. American-style prejudice did not infect Cuba. "White and colored soldiers in the patriot army fight side by side for liberty, are not divided off into colored and white regiments, stand shoulder to shoulder in the same ranks." The rebel commander, Policarpo Rustán, "one

15 *Cong. Record*, 43rd Congress, 1st Session: 5239–5245.

16 See Gerald E. Poyo, "Cuban Revolutionaries and Monroe County Reconstruction Politics, 1868–1876," *Florida Historical Quarterly*, 55 (1977): 408–413.

17 Purman's Free Cuba speech, *Cong. Record*, 43rd Congress, 1st Session: 5239–5245.

18 Poyo, "Cuban Revolutionaries," 414–416.

of the bravest generals," was a black man. From Washington Purman made a detour to New York City, where he called upon the Junta, the supreme council of Cuban revolutionary leadership, at its headquarters in exile. He returned home with the Junta's blessing in his hand.[19]

Too late Democrat Henderson realized the error of his complacency. A hurried trip to Key West followed. On the campaign's final day he telegraphed Tallahassee: "Glorious reception here. I am assured a three hundred majority in Monroe."[20] The assurance was excessive. Henderson carried Monroe County, but with only 12 votes to spare.

William Purman returned to Congress, one of just five southern white Republican incumbents to win reelection. He took only four counties, Gadsden, Jackson, Leon and Jefferson. His erasure of 340 Democratic votes in Monroe pulled him through. Some Democrats blamed perfidious Cubans. "What nobler specimen of valorous patriotism can be imagined," growled the Savannah *News*, "than a Cuban who bravely refugees from his own country in her hour of peril and votes the Radical ticket in Key West?"[21] The *Floridian* blamed lazy white men. It was "criminal apathy." They failed to register. If registered they failed to vote.[22] They failed to panic at the mention of civil rights.

Florida, Second District
Josiah Walls (R), Jesse Finley (D)
Population: 52% black

Civil rights played quietly in the 2nd District as in the 1st. Incumbent Josiah Walls was black. He had voted for and spoken for the Civil Rights Bill. But Walls was Congress' most precarious black member. Barely 52% of his constituents were black. He preferred, even in apathetic Florida, to avoid a civil rights confrontation.

Congressman Walls found the road to re-nomination no smoother than did his colleague Purman. He had served two terms. Many considered that sufficient. "Mr. Walls has secured some $24,000 in the way of salary," wrote the Tallahassee *Sentinel*. Others would like "a hack at the same butter."[23] Two population centers, the cities of Gainesville in Alachua County and Jacksonville in Duval County, vied for political influence. Jacksonvillians, particularly their

19 Tallahassee *Floridian*, November 3, 1874.
20 Tallahassee *Floridian*, November 3, 1874.
21 Savannah *News*, November 17, 1874.
22 Tallahassee *Floridian*, November 10, 17, 1874.
23 Quoted in Tallahassee *Floridian*, July 28, 1874.

Republican organ the Jacksonville *Florida Union,* denounced the Gainesvillian Walls.[24] Walls faced rivals, fellow black politicians. John Willis Menard announced his candidacy on June 23. Rev. John R. Scott, Jacksonville Collector of Customs, emerged as the favorite of the *Florida Union.*[25] When the 2nd District Republican convention met at Jacksonville on August 10, Josiah Walls nevertheless beat back all comers.[26] The triumph came at a price. Menard and Scott joined the Walls re-election team. Other Jacksonville Republicans, including the *Florida Union,* bolted.

Josiah Walls cultivated an image of inclusiveness. He represented all Floridians, he declared. That mantra rankled some. Walls, Menard complained, conciliated too many Democrats.[27] Even Democrats agreed. His tenure "has been marked by more than common liberality."[28] He voted for the Amnesty Bill. He spread patronage evenhandedly. He secured appointments for Democrats as well as Republicans. When the time came for Florida's congressmen to name constituents for West Point cadetships, Purman chose a black youth, Reuben S. Smith. Walls selected a white boy, son of former Democratic governor David Shelby Walker.[29] Josiah Walls' journalistic organ, the Gainesville *New Era,* of which he himself was proprietor, defined his doctrine.

> I would sincerely deprecate any movement looking to the division of the people of our fair State upon sectional hatred or prejudice to race.... Colored men, we have nothing to gain by an issue with the white race, nor has the interest of the State anything to gain by an open political issue between its citizens based on sectional hatred, and in no way will I be a party to such an issue.[30]

Every instinct prompted Congressman Walls to mute the issue of civil rights. His Democratic opponent might have chosen to advertise his opposition. He did not. Gen. Jesse J. Finley of Lake City was one of Florida's Confederate heroes. A lifelong civilian, he volunteered as a private soldier at age 51. He earned a general's insignia, leading one of Florida's two infantry brigades until bullets felled him at the battle of Jonesboro. Finley viewed matters much as did Walls. The district was close. There was no need to energize the other side or reunite

24 Jacksonville *Florida Union,* June 2, August 1, 1874.
25 See Canter Brown, Jr., *Florida's Black Public Officials, 1867–1924* (Tuscaloosa: 1988), 110, 123–124.
26 Savannah *News,* August 15, 1874.
27 Jacksonville *Florida Union,* June 23, 1874.
28 Ocala *Banner,* quoted in Jacksonville *Florida Union,* October 8, 1874.
29 Tallahassee *Floridian,* June 2, 1874.
30 Quoted in Tallahassee *Floridian,* June 2, 1874.

an opposition for the moment delightfully disunited. Civil rights hysteria, even if it could be manufactured, did not suit his interests.

Finley referred respectfully to his black competitor: "I propose to treat him with courtesy, and if I should be elected I trust I shall not be indebted for my success to any disparagement of my adversary."[31] He managed to disparage fairly well, albeit with no names named. It was time, his platform declared, to return government to "capable and responsible hands." It quoted a Republican, Edwards Pierrepont: "Liberty cannot survive in States where ignorance and iniquity can prevail." Wherefore, "we are only striving to establish the rule of virtue and intelligence." It promised to uphold the rights of all Floridians: "We are in favor of the recognition and protection of all citizens in the enjoyment of their constitutional rights and of the impartial enforcement of the Laws."

General Finley took that message on the road. At the locality of Picolata he spoke. A bucolic setting amid piney woods near the St. John's River, a picnic in the offing, men and women sat on the green, carriages tethered in the trees. Children played round about. The candidate's restful words suited the serenity. "Suffice it to say that he denounced no one, no party nor no section of the country," reported the *Florida Union*. "We heard no sentiment advanced, nor no principles enunciated but what an old fashioned Republican could respond to."[32] The *Union*, to be sure, mouthpiece of Walls' Jacksonville rivals, was by now thoroughly pro-Finley. Candidate and journal harmonized. The former provided the latter no reason to report unpleasant notions. The latter gave Republicans no reason to regret a Democratic vote. Finley spoke at Ocala on October 20. Intelligent men must govern, rather than those who (no names named) until recently could neither read nor write. Civil rights? He opposed it because "it was sure to introduce a state of ill feeling between the races that might otherwise be avoided."[33]

Final returns gave Walls the victory. Democrats charged fraud. The 44th Congress, now dominated by Democrats, agreed. The House Elections Committee reversed the decision. General Finley took his seat on April 19, 1876.

2 Louisiana

In Louisiana black people had achieved equality, in one respect: prison punishment. "The guards generally were competent men," a commission of inquiry into penitentiary conditions reported in 1873. "White as well as colored convicts

31 Jacksonville *Florida Union*, September 19, 1874.

32 Jacksonville *Florida Union*, October 30, 1874.

33 Tallahassee *Floridian*, October 27, 1874.

were whipped; they made no discriminations as to race in the punishments inflicted."[34] In other respects Louisiana had a way to go. State civil rights statutes had operated officially for the better part of a decade. Despite Democrats' screaming end-of-the-world prophecies, those laws had not overturned the hierarchy of the races. Louisiana's statutes had undergone a thorough test. They failed. Attempting to prove their power, the testers proved their powerlessness. Testing nevertheless grew more determined as the elections grew closer.

The author of Louisiana's civil rights tests was an uncommon man with a gift for blazing trails: Thomas Morris Chester, the only black member of the Louisiana bar, journalist, war correspondent, general of the militia. Chester had his eye on a congressional seat. He became a civil rights pioneer. From his base in New Orleans he orchestrated a fully-fledged desegregation campaign. He inaugurated a movement that prefigured the lunch-counter protests and sit-ins that swept the South a century later. His efforts fell short, but he pointed the way in the 1870s for his successors of the 1960s. He relied on state statutes and on the help of a friendly judge to give Louisianans a taste of the future.

Foretastes had occurred. Josephine DeCuir recovered impressive damages when the officers of the steamboat *Governor Allen* denied her first-class amenities. Louisianans also remembered the case of Sauvinet *v.* Walker in 1871. Charles Sauvinet, black Sheriff of Orleans Parish, had sued the proprietors of the Bank Saloon after it refused him a drink at the bar. The court awarded Sheriff Sauvinet $1,000 for violation of his civil rights. That judgment eventually reached the United States Supreme Court. It was upheld. Sauvinet and DeCuir relied on Louisiana's civil rights enactments, namely Article 13 of the Louisiana constitution and the enforcing statute of 1869. Nothing prepared white people for the wave of agitation that swept upon them in 1874. "A rain of litigation," reported the New Orleans *Abeille*.[35] A swarm of cases, cried the Alexandria *Democrat*.[36] Black people, the Shreveport *Times* warned, had become alarmingly insolent.[37] Gen. Chester, "the sable limb of the law," declared the New Orleans *Bulletin*, has unleashed a civil rights tempest "that threatens to sap and destroy our whole social fabric."[38] The tests began in March, accelerated in May and continued into the summer.[39]

34 Mark Carleton, "The Politics of the Convict Lease System in Louisiana: 1868–1901," *Louisiana History: The Journal of the Louisiana Historical Association*, 8 (1967): 10.

35 New Orleans *Abeille*, May 2, 1874: *une pluie de procès en dommage*.

36 Alexandria *Louisiana Democrat*, May 27, 1874.

37 Shreveport *Times*, June 4, 1874.

38 Quoted in Quitman, Georgia, *Independent*, July 25, 1874.

39 See John W. Blassingame, *Black New Orleans, 1860–1880* (Chicago, 1973): 182–186.

On March 11th Peter Joseph, a black man, captain in the New Orleans Metropolitan Police, sued David Bidwell, director of the New Orleans Academy of Music. The plaintiff alleged that he had presented a ticket to the parquet of this grandly-named establishment (actually a comic theater and music hall).[40] The defendant's ticket agent refused him admission, injuring him thereby in his statutory civil rights. He asked for $5,000 in damages. The case, the *Abeille* huffed, was a put-up job. The music hall's tickets, as anyone could read ("though it is possible that Monsieur Joseph, captain of police, knows not how to read"), clearly stated the terms of sale: "Management reserves the right to refuse entry to the bearer on condition of reimbursement of the full price."

The Joseph case headed for the tribunal of the 4th District, Judge Barney L. Lynch presiding. Lynch was a thorough Radical. "Pseudo-Judge Lynch!" the *Abeille* screamed. "He dreams the dream of demagogues, who want to abase their superiors, to drag all down to their own level."[41] Only the thin white line of an upright jury could prevent disgrace.

> It is too much. They force us to mingle shoulder to shoulder with people who disgust us. The public will not stand for it, if the thing becomes general.... One more drop and the pot will overflow – and we have heard already, for several weeks now, hushed rumors; they portend no good.[42]

The *Abeille's* forebodings were justified. Joseph v. Bidwell was only the beginning. Lawyer Chester counted on a confluence of circumstances. He had the law, the Louisiana civil rights statute of 1869. He had the judge, Barney Lynch. And he had Act no. 23, the factor uniquely calculated to make the operation work. A cascade of cases followed: Davis v. Kuntz; then Clermont v. O'Neal; next Lewis v. O'Neal; Washington v. McCloskey; Lewis v. McCloskey; Smith v. Pellegrini; Moore v. Kuntz; Jourdain v. Frederickson; Labère v. Lopez; most spectacular, the case of Pinchback v. Redwitz. Soda shops and beer halls were the targets, just as lunch counters and cafeterias would be a century later.

The operation was straightforward. The plaintiff, if possible accompanied by a white companion to prove discriminatory conduct, entered the targeted establishment. He (or she) demanded to be served. After the inevitable ejection, he or she filed suit. The problem was how to get by the jury. No white jury

---

40 Currently appearing, acclaimed trapeze artists Leopold and Geraldine; a drama, "Forsaken, or, Miseries of Gotham"; a burlesque, "Cupid's Victims," by the Waite sisters; a farce, "The Mad Hamlet"; variety of dances and comic songs. New Orleans *Abeille*, March 15, 1874.

41 New Orleans *Abeille*, May 2, 1874.

42 New Orleans *Abeille*, March 12, 1874.

would convict, no matter how clear the violation. Louisiana's Reconstruction regime permitted black men to sit on juries. Yet even a racially-mixed jury, be there a single white vote, would return a hung verdict. Here Chester played his decisive card. Act 23 of the State Provisions of 1871 provided that if, exclusively in civil rights cases, a jury were unable to reach a verdict, the decision reverted to the judge. That meant Judge Lynch. The plot was laid. Plaintiffs caused lawsuits. Juries hung. The judge would deliver decisions for the plaintiffs. T. Morris Chester and Barney Lynch prepared to jolt Louisianans out of their civil rights complacency.

At noon of April 22nd Cynthia Davis, a citizen of dubious color (yellowish, "*de couleur isabelle*") approached the confectioner's shop and soda fountain of Mr. N. Kuntz at the corner of Carondelet and Canal streets. Attracted by a sign advising "Ladies' lunch and refreshment saloon, down and up stairs," she stepped in. She requested a glass of soda water advertised for the price of 5¢. The establishment, she was informed, had no soda water. She asked for plain water. No water was available. She repaired to lawyer Chester and filed suit against N. Kuntz in the amount of $500 for violation of her civil rights.[43]

On the same day Richard Moore, a person of color, and escorting a lady companion, entered Kuntz's shop. They requested soda water. This time refreshment was available. But the price rose suddenly tenfold, from 5¢ to 50¢. Moore called for a whiskey instead. Refused. He asked for Vichy water. He was served with eviction; another suit for $500.[44]

On April 9, William H. Smith entered G. Pellegrini's shop at 209 Canal Street. He too asked for a 5¢ drink of soda water. He found the charge inflated twentyfold, to $1. He objected emphatically, pointing to white customers being served for the price of a nickel. Among those customers sat Edwin Jewell, editor of the New Orleans *Bulletin*. Jewell chose to resent Smith's observation. He ordered Pellegrini to eject the intruder from his presence.

T. Morris Chester handed Smith's complaint to the 4th District Court. He also handed a copy to the press. The establishment of Pellegrini, Chester asserted, was licensed by the State of Louisiana and the City of New Orleans, "where the public is explicitly or impliedly invited to purchase soda water and other refreshing drinks, also cakes, pies and pastry in general." The Revised Statutes of New Orleans, Sec. 458, required that all customers be served. Mr. Smith had not been served. "This indignity and contempt has distressed

---

43 New Orleans *Republican*, May 1; New Orleans *Abeille*, May 2, 1874.

44 New Orleans *Republican*, May 28, 1874.

the mind, wounded the pride and aggravated the feelings of your petitioner so as to cause him damage in the sum of $500."[45]

The rain of cases continued to fall. John F. Clermont v. John O'Neal came next.[46] Clermont, a corporal in the Metropolitan Police, appeared at O'Neal's café, corner of Tchoupitoulas and Delord. He requested whisky. O'Neal decided against it: "He would not bother himself, and suggested he quench his thirst elsewhere." Clermont remonstrated. O'Neal removed him "with the utmost politeness" into the street. Clermont sued for $500.

McCloskey's soda shop on St. Charles Street took a double hit. First George Washington, a person of color, asked for the customary 5¢ glass of soda water. He objected to being charged $5 "in advance."[47] Charles Lewis followed. He found his carbonated beverage forbidden at any price.[48] In May these cases came to trial. They followed the trajectory plotted by Chester and Lynch.

Joseph v. Bidwell arrived first before the court. Testimony showed Capt. Joseph's foray into the music hall to have been a calculated scheme. Joseph had provided himself a white accomplice, James Riordan. Riordan purchased both admissions, paying $1 each for adjacent seats in the parquet. Joseph and Riordan stepped up to the door together. Riordan's ticket was honored, Joseph's rejected. Joseph also alleged that ticket agent David Owens had pushed him, thereby committing an act of assault and battery. Defense counsel objected. Judge Lynch ruled the assault immaterial.

David Bidwell offered no defense. He had been ill, confined to his bed. Owens had acted without his approval. Had he known, he would certainly have admitted the gentleman, for he had never in his life refused colored men admission. He admitted them, he explained, to a special section of seats "in what is known as the Family Circle." He had arranged this privilege with a committee of black leaders. "They selected that place; he fixed it nicely, carpeted it etc.; they stated to him that they wanted to be by themselves." Even so, he would not have denied Captain Joseph the right to sit where he desired.[49]

---

45 Revised Statutes Sec. 458: "All licenses hereafter granted ... shall contain the express condition that the place of business or public resort shall be open to the accommodation and patronage of all persons without distinction or discrimination on account of race or color.... Any such person who shall violate the condition of such license shall, on conviction thereof, be punished by forfeiture of his license, and his place of business shall be closed, and moreover he shall be liable at the suit of the person aggrieved to such damages as he shall sustain thereby." New Orleans *Republican*, March, 26, 27, 1874.

46 New Orleans *Republican*, March 27, 1874.

47 New Orleans *Abeille*, May 13, 1874.

48 New Orleans *Abeille*, May 13, 1874.

49 New Orleans *Abeille*, May 13, 1874.

The case went to the jury. For five hours those citizens deliberated. At 7:30 they grew tired. Lynch had them sequestered. The vote stood at 11 to 1 for acquittal. Discussions resumed the next day. One hold-out held out. The jury reported itself hung. Lynch discharged the jurymen. Pursuant to Act 23, he prepared to render judgment. Bidwell's lawyers appealed, viva voce, to the State Supreme Court. Act 23 violated the 14th Amendment. It denied their client due process of the law.[50] Lynch suspended his ruling.[51]

Meanwhile he commenced the case of Clermont v. O'Neal.[52] Thirty-eight jurors were examined, and dismissed. Some expressed doubts about the constitutionality of the civil rights statute. Lynch excused them. Defendant's counsel eliminated others: "He was exceedingly particular in asking if, supposing such a law existed and the juror believed in its constitutionality, he would enforce it. And when the answer was yes, he gravely submitted to the court that the juror was incompetent." Lynch called up another sixty potential jurymen. Finally the trials began.

The Clermont jury was mixed. It deadlocked. Black jurors, it was reported, tried every means to reach a verdict. For them the principle was essential, damages secondary. The plaintiff had asked for $500. They agreed to accept an award of $50, if the white jurors agreed to find the defendant guilty. They offered to take $37.50. They suggested $25. They came down to $5 on principle. The jury hung. Judge Lynch invoked Act 23.

In the last case, Lewis v. McCloskey, T. Morris Chester delivered a summation. He begged the jury to conceive the larger picture. A frivolous quarrel it seemed, a glass of soda. It touched fundamental issues, "the dignity of manhood and the rights of citizenship."

> Charles Lewis, a resident of New Orleans, an elector of Louisiana and a citizen of the United States, a man in the image and likeness of his Creator ... entered the place of public resort kept by Hugh McCloskey, situated at No. 76 St. Charles Street, and respectfully asked for a glass of

50 Act 23, Provisions of 27 February 1871: "An act to regulate the mode of trying cases arising under the provisions of article thirteen (13) of the constitution of Louisiana or under any acts of the Legislature to enforce the said article thirteen of the said constitution, and to regulate the licenses therein mentioned."

51 New Orleans *Abeille*, May 9, 10–12; New Orleans *Republican*, May 8, 1874. The question of Act 23's constitutionality reached the United States Supreme Court in the appeal of Walker v. Sauvinet and was decided in the October term of 1875. The ruling, written by Chief Justice Waite (Justices Field and Clifford dissenting) sustained the legality of Louisiana's provisions.

52 New Orleans *Republican*, May 14, 1874.

> soda water.... He was refused with indignity and reproach, in which his manhood was insulted and his citizenship was outraged.[53]

America alone sanctioned prejudices that everywhere else made civilized men blush.

> In no country throughout all God's Creation, leaving out the United States of America, would such an outrage as Charles Lewis has suffered be tolerated, and even here it is perpetrated in violation of law. Under any other flag than our own, whether Pagan or Christian, black and white men are equal before the law, not only in theory but in practice.... I have sat at the imperial table in the Winter Palace at St. Petersburg, in company with the Emperor of all the Russias.... I have been received at the throne of England on the occasion of a royal reception; and with all the self-respect and manhood inspired by such illustrious associations I could not, if this outrage is sustained by you, in this city obtain a glass of soda water, if I was dying of thirst.[54]

The Lewis jury hung. On May 24 Barney Lynch delivered his verdicts. He ruled for the plaintiffs. He lowered the awards, but upheld the principle. Peter Joseph had asked for $5,000. He received $1,000. John F. Clermont took $200, as did George Washington and Charles Lewis. On June 5, the defendants in the case of Alfred Jourdain pleaded no contest. They renounced the action of their barkeep in refusing to serve the disputed glass of Vichy water. Lynch fined the café's proprietors $25 and costs.[55] The most remarkable conclusion came in William Smith v. Pellegrini. The jury itself declared the defendant guilty. Smith

---

53 New Orleans *Republican*, May 24, 1874.

54 The Alexandria *Democrat* was not impressed. T. Morris Chester, it observed, "who was permitted the other day to play lawyer," demonstrated nothing so clearly as the Negro's propensity for lying. He had never taken tea with the Czar. And if he had, who cared? No matter what silly customs Europeans indulged, the best answer was still that given, in happier times, by John Y. Mason when, as ambassador in Paris, he encountered a fellow diplomat, the ambassador of Haiti: "Asked what he thought of him, 'I think he will bring fifteen hundred dollars,' was the reply of the insouciant Virginian." Alexandria *Louisiana Democrat*, June 3, 1874.

55 New Orleans *Abeille*, June 6, 1874. The whole exercise, the *Abeille* sneered, served only to fatten the purse of lawyer Chester: "Le montant que les malheureux propriétaires de cafés sont condamnés à payer passe toujours dans la poche béante de l'avocat nègre. Le plaideur n'a jamais que les coquilles de l'huitre avalée par Morris Chester." New Orleans *Abeille*, July 10, 1874.

left court with $30.[56] One plaintiff did not long enjoy his victory. On September 14th White League marksmen killed Corporal Clermont, a casualty of the Battle of Liberty Place.[57]

Meanwhile harassed refreshment-shop operators devised countermeasures. John O'Neal displayed the technique when his precincts were invaded again on May 15. Another black Metropolitan policeman approached, arm in arm with a white accomplice.

> The white man, speaking up in his name and that of his companion, ordered two glasses of beer. Mr. O'Neal, who is Irish by birth and who thus lacks no refinement of spirit, turned with comic gravity to the white and informed him that his establishment served only respectable men, gentlemen only. Consequently, since he appeared neither respectable nor a gentleman, he requested him to drink elsewhere. Turning to the astonished black policeman, and staring with the whites of his eyes, "I am ready to serve *monsieur*," he said with the most exquisite courtesy, "if he will have the kindness to place an order."[58]

The white intruder protested. He was introduced to O'Neal's Irish fist. He fled. His black companion fled with him, their civil rights scheme utterly disrupted.

A similar scene unfolded at 132 Common Street, the site of Hugo Redwitz's beer hall. A black man named Sam and a white man named Grafton asked for beer. Bartender Alexander Hoffman leaped across the counter and propelled Grafton into the street. Sam announced he was no longer thirsty. Hoffman disagreed. Drink, he insisted, "nailing him to the place" until he emptied the glass.[59]

At noon on May 19 Redwitz's beer-garden witnessed an extraordinary incident. Two former Governors of Louisiana entered side by side: Henry Clay Warmoth (white) and Pinckney Pinchback (black). Accompanying them was another black man, John W. Roxborough, Clerk of the Assembly. They ordered beer. Hoffman, again on duty, refused. It was too early; he had not set up the tap. Pinchback replied. They would take whiskey, "our national liquor." Hoffman produced a bottle. He set it directly before Roxborough. "The *gentleman* is served. I see no one else present who can pretend to that title."

---

56 New Orleans *Republican*, June 25, 1874.

57 Capt. Joseph survived, leading his detachment to join the governor's forces besieged in the Custom House.

58 New Orleans *Abeille*, May 19, 1874.

59 New Orleans *Republican*, May 21, 1874.

> Ten seconds of terrible silence.... Warmoth looked at Pinchback. Pinchback looked at Warmoth. They looked at each other. Then, in a faint voice, a sigh, they mumbled together, "We are not thirsty; let's go."... Mr. Alexander Hoffman also let go, with an irrepressible laugh, which served even more to hasten the retreat of the noble trio. He is still laughing at the picture of the diminishing figures of Warmoth, Pinchback, and Roxborough well-named, *Lenoir*. Bravo![60]

"When the party left," reported the *Bulletin*, "a cheer from the guests broke upon the ears of the departing trio," and its echo chased them down the street.[61] For Pinchback it will have been mortifying. He was officially black, but notably light-skinned. White society insulted him anyway. Now white society told him he was not black enough, and insulted him. Pinchback gave his own account. Neither he nor Warmoth, he said, wanted to test Louisiana's civil rights laws. They wanted a drink. They entered Redwitz's beer hall because they expected no difficulty. He regularly patronized Redwitz's saloon. Nothing would have induced him to enter "if he had not been under the impression that it was the disposition and habit of the proprietor to welcome all customers."[62]

Henry Warmoth too appealed for understanding. On Decoration Day, a week after his beer-hall humiliation, he stood in the Chalmette Cemetery. A crowd of citizens waited, and wilted, under a blazing sun. They heard a plea for civil rights:

> The last remaining cause of irritation growing out of the changes produced by the war relates to the civil rights of our colored fellow-citizen.... He longs for the time when he can go anywhere his fellow-citizens can go, and enjoy all the privileges and courtesies extended to them. He sees in his refusal humiliation: an evidence of contempt which, poor and ignorant as he may be, wounds his pride, hurts his feelings, and excites him to

---

60 New Orleans *Abeille*, May 20, 1874.

61 Quoted in Mobile *Register*, May 22, 1874.

62 New Orleans *Louisianian*, May 23, 1874. Redwitz's conversion to racism left racists unimpressed. "Mr. Hugo Redwitz," the New Orleans *Bulletin* reported, "is making a good deal of cheap reputation on some extraordinary conduct on his part in refusing to wait on white people when accompanied by negroes.... This saloon has entertained negroes, and was among the very first to permit them to receive that attention which is denied them by every first-class house in this city. This demonstration, then, of his at this hour of the day, is obvious and will not deceive anyone." Quoted in New Orleans *Louisianian*, May 23. Redwitz, a tolerant man, surrendered to intolerance, caught in the polarizing vortex of a civil rights campaign.

> acts of retaliation. Will not our white fellow-citizens consent to this [civil rights]? … Then the next generation would be so intelligent, so virtuous and so good that the history of the past and the present would be read and laughed over like the contests of Don Quixote over the wind-mills of Spain.[63]

Governor Warmoth's quixotic plea fell flat. So did Morris Chester's civil rights campaign. The "rain of cases" became a drizzle and stopped. Even the *Abeille* saw the futility. "All these lawsuits, all these chicaneries accomplish nothing."[64] Newspapers mocked Chester. Bartenders turned Warmoth and Pinchback into laughingstocks.

Then came the elections. They were no laughing matter. Statewide a bare majority of black voters combined with a scant measure of white support allowed Republicans to control the administration. Each election grew tighter. In the Republican split of 1872 Louisiana Democrats had followed the lead of their national party. They built a fusion campaign, an alliance with the Liberal Republicans. Democrat John McEnery ran for the governorship, Liberal Republican Davidson Penn stood for the lieutenant-governorship. A black man, Samuel Armistead, took the nomination for Secretary of State. That road led to frustration. Black voters did not rally to the fusion ticket. White voters mistrusted it. Liberals blamed Democrats.[65] Democrats blamed fusion, the fuzzy notion of such men as Warmoth and Penn that cooperation could achieve success.[66]

Cooperation nevertheless uttered one last gasp before expiring. This came in the form of the "Unification Movement" of 1873. Moderate black leaders joined pragmatic whites. Those pragmatists largely represented the merchant class. For capitalists a customer was a customer. Race turmoil was bad for business.[67] At their head unificationists placed a white man of impeccable credentials: Pierre Gustave Toutant Beauregard, Louisiana hero, full general of the

63 New Orleans *Republican*, May 31, 1874.

64 New Orleans *Abeille*, July 10, 1874.

65 Henry Clay Warmoth, *War, Politics and Reconstruction* (New York: 1930), 199–200.

66 "At the late election the Democrats made every possible concession to the negro element. They agreed to accord them all their rights.… The negroes were evidently much obliged to the Democrats for their condescension, but voted the Republican ticket in a body." Alexandria *Louisiana Democrat*, July 2, 1873.

67 Moderate blacks included Louis C. Roudanez, Aristide Mary, James Lewis. Among the merchants were Isaac N. Marks, owner of the New Orleans, Florida and Havana Steamship Company and the Sun Mutual Insurance Company, James I. Day of the Bank of Louisiana, Auguste Bohn, president of the Mechanics' and Traders' Bank and the Mutual Insurance Co. See T. Harry Williams, "The Louisiana Unification Movement of

Confederacy. Under Gen. Beauregard's imprimatur they issued "An Appeal for the Unification of the People of Louisiana." Charles Sumner could have written the unification manifesto word for word into his civil rights bill:

> Whereas, we have an abiding faith that there is love enough for Louisiana among her sons to unite them in a manful and unselfish struggle for her redemption, be it therefore resolved, That henceforward we dedicate ourselves to the unification of our people; That by "our people" we mean all men, of whatsoever race, color or religion, who are citizens of Louisiana, and who are willing to work for her prosperity; That we shall advocate ... every civil and political right guaranteed by the constitution and laws of Louisiana, by the constitution and laws of the United States, and by the laws of honor, brotherhood and fair dealing ... the right to frequent at will all places of public resort, and to travel at will on all vehicles of public conveyance, upon terms of perfect equality with any and every other citizen. We shall recommend to the proprietors of all places of licensed public resort in the State of Louisiana the opening of said places to the patronage of both races inhabiting our State. That hereafter no distinctions shall exist among citizens of Louisiana in any of our public schools ... That as an earnest of our holy purpose we hereby offer upon the altar of the common good all party ties, and all prejudices of education which may tend to hinder the political unity of our people.[68]

General Beauregard's plea pleased neither Democrats nor Republicans. Unification faded. Fusion failed. One option remained. White men must rally to a "White People's Party." No journalistic voice stated the case more honestly than the aptly-named campaign paper the Alexandria *Caucasian*. Its editors Wilbur F. Blackman, Robert P. Hunter and George W. Stafford launched their sheet as a mouthpiece for the movement: "It will lend its aid and espouse the cause of that white man's party – by whatever name it may be called – which shall seem most likely to relieve our downtrodden State."[69]

1873," *Journal of Southern History*, 11 (1945): 349–369; "An Analysis of Some Reconstruction Attitudes," *Journal of Southern History*, 12 (1946): 479–483.

68 Full text of the unification manifesto: Williams, "Unification Movement," 359–361.

69 The *Caucasian* advertised its arrival with a prepublication prospectus: "The *Caucasian* will be a white man's paper, devoted to the interests of the whole people of the Parish and the State, and opposed to the aggrandizement of the negro to the prejudice of the Caucasian race, the superior of the African race in every particular, except the endurance of physical labor for which the latter was created and designed by Providence." Alexandria *Louisiana Democrat*, March 25, 1874.

The *Caucasian's* maiden edition of March 29, 1874, featured civil rights. Directly under its masthead motto – "The Truth Crushed to Earth Will Rise Again" – it printed the first half of North Carolina Congressman William Robbins' anti-civil rights speech in the House. Its second weekly edition completed the text. White people's misery must end.[70]

The *Caucasian's* May 23 edition again addressed civil rights. "A Civil Rights bill which shall attempt to make white and black companions at the table, in hotels and railroads, at theaters and the race track, will never be executed in the South." If reason did not avail, let violence perform the purification.

> Now, when we, having grown weary of tame submission to this most desolating war of the negro upon us, propose to take a bold stand, to assert the dignity of our manhood, to say in tones of thunder and with the voice of the angry elements STOP! THUS FAR SHALT THOU GO, AND NO FURTHER! we are met with the babyish wail and old maidish horrified whine of, *"Oh! Please don't! You will array the two races in conflict."* ... And what do we care if it does become necessary to array them in conflict? ... We would counsel a resort to violence only when it was forced upon us, as it was at Colfax, but we are not to be deterred from a bold and outspoken advocacy of our ideas because such a conflict might take place.

Louisiana's elections took shape: redemption through violence. Violence, "the assertion of manhood," took varied forms. Terror, deadly force, certainly. Or it could adopt gentler means: starvation, for instance. The New Orleans *Morning Star and Catholic Messenger* liked that idea. It printed the advice of Father Abram J. Ryan, the "poet-priest of the Confederacy." Hunger, he hoped, would humble black people's hubris.[71]

> There is but one way to manage the negro. He is, as a class, amenable to neither reason nor gratitude. He must be starved into the common perceptions of decency. Let him go to his own race or his carpetbag friends

70 Alexandria *Caucasian,* March 29, April 5, 1874.

71 On Father Ryan, see Charles C. Boldrick, "Father Abram J. Ryan, the 'Poet-Priest' of the Confederacy," *Filson Club Historical Quarterly*, 46 (1972): 201–218. Father Ryan's odes, "The Sword of Lee" and "The Conquered Banner," were popular favorites. So intensely did their author identify with the cause that he underwent a name change (reversing the Biblical switch) from Abraham to Abram, apparently so as not to be connected, even praenomenally, with the hated Lincoln.

> for employment.... Without cutting as deep as this, the White Man's party will not reach the root of the evil.[72]

Republicans objected, a genocidal notion. The *Catholic Messenger* explained: "Nobody ever proposed to starve the negro to death; only to the point of common sense."[73] The New Orleans *Bulletin* approved. Black field-hands, unavoidably, must continue to labor for the sake of the general economy. Black persons otherwise, maids and house-servants, porters and draymen, bootblacks, charcoalmen, washerwomen, could easily be replaced by white menials who did not presume to rise above their station.[74] Destitution as a political weapon was not unique to Louisiana. But in Louisiana it enjoyed a most efficient application. The White League pressured planters in De Soto, Caddo and St. Landry Parishes. It harried businessmen in Shreveport; fire any employee who votes incorrectly.

Louisiana Democrats renamed themselves, the White People's Party. They met on August 24 at Baton Rouge. Resolution 2 drew the race line: "The Radical party in this State has, by false and fraudulent representation, inflamed the passions and prejudices of the negroes as a race against the whites, and has thereby made it necessary for the white people to unite and act together in self-defense and for the preservation of white civilization." Resolution 8 reached out to white folks everywhere: "We extend to all our race, in every clime, the right hand of fellowship and a cordial invitation to come and settle among us, and unite their destinies with ours." Article 3 denounced the Civil Rights Bill.[75]

Republicans met on August 5. Resolution 11 stated: "We approve and indorse the civil rights bill now pending before Congress."[76] The elections began. (see Map 7, below)

Louisiana, First and Second Districts
J. Hale Sypher, Henry C. Dibble (R), E. John Ellis, Randall Lee Gibson (D)
Populations: 52% black

Louisiana's 1st and 2nd districts shared the city of New Orleans. The 1st covered that portion of the city below and east of Canal Street, and also St. Bernard and Plaquemines Parishes to the south. Its not-quite-incumbent incumbent, Jacob

---

72 Quoted in Alexandria *Caucasian*, June 20, 1874; also Monroe *Ouachita Telegraph*, June 26, 1874; House Report 261, Part 2, 771.

73 New Orleans *Republican*, June 18; Alexandria *Caucasian*, June 27, 1874.

74 New Orleans *Republican*, July 26, 1874.

75 Monroe *Ouachita Telegraph*, September 4, 1874.

76 New Orleans *Republican*, August 8–9, 1874.

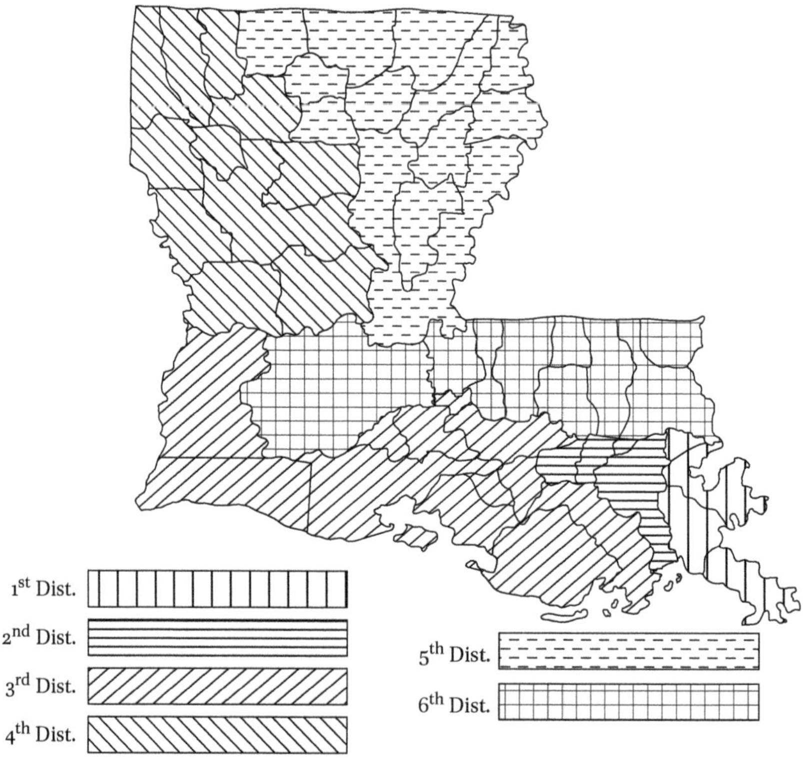

MAP 7 Congressional Districts, Louisiana
SOURCE: AUTHORS OF *WELCOMING RUIN*.

Hale Sypher, was a carpetbagger, born in Pennsylvania, educated in New York. In war he had commanded black soldiers, the 11th United States Colored Heavy Artillery. In peace black constituents praised him. "In the darkest hours he never wavered in his allegiance," Pinchback's *Louisianian* declared. "Never has he deserted his post."[77] He held his seat from the 40th almost through the 43rd Congresses. Sypher's constituency, however, was barely black. The 1870 census counted 18,000 of the city's 48,000 residents as in some degree "colored." Only two wards, the 7th and 15th, possessed a non-white majority.[78] Republicans relied on the rural parishes to outvote the city. St. Bernard had an excess of 273 colored persons, Plaquemines a surplus of 3,100.[79] Democrats contested Sypher's 1872 election. He had won, they claimed, only by fraud. Congress eventually

77 New Orleans *Louisianian*, August 15, 1874.
78 New Orleans *Abeille*, October 24, November 4, 1874.
79 New Orleans *Republican*, November 1, 1874.

agreed. Liberal Republican Effingham Lawrence took his seat on the last day of the 43rd Congress. He enjoyed a congressional career of three hours.

The remainder of New Orleans, along with the parishes of St. James, St. Charles, and St. John the Baptist, formed the Second Congressional District. Its occupant was another transplanted northerner with a military title, Gen. Lionel Sheldon. After three terms, Republicans denied Sheldon re-nomination. He seemed apt to make compromises with Democrats. His ingrate party, said the Shreveport *Times*, "shelved him ignominiously."[80] As in the 1st District, Republicans relied on the rural parishes. Of the district's urban wards, only the 16th and 17th contained a small majority of black residents. Nevertheless, with Sheldon shelved, T. Morris Chester paused in his soda shop campaign to announce his candidacy. Chester made civil rights his theme: "Louisiana will only reach that exalted destiny which she is capable of attaining when the rights of all men shall be equally respected."[81] At the convention Pinchback presided. Two black men, Chester and State Senator T.B. Stamps, were put in nomination. A white man, however, Judge Henry Dibble, took the prize.[82]

Dibble, as Sypher, had arrived with the conquering army. He arrived incomplete, having left a leg on the battlefield of Port Gibson. Disability did not diminish his determination. "A pronounced Radical," the New York *Tribune* warned, "an ardent party man and an enthusiast in his advocacy of centralization and strong government."[83] Dibble boasted ardent civil rights credentials. As judge of the 8th District Court in 1871 he was the first magistrate to deploy the power of Act 23, handing down his decision in Sauvinet v. Walker. "He gave us our first gleam of hope," said the *Louisianian*.[84] "A peg-legged devil," the *Abeille* snarled, "one of the worst, most hateful, implacable Radical agitators."[85] Currently Dibble served as New Orleans' superintendent of public schools.

To oppose Judge Dibble the Democrats advanced their most attractive candidate, dashing Gen. Randall Lee Gibson, flower of southern gentility, born on his ancestral plantation "Live Oaks" in Terrebonne Parish, a Confederate general at 31. He had barely failed in his first attempt at the congressional seat in 1872.[86]

80 Shreveport *Times*, August 15, 1874.
81 New Orleans *Republican*, July 9, 1874.
82 New Orleans *Republican*, August 8, 1874.
83 New York *Tribune*, October 27, 1874.
84 New Orleans *Louisianian*, August 15, 1874.
85 New Orleans *Abeille*, October 30, 1874.
86 See Mary Gorton McBride, *Randall Lee Gibson of Louisiana: Confederate General and New South Reformer* (Louisiana State University Press: 2007).

A Democratic challenger also appeared in the Second District. Ezekiel John Ellis could not match Gibson's wartime glamour. He had fallen into enemy hands early on and spent most of the time a prisoner. Ellis' name leapt to postwar prominence in the Colfax Massacre case, in which he acted as an attorney for the defense.[87] He brought his courtroom brilliance to the stump, "sparkling with wit, just as the people like it."[88] He also sparkled as a senior officer of New Orleans' White League militia.

Neither the gallant Gibson nor the eloquent Ellis spoke much about civil rights. This neglect resulted not from indulgence. In part it arose from familiarity with the state statute, and in part from a strategic calculation peculiar to the urban districts of New Orleans. In a multi-hued metropolis, Democrats preferred to draw voters away from the Republicans rather than alienate them. Across the city black Democratic clubs emerged. They appeared in the 3rd, 7th, 8th and 9th wards in Sypher's district, in the 1st, 2nd and 13th wards in Dibble's. The clubs attracted 150 participants to a meeting in the 7th ward and drew 250 to a rally in the 3rd. Black clubmen paraded at night through the 1st ward under protection of White League militias. Their banner bore a succinct slogan: "E. John Ellis, candidate for Congress in the Second District; Henry C. Dibble is our political enemy."[89]

Republicans questioned the spontaneity of these assemblies. Despite skepticism, the movement, partly at least, was genuine. William Alexander, organizer of the First Ward Democratic Club, spoke to members of the congressional investigative committee in 1875. Black people, he said, had proposed the alliance. Unemployment was high and Republican promises unfulfilled: "The Republicans used us for their benefit on election-day, and afterward they had no use for us – gave us no work." As White League agitation grew in August fear gripped black people. They sought to place themselves preemptively under the enemy's protection. In return they promised to vote the enemy's ticket. Three times, Alexander recalled, they appealed to the Crescent City White League. Twice they were rejected: "We told them that we had a number of men that wished to come under their platform if they would accept of us, and they laughed at me and made fun of me." The third try succeeded. Rebellion erupted on September 14. No massacre of black people (except black policemen) occurred. Grateful clubmen voted Democratic. Their leaders reaped rewards. William Alexander found employment as foreman of a work gang hired by the

87 Ellis' participation in that case, see Charles Lane, *The Day Freedom Died: The Colfax Massacre, the Supreme Court, and the Betrayal of Reconstruction* (New York: 2008), 180–181, 202.

88 New Orleans *Abeille*, September 2, 1874.

89 New Orleans *Abeille*, October 16, 1874.

City Supervisor of Improvements, Maj. E.A. Burke, coincidentally chief-of-staff to White League commander-in-chief Gen. Fred Ogden.[90]

Black Democratic clubs marched in the streets. Civil Rights played in the courts. Ezekiel Ellis won the 2nd District by 3,611 votes. Randall Gibson won the 1st by 4,700.

Louisiana Fourth District
George L. Smith (R), William Levy (D)
Population: 60% black

Beyond New Orleans the war zone commenced. Nowhere did blood flow more freely than in the 4th District. Indeed, if there was a sickness gnawing at the heart of American democracy in 1874, the Fourth Louisiana District was the poster-child of that disease. No southern district should have remained surer in the hands of the Republican Party. None was wrenched more brutally from those hands. Violence, murder, economic persecution stalked the frenzied Fourth. Civil rights lurked in the wings.

The 4th District's twelve counties ran from the state's northwest corner with Caddo, Bossier and Webster Parishes, south along the Texas border through Sabine and Vernon, and east into Louisiana's center, Rapides, Grant and Winn Parishes. It included the city of Shreveport and the town of Alexandria, heart of the White People's Party movement. Even in a state noted for mayhem, the 4th District stood out, site of celebrated massacres, Colfax in Grant Parish and Coushatta in Red River. Caddo Parish had won its own infamous appellation, "Bloody Caddo": 566 homicides distinguished that county in the first post-war decade, a quarter of the total for the whole state; 105 murders occurred in 1874 alone. Nearly all the victims were black. Almost all the assassins were white.[91]

Body counts rose in election years.[92] The presence of a nearly two-thirds black majority terrified white inhabitants. If black people voted, as the

90 Testimony of William Alexander, House Report 261, 677–682. Another black witness told a different story. William Riley, a house-painter, led the 13th Ward Democratic Club. White Leaguers, he said, threatened to evict him from his apartment and promised him a future of unemployment unless he organized the club. They gave him $175 with which to persuade his neighbors. This money he distributed to recruits in small amounts ("some wanted it to buy shoes, some wanted it for family use, some to pay house rent"). In return they pledged to vote as instructed. House Report 261, 304–307.

91 Gilles Vandal, "'Bloody Caddo:' White Violence against Blacks in a Louisiana Parish, 1865–1876," *Journal of Social History*, 25 (1991): 373–377.

92 Vandal, "Bloody Caddo," 379: "It was indeed impossible to be a Republican and to survive in Caddo during the fall of 1868 and the summer of 1874."

Fifteenth Amendment encouraged them to do, redemption would never come to the 4th District. It was necessary to discourage them from voting, or to persuade them to vote correctly. The task was daunting. But with the help of a full assortment of White League tactics it would be done.

The Republican incumbent George Luke Smith seemed, before the storm came upon him, assured of a continued and comfortable congressional career. Born in New Hampshire, educated at Union College in New York, he settled in Shreveport. He edited a Republican paper, the *Southwestern Telegram.* Smith's rise to Congress was fortuitous. The 1872 election had given the seat to a black man, Samuel Peters. Yellow fever struck down Peters just weeks before he would have taken his seat as the eighth black member of the House.[93] Democrats boycotted the special election. George Smith won the seat unopposed. Frederick Douglass' *New National Era* greeted him warmly: "Shrewd, independent, determined, cultivated, and self-possessed. He needs only the experience of a session to do noble work for his constituents."[94] "Few young men have a brighter future before them," the New Orleans *Republican* declared.[95] That future darkened quickly.

In the Fourth Congressional District was laid the egg of the White People's Movement. Partisan papers, the Alexandria *Caucasian,* the Shreveport *Times* and the Natchitoches *People's Vindicator,* incubated it. On July 4 the *Times* announced itself officially "The Organ of the White League." The White League announced itself the arm of the White People's Party. Together they announced an armed strategy: death to white Republicans. The *Vindicator* spelled out the idea:

> The white man's party is determined to rescue Louisiana from the polluting embrace of a hybrid pack of lecherous pimps.... They were conceived in sin, brought forth in pollution, nursed by filthy harpies, and dropped into Louisiana to show the world to what depth of corruption, disgrace and infamy human nature can stoop. We intend to clean out that Augean stable ... if we have to turn a river of liquid fire through it.[96]

The Shreveport *Times* put it plainly: "Any white man, be he carpet-bagger or renegade, who is detected [organizing Negro voters] ought to be dispatched

93 Monroe *Ouachita Telegraph,* October 3, 1873.
94 Washington *New National Era,* December 18, 1873.
95 New Orleans *Republican,* January 9, 1874.
96 Natchitoches *Vindicator,* August 29, 1874, quoted in House Report 261, Part 2, 283.

at once, and in the most summary manner."[97] The Coushatta killings provided a model. Black people too were targeted. In Caddo, Negro laborers and field-hands were reported slain around the countryside. In De Soto Parish whole families fled to the woods and swamps.[98] Lt. Gerlach reported from Red River Parish. Black people could hardly be found anywhere. They hid as fugitives in the woods, emerging only when blue-coated troops approached.

After the elections Congress delegated a committee of investigation to sort out the mess. George Frisbie Hoar led that inquest.[99] Even before leaving Boston, he received a disturbing letter. It was signed by 76 black citizens of Shreveport. Voting, they explained, was a hazardous enterprise in their vicinity.

> We the undersigned colored citizens of Caddo Parish … in the first place we will say very near every white man of this parish was an Officer of the [election] day, and at the same time well armed from one to two six shooters. In the second place whenever a colored man be led by a white man into the ballot-box with the white peoples ticket he would be shoved in either side of the door by one white man and pulled in by another. And the third is this. At the two ballot boxes at the Court House in Shreveport ropes was tied before the door so as to keep the Republicans back from voting, and white men placed there with great sticks in their hands and six shooters belted around them.[100]

Life itself, they further explained, was a hazardous enterprise.

> There are plenty of White Leguers here yet, thousands of them and hates a colored man on top side of the earth all to his labor and after that they will kill him, as quick as you can wink your eye and think they have done no harm and no law to protect them. And in regards of the colored men getting justice before a white jury, that thing is dead … the colored man's

97 Shreveport *Times*, June 20, 1874.

98 New Orleans *Louisianian*, August 22, 1874. House Report 261, Part 2, 178 (testimony of Lewis Merrill).

99 Hoar's committee provided him a congenial group of companions, including William Wheeler, William Frye and, on the Democratic side, his friend Clarkson Potter. For the journey, Potter sent him some advice. Pack a goodly supply of tea. Avoid at all costs the abominable mixture that resembled coffee at southern train stops and eateries. Clarkson Potter to George Frisbie Hoar, January 1, 1875. George Frisbie Hoar Papers, Massachusetts Historical Society.

100 "We the Undersigned" to George F. Hoar, January 5, 1875. George Frisbie Hoar Papers, Massachusetts Historical Society.

> life was not safe in jail nor no leading Republican life was not safe out of jail not in the Parish of Caddo.... Our ablest and best men, and Republican voters be sassinated our wives and our children and our fellow-men by thousands, clothless, hungry, stark naked, out of employment on account of supporting their Republican principal which we know is divine rights.... We the purposes of this statement do solemnly declare that we wright nothing but the truth, so help us God.

George Boutwell called it sedition, "as treasonable in purpose as the plans of the leaders in 1860 and 1861."[101] The New York *Tribune's* correspondent passed through the district in October. Black people had lost hope, "disheartened and disgusted," he wrote, "realizing the powerlessness of their protectors."[102] George Smith resigned himself to defeat. The black population of Bossier Parish, he reported, was thoroughly demoralized, "driven off and compelled to seek the protection of the Federal troops in Shreveport."[103]

Democrats left nothing to chance. To supplement physical coercion they unsheathed economic coercion. This took a properly businesslike form in the appearance of the Merchants' Pledges. They brought to life Father Ryan's dream: starve the Negroes into line. Loyal merchants promised to fire uncooperative employees. They promised to boycott other merchants and planters who failed to honor the pledges. The pledges circulated officially "in obedience to" the Shreveport (Democratic) Campaign Club.

> We the undersigned merchants of the city of Shreveport ... agree to use every endeavor to get our employees to vote the People's ticket at the ensuing election, and in the event of their refusing to do so, or in case they vote the Radical ticket, to refuse to employ them at the expiration of their present contracts.... [We] agree and pledge ourselves not to advance any supplies or money to any planter, the coming year, who will give employment or rent lands to laborers who vote the Radical ticket in the coming election.[104]

An initial wave of 130 businessmen swore to uphold the Merchants' Pledge. The *Times* printed their names. "It is to be hoped the example they have so

---

101 George Boutwell to William W. Clapp, January 15, 1875. George S. Boutwell Papers, Houghton Library, Harvard University.

102 New York *Tribune*, October 27, 1874.

103 Louisville *Courier-Journal*, October 13, 1874.

104 Shreveport *Times*, October 16, 1874.

nobly and fearlessly given will be everywhere followed."[105] Posters notified Louisianans. *Avertissements* appeared in French. Warnings informed readers of English.[106] Bilingual versions circulated.

Merchants, of course, who participated risked criminal charges, as one Shreveport businessman wrote the St. Louis *Republican:* "If all the merchants are arrested and carried away it will stop the trade of the town for the year."[107] Coercion or blacklisting of employees for political purposes violated the Enforcement Act of 1870 and also Section 5574 of the United States Code, Chapter 7, which mandated a $500 fine and imprisonment of one year for individuals guilty of such offense. Section 5575 increased the penalties to $5,000 and imprisonment for not more than ten years for those found to have conspired to accomplish such ends. Pledges sworn "in obedience" to the political club of Shreveport constituted a clear case of conspiracy. The press printed the pledges and identified the signatories. Conspirators conspired in the full light of day. No arrests came.

Finally President Grant acted. The army moved. Federal troops already garrisoned parts of Louisiana under overall command of Col. William Emory. Now reinforcements headed out, a full battalion of the 7th Cavalry, relieved of duty on the Dakota frontier. Four companies under command of Major Lewis Merrill disembarked at New Orleans on October 8. One rode for Alexandria. Detachments settled at Natchitoches, St. Martinville and Homer. Merrill himself occupied Shreveport.[108]

The major was not a favorite of white leaguers. He knew how to sweep for terrorists. He had polished his skills during the war. Commander of the 2nd Missouri Cavalry, dashingly known as "Merrill's Horse," he tracked down and dispatched guerillas in the lawless western theater of conflict. Post-war in South Carolina Merrill had led the army's operations against the Ku Klux

105 Shreveport *Times*, October 16, 1874.

106 Hoar preserved one specimen. He transcribed it into his committee's final report. He saved the original among his Louisiana souvenirs:

"Louisianais! Pour sauver votre patrie
il faut renvoyer les nègres.
(Par la faim l'animal le plus féroce est dompté.)
Louisianians! To save your country,
do not employ the negro.
(Wild beasts can only be tamed by hunger.)"

House Report 261, Part 3: 15. Original in George Frisbie Hoar Papers, Massachusetts Historical Society.

107 St. Louis *Republican*, October 27, 1874.

108 James E. Sefton, *The United States Army and Reconstruction, 1865–1877* (Baton Rouge: 1967), 226–228.

Klan.[109] Where Lewis Merrill appeared masked vigilantes disappeared. Democrats detested him. Senator Bayard demanded a court martial.[110] Republicans rather appreciated Merrill's conduct. "He was just the man for the work," Attorney-General Amos Akerman wrote in 1871 as the South Carolina cleanup took effect.[111] White Shreveporters unhappily agreed. "Insolent, domineering, brutal and heartless, he is precisely the sort of man to tyrannize over a defenseless people."[112]

Merrill ignored Order 75. He ignored Colonel Emory's order to keep his forces in barracks. He deployed detachments in Claiborne Parish, in Iberia and Iberville. The major devoted his efforts to undoing the merchants' pledges. On the 20th reports circulated. U.S. marshals were initiating arrests, beginning in Coushatta. "It is a most dastardly and barbarous business," cried the *Times*, "and should damn, in the opinion of the civilized world, all connected with it."[113] Reports were premature. Judge Aaron B. Levissee, United States Commissioner at Shreveport, drew up a list of suspect merchants. But he could not act. He held no warrants. No one had filed a complaint. Merrill reportedly was disgusted.

As the major feared, judicial dallying emboldened the White People's partisans. At Spring Ridge they prepared another pledge. "Even the negroes, when the matter is explained to them, admit its justice and fairness, and will avert the evil consequences to themselves by voting the people's ticket."[114] On the 23rd a new pledge appeared in Shreveport. Its 172 adherents represented "nearly every business house in the city." Planters in the countryside appended another 600 signatures. Women caught the spirit. "A large number of ladies signed an obligation to hire no servants whose husbands affiliated with the

109 See Lou Falkner Williams, *The Great South Carolina KuKlux Trials, 1871–1872* (Athens: Ga., 1996).

110 *Cong. Record*, 43rd Congress, 1st Session: 1378–1381. The New York *World* inveighed against Lewis Merrill. After one particularly abusive column, Merrill demanded satisfaction. He wrote Editor Manton Marble: "I ask as a matter of fact that you give me the author of this article or of the person who is responsible for its appearance in your columns." Marble replied coolly: "Your right to know the name of the writer of any article in the World is not conceded. Your right to know the name of the editor and proprietor of the World is not contested by, Your obd't sev't Manton Marble." Lewis Merrill to Manton Marble, April 9, 1874; Manton Marble to Lewis Merrill, April 20, 1874. Manton Marble Papers, Library of Congress.

111 Williams, *The Great South Carolina KuKlux Trials*, 45.

112 "A fitter and dirtier tool of despotism could not be found ... as prompt to wring tears of agony from a Southern woman's heart as his tongue is to command the imprisonment of a Southern gentleman." Shreveport *Times*, October 27, 1874.

113 Shreveport *Times*, October 20, 1874.

114 Shreveport *Times*, October 20, 1874.

Radical party." The *Times* was overjoyed. If Merrill wanted to arrest citizens, "he will have to arrest three-fourths of the white population of the parish." On October 24 yet another pledge joined the parade: 104 participants signed on in Summer Grove.[115]

Lewis Merrill filed the affidavit personally. Commissioner Levissee issued warrants for the arrest of five citizens: Edward Jacobs, of the firm of E.& L. Jacobs, John J. Horan, of the firm of Horan & Looney, George A. Pike, banker, W.P. Ford of Baisseau & Ford, and J.G. McWilliams. Behind these first victims stretched a great list, "merchants, professionals, and property holders." The major cited them for conspiracy to violate the Enforcement Act.[116] The Democratic Central Committee fired off a protest to Colonel Emory. Merrill had no standing, being neither a resident nor a voter of Louisiana. As an officer in uniform he had thrust the United States military into civil matters.[117] Merrill defied them. Everyone else was so cowardly, or so cowed, that they left him no option. "It would have been certain death for any citizen to have done this," he told reporters, "so I took upon myself the responsibility, and made the affidavit."[118] Col. Emory was displeased. He ordered a halt. Commissioner Levissee withheld further warrants.[119] A new pledge of 108 names emerged in De Soto Parish.[120]

A pledge, of course, was only as good as its enforcement. White League troopers saw to that. On election day black voters approached Shreveport. Armed outriders stopped them for inspection. Those permitted to proceed found poll-workers waiting who formed them into line and provided them with White People's Party tickets. All tickets must be held openly in the hand, palm up. After a voter deposited his ballot he received his reward, a certificate signed by the White People's Party, his license to return to work.[121] Recorders drew up an exit roll containing the names of all voters and a report of how they had voted.[122] Results were excellent. Spring Ridge poll in 1872 had given

115 Shreveport *Times*, October 25, 1874.

116 St. Louis *Republican*, October 26, 1874.

117 St. Louis *Republican*, October 27; Altoona *Morning Tribune*, October 27, 1874.

118 Chicago *Inter Ocean*, December 19, 1874.

119 Shreveport *Times*, October 28, 1874.

120 Harrisburg *Patriot*, October 30, 1874.

121 Senator Logan displayed one such certificate and had its facsimile reproduced in the Congressional Record. It was an exemplary document, preprinted, a blank space left for the voter's name and another for White League countersignature. *Cong. Record*, 43rd Congress, 2nd Session: 423.

122 Sheriff John de Lacy of Rapides Parish described the situation at Alexandria. Uncooperative voters were searched. "I saw them calling a man by his name, and I saw a man pull up his sleeve and ask him what was his name and where he lived; and he said 'my name is so

Republicans 160 votes. This time 11 Republican tickets somehow forced their way into the ballot box.

Major Merrill was reprimanded by his superior, Col. Emory. Ulysses Grant received the strangest souvenir. Black citizens of Caddo Parish wrote to apologize. "They [Democrats] swore by the God who made them that they would not give no one any work, who voted the Republican Ticket, and they have turned off a great many who voted the Republican Ticket, and we who voted the Democratic Ticket is still working."[123]

Nonsense, the Shreveport *Times* huffed. No one was "turned off." No lists of proscription existed.[124] That protest might have been more convincing had the *Times* not printed the proscriptions. After the election merchants of Summer Grove met to implement their pledge relative to the "labor question." They referred all inquiries to the list.[125]

Amid these events the 4th District's candidates seemed to recede into an afterthought. Democrats convened on August 25. Col. William Levy of Natchitoches took the nomination. He spoke at Shreveport on October 12: "Those who were not for us in this contest were against us; the disgrace of proving recreant now would attach to traitors and to their children, even to the third and fourth generations."[126] White League posters informed Congressman Smith: if reelected, he would be shot.[127] Smith was not shot. He was not reelected, despite a majority of 60% in his favor. Favorable voters feared to vote, or kept their jobs

and so; I live at such a place'; and a man said: 'I will put a black mark before your name.' I saw that done." House Report 261, Part 2, 373.

123 "How on Earth can we call our-selves Free People? when we was driven to the Polls, and made to vote the white man's Ticket, like hogs & dogs, and like beef cattle, with revolvers, and made to vote the white man's Ticket, the majority of colored people who voted the Republican in this parish, their lives aint worth $10." E. Allen et al. to Ulysses Grant, November 9, 1874. Simon, *Papers of Ulysses S. Grant*, vol. 25, 240.

124 Shreveport *Times*, December 29, 1874.

125 "We call upon the presidents and secretaries of the various clubs in the parish to furnish complete *alphabetical* lists of all the Radical voters whose names were taken down at the polls, and that said lists be forwarded at once to the office of the Shreveport TIMES. Resolved, That the TIMES be requested to print the said lists by wards and precincts for the benefit of the merchants and planters, and that the people be requested to purchase the said lists at such a price as will pay the paper the expense of publishing them." Shreveport *Times*, December 11, 1874. Other newspapers performed similar service. The Attakapas *Sentinel* printed a post-election list of white men who had failed to vote the white man's ticket, and also Negroes who were to be rewarded for voting as instructed. House Report 261, Part 2, 868.

126 Shreveport *Times*, October 13, 1874.

127 *Cong. Record*, 43rd Congress, 2nd Session: 424. Lewis Merrill testified later before Hoar's investigative committee. Could he, William Wheeler inquired, enter west Louisiana? Merrill's reply: "He would probably have the top of his head shot off." Would he, Merrill,

and voted unfavorably. Sabine Parish presented a case in point. It possessed 1,847 black residents. It recorded precisely 2 votes for George L. Smith.

Louisiana, Fifth District
Frank Morey (R), William B. Spencer (D)
Population: 63% black

The 5th District occupied the state's northeast, from Claiborne and Bienville Parishes to the banks of the Mississippi, through Carroll, Madison, Tensas and Concordia. Monroe in Ouachita Parish was its principal town. Seven of the fourteen parishes held a white majority. Those majorities were overwhelmed by immense black numbers in the fertile Mississippi River districts. In Concordia 700 whites dwelt among 9,000 blacks. In Madison 900 whites lived alongside 7,000 blacks. Tensas was home to 1,400 white and 11,000 black residents. Overall black persons held nearly a two-thirds majority.

Incumbent Congressman Frank Morey was white, 34 years old, a native of Boston. A clean-shaven young man, he had held the 5th District seat in the 41st, 42nd and 43rd Congresses. Democrats found him a person of no account: "an insignificant man, who has never been anything but a pack-animal for the Radical ring."[128] In the civil rights pack he was not insignificant. Even before Ben Butler introduced H.R.796, he had proposed an independent version, H.R.473. Frank Morey's name sprang to the forefront of civil rights.

White people believed they could regain the 5th District, despite its enormous black presence. Chief among the hopeful redeemers was George W. McCranie, publisher of the Monroe *Ouachita Telegraph.* Twice before, in 1870 and 1872, he had run for the seat. Twice Congressman Morey returned to Congress and George McCranie returned to his newspaper office. While he did not run again, McCranie devoted himself to ending his antagonist's congressional career. He disavowed the meretricious attractions of Gen. Beauregard's Unification Movement.[129] Violence would lead the way.

White League operations fit comfortably in the 5th District. A half-century later, Henry Clay Warmoth recalled Ouachita Parish, "one of the most extreme and relentless of all localities in the State."[130] Republicans in Ouachita, Union,

---

venture there in civilian attire? The reply: "I should want to borrow a Gatling gun at least." House Report 261, Part 2, 181.

128 New York *Tribune*, October 27, 1874.

129 Williams, "Unification Movement," 363.

130 Warmoth, *War, Politics and Reconstruction*, 199–200.

Lincoln, Jackson, Claiborne and Franklin Parishes were terrorized, the Nashville *Banner* reported; they could hardly be induced to register, let alone vote.[131]

The 7th Cavalry tried to help. Second-Lieutenant Benny Hodgson took charge. He was short on years, only four years out of West Point. He was short on experience, despite the adoption of a fierce mustache, but full of zeal. Hodgson and his heartless dragoons, so the *Telegraph* cried, scoured the district. He led his men to the town of Homer in Claiborne Parish where White League operatives had disrupted political meetings. He advanced to Vienna in Lincoln Parish where White Leaguers menaced United States Commissioner David Jewett. Everywhere, white people's partisans bemoaned, the lieutenant pursued his mission with inhumanity. He allowed not even a farewell to wife or loved one. Asked by one victim to show his warrant, he "drew his [Colt] repeater, saying 'This is my authority.'" He tore up writs of habeas corpus. He was also (the *Telegraph* declared) a coward. To cover his escape from Vienna he ordered his men to cut the telegraph wires. Hodgson's conduct – forcible arrests, destruction of public property – led to a court martial. The court, Col. Philippe de Trobriand presiding, dealt gently with the young officer. It reprimanded him, but released him in time to find death at the hands of Lakota warriors.[132]

Republicans convened on August 20 at the town of Delta. They united behind Frank Morey. Yet they prepared for the worst. Returning from the convention, former congressman Jasper Blackburn paused to purchase two new Winchester repeating rifles – as if, the *Telegraph* remarked, he feared for his life.[133]

The Democratic/White People's Party gathered at Vienna. William B. Spencer became the nominee by acclamation. Captain Spencer was 39, a noted lawyer, later a justice of the State Supreme Court.[134] He was not a fiery orator. White League militias supplied the fire. White League papers supplied the oratory. "Now hath Caesar crossed the Rubicon," the *Telegraph* declaimed. "Rome united in defense will give him welcome." Beware the curse of civil rights. "All the rascality and villainy the Radicals have done before might still have been endured … but in its stead is set up the horrid, repellent, hideous monster of *Negro Equality*!"[135]

131 Nashville *Banner*, October 9, 1874.

132 Findings of the court martial, December 30, 1874, House Report 261, Part 2, 950–952.

133 Monroe *Ouachita Telegraph*, August 21, 1874.

134 Monroe *Ouachita Telegraph*, September 25, 1874.

135 Monroe *Ouachita Telegraph*, August 14, 1874. Caesar's invasion, one might have said, was not the happiest historical allusion, Caesar having gone on from the Rubicon to triumph over the citizens of Rome.

Democratic champion John McEnery toured the district. Violence was the order of the day. "I should prefer to go to war rather than submit to the Civil Rights Bill if it should become a law.... Get every public opinion up to a white heat. Make every carpet-bagger, scalawag, radical or negro vote our ticket or leave the State. Let it be peaceful if we can, but if necessary apply force in all cases."[136]

Congressman Morey urged calm. At Monroe his rally featured a speech by P.B.S. Pinchback. Pinchback's words, even the *Telegraph* admitted, were "free from rant and had the semblance of fairness and moderation." Looking to black people in the audience, "'There are many of you here who bear the scars of the lash upon your back,' [he said], and then he added deprecatingly – 'But I hope you will forget those scars.'"[137]

With a two-thirds black majority Frank Morey should have won by several thousand votes. He eked out a margin of 1,221. Just enough black voters, thanks perhaps to Benny Hodgson's "inhumanity," managed to vote. The Democrats, however, were not to be denied. Where the White League failed the 44th Congress succeeded. Hodgson's zeal saved and lost the election. His rough-riding provided Democrats grounds to contest. The newly-Democratic House Elections Committee cast out the result, cast Congressman Morey from his seat, and presented that seat to William B. Spencer.

Louisiana, 3rd District
Chester B. Darrall (R), Joseph A. Breaux (D)
Population: 52% black

White League tactics bore fruit in Louisiana's most heavily black districts. In its least black district they failed. Democrats in the 3rd District faced a difficult task. Their efforts in 1874 added to a record of disappointment. The district had elected Republican Chester B. Darrell to the 41st, 42nd and 43rd Congresses. It elected him to the 44th. It very nearly returned him to the 45th; it did return him to the 47th Congress. The 3rd proved a frustrating district. White people seemed inclined to tolerance and moderation.

The 7th Cavalry again provided a presence. Its representative was the elegant Italian, First-Lieutenant Carlo Camillo di Rudio or, as he called himself in his new home, Charles De Rudio.[138] He held his post at Breaux Bridge.

136 *House Report* 261, Part 2: 298–299.

137 Monroe *Ouachita Telegraph*, October 23, 1874.

138 The lieutenant came complete with waved hair and waxed mustachios. He had already led a hopelessly adventurous life: from the ranks of the Risorgimento to the back alleys

St. Martin Parish stood out as a stronghold of White League activity. The 3rd Infantry's Capt. James Gageby, commanding the area, ordered extra detachments to Breaux Bridge where the resident white people, the "swampers," had thoroughly terrorized the black population. Lt. Lorenzo Cook of the 3rd Infantry supported De Rudio. Cook too was a veteran of the frontier wars. Indians, he concluded, were a civilized enemy, compared with white men of Louisiana. "If I could go back to the plains, I would rather pay my own expenses. I would rather be among the Comanches." Let black people vote carefully, he advised. Only "young men who had not heavy families" should cast a ballot.[139] De Rudio nevertheless, having been an insurgent himself, understood counterinsurgency work.

The 3rd District had been redrawn. Shorn of its northerly appendages, Baton Rouge, East and West Feliciana Parishes, it stretched across the southern coast from Lafourche and Terrebonne through Cameron and Calcasieu to the Texas border. At its heart lay the parishes of Lafayette, St. Martin, Iberville and Iberia. The population held some 62,500 black persons and just under 57,000 whites.

Chester Darrall was, at 32, the youngest member of the Louisiana delegation. "One of the weakest most undeserving and insignificant carpet-baggers who ever misrepresented a decent State in Congress," the New York *Tribune* concluded.[140] On the Civil Rights Bill Congressman Darrall misrepresented nothing. Civil rights statutes, he informed the House, would work as they worked in Louisiana. "We paid the penalty for holding a people for years in a cruel bondage.... Let us as a nation be fair and just to all our people, or else divine Providence will again chasten us in wrath."[141]

Democrats struggled to overcome the voters' tolerance. The Civil Rights Bill might wake them up. The Thibodaux *Sentinel* sounded the alarm. True, Louisiana already possessed a civil rights law. It seemed harmless. But federal

---

of Paris' revolutionary underground to America's Civil War, with a stop-over on Devil's Island. He had hunted down Ku Klux in South Carolina. Later he found himself hunted down by Native Americans along the Little Big Horn River. According to one's perspective he was an idealist and a patriot, or a terrorist and a murderer. Democratic sheets preferred the latter characterization. To wit, they cited his participation in one of Europe's most spectacular political conspiracies, the attempted assassination of Napoleon III in 1858. The bomb-throwers struck the imperial carriage on its way to the Opera. They succeeded in mangling 150 bystanders, as the emperor stepped from the wreckage unharmed. The leader of the plot, Felice Orsisi, went to the guillotine. Carlo went to Guiana, whence he engineered a sensational escape. He did not even give Louisianans the satisfaction of dying at the Little Big Horn. Surrounded by hostile warriors, hidden in reeds for a day and a night, he crawled to safety.

139 House Report 261, Part 2, 342–344.

140 New York *Tribune*, October 27, 1874.

141 Darrall's speech, *Cong. Record*, 43rd Congress, 1st Session, App., 477–480.

statutes were worse, far worse. "Let it once become a United States law, and its infernal objects will be consummated in a style much more effectual than ornamental."[142] White people beware. "Any man who keeps a hotel, or any poor woman who takes a few boarders by which she earns a subsistence for her hungry children ceases by that action to have any control in his or her own home." An innkeeper could refuse accommodation to a white person. He might turn away President Grant, but not a Negro. They would overrun hotels. Then they would swarm into white people's homes, into their parlors, even their bedrooms. One might wake to find a black face snoring on the same pillow.

> If the civil rights bill can force a negro into a coffee house kept by a white man and compel the proprietor to sell him a dram at the bar, or compel a hotel keeper to furnish a dirty ragged negro with a dinner or bed, cannot the same or a similar bill compel his admission into a private house and make the owner furnish the vagabond a meal and a bed, and if there should be a double bed will it not give the loafer a right to the half of that bed, no matter who occupies the other half?[143]

The White League proposed a simpler message. An exalted plea: unity or treason! La Ligue Blanche placed its call to arms in the *Sentinel's* French language edition.

> The White League believes that one cannot serve two masters. Therefore those who are not for us – no matter what reasons they may profess – are against us.... There can be no equivocation; we must win, do you understand, at any price. We are pure. We are free. We are Caucasians, most of us with the ancient Gallic blood in our veins. We stand for truth, justice, and civilization! ... If the enemy throws down the gauntlet and war begins, so be it! God's will be done! Let us rise, thrilled, trembling, as one people, and let us utter from the bottom of our lacerated hearts that noble and fearsome cry: "Live Free or Die."[144]

The Democratic nominee preferred a quieter tone. Joseph A. Breaux of Iberia, formerly a Liberal Republican, sought unity in appeasement. Voters displayed a moderate streak. He moderated his message. He disliked the state debt, he said. Taxes, he thought, were too high. He failed to echo the White League's cry of race, purity and civilization.

142 Thibodaux *Sentinel*, August 29, 1874.
143 Thibodaux *Sentinel*, September 19, 1874.
144 Thibodaux *Sentinel*, August 29, 1874.

Congressman Darrall also soothed the district's centrist voters. At the Thibodaux Court House Pinchback joined the rally. The *Sentinel's* reporter observed. He could find nothing outrageous to relate, no affront to white men or women. He found Pinchback quite gentlemanly, "a very fluent and pleasing speaker."[145]

Democrats resorted to economic repression. Planters at St. Martinville and New Iberia, Lt. De Rudio reported, dispossessed a hundred black tenants. They exiled a further 160 families in Iberia Parish.[146] Merchants' Pledges caused the unemployment of workers in St. Martin Parish.[147] It was not quite enough. Chester Darrall joined a select company, a handful of southern white Republicans who returned to the 44th Congress.

Louisiana, Sixth District
Charles E. Nash (R), Joseph M. Moore (D)
Population: 61% black

Redemption endured an irritating setback in the 3rd District. In the 6th it suffered an unconscionable betrayal. In the 3rd supine white voters allowed a small black majority to outvote them. In the 6th civilized white people, those for whom the White League existed, opposed its existence.

The 6th was a new creation, drawn to replace the state's at-large seat. Republicans drew it to provide a large black majority. A marvel of gerrymandering, the Opelousas *Courier* dubbed it, "a tongue of earth" running west from the Mississippi line in Washington and St. Tammany Parishes.[148] It incorporated the capital city, Baton Rouge, and its surrounding parishes filled with black folk: East Baton Rouge Parish, with 11,000 blacks to 6,000 whites; East Feliciana with a ratio of two to one; West Feliciana, with 9,000 black residents to barely 1,500 whites; Pointe Coupee Parish with an almost three to one black majority. Against such odds the White People's Party struggled manfully. Voter intimidation, employment threats, economic sanctions, all must be brought to bear. To its dismay, it met resistance. White men defied their white brethren.

145 Thibodaux *Sentinel*, November 7, 1874.

146 New Orleans *Republican*, January 26, 29; Louisville *Courier-Journal*, January 29, 1875. Lt. De Rudio, having planted bombs in Paris, spoke fluent French, allowing him to eavesdrop on unsuspecting natives. Doctors, he reported, informed black patients: expect no medical services if they voted incorrectly. White Leaguers warned black men: once the army departed, "then we will fix you." House Report 261, Part 2, 168.

147 House Report 261, Part 2, 346–347.

148 Opelousas *Courier*, June 27, 1874.

The White People's Party inaugurated its campaign early enough. It held its organizational meeting in St. Landry Parish on April 27. Its leaders, future Congressman Edward T. Lewis and Alcée Dupré, observed that fusion had failed. Only a race line campaign could succeed. Starvation was the plan. Destitution would bring the Negro to heel. Most black people were already destitute, or very nearly. Destitution therefore must be made utter and complete. Servants must be discharged, menials must be dismissed – no commercial contact at all. Field-hands must be chased from the plantations.

> The negroes must not only be excluded from clerkships in white stores, but they must not be allowed to trade there in any manner – to buy or sell. They must be driven from the cabins and decks of steamers, and from serving in hotels, and from all such employment generally. They must not be allowed to drive drays, wagons, carriages or carts.... Above all let negroes be driven out of our fields and the whites driven in.[149]

The plan seemed promising. White League militia were set to enforce it. Then, most unexpectedly, white men objected to the White League. Farmers needed labor. There was no supply of white field-hands to be "driven in" if blacks were driven out. Landowners preferred not to see their crops rot in the fields. Somebody had to drive the drays, or even rotten crops would not reach market. Storeowners required customers. Black customers paid with the same coin as whites. Steamboats needed deckhands.

White People's papers pleaded. Greedy planters, could they not see beyond narrow self-interest? "Read the Bible, friend planter," the Opelousas *Courier* counseled, "for in it you will find that 'no man can serve two masters.' He will love one and hate the other, says that good book; and if these white men love the negro they have no love for us."[150] A cabal of planters, serving mammon not God, spurned the biblical wisdom. They professed to be white men. They claimed to be Democrats. But they refused to commit economic suicide for the sake of white civilization. Distinguished persons led them: Henry L. Garland, George W. Hudspeth, and Judge Edmond Estilette, later Speaker of the Louisiana Assembly. As the White League prepared operations in St. Landry Parish, they proposed a parlay: "to meet with the partisans of this organization at those times and places they may be pleased to name, so as to debate in the presence of our co-parishioners the propriety of establishing such said organization."[151]

149 Opelousas *Journal*, quoted in New Orleans *Republican*, June 24, 1874.
150 Opelousas *Courier*, May 30, 1874.
151 Opelousas Courier, May 30, 1874.

White League representatives agreed to meet the malcontents in a public forum. But the League imposed conditions. Ladies must be invited. Dissident planters must state their political affiliations. White League speakers must have the rebuttal. A firm vote would settle the question. The planters declined to enter a lion's den designed by the lions. They recoiled especially at the presence of women, females guaranteed to react hysterically to suggestions of a Negro invasion of their hearths, their homes, their bodies.

The League took charge of the local paper. On May 30 Léonce Sandoz, proprietor of the Opelousas *Courier,* informed his readers. He yielded control of his editorial column henceforth and until the election to the voice of the White League. The voice promptly announced its rally would assemble at the Opelousas Court House on the Fourth of July. The planters yielded. They accepted their opponents' preconditions.

The anniversary of the nation's birth, a unique spectacle unfolded. White men argued with white men over the means of achieving white men's supremacy. Henry Garland spoke first. He declared that he was a Democrat. He adhered to the principles of the party – those principles, that is, it had declared in its Baltimore platform of 1872: equal rights under the law for all citizens. The White League intended to betray that platform, to deprive Negroes of their rights. George Hudspeth followed. A Fusionist, he could not agree to the politics of exclusion. An army outnumbered operates tactically, "by maneuvering, strategy, &c." White people must maneuver, seek accommodation rather than insist on antagonism and alienation. White League orators insisted on alienation and antagonism. According to the *Courier,* now under League control, those orators won a glorious victory. "Every White League speaker was vociferously cheered throughout."[152]

The victory proved less glorious than the *Courier's* partisan reporter reported. The debate left the White League shaken. Its leaders thought it wise to lower their tone. They published a clarification the very next day.

> While we unite as white people so as to secure the supremacy of the white race in this State, our purpose is to place the lawgiving power in the hands of men who will protect our property, who will not rob us ... men who know how to read and write and understand the rights of person and property; it is not to destroy any rights that the law has conferred upon the negro. Let him vote as he wants and work as he may.[153]

152 Opelousas *Courier,* July 11, 1874.
153 New Orleans *Republican,* July 5, 1875.

Republicans chose a black man as candidate. Charles Edmund Nash of Opelousas won the nomination over J. Henri Burch.[154] Nash was a solid establishment choice. In pre-war days he had been a bricklayer, later an inspector in the New Orleans Custom House. He saw his advantage. He did his best not to ruffle or reunite a disunited opposition.

Democrats nominated Joseph M. Moore, also of Opelousas, a lawyer and former state legislator. He ran a vigorous campaign. But it was not the White League campaign. Confronted by the division between the planters and the League, he chose the planters. Only two weeks after the Fourth of July forum the *Courier* reported the birth of a new political organization. In opposition to the Opelousas White League Club, it called itself the Opelousas Democratic Club. It supported the party but not the party's white knights. Henry Garland and E.D. Estilette signed its list. Newsman Léonce Sandoz joined them. He liberated his editorial page. Topping the list appeared the name of Joseph Moore.[155]

Charles Nash proceeded to Congress. What should have been an enormous margin was reduced to a fraction, 1,071 votes. But it held. The *Courier* fumed. White people offered Negroes friendship. Negroes handed them humiliation. "With the help of blind and benighted voters even the most worthless Negro can gain the highest honors."[156]

Louisiana's elections ended. In January George Hoar's investigative committee arrived. In February Hoar concluded his hearings. Capt. J.H. Gageby of the 3rd Infantry was the final witness. Republican counsel Hugh Campbell posed the final question.

> If in any northern State all the strong and intelligent and rich men were on one side, and all the weak and poor and ignorant were on the other side, and if the strong and the intelligent and the rich combined together in leagues and conspiracies, and secret societies, and open societies, and had all the press, and all the merchants, and all the banks, and all the avenues to employment in their possession, and if they should form stringent combinations for the non-employment of the poor men unless they should vote at their dictation, and then, not satisfied with that, would murder them by thousands, or hundreds, and then, not satisfied with that, would drive hundreds of them from the polls, and then have a very

154 New Orleans *Republican*, August 9, 1874.
155 Opelousas *Courier*, July 18, 1874.
156 *Courier des Opelousas*, November 14, 1874.

> peaceable election on the day of the election, would that be considered a fair, free, and peaceable election in the North?[157]

Before the no doubt astonished captain could reply, Hoar came to his relief: "I think the committee might possibly be left to judge of that." The committee judged. It judged the elections free and fair. Two Republicans, William Walter Phelps and Charles Foster, joined Democrats Samuel Marshall and Clarkson Potter to write the majority report. The White League, they decided, did no harm, an inoffensive political club. Black voters voted freely. Murders were incidental, a natural byproduct of electoral effervescence. Chairman Hoar, joined by William Frye and William Wheeler, submitted a minority report: "The free institutions of the whole United States will not long survive the destruction of those in the South."[158]

---

157 House Report 261, Part 2, 711.
158 House Report 261, Part 3, 29.

CHAPTER 10

Greeley's Ghost: Elections in Arkansas, Texas, Missouri and Maryland

1 Arkansas

Arkansas Democrats rejected the call for a White League-style racial campaign. They relied on arithmetic. The state was white. Victory was assured if white men voted. There was no need for violence. Violence would benefit only Republicans, allowing them to contest and overturn the results. Arkansas Democrats walked softly and carried a twig. Some even gave civil rights a friendly nod. Should Congress in its wisdom enjoin Sumner's Civil Rights Bill upon them, they raised no objection.

One man primarily was responsible for this situation, and he was not a Democrat: Hon. Powell Clayton, Republican, once governor, currently United States senator, perhaps the most forceful "carpetbagger" to dominate a southern state. In 1871 he had relinquished the governorship to take his seat in the Senate. He left his place in the friendly hands of a Republican, Ozra Hadley. Events upset his plans. The election of 1872 commenced the destruction of the Republican Party in Arkansas, a downfall for which Sen. Clayton was honest enough to blame himself. The Liberal Republican movement tore the party's vote apart. Democrats emerged the only ones to gain.

In that year's election for governor the genuinely radical candidate, Joseph Brooks, ran as a Liberal Republican. Brooks, an Abolitionist before the war, a chaplain of the Colored Infantry during the war, owned radical beliefs, but he had developed a contentious dislike of Powell Clayton. The senator handpicked a rival. Elisha Baxter had been a Whig. Now he professed Republican allegiance. He could, Clayton hoped, attract Democratic votes. It was a monumental miscalculation.[1]

In an election rife with fraud, Baxter emerged a much-disputed winner. He turned at once to bite the hand that fed him. "I discovered," Clayton recalled, in a considerable understatement, "that we had made a bad political deal."[2] Baxter reached out to Democrats. A referendum ended the disfranchisement

1 Powell Clayton, *The Aftermath of the Civil War in Arkansas* (New York: 1969), 346–347.

2 Clayton, *Aftermath*, 347; see also Thomas A. DeBlack, *With Fire and Sword: Arkansas, 1871–1874* (Fayetteville: 2003).

of the white masses. Special elections swept Democrats into the legislature. Another referendum authorized a convention to rewrite the Reconstruction constitution of 1868, effectively to undo Republican control of Arkansas. Clayton reconciled with Brooks. Brooks seized the governor's mansion. Baxter mobilized to take it back.

In the spring of 1874 the Brooks-Baxter War became a shooting affair. Earthworks surrounded the capital. Baxter forces won a pitched battle at New Gascony. Brooks' men killed a score of the enemy in the ambush of the steamboat *Hallie.* After a month of chaos, President Grant ordered federal troops to intervene. He decided in favor of the officially-elected Governor Baxter. Democrats recognized Baxter's victory as their own. They also acknowledged that that victory had occurred courtesy of the indulgence of the Republican administration in Washington. They must do nothing to jeopardize that indulgence: no violence against black people; no agitation against civil rights bills. All that could wait for another day.

The immediate result of the Brooks-Baxter War was the creation of a new state constitution. Baxter's victory ensured its consummation. A constitutional convention assembled. Voters ratified its handiwork in October. A new election for governor commenced. Democrats offered Baxter the honor. He declined. They nominated Augustus Garland, one of their own. His election would signal Arkansas' redemption.

For Republicans salvation could come only one way: federal intervention.[3] If they could show that Democratic success was tainted by violence, Congress might reverse the course of events. As the election approached Clayton fine-tuned his antennae, searching for Democratic "outrages." He organized the Southern Republican Convention to dramatize the situation. Arkansas Democrats understood. They must commit no misdeed. The elections of 1874 found them on their best behavior. Extend the hand of friendship to Republicans equally and to black people. Thus Arkansas Democrats, alone among their southern kin, gave the Civil Rights Bill not merely kind treatment but practical endorsement. What they confessed in their hearts nobody knows. What they professed on the stump we know. Politics obliged. Democrats obeyed.

Arkansas' Republicans, faced with opponents who refused to fight, were reduced to taunting. They denied the validity of the new constitution. They refused to participate in the gubernatorial election. They assembled in state convention at Little Rock on September 15. By then Baxter rested safely in the governorship. The constitutional convention had met. The constitution lay

3 DeBlack, *With Fire and Sword*, 224–225.

ready for the voters' approval. In a few weeks that approval would signal the end of Republican ascendancy in Arkansas.

Party faithful showed up for a last hurrah.[4] Senator Stephen Dorsey presided. Rhetoric remained defiant. "One good man after another is falling all over the South," declared Sidney M. Barnes. "How many of our friends have been murdered, how many school-houses burned in the Southern States? Language cannot express." Black delegate William C. Grey reminded his colleagues: "This is not a war of races, but a war of liberty."[5] Powell Clayton looked northward for help: "The north will not see its defenders massacred and murdered." He all but pleaded with Democrats to commit some bloody outrage, something, anything that would allow him to turn to Congress. "Fear of Congress now causes the Democracy to hold back their hordes of cut-throats. When these Democrats dip their hands into the blood of the colored race, you can't break them until you break their necks." Congress, he hoped, would accomplish the neck-breaking – if only he could stir it into action.[6]

Democrats refused to take the bait. The Little Rock *Gazette* warned white people. The Republicans' "outrage" scheme had Arkansas in its crosshairs.[7] To foil the plot there must be no violence, or even violent rhetoric, no matter what provocation Republicans applied. The Democratic convention met at Little Rock on September 9. Delegates called thunderously for Elisha Baxter. He declined to be their candidate. Augustus H. Garland took up the standard. The convention made no false step into the pit Powell Clayton had dug. The resolutions drew no race line, no call for white men to rally and crush the Negro in their midst. Unite in good fellowship.

> We do and will forever discountenance, reprobate and unqualifiedly condemn lawlessness, violence and outrage, wheresoever and whensoever found, and we demand in the name of the State equal protection, equal justice and equal rights to all, from the highest to the lowest, and without regard to race, color, or previous condition, and we unqualifiedly and unreservedly pledge ourselves to the same.[8]

On September 23 Garland appeared at the town of Monroe. Black people came out to hear him. The new constitution, he said, gave those people "all the rights

4 Little Rock *Gazette*, September 16–17; Chicago *Inter Ocean*, September 20; New York *Times*, September 28, 1874.
5 Little Rock *Gazette*, September 16.
6 Little Rock *Gazette*, September 17.
7 Little Rock *Gazette*, August 29, October 21, 1874.
8 Little Rock *Gazette*, September 25, 1874.

and immunities under the law which we ourselves enjoy." He was, the Little Rock *Gazette* observed, overcome with emotion. His "big heart almost swelled to bursting, and his eyelids could scarcely retain the tears gushing from his manly and noble bosom."[9]

Continuing on to Forrest City, Garland's smooth delivery encountered some turbulence. Another speaker, Col. R.A. Howard, addressed the crowd. Howard, once a Republican, was an old adversary of Powell Clayton. Unfortunately, he mentioned one cause of his disaffection: the Civil Rights Bill. His remarks produced precisely the effect Democrats did not desire. Excited black spectators interrupted him. Hoots and cries resounded. Garland hastened to repair the damage. After the speeches he took black people aside to provide reassurance. Democrats wished no harm, not to them nor to "their civil and political rights and interests."[10]

Finally Garland performed the ultimate pirouette. He pledged not only to accept but to honor the legacy of the late beatified Charles Sumner. At Lewisburg on October 7, he spoke. One of the largest gatherings people could remember in Conway County attended. He defended the new constitution: "Our opponents predicted that when the constitutional convention met in Little Rock last July it would be but the assembly of ku-klux or white leaguers, and they would at once proceed to take from the colored man every right he had, even to put him back into slavery." On the contrary, the constitution loved all men. Article 2 guaranteed equality before the law. "And if I am the executive to enforce that constitution he [the black man] shall have his rights as completely as I have mine." Article 27 outlawed slavery. "And if I am your governor, and the effort is made [to re-enslave black people], I shall use all the power I have under this constitution to prevent it." Article 3 guaranteed the right to vote. Article 14 mandated public education (integrated schools not included). "And if in this race of education, the colored boys learn better and faster than my boys I will not cry at all, nor will I feel the least jealousy."[11] He praised Arkansas' Civil Rights Act. He welcomed the prospect of a federal companion.

> In the acts of the legislature of 1873, pages 15–19 (No. 12), we have a "civil rights bill" which is now in force – almost a copy, if I mistake not, of the bill Mr. Sumner shortened his life in vainly trying to get Congress to pass. If Congress next winter can get up one more definite, more minute and more specific in giving rights to the colored man, I would be pleased to look upon and observe it. That [Arkansas] act is now in force, as I said,

9 Little Rock *Gazette*, September 30, 1874.
10 Little Rock *Gazette*, September 23, 1874.
11 Little Rock *Gazette*, October 9, 1874.

> and I know of no one who wants to repeal it, and certainly I do not want it repealed, and will not favor its repeal.... If there is any complaint among our colored friends as to the terms of this act, or as to its not being enforced, I have not heard of them, and I am persuaded there have been none.... If elected I mean to be true to that platform and that constitution in spirit and letter, and every right held by the colored man shall be as carefully handled and protected as those of the white citizen.[12]

Republicans found their positions maddeningly co-opted. Joseph Brooks spoke at Little Rock on the 27th. Garland's Lewisburg speech infuriated him.

> In 1868, January, a constitutional convention assembled in this hall, and here are the resolutions presented by Hon. M.C. Rose [Democrat] calling for a white man's government in a white man's country.... This is how these Bourbons started out.... Brother Garland asserted that there was a good civil rights bill on the statute books, and there was no disposition to repeal it.... Is that the attitude of the Bourbon party now, before God and before man on the civil rights question? ... Which represents the southern people, Mr. Rose's resolutions, or Mr. Garland's speech?[13]

The *Gazette* answered: Garland's speech. Governor Baxter had validated the state statute. Augustus Garland pledged to uphold it. What more did Republicans want? "What better guarantees could we give? These issues are things of the past in Arkansas."[14] Congress sent an investigative committee in 1875. Among its members was Jasper Ward. It found no cause to undo Democratic triumph. Arkansas Republicans occupied three of four seats in the 43rd Congress. They occupied none in the 44th. (see Map 8, below)

> Arkansas, Third District
> William Hynes (R), William Wilshire (D), Hugh Thomason (I)
> Population: 81% white

In the topsy-turvy world of Arkansas politics politicians spun allegiances with dizzy abandon, none more dizzily than dark-bearded William W. Wilshire. In 1872 he had been elected to Congress from the 3rd District as a Republican.

---

12 Little Rock *Gazette*, October 9, 1874.
13 Little Rock *Gazette*, October 28, 1874.
14 Little Rock *Gazette*, October 29, 1874.

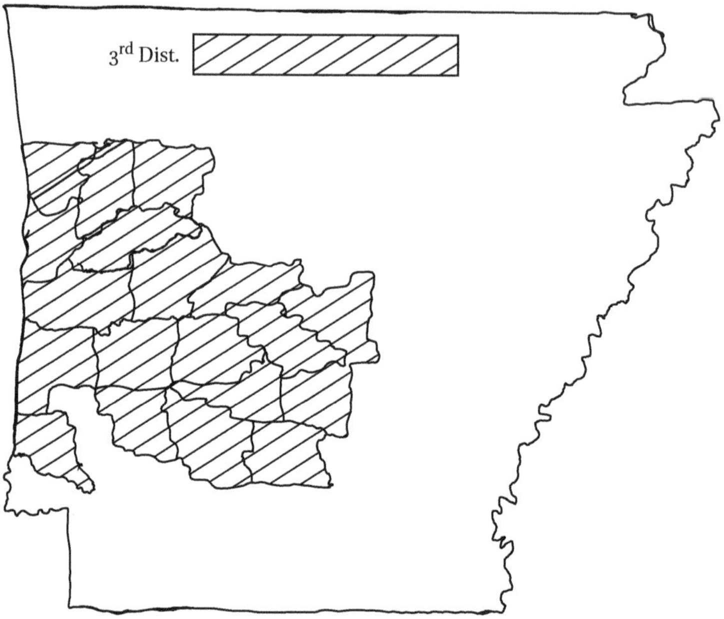

MAP 8 Congressional Districts, Arkansas
SOURCE: AUTHORS OF *WELCOMING RUIN*.

A Republican Congress threw him out. It gave his place to a Democrat. Redistricting reshuffled Arkansas' congressional seats. The Democrat, Thomas Gunter, sought reelection in a new 4th District. Republican Wilshire deftly became a Democrat to run again in the 3rd – though Democrats suspected him of remaining at heart a Republican. His opponent was William Hynes, previously a Liberal Republican. Now he became a Republican, in order to oppose Wilshire, once a Republican now a Democrat.

Civil rights also presented a looking-glass world. Wilshire, while a Republican, failed twice to vote for his party's bill. Hynes, as a Liberal, voted for the Republican measure twice. Nevertheless, when civil rights came up in the campaign, the Republican-turned-Democrat, who had abstained, endorsed it. The Liberal-turned-Republican, who had endorsed it, denounced him for endorsing it.

Judge William Wilshire qualified as a carpetbagger, having entered his southern home as major of the 126th Illinois regiment. For three years he served Governor Clayton as Chief Justice of the State Supreme Court. His election against ex-Confederate Colonel Thomas Gunter ended in uncertainty, charges of fraud flying back and forth. Not until February did the House accept Wilshire's credentials by a razor-thin vote of 135–129. Wilshire might yet have finished his term but for a wrong turn on the Brooks-Baxter road. Initially he had followed Powell Clayton to endorse the regular Republican ticket, but when Clayton bolted Wilshire refused. He stood by Elisha Baxter. He criticized Senators Clayton and Dorsey. He sent his criticisms to the national papers[15] and to President Grant. His memorandum denouncing the machinations of Clayton's "ring" reached the White House in May.[16] Wilshire's exposé, sources said, persuaded the president to favor Elisha Baxter.[17] Clayton took revenge. The House reconsidered its seating of William Wilshire. In June Republicans expelled the renegade Republican.

The 1874 elections offered Judge Wilshire his chance to avenge Powell Clayton's revenge. Gunter moved up to the 4th District. Wilshire had to convince Democrats to nominate him, their old enemy, to take back the 3rd. He won the support of the Little Rock *Gazette* and its influential editor William Woodruff. But party regulars viewed him with suspicion. The nominating convention met at Clarksville. It deadlocked. After two days of wrangling, Wilshire prevailed. Rumblings of discontent followed.[18] A bolter, Hugh Thomason of Crawford County, declared an independent candidacy. He urged Democrats to beware pseudo-Democrat Wilshire. He arraigned the convention, a fraud upon the "true masses of the party."[19]

For once no such quarrel troubled Republicans. William Joseph Hynes, currently congressman at-large, won nomination at the state convention. Hynes, with elegantly waxed whiskers and an ovoid physique, hailed from New York and Massachusetts. Democrats, having nominated a carpetbagger, could not fault him for that. They faulted him for corruption, and for corpulence: "Large Congressman Hynes," laughed the Clarendon *Age,* "a faint representation of the scriptural sow who was washed but went again to her wallow in the mire.... Hynes never has had all the dirt washed off him or out of him."[20] The election hinged on uncertain factors. Would Republican voters support repentant Liberal-Republican Hynes? Would Democrats rally to a converted Republican? Would Independent Thomason pose a threat? Would civil rights disturb the campaign?

The new 3rd District extended from the center of the state, Faulkner, Pulaski, Grant and Dallas Counties, to the border of Indian Territory. It included the city of Little Rock and the towns of Fort Smith and Van Buren. Some 26,000 black persons lived within its borders, among 110,000 whites. Half those black

15 Clayton, *Aftermath of the Civil War in Arkansas*, 356–358.
16 *Papers of Ulysses S. Grant*, vol. 25, 96–97.
17 St. Louis *Republican*, May 14, 1874.
18 Little Rock *Gazette*, October 1, 1874.
19 Little Rock *Gazette*, October 13, 1874.
20 Quoted in Little Rock *Gazette*, September 30, 1874.

residents (13,708) resided in Pulaski County. Even there 18,000 white people outnumbered them. Wilshire, nevertheless, adhered to Augustus Garland's strategy. Race-friendly issues must control the debate. This approach also appealed to Judge Wilshire's convictions. Suspicious Democrats were right. He had changed parties. He had not changed beliefs. In Congress he remained mute on civil rights.[21] The election gave him a chance to speak. His words gave Charles Sumner's spirit no cause to complain.

Wilshire began at Little Rock on September 26. He had lived in the enemy's camp, he warned his new party. He knew Powell Clayton and the trap he had prepared: "In the Northern papers you will find the basest slanders on Arkansas, and I know pretty well who they are written by.... They are sending through the State for accounts of murders, and whether arrests are made. This is to present to Congress as a 'horror,' and in this Congress is expected by them to reconstruct the State." Avoid the trap. Give Clayton no ammunition. Respect the rights of black citizens.[22] He spoke again at Arkadelphia. Democrats and Republicans, join hands: "equal and exact justice to all."[23]

For Democrats not enchanted with Wilshire, the independent candidate offered attractions. Hugh F. Thomason was a popular figure, a barn-burning orator, "The Wild Bull of the Woods," as he was known to the public. Once a Whig, then a Democrat, then a Know-Nothing, he was now a Democrat again. Wilshire's partisans charged he was actually a creature of the Republicans, set up to cause Democratic disarray. Many Democrats, however, considered Thomason the true Democrat in the race. "Personally," wrote future governor William Fishback, "I would prefer him to either of the others if I were allowed to consult my personal preference." But the party had nominated Wilshire. So be it: "As to the objection urged by some that a mistake had been made in giving Judge Wilshire the nomination, let it go, and in two years it could be rectified, if it should be found there was a mistake."[24]

Wilshire meanwhile stuck to his principles. He spoke at Hot Springs on October 28. He had indeed been a Republican. He had not quit that party. It had quit him. As for the Civil Rights Bill, he had but one objection: the mixed-school clause. If he returned to Congress "he would work to have it changed."[25] Otherwise he found no fault in the bill.

21 When the House's civil rights votes came up on May 25 and June 8, Wilshire still sat as a Republican. He was recorded both times as Absent. Before the third vote arrived he had been expelled.

22 Little Rock *Gazette*, September 27, 1874.

23 Little Rock *Gazette*, October 13, 1874.

24 Little Rock *Gazette*, October 16, 1874.

25 Little Rock *Gazette*, October 31, 1874.

The campaign concluded at the Little Rock Opera House. Wilshire repeated his message: if Republicans wanted civil rights, let them read the new state constitution. "It secures the rights of the colored people as firmly as they can be secured. It is your own fault if you do not stand by it." He turned to the black people. "As one who fought for your freedom and one who believed in reconstruction, I am your friend and I propose to stand there."[26] Finally William Wilshire spun completely around the circle. Hynes the Republican, not he, begrudged black people their rights.

> Colored men of Pulaski! W.J. Hynes was appointed a delegate to the Chattanooga convention. That convention refused even to indorse Sumner's Civil Rights Bill.... Can you vote for a man who is pledged to throw your cherished hopes overboard the first opportunity that presents itself? ... Colored men of Arkansas, what do you think of the men who openly avow these sentiments?[27]

In the last weeks of the campaign a notice circulated informing the public of sad news. William Wilshire was dead. Democrats, therefore, be advised. Vote for Hugh Thomason.[28] The news was exaggerated. Wilshire (he expired in 1888) won by 5,000 votes. The Republicans' last trick had failed. Four months later the Civil Rights Act became law. The Little Rock *Gazette* was unperturbed. "This bill has no particular terrors for us," it concluded. "We have on our statute books a civil rights law more stringent by far than this, and as yet we have heard of no trouble growing out of it. If the people of the north can stand it we can."[29]

2 Texas

Even among her sanguinary sisters, southern states suffused with violence, Texas stood out. Hollywood dramatized but did not imagine the scene. Newspapers in 1874 regaled readers with tales of Texas terror. Thus New Jersey gentlefolk, sitting down to morning coffee on February 10, and taking up the latest edition of the Paterson *Press,* could peruse a "Summary of Texas News," a résumé of recent items from that quarter.

---

26 Little Rock *Gazette*, November 3, 1874.
27 Little Rock *Gazette*, October 31, 1874.
28 Little Rock Gazette, October 25, 1874.
29 Little Rock *Gazette*, March 5, 1875.

> Paola County: a negro found murdered in the woods; Nueces County – a man killed by a Mexican; Limestone County – horse thieves on the rampage; Washington County – horse thieves have robbed Col. Alcorn; Travis County – another man knocked down and robbed; Cameron County – cattle thieving operations continue; Marion County – district court suddenly suspended and the judge indefinitely absent.[30]

Horace Redfield devoted the longest chapter of his book, *Homicide, North and South,* to Texas. Seven thousand murders, he estimated, had distinguished the state in the decade since the Civil War. Even school children carried firearms, so as to shoot armed classmates in the classrooms.[31] Texas was out of control, the Galveston *News* conceded. Under an idolatrous veneration of individual liberty mob rule ruled.

> They [the people] exult in the glories of mob law and its Draconian code, and its ferocious confusion of great and small offenses, of revenge and justice, of innocence and guilt ... a deep-seated and systematic repugnance to the claims of civil government, a principle that would plant the volcanic frenzy of the Commune in every city, in every village, in every neighborhood.... They make the world believe that civil government, as now constituted, is a failure, and unfortunately our highest State functionaries are, apparently, in no haste to demonstrate the contrary.[32]

In a state where merely the polite suggestion of civil control excited objection, government dicta mandating the regulation of public behavior – for instance civil rights bills – appeared absurd. Sources recall not even a debate. The state was overwhelmingly white. Its politics were overwhelmingly Democratic. Republicans seated no members in the 43rd Congress, apart from holdover Senator Flanagan. For the 44th Congress Republicans did not bother to run candidates in three of the state's six districts. In two of the remaining three,

30 Paterson, New Jersey, *Press*, February 10, 1874.

31 Horace Redfield, *Homicide, North and South* (Columbus: 2000), 63–85. Virginia's Rev. Dabney ended his life self-exiled to Texas. Even he could not reconcile himself to the libertarian lawlessness he found, "the brutal ignorance, superficiality and egotism of the people." Charles Wilson, "Robert Lewis Dabney: Religion and the Southern Holocaust," *Virginia Magazine of History and Biography* (1981): 88.

32 Galveston *News*, June 14, 1874. Itinerant observer Edward King, taken to visit a typical east Texas chain gang, puzzled over the number of men condemned to a life sentence – puzzled until he noted, on examining the convict rolls, the frequency of the crime of murder. Edward King, *The Great South*, 120.

candidates were a formality. No Democrat had a kind word to say about the Civil Rights Bill. Few Republicans had the temerity to say a word.

Some Democratic papers effervesced with rage against the bill. "An outrage upon [white people's] God-given social rights and privileges," fumed the Sherman *Register*.[33] The state's most influential Democratic paper, the Galveston *News*, found it simply silly. Texans would not allow the thing. Only black people would suffer. "We have no fear that the white race of the South will consent to be snuffed out by an act of Congress."[34]

Texas was redeemed. The election of 1872 removed the last Republican administration. The state did not see another for 105 years. Republicans faced the voters with a feeling of hopelessness, the Dallas *Intelligencer* observed: "as yet, no Republican candidates have been spoken of in any part of the State, and it looks as though there was a scarcity of aspiring men in the party."[35] Fourth District Republicans tried twice to organize a nominating convention. Their first attempt, at Waco, "fizzled." Their second, at Houston, fizzled again.[36] By October Democrats had begun to suspect a trick. Perhaps the enemy hoped to lull them into "a fatal degree of indifference and carelessness." How else could one explain such incredibly supine behavior?[37] Democrats denounced the Civil Rights Bill so as to have something to denounce in the absence of flesh and blood opponents. Republican candidates, those who existed, remained mum.

The state had redrawn its political map. Two at-large seats, held currently by Democrats Roger Mills and Asa Willie, were absorbed into the geographical landscape. The party disdained to re-nominate four of its incumbents, among them Congressman Willie. Their replacements included two distinguished statesmen, former Governor James Throckmorton and former Confederate Secretary of the Treasury John H. Reagan. Reagan took up the banner in the 1st District, the southeastern zone bordering Louisiana and Arkansas. His nomination, despite his fame and Confederate pedigree, did not come easily. Incumbent William Herndon retained support. His constituents noted that he had risen on the House floor to denounce the Civil Rights Bill. That praiseworthy act failed to compensate for Herndon's association with the infernal salary-grab.

The Democratic nominating convention met at Nacogdoches.[38] For fifty ballots Reagan held a lead but fell short. Stalemate continued. First Reagan

33 Quoted in Galveston *News*, June 3, 1874.
34 Galveston *News*, June 13, 1874.
35 Quoted in Galveston *News*, August 26, 1874.
36 Galveston *News*, September 19, 1874.
37 Corsicana *Observer*, quoted in Galveston *News*, October 6, 1874.
38 Account in Galveston *News*, September 5–6, 1874.

then Herndon chivalrously offered to withdraw. Col. Tom Banner jumped up. They should nominate Reagan by acclamation – which was done, in a burst of wildest Texas enthusiasm. Republicans nominated no one. A few weeks before the vote Judge William Chambers stepped up as a sacrificial victim. He called himself an Independent Radical.[39]

Notwithstanding the absence of a viable opponent, John Reagan ran a vigorous canvass. He defined his theme: "Constitutional Government and the Rights of the People in a Free Republic." On September 23 he brought that discourse to the citizens of Cherokee County at Jacksonville. He came, he said, "not as John H. Reagan but as the candidate of the Democracy … a Party whose doctrines must prevail or you can have no republic." The republic was dying: "We live in a day when the officers are above the law and people, when private rights are disregarded and public wrong is the rule." The greatest wrong was the Civil Rights Bill. It violated the values of humanity, the values of Texas. It told the people how to live. "It punished men for being free."[40]

The 2nd District occupied the northeast quarter of the state. Democratic incumbent William McLean also yielded to a new man. David B. Culberson won the nomination and his first of eleven terms in Congress. Culberson faced no Republican opposition. Yet he prepared a mighty speech, a jewel of rhetorical turgidity which he delivered to the townsfolk of Marshall and Kilgore. He put civil rights into historical context. It was the latest link in a chain of servitude that despots tried ever and ever to fasten on the people. The first President Adams was the first aspiring dictator "who claimed that the government could interfere with the rights of its citizens." Adams' tyranny had failed. Its seed only slept. Republicans watered it again. The South had lost the war. Unutterable sadness: "the tears – and they flowed like streams of water; the sorrows – and they were mountain high; the blood – and it was an ocean that crimsoned the nation's body – the graves … in every house there is a vacant chair." Gallantly the South had surrendered its slaves. "We gave up slavery because we lost the wager of battle. We surrendered our institution … The world, perhaps, never saw such an example of forbearance." Now slavery returned. It was called "Civil Rights."

> The negro shall meet you on a common plane, schoolhouses to be opened to all alike, cars, churches, theaters, hotels, and all places where people assemble shall be thrown open to the occupancy of negroes and that you

39 Galveston *News*, September 29, 1874.
40 Galveston *News*, September 24, 1874.

> and they shall meet together in such places.... All alike shall stand upon a level, and that the basest in the walks of life.[41]

Democrats experienced their most contentious nomination in the 5th District, with Galveston, the state's metropolis. Redistricting forced incumbents John Hancock and D.C. Giddings to vie for the seat. Hancock's problem was salary-grabbing. He stood out as one of the most unapologetic grabbers. That should have sunk his candidacy. But fortune favored him. Hon. DeWitt Clinton Giddings had also banked his increased salary and taken "back pay." The Democratic convention opened on August 19 at Brenham.[42] On the 53rd ballot Giddings gave up. Hancock left with the nomination, but he left behind much bad feeling. With Democrats in disarray Republicans, it seemed, could finally take advantage. They took no advantage. They managed to assemble a convention at Austin on September 25. It nominated no one.[43]

Candidate Hancock nonetheless campaigned vigorously. Lacking a Republican with whom to dispute, he disputed the Civil Rights Bill. He spoke at Galveston on October 13. He denounced the bill as usual: government meddling in social affairs, destruction of the common school system. Hancock did offer one original contribution, an idea no one else in 1874 considered, a burst of prescience validated a century later. If this bill became law, he warned, the government would surely establish an agency to oversee its enforcement. He predicted a Civil Rights Commission.

> This supplemental Civil Rights bill will be followed up by another one equally evil in its embodiments. Its provisions will embrace the appointment of commissioners to see that the Civil Rights bill is administered in all of its requirements – to see that the colored man is put in possession of all the rights and privileges conferred upon him. The colored man himself should take warning here. The well-wishers of the human family should pause ere this is accomplished. It bodes but evil for both races.[44]

In the 3rd District, running across north Texas, Democrats nominated former governor James Throckmorton. The convention at Fort Worth was a harmonious affair. Col. Edward C. McClure, editor of the Dallas *Herald,* addressed the gathering. The colonel was a recent refugee from the civil-rights-infested state

41 Galveston *News*, October 20, 1874.
42 Galveston *News*, August 20–21, 1874.
43 Galveston *News*, September 26, 1874.
44 Galveston *News*, October 14, 1874.

of South Carolina. "He thanked God that he was among white men and freemen, and no longer where the heel of the negro was on the neck of good and true men. He believed that Texas would become the Evangel of Liberty to the oppressed."[45] Republicans actually nominated a candidate. Frederick W. Sumner, a Connecticut Yankee, had come to Texas before the war, but left during it. His candidacy posed no threat. He made no issue of civil rights.

The 4th District stretched through the center of the state, including Waco and the nascent town of Houston. Democrats united behind veteran congressman at large Roger Q. Mills. After two failed attempts, Republicans found a candidate. Judge Pleasant M. Yell of Montgomery County was, so the Galveston *News* said, a good man in bad company.[46] His candidacy posed no threat. He made no issue of civil rights.

The 6th District provided the only contest. Larger than many states, the 6th encompassed the vast reaches of west Texas. It contained the towns of San Antonio, Brownsville and El Paso, a great deal of sagebrush, and empty space. It was home to very few African Americans but very many Mexican Americans. They substituted neatly as objects of discrimination. Republicans nominated Brownsville's Tejano millionaire, Jeremiah Galvan. He proposed to protect his compatriots' civil rights. He preferred, however, to do it not through a civil rights act but by the establishment of a new state. If elected to Congress, he promised, he would offer a bill for west Texas secession from Texas. In their own state citizens of Mexican descent could define their destiny and defy discrimination.[47] "A commonwealth of cow-stealers," chuckled the Victoria *Advocate*.[48] Democrats also ran an ethnic candidate, Gustave Schleicher, a son of the German immigrant population. He promised to protect Texans from the cow-stealers.

As the election approached, Democrats fretted. Jerry Galván, grumbled the Austin *State Gazette*, "the frontier Croesus," was spending his fortune lavishly. His agents crossed the border to purchase hordes of shiftless Mexicans and ship them in to vote on his behalf. A battery of printing presses cranked out his propaganda. "Documents of the foulest nature are being circulated, printed in Spanish, to lead the minds of Mexicans astray on political subjects."[49] Jerry Galván himself, complaining of physical infirmities, crisscrossed the district on jolting prairie roads to pursue his quest. The efforts of the frontier Croesus

45 Galveston *News*, July 31, 1874.
46 Galveston *News*, October 3, 1874.
47 Galveston *News*, October 13, 1874.
48 Galveston *News*, October 15, 1874.
49 Quoted in Galveston *News*, October 30, 1874.

did not avail. Civil rights for Mexicans proved as unpopular as civil rights for African Americans. Sixth District voters sent Gustave Schleicher to Congress. Freedom, as John Reagan had proclaimed, the beating heart of Texas, lived.

3 Missouri

In Arkansas Republicans were disheartened, in Texas downtrodden. In Missouri they disbanded. They contested some congressional districts. Some they did not bother to contest. The governorship they abandoned. Missouri retained traces of the once-vital Liberal Republican movement. Senator Carl Schurz personified the remains of that diminished party, but he had no hope of re-election by a Democratic legislature. Missourians disenchanted with the present state of affairs coalesced around a new political organization. The People's Party assembled malcontents of all stripes. Schurz joined it. The Republican State Committee set its voters free to vote the People's Party ticket. As to the Civil Rights Bill, those Republicans who remained Republicans hesitated to advertise their support. People's Party partisans ignored it. Democrats sowed the seeds of passion and prejudice. They reaped a harvest of rewards.

Missouri Republicans threw in the towel remarkably early. On March 19 their members of the General Assembly caucused. They denounced the Democrats, particularly the current administration of Governor Silas Woodson, "a faction fitted rather to represent some form of semi-barbarism than any form of modern civilization." Then they surrendered to the barbarians. They urged the State Executive Committee to call no convention and make no nominations for state offices, to "open the way" for a united opposition movement to develop. Ex-United States Senator John B. Henderson composed the resolution. He began with a bang: "The Republican party is not discouraged." He ended with a whimper. Let Republicans support some other political organization.[50]

In July the Central Committee met at Jefferson City. It released party members "to act as to them may seem best." It did not dissolve the party, but floated it free. "We are in all fundamental principles Republicans," the Committee insisted, "but we are willing to forego present partisan advantage for the public good."[51] On September 23 Republicans held a brief convention. They passed no resolutions. They nominated no candidates. They directed voters to vote their consciences.[52]

50 Springfield, Missouri, *Patriot*, March 26, 1874.

51 Springfield *Patriot*, July 30, 1874.

52 St. Louis *Republican*, September 24, 1874.

The People's Party alternative meanwhile had taken shape. Its members included downcast Republicans, discontented Democrats, and rudderless Liberal Republicans. Black persons were not abundant, although some did attend the People's Party Convention. That assembly met at Jefferson City on September 2. Farmers predominated. They were a serious conclave. (They were also an abstemious lot, as one Jefferson City saloon-keeper was heard to mutter: "D – n such a convention – they don't drink anything.")[53] St. Louis Republican Congressman Edwin Stanard addressed the sober sodbusters. He admired Republicans embracing Democrats, Radicals clasping hands with Liberals "and even some who were in the Confederate army." He invited fellow Republicans to join the People's Party ranks: "We would leave the Republican car on the side track for the time being. If Republicans desire to come into this grand organization, gentlemen [let them come]."[54]

The Republican-People's Party alliance left civil rights on the side track. The People's Party disavowed interest in national affairs. It took no position on a federal civil rights bill. The farmer-filled convention nominated for governor a farmer, William Gentry. Major Gentry was a farmer in the plantation sense. His sprawling spread covered 6,000 acres in Pettis County. Most recently he had affiliated with the Democrats. To balance the ticket a Republican, Samuel W. Headlee, stood for lieutenant-governor. Foremost on the People's Party concerns was repression of banditry. Gov. Woodson's pathetic or even (Carl Schurz alleged) deliberate failure to suppress roving highwaymen had given the state a sorry reputation. The Democrats' criminal collusion with outlaws such as the James gang, actually rejuvenated ex-Confederate guerillas, must cease. The People's Party called for lower taxes and regulation of railroads. It suggested one quadrennial meeting of the state legislature should suffice for the public's needs.

Democrats mocked the People's Party, half-formed "Tadpoles." "The idea of taking the sore-heads, the broken-down tricksters, malcontents and scalawags that have been kicked out of either party as too vile for further use," laughed the Gallatin *Democrat*, "and mixing them up and giving them the title of reformer is simply preposterous."[55] Democrats gave their voters a fully-formed frog. They broadcast a manly appeal to the hatreds of the past. Remember the Lost Cause. Honor the name of Slavery:

> When dead men come back from their graves who were slain because of the Democratic garments they wore; when the land that Missourians

53 Account of the People's Party Convention, Springfield *Patriot*, September 10, 1874.

54 St. Louis *Republican*, September 2, 1874.

55 Gallatin *Democrat*, May 21, 1874.

> own passes away from an offspring taught how to revere the cause their fathers worshipped; when stranger feet tread the battle-fields made precious with the blood of slave-holding Democracy ... when the millennium comes, indeed, and the lion and the lamb lie down together, then the new party born of a race that has neither wrongs to remember nor monuments to build may come into Missouri.... When there are sharp swords in the hands of prejudiced men, blood is spilt and opposition perishes as the dew in the morning.[56]

Despite the bravado, Democrats worried. Tadpoles might grow teeth. Party leaders conceded that their record left much to be regretted. Fiscal mismanagement had run up the state debt, yet taxation remained high. Outlaws indeed scoffed at authority. They disrupted commerce. The economy suffered.[57] Edward King passed through central Missouri. He found farmers "savagely discontented," squeezed by high costs of production, high costs of transportation, and low market prices. "They conversed with great bitterness of the difficulty of obtaining proper representation in Congress on the subject of their grievances."[58]

Democrats struggled over their nomination for governor. Charles H. Hardin prevailed over ex-Confederate General Francis Marion Cockrell, whose colleagues consoled him with Carl Schurz's Senate seat instead.[59] The party faced a rebellious public. It could not stand on its record. Voters were restless. What to do? Distract their restlessness. Displace it to their fears – fear of black people; fear of civil rights. At the state convention future U.S. Senator George G. Vest struck the tone:

> My friends and fellow Democrats, speaking for one Democrat alone, I say ... this is a government of white men and made for white men – [great applause] – and to be administered by white men and their children forever [applause].[60]

The heteroclite "People's Party" reminded him of another degrading partnership, the union of Democrats and Liberal Republicans in 1872. He had attended that mongrel convention at Baltimore.

56 St. Louis *Dispatch*, quoted in St. Louis *Republican*, May 14, 1874.
57 St. Louis *Republican*, May 21, 1874.
58 King, *The Great South*, 189.
59 St Louis *Republican*, August 27–28, 1874.
60 Account of Democratic convention, St Louis *Republican*, August 27–28, 1874.

> There we sat, one-armed and one-legged Confederate soldiers, and the first thing they did was to play "John Brown's soul is marching on" … They ran up a picture of old Greeley, with spectacles on, looking for all the world like a Tom-cat looking through a dairy window. Then we hallooed…. Then they tendered thanks to the gallant soldiers and seamen of the army and navy of the Union for their labors in suppressing the late unholy and wicked rebellion…. I turned to a brother delegate and said: "I expect the next thing they will offer a resolution thanking Ben Butler for his treatment of the women in New Orleans."[61]

He turned to the Civil Rights Bill.

> God … has for three thousand years appointed to the white race the power and the black races as subsidiary and subservient to them. And yet we have it now in direct violation of the teachings of history – of the voice of God himself – that the negro race is to be elevated and forced almost against their own will to an equality with the white man.

Charles Hardin, for his part, refought the Civil War. At Lebanon in Laclede County he warned white voters. Don't let Radicals hide behind a "People's Party" façade. A vote for the People's Party was a vote for civil rights. "He showed up the civil-rights bill in all its hideous deformity, and proved beyond dispute that all who are not on the Democratic platform are indirectly supporting this infamous measure."[62] People's Partyers retorted. Hardin was a "haystack rebel." He hid behind a haystack when bullets were flying. Now, once the cause was safely lost, he raised the rebel yell.[63] Carl Schurz stumped the state for the People's Party. On September 23 he delivered his great speech at St. Louis. Put away the Confederate flag. Put down the southern bloody shirt.

> What spirit is it that now again boisterously appeals through the organ of your leading men to ceaseless yearnings for revenge? What spirit is it that thus sedulously strives to revive the bitterest passions of the civil war to new acrimony? … Those who still speak of "ceaseless yearnings for revenge" should be emphatically informed by our votes that, in the opinion of the people of Missouri, the war is over.[64]

---

61 St Louis *Republican*, August 28, 1874.

62 St. Louis *Republican*, September 9, 1874.

63 Springfield *Patriot*, September 3, 1874.

64 Carl Schurz, *Speeches, Correspondence and Political Papers of Carl Schurz*, ed. Frederic Bancroft (New York: 1913), vol. 3, 100–101, 108.

Schurz denounced the Democrats' tactics. He also renounced his friend Sumner's Civil Rights Bill. As he continued to campaign he erased that topic from his agenda. On September 30 he joined Major Gentry at Chillicothe. He repeated the very same speech he had made one week earlier at St. Louis, but in a shortened version, "with the exception, however, that he avoided alluding to the civil-rights bill."[65] On October 18 he debated Democrat Hardin at the town of Louisiana in Pike County. Hardin eagerly brought up the issue: "Though he was speaking to an audience where there were two hundred and fifty negro votes, he declared his unalterable opposition to the civil-rights bill." Schurz's reply occupied an hour and forty-five minutes. On civil rights "he was as silent as the house of death or the valley beyond."[66] (see Map 9, below)

Missouri, First District
Edwin O. Stanard (R/PP), Edward C. Kehr (D)
Population: 90% white

Missouri Republicans held four seats in the 43rd Congress. They lost all four. Their incumbent in the 1st District, incorporating part of St. Louis and

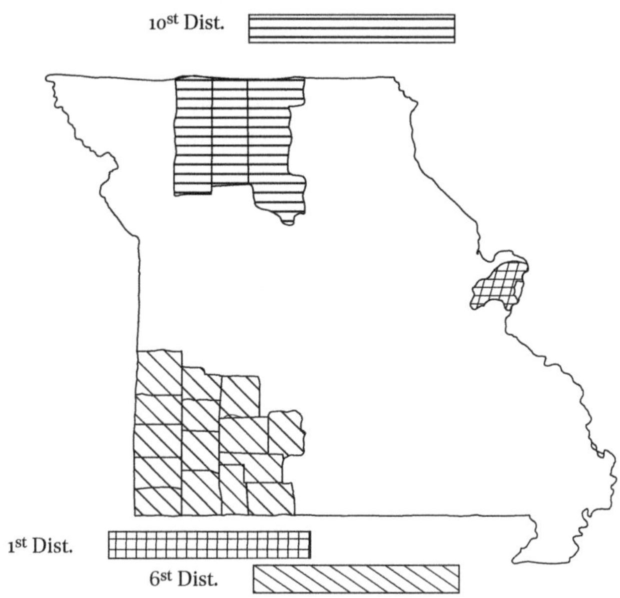

MAP 9 Congressional Districts, Missouri
SOURCE: AUTHORS OF *WELCOMING RUIN*.

65 St. Louis *Republican*, October 3, 1874.
66 St. Louis *Republican*, October 20; Kansas City *Journal of Commerce*, November 3, 1874.

surrounding areas, was the elegant, affluent Edwin Obed Stanard. Born in New Hampshire, he had gone west to make his fortune along the Mississippi. Stanard was one of the city's outstanding capitalists: president of his own grain-milling concern, E.O. Stanard & Co., president of the Citizens' Insurance Co., a director of the Missouri Pacific Railroad, the Mississippi Valley Transportation Co., the 2nd National Bank, the St. Louis Elevator Co. He rose through Republican ranks to serve as lieutenant-governor from 1869 to 1871. After an unsuccessful Liberal Republican run for mayor of St. Louis, he entered Congress as a Republican.[67] He found civil rights impractical and politically dangerous. He joined the Republican road-blockers. His initial House vote, on May 25, saw him rise in favor of the bill. Then he changed his mind. He voted No on June 8. He voted No on June 20. In the final debate in 1875 he apologized to black people. Again he voted No.

Stanard's 1st District contained a portion of St. Louis city (wards 1, 2, 3 and 4) and a portion of surrounding St. Louis County. It included the heavily industrialized township of Carondelet and a slice of St. Louis Township. Its racial demographics reflected the state's decisively white nature. His margin of victory over Liberal Republican William M. Grosvenor in 1872 had amounted to 142 votes. Stanard rallied early to the People's Party coalition. When that party's convention in the 1st District met on September 30, Stanard took the chair. When the convention closed on October 2 he held its nomination in his pocket. The next day the regular Republicans assembled. They found themselves preempted. If they did not second his candidacy they would split the vote and hand the district to a Democrat. The preferred Republican candidate, Louis Gottschalk, withdrew. Republicans re-nominated Edwin O. Stanard.[68]

Democrats appealed to St. Louis' German constituency. Edward C. Kehr, youthful, bespectacled, in appearance not unlike a juvenile Carl Schurz, was a second-generation immigrant, fluent in the old native tongue. Neither he nor Stanard had a friendly word, in any tongue, for Charles Sumner's legacy. Stanard had already declared his opposition. That did not prevent Democrats from tagging him as a civil rights man. Many issues concerned the voters: the Currency Bill (which Stanard had favored), tariff reform, the decline of industrial trade.[69] The Democrats ignored them all. Their platform produced precisely one resolution: rejection of the Civil Rights Bill.[70] Stanard refused to be flanked. He denounced the bill with equal vigor. Schurz joined him. Schurz's

67 Barnes, *The American Government*, vol. 3, 172.
68 St. Louis *Republican*, October 4, 1874.
69 St. Louis *Republican*, October 21, 28, 1874.
70 St. Louis *Republican*, September 30, 1874.

Westliche Post warned of dire consequences for Germans should civil rights prevail. What began with streetcars might end with beer. "Those who would compel us to-day to admit a negro as a guest, might with quite as much show or right prohibit us to-morrow from drinking a glass of beer or wine."[71]

Francis Cockrell, Democratic senatorial aspirant, spoke. Beware mixed schools, mixed graveyards, Negroes sitting in one's parlor: "He appealed to the nobler feelings of the people."[72] Civil rights, Kehr insisted, was a Republican evil. Stanard was stuck with it. "It undertakes to dictate to one class of citizens what company they shall keep in their houses, their hotels, their schools and their public conveyances ... to dictate what we shall eat or what we shall wear."[73] In St. Louis, candidates vied for the right to oppose civil rights most righteously. Edwin Stanard returned to Congress a lame duck.

Missouri, Sixth District
Charles W. Thrasher (R), Charles H. Morgan (D)
Population: 97% white

The Missouri 6th District's fifteen rural counties nestled in the state's southwest. In 1870 it possessed 149,598 inhabitants; 145,639 were white. Of the 3,959 black people, 2,156 inhabited Greene County with the town of Springfield, 1,400 within Springfield itself. Elsewhere black persons all but disappeared. In Taney County there were 10, among 4,407 residents. Stone County had 20; 37 existed in McDonald County; 52 lived in Barry County. Barton County, population 5,087, was home to 5,068 whites and 19 blacks. Unlikely were white people to find their parlors besieged by vagrant black hordes. Barely a black child outside of Springfield clamored to corrupt the sanctuary of the schoolroom. Civil rights should cause no fear. Fear played well in the 6th District.

The incumbent Republican, Harrison E. Havens, had arrived in Missouri from Illinois. He settled in Springfield, where he edited a Republican journal, the *Patriot*. During two terms in Congress he had acquired some influence, becoming chairman of the Committee on Public Expenditures. On the matter of civil rights, Havens trimmed. In the first showdown, on May 25, he managed to be recorded as absent, although the Record noted his presence in the chamber only shortly before. On June 8 he gathered up his courage and voted Aye. Twelve days later he arranged to be absent again, though he paired an

71 Quoted in Mobile *Register*, June 10, 1874.
72 St. Louis *Republican*, September 12, 1874.
73 St. Louis *Republican*, October 28, 1874.

affirmative vote with an opponent. When the final vote came on February 5, 1875, Harrison Havens, true to form, abstained.

Salary-grabbing also troubled Congressman Havens. His own paper, the *Patriot,* reported his prospects for re-nomination dim.[74] A rival appeared. Former congressman Sempronius H. "Pony" Boyd came from a large and popular Greene County family. Some of his half-dozen brothers fought for the Confederacy. He adhered to the Union, raised the 24th Missouri regiment and commanded it under Missouri's Gen. Franz Sigel. Boyd had twice been elected to Congress, sitting in the 38th Congress as an Unconditional Unionist and in the 41st as a Republican. In 1874, declaring himself "financially flattened," he begged Ulysses Grant for a job.[75] He dipped again into politics.

The Republican nominating convention opened on September 5 at Pierce City.[76] Boyd appealed to black voters and for civil rights. Their support was insufficient. He dropped out. The salary grab demolished Havens, though he protested. If congressional pay raises were to be condemned, then they must condemn such men as Henry Clay, Stephen Douglas, William Seward, for they all had accepted pay raises in their time. Havens dropped out. A dark horse, Charles Thrasher, won the nomination. Col. Thrasher was a northerner. He had arrived in military style with the 11th Rhode Island infantry, and settled at the town of Neosho. Havens' partisans vowed revenge.[77]

The Democrats also met at Pierce City. State Assemblyman Charles Morgan of Barton County accepted the nomination.[78] His selection at least removed the carpetbagger issue from the table. Born in New York, he had wandered west, performing his wartime service with the 21st Wisconsin regiment. He landed in Missouri in 1868. He promptly asked his new neighbors to send him to Congress.[79]

Charles Thrasher had not, as Pony Boyd, appealed for civil rights. Civil rights appealed to him. Personal feeling inclined him to favor Charles Sumner's dream. Political reality woke him up. In a speech at Neosho he endorsed the Civil Rights Bill. Public reaction was swift, sharp, and negative. Next, at Marshfield in Webster County, he tried a different approach. He supported the

74 Springfield *Patriot*, June 25, 1874.

75 Sempronius Boyd to Ulysses Grant, April 24, 1874. *Papers of Ulysses S. Grant*, vol. 25, 370–371.

76 Accounts in St. Louis *Republican*, September 10–11; Springfield *Patriot*, September 17, 1874.

77 St. Louis *Republican*, September 11, 1874.

78 Springfield *Patriot*, September 17; St. Louis *Republican*, September 17–18, 1874.

79 He asked them repeatedly. After serving in the 44th and 45th Congresses, he was defeated for election to the 46th. He was elected again to the 48th, defeated for the 49th, elected to the 53rd, defeated for nomination to the 54th. He was elected once more to the 61st. Congress, and defeated for the 62nd. He died the next year.

bill but not mixed schools. "His speech fell like a wet blanket," the St. Louis *Republican* reported, "and he left the stand amid the most profound silence.... He will probably be sent home with positive instructions not to open his mouth again until a speech is prepared for him in accordance with the known wishes of the people of this district."[80]

The candidates debated at Springfield. Morgan threw civil rights directly into the fray: "an infamous measure ... Mr. Thrasher was especially invited to define himself distinctly on that issue." Thrasher emitted uncertain sounds. "He commenced skirmishing ... and everyone saw he was trying to dodge, and a voice from the audience demanded him to come to the front." Finally he announced himself opposed.[81] Morgan pounced. "He referred in a happy manner to Mr. Thrasher's Neosho speech, in which he had indorsed the bill as a whole, and then to his Marshfield speech in which he indorsed it with the exception of the clause relating to mixed schools, and now congratulated him upon his advancement in coming out square against it." Black persons sought out Pony Boyd. "The colored citizens are all greatly incensed at Thrasher," the *Patriot* reported. "Some fifty of them waited on Col. Boyd this forenoon and requested him to become an Independent candidate."[82] Pony declined the offer. The Republicans' campaign collapsed. They carried only three counties, Dade, Christian and Jasper. Jasper County in 1872 had provided Harrison Havens a majority of 600. Thrasher won it in 1874 by all of 3 votes.

Missouri, Tenth District
Ira Hyde (R/PP), Rezin DeBolt (D)
Population: 96% white

Republicans held two more of Missouri's thirteen congressional seats: the 9th District in the northwest, centered on the town of St. Joseph, and the 10th, in the north-center. In the 9th Republicans ran no candidate. They passed the baton to the People's Party. That concession cost civil rights one of its champions, Republican incumbent Isaac Parker. With Parker's disappearance civil rights disappeared from the race. The People's Party's Philip A. Thompson wanted nothing to do with it. Democrat David Rea won by 2,000 votes.[83] Chances seemed more encouraging in the 10th District.

80 St. Louis *Republican*, September 16, 1874.

81 Account in St. Louis *Republican*, September 24, 1874.

82 Springfield *Patriot*, September 24, 1874.

83 Judge Parker found consolation. Ulysses Grant awarded him the United States District Court for Western Arkansas. There he enacted the People's Party's pledge to eradicate banditry, "hanging 'em high'" in large numbers.

The area was entirely rural, its market towns merely adjuncts of the farm-based economy. The People's Party platform found a favorable appeal. The district also contained many Republicans, among them its incumbent Ira B. Hyde. Hyde was 36. He exuded youth and vigor. He had not been present in Congress for the salary grab; his hands were clean. He was born in New York, raised in Cleveland. But his wartime service with the 1st Minnesota Mounted Rifles allowed him to avoid killing Confederates, that unit having engaged only in border campaigns against the Sioux. Hyde had been a popular public prosecutor in Mercer County. He won his 1872 election by more than 1,600 votes. The St. Louis *Republican* considered Ira Hyde a likely winner: "His record is clear and his votes on all questions have been in close harmony with the sentiments of his constituents, and with all his popularity with the Republicans there is added a powerful support from the Grangers, which he has successfully captured."[84]

Hyde presented a difficult target. He had covered all his bases. If people voted their interests they would return him to Congress. They must be made to vote their fears. In the 10th District, as in the 6th, there seemed little to fear. The district formed a block of nine square-shaped counties that ran from the Iowa border (Harrison, Mercer and Putnam Counties) south to Caldwell, Livingston, and Linn, plus one irregular appendix, Chariton County, pointed southeast. Few towns of any size marked its agrestic landscape. A total of 5,375 black persons resided within the ten counties, amid 132,074 whites. Chariton County possessed most of that black population. Nine black persons lived somewhere in Putnam County. Ten existed in Harrison County. Sullivan County hosted 42. It was enough to generate fear.

Tenth District Republicans maintained their party's identity. They aligned it with the People's Party. Both organizations held conventions simultaneously on October 7. Both conventions assembled at the town of Trenton in Grundy County. Both agreed to nominate Ira Hyde.[85] The Gallatin *Democrat* sneered at the Republican nomination; all the sins of the party would plague its candidate. But the paper found the People's Party endorsement troubling. Its platform was popular. It was clear of corruption. Its organizers locally were prominent men: Gallatin lawyer William C. Gillihan, county attorney S.T. Brosius, and David L. Kost, ex-Republican populist.[86] The *Democrat* did its best. Its editorials mocked the People's Party's obsession with law and order. Bandits beware! "A resolution passed by the 'people's' convention might catch them;

84 St. Louis *Republican*, June 18, 1874.

85 Gallatin *Democrat*, October 8, 1874.

86 Gallatin *Democrat*, July 2, 23, 1874.

they should not forget it."[87] Such persiflage was unlikely to impress seriously discontented farmers. Democrats pinned their hopes on civil rights.

Democrats met at the town of Chillicothe on September 24. The nomination fell to Judge Rezin A. DeBolt of Grundy County. He, like Hyde, was an immigrant, having come down from Ohio before the war. He too served the Union, but, as captain in the 23rd Missouri regiment, he had shot at Confederates. Those Confederates captured him at the battle of Shiloh.[88] Republicans jeered. Democrats ended every rally with the rebel yell. They mourned for the Lost Cause. Then they put their banner in the hands of a man who had fought against it. The *Democrat* replied huffily: "It matters not to us where he has been, whether he followed Sherman in his terrible march to the sea, or surrendered with Lee at Appomattox."[89]

Facing a popular incumbent, saddled with a shaky candidate, Democrats rushed to raise the civil rights specter. The congressman was vulnerable. Hyde had been educated at Oberlin College, a hot-bed of racial-equality ideals. He favored Charles Sumner's project. He voted for it twice. He voted, the *Democrat* declared, "for the humiliation and degradation of the Caucasian race." He voted "virtually to place your children side by side with the colored children in our common schools." He had "sealed [his] fate beyond the hope of political resurrection."[90] Ira Hyde, who thought himself safe, began to squirm. When the third civil rights vote arrived on June 20 he voted no. It was too late. Democrats awarded him a nickname: "Civil Rights Bill Hyde." "Democrats!" the Gallatin *Democrat* implored. "We have warned you, so now beware.... The blood of liberty is at stake, and if the only bosom friend I had on earth were to prove traitor now, I would sign his death warrant with one hand though I should have to dash off tears of blood with the other."[91]

Rezin DeBolt toured the district. As a former Federal officer, he refrained from giving the rebel yell. But he advertised himself as the "white man's candidate." Advance-men prepared the way. Citizens of Trenton awoke in early October to find their streets placarded with notices of the candidate's imminent arrival. He would, the posters explained, discuss the civil rights bill.[92] The candidate moved on to Gallatin. "He showed conclusively that Mr. Hyde voted for the bill along with Ben Butler every time, and his last vote on the motion to refer to the judiciary committee in which he voted No, was but a vote to save

87 Gallatin *Democrat*, September 3, 1874.

88 St. Louis *Republican*, September 25, 1874.

89 Gallatin *Democrat*, October 15, 1874.

90 Gallatin *Democrat*, June 11, 18, 1874.

91 Gallatin *Democrat*, September 24, 1874.

92 Kansas City *Journal of Commerce*, October 6, 1874.

the bill from an utter defeat, it lying now on the Speaker's table, where it can be taken up any day and passed by a simple majority."[93] The *Democrat* summed it up. Voters had only to remember four things. Three of those things were civil rights:

> *Vote For DeBolt* – Hyde voted against enfranchisement and don't deny it.
> *Vote For DeBolt* – If you are opposed to mixed schools vote for DeBolt.
> *Vote For DeBolt* – DeBolt is opposed to the Civil Rights Bill – vote for him.
> *Vote The Straight Ticket* – A vote against Hyde is a vote against the infamous Civil Rights Bill.[94]

Hyde carried Harrison, Putnam and Mercer Counties, along with Grundy and Caldwell. Chariton County was his downfall. Even with People's Party reinforcement, he forfeited 2,000 votes from his 1872 total. Democrats completed their sweep of Missouri's congressional seats. Republicans had blessed them with the issue of civil rights.

4 Maryland

Democrats, as a rule, ruled Maryland. No Republican had held the governorship. None sat in the 42nd Congress. But Democratic serenity shattered in 1872 when Horace Greeley became the party's presidential candidate. Maryland's Democratic masses did not flock to the polls to vote for the quaint old Abolitionist. Barely a thousand votes statewide separated Greeley from Grant. Safe congressional districts wavered. The 1st District elected Ephraim Wilson by only 600 votes. The 2nd returned Stevenson Archer by 288. In Baltimore, incumbents Thomas Swann and William O'Brien faced no Republican opposition; they eked out 1,200 vote margins over weak independent rivals. Two districts, the 5th and 6th, fell outright to Republicans. "The result," the Baltimore *Gazette* concluded, "was entirely and altogether owing to the remarkable fondness exhibited by some of our friends to stay at home on election day."[95]

Now Greeley was gone. Moreover he had died. It behooved Democrats to exorcise his phantom, to bid his spirit depart forever. No ghost must remain – no taste or aftertaste, especially, of Greeley's sympathy for blacks and civil rights.

93 Gallatin *Democrat*, October 8, 1874. DeBolt lied. The vote was not to refer but to pass the bill. It could not be reached by a simple majority. Voters, he assumed, seldom fact-checked the Congressional Record.

94 Gallatin *Democrat*, October 8, 1874.

95 Baltimore *Gazette*, quoted in Frederick *Maryland Union*, November 21, 1872.

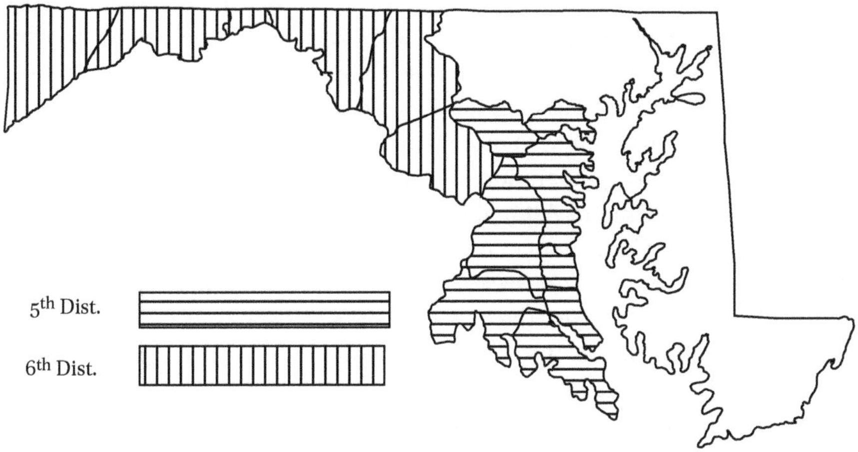

MAP 10 Congressional Districts, Maryland
SOURCE: AUTHORS OF *WELCOMING RUIN*.

Then, Democrats hoped, their friends might venture from their homes and vote. (see Map 10, above)

Maryland, Fifth District
Alexander Hagner (R), Eli Henkle (D)
Population: 54% white

Horace Greeley's ghost hovered over the 5th District. It transformed a contest between two moderate candidates into a referendum on race. The district began in Howard County. It included a small slice of Baltimore city (the 17th Ward) and districts 1 and 13 of Baltimore County. It extended through Anne Arundel County with the city of Annapolis to the state's southern tip, St. Mary's County. Black people were a distinct, though significant minority. They predominated in Charles and Calvert Counties. The balance was close in St. Mary's and Anne Arundel. Howard County and the Baltimore annexes contained the largest preponderance of white persons.

Republican William J. Albert had won the 5th District in 1872. Democrats itched to reclaim it. Calvert, Charles and St. Mary's, along with Prince George's County, favored Republicans. Anne Arundel swung Democratic, though the city of Annapolis remained Republican. Democrats enjoyed their heartiest support in Baltimore's 17th Ward, Baltimore County and Howard County. In 1872 Greeley's deadening hand helped Republicans carry Anne Arundel and secure a 97 vote margin in Howard County.

William Albert was a banker, president of the First National Bank of Maryland and director of other banks and enterprises. In 1861 he helped save his state for the Union. He worked to cleanse slavery from the state constitution. He was a philanthropist. He spent his fortune for the welfare of the freed people, benefactions that endowed more than 100 rural schools and the Baltimore Normal School for the preparation of black teachers.[96] He had lobbied in support of the first Civil Rights Act in 1866. He voted three times for its supplementary successor. But Congressman Albert's health, at 58, was precarious. On July 1 he announced he would not seek reelection. "Advancing years and declining health admonish me to leave the field of politics."[97]

The Annapolis *Gazette,* the district's leading Republican sheet, considered potential replacements. Local party chairman William R. Wilmer appeared a favorite. Gradually another name rose. Alexander B. Hagner was a lawyer, a native of Washington D.C., educated at Princeton. He settled at Annapolis. Though he never found his way into Congress, he enjoyed a distinguished career. President Hayes nominated him to a prestigious bench, the United States District Court for the District of Columbia. There he resided for a quarter century, until he stepped down in 1903.

In politics Alexander Hagner had traveled a circuitous route. Once a Whig, he flirted with the Know-Nothings. He supported the ticket of Bell and Everett in 1860. Finally he came around to the Republicans. His conservative leanings recommended him to Republicans in a Democratic-leaning district. The *Gazette* applauded his "pure record and character."[98] When the convention met at Annapolis Junction on September 23, Hagner took the nod over William Wilmer. In his remarks Wilmer made favorable mention of the Civil Rights Bill. Hagner did not.

Democrats meanwhile wrestled with Greeley's ghost. Party leaders preferred a cautious approach. But an agitator appeared, forcing them to confront the phantom, and to confront civil rights. Benjamin G. Harris had represented the district during the war. He was an uncompromising partisan. The 38th Congress censured him for "treasonable utterances." The 39th Congress expelled him for outright treason, concealing un-paroled Confederate officers in his home. He earned a sentence of imprisonment and loss of citizenship. President Johnson pardoned the offense. Now Harris emerged, ready to challenge his wayward political party. He announced he would run again for Congress. If Democrats denied him, he would run as an Independent. On only one condition would

---

96 Barnes, *The American Government,* vol. 2, 230–232.

97 Annapolis *Gazette,* July 7, 1874.

98 Annapolis *Gazette,* August 11, 18, 1874.

he desist. They must agree to a platform of his dictation: white supremacy; no Greeleyesque notions; no "equal justice to all."

"Turn back the clock," the Republican Annapolis *Gazette* sneered, "and set Sambo hoein' 'taters for old Mars."[99] Democrats worried. Harris' extremism, the Anne Arundel *Advertiser* warned, would sink the party.[100] The party, Harris replied, had sunk itself by the adoption of Greeleyism. "My policy is to throw Greeley to the dogs.... I will not agree that the party shall make another attempt at suicide." He pledged never to admit the 14th and 15th Amendments. He swore to repeal the Ku-Klux Act. If he got to Congress he would expel all non-white members from those halls.[101] Benjamin Harris dictated. Democrats capitulated.

The nominating convention met at Annapolis on September 16. Ex-governor Oden Bowie presided. On the 104th ballot Dr. Eli J. Henkle emerged the winner. That was it. The convention adjourned. It produced no platform, no resolutions, no statement of principles. It left a candidate free to adopt any set of principles he wished: to adopt the principles of Benjamin Harris.[102] Dr. Henkle was a prosperous person. He supplemented his physician's fees with an appointment as a director of the Baltimore and Potomac Railroad. He had served in the State Senate and House of Delegates. Even the Annapolis *Gazette* liked him.[103] He had supported Horace Greeley in 1872. Now he shed all trace of Greeley. It was bitter wine he served. Eli Henkle took a sharp right turn.

Henkle inaugurated his campaign at Leonardtown, coincidentally Benjamin Harris' hometown. Harris was at home. He warmed up the crowd with a rousing speech. Repeal the 15th Amendment. Disfranchise black people. He waved forward the candidate. Henkle embraced the theme. "He was a States' Rights Democrat, a Democrat of the old school. This government was made by white men, for white men, and should now be controlled by white men.... White men shall rule, the white superior, the white man supreme." Greeley be damned. "The Democratic candidate for the Presidency might with as much propriety have been a negro as Horace Greeley." He congratulated the people on their fine new county jail; he had been glad to notice in passing only black faces peering through the bars.[104]

---

99 Annapolis *Gazette*, June 16, 1874.

100 In Annapolis *Gazette*, August 4, 1874.

101 Annapolis *Gazette*, June 16, 1874.

102 Annapolis *Gazette*, September 22, 1874.

103 Henkle amiably sent the Republican paper his recipe for home-made blackberry wine. "Try it," the *Gazette* urged its readers, "and send us a bottle." Annapolis *Gazette*, July 7, 1874.

104 Annapolis *Gazette*, June 16, 1874.

As Dr. Henkle continued, a twinge of conscience seems to have intruded upon his thoughts. He spoke next at Port Tobacco. He wanted it known that he had voted in the State Senate to allow Negroes some rights, for instance the right to testify in court. He had voted subsidies for colored schools. But that was enough. As to the Civil Rights Bill, "every man knows it means social equality and mixed schools, and these will come upon us if we allow Radicals enough to be returned to Congress."[105]

He thoroughly banished Horace Greeley. Here he felt compelled to apologize. He had attended the Democratic National Convention of 1872. He had supported the Greeley ticket. But, he was pleased to say, that was only a political maneuver, "a policy affair merely." No Democrat really believed in Greeley's doctrines, equal rights, not then and not now. Finally, following Harris' lead, he disowned the 14th and 15th amendments, "the offspring of force and fraud.… They were de facto amendments, and we are compelled to submit to them, but he would blot them out if he could."[106]

Henkle's conversion accomplished its purpose. Benjamin Harris called off his independent campaign. "Greeleyism is, I think, completely repudiated by candidate and people," he announced, "and the contest can now be carried on under a pure white banner." On October 22 at Annapolis Henkle again demanded repeal of the 14th and 15th amendments. He tied the 14th Amendment to its legitimate offspring, the Civil Rights Bill. For that reason alone the amendment deserved blotting out. Civil rights served Eli Henkle as a constant campaign motivator. "A shibboleth," the *Gazette* complained, "a bugaboo to frighten the ignorant."[107]

The "bugaboo" frightened Republicans, ignorant or wise. "The Civil Rights Bill is an ill-advised one, and meets our entire disapprobation," the *Gazette* pronounced, "impractical and mischievous legislation, repugnant to four-fifths of the people … humbug and political claptrap, and as such all sensible people regard it."[108] Alexander Hagner repeated that line in rallies at Annapolis, St. Mary's, Upper Marlboro.[109] He grew so insistent upon the matter that he left Dr. Henkle exasperated. His opponent's assurances, Henkle declared, would not last. Party pressure would force him into line.

For black voters Hagner developed a separate theme. He opposed the Civil Rights Bill but he favored civil rights. "He was for maintaining to the fullest

105 Annapolis *Gazette*, October 27, 1874.
106 Annapolis *Gazette*, October 27, 1874.
107 Annapolis *Gazette*, October 13, 27, 1874.
108 Annapolis *Gazette*, June 2, September 29, October 6, 1874.
109 Annapolis *Gazette*, October 20, 1874; Baltimore *Sun*, October 23, 1874.

extent every civil and political right of the colored man, and he was also willing to vote for whatever measures requisite to secure their rights to the full."[110] Baltimore's black leader John H. Butler came out to support that message, whatever it meant. Vote for Hagner.[111]

Alexander Hagner's vote matched that achieved by William Albert under far more favorable circumstances. Black voters ignored civil rights apostasy. They voted as they had before. White voters voted as they had not before. They exorcised Greeley's ghost. They expelled the shameful shadow of equal rights.

Maryland, Sixth District
Lloyd Lowndes, Jr. (R), William Walsh (D) James Montgomery (I)
Population: 87% white

The 6th District presented Democrats a puzzle. It possessed an electorate that was white but sympathetic to Republicans. Its Republican congressman repudiated civil rights bills. Democrats denounced him for complicity with his party's measure. He renounced complicity. They denounced him for duplicity because he renounced complicity.

Maryland's 6th stretched north and west from Washington, D.C. It passed through Montgomery, Frederick, Washington, Allegany to newly-formed Garrett County, the end of the state's panhandle. It did not contain a large black population, only 19,000 of 142,000 inhabitants, but it did contain a significant population of white Republicans. Four of the district's five counties, Frederick, Washington, Allegany and Garrett included the most active Republican areas in the state.[112] Montgomery County remained the most reliable Democratic bastion.

The incumbent, Republican Lloyd Lowndes, was a man in the middle of a civil rights muddle. In the House he sat in the very middle of the civil rights contingent – seat 100 west, just to the left of Ben Butler and Josiah Walls, almost alongside Joseph Rainey in seat 97. At home a civil rights muddle confronted him. He was not unsympathetic to civil rights. But his political instincts deduced that civil rights damaged his chances to remain in office. On all votes, except that of June 8 when he was absent, he voted No. He underlined his opposition with an amendment explicitly to strike out the mixed-school clause. No one could mistake Lloyd Lowndes' position.

110 Annapolis *Gazette*, October 20, 1874.

111 Baltimore *Sun*, October 23; Annapolis *Gazette*, October 27, 1874.

112 Margaret L. Calcott, *The Negro in Maryland Politics, 1870–1912* (Baltimore: 1969), 66–67.

The congressman arrived at that position through easy calculation. His district was white. Many of its residents had resisted secession. They could be induced to support Republicans. That did not mean they supported notions of racial equality. The Frederick *Maryland Union* understood: "The truth is the sentiment of the Sixth Congressional District of Maryland is Democratic and Mr. Lowndes has sense enough to know this, and hence it is not likely that he will pursue such a course in Congress as will please the three thousand negroes [voters] of his District and displease all the white men."[113]

The Cumberland *Times* (Democratic) congratulated the congressman on his betrayal of his black constituents: "Mr. Lowndes has swallowed about as much of the colored man and brother as he finds consistent with a robust state of political health."[114] Still Lloyd Lowndes worried about his political health. Thousands of "honest Republicans" the *Maryland Union* predicted, would abandon their party. "Their honest convictions and their high sense of duty will urge them to strike hands with those who are opposed to the Civil Rights Bill."[115]

Mixed schools, of course, were the ultimate horror. Here Lowndes saw a chance to break free. On January 2, just as the House prepared to debate, a letter reached him. Dr. McFadden A. Newell, President of the Maryland Board of Education, wrote urgently. Do something. Save public education in Maryland. Already the legislature was preparing plans to shut down the schools. "It cannot be concealed that if the issue were presented to the Legislature of 'mixed schools' or 'no schools' there would probably be a majority of 'no schools.'" The state supported 210 colored schools; 12,000 black children attended. All that noble work would end. "In Maryland, for the present at least," Dr. Newell advised, "we must have separate schools or no schools."[116]

Four days later Lowndes presented his amendment, a proviso insisting on the sufficiency of separate-but-equal in public education.[117] One day after that Ben Butler withdrew the Civil Rights Bill. Lowndes' courageous act, reports said, had stopped the bill's passage. But it attracted Republican discontent. Challengers rose. State Senator Dr. Lewis Steiner, a Radical stalwart, announced himself a candidate for the congressional nomination, as did another aspirant,

113 Frederick *Maryland Union*, November 21, 1872.

114 Quoted in Frederick *Maryland Union*, June 4, 1874.

115 Frederick *Maryland Union*, June 11, 1874.

116 Frederick *Maryland Union*, January 22, 1874.

117 *Cong. Record*, 43rd Congress, 1st Session: 407: "Provided, That when separate schools are provided for white and colored children, the children of each race shall have admission only to the schools for that race."

Captain Henry Clay Naill.[118] Naill committed himself to the Civil Rights Bill. Frederick Douglass and John Mercer Langston endorsed him. The *Maryland Union* took note. If 6th District Republicans stood by their principles they ought to stand by Capt. Naill. But, the *Union* concluded, they would not. White votes would vanish if they stood by their principles.[119]

Lloyd Lowndes had an answer. He dropped out of the race. If the party preferred to seek a principled candidate, let it do so. After it had finished seeking, it would return to him. Lowndes made that announcement on July 14 in a letter to district chairman Charles Gilpin.[120] Ten days of seeking seemed sufficient. On the 24th he hinted he might reconsider, if Republicans offered him the nomination unanimously.[121] "He has changed his opinion," the *Union* chuckled, "and will graciously consent to go it once more."[122] Republicans met at Hagerstown on September 10. Steiner and Naill withdrew. Lloyd Lowndes received the party's gracious consent.[123]

Democrats also traveled a twisty road. Ex-congressman John Ritchie, having lost to Lowndes in 1872, wanted his job back. The *Maryland Union* endorsed him, as did the Cumberland *Times*.[124] Other hopefuls included Andrew K. Syester of Washington County, currently Maryland's Attorney-General. A Confederate hero rode into the race: Major Henry Kyd Douglas, erstwhile aide-de-camp and tireless adulator of Stonewall Jackson. Syester was a solid establishment creature. Douglas inspired the rebel vote, but he threatened to alienate the district's unionists. There was also a 46 year old Cumberland lawyer, William Walsh.

Party leaders had a better idea. They circulated the name of Montgomery Blair. Reports began early in June.[125] Blair, a Democrat, yet one-time member of Abraham Lincoln's cabinet, would unite all factions. "Mr. Blair's name is a tower of strength," the *Union* proclaimed.[126] His move seemed promising. Ex-governors Thomas Swann and William Pinckney Whyte supported him. But the rank and file demurred. There was the smell of a fix. Party boss Arthur Pue Gorman, rumors reported, had set up Blair's candidacy in furtherance of one of his (Gorman's) lucrative "jobs," the Trans-Alleghany Canal extension.

---

118 Frederick *Maryland Union*, June 11; Baltimore *Sun*, July 18, 1874.
119 Frederick *Maryland Union*, July 23, August 6, 1874.
120 Annapolis *Gazette*, July 14; Frederick *Maryland Union*, July 16, 1874.
121 Annapolis *Gazette*, July 24; Baltimore *Sun*, July 24, 1874.
122 Frederick *Maryland Union*, July 30, 1874.
123 Martinsburg *Independent*, September 12; Frederick *Maryland Union*, September 17, 1874.
124 Frederick *Maryland Union*, July 23, 30, August 20, 1874.
125 Annapolis *Gazette*, June 9; Baltimore *Sun*, June 10, 1874.
126 Frederick, *Maryland Union*, June 18, 1874.

A mere several millions in government subsidies, facilitated by a Congressman Blair, would put the waterway through to the Ohio River – and put money in Gorman's pocket. Blair, coincidentally, sat on the canal project's board of directors.[127]

The Democratic convention opened at Hagerstown on September 2. Blair held the delegates of Montgomery County. Frederick County favored Ritchie. Washington County supported Syester. Allegany County voted for William Walsh. One hundred thirteen ballots brought no decision. On the 114th Frederick County came over to Walsh. The great man fell. Walsh emerged the Democratic choice. The platform proposed only three resolutions. The very first item contained its denunciation of the Civil Rights Bill.[128]

Congressman Lowndes, of course, had repudiated civil rights. "Believe him not," said the Cumberland *Times*. "Trust him not." He had betrayed the Negroes. He would betray the whites. In fact he had already betrayed them. A secret deal was in the works. Lowndes had assured the blacks: "If they will vote for him this time, he will vote for the Civil Rights Bill at the next session of Congress." Lowndes denied it. His denial, the *Union* returned, proved it was true; why else would he deny it?[129]

The logic was tortured. But it tortured Lloyd Lowndes. Black voters meanwhile did feel betrayed. In August a large and angry assembly gathered in Baltimore. They singled out Mr. Lowndes. "They denounced him in the bitterest terms for his opposition to this [civil rights] measure, and the feeling appeared to be unanimous not to support him or any other man who either voted against it, or is in any manner opposed to it."[130] Finally, it seemed, black people would mount a serious revolt against a Republican renegade. Mutiny had fizzled at Savannah, at Raleigh, at Fredericksburg. It failed at Nashville and Knoxville. Would it succeed in Maryland?

Lowndes tried to head off insurrection. He circulated a letter. "Personally," he explained, he favored the Civil Rights Bill. But the majority of his constituents opposed it. He had to respect their opinion.[131] He imported black leaders for

127 Frederick *Maryland Union*, March 26; Annapolis *Gazette*, June 9; Chicago *Tribune*, September 26, 1874. See Walter S. Sanderlin, "Arthur P. Gorman and the Chesapeake and Ohio Canal: An Episode in the Rise of a Political Boss," *Journal of Southern History*, 13 (1947): 323–337.

128 Baltimore *Sun*, September 3; Frederick *Maryland Union*, September 10, 1874.

129 Frederick *Maryland Union*, September 17, 1874.

130 Frederick *Maryland Union*, August 6, 1874.

131 Baltimore *Sun*, August 12, 1874.

support. John H. Butler, having helped the similarly-afflicted Alexander Hagner in the 5th District, arrived in the 6th. Isaac Myers of the Colored National Labor Union also hurried over from Baltimore. Myers and Butler confronted black voters in Cumberland. Before they could finish their remarks the crowd hooted them down.[132] Myers spoke at Frederick. Sumner's bill, he insisted, "would do the negro more harm than good if it passed – Mr. Lloyd Lowndes did right in opposing it, and it was only the stupid and ignorant negroes, who did not understand what was good for themselves, who were clamoring for its passage."[133] The audience turned a deaf ear. The revolt grew.

On September 21 the mutineers met at Cumberland. A crowd filled the Good Templar's Hall on Baltimore Street. Their organization, the Frederick Douglass Club, led the way. Chairman Emanuel Martin put Republicans on notice:

> A great many leading Republicans think we are bound to come down and vote for them anyhow.... We do not intend to be considered as safe to vote for any party right or wrong, nor do we intend to be led into a campaign where such rank injustice is contemplated against us.... Some say we are going to butcher the party. No! But we do not intend to let the party butcher us.[134]

Other speakers counseled caution. It was futile, argued Rev. A.B. Wilson. If they expectorated a Republican they must swallow a Democrat: "Two candidates are announced for your suffrages. You must make your choice of one or the other. Some say they won't vote. That is not the part of good citizens. You must make up your minds to support either Mr. Walsh or Mr. Lowndes." The Frederick Douglass Club made up its mind. It spat out Lloyd Lowndes. His conduct "indicated an almost malicious hostility to the rights, interests and feelings of the colored people."[135] A voice called out: "Who are you going to vote for?" Voices answered: "Nary one! Nary one!"

Lowndes opened negotiations with the malcontents. Once again, according to the Democratic Cumberland *Times,* he promised he would vote for the Civil

132 Frederick *Maryland Union*, September 24, 1874.

133 Frederick *Maryland Union*, October 1, 1874. Myers was consistent. In January he had written to Ben Butler: "We recognize in you one of the best friends of our race in this country." But, he warned, drop the Civil Rights Bill. "We stand in danger of losing much that we have gained, without hope of recovery." Isaac Myers to Benjamin Butler, January 8, 1874. Butler Papers, Library of Congress.

134 Frederick *Maryland Union*, October 1, 1874.

135 Frederick *Maryland Union*, October 8, 1874.

Rights Bill if black voters would vote for him. But they must keep it secret until after the election. Its source, the *Times* claimed, was trustworthy, a bona fide member of the Fred Douglass Club, "one of the most responsible colored men of this city." The club, the informant said, had declined the congressman's slippery promises. Democrats spread the word: "How can he [Lowndes] explain such disreputable double-dealing? Is he willing to vote for the civil rights bill as a price for colored votes? Were his votes recorded against that instrument a sham and a trick? ... Who is he deceiving, the white people or the colored people?"[136] Republicans denied the whole thing. There was no secret deal. Where was the proof? No proof needed, the *Union* replied. A secret was necessarily secret.[137] The Frederick Douglass Club declared a bolt. It named its own congressional candidate, a black man, James H. Montgomery. The Cumberland *Times* published its announcement:

> The Fred Douglass Club of Allegany County, Md., has requested Mr. James H. Montgomery, a colored man, to be an independent candidate for Congress in the Sixth District of that State, and he has consented.... Mr. Lowndes, the Republican nominee is not thoroughly a Republican, and if he should be elected he could urge in Congress the fact that he was opposed to the Civil Rights bill, and was supported by colored voters in spite of that opposition, as a significant proof that the colored people do not desire the passage of the bill.[138]

For the first time a black Marylander stood for federal office.[139] The Frederick *Examiner* (Republican) urged voters to give the bolter a cool reception.

> A contemptible negro named James Montgomery, who left this city for Cumberland, Md., some twelve months ago (between two days) is now in this county circulating republican tickets with his name on them as a candidate for Congress. Colored men, don't be deceived by this villain who has been hired by the democracy to do this dirty work. A coat of tar and feathers might be serviceable.[140]

136 Cumberland *Times*, quoted in Frederick *Maryland Union*, October 15, 1874.
137 Frederick *Maryland Union*, October 22, 1874.
138 Cumberland *Times*, quoted in Frederick *Maryland Union*, October 22, 1874.
139 Baltimore *Sun*, October 28; New York *Times*, October 31, 1874.
140 Quoted in Baltimore *Sun*, October 29, 1874.

Rev. Wilson warned again. Think carefully. A bolt would do more harm than good. Montgomery's supporters refused: "If he [Lowndes] is not to be catechized for his voting with Democrats in Congress, we ought not to be at the polls."[141] A black voter rebellion, finally, had caught fire. Then, from the most unexpected quarter, a fireman arrived to snuff it out. Frederick Douglass, hero and eponym of the Frederick Douglass Club, reprimanded his club for its presumption. He sent a letter to the Cumberland *News.* He left his clubmen aghast. Stop! Black voters must return to party discipline. Lloyd Lowndes, Douglass agreed, is a scoundrel. But he's our scoundrel. Keep him in Congress.[142] Such was the real Frederick Douglass' command.

Democrats, savoring Republican fratricide, were incensed. The *Maryland Union* exploded with contempt for the nation's preeminent black leader: "a demagogue and a base hypocrite besides ... like a filthy dog he turned and swallowed his own vomit." James Montgomery refrained from vilifying his hero. He continued his campaign. That campaign languished and died.

Results came in. Lowndes carried Frederick County and Allegany County. He took Garrett County by 20 votes. He fell 19 short in Washington County. Montgomery County defeated him. Walsh carried it with 500 to spare. He went to Congress by 77 votes. James Montgomery, for his part, attracted exactly 25 votes.[143]

The election in Maryland's 6th District put to the test the Democrats' most cherished axiom, that Republicans needed the Civil Rights Bill, that they had designed the Civil Rights Bill for one purpose: to retain the votes of their black adherents. The Sixth District race, more clearly than any other contest, laid that theory to rest. No Republican candidate maintained his civil rights opposition more emphatically than did Lloyd Lowndes. No black constituents seemed more determined to punish a renegade. James Montgomery exhorted them to stand up and deliver an unmistakable message. Give us the bill or lose our votes. Precisely two dozen black voters stood up. Frederick Douglass himself ordered his people to desist.

Black people remained loyal. Black voters voted.[144] There was no reason to abstain. James Montgomery provided them a perfect opportunity to express their discontent at the polls, to vote for a black man and affirm their

141 Frederick *Maryland Union*, October 15, 1874.

142 Chicago *Inter Ocean*, October 29; Frederick *Maryland Union*, November 5, 1874.

143 Calcott, *The Negro in Maryland Politics*: 58.

144 Black voter turnout was consistent with other years. It fell slightly in Washington County, Montgomery and Frederick. It rose in Allegany County. See Calcott, 167–187.

enthusiasm for the Civil Rights Bill. They affirmed neither. Lowndes, the *Union* concluded, had played his hand brilliantly.[145] The Baltimore *Sun* agreed. "It is alleged that repudiation of the civil rights bill by those gentlemen [Lowndes and Hagner] caused their defeat. Nothing is more obvious than the fact that their avowed hostility to that odious measure was the only reason why they received so respectable a measure of the suffrage in their respective districts, and was the only card they played with astuteness."[146]

145 Frederick *Maryland Union*, November 5, 1874.

146 Baltimore *Sun*, November 6, 1874.

CHAPTER 11

Taliaferro's Ghost: Border States and the North; Obituary

1 Delaware

Delaware, At-large
James R. Lofland (R), James Williams (D)
Population: 78% white

Delaware balanced on the edge of the north. It tilted, temperamentally and politically, southward. Not until 1901 did its legislature ratify the Thirteenth, Fourteenth or Fifteenth Amendments.[1] Its governorship remained in Democratic hands. The senatorial seats were fiefdoms shared by Saulsburys and Bayards. For the moment Eli Saulsbury and Thomas F. Bayard held sway. The state's single congressional seat was coterminous with the state. Only one Republican, James Lofland, the present incumbent, had ever occupied it; another did not arrive for two decades. The state had been slave-owning, but by the time of emancipation that shackled population had declined.

African Americans represented a distinct minority; 23,000 appeared among 125,000 Delawareans in 1870. Ten thousand resided in New Castle County with its city of Wilmington. Kent County held a further 7,000, the rest being found in southern Sussex County. Their numbers, small in relation to the state's entire population, were considerable in relation to its Republican population. Delaware's Assessment and Collection Act of 1873, allowing politically-motivated officials to disenfranchise delinquent taxpayers, effectively reduced the number of black Republicans who could be expected to vote. Most of Congressman Lofland's votes must come from white people. He could be certain his opponent would use the Civil Rights Bill against him. "However dead an issue the negro question may be in other States," noted the New York *Tribune*, "Delaware Democracy still clings to the old issues of opposition."[2] The Wilmington *Every*

1 Harold B. Hancock, "Reconstruction in Delaware," in Richard O. Curry, ed., *Radicalism, Racism, and Party Realignment: The Border States During Reconstruction* (Baltimore: 1969), 191–192; John H. Gauger, "A Delaware Experiment with Reconstruction Nullification," *Delaware History*, 21 (1985): 166–168.

2 New York *Tribune*, August 14, 1874.

Evening expected civil rights to lead the Democratic campaign. "Such a line of attack will be likely to prove very embarrassing to the Republicans."[3] It embarrassed James Lofland, and confounded him when the civil rights votes arrived in Congress. On May 25 he voted Aye. On June 8 he voted No. On June 20 he was nowhere to be found.

Lofland came from a noted Delaware family, whose pedigree recalled the poet John Lofland, "The Bard of Milford." He had served in the State Senate and then as Secretary of the State. He did not impress observers with force or clarity of character. Democrats, perhaps unjustly, attributed his intermittent befuddlement to insobriety. During the campaign reporters spotted him drinking liberally, "and it was not water." The congressman denied it; he had been on the wagon for seven years.[4]

Black Delawareans targeted Lofland, drunk or sober. In June Wilmington's black people assembled at the Bethel African Methodist Church. Sojourner Truth, 77 years old, spoke "in her quaint and forcible manner." John W. Eaton, a young lawyer, graduate of Howard University, rose. "The weak-kneed action of Major Lofland on the Civil Rights bill" was treason. "Better to send a Democrat to Congress than such a man."[5] Eaton's associates formed an Equal Rights League, "to declare their unalterable devotion to the great principles of Human Liberty ... the civil, political and public equality of all men."[6]

Democrats struck from the opposite direction. Former congressman and future governor Benjamin T. Biggs outlined their race-based campaign.

> There is something innate in the heart of every true white Delawarean that leads him instinctively to the Democratic party.... I welcome all white men to its ranks. I want no man of African descent to help swell its triumph. If the Civil Rights bill should pass, as I hope it may not, and as I believe it will not, the attempt will then have been made to force the complete equality of the races. The slave of yesterday is made our equal at the polls to-day, and to-morrow will be our equal in all respects ... but he is not the white man's equal and cannot be made so.[7]

With that succinct statement Democrats opened their state convention at Dover on August 27. Nominations went to John P. Cochran for governor and

3 Wilmington, Delaware, *Every Evening*, August 13, 1874.
4 Wilmington, Delaware, *Commercial*, October 24, November 2, 1874.
5 Wilmington *Every Evening*, June 24, 1874.
6 Wilmington *Every Evening*, August 26, 1874.
7 Wilmington *Every Evening*, June 8, 1874.

James Williams for Congress. Williams was an unassuming man, a farmer, who did not much take to public speaking. The party spoke for him. The platform contained ten items; three condemned the Civil Rights Bill, "a wild, cruel, reckless measure ... an intermingling of those races whose essential differences have been marked and established by Almighty God."[8] The Georgetown *Sussex Journal* ran the text of the Senate bill under its masthead for the entire campaign. Copies of Sumner's infamy should be passed out everywhere, it advised, "hand-billed by the thousands, placed and replaced into the hands of every man, woman, and child." Distribute them at the schools. Little ones could bring them back as homework for their parents to study. "The more the infamous thing is read by the fireside, the better it is understood by the mother as she dandles her infant upon her knee, the more intelligently will the head of the family vote."[9] Senator Bayard took to the stump. Dandling mothers beware. Civil rights meant mixed marriage. Marriage was a civil, licensed contract, was it not? The bill mandated civil equality, did it not? Mixed marriages would be mandatory.[10]

Republicans gathered at Georgetown on July 28. They re-nominated James Lofland and chose Dr. Isaac Jump for governor. The platform arraigned Democrats for every species of wrongdoing.[11] Democrats, Dr. Jump declared, had accumulated a state debt of one and a half million dollars, "and we have nothing to show for it." Their resolutions were diversions. "They commence with an admiration of themselves and end with the suffering of Louisiana.... They talk about the 'plundered and misgoverned South' but have nothing to say regarding the wrongs of the people of Delaware."[12]

Dr. Jump mentioned civil rights kindly. James Lofland did not. It was "an assumption of power not warranted by the Federal Constitution." The Wilmington *Every Evening* applauded the congressman's move, "the smartest from a politician's standpoint." He might lose a few Negro votes, but to do otherwise would cost him "three-fourths of the votes of the white Republicans." And furthermore, "the niggers have got to vote with us anyway."[13] Lofland too mocked the Democrats' campaign. "Their resolutions are as applicable to the Fiji Island as to Delaware. They dodge every state issue and fly off to Louisiana and the Civil Rights bill."

8 Wilmington *Every Evening*, August 28, 1874.
9 Quoted in Wilmington *Every Evening*, August 28, 1874.
10 Wilmington, *Every Evening*, September 7, 1874.
11 Wilmington *Commercial*; Wilmington *Every Evening*, July 29, 1874.
12 Wilmington *Commercial*, October 17, 19, 1874.
13 Wilmington *Every Evening*, September 30, October 1, 1874.

> They tell you that we are in favor of negro equality, and that I am an equal rights man. I tell you I am not in favor of the Civil Rights bill, mixed schools, nor mixed breeds. [They tell you] that I voted for the bill. This all intelligent men know is not true.... When General Butler moved to take that bill from the Judiciary Committee and put it upon its final passage I voted against it. This is the whole case.[14]

Republicans resorted to the fading bloody shirt. They poured fresh blood and waved it frantically: "Rebels and traitors band together under the catch word of Democracy," the Wilmington *Commercial* pleaded. "The slain of every battle field call upon you to honor their memories by perpetuating at the polls what they died to build up."[15] The slain called in vain. Nor did it help when murky stories circulated. Ante-bellum, Lofland had owned slaves, stored for safe keeping in Maryland. Some of his property escaped. He had them hunted down and resold in the Richmond market, along with them a free Negro who had sheltered the fugitives. Lofland himself purchased this person, as per the bill of sale recorded: "Elijah Prates, sold, on the eleventh day of May, 1859, after due notice given, to James R. Lofland Esq., for the term of seven years, for the sum of five hundred dollars, he being the highest bidder."[16]

Sordid slave-owning past, present civil rights rejection, Democrats hoped would give black voters pause. Black voters ignored James Lofland's past. They ignored his civil-rights-bill-opposition present. Once again they supported a civil rights renegade. Lofland took just 350 votes fewer in 1874 than he had in 1872. He lost to Williams by five times that number. A wave of white men, whipped up by civil rights fear, swamped him.

2 West Virginia

Congressional alignment divided West Virginia into three districts. Democrats held the 1st, including the northern panhandle, and the 3rd, occupying the center and south of the state. There the incumbent, bespectacled lawyer Frank Hereford, was a salary grabber. But he had donated the money away. His constituents accepted his mea culpa. He survived to win re-nomination, re-election, and eventually a seat in the United States Senate. Republicans ran a candidate against him, only to see their champion withdraw in the last weeks of the campaign. A replacement took up the fallen banner. He disappeared

14 Wilmington *Commercial*, October 24, 1874.
15 Wilmington *Commercial*, November 2, 1874.
16 Wilmington *Every Evening*, November 2, 1874.

beneath an avalanche of 6,000 votes. The race, concluded the Republican Wheeling *Intelligencer,* was hopeless from the start. "The people as a matter of course are governed largely by their prejudices. The Civil Rights bill is what did the work."[17] In the 2nd District Republicans preemptively surrendered. Civil rights did its work anyway. (see Map 11, below)

West Virginia, Second District
Charles James Faulkner (D), Alexander Boteler (I)
Population: 96% white

Two hundred ninety-two men sat in the U.S. House of Representatives. Some rejoiced in their constituents' support. Some clung to shaky seats. Others arrived unaccountably, an electoral happenstance, a fluke, a split vote. They were accidental congressmen. None was more accidental than Republican John Marshall Hagans, temporary occupant of West Virginia's 2nd District. From the

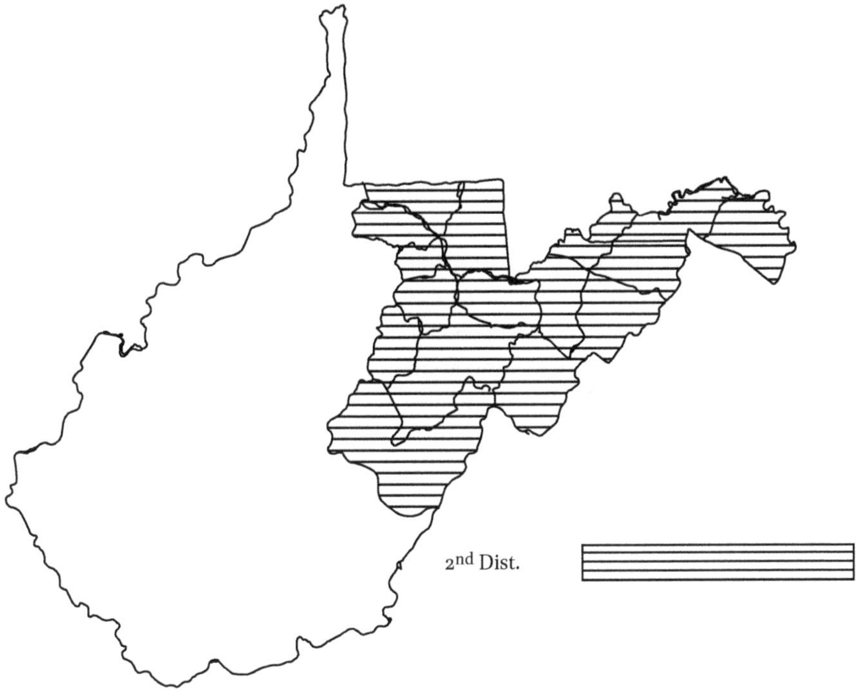

MAP 11 Congressional Districts, West Virginia
SOURCE: AUTHORS OF *WELCOMING RUIN.*

17 Wheeling *Intelligencer*, October 19, 1874.

moment of his election he was a lame duck. No one knew it better than John Marshall Hagans. Hagans was the product of a strange double election, an election in one half of which Democrats did not participate.

West Virginia's legislature, having come under Democratic control in 1872, rewrote the state constitution. It provided for congressional elections on August 23 of that year, the vote to coincide with a referendum ratifying the constitution. Many counties objected to the eccentric election date, preferring to abide by the traditional fall schedule. Two separate votes occurred. August turnout was low. More people voted in October. Winners and losers called upon Congress to decide. Congress accepted the first results, seating Independent Democrat John J. Davis in the 1st District and giving Republican Hagans the 2nd.[18] There in the August contest only 4,179 votes were cast. Hagans accumulated 3,441. Democrats ran no candidate. Independents Alexander Boteler and Ward Hill Lamon shared the residue. In October 10,000 voters voted. Almost all were Democrats.[19] None of those votes counted.

On civil rights, Congressman Hagans, having no possible worry about re-election, ought to have been the most liberated of gentlemen. No one, theoretically, was freer to vote as he chose. He chose not to vote. The first two calls marked him absent. The third marked him absent again. He awoke from his trance in time for the final civil rights vote in 1875. He voted Aye, a fitting conclusion to an accidental congressional career.

Hagans' 2nd District ran through the eastern panhandle, Jefferson, Berkeley and Morgan Counties, along the Pennsylvania line to Monongalia County, south to Webster and Pocahontas Counties. Fully 115,000 of its 120,000 inhabitants were white. The 1870 census located 231 persons of color among 13,000 residents of Monongalia County; 118 existed in Preston County, with 14,000 whites; 78 dwelt furtively among 12,000 whites in Marion County. Census takers detected 27 in Tucker County. None at all emerged in Webster County. Berkeley County, with the town of Martinsburg, had 1,672 in a population of 15,000. Racial tension, of course, ran high. In the summer of 1874 a lurid incident ran it higher. Grisly events, the Taliaferro murder case and its disturbing aftermath, gave the public a lesson in the turmoil civil rights acts could bring.

---

18 Chester H. Rowell, *A Historical and Legal Digest of All the Contested Election Cases in the House of Representatives of the United States from the First to the Fifty-Sixth Congress, 1789–1901* (Washington: 1901), 284–286. A majority of the House Elections Committee, including its Chairman Horace Boardman Smith and North Carolinian Charles Thomas, decided in favor of the October results. The full House preferred to adopt the committee's minority report, giving precedence to the August canvass.

19 Wheeling *Intelligencer*, February 2, 1874.

On the night of October 6, 1873, in the woods beyond Martinsburg, men moved in the undergrowth. Lanterns in hand, they searched the darkness. Their light fell upon a small tortured body – all that remained of a little white girl, Annie Butler, 12 years old, raped and murdered. The murderer had left his handiwork. He also left forensic traces. They pointed to a black man, John Taliaferro. He fit the profile: active, 24 years old, an itinerant farmhand, "powerfully built, six feet in height, with a forbidding expression of countenance," so the Martinsburg *Independent* described him.[20] After one suspended hearing, authorities set him in the Martinsburg jail to await the return of the Third District Circuit Court. Proceedings promised to be routine. The public looked forward to a springtime hanging. Spring came. Nothing hung. Lawyers interfered.

The vexatious attorneys were a local pair, Lamon and Blackburn. Ward Hill Lamon, companion and once law-partner of Abraham Lincoln, was Martinsburg's most famous citizen. A new associate, H.H. Blackburn, assisted him. Railroad litigation occupied their business. But they shared an enthusiasm for justice and equality. The partners took up John Taliaferro's cause. They turned it into a test case of civil rights.

The court, in the person of Judge John Blair Hoge, arrived in Martinsburg on May 12. On the 13th came the call: State v. John Taliaferro. The affair was racially charged. The public was aroused. County Attorney R.M. Price headed the prosecution. Two lawyers sat with him: Charles James Faulkner, Sr., formerly four-times congressman from an undivided Virginia, and his son, congressman-to-be Charles James Faulkner, Jr. Attorney Blackburn led off for the defense. He presented an immediate appeal. The proceedings were improper; they violated his client's civil rights.

On Thursday, May 14 Taliaferro appeared. "The prisoner presented the same dull, stolid appearance as at the last term of the court," wrote the *Independent*. "The only change in him is he is a little thinner, and his mulatto appearance is changed from confinement to a sickly, paleish color." Unfortunately for the pale defendant, John Blair Hoge was not only a Democrat but a man with political ambitions. He satisfied those ambitions ultimately by election to the 47th Congress in 1880. The judge was in no mind now to jeopardize future popularity by entertaining civil rights appeals on behalf of a black man accused of the vilest crime imaginable to white men and voters. He wasted no time in dismissing the defense motion. That motion, nonetheless, and Judge Hoge's ruling, occasioned a remarkable digression into civil rights theory and practice.

---

20 Details of the Taliaferro affair: Martinsburg *Independent*, May 16, 23, June 6; Frederick *Maryland Union*, August 20, 1874.

Blackburn and Lamon asked the judge to transfer the case to the United States Circuit Court. They argued on two grounds – the equal protection clause of the 14th Amendment and the Civil Rights Act of 1866. That latter statute, though preceding the amendment, had defined for the first time that all persons born or naturalized in the United States were citizens of the United States. It also guaranteed citizens the "full and equal benefits of all laws and proceedings for the security of person and property." Lamon and Blackburn pointed to the third section of the 1866 Act:

> That the district courts of the United States, within their respective districts, shall have, exclusive of all courts of the several States, cognizance of all crimes and offenses committed against the provisions of this act, and also, concurrently with the circuit courts of the United States, of all causes, civil and criminal, affecting persons who are denied or cannot enforce in the courts or judicial tribunals of the State or locality where they may be any of the rights secured to them by the first section of this act; and if any suit or prosecution, civil or criminal, has been or shall be commenced in any State court against any such person, for any cause whatsoever ... such defendant shall have the right to remove such cause for trial to the proper district or circuit court in the manner prescribed.

The State of West Virginia, by act of its legislature in 1873, denied black people the right to sit on juries. Thus, Blackburn argued, the present prosecution of John Taliaferro in the tribunal of his state or locality constituted a denial of right such as the Civil Rights Act conceived, and it violated in addition the equal protection clause of the 14th Amendment. The defendant's case must be removed to the United States court properly prescribed, as in Section 3 of the Act of 1866.

Judge Hoge would have none of it. He would not, he said, "discuss the constitutionality of the Civil Rights Act, or the jurisdiction of the Federal Courts in cases arising under it." He rejected the whole idea. Excluding black persons from juries constituted no denial of equal protection to a black defendant. "If by the laws of West Virginia a discrimination is made against certain citizens because not liable to serve on juries, such discrimination is not against the petitioner." John Taliaferro could enjoy full and equal benefit of the law in the present court in Martinsburg.

> The petitioner will be tried here precisely as any other citizen of any age, sex, or color. He has the same tribunal before which he must appear; he has the same right to challenge, and the benefit of the same constitution-

> al provisions for obtaining witnesses through the process of the courts. No right granted to a white man is denied to him. There is no privilege or indulgence given to other citizens he does not share.... Indeed, the more friendless and helpless his condition, the more carefully assured to him will be every right belonging to one in his unfortunate position.... The purpose of the Civil Rights Act, to use the language of the Supreme Court, was to guard all the declared rights of colored persons in civil actions, and to afford a like protection in criminal prosecutions. None of these declared rights are or can be endangered here.[21]

Hoge anticipated the reasoning the United States Senate itself would hear a few months later from its great constitutional lawyer Allen Thurman. Jury service is not a right. It is not a privilege. It is a duty, "a duty required by the State from some of its citizens, analogous to military service." The state could exclude whom it pleased from military duty – women, for instance, and children – if it found them unfit. It could exclude whom it pleased from jury duty. Selectivity denied no citizen protection of the laws. The army protected woman and children who did not serve. Juries protected black people equally, though they did not serve. Moreover, Hoge added, if Congress had intended to cover such discrimination in its old civil rights act, why had it inserted a jury clause into its new bill?

Blackburn and Lamon filed for a change of venue; the panel of jurors had been assembled improperly because the court had not issued the summons *venire facias* thirty days in advance of the trial. Denied. Jury selection began. Thirty jurors appeared. Eight were empanelled. Judge Hoge ordered up twenty more. Blackburn presented a motion in abatement of the indictment because black persons had been excluded from the grand jury. Prosecutor Price demurred. Hoge sustained the demurrer.

Friday, May 15, the trial of John Taliaferro commenced. The defendant sat quietly, the *Independent* reported, showing no emotion. "He usually inclines his head to the right side after taking his seat, and maintains that position throughout the day." Inclined in posture, he heard Attorney Price outline the prosecution's case. On Saturday witnesses appeared. Prof. Berthollet of Philadelphia explained the forensic evidence. On Sunday the court rested. On Monday it finished. Ward Hill Lamon spoke. For an hour and a half, in words we cannot hear, Lamon pleaded with the jurors. Put aside prejudice. Forgo prejudgment. Evidence was circumstantial. Admit a reasonable doubt. Venerable

21 Martinsburg *Independent*, May 16, 1874.

Charles Faulkner, Sr. summed up for the State. Evidence was circumstantial. But it was not inconsiderable. It pointed reasonably to John Taliaferro's guilt.

Tuesday, May 19, the jurymen retired to deliberate. At 11:00, not waiting for lunch, they returned. They found John Taliaferro guilty of murder in the first degree. Lamon demanded a poll of the jury. He moved to set aside the verdict. The gavel brought Taliaferro's trial to an end. Justice had prevailed, the *Independent* concluded, but Lamon and Blackburn deserved praise: "Without reward, in the face of a settled public opinion, and sometimes open censure, they nobly performed their duty. All honor to them for their fidelity and manliness, say we, be their cause ever so bad."

Monday, June 1, sentence was passed in the Martinsburg courtroom. John Taliaferro declined to speak. He maintained his attitude of "defiant indifference." John Hoge basked in the moment. The crime was unpardonable.

> That poor child, Annie Butler, on that sad October evening, in the dim wood around which the shadows and silence of the night were gathering, poured out her young life – the victim of your murderous purpose.... The lesson which this hour teaches is not for you alone. It speaks with impressive tone to others in whose hearts vicious impulses have not yet ripened into the perpetration of actual crime.... Speaking to them of life and its obligations, its laws and its penalties, it speaks to you, only, of DEATH.[22]

Sheriff A.J. Thomas received the order to execute the prisoner on July 31 between 10 and 2 o'clock. Lamon and Blackburn filed a motion to the State Court of Appeals. Exclusion of black people from the jury, they insisted, abridged their client's equal protection of the law.[23] On July 25, six days before the date of execution, the Court of Appeals issued a writ of *supersedeas*. It agreed to reconsider John Taliaferro's case.[24]

The lynch mob waited some time. On Thursday, August 13, just at midnight, it arrived. Participants wore appropriate attire, "some of them fully and others partially disguised." They backed a wagon to the jail and conveyed the prisoner out of town. They chose a conspicuous spot where the Warm Spring Road crossed the Cumberland Valley Railroad. A locust tree stood on open ground, with a conveniently overhanging limb. At 1 a.m. proceedings commenced. The victim enjoyed fifteen minutes to pray. He protested his innocence. The body, suspended 25 yards from the railroad tracks, remained available for sightseers.

---

22 Martinsburg *Independent*, June 6, 1874.
23 Martinsburg *Independent*, July 13, 1874.
24 Martinsburg *Independent*, July 25, 1874.

Some came on foot. Some came in buggies. Passengers peered from passing trains. The corpse swung through Friday and the following night. Saturday a coroner's jury examined the scene. Its conclusion: "John Taliaferro came to his death at the hands of an organized band of men unknown."[25]

The Taliaferro events established immediately, and for months to come, a climate of racial anxiety across the 2nd District.[26] Civil rights statutes rose to voters' minds. Death threats descended upon H.H. Blackburn and Ward Hill Lamon. In an atmosphere thus charged, the congressional campaign began. White voters found a candidate eager to stoke their fear, and to remind them of the civil rights acts connected to it: Charles James Faulkner, senior, fresh from a triumphant prosecution of John Taliaferro, deceased.

Faulkner was a man in search of political rehabilitation. Once he had walked the corridors of power in a united nation. That nation had forced him out, unjustly he claimed, into the arms of rebellion.[27] He yearned to stand again in the United States House of Representatives. In the glow of the Taliaferro trial he seized his moment.

Party regulars, however, preferred one of their own. Benjamin Franklin Martin had won the second election in 1872, only to have his victory disallowed.[28] Faulkner, Martin's supporters charged, was a meddler with a muddled message. Ben Martin professed pure Democratic values. He announced contempt for a variety of un-American individuals: "carpetbaggers, negroes, and mulattoes, Chinese, Dutch, Irish, coolies, Norwegians, and scalawags" – all apparently infesting eastern West Virginia.[29] Black people had been emancipated, unfortunately; fortunately they could still be disfranchised.

---

25 Martinsburg *Independent*, August 15, 1874. The Taliaferro affair served as a precursor to a celebrated decision: the case of Strauder v. West Virginia. Even as John Taliaferro sat in his Martinsburg cell awaiting trial, another black man, Taylor Strauder, entered an Ohio County jail, charged with the murder of Anna Strauder, his wife. On October 20, an all-white jury convicted him. He too appealed. Strauder wisely had involved himself only in the death of a black person. Lynch mobs showed no interest. In 1880, the United States Supreme Court, Mr. Justice Strong writing for a 7–2 majority (Justices Field and Clifford dissenting) overturned West Virginia's exclusionary jury rule as a violation of the 14th Amendment. Three years later the Supreme Court struck down most of the Civil Rights Act. It retained the jury clause as consistent with that ruling. See Earl M. Maltz, "The Civil Rights Act and the Civil Rights Cases: Congress and the Constitution," *Florida Law Review*, 44 (1992): 628–632.

26 Martinsburg *Independent*, August 22, 1874.

27 Donald McVeigh, "Charles James Faulkner: Reluctant Rebel," Diss., University of West Virginia, 1955.

28 Martinsburg *Independent*, July 18, 1874.

29 Stephen D. Engle, "Mountaineer Reconstruction: Blacks in the Political Reconstruction of West Virginia," *Journal of Negro History*, 78 (1993): 153.

Faulkner, in contrast, seemed a weak-kneed waffler. "He is a time-server and not a statesman," wrote the Wheeling *Intelligencer*. "He now aspires to return once more to the old haunts at Washington, and should he get there will no doubt be the same French gentleman in politics he was before."[30] The Richmond *Dispatch* remembered Faulkner: "He has seen a great many changes during his life, but has, with remarkable sagacity, kept himself out of harm's way."[31] The Parkersburg *Journal* summed up the candidate:

> I was once a Whig, then a Democrat, now I am neither. I was once a Confederate, now I am a Federal. I am for gold and silver, but rather opposed to specie payment. I am opposed to civil rights, but in favor of giving the negro all he asks for.[32]

A man whose image appeared shifty required definition. In one way at least Faulkner adopted a definitive attitude. What the Negro asked he should not receive, be it civil rights or the right to kill little white children. Those requests went hand in hand.

Republicans mounted no campaign. They assembled a convention on September 9 at Cranberry Summit in Preston County. They hoped to lure the one man whose stature gave him a chance, former United States Senator Waitman Willey. Willey fled the convention. The convention pursued Willey. Willey notified the convention: if nominated he would not run. The convention insisted. "He cannot certainly refuse to answer the spontaneous call of his fellow citizens."[33] Waitman Willey refused.

Charles Faulkner heard a call, spontaneous or not. He defined his wobbly principles. He disliked centralized government. He opposed corruption. He favored specie payment. And he condemned the Civil Rights Bill.[34] The Democratic convention met at the town of Piedmont. By a vote of 76 to 63 it nominated Faulkner.[35] Ben Martin resigned himself to wait. "Honors deferred," Faulkner smarmed, "are not honors denied."

With no Republican candidate, Charles Faulkner's path to Congress seemed clear. But a rival emerged, an old rival of antebellum days, ex-congressman Alexander R. Boteler. They had run against each other in 1852 and again in 1856. Faulkner went off as ambassador to Paris in 1858. Boteler finally took the seat.

30 Wheeling *Intelligencer*, August 22, 1874.
31 Richmond *Dispatch*, July 29, 1874.
32 Quoted in Martinsburg *Independent*, August 8, 1874.
33 Wheeling *Intelligencer*, September 12; Martinsburg *Independent*, September 19, 1874.
34 Martinsburg *Independent*, July 18, 1874.
35 Wheeling *Intelligencer*, August 22, 26, 1874.

Boteler and Faulkner did not like each other. A duel once had almost settled matters between them. "Aleck" Boteler announced his independent candidacy in August. He hoped for Republican votes and for the support of Ben Martin's disappointed friends. In the end he took 8,000 votes, including a majority in four counties. He fell short by 3,500.

The candidates had no disagreement on the Civil Rights Bill. Boteler condemned it as did his competitor. But, he insisted, his opposition was sincere. Faulkner's was a matter of convenience. Faulkner denied it. At Mannington in Marion County he delivered terrifying news. Charles Sumner's bill was law; it had been passed and signed. The county's black people (78 of them) were poised to leap out and wreak havoc on the 12,000 whites.[36]

Faulkner appeared at the town of New Creek in Mineral County. United States Senator Henry Gassaway Davis, "the smiling Senator," accompanied him to the rally. The candidate reminded his audience of the deed committed in the Martinsburg woods. There were woods in Mineral County. The villain, Taliaferro, had tried to escape retribution through legal chicanery, appeals to "civil rights." Fortunately the mob had voided his appeal. At such times, said Faulkner, "judge lynch" might rule.[37]

The New Creek remarks proved an embarrassment. The candidate, it seemed, had set vigilantes above the majesty of the law. Faulkner protested. He had been misunderstood. He did not approve the lynching of prisoners. A mob had hanged a man, true. Truly it had lynched a thing, the Civil Rights Bill. A man had murdered Annie Butler, yes. Truly the Civil Rights Bill had murdered her. That enactment (not yet enacted) released vicious persons' inhibitions. In the name of equality it bred criminality. It unleashed "bad passions," libidinous license: John Taliaferro unchained. Charles Faulkner sent his clarification to the press.

> Mr. Faulkner authorizes us to say that in his speech at New Creek … he was commenting upon the evil and pernicious influences of the Civil Rights Bill now pending before Congress. He spoke of the extent to which it was stimulating the bad passions of the colored race … of the unfortunate prevalence of the crime of rape by colored persons upon white girls and women as one of the evils resulting from this social anarchy, engendered and stimulated by that bill. He said such crimes necessarily awakened much excitement and led to violence and danger.[38]

36 Wheeling *Intelligencer*, September 21, 1874.

37 Wheeling *Intelligencer*, August 19, 1874.

38 Wheeling *Intelligencer*, August 29, 1874.

Rape, murder, mob justice, and civil rights mixed a noxious cocktail in the 2nd West Virginia District. The district rested far from the deep South. Few black persons disturbed its racial symmetry. Charles Faulkner nevertheless stirred that cocktail vigorously, in an election with no Republican in sight. He poured it out for the voters' delectation. Opponents accused him of being soft on black people. He hardened himself. The civil rights antics of Lamon and Blackburn gave him an opportunity. He took it.

3 Illinois

Republicans held fourteen of Illinois' nineteen districts. Six remained after the voters had spoken. As in Missouri, an independent People's Movement arose, representing "the farmers, mechanics and laboring men." Ex-governor John M. Palmer, migrating slowly from Republican to Democrat, addressed its convention at Springfield.[39] The Independents nominated candidates. Two, William B. Anderson in the 19th District and Alexander Campbell in the 7th, won election to Congress. Democrats meanwhile played on civil rights. Republicans faced it squarely. Their convention met at Springfield on June 17. Congressman Charles Farwell presided. Black Jack Logan gave the oration.

> Wherever any lingering prejudice exists on account of race or color, the full measure of rights will never be conceded until by the laws of the country the power to enforce them is fully given. We know that the rights so guaranteed by the Fourteenth Amendment in many instances and many communities are trampled underfoot with impunity; therefore I believe it [the Civil Rights Bill] to be the duty of Congress.[40]

In Chicago, Republicans held all three districts. They lost all three. First District incumbent John B. Rice, terminally ill, declined to run again. Democrats easily took the seat. Farwell in the 3rd District appeared to win. But his opponent contested the results. The newly-Democratic 44th Congress seated him. The 2nd District had sent Jasper Ward to Congress. He faced a Democratic machine on the city's west side: the "Irish-Democratic-Vote-Brokering Company," the Chicago *Tribune* sneered, whose board of directors included such notorious wire-pullers as Barney Caulfield and "Honest John" Comiskey. Caulfield preferred to take the 1st District seat. Ward's opponent was Carter Henry Harrison, Sr., destined to become the city's most popular 19th century mayor. Jasper

39 Chicago *Tribune*, June 11, 1874.
40 Chicago *Inter Ocean*, June 20, 1874.

Ward campaigned for civil rights. Distressed workers failed to appreciate the message. Dr. F.A. Hoffman, candidate of the Communist Party, unfurled the red banner. He took 318 votes. Ward lost by 8 votes, the second closest contest in the nation. He returned to the Judiciary Committee a lame duck, but with his civil rights fire undimmed. Other Republicans dimmed their fire frantically. (see Map 12, below)

MAP 12 Congressional Districts, Illinois
SOURCE: AUTHORS OF *WELCOMING RUIN*.

Illinois, Eighteenth District
Isaac Clements (R), William Hartzell (D)
Population: 94% white

The 18th District covered the state's south, the land known popularly as "Egypt." Once it had been the bailiwick of Senator Logan. His protégé, Isaac Clements, "little Ike," took the seat in 1872. Ike's occupancy was brief.[41]

Ten counties shaped the district, running from the town of Cairo at the tip of Alexander County through Pulaski, Massac and Pope Counties, then north to Johnson, Williamson, Union, and Randolph. Only Alexander and Pulaski Counties contained an appreciable number of black people. Johnson County sheltered 52. In Williamson County 106 lived fearfully in a population of 17,000.

Egypt was an inhospitable place for those isolated black persons. In 1858 Abraham Lincoln and Stephen Douglas debated at Jonesboro in Union County. "The very notice that I was to take him down to Egypt," Douglas crowed, "made him tremble in the knees."[42] Sixteen years passed. The situation had hardly changed. Racial violence, the Cairo *Bulletin* lamented, ran rampant in Williamson, Jackson, Randolph Counties, "and generally all over Southern Illinois ... the story of Egyptian Ku-kluxism."[43]

Williamson County built a particularly sinister reputation, "the scene of many dark and mysterious deeds of blood," the *Inter Ocean* reported. "Men have been waylaid and murdered, have been assassinated in their own dooryards and on their own thresholds; others have been dragged from their beds at night and hung upon trees."[44] The Chicago *Tribune* agreed: "There is no part of the South that has been disgraced by lawlessness more outrageous. Ku-kluxism has been rampant for years." Governor John L. Beveridge ordered the legislature to open an investigation of mayhem in Williamson County.[45] Perhaps, suggested the Chattanooga *Times* sarcastically, the government ought to deploy its army to save the oppressed black people of Illinois:

> They make a fuss about it in the Egyptian counties of Illinois. In Williamson, for example, where the conventional Democrat abounds, they shoot a nigger or a Republican once or twice a week and send his body home in

41 Chicago *Tribune*, April 11, 1874.

42 Lincoln/Douglas, 3rd Debate, *Life and Works of Abraham Lincoln*, vol. 3 (New York: 1907), 275.

43 Quoted in Alexandria, *Louisiana Democrat*, February 17, 1875.

44 Chicago *Inter Ocean*, May 13, 1874.

45 Chicago *Tribune*, November 20, 1874.

> a wagon ... they catch a nigger that has not heeded their warning to quit the State, tie him to a tree and slash his back with butcher knives, leaving him to die.... Is not Illinois entitled to a little respect, if not a few troops, from the Southern outrage factory?[46]

On the Civil Rights Bill Ike Clements naturally displayed a nervous indisposition. His personal disposition was to vote for it. Political sense disposed him not to. Yet he could not bring himself to oppose it. On May 25 and on June 8 he whispered an affirmative, both times paired with a nay-saying Democrat. On June 20 he said nothing. Democrats were not deceived. "Mr. Clements, our present congressman," wrote a correspondent to the St. Louis *Republican*, "evaded the bill and kept from voting. Since his return home many of his supporters have demanded his opinion in reference to the bill. So far he has eluded them, and reserved his opinion to himself. Clements' object is to make a still fight, and steer away from the reef which he knows will inevitably wreck his frail craft."[47] In Cairo, the *Inter Ocean* reported, Republicans deserted in droves.[48] "Republicans say that if they must concede to such [civil rights] proceedings they are no longer of the party.... They assert they will support no man in favor of the bill."[49] Isaac Clements struck the reef. Egypt returned to the Democrats.

4 Indiana

Indiana presented Republicans a crucial challenge. Its governor was a Democrat. Its senators were Republican. Republicans held ten of thirteen congressional districts. They were shaky. Their margins were slim. Only one, Henry Sayler in the 10th District, held his seat by more than 1,000 votes. The Indianapolis *Journal* grumbled. Indiana harbored a stubborn reactionary streak: "In old times it was one of the stiffest and staunchest in its Democracy; and when the new order of things began to be ushered in it was still one of the most abject in its devotion to the interests of slavery."[50] Republicans took heed. Their state convention omitted all mention of civil rights.

Democrats mentioned it loudly. In August Daniel Voorhees, their champion, spoke at the Terre Haute Opera House. "Four millions and upwards of

46 Chattanooga *Times*, October 20, 1874.
47 St. Louis *Republican*, August 14, 1874.
48 Chicago *Inter Ocean*, October 30, 1874.
49 St. Louis *Republican*, August 14, 1874.
50 Indianapolis *Journal*, July 14, 1874.

negroes in the United States," he thundered, "are suddenly and imperatively, by the force of law, thrust into an absolute equality with the white race." It was unbearable: "the most extensive and remarkable social revolution ever attempted by legislation in the history of the world." It was unprecedented. "I know of no parallel to it in the history of the nations of the earth." It was unwise. "Senator Morton says it is only a prejudice which opposes this vast measure.... In fact, what is often denominated prejudice as often proves to be the highest instinct of wisdom."[51]

Morton was ill. His colleague Senator Daniel Pratt took up the fight. The Chicago *Tribune* regarded him, even next to the dynamic Morton, as "one of the most forcible and effective stumpers on the Radical side in the West."[52] Pratt had entered the Senate with a moderate reputation. He grew a radical streak. Service on the Ku Klux Commission in 1871 gave him a taste of southern violence. He evolved into a supporter of the Civil Rights Bill. In the Senate he rose to deliver a plea for its passage.[53] In Indiana he traveled tirelessly, speaking in big towns and small: Connersville, Winchester, Eaton, Lagrange. He reached Kendallville on August 28. Black people, he told the crowd, asked only for what was right, for their rights as citizens: "If you will define to me what is the measure of a citizen's rights I will tell you what is the measure of a colored man's rights.... What more than a citizen are you? There is no higher title in this country than that of a citizen of the United States." He scolded fellow Republicans. "I address my remarks to the weak-kneed men of the party.... This is the time to do that act of justice." He defied the Democrats. "When this bill, which has passed the Senate, shall have passed the House of Representatives, as it will as sure as the sun rises, the last bulwark of the Democracy will have passed away. They have been trading on this capital long enough." He invoked the Bible: "The colored man – recognize him we must as a man – and if so he is the image of God.... What authority have I to say whether Adam was black or white?"[54]

In September, overweight, overworked, and exhausted, Pratt retired from the field. But the battle was joined. Republicans strode into the contest with ten of the state's thirteen districts. They staggered out with five. Democrats

51 Terre Haute *Express*, August 8, 1874.

52 Chicago *Tribune*, August 18, 1874.

53 Joseph E. Holliday, "Daniel D. Pratt: Senator and Commissioner," *Indiana Magazine of History*, 58 (1962), 25–26.

54 Indianapolis *Journal*, August 29, 1874.

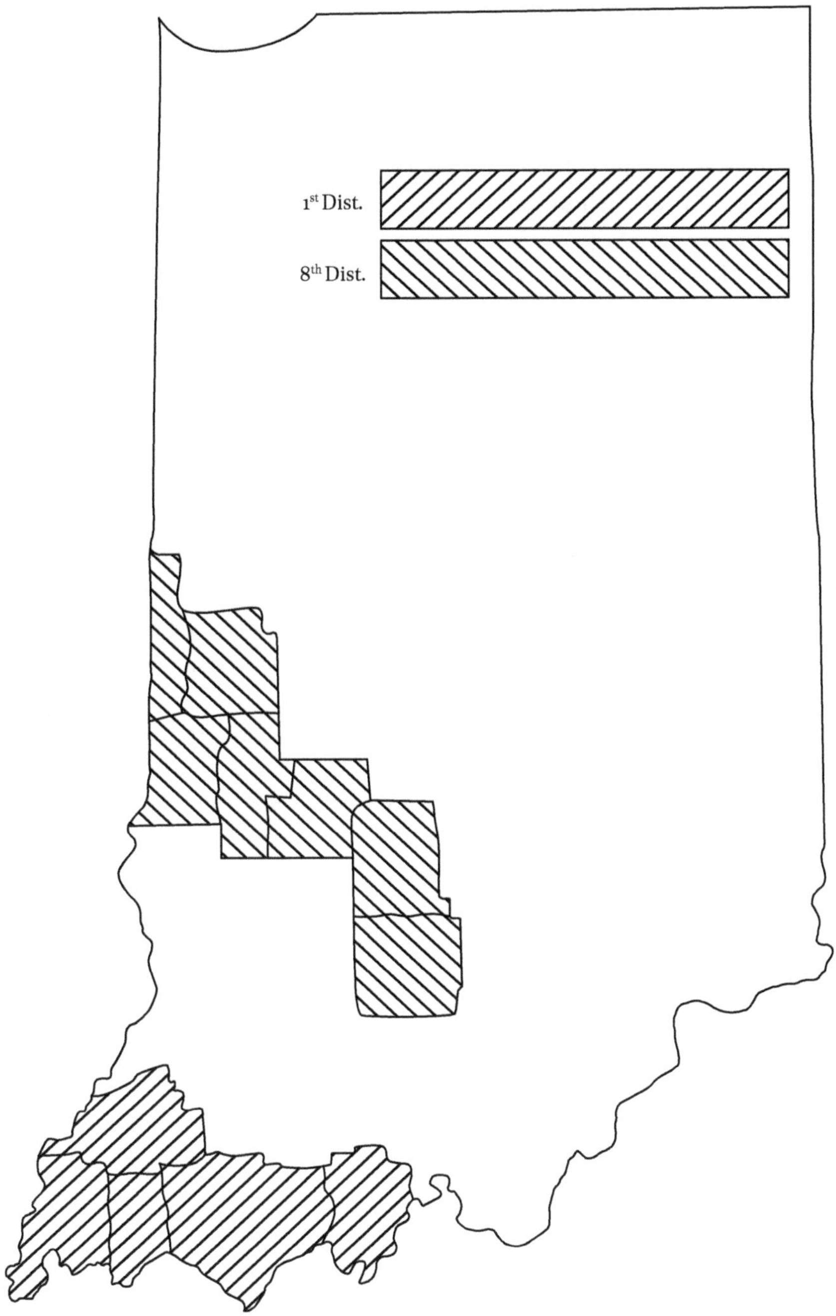

MAP 13 Congressional Districts, Indiana
SOURCE: AUTHORS OF *WELCOMING RUIN.*

captured the legislature. Pratt's term expired. He cast his last senatorial vote for passage of the Civil Rights Act. (see Map 13, below)

Indiana, First District
William Heilman (R/I), Benoni Fuller (D)
Population: 96% white

Indiana's 1st District occupied the state's lower angle – Posey, Vanderburgh and Gibson Counties. It extended east along the Ohio River to Warrick, Spencer and Perry Counties. The population was nearly-pure white but sharply divided. In the midst of a long-settled rural and agricultural constituency sat the industrial city of Evansville, a boisterous community of workers and immigrants. The six counties held 123,000 people; 4,700 were black. Half those black persons huddled in Vanderburgh County, the majority in the city of Evansville.

The 1st District had elected Democrat William E. Niblack for seven terms. Niblack was a salary grabber. That finished his distinguished career. The seat came open. Despite Niblack's longevity, it was a competitive seat. He had barely held it in 1872 against William Heilman, a son of Evansville's German community. Heilman was eager to run again. His prospects seemed bright. Civil rights and beer ruined him.

Wilhelm Heilman validated the American dream. Emigrant from the old world, he made his fortune in the new. He began as a poor Hessian farmer, ended as an American millionaire. In Evansville his factory, the City Foundry and Machine Works, forged the mechanical engines that drove the region's economy. His mansion, complete with marble floors and hot water in its pipes, became a landmark.[55] Defeated for Congress in 1872 by 132 votes, he tried again in 1874. He reached Washington on his third try in 1878.[56]

Conditions seemed favorable as the enterprising businessman approached his second run for Congress. His opponents were in disarray. Grangers organized to oppose the regular Democrats. Posey County farmers denounced party bosses. They designated themselves the "Anti-Ring Democrats."[57] The Ring chided the farmers: "We cannot sit quietly by and see our bucolic friends, the Grangers, made the victims of a diabolical conspiracy," wrote the Evansville *Courier*.[58]

---

55 See Mary Rose Heilman Johnson, *William Heilman: Immigrant's Outstanding Achievements* (n.p.: 1982), biographical sketch and William Heilman's diary.

56 He found Congress disappointing, palsied by pointless palaver and empty of enterprise: "The people," he complained, "will elect such men it seems in preference to businessmen." Johnson, *Heilman*, 38.

57 Evansville *Journal*, July 20, 1874.

58 Evansville *Journal*, August 11, 1874.

Ultimately, party bosses thought it best to appease the bucolic element. The nominee, after much wrangling, was Benoni S. Fuller. A farmer, formerly a school teacher and sheriff of Warrick County, he bore an uncanny resemblance to a younger Ulysses Grant. Thus a farmer opposed a manufacturer of farm equipment in a district where agriculture and industry resided in uneasy proximity. Civil rights injected itself uneasily into the mix.

Heilman's strength ought to have rested in Evansville, but civil rights rose up against him. The city contained 1,500 Negroes. Already Evansville had witnessed two notable race riots. One rocked it in 1857, the other in 1865.[59] Democrats commenced the attack. Their platform singled out the Civil Rights Bill, "unwise, unnecessary, and not within the purview of Federal legislation."[60] Candidate Fuller's stump speech featured a description of mixed schools: Negro children playing with white children; Negroes reciting their lessons; Negroes sitting on the school bench.[61] William Heilman had not sat in Congress, voted for or pronounced upon a civil rights bill. The Evansville *Courier*, the district's Democratic sheet, demanded to know nevertheless how he intended to vote, if elected – all the while assuring its readers he planned to vote for it, no matter what else he might say.[62] Heilman said nothing.

The *Courier's* suspicions were justified. William Heilman never had the chance to vote for a civil rights bill. But he would have voted for it. To his diary he confessed. President Lincoln had lit the torch: "All men are born free and equal. So they are, and trust they always will be."[63] Such thoughts were a dangerous political doctrine. Heilman wisely confined them to his diary. Generally he avoided public speaking. He avoided speaking about civil rights. He avoided speaking about the Republican Party. Along with civil rights associations came an additional liability: Temperance. The Republican Party was for it; many voters disagreed, wherefore the candidate dropped his party affiliation. He ran officially as an Independent. Civil rights and alcohol pursued him anyway.

At the heart of the temperance controversy in Indiana lay the Baxter Law. This enactment, passed by a Republican legislature, provided that the people of a given district might decide upon the sale or prohibition of liquor by petition. Despite their own Democratic governor's signature, Democrats put repeal of the Baxter Law, along with hatred of civil rights, at the top of their platform:

59 See Emma Lou Thornbrough, *The Negro in Indiana before 1900: A Study of a Minority* (Bloomington: 1993), 130–131, 209–210.

60 Evansville *Journal*, July 9, 1874.

61 Evansville *Journal*, October 9, 1874.

62 Quoted in Evansville *Journal*, October 3, 1874.

63 Johnson, *Heilman*, 19.

"They piled on a whisky and negro plank to fix the voters, and we will venture to say that they have succeeded."[64]

The "negro plank" tied Heilman's tongue in silence. The liquor question tied him in knots. Republicans looked favorably upon the Baxter Law. His German compatriots did not. Having cut off the Republican label, he hoped to cut off that dilemma. Democrats responded by throwing beer. "Beer and Bribery!" screamed the Evansville *Courier*. With his vast resources of money he bought beer. With beer he bribed the thirsty voters.[65] Heilman poured brew on the Democrats. Their agents, declared the Evansville *Journal*, prowled the factories inviting workers to share a keg of "Fuller beer" at the close of their shifts. "The only ground on which it could be argued that Mr. Heilman bought more beer than Mr. Fuller is that he had more friends to drink the beer."[66]

Results emerged slowly from the 1st District's spirituous election. Early returns favored Heilman. He fell short in the end by 337 votes. He won Posey, Spencer and Gibson Counties. Vanderburgh County, where whites met most with blacks, gave Fuller a 2,000 vote majority. Temperance troubled William Heilman. Civil Rights proved fatal. He disassociated himself from his party. He refused to disassociate himself from his party's principles, those principles he confided to his diary. "He lost votes," the *Journal* concluded, "because he would not declare his opposition to the Civil Rights bill." Fuller had no such worries. "His party was a unit against Civil Rights, and he could alienate nobody by treating to a glass of beer or 'red eye,' the latter generally preferred."[67]

Indiana, Eighth District
Morton Hunter (R), Harrison Rice (D)
Population: 98% white

Indiana's 8th District planted itself firmly in the North. Its seven counties cut a zigzag through the center of the state from Vermillion and Vigo on the Illinois border across to Clay County then diagonally east to Monroe and Lawrence. Vigo County, with the city of Terre Haute, was its heart, the population almost completely white. Lurking somewhere in Parke County were 48 African Americans; 59 called Owen County home. Clay County possessed 26 black residents, all apparently residing in the town of Brazil. It wasn't much. It sufficed to distress the white people of the 8th District.

64 San Jose *Mercury*, July 23, 1874.
65 Evansville *Journal*, September 22, 1874.
66 Evansville *Journal*, October 7, 1874.
67 Evansville *Journal*, October 16, 1874.

In political sentiment the district was volatile. Its current congressman was a Republican. Its greatest citizen was a Democrat. Daniel Voorhees, "The Tall Sycamore of the Wabash," orator and statesman, had held place for four terms, in the 37th, 38th, 41st and 42nd Congresses. Angling for Daniel Pratt's Senate seat, he informed his former constituents that he declined to run again.[68] But he remained a force. In August he thrilled the Democratic faithful with his Terre Haute speech, defying civil rights and Oliver Morton. His absence from the ballot, nevertheless, gave Republicans a break.

The incumbent was Gen. Morton C. Hunter. His military brevet was not honorific. He had taken his men, the 82nd Indiana regiment, through bloody battles. He led a brigade in Sherman's march through Georgia. He had been a popular and a humane officer. He chose to face a court martial in 1862, violating orders to save the life of one of his men; the court not only acquitted but commended him.[69] Having felt the rigors of war, Morton Hunter enjoyed the comforts of peace. His frame grew round, but his hair still black, his beard curling and luxuriant. He continued to show a humane character, a sympathetic regard for the rights of black people.

Republicans met at Brazil on July 16. They re-nominated the incumbent. Hunter declared himself in favor of monetary expansion and against a protective tariff. He endorsed the Baxter Law, defying the 8th District's drinkers. For its finale the convention called upon a black delegate. Samuel A. Malone, "an old colored gentleman," pledged his people's loyalty: "Democrats speak of the negro and associate him with the ape and the monkey, but apes and baboons are far better than some of the white people who render themselves ludicrous by stigmatizing the negro on account of his black skin."[70] The convention cheered. The campaign in Indiana's 8th District, a district almost devoid of racial division, became a battle of racial division.

Democrats convened at Terre Haute on July 23. Dr. Harrison J. Rice of Rockville won the nomination. He ran immediately to embrace the color line. Tariffs could wait. Negroes were the problem. Negro equality, civil rights, an abomination! ("Here a thrill of convulsive joy shot through and pervaded the convention, culminating in applause.")[71]

Dr. Rice took his show on the road. He campaigned at Bloomington on September 19. Civil rights was a denial of rights: "It goes back on the prejudices of the white man.... The God of the universe has made the white and black

68 Terre Haute *Express*, June 21, 1874.

69 Thomas P. Lowry, *Curmudgeons, Drunkards and Outright Fools: Courts-Martial of Civil War Union Colonels* (Lincoln: 2003), 28–33.

70 Terre Haute *Express*, July 16, 1874.

71 Terre Haute *Express*, July 24, 1874.

man to differ. It is against the laws of nature." Few black people, Rice admitted, presently plagued the district. But they would come. Once the Civil Rights Bill passed, Kentucky would commence to unload unwanted Negroes on Indiana. The bill allowed blacks into white schools. School facilities were better in Indiana than in Kentucky. Therefore Kentuckians would push their riff-raff away across the border. The 8th District had no border with Kentucky. That did not deter Dr. Rice. "Worthless, vagabond negroes will come over here in hordes, to swelter and swarm around our schools and firesides."[72] He repeated the message at Brazil. White citizens there had already panicked at the swarming of five black children into their schools. He delivered the word at Terre Haute: "A mongrel race" would emerge once schoolchildren mingled, "a race such as are found outside and on the edge of the races of people on the earth."[73]

Morton Hunter faced the enemy boldly. He visited Rockville on August 8. His opponent said the Civil Rights Bill would pass. That was correct. It would pass. It should pass: "He stood by the civil rights bill."[74] He tried to calm the fears of white folks. The state constitution already guaranteed equality to all citizens. "The fate of the civil rights bill cannot affect the State of Indiana. It does not affect a single right of its people." Why then was it wanted? It was wanted because there were states that *did* deny equal rights to their citizens. "This bill is for the purpose of giving all an equal chance." General Hunter marched where few politicians dared to go. He defended mixed schools.

> Now when Mr. Rice comes around, I have no doubt he will hold up this negro equality, this forcing the negro into the public schools, and tell you what a terrible thing it is; he will tell you that children of weak nerves cannot stand it. There are now several colored men in Congress, and when he says that, you can tell him that if he is so bitterly opposed to associating with colored men, that he should not go to Congress. [Laughter] I have been there and associated with them, because they have the same right there that I have. I do not know whether I am any the worse for it or better. You can judge for yourselves. I do not believe it will make any material change with me and I think I can stand it if he can. [Much merriment][75]

Hunter's journalistic ally, the Terre Haute *Express*, recalled Voorhees' oration. Prejudice, Voorhees asserted, was the instinct of wisdom. No! Wisdom ab-

72 Terre Haute *Express*, September 23, 1874.
73 Terre Haute *Express*, October 10, 1874.
74 Terre Haute *Express*, August 15, 1874.
75 Terre Haute *Express*, September 18, 1874.

horred prejudice. Wisdom destroyed prejudice. Prejudice was the instinct of ignorance.

> Every martyr burned, every sufferer for principle, went down before the prejudices of the people; and every battle for freedom, every movement for the amelioration of man has found in man's prejudice its subtlest and most formidable foe. It feeds the tyrants and fattens the priests.... It will be a puzzling contradiction to future generations to read of men of Mr. Voorhees' capacity upholding in the latter half of the nineteenth century the cause of caste.... The denser the ignorance the more intense the prejudice, or, as Mr. V calls them, the "highest instincts of wisdom."[76]

Dr. Rice, when not dwelling on civil rights, ran a populist race. He damned the rich, "the capitalists, the bond-holders, the railroad kings and bankers and monopolists." He saluted the true men, "the agriculturalists, the mechanics and laboring men of the country." For railroad kings he had a special request: please do not vote for his ticket. He wanted only the votes of honest people.[77]

Morton Hunter hung on to his congressional seat, but barely. He saved the 8th District by 181 votes. Indiana Republicans saved only four others. As to the cause of the collapse, Democrats and Republicans agreed. Temperance hurt. Civil rights killed. "The prejudice of the low and ignorant white people against the blacks has not died out," the Terre Haute *Express* lamented, "and it has been appealed to with vigor by every Democratic orator possessed of so little self-respect as to invoke the lowest passions of men."[78] The Indianapolis *Journal's* Editor Elijah Halford, poured out his frustration:

> "Fathers, save us from nigger husbands!" – Democratic papers taught it ... that giant of distorted rhetoric, Voorhees, preached it, and all the mud-crawlers talked it, drank it and swore it.... Nobody knows better than those who pull the strings what an empty thing of pasteboard and bran it is, but with the ignorant it serves their turn as effectually as a scare-crow in a corn-field.... Oh, the depth and density of their stupidity that can believe this, and the immeasurable impudence that can assert it without believing it.[79]

76 Terre Haute *Express*, August 9, 1874.
77 Terre Haute *Express*, September 23, October 10, 1874.
78 Terre Haute *Express*, October 15, 1874.
79 Indianapolis *Journal*, October 31, November 2, 1874.

5 Ohio

Ohio possessed a Republican legislature and a Democratic governor. The elections swept away the Republican legislature. Republicans held thirteen of twenty congressional seats, Democrats seven. The elections reversed that arithmetic. Ohio Republicans nevertheless endorsed the Civil Rights Bill with suicidal zest. At the state convention Senator John Sherman spoke.

> I have seen, one by one, the narrow prejudices of caste which denied to the black race the rights of human nature melt away without evil results, and I wish to see this work complete and perfect by securing to all men who are citizens of the United States precise equality in all civil and political rights, whether they tend to protect his person and property, or lift him above degradation by local or State authority.[80]

Ex-governor Edward Noyes followed Sherman: "It is the genius of this country to give every man a fair chance in life ... yet we find the Democracy of Ohio in the exercise of their hatred appealing to the passions and prejudices of ignorant white men."[81] United States Secretary of the Interior, Ohio native Columbus Delano, followed Noyes: "The mission of the Republican party will not be ended until the civil rights of the emancipated race are fully secured."[82]

Ohio Republicans stood up for civil rights. Their campaigns sank beneath it. Various factors contributed to the disaster. Charges of corruption alienated usually loyal Republican voters. James Garfield survived in the 19th District, but with a margin much reduced. Allegations of malfeasance torpedoed Cleveland's Richard Parsons in the 20th District. Suction from that shipwreck took down Garfield's friend John Quincy Smith in the 18th. Whiskey wars, as in Indiana, worked against Republicans. But civil rights hatred served Democrats. It worked well even in Ohio's northernmost regions, where very few African Americans existed.

The 6th District at Toledo presented a perfect picture of Republican woes: hapless candidates; spiritless voters, their spirit haunted by civil rights fears. Republican incumbent Isaac Sherwood was young and vigorous. He failed to secure re-nomination. His replacement, Albert M. Pratt, floundered. To generate enthusiasm he organized a rally. A flotilla of boats, led by the brand new steamer *Chief Justice Waite,* prepared to ferry voters across Lake Erie to Put-in-Bay on South Bass Island. There the pleasures of a picnic would add

80 New York *Times*, September 5, 1874.
81 Dayton *Journal*, September 3, 1874.
82 Chicago *Tribune*, October 12, 1874.

to the excitement of political speeches. Tenth District Congressman Charles Foster promised to bring supporters from Sandusky. Nothing went right. The day dawned chilly. Foster failed to arrive. The sky turned grey. It drizzled. Few people relished the boat ride. A limp, damp crowd heard Pratt's appeal.[83]

Democrat Frank Hurd accepted the nomination in August. Then he left for a prolonged vacation. A few weeks before the vote he returned. He promptly deployed civil rights fear. He denounced Negroes. He assailed Negro suffrage. He deplored Negro citizenship. He abhorred equal rights. He condemned the Civil Rights Bill.[84] He won. The Republicans' soggy setback in Toledo reflected their sodden fortunes across Ohio. (see Map 14, below)

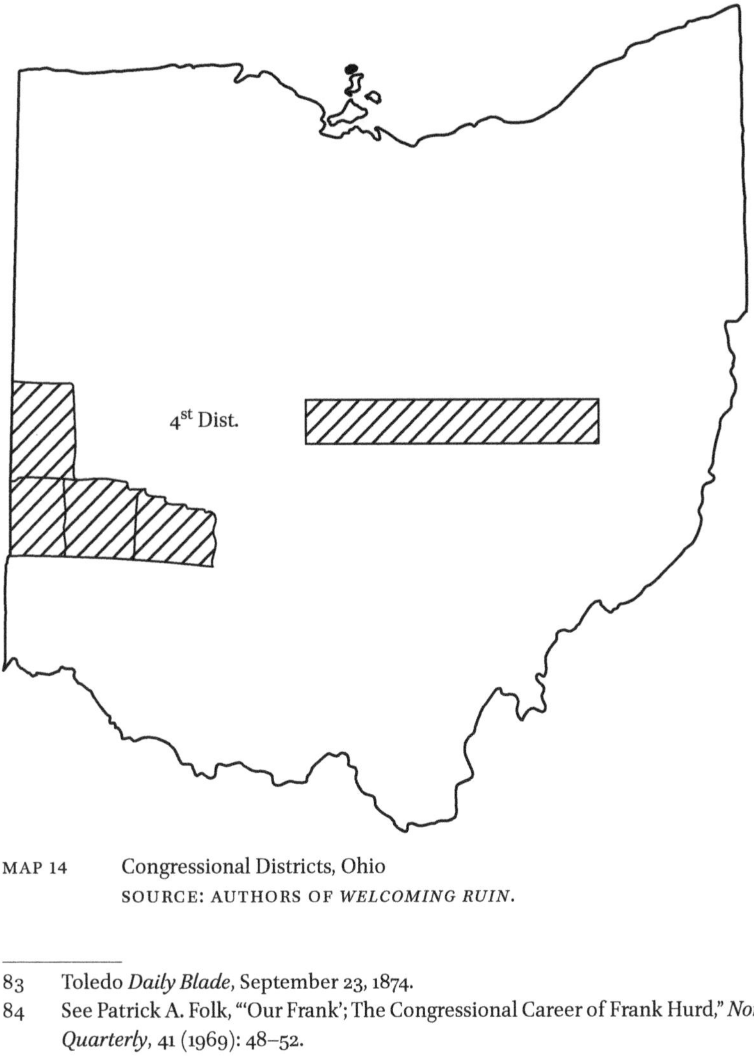

MAP 14 Congressional Districts, Ohio
SOURCE: AUTHORS OF *WELCOMING RUIN*.

83 Toledo *Daily Blade*, September 23, 1874.
84 See Patrick A. Folk, "'Our Frank'; The Congressional Career of Frank Hurd," *Northwest Ohio Quarterly*, 41 (1969): 48–52.

Ohio, Fourth District
Lewis B. Gunckel (R), John A. McMahon (D)
Population: 96% white

The 4th District formed a block of four counties, Darke, Greene, Preble, and Montgomery, in Ohio's west-center. Embedded in its midst was the city of Dayton. In 1870 some 5,600 black persons coexisted with 140,000 whites; 4,000 of those black people resided in Greene County with the town of Xenia. But black immigration had risen since 1870, bringing an influx of newcomers especially to Dayton and surrounding Montgomery County. White workingmen worried about competition for their jobs. Black people worried about white people. Dayton had been the home base of the great Copperhead, Clement L. Vallandigham. Democrats chose the late congressman's nephew to reclaim his uncle's seat.

The Republican was Lewis Gunckel, a Dayton lawyer, partner in the firm of Gunckel & Gunckel. He also dabbled in real estate. He had won the seat in 1872 by 2,000 votes, taking three of the four counties. Once in Washington, Gunckel discovered a passion for fiscal responsibility. He appointed himself watchdog of the public treasury.[85] This led him to propose various economies, among them a bill to reduce the size of the capitol police force. Its 39 men – one captain, three lieutenants, 27 officers and 8 night-watchmen – cost the nation the insupportable sum of $58,256 annually.[86] Other sums, nonetheless, which benefited him, Congressman Gunckel considered quite supportable.

A unique feature of the 4th District was the "Soldiers' Home," the National Asylum for Disabled Veteran Soldiers, located near Dayton. Filled with 2,000 handicapped Union war veterans, it was a boon to any politician. Lewis Gunckel not only possessed the Dayton soldiers' home, he sat on the National Board of Managers for the care of all soldiers' homes. The president of that board was none other than Benjamin F. Butler. Detractors found excessive Congressman Gunckel's solicitude for his disabled veterans. He begrudged capitol policemen their pay. He pursued twice the appropriation for his Homes, including a disbursement of $2,000 for the upkeep of Manager Gunckel.[87]

---

85 Dayton *Journal*, July 11, 1874.

86 Dayton *Journal*, March 25, 1874.

87 Ben Butler, after his defeat, was greeted with a note from inmates of the Veterans' Home at Ward's Island, New York: "Chickens will come home to roost. Gunckel is in the same boat.... You have got all the money you will ever get out of us." Many Soldiers to Benjamin Butler, December 18, 1874. Butler Papers, Library of Congress.

Gunckel's ethical probity left room for doubt. His votes on the Civil Rights Bill did not. On every call in the House Lewis Gunckel spoke Aye. Democrats prepared to make him pay. Those Democrats met on September 3 at Dayton's Beckel Opera House. They chose John A. McMahon, nephew and protégé of Clement Vallandigham. Race consumed the 4th District race. Civil rights beat down on Lewis Gunckel. McMahon spoke at Greenville. "He assumed the mantle of Vallandigham," the Dayton *Journal* reported. He delivered a diatribe on the Civil Rights Bill, "singing the old song of 'nigger equality.'"[88] He proceeded to Xenia. "McMahon is down with Negrophobia," the *Journal* despaired.[89] At every stop the Civil Rights Bill was "bitterly cussed and discussed":

> He gesticulates and beats the air so violently and becomes so "tore up" in the course of a day's labor ... that at the sound of a bell, the bark of a dog, or the braying of an ass, he clears his bed at one bound and sallies forth with tomahawk in hand in search of the "black scoundrels" who are threatening the overthrow of the Constitution.[90]

The *Journal's* raillery rang hollow. Republicans struck at McMahon's Copperhead past. "Will you take Gunckel, who has always been on the side of his country and the perpetuation of the Union, or McMahon, who took sides with the enemies of the nation?"[91] Ex-governor Noyes stumped the district: "Our soldiers remember that in that conflict these colored people were the most faithful allies, and their bones sleep on many a battle field beside those of our dearest friends."[92]

On civil rights Lewis Gunckel proved faithful. He had voted for the bill. He stood by his votes. He pleaded against irrational fear. It would make no difference in Ohio. It aimed at the South. "It bestowed no new rights upon the colored man – it merely provided for the enforcement of the rights he already possessed." He offered to have the bill amended. "If the bill as it stood was not acceptable to the people, he was in favor of its modification." But he would not disown it. Something had to be done, something, so that black people did not eat in cow yards or ride the train in cattle cars.[93]

On September 22, Emancipation Day, black people gathered at Oakwood Grove outside Dayton. Trains brought hundreds from Cincinnati, Lima, Xenia

88 Dayton *Journal*, September 11, 1874.
89 Dayton *Journal*, September 22, 1874.
90 Dayton *Journal*, October 8, 1874.
91 Dayton *Journal*, October 13, 1874.
92 Dayton *Journal*, October 1, 1874.
93 Dayton *Journal*, September 26, 1874.

and Springfield. The Soldiers' Home Band serenaded the crowd. Portraits of Lincoln, Frederick Douglass and Senator Hiram Revels overhung the stand. The principal speaker was Solomon Day.

> It was not until after a baptism of blood during the rebellion that freedom came. It was not until after another baptism of blood by ex-rebels and Kuklux Klans that we got the 15th amendment; and now we are receiving another baptism of blood at the hands of the "White Leagues" of the South before we get the Civil Rights bill. It may be that this is the only way that the rights of the negro can be secured, but he is paying a terrible price, and the exacting of this price by the party he supports is a dear kind of fealty.[94]

Lewis Gunckel, campaigning in Darke County, did not attend this lecture. He wired a telegram of support. On his return to Congress he did what he could. He voted "aye" one more time, for passage of the Civil Rights Act. He voted as a lame duck. Clement Vallandigham's nephew easily took the 4th District. Sadly, the Dayton *Journal* admitted, "the ghost of negro and social equality stalks forth at the dead hour of night."[95]

6 Pennsylvania

The Democratic tide swept east through Pennsylvania. The state did not boast an abundance of African-American citizens: 65,000 mingled with a multitude of three million and a half whites. One third of that miniscule minority resided in the city of Philadelphia, leaving an almost imperceptible residue elsewhere in the commonwealth. Scarcity notwithstanding, Democrats made sure they scared white people.[96]

Both parties took unambiguous stands. Republicans met at Harrisburg on August 19 under the guiding hand of State Party Chairman Russell Errett. Their platform called upon Congress to pass the guarantee of civil rights.[97] Lieutenant-Governor nominee Arthur Olmstead campaigned for the bill. Philadelphia District Attorney William B. Mann told audiences he hoped it would pass, "so

94 Dayton *Journal*, September 23, 1874.
95 Dayton *Journal*, September 23, 1874.
96 See David Montgomery, "Radical Republicanism in Pennsylvania, 1866–1873," *Pennsylvania Magazine of History and Biography*, 85 (1961), 443.
97 Harrisburg *Patriot*, August 20, 1874. See above, Chapter 6.

that it might be his great privilege to try the first case of a violation of its provisions." Congressman William Kelley linked civil rights and labor: "Let me tell you, workmen, that it is not only the colored men's rights that are at issue, it is your right to labor and liberal pay for labor."[98] State Senator Harry White introduced an amendment to the state constitution banning discriminatory use of the word "white" in all legislation.

Democrats assembled at Pittsburgh on August 26. Civil rights topped the agenda. "The Republican party since its accession to power has dominated the white by the negro race … and by its proposed civil rights bill made a war of races imminent." The platform devoted three full articles to a denunciation of the measure.[99] Democrats supplemented that with an address, "To the People of Pennsylvania." Voters beware. The Republicans' aim was clear: "to degrade the white race by enacting into law what is known as the 'odious civil rights bill.'" White men and women will be "degraded to the level of the negro, since no legislation can ever elevate the negro to that of the white."[100]

Republicans might have taken heed and pulled back. They echoed Danton: *l'audace et encore de l'audace*. They dared the voters to swallow nothing less than desegregation of the public schools. State Senator James Graham introduced his measure on April 14.

> From and after the passage of this act all children over six years of age shall be admitted into the common schools of this commonwealth without regard to color, and colored children shall have and enjoy the same rights and privileges of said schools now allowed or which may hereafter be allowed to white children.[101]

Graham's bill imposed a maximum penalty: $500 and a year of imprisonment, "or either or both at the discretion of the court." Senator George H. Anderson added a supplement, "repealing all laws requiring school boards to maintain separate schools for the exclusive use of children of color."[102] Both bills passed the State Senate. Companion measures passed the House.[103] Demo-

98 Philadelphia *Inquirer*, October 12, 19, 28, 1874.
99 Harrisburg *Patriot*, August 27–28, 1874.
100 Harrisburg *Patriot*, October 1, 1874.
101 Harrisburg *Patriot*, April 15, 1874.
102 Harrisburg *Patriot*, April 17, 1874.
103 Harrisburg *Patriot*, April 21, 28, May 6, 1874. All Republican senators present voted for the bill, as did the one Liberal Republican, Alexander McClure of Philadelphia. Before the measures could be reconciled the legislative session ended; the elections cost Republicans control of the legislature.

crats were delighted. Voters would exact fitting revenge. "The white men and women of Pennsylvania who must perforce send their children to common schools will know without telling whom they are to thank for this latest social innovation."[104]

Republicans forged ahead. Next came a Compulsory Education Bill. "Constabulary education!" screamed the Harrisburg *Patriot*: "If white children will not attend the mixed schools enjoined by the civil rights bill, they are to be taken to school in charge of a state constable."[105] "If this bill becomes a law," the Clearfield *Republican* (Democratic) declared, "a complete Russian serfdom will be inaugurated."[106]

Internal discord weakened Republican efforts. Conventions deadlocked for weeks in the 24th District and in the 25th. In the 26th, delegates struggled through 500 ballots. Three weeks before the election they found a candidate, who promptly lost. In the 22nd District, James Negley secured re-nomination. Rivals ran an independent candidate. Democrats won the seat. Carlton Curtis in the 27th District managed to be re-nominated. He lost by 11 votes. Redistricting eliminated three at-large seats, all held by Republicans. Incumbents Leonard Myers and Alfred Harmer in the 5th District and John Packer and John Killinger in the 14th devoured each other in cannibalistic competition.

Civil rights chased the survivors. "Are the sober-minded and order-loving men in the Republican party prepared to lend a hand in hurling the firebrand of Civil Rights?" demanded the West Chester *Jeffersonian*. "Are they willing to aid the carpet-baggers in inciting the negroes to riot and bloodshed in order that through a second San Domingo their party may maintain power? If not they will repudiate the candidates nominated on the Civil Rights platform."[107]

In Pennsylvania's deepest recesses civil rights roamed. The 25th District sat squarely in the state's center: Indiana, Armstrong, Clarion, Forrest and Jefferson Counties. Black persons were practically nonexistent. Precisely 466 "colored residents" appeared in the 1870 census, lost in a population of 131,722. Republicans nonetheless nominated an outspoken friend of that microscopic minority, State Senator Harry White, advocate of mixed schools and social equality. Harry White, Democrats screamed, was a fanatic, a Ben Butler wannabe, a minor-league clone of the Beast prowling Pennsylvania.[108] The

104 Harrisburg *Patriot*, May 6, 1874.
105 Harrisburg *Patriot*, August 22, 1874.
106 Clearfield, Pennsylvania, *Republican*, March 25, 1874.
107 Quoted in Clearfield *Republican*, October 14, 1874.
108 Clearfield *Republican*, October 7, 1874.

Republican campaign, judging from surviving sheets of the Indiana *Progress,* collapsed. Democrat George A. Jenks cruised to victory. "Two years ago," joked the (Democratic) Clearfield *Republican,* "Harry White and James A. White [unsuccessful Republican candidate in the 26th District] both voted to strike the word *white* out of our State Constitution. Last week both these gentlemen went before the people and asked to be sent to Congress, but the people struck both these *Whites* out of that body. A little rough on the *Whites,* but they began it."[109] Nearby in the 17th District another Republican campaign crumbled. It repeated the lesson of the Whites. (see Map 15, below)

Pennsylvania, Seventeenth District
Samuel S. Blair (R), John Reilly (D)
Population: 99% white

The redrawn and renumbered 17th District covered four counties, Bedford, Blair, Cambria and Somerset. In the midst of sylvan solitudes it hummed with clamorous centers of mining and industry, the manufacturing city of Johnstown and the railroad hub of Altoona. It was home to Republican Congressman John Cessna, champion of the Civil Rights Bill. But the odor

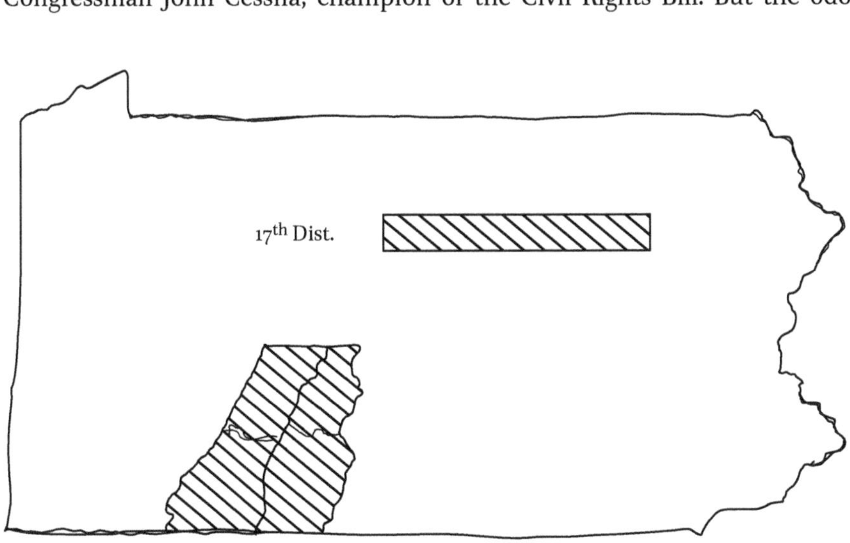

MAP 15 Congressional Districts, Pennsylvania
SOURCE: AUTHORS OF *WELCOMING RUIN.*

109 Clearfield *Republican,* November 11, 1874.

of corruption hung about "Honest John" Cessna.[110] He failed to survive the nomination. Three former congressmen, Abraham Barker, William Henry Koontz and Samuel S. Blair, vied for a return to office. The convention wrangled for two weeks. It adjourned. It reassembled. On the 277th ballot Blair won. He had no civil rights record. Democrats were undeterred. With Cessna gone, they attacked his stand-in.

Depression stalked the district. At Johnstown, the Cambria Iron Works had just shut its doors. Out in the coal fields miners struck for better wages. Mine owners brought in desperate, destitute black men to replace them. Unemployment, scab labor, hard times, hardly generated enthusiasm for social equality, for black people, or Republicans who sympathized with black people. Race and class conflict combined in the 17th District.

Democrats nominated John Reilly, a poor farmer's son who had risen to become a supervisor on the Pennsylvania Railroad. They anointed him the workingman's friend, as against lawyer Samuel Blair, "the aristocratic-Republican-kid-glove-third-term-hard-times candidate."[111] Republicans sensed a disadvantageous matchup. They turned to the boss, Thomas A. Scott, President of the Pennsylvania Railroad. Scott summoned Reilly to his Philadelphia boardroom. He invoked a clause in the company's contract forbidding employees to seek elective office. Reilly defied the boss. Fire me if you dare. He returned to Altoona in triumph, riding the cars of the Pennsylvania Railroad. Cheering crowds met him. At every station he stepped out to brass bands' blare and white men's salutes.[112]

Few black people could have saluted, had they wanted to. Few inhabited the 17th District: 485 appeared in Bedford County; 386 in Blair; 98 in Cambria; 45 in Somerset County; altogether 1,014 among 131,467 whites. Few as they were, they infuriated white people. In May police raided a cathouse in one of Altoona's seedier haunts. They found civil rights: "seven buck negroes and two white

110 That scent arose most pungently from the Chorpenning Claim. This tangled affair featured the complaint of George Chorpenning, Jr., who demanded half a million dollars from the United States Treasury. Congressman Cessna championed his cause. The case went back twenty years, to 1853. At that time the government canceled its contract with the firm of Chorpenning and Woodward, engaged to carry the mails on Route 12,801, from Sacramento, California, San Pedro and Carson's Valley to Salt Lake. Congress thought it had resolved the matter in 1857, agreeing to a payout of $30,000 per year of annulment. Chorpenning thought otherwise. Cessna renewed his claim in the 41st Congress, and again in the 43rd. By then Chorpenning's request had grown to the princely sum of $443,000. An act of justice, Cessna said. Highway robbery, his critics insisted, another example of "Honest John's" dishonesty.

111 Hollidaysburg, Pennsylvania, *Register*, October 28, 1874.

112 Altoona *Morning Tribune*, October 28–31, 1874.

women (white outside)," including the proprietress Mrs. Jennie Robinson, all engaged in amorous activities. "How elevating!" commented the Clearfield *Republican*. "But then these creatures are just practicing what Garrison, Seward & Co. preached and theorized about for forty years."[113]

John Reilly understood. He understood the white working people. He understood their distress. He understood their prejudice. Civil rights, he explained, conspired with capitalist oppression. Together they aimed to bring down the laboring man and bring degradation upon his family. "If the Civil Rights Bill should pass, what will be the penalty for one of our fair daughters or sisters refusing a negro's invitation to dance, or to an evening's entertainment, or ten years hence refusing his offer of marriage?"[114] John Reilly rode the Pennsylvania Railroad to Congress. "The Ku-Klux are jubilant," sighed the Republican Hollidaysburg *Register*. "Jeff Davis is jubilant."[115]

So it went across Pennsylvania. Democratic State Chairman John Miller surveyed the scene. "The white race in this State has risen up in its majesty to assert its supremacy." Republicans had learned a lesson, he hoped. "The Civil Rights Bill ought never to be passed in mercy to the negro. My God! Sir, if they keep on the state of things will be similar to that which produced the Sicilian Vespers, for it is nearly that now."[116]

7 New Jersey

New Jersey Democrats beheld a magnificent target: New Jersey's own Frederick Frelinghuysen, sponsor of the Senate Civil Rights Bill. Frelinghuysen sat in a bulls-eye. Fourth District Democrats met at the town of Washington in Warren County to re-nominate the party's only incumbent congressman, Robert Hamilton. Their platform resolved: "the special efforts of Senator Frelinghuysen to impose upon the people of New Jersey the Civil Rights bill should receive the unmistakable condemnation of the people of this State." Sixth District Democrats met at Orange in Essex County. They opposed "the forcible establishment of social equality as proposed by the 'Civil Rights' bill introduced by a New Jersey Senator."[117]

---

113 Clearfield *Republican*, May 27, 1874.
114 Altoona *Sun*, quoted in Shreveport *Times*, June 18, 1874.
115 Hollidaysburg *Register*, November 11, 1874.
116 Clearfield *Republican*, November 11, 18, 1874.
117 Newark *Journal*, August 14, 1874.

Freedmen did not swarm New Jersey to terrorize its population. Unemployment, however, hunger howling at the door, produced a suitable terror. New Jersey Democrats, as their colleagues in Pennsylvania, crafted their message, merging economic and civil rights fear to fit a manufacturing state sunk in an industrial depression. A simple equation: Frelinghuysen's civil rights bill oppressed the South. An oppressed South did not consume consumer goods. The market for New Jersey's manufactures declined. The result: privation, homelessness, and hunger. Mayor George J. Ferry of Orange explained.

> Time was when the Southern merchant came to your city and purchased $10,000,000 worth of your labor and products yearly. But now many of you are out of employment, unable to feed your wives and children. All this comes because the South is so ground down that it has no purchasing power.... Many a time you men have gone home and found your children pinched with hunger, and not a dollar in your pocket. Why is this? Because the people of the South are so oppressed that they cannot buy your goods.... How long is this state of things to continue? Just so long as the Republican party is kept in power.[118]

Mayor Ferry's argument did not preclude an appeal to racism. New Jersey Democrats, perhaps a trifle squeamish, seemed reluctant to pursue that line of rhetoric. A champion crossed the Delaware. Senator Thomas Bayard, secure in his home state, rallied the Jerseymen. At Jersey City on the banks of the Hudson Bayard delivered a harangue fit to warm the hearts of multitudes on the broad flowing Mississippi.

> I want New Jersey to give her answer to Frelinghuysen. Charles Sumner's mantle, somewhat too large for him, he imagined was on his shoulders, and he took up the law enacting social equality. If in any way it is passed, roll up the map of your State, blot out her fair name.... A negro may be greasy, he may be impudent, he may be, as they sometimes say, fragrant; but if he goes to any hotel and is refused equal accommodation, in a week

---

118 Newark *Journal*, September 30, 1874. The argument was not new, nor did it go out of style. "Any legislation in Washington based upon the assumption that the negro is wronged," said Alabama's Hilary Herbert in 1889, "would tend towards a conflict of races in the South.... How appalling the prospect! And not only the properties of Southern, but of Northern men also – ruined stocks, state bonds, city bonds, county bonds, mining and manufacturing interests – all would be in peril. It is amazing that capitalists, proverbially sagacious in their foretastes, should be so quiescent and complacent." Hilary A. Herbert, *Why the Solid South? or, Reconstruction and its Results* (Baltimore: 1890), 440.

> he can collect \$3,000.... This bill goes farther; it attacks the children of the South, forcing on the children of the poor white man a contact which those who voted for the bill know their wealth would enable them to avoid. I ask you, white men of the North, will you permit this? [Cries of "No! No!"] ... Knowing the South as I do, I say here to-night that if I must choose between living at the South with the children I love and standing against yonder blank wall to be shot to death with musketry, I should thank God for the musketry.[119]

New Jersey Republicans scattered and dove for cover. The state convention made no mention of civil rights. Frelinghuysen at least stood firm. Wrapped in Sumner's mantle, he replied with religious fervor.

> The foremost principle of government is elementary, and it lies at the foundation of the Union. It is the principle which teaches that it is well to do right and ill to do wrong. The Gospel is an elucidation of this principle. In the violation of it we read the downfall of nations. What will our children say if we fail to place this nation on the rock of eternal right? ... Let it be decreed that any class of men in this country shall enjoy a secondary citizenship; that they may, no matter how tidy and respectable, be pushed into a cattle-car or denied equal privileges in the schools for which they pay taxes, or, tried for life, be excluded from the jury-box. Let such things exist and that race are slaves in everything but the name, and they rest under the weight of degradation.[120]

Frelinghuysen was not finished. "Let the men of the South understand that we are tired of this. It is only by the forcible enforcement of the law that they can be made to obey it."

> Northern men have in them the enthusiasm of freedom. Southern men feel that some one was born to be their subordinate. Northern men are industrious and self-reliant; Southern men are dependent on the colored race for subsistence.... They would drive the colored men from the polls and then take control of the ballot box. They are doing it now.... They would inaugurate a reign of terror and crystallize it into a permanent state of things. They would perpetuate by State enactments, by tax laws, etc., a system of practical disfranchisement for the colored man.... If that

119 Newark *Journal*, October 22, 1874.
120 Newark *Journal*, October 17, 1874.

> can be done with impunity – if the amendments to the Constitution can be violated, then have we destroyed the Republic.[121]

The senator "caused the blood to boil in the veins of his hearers," so the Jersey City *Journal* reported.[122] Ebullition did not mean votes. Democrat Joseph Bedle handily won the governorship. Democrats retained control of the legislature. Two of six Republican congressmen survived. A fresh candidate, Clement Sinnickson, helped them hold the 1st District. Amiable Samuel "Uncle Sammy" Dobbins retained the good will of his constituents in the 2nd. Elsewhere incumbents fell. Amos Clark in the 3rd District was an influential man, a friend of President Grant. Democrats swept him away. Voters retired ex-governor Marcus Ward in the 6th District. Isaac Scudder of the 7th (Hudson County) was "portly, gregarious, a jolly bachelor and very popular with the ladies." Those qualities failed to save him.[123] Their most celebrated colleague, chic, cultivated, William Walter Phelps, held the 5th District. Democrats all but conceded his reelection. Phelps, too, fell from his perch. Civil rights delivered the fatal blow. (see Map 16, below)

New Jersey, Fifth District
William Walter Phelps (R), Augustus W. Cutler (D)
Population: 97% white

Hon. William Walter Phelps had risen from the top to the tip-top. His family planted its roots in the New World in 1630. It traced its bloodline in the Old World to the 11th century, a pedigree William Walter was not reluctant to mention.[124] Phelps' brilliance was plain in all worlds. He entered Yale at 15,

---

121 Newark *Journal*, October 17, 1874.

122 Jersey City *Journal*, November 2, 1874.

123 Paterson *Press*, April 27, June 15, 1874.

124 See Hugh M. Herrick, *William Walter Phelps, his Life and Public Services* (New York: 1904). Mark Twain recalled an evening spent with Phelps, then U.S. Ambassador to Germany. "After dinner he took us about his drawing-room, showing us the pictures, and finally stopped before a rude and ancient engraving. It was a picture of the court that tried Charles I. There was a pyramid of judges in Puritan slouch hats, and below them three bare-headed secretaries seated at a table. Mr. Phelps put his finger on one of the three and said with exulting indifference – 'An ancestor of mine.' I put my finger on a judge and retorted with scathing languidness – 'Ancestor of mine. But it is a small matter. I have others.' It was not noble in me to do it.... However, it made no difference in our friendship. I always treated him as an equal." Mark Twain, *Autobiography of Mark Twain* (Berkeley: 2010), vol. 1, 204–205.

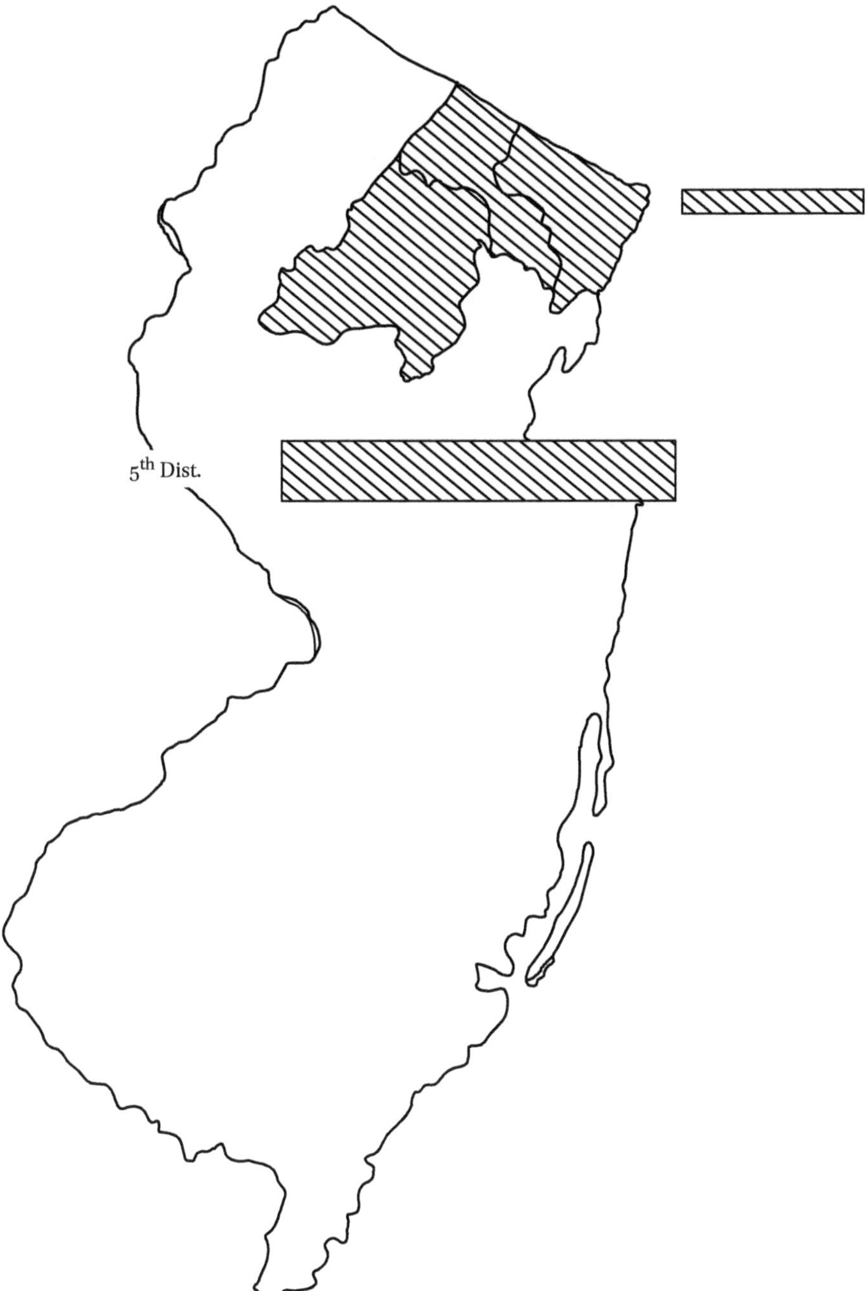

MAP 16 Congressional Districts, New Jersey
SOURCE: AUTHORS OF *WELCOMING RUIN*.

graduated second in the class of 1860, a member of the Senior Society of Skull and Bones. He devoted his further efforts to growing increasingly rich. He sat on the board of a dozen railroads, including the New Haven in the east and the International and Great Northern Railroad in the west. He acquired title to 3,000,000 acres of real estate in Texas. Banking provided a supplementary income. He took a part interest in the New York *Tribune*. He inherited the ancestral domains in Connecticut. His New York City townhouse and gardens enclosed the block of 36th St. and Madison Ave. His New Jersey estate stretched from the Hackensack River to the Hudson. "He would look with the pride of ownership over the fair lands of his home," his biographer wrote, "so far as sight carried, the wide and rolling fields, the vivid green of the meadows, the blue range of the Palisades beyond, and the cottages of his dependents half-hidden by the trees."[125] A tree-enshrouded private road ran for three miles from the town of Englewood to reach his secluded mansion, "Teaneck Grange." The wunderkind entered Congress at the age of 33 in 1873.

For all his brilliance, Phelps failed to feel the political headwind rising against him. His district offered him a rude awakening. New Jersey's 5th contained three counties: Morris, Passaic and Bergen. He had won the seat comfortably over Democrat-Liberal Republican Absalom B. Woodruff. Phelps, Woodruff said, was a foppish interloper, hair parted in the middle, a slick New Yorker too rich to understand the needs of Jersey folk.[126] In 1872 Phelps was elected anyway. In 1874 unemployed workers in Paterson and Passaic felt less fond of fops.

Phelps disdained party discipline. He declared himself a maverick, an independent thinker, responsible to his own wisdom. He defied his party when he saw fit, which was often: on the Currency Bill, on the Franking Privilege Bill, on the Centennial Bill, on the Civil Rights Bill. Most gallingly he sided with Democrats on the Louisiana elections question. Early in 1875 he toured New Orleans as a member of Frisbie Hoar's investigative commission. Democrats stroked his ego. Congressman-elect Gibson toasted him at a reception at Moreau's Restaurant.[127] Phelps joined the commission's Democrats to declare the recent elections free, fair, and innocent of White League murderousness.

---

125 Herrick, *William Walter Phelps*, 30.

126 Herrick, *William Walter Phelps*, 38.

127 Paterson *Press*, January 6, 1875. Pinchback's *Louisianian* bade him good riddance: "We lay no claim to this dandy and affected statesman from New Jersey, and cheerfully pass him over, eye-glasses and all, to such uses, or even abuses, as may suggest themselves to our Democratic friends... We never had so much respect for New Jersey as we have cheerfully cultivated since it expectorated from its bowels this renegade Republican." New Orleans *Louisianian*, April 10, 1875.

The congressman's supporters extolled his maverick stand. "It has been many years since the voice of a New Jersey member of Congress has resounded throughout the country, creating such electric emotions," proclaimed the Orange *Journal*. "He had the moral courage to defy the denunciations of an aggressive majority in Congress – while he did not fear to rebuke the errors of popular delusion."[128] A thin line, however, separated maverick from renegade. Many considered Phelps to have crossed it. A fawning press "has made him a great man before his time," one constituent wrote Ben Butler. In fact he was a posing mediocrity.[129] Others saw an empty suit, "an imitator of the English gentleman ... cynical, purposeless and passive."[130]

Phelps' 5th District was redrawn, most of it a remnant the former 7th District. That area had a Republican edge. Republican John Hill had held it for three terms. Republicans Charles Voorhis and Hill again recovered the 5th District after Phelps lost it. Phelps himself returned in the 48th Congress. Democrats hesitated to put a candidate in the field. "There is the best reason to believe," the Paterson *Press* reported, "that it will be difficult for the Democracy to find a candidate who will make anything like a promising show of opposition."[131] The Morris *Jerseyman* deplored its party's cowardice: "Where is the self-sacrificing individual in these three counties who will come to [our] relief?"[132] Well into October Democrats remained without a candidate.

Phelps disdained to worry about reelection. Congress adjourned. He left for a leisurely vacation on the Connecticut shore. He observed commencement at Yale, standing under the gate that bore his family's name. The congressman idled. His district boiled. Heat rose from the Civil Rights Bill.

Phelps had chosen that issue to stamp his maverick reputation. Alone among northern Republicans he opposed it, deliberately, and on every occasion. In the opinion of black people William Walter Phelps committed an uncommon betrayal. Back in December when the National Civil Rights Convention gathered at Washington its delegates had approached the congressman. He pledged his

128 Quoted in Paterson *Press*, August 26, 1874.

129 Thomas D. Horsey to Benjamin Butler, December 17, 1874. Butler Papers, Library of Congress.

130 Springfield *Republican*, May 22, 1874. Even his duplicate first name irritated detractors. "Why William Walter Phelps?" inquired the Brooklyn *Eagle*, "that surplusage of nomenclature which makes good young men so nice and detestable.... He should be baptized at intervals and put by to shrink. We admit that Mr. Phelps is an exception; but he knows well enough that, ordinarily, a brace of names distinguishes pimply students, and not men with real stuff in them." Quoted in Paterson *Press*, August 20, 1874.

131 Paterson *Press*, August 11, 1874.

132 Quoted in Paterson *Press*, August 20, 1874.

honor to support Charles Sumner's bill. Now he outdid the Democrats in rejecting it. Phelps acknowledged the fact. He had changed his mind. "I have not that conceit in the accuracy of my own judgments that would lead me to think that my ninety-nine associates thought incorrectly and I alone correctly.... But when it comes to a matter of conscience and right like this, all domination of party I spurn, and the crack of the party whip falls on a deafened ear."[133] Some Republicans granted him his conscience. "His vote on the civil rights bill was not the one we would have given," wrote the Jersey City *Journal,* "but if Mr. Phelps really deemed the bill to be of doubtful constitutionality he did right to vote against it."[134] Phelps' black constituents meditated revenge.

Rumbling came first in Newark. That city lay outside the 5th District, but its message resonated within. Black citizens met on July 13 under the leadership of Col. John Taylor. They put their resolution plainly:

> Resolved, That we denounce the name of W.W. Phelps of New Jersey, who voted against the Civil Rights Bill on June 20th, 1874, and earnestly recommend that no colored voter in this district recognize him as a true friend of the colored men of New Jersey.[135]

Such impudence disagreeably ruffled the congressman's feelings. He laughed it off. "When I give up my present motives to do right and please my constituents I shall not make it a motive to please one whose chief merit is his color, whose only boast is a military title which he has assumed.... No, I cannot please 'Col.' Taylor."[136] The revolt spread. Black citizens of Hackensack, this time within Phelps' district, organized a club dedicated to his defeat. Phelps began to fret. He solicited the help of black supporters. A letter appeared in the Paterson *Press.* New York's Samuel R. Scottron upbraided his New Jersey brethren. Do not abandon the congressman.

> The colored people of the United States, having been lifted up to the common platform of citizenship, have as a consequence a like interest with others in every able man in the nation.... We cannot afford to act as though we were building for ourselves alone, but our actions should be

133 *Cong. Record,* 43rd Congress, 2nd Session: 1001–1002.

134 Jersey City *Journal,* August 14, 1874.

135 Newark *Journal,* July 14, 1874.

136 Paterson *Press,* August 12, 1874. His rank in the New Jersey militia, Taylor replied, was legitimate. And, unlike some foppish war-profiteering millionaires, he had served as a soldier in the real conflict.

> guided by that wisdom and liberality which shall redound to the welfare of our country.[137]

As a black man, Scottron declared, he knew the sting of prejudice. "I yield not the first place to any of my people in an earnest desire for the early acquisition of all the civil rights common to American citizens." But they must put citizenship first, and the needs of the nation. Scottron's words drew a cutting reply. William H. Hopper of Paterson shot back. To ask black voters to support Phelps "is to insult our Republican principles, our manhood." Scottron professed to understand the experience of prejudice. Very well. Prejudice meant nothing. Prejudice would always exist. Injustice must end. "Allow me to say to him that we are not troubled at all about the prejudices against color. It is the discrimination against color to which we protest."[138]

The Republican convention met at the Paterson Opera House on August 12. It opened at noon and closed two hours later. William Walter Phelps accepted re-nomination. Resolutions danced around the Civil Rights Bill. "We affirm our belief in the doctrine of equal civil and political rights for all men," the fifth resolution declared, "and we trust that as the latter have been achieved through the agency of the Republican party, the former will soon be also." But, the resolution continued, black people must wait, wait until objections were met, "objections which have constrained many conscientious men, earnestly in favor of the great principle involved, to oppose what they deemed an injurious, partial and inoperative application of it."[139]

The nominee spoke, a supremely Phelpsian oration. He congratulated himself. "After being in the fierce contest of the capital, where my merits and demerits – the latter, alas, too many – have been freely canvassed … I have a right to accept this nomination as to a certain extent due to myself." He wagged a finger at ill-mannered critics. "They found fault with me if I were silent, or if I spoke … and I have never found the reason." His constituents knew he knew what was best for them. "The intelligence and fairness of my people was my chiefest delight and strength. I had only to ask, 'is any measure right?' I had never to ask, 'will my people understand it?'" He applauded his civil rights courage. "I dared to vote against a bill which violated the Constitution and would injure the national welfare and permanently check the progress of the colored race."[140]

---

137 Paterson *Press*, September 30, 1874.

138 Paterson *Press*, October 3, 1874.

139 Paterson *Press*, August 12, 1874.

140 It was a congressman's lot, he lamented, to suffer the importunities of his people, the whining, for instance, of disabled veterans forever seeking a government job: "Alas! If they would only think how hard it is … when every mail-bag is already divided between a one-

Phelps retired to rest at Long Branch, then to vacation again in Connecticut. He did pause to pay a visit to distressed workers. He put in a quick call at Prall's Silk Factory in Paterson, "at the urgent invitation of the workmen there employed." He expressed "sympathy with their difficulties."

Democrats continued to dither. No candidate appeared. Party leaders asked ex-governor Theodore Randolph to run. He had his eye on a nomination to the Senate and so declined.[141] They turned to Col. Thomas Miller, millionaire industrialist of Mahwah (inventor of Miller's Patent Railroad Coupler and Buffer). He too declined. Next proposed was Abram Hewitt, the great scientific iron-monger. Though a New Yorker, he maintained a residence in New Jersey. Hewitt had his eye on a New York seat, the 10th District, to which he was elected. Democrats entered their convention at Paterson on October 10 still undecided. Several more candidates were sounded. Each declined. A resolution to unite behind Phelps failed after a stormy debate. At last a nominee emerged. State Senator Augustus Cutler of Morristown accepted the challenge. Behind a great wide-spreading beard, he was by all accounts an amiable gentleman. He rivaled Phelps at least in pedigree. His great-grandfather Silas Condict had sat in the Continental Congress. His grand-uncle Lewis Condict served nine terms a congressman and a trustee of Princeton. Cutler remarked nevertheless that he expected to lose. The Paterson *Press* agreed: "The poor dupe is only set up to be knocked down ... the most good-natured man in the party, whom it is a shame to impose upon."[142] It soon became clear that Augustus Cutler was not a dupe, or a sacrificial lamb.

The 5th District's three counties tilted in different directions. Bergen County was Democratic. Passaic voted Republican. Morris County held the swing position. Cutler had strength in Morris. Republican swagger slumped. On October 19 the New York *Herald* considered the race too close to call. Only 3,040 black persons resided in the district. They could manage a few hundred votes. Suddenly every vote counted.

Democrats zeroed in on Phelps' civil rights quandary. On the 23rd Cutler appeared at Hackensack, accompanied by his supporters, State Attorney-General Robert Gilchrist, Absalom Woodruff and Judge Ashbel Green. The Grant Locomotive Factory had just shut its doors in bankruptcy. Judge Green reminded unemployed workmen which party they had to blame for their misery; it was

---

armed soldier and a one-legged soldier, the honest applicant would leave his congressman filled with pity for him rather than anger."

141 Paterson *Press*, August 13, 1874.

142 Paterson *Press*, October 10, 1874.

certainly not the party out of power. Then he turned to civil rights. Phelps had voted against it. He was guilty nonetheless.

> A Republican is a man who believes in the Civil Rights Bill…. Mr. Phelps apologized in Paterson and told why he did not vote for the Civil Rights Bill. I don't know of but one animal on this earth that was in such a predicament as Wm. Walter Phelps is, and that was Ben Hardin's heifer, who straddled the stream and walked down on both sides until it split to pieces.[143]

Congressman Phelps, as the proverbial heifer, commenced to break apart. Black voters held the balance of power. It was too late to please Col. Taylor now. He could only defend his stand. He did so, with increasing irritation, at each occasion. He appeared at Passaic on October 15. Ex-Speaker of the House Galusha Grow, a fellow speculator in Texas railroads, came to his aid. The candidate delivered an apologia for his vaunted independence. Yes, he had voted against his party on the civil rights question. But "he had done so conscientiously, and he tersely and forcibly stated his reasons therefore."[144]

He appeared again with Speaker Grow at Paterson on the 21st. Reinforcements arrived: gubernatorial candidate George Halsey, New York's Stewart Woodford, and E.B. Conover, a black man.[145] Phelps' greatness, said Grow, was the exercise of free will, "acting according to his conscience and not under the party lash." Conover urged black citizens to see civil rights the Phelps way. Civil rights bills failed everywhere they were enacted. He, Conover, had fought to pass the New York Civil Rights Act. What had it accomplished? "It has always been a dead-letter." Louisiana had passed one. Result? "Colored people are trampled and murdered in every part of the State."

The candidate spoke, defiant and petulant as ever. "Fellow citizens, I am here to-night not to make any defense of my acts." He proceeded to defend his acts. The Civil Rights Bill was unconstitutional. It would lead to a war of races. It would destroy the common school system. Senator Brownlow agreed with him. So did Dr. Sears. So did President Grant. It saddened him to oppose a humane measure. But he obeyed his conscientious objection.

> I voted against the whole natural impulse of my character. My natural desire was to vote for it…. I submit that I proved myself a better friend to

143 Paterson *Press*, October 23, 1874.

144 Paterson *Press*, October 16, 1874.

145 Paterson *Press*, October 22, 1874.

> the colored man by my adverse vote on the Civil Rights Bill. What reason had I not to do it unless I was actuated by an honest principle? No one would have blamed me, and I might easily have swung with the tide. In voting against it I expected to be misunderstood.[146]

Phelps' black constituents understood perfectly. They took the final step, a bolt against the Republican ticket. Their leader was Alfred P. Smith, political activist and sometime journalist of Saddle River in Bergen County. Smith launched his coup on October 12. A circular letter addressed black voters. Two years ago they had voted for Phelps against Absalom Woodruff. "Have we gained anything in any way by the results? Had we voted differently, and had Woodruff instead of Phelps been elected, would we have lost anything by it?"

> William Walter Phelps has betrayed us, and on the altar of his supposed self-interest has sacrificed our dearest rights. His honor as a man and as a Republican, in which we kindly trusted, has proved, like his word, which was expressly pledged, a broken reed. Stripped of all disguise, he stands before the country false to us who placed him in the high position he occupies, false to every distinctive principle of the party whose name he bears, and false to his own plighted word.... As true as he has been to us and to the suffering people of our blood in the South we will be to him.[147]

A thousand black votes, Smith claimed, would turn against the incumbent.[148] That seems unlikely, given a population of only 3,040 black persons.[149] Circumstances did not require so large a number. As the election tightened every lost vote portended the loss of a congressional seat. Phelps fled to speak in neighboring Hudson County, the 7th District. Black men heckled him from the audience.[150] He returned home. Black people organized a rally at Westwood in Bergen County. Phelps agreed to appear. Then he disappeared. He had missed the train, he said.[151] Republicans begged the candidate to set matters right with his black constituents. The Paterson *Press* was beside itself.

---

146 New York *Tribune*, October 22, 1874.

147 New Orleans *Republican*, January 24, 1875.

148 New Orleans *Republican*, February 5, 1875.

149 That population remained static. The 1880 census, a more rigorous count than that of 1870, found only 3,778 colored persons: 1,891 in Bergen County, 1,077 in Passaic, 810 in Morris.

150 Indianapolis *Journal*, October 30, 1874.

151 Paterson *Press*, October 28, 1874.

> Some of our colored people are in a fair way of doing more by a single foolish, selfish and narrow-minded act to injure themselves and to put back the current of their progress to equal civil rights, and to render further advance impossible, than all the resistance the Democratic party has ever made to it. We have no patience with this crazy element among the colored voters, and for our part we propose to let those who are fools enough to walk into the web of the gloating Democratic spider do so, and take the responsibility for the consequences.... For such ingratitude and folly they deserve the worst fate.[152]

Black voters embraced their fate. Democrats rallied at Paterson on October 29. Black guests, former Republicans, took seats prominently reserved in the front row. They applauded as speakers condemned "the audacious stripling from Yale."[153] On the 31st A.P. Smith spoke at Paterson. He urged black people to vote down William Walter Phelps.[154] The *Press* warned of dire consequences: "Do you remember the nursery rhyme? 'For want of a nail the kingdom was lost.' The nail that you drive, or fail to drive, on election day may be the very nail that will win or lose for us our District in Congress."[155]

The *Press* could not have imagined how truly the nursery rhyme spoke. Returns came in swiftly. Cutler won Bergen County. Phelps took Passaic. The difference was five votes in Phelps' favor. A preliminary count gave Cutler Morris County by 39 votes, and the election by 34. But tallies were disputed. Forty-three ballots had been discounted in Bergen County. They appeared to record votes for the Republican, enough to put Phelps ahead by 9. The marking, however, was irregular. Democratic canvassers disqualified variant versions of Phelps' tripartite appellation. In Palisades they rejected 27 ballots marked for W.W. Phelps. The board of elections in Franklin Township refused to accept 16 inscribed in the name of Wm. Walter Phelps. The *Press* cried foul. The voters' intentions were clear. One Democratic member of the board in Franklin was heard to declare "he'd be damned" before he admitted the disputed ballots. The Bergen County Board of Canvassers re-counted all the ballots. They awarded some to Phelps. But they discovered others overlooked for Cutler. Cutler's majority held at 596. Phelps had carried Passaic County by 631. Morris County

152 Paterson *Press*, October 29, 1874.
153 Paterson *Press*, October 30, 1874.
154 Paterson *Press*, November 2, 1874.
155 Paterson *Press*, October 31, 1874.

recorded an official majority of 40 for Cutler. The 5th District went Democratic by five votes, the closest result in the nation.[156]

No one would have faulted Phelps for filing a contest. That act was beneath him. He refused to dignify the voters' insult by groveling for the privilege of representing them. He wrote Augustus Cutler: "A majority of the citizens who went to the polls preferred another. And I should be the last one to question or impede their choice." Such gallantry, of course, required the winner to thank the loser for condescending to concede. The amiable Cutler replied with a twist of humor: "I doubt if any Congressman-elect can boast of a constituent more chivalric and high-minded than yourself, and I know that none can feel more honored than I do when I remember that among *my* [emphasis assumed] constituents I can number you."[157]

Various factors – economic depression, the candidate's effete temperament, his irrepressible "independence" – contributed to William Walter Phelps' defeat. Civil rights topped the list. "But for his plucky vote on the Civil Rights Bill," wrote his New York *Tribune*, "it is plain that Mr. Phelps would have ridden out the typhoon in triumph."[158] How many black voters actually joined the revolution? Perhaps only a few. They were enough. Alfred Smith was ecstatic.

> His boasted abilities have been tried and found to be nothing more than the vaporings of a sophomore who imagines he knows everything.... He proved an ingrate and a traitor, and this fall we gave him a majority of less than nothing. He was tried and found wanting and branded as a wretched failure, mistrusted and rejected by men of all parties. He goes dishonored to the limbo of departed politicians.[159]

Phelps did not fade forever into political limbo. He returned to his railroads and banks. Trees obsessed his esthetic sense.[160] He busied himself with reforestation, planting thousands of trees on his Englewood estate. The party recalled him from exile. He sat again in the 48th, 49th, and 50th Congresses. President Hayes employed him as Minister to Austria, where he chatted with Emperor Franz Joseph in French. President Harrison gave him a chance to

156 Paterson *Press*, November 4–5, 7, 1874.

157 Herrick, *William Walter Phelps*, 60–61.

158 New York *Tribune*, November 4, 1874.

159 New Orleans *Republican*, February 20, 1875.

160 "He respected [trees], admired, and cherished as he would human beings; they seemed to have for him an intelligent presence, and in his adoration he almost believed they could think." Herrick, *Phelps*, 76.

serve the cause of peace, appointing him envoy to the Samoa arbitration conference at Berlin and then Minister to the German Empire. His magnificent mansion burned in 1889. Someone let gas jets leak in the portrait gallery. Servants sent to investigate imprudently opened the door to a hallway lit by other gas jets. The inferno left little behind. William Walter Phelps died in 1894. He lived long enough to enjoy one satisfaction. In 1883 he saw the Supreme Court strike down the Civil Rights Act.

8 Obituary

The elections passed. Members of the 43rd Congress returned to reconsider the fate of the Civil Rights Bill. They considered it in the wake of an unprecedented electoral earthquake that ended a political era. Thirty-seven states made up the Union. The Civil Rights Bill crippled the Republican Party in at least a third of them. It obliterated Republicans all across the South. The effect was muted in Florida, to some extent in Louisiana and Arkansas. It raged in Alabama, in Tennessee, Georgia, Virginia, North Carolina and Missouri. It helped Democrats sweep Maryland, Delaware and West Virginia. It performed its mischief in the North. In swing states it swung the balance: Ohio, Indiana, Pennsylvania and New Jersey. "Greasy, impudent and fragrant" Negroes, Senator Bayard told the people of Jersey City, would overrun their state, "blot out her fair name." Even where the Civil Rights Bill did no harm it did Republicans no good. Nowhere did it benefit their cause.[161] White candidates fled in terror. Black candidates feared its apparition. James Rapier avoided it. Josiah Walls barely mentioned it. Jeremiah Haralson all but repudiated it. John Hyman in North Carolina did repudiate it. James Harris and Stewart Ellison denied the need for a civil rights act.

Why then did Republicans support it? They had no choice, it is assumed. They were caught in a trap. They could not abandon their quest for civil rights – they had to stick with it – because they needed to retain the support of black voters. The elections put to rest that pervasive myth. Or rather, they ought to have put it to rest. The myth persists. Historians have repeated it solemnly. Black voters were mutinous. They needed to be "rallied," to be "reunited"; their

161 See William Gillette, *Retreat from Reconstruction, 1869–1879* (Baton Rouge: 1979), 216–228, 256–257.

loyalty required "renewal."[162] No hint of mutiny or a need for renewal appears. Still the refrain continues to echo as it echoed in 1874.[163] It has no more validity now than it did then.

Black leaders, to be sure, muttered the threat of rebellion. Frederick Douglass menaced as early as 1871, when the Senate tabled Sumner's first civil rights proposals.[164] Nothing came of that. Black delegates threatened mutiny at the National Colored Convention in 1872. No mutiny occurred. They spoke darkly of desertion in 1874. George Downing made the threat formal.[165] No one deserted. Indeed, the *New National Era* admitted, they could not desert. They had no refuge. "Can we as a people afford to have the party disintegrated and destroyed? ... We are poor, landless, and uneducated. If we break with the Republican party and it breaks from us, we have nowhere to go."[166] The San Francisco *Elevator* agreed. "If we leave the Republican party, where will we go?"[167] John Roy Lynch assured the Republican caucus. They would not go. Failure to pass a civil rights bill disappointed black voters. It did not displace their loyalty.

Shrewd observers understood. Black people would not abandon their party because of some civil rights disillusionment. If the Civil Rights Bill failed, *Harper's Weekly* concluded, "the Republicans will theoretically bear the responsibility. But at the polls, where the facts will be considered, this theory will not harm them."[168] It did not harm them. Black voters marched to the polls. They supported Jacob Thornburgh, who made a point of dismissing the Civil Rights Bill. They endorsed Horace Harrison; they stuck with David Nelson, who abandoned it. They voted for James Sener, who voted against it. They came out for James Lofland, who disowned it, and agreed with James Headon who denounced it. In Richmond Rush Burgess found, to his dismay, that civil

162 Gillette, *Ibid.*, 261: "The only way to rally and reunite that bloc of voters – in order to keep the power and electoral votes of the few southern states that still remained in the Republican camp – was to make civil rights the law of the land, thereby renewing the Negro voter's loyalty to the party."

163 It echoed in the civil rights debate's twentieth-century revival. "Political power seekers!" cried South Carolina's Albert Watson in 1963. "They are more interested in votes than in solutions. Solutions would kill their golden goose." *Cong. Record*, 88th Congress, 1st Session: 11,211. Watson knew which geese were golden. It was not the gaggle of black voters. He fled the Democratic Party. He resigned from the 88th Congress, endorsed Barry Goldwater, and returned to the 89th Congress as an anti-civil rights Republican.

164 James M. McPherson, "Abolitionists and the Civil Rights Act of 1875," *Journal of American History*, 52 (1965): 501.

165 New York *Tribune*, July 4, 1874.

166 Washington *New National Era*, May 7, 1874.

167 San Francisco *Elevator*, June 13, 1874.

168 *Harper's Weekly*, July 11, 1874, p. 574.

rights could not unite disunited black voters. At Annapolis Alexander Hagner found the opposite; renunciation of civil rights bills did not diminish the vote of black voters. Independent black candidates, Jesse Wimberly, Robert Norton, James Montgomery, appealed for votes on behalf of civil rights. They failed. No Republican cast aside the Civil Rights Bill more callously than Lloyd Lowndes. When his black constituents finally seemed ready to revolt, Frederick Douglass commanded them to stop. Only the unlamented William Walter Phelps, trapped in an excruciatingly close election, paid a price: the exception that proved the rule.

Was the Shirt of Nessus poisonous to black voters if one tore it off? Hardly. Was it poisonous to white voters if one put it on? Highly. Rarely had the American people sent their representatives in Congress such manifest instructions for the disposition of a pending issue. Why would the Republican Party, in the name of political sanity, disregard such clear instructions? Democrats surveyed the smoking wreckage their civil rights blitzkrieg had wrought. They presumed that, for all their faults, Republicans were not insane. Nor were they suicidal. Hence they would jettison the Civil Rights Bill and seek survival. Citizens of Montgomery, Alabama, painted banners for their victory parade: "Civil Rights Bill – Requiescat in Pace." It did not rest in peace. Stricken by sincerity, defiant of political logic, the Republican Party revived its tormenting wraith. Principle prevailed over politics.

CHAPTER 12

Suffer the Little White Children: *Vox Populi* Reconsidered

Members of the House of Representatives returned to their seats as Congress convened on December 7, 1874: the second meeting of the Forty-third Congress, in the truest sense a lame duck session. The elections had seen to that. Ninety-four Republicans qualified as limping aquatic fowl or, as Sunset Cox called them, "mortuary monuments."[1] Only hotel-keepers and restaurateurs seemed truly happy at the return – along with the bootblacks, "those scions of emancipation rejoicing that the 'gemmen who don't black their own boots' are coming to Washington."[2] As to the Civil Rights Bill, its prospects seemed equally forlorn. The elections had seen to that, too.

The 44th Congress promised to be a duller place. Ben Butler had lost, beaten by Democrat Charles P. Thompson; no chamber could be the same without his presence.[3] Gone soon would be Luke Poland's cerulean swallowtail coat. The salary grab and press-gag bill had done him in. He lost to an Independent, Dudley Denison. Tennessee's William Crutchfield, he of muddy boots and bibulous habits, was now a lame duck. The gaunt silhouette of the Narragansett, Horace Maynard, would cease to haunt the hall. Good-bye humorless Moses Field of Michigan, beaten in Detroit by Democrat-Liberal Republican Gen. Alpheus Williams. Black members maintained a presence. Joseph Rainey was returned. John Roy Lynch would join him. Josiah Walls appeared, but was unseated by Jesse Finley's contest. Charles Nash, John Hyman and Jeremiah Haralson prepared to assist them. Robert Elliott had resigned. His replacement was a Republican, but a white man, Lewis Cass Carpenter.

New York's David Mellish had died. He appeared for the last time in the House on May 11, moving erratically on the floor. Fellow New Yorker Stewart Woodford led him gently into the lobby. That evening, cradling his two

1 Samuel Cox, *Why We Laugh* (New York, 1969), 184.

2 New York *Herald*, November 6, 1874.

3 "A man by the name of Thompson, we believe, is elected in the Sixth District, and will doubtless run his sleepy course in Congress without difficulty," wrote the Chicago *Inter Ocean*. "The House will not gather round him as they were wont to do about Butler. The sight of a hundred members, all talking and gesticulating at once, and all in reply to one man, who defied the entire body, will not meet us in the Forty-fourth Congress." Chicago *Inter Ocean*, November 6, 1874.

daughters, he drove his carriage through town, shouting to crowds on the street. He was taken to the Government Insane Asylum. There he refused nourishment; Horace Greeley, he said, appeared to him and advised him not to eat. He died on May 23.[4] Among the mourners at his funeral was Thomas Acton, the former New York City Police Commissioner whose civil rights victory he had recalled. He also received the tribute of New York's Women's Suffrage Society for his "ardent and faithful" support of that cause.[5] His seat, the 9th District on Manhattan's west side, returned to the Democrats. Tammany Hall sachem Richard Schell replaced him for the term.

Before the Civil Rights Bill came to its crucial votes, four more Republican supporters departed. Stewart Woodford resigned on July 1. He had never been happy in Congress.[6] His seat went to the great merchant Simeon Chittenden. Though a Republican, Chittenden ran an independent campaign. His victory in the north Brooklyn district rested upon many Democratic votes. The New York *Herald* speculated he might caucus with the opposition.[7] He did not. But in the matter of civil rights he joined his friend William Walter Phelps, the only northern Republicans to vote against the bill on its final passage.

John Rice of Illinois, actor and congressman, died on December 17. Massachusetts' Alvah Crocker succumbed to a long illness on December 26. Pennsylvanian Ebenezer McJunkin, elected to a judgeship, resigned effective January 1. Crocker had declined to run again. His seat was already lost. In the special election Republican Charles Stevens tried again and received the consolation of a short tenure. Republicans saved McJunkin's seat. Rice's was lost. Democrat Barney Caulfield, who had won the election for the next full term, also won the special election. He took his place on February 1, just in time to vote against the Civil Rights Bill. Alexander Stephens reappeared, reinvigorated. "He tipped the scales at 80 lbs.," quipped the *Sunday Chronicle*. "The natural exclamation

4 New York *Times*, May 12, 21, 24; New York *Herald*, May 24, 1874. During his brief career Mellish had built a reputation for the intensity of his work, especially on questions of fiscal policy. Hence unkind wits joked: "Poor Congressman Mellish! He went crazy from too much study of the finances, and didn't get the first moiety." Hartford *Courant*, May 21, 1874.

5 New York *Herald*, October 2, 1874. Mellish's fate awoke Congress' better angels. Mellish was one of its poorest members. Ben Butler organized a fund for the relief of his fatherless family. Congressmen and senators contributed $25 each, collecting $7,500. They found his widow a government position at $900 a year. "They have done a good deed," wrote the Jersey City *Journal* (May 28).

6 Questioned by reporters on the madness of Mellish, he replied glumly: "A man who has left a good home, wife and two children, and a good business that supports him, to come up to Congress is not, in my opinion a person suitable to pass judgment on the sanity of his colleagues." Wheeling *Intelligencer*, May 25, 1874.

7 New York *Herald*, December 9, 1874.

of the world will therefore be, 'What ate he?'"[8] His first act was to pay a friendly visit to the White House.[9]

Given the exquisitely thin margins that had attended every vote on the Civil Rights Bill, the loss of even one Republican seat increased the difficulties exponentially. A far greater change, however, affected the members who returned. For the first time since the war Republicans faced the prospect of minority status. What sins had brought on this downfall? How badly had the unpopularity of civil rights legislation harmed the Republicans' vote? Was it a liability, best abandoned in the interests of all? Or did its value as a party principle overcome its malignance?

Exhilaration overcame Democrats. "At last! At last!" ex-senator Eugene Casserly exclaimed when news reached San Francisco over the wires. "After long years of weary waiting – storming against the immutable – hoping against hope – the day of deliverance has dawned. Like a sign in the heavens."[10] Former Philadelphia mayor Richard Vaux wrote the Judiciary Committee's John Stevenson: "It is a great blessing, a great manifestation of the ways of God's dealings with nations." He thanked God particularly for His hatred of civil rights. "This strikes at the Civil Rights Bill, the gag law, negroes ... I have great hope for the future."[11]

Some viewed the Democrats' resurgence calmly. "Here and there a blind and obtuse Bourbon, who has learned nothing from the experiences of the past, may exhibit the old pro-slavery spirit," concluded the *Christian Union.* "But these will be powerless to turn backward the greatest Revolution in modern times.... Politicians of all parties must hereafter worship at the shrine of Justice and Equality."[12] Others worried about justice and equality. Mississippi's Governor Adelbert Ames felt consternation: "The great reaction at the North is an enigma to me. I cannot understand it.... A Democratic Congress! And the war not yet over. The old rebel spirit will not only revive, but it will make itself felt. It will roam over our land, thirsty for revenge, and revenge it will have."[13] Among black people panic set in. They would be remanded to slavery. Ante-bellum Senator David Yulee of Florida, like Chichikov in search of

8 Washington, *Forney's Sunday Chronicle*, November 22, 1874.

9 Harrisburg *Patriot*, November 23, 1874.

10 Eugene Casserly to Manton Marble, December 5, 1874. Manton Marble Papers, Library of Congress.

11 Richard Vaux to John Stevenson, November 10, 1874. John W. Stevenson Papers, Library of Congress.

12 *Christian Union*, November 18, 390.

13 Blanche Butler Ames, *Chronicles from the Nineteenth Century: Family Letters of Blanche Butler and Adelbert Ames* (Clinton, 1957), vol. 2, 52.

dead souls, had been reported buying up slave claims in the expectation that owners would receive compensation for their former property, living or deceased.[14]

White southerners celebrated. The elections marked their restoration to the United States of America: yesterday outcasts, today once more citizens of a common nation. In Atlanta, former Confederate General George Anderson led a torchlight parade. Banners featured caricatures of defeated Republicans, J.G.W. Mills and the hated Ben Butler. They bore messages: "Butler Bottled"; "White Man's Government." One of the largest displayed three female figures personifying States of the Union. Georgia stood between two of her sisters, at her feet the words: "Georgia Joins the Reconstructed States, New York and Massachusetts." The procession stopped at the square on Alabama Street. Flaming tar barrels spread a lurid light. Senator John B. Gordon spoke:

> But a few years ago you were aliens and strangers in the land of your fathers. Now you find yourselves recognized as a part of the great body of a great people. But a few years ago you stood like a band of stricken brothers by the cross upon which your liberties were crucified, or around the grave in which they were buried. Now you stand by the open, empty grave and know that liberty is risen.[15]

Horace Redfield rode the rails. He interviewed the engineer of his train on the Nashville and Chattanooga Railroad. Mr. T.B. House, ex-soldier of the Confederacy, declared that he felt himself, for the first time since the war, an American. "All rejoice in one great nationality, and the stars and stripes is the flag to which all do honor."[16] On the northern side, well-wishers serenaded Democrat Benjamin Willis, congressman-elect from New York's 11th District, in front of his hotel on Fifth Avenue. He returned the compliment with a tribute to the gallant voters of the South: "We rejoice at the spectacle presented by our brethren at the South giving praise to Almighty God that their chains are at last broken." From the unchained South, congressman-elect Jesse Yeates of North Carolina clasped the fraternal hand: "An era of good feeling is established by the late elections."[17] A crowd serenaded Senator Thurman outside his Washington residence. Pressed to name the cause of the Republicans' downfall, Thurman held to a lofty line:

14 Montgomery *Advertiser*, December 1; Altoona *Morning Tribune*, November 30, 1874.

15 Atlanta *Constitution*, November 6, 1874.

16 Cincinnati *Commercial*, November 23, 1874.

17 New York *Herald*, November 13, 21, 1874.

> Americans are a constitution loving people, but no regard has been paid to the constitution by our rulers. Americans are a liberty loving people, but liberty has been remorselessly trampled underfoot. Americans are a home rule loving people, but home rule has been treated with scorn. Americans are an honesty loving people, but Credit Mobilier, custom house frauds and Washington rings have made corruption almost a synonym for government.[18]

The Senator neglected to mention that Americans were not a civil-rights bill loving people. Many put that at the top of the list. Congress, said the Baltimore *Sun,* ought to think long and hard before it plunged the Republican Party deeper into the "civil rights abyss."[19] Redfield ended his long season of travels.

> Without any exception whatever, the Civil Rights Bill was the most harmful, mischievous and dangerous piece of legislation ever attempted upon the American Continent. The Government that stood the shock of four years of war can not stand such legislation as this, and if it is persisted in I fear the end of the first century of the Republic will be the end of the Republic itself.[20]

William Lloyd Garrison admitted it sadly. The party had misread public opinion, "proclaiming liberty throughout all the land, endeavoring to pass the Civil Rights Bill ... it has obviously attempted more in these matters than the popular sentiment is disposed to tolerate."[21] In Ohio Benjamin Wade urged fellow Republicans to abandon civil rights legislation. It was right in principle. But it unleashed uncontrollable prejudices. "True statesmanship keeps abreast of public opinion."[22] Such words from a radical's radical could not be disregarded.[23]

Republican Congressman Washington Townsend, re-elected in Pennsylvania's 6th District, wrote to fellow-survivor George Frisbie Hoar. He listed a litany of woes, wherefore the nation's discontent: economic downturn, corruption, "Butlerism, Prohibition, drought, the cotton worm ... locusts." Also

18 Harrisburg *Patriot,* November 6, 1874.

19 Baltimore *Sun*, November 12, 1874.

20 Cincinnati *Commercial*, November 30, 1874.

21 William Lloyd Garrison, *The Letters of William Lloyd Garrison* (Cambridge, 1981), vol. 6, 371.

22 New York *Tribune*, December 3, 1874.

23 Wade's radicalism declined as the 1870s progressed. See Patrick W. Riddleberger, "The Radicals' Abandonment of the Negro during Reconstruction," *Journal of Negro History*, 45 (1960): 89–90.

on Townsend's list, just between boll weevils and locusts, was the Civil Rights Bill.[24]

Other commentators exonerated the grasshoppers (currently wreaking havoc on the central plains). They mounted a mosaic of isms: "Grantism, nepotism, favoritism, absenteeism, salary-grabism, credit-mobilierism, land-swindleism, fanaticism, one-ideaism, charlatanism," according to the Dayton *Democrat.*[25] "Credit-Mobilierism, carpet-bagism, Kelloggism, Butlerism, ringism, Grantism, and Hard Times," in the opinion of the Harrisburg *Patriot.*[26] The Boston *Commonwealth* applied arithmetic: "The sum of all the littles made a mickle which had revolutionary results."[27] Members of Congress blamed the president: "When asked what was the cause of their untimely taking off, they reply in one portentous monosyllable – 'Grant.'"[28] The president blamed Congress: "Leaders without any element of leadership ... they had the destiny of the party in their hands, but they threw it away."[29] Astute observers focused on the voters. "The people have gone crazy," James Garfield concluded.[30]

One toxic dose that had crazed the voters emanated from the Civil Rights Bill. That was certain. At best it was an irritant. At worst, as Congressman Townsend implied, it was a pestilence. "We cannot perceive the necessity or desirability of the passage of the bill," declared the New York *Times*. "From the standpoint of party policy the measure is a mistake.... It makes any considerable reinforcement of the Republican party from among the whites of the South a moral impossibility, and without such reinforcement the party is doomed to lose the Southern States which it already holds."[31]

Few congressmen will have subscribed to the Elizabeth City, North Carolina, *North Carolinian.* In it, nevertheless, they might have found a most succinct summation. "Inexplicable folly," wrote Editor Palemon John. Republicans had persisted in agitating the Civil Rights Bill "but not disposing of it."[32] They had

24 Washington Townsend to George F. Hoar, November 6, 1874. George F. Hoar Papers, Massachusetts Historical Society. Townsend took a relaxed view: "You and I will be relieved of some responsibility in the next Congress and from the back seats that will be assigned to us we can overlook the antics of the Democracy, with philosophic eye, as they endeavor to inaugurate their wild schemes of finance, revenue and Southern regeneration."

25 Dayton *Democrat*, November 7, 1874.

26 Harrisburg *Patriot*, October 31, 1874.

27 Boston *Commonwealth*, November 14, 1874.

28 New York *Tribune*, December 11, 1874.

29 Washington *National Republican*, October 31, 1874.

30 James D. Norris and Arthur Shaffer, *Politics and Patronage in the Gilded Age: The Correspondence of James A. Garfield and Charles E. Henry* (Madison, 1970), 119.

31 New York *Times*, January 28, 1875.

32 Elizabeth City *North Carolinian*, August 12, 1874.

opened that venomous issue to public scrutiny but had not resolved it. Obey the public's pronouncement or defy it. It could not be left to linger, a plague pool spreading political death.

Simplest would be to drain the pool. Kill the Civil Rights Bill. The black vote was secure without it. The white vote was lost with it. Why would the Republican Party pass it? Redfield's *Commercial* pronounced the obituary: "The Civil Rights Bill may be regarded as dead. With the results of the election before them, it is doubtful whether it would stand a ghost of a chance."[33] The paper was disabused. Civil rights did not die. Republicans refused it burial. The election was lost. So be it. If it stood by its principles the party reclaimed its right to govern. If it did not, it lost its soul. Gerrit Smith, almost at the end of his life, wrote one last time to his friend Vice-President Henry Wilson:

> What a precious opportunity the Republican Party has to redeem itself & regain its lost power! I fear it has not the courage to improve it. If, in stern defiance of the enemies of God and man, it shall pass the Civil Rights Bill, it will, by force of such justice and bravery, be stronger than ever. If, on the other hand, it shall succumb to those dastardly enemies, its weakness resulting from its unprincipledness and cowardice, will make it utterly contemptible. God forbid that the Republican Party should prove itself to be both a knave and a fool![34]

Vice-President Wilson wrote to the press. "Unprincipled" must not be the party's epitaph.

> When the country sees where they stand who believe in the perfect equality of the races, and who, come victory or defeat, life or death, mean to maintain in its completeness the equal rights of American citizens, of every race, nationality and faith, then will the republican masses rally again, achieve new victories, and give the party a new lease of power.[35]

Congress reconvened. The choice had been made. Even Democratic organs caught the drift. "Word has been passed around among the faithful that the civil-rights bill must be passed," reported the Louisville *Courier-Journal*.[36]

---

33 Cincinnati *Commercial*, December 7, 1874.

34 Gerrit Smith to Henry Wilson, December 20, 1874. Henry Wilson Papers, Library of Congress.

35 Springfield, Massachusetts, *Republican*, January 19, 1875.

36 Louisville *Courier-Journal*, December 11, 1874.

Republicans have determined to remain loyal to their principles, the New York *Journal of Commerce* confirmed, even in defiance of the people's will, "a wanton and studied insult to the public sentiment of the country."[37] Reporters questioned Sunset Cox. "Well, let them pass it," he yawned. "It will be a dead letter, only vital in helping our future."[38]

Whatever path Congress chose, the final word belonged to Ulysses Grant. He had toyed with a veto before the elections. The elections had come and gone and wrecked the party. At first the administration's journalistic mouthpiece, the *National Republican,* credited with bearing the president's imprimatur, laid blame squarely on the economic collapse. "History teaches us," declared its editorial post-mortem, "that financial revulsions in this Republic which result in 'hard times' have always been followed by political revolutions. The Republican party had no right to expect that it should escape such a sequel."[39] The president seemed to take the results with equanimity: "He said that there had always been two parties in the country, and doubtless always would be, that one was a check upon the other and opened to the people a prompt means of redress. He hoped that they would always avail themselves of the privilege."[40]

Then another message began to spread. The president, speaking to unattributable friends, assured said friends that he held the Civil Rights Bill supremely responsible for the debacle. He vowed to veto it. This time the threat was formal:

> [The President] unreservedly admits that although he fully expected the large republican losses, he was not prepared for the crushing defeat which has come upon the party. He does not for one instant sanction the idea that his policy or his personal acts have contributed in any degree to the party defeat.... The President thinks that the great element of discord in the republican party was the unwise attempt to force upon the American people the impracticable and utopian theories of Senator Sumner as embodied in the civil rights bill last spring.... He is firmly convinced that the civil rights bill had more to do with the defeat of his party than all other causes combined, and he has expressed himself in such a manner as to leave no doubt upon the minds of those with whom he has conversed, that if the bill shall be passed at the next session, he will interpose his veto.[41]

37 Quoted in Wilmington, North Carolina, *Journal,* December 9, 1874.

38 New York *Tribune,* December 7, 1874.

39 Washington *National Republican,* November 5, 1874.

40 Baltimore *Sun,* November 12, 1874.

41 Atlanta *Constitution,* November 9; also Baltimore *Sun,* November 7; New York *Tribune,* November 8; New York *World,* November 21, 1874.

Papers in all sections ran the news. The earliest story was dated November 7th. On the previous day the president had met with his political advisors. He held a long talk with Senator Morrill of Vermont. Then he called in his cabinet. He seemed to take the defeat in stride, "in an admirable temper ... a good-natured spirit"[42] – until it came to civil rights bills. A second report followed. The president continued his candid conversations with clandestine cronies. Now he rejected the whole concept of civil rights.

> He has always looked upon some of the measures advocated in that connection as exceedingly unwise. He does not think that legislation designed to regulate the social relations of any class of people is judicious.... So far he has favored civil rights, but when it has been brought up as a social question, in which Congressional interference can effect no beneficial results, and only annoy a very large, influential and intelligent class, he has opposed any further steps. Had the bill before Congress been presented for his signature, as already known, he would have vetoed it, and that he will do with any other bill of a similar nature with similar provisions on social questions.[43]

Some journalists expressed doubt about anonymous disclosures. Washington's *Sunday Chronicle* prefaced its account with "if reports are true."[44] The Chicago *Tribune* noted that the story was based on "what appears to be good authority."[45] The Nashville *Banner* offered it on the word of its Washington correspondent. He had heard it from a friend of the president. Guarded by anonymity, that friend had spoken (privately) to Secretary of State Hamilton Fish who assured him (privately) that every member of the cabinet advised the president to veto the Civil Rights Bill (privately).[46] One source winked. Another nodded. The *National Republican* spoke. It repudiated all the private winks and nods. The president's journal adverted to the first report as it had appeared in the New York *Tribune.* "Mad as a March Hare," it titled its column.

> The Tribune must have known that the above assertions were entirely gratuitous on the part of somebody. It knew that the President stood committed to the principle of "better security of the civil rights which freedom should secure but has not effectively secured to the enfranchised

42 New York *Tribune*, November 7, 1874.
43 Atlanta *Constitution*, November 28, 1874.
44 Washington *Forney's Sunday Chronicle*, November 22, 1874.
45 Chicago *Tribune*, November 8, 1874.
46 Nashville *Banner*, November 28, 1874.

> slave." It knew or ought to have known, or might just in common charity have believed, that he had not changed front on this question any more than he had on that of finance and currency.... From this fact alone it might have known the falsity of the assertion that he had menaced the Republican leaders of the House with a veto of the civil rights bill.... Mad as a March Hare![47]

An air of unreality hung over the situation. Ulysses Grant, as in days past, permitted rumors to form stating his antipathy to an important party measure. The organ of that party denied the rumors. Its chief allowed them to grow and to spread. As before, sources professed to detect the spinner of the web. On Friday, November 6, the day the president met with his cabinet, the day before the rumors began, Colonel John S. Mosby paid a visit to the White House. An hour later Mosby emerged smiling.[48] Subsequently the cabinet departed through the front door. Unofficial revelations to unnamed "friends" filtered out the back door.[49] Third-termism flared. Then it faded.

In Georgia, the Atlanta *Constitution* tried to sort it out. It took a poll of the state's Democratic congressmen. If Grant stood for reelection as a Democrat or as an independent would they support him? Four of the six declared themselves opposed under any circumstances. Alexander Stephens equivocated. It were better to consider the platform than the man: "Give him a good platform, such as the country needs, and he will vote for it, he does not care who is nominated." Only one remained open to the third-term idea. Third District Congressman Phil Cook was positively enthusiastic. He wanted Grant. He wanted him as a Democrat: "The only third term Grant can possibly have is to be the nominee of the democratic party next time. His thirst for office is so great he will undoubtedly be our candidate, and if we can beat a republican partisan with Grant I am in favor of his having a third term and will support him – you bet."[50]

Congressman Cook was one of the last to entertain those sentiments publicly. The third-term bubble had gone flat. Democrats, in the euphoria of their

---

47 Washington *National Republican*, November 18, 1874.

48 New York *Herald*, November 7; Springfield *Republican*, November 9, 1874.

49 Republicans made no secret of their annoyance. "The great influence of Col. Mosby with the President continues to be the most interesting and alarming topic in the circles of the faithful," reported the Baltimore *Sun*. "It is the cause of much lamentation that, as it is said, Mosby has more influence with the President than any other living person, not excepting a member of the cabinet or a Senator. It is openly said on the streets to-day by prominent radicals that the President must break with Mosby. The President is, however, not the man to be dictated to." Baltimore *Sun*, November 11, 1874.

50 Atlanta *Constitution*, October 18, 1874.

election sweep, saw no reason to compromise with a borrowed candidate. The crisis in Louisiana, Grant's suppression of the Penn Rebellion, served to disillusion many. The Richmond *Dispatch*, which once had considered a third term favorably, now declared it unthinkable: "It is possible ... that we may have to take Grant for another term, but it will be as an enemy, not as a friend as we would fain have had him."[51] A quid pro quo on civil rights no longer enticed the South. "The market for vetoes has lost its buoyancy," the New York *Tribune* concluded. "The deluge has come and gone and arks that were worth their weight in gold are now good for nothing but kindling wood."[52]

Congressmen returned to the capital. The first guest given entrée to the presidential presence was Ben Butler. When Butler reemerged he seemed entirely pleased with himself: "he fell in with a good many of his friends, with whom he interchanged the compliments pertinent to the occasion."[53] Butler's White House conversation has not come down to us. It appears nevertheless that he and the President reached an understanding. The Civil Rights Bill would pass. Grant would sign it, as Tom Swann had said. But changes would have to be made.

Butler convened his Judiciary Committee. The focus again fell on the most contentious issue, desegregation of the public schools. And now the bill itself became enmeshed in the coils of even deeper political maneuvering. As congressmen gathered at the beginning of December Republicans seemed dispirited, "sadly demoralized," the *National Republican* reported. Speaker Blaine predicted the session would be "quiet and uneventful."[54] Alexander Stephens had a different feeling. The present meeting would be "the liveliest or the dullest session on record ... a tornado or a farce."[55] What followed proved to be on occasion farcical. It was seldom dull.

Returning members assembled on the morning of December 7. At noon James Blaine gaveled the House to order. Chief Clerk Edward McPherson read the president's Annual Message. Most members listened respectfully. Some dozed. Pennsylvania Democrat Robert Speer, visible in his front row seat, ostentatiously struck a defiant pose, feet on desk, an unlit cigar in mouth, while an unidentified New Jersey Republican promptly went to sleep.[56] From that moment time began to tick.

---

51 Richmond *Dispatch*, September 19, 1874.
52 New York *Tribune*, November 9, 1874.
53 Baltimore *Sun*, November 30, 1874.
54 Washington *National Republican*, December 7, 1874.
55 Charleston *New and Courier*, January 8, 1875.
56 New York *Tribune*, December 8, 1874.

Time was the Republicans' enemy. Twelve weeks remained before they yielded power they had held for fifteen years. Unfinished projects lay upon the table. They no longer had the leisure to pursue them with deliberation. Time was the Democrats' ally. Delay was their weapon, Republican disunity their aid. The outgoing majority, suddenly pressed to act, could agree neither on the agenda to pursue nor on the priorities with which it should be pursued. Civil Rights competed with other measures in a rapidly-closing window of opportunity. Its competitors included a package of legislation desired particularly by southern Republicans. This had the clear support of President Grant. In his estimation it merited the first priority in the time left to the Forty-third Congress.

The package comprised measures designed to support the crumbling Republican Party in the South: a new Enforcement Act (the Force Bill) and an Army Appropriation Bill. As the president and southern Republicans could plainly see, the forces of white "redemption" were marching to victory in state after state. Violence cleared their path. In his Annual Message the president omitted mention of civil rights bills, but he emphasized the need for political protection of black people. He spoke of the White League terrorism at Shreveport; even Major Merrill had failed.[57] The Force Bill gave government the authority to intervene. It allowed federal monitoring of elections. It prohibited the bearing of arms at polling places. It granted the president the right to suspend the writ of *habeas corpus*. The Army Bill funded the maintenance of troops across the south for two years. Southern Republicans supported these measures with one voice. For many northern Republicans however the Force Bill went too far. It seemed to construct an imperial presidency, and a third term for Grant.[58] It drove a wedge between southern and northern Republicans. Where should the party place its priorities, civil rights or force bills?

This new political dynamic brought to the fore one member of the Judiciary Committee, Alabama Republican Alexander White. Sumner's vision had to be modified. White revived his cherished notion, incorporating separate-but-equal into the fabric of the bill. The committee had considered that option almost a year before, and rejected it. His idea, White suggested, might have more appeal now. He embodied it in a proviso:

---

57 Failure in Louisiana did not harm Lewis Merrill. While his regiment rode off in 1876 to be slaughtered in the Dakota he remained behind, called to command the guard of honor accompanying the President as he attended the Centennial Exposition in Philadelphia. He retired in 1886 with the brevet of brigadier general.

58 See Alfred H. Kelly, "The Congressional Controversy over School Segregation, 1867–1875," *American Historical Review*, 64 (1959): 556–557.

> *Provided,* that nothing in this act shall be construed to require mixed accommodations (by sitting together,) facilities, and privileges at inns, in public conveyances on land or water, theaters, or other places of public amusement, for persons of different race, or color, nor to prohibit separate accommodations, facilities, and privileges at inns, in public conveyances on land or water, theaters, or other places of public amusement; such separate accommodations, facilities, and privileges being equal in equipment and kind for persons of every color, regardless of any previous condition of servitude.[59]

A separate proviso extended this principle to the requirement of the school clause. White submitted his amendments at the Judiciary Committee's first meeting. He left Chairman Butler in an awkward position. Butler faced pressure to soften the text. The president had made that clear. But Alexander White's provisos were excessive. The National Civil Rights Council protested at once. And now the president's ever-shifting messages shifted again. On December 14 the *National Republican* put forth an editorial. Sound the reveille! Carry the Civil Rights Bill!

> Great political generalship is shown in making the most of a defeat.... Great measures, coming home to the whole people, are required; measures which shall secure speedily soundness of finance, the inauguration of transportation reform, the restoration of material prosperity ... the more complete establishment of civil rights to all citizens.

Butler understood. A bill must reach the president's desk. Somehow it must satisfy the moderates. But it could not eviscerate the very principle it proposed to embody. Two days later the *National Republican* published another exhortation, a letter to the editor. Its pseudonymous author was a black man. He called himself Vindex, the avenger. "At this time, when even chains do not fetter our bodies, nor the lash lacerate our skins," Vindex declared, "the law knows no distinction of citizens."

> The substituted bill of civil rights by Mr. White, of Ala., is an insult to a loyal class of American citizens, and every honest Republican knows this.... We do not desire to hamper the Republican party; nor will we brook an insult. Modify and modify your civil rights bill as much as you

59 *Cong. Record,* 43rd Congress, 2nd Session: 939.

> please, but make what remains of it defensible law, a credit to the head and heart and principles of the Republican party.

Benjamin Butler, pulled in contrary directions, faced the Judiciary Committee. Ten of the eleven members were lame ducks. Only William Frye had managed to be reelected. Luke Poland, beaten by an Independent, had suffered a spectacular fall. Cessna had lost his re-nomination. Jeremiah Wilson and Lyman Tremain simply declined to run again. Alexander White's hopes perished in the flames of Alabama. Jasper Ward, the committee's radical conscience, had suffered his nightmarish defeat by eight votes in Chicago. No Democrat survived. Clarkson Potter had miscalculated. Not foreseeing the dimensions of the Democratic sweep, he imagined he would return to two more years in the minority. He preferred to retire. Charles Eldredge succumbed to the salary grab. He failed to win a single delegate at his Fond du Lac nominating convention. Hugh Jewett had left in June, following the trail of money into the boardrooms of the Erie Railroad. His replacement, William Finck, brought the committee a fresh face. But Judge Finck too had one foot out the door. He took the seat for the short term only, to complete the remaining days of the present session.

An unhappy Judiciary Committee assembled on December 10. Its first order of business was to consider the amendment of an unhappy bill. It failed to accomplish that task. Hours passed. Congressmen bickered. No consensus emerged, even among Republicans.[60] Butler struck a new tack. A subcommittee – he himself, White, and Poland – would stand aside, weigh the options and report. Perhaps the full committee could agree on their recommendations. Butler chose his collaborators shrewdly. White spoke for Republicans of the South. A solution acceptable to him might satisfy the moderates. Poland stood well with the radicals. But his experience heading the Ku-Klux Commission had shown him the problems Alexander White insisted a civil rights act would worsen.

The subcommittee met on December 11th. White agreed to set aside his separate-but-equal suggestion, but only in favor of striking out the mixed-school clause. The committee had debated that notion the previous January and decided against it. The subcommittee hesitated to renew the argument. The Senate, moreover, following the Frelinghuysen doctrine, had declared a school clause indispensable. And the mixed school controversy did not remain as it had been. New, disturbing events jolted the issue. They left the puzzle more baffling than ever.

---

60 New York *Tribune*, December 11, 1874.

First came the report of the Peabody Fund for Education. That august body issued its pronouncement on October 16. Executive Agent Dr. Barnas Sears had made his views known. Now the Peabody Trustees spoke, the nation's most distinguished educational commission. The gravitas of its signatories alone demanded deference. On the Peabody Board sat the President of the United States, the Chief Justice of the United States, the Secretary of State. Ex-governors and senators assisted them. The wise men gathered in suitable luxury at the Fifth Avenue Hotel in New York City. Dr. Sears handed them the Eighth Annual Report of the institution's progress.[61] He had tried to warn a misguided Congress. Congress ignored him. It must be warned again. "The Civil Rights Bill," he told the Trustees, "would undo nearly all that you have done at the expenditure of so much treasure and assiduous labor." The South desired the death of common schools.

> They [southerners] look with pride upon the past, with disdain upon the present, and with distrust into the future.... Stung by wounded pride and aroused to a high pitch of excitement by an appeal to their prejudices and passions ... they only wait for an opportunity to combine their strength ... that is all they would need to crush out the school system. Such undoubtedly would be the immediate result in at least half the States; and in the others nothing would remain but a sickly system struggling for existence.[62]

The Trustees found Dr. Sears' words insufficient. The Board itself must speak. Former Attorney-General William Evarts composed a definitive declaration.

---

61 Twelfth Annual Meeting of the Peabody Trustees, *Proceedings of the Trustees of the Peabody Education Fund*, vol. 1 (Boston, 1875), 398–442. Those present included Secretary of State Hamilton Fish, future Secretary of State and ex-Attorney-General William Evarts, former Governor of South Carolina William Aiken, former Governor of North Carolina William Graham, former Governor of Massachusetts John Clifford, former Secretary of the Interior Alexander H.H. Stuart, Gen. Richard Taylor, son of Zachary, United States Surgeon-General Joseph Barnes. Absent were Chief Justice Morrison Waite, newly elected to the Board, and President Grant, attending his son's wedding to Miss Ida Honoré in Chicago. The most detailed newspaper account, Richmond *Dispatch*, October 24, including an interview taken from the Staunton *Vindicator* of Peabody trustee and Staunton native Alexander Stuart.

62 *Proceedings*, 408. "They [the people] have been educated to look with jealousy upon all improvements made at their expense for the public good. The domain of individual rights has been made as wide, and that of public interest as narrow, as possible." Dr. Sears acknowledged a perennial American truth.

> The Board, after the most careful comparison of opinions ... have unanimously come to the conclusion that the prospects and hopes of the public systems of education at the South will receive a serious, if not a fatal, blow.... Compulsory legislation by Congress in favor of "mixed schools," as the system of public education, will be most pernicious to the interests of education.[63]

Such a solemn, sententious statement sent to the nation by men of such stature commanded consideration. A few desegregationist diehards, Louisiana's Thomas Conway, to be sure, protested – a feeble whine, drowned out by the voice of authority.[64]

Then, when night seemed darkest, a beacon shone. It had never been a simple choice, a matter of segregation only or integration. The mixed school clause existed, Frederick Frelinghuysen insisted, not to guarantee mixed schools but to guarantee education. For that reason the Senate had retained the feature. Now, just as the House contemplated a move to cut it, it heard a decision that proved the Senate's case. Whatever Peabody patricians might say, a school clause was needed. Without federal safeguard states could, and would, deny black children access to public education. They would do it with the full sanction of the law. The bombshell dropped from the Supreme Court of Indiana on November 25: the decision in the Corey-Carter case, the appellate ruling in the case of Samuel Corey, John Beaver and Worthington Craig v. Carey Carter.

Corey-Carter had been making its way through the Indiana courts for nearly a year. Its implications were breathtaking, a test case, the Indianapolis *Journal* admitted, designed to take the issue of mixed schools to the highest judicial tribunal. Commentators compared it to the case of Dred Scott. The comparison might have been apt, had it reached the U.S. Supreme Court as its designers hoped it would.[65]

---

63 *Proceedings*, 438–439.

64 Conway sent yet another plea to the press: "If I exclude these children now, then I help put upon them and their posterity a brand of disgrace which has its birth in wrong, which is at war with the spirit of equality that inspired the makers of the Declaration of Independence ... utterly in conflict with the spirit and teachings of Christianity." New York *Tribune*, October 5, 1874.

65 See Emma Lou Thornbrough, *The Negro in Indiana before 1900: A Study of a Minority* (Bloomington, 1993), 326–328; J. Morgan Kousser, *Dead End: The Development of Nineteenth-Century Litigation on Racial Discrimination in Schools* (Oxford, 1986), 20–21; Robert J. Kaczorowski, *The Nationalization of Civil Rights: Constitutional Theory and Practice in a Racist Society, 1866–1883* (New York, 1987), 293–294. Details of the case, Indianapolis *Journal*, January 29, April, 7, November 25–27; Terre Haute *Express*, October 11, November 25, 1874.

Carey Carter, a person of color, resided in the township of Lawrence, northeast of Indianapolis. Few black people inhabited the area. The district maintained one public school; only white students attended. The Carter household included two children, Mary and Emma Carter, aged 19 and 16, and two orphaned grandchildren, Lucy Carter, 12, and John Carter, 9. Carey Carter applied for their admission to the common school. The board refused. He walked them to the schoolhouse door. They were ejected bodily. He filed suit, naming school director Beaver, teacher Craig, and Samuel Corey, trustee of the township school board. The case presented the problem in perfect form: an isolated black population; a community unwilling or unable to afford duplicate, separate facilities; denial of education to black citizens. Carter obtained a writ of mandamus which ordered the defendants to appear before the Superior Court of Marion County to show cause why the plaintiff's children should not attend the only school available.

The law firm of Gordon, Lamb and Brown took Carter's case pro bono. Its argument cited the citizenship provision of the Fourteenth Amendment and the Indiana Constitution, article eight. That document required the state to provide a general and uniform system of common schools open to all citizens. On May 13, 1869, however, the Indiana legislature passed a statute mandating separate schools for blacks and whites. The trustees of each city, town or township must organize said schools. All citizens should be taxed for their maintenance. If the population in a given district was deemed insufficient to sustain separate schools, two or several districts might consolidate. If, even after consolidation, numbers remained insufficient, then, said the statute, the local districts "shall provide such other means of education for these children as shall use their proportion, according to the numbers, of school revenue to the best advantage."

Carter's suit argued that he was a citizen of the United States and a citizen and taxpayer of the State of Indiana. His children were denied the benefit of the schools for which he was taxed. The state constitution guaranteed access to public education. Lawrence Township provided no access. It established no separate school. It arranged no consolidation. It must admit his dependents to the one existing common school.

The Superior Court of Marion County rendered a decision on April 6. Its author, Judge Samuel E. Perkins, was a justice of the State Supreme Court serving a term on the lower bench. Judge Perkins was a Democrat. He was a Democrat of decidedly conservative cast. He was a pronounced racist.[66] Even he upheld

---

66 Kousser, *Dead End*, 48, n. 65: "one of the most bitterly partisan and racist judges who ever sat on the Indiana Supreme Court."

the plaintiff's case. Segregation could not be an excuse to deprive citizens of their rights. It was obvious: "[The State] cannot, when she has not provided such separate schools, deny the right of attending such common schools as may be then in operation." Perkins found the last clause of the 1869 statute "unconstitutional and void." Leaving districts to concoct some vague "other means" of education for unwanted minorities was nothing but a deceit.

On November 25 the Supreme Court of Indiana overruled Judge Perkins. Republican Justice Andrew Osborn dissented on the court's reasoning but accepted its conclusions. Chief Justice Samuel H. Buskirk wrote the ruling. He left Carey Carter without a remedy. He left Mary, Emma, Lucy and John Carter without an education.

Justice Buskirk dealt first with the Indiana Constitution. That document, despite appearances, did not allow black people access to public schools. "All citizens" were entitled to education. All citizens meant white citizens only. The court, he wrote, must "look to the history of the times and examine the state of things existing when the constitution was framed." Indiana's constitution, ratified in 1851, accorded black persons no rights, no citizenship. It prohibited them from settling in Indiana. It could not have meant to include them in its educational provisions. "Persons of African descent were not in the minds of the framers of our constitution ... nor can it be maintained that the provisions of section one article eight were intended for children of African descent."

Now, it was true, persons of African descent were citizens, thanks to the 14th Amendment. Buskirk discarded that too. The amendment did not override the statutes of Indiana. Its privileges referred only to privileges defined in the United States Constitution. The right to an education at public expense was not among them.

> The Federal Constitution neither provides for a general system of education under control of the national government, nor vests Congress with the power to exercise general or specific supervision over the States on the subject of education.... In this State the common school system is purely a domestic institution.... The Legislature is left free to fix the qualifications of pupils as to age, sex, advancement, etc. ... This being settled, what is there to prevent the classification of children equally entitled to the privileges of the system of common schools with reference to difference of race or color, if the judgment of the Legislature should hold that such classification was likely to be conducive of the good order and discipline of the schools, and the interest of the public?[67]

---

67 Judge Buskirk's ruling, Indianapolis *Journal*, November 26, 1874.

One possibility remained to Carey Carter. Lawrence Township had not provided the mysterious "other means" of education to which his children were entitled.[68] Buskirk voided that argument. The suit complained only of exclusion from the white school. The court passed no judgment on the school board's failure to provide alternatives. "Even if such allegation had been made, it would not have entitled the children to admission into the white schools, because the Legislature has not provided for the admission of colored children into such schools in any contingency."[69]

Reaction transcended party lines. The most uncompromising southern organs praised Justice Buskirk's wisdom. But most journals, even Democratic sheets, deplored it. Children everywhere could legally be deprived of education. A Democratic court had validated the very point Republicans used to justify their mixed school clause. Buskirk had injected a powerful stimulant into the cause of civil rights, the Baltimore *Sun* lamented.[70] For the New York *Times* it was an atavistic atrocity:

> It is as black as Erebus ... practically to prevent colored children in sparsely settled localities from the enjoyment of the free common-school system, wherever men mean enough can be found to object.... It is strange and suggestive that no sooner does the Democracy attain to power than it puts its hand to the throat of popular education.[71]

Friends of civil rights found Judge Buskirk's words a godsend. He had set up a target they could hardly miss. Former Congressman George W. Julian discharged a volley of rhetoric: "[It is] the bursting of the festering pustule of the rottenness of the old, unregenerated Democracy ... rotten to the core.... They furbish up their old, rotten and stinking theories which animated them in the

---

68 State officials did describe some expedients to satisfy the "other means" requirement. These included a subsidy for the purchase of books, which could be supplied to parents for children to read at home (provided they and their parents first had learned to read), or a donation of money, which indigent parents could spend to the "best advantage" of their offspring. Thornbrough, *The Negro in Indiana*, 326.

69 Carter's supporters hoped to pursue an appeal. On December 14 Oliver Morton introduced a joint resolution, S.R. 12, directing Congress to provide for a writ of error sending the case to the United States Supreme Court. The Supreme Court ultimately did not review the case. Carey Carter did (if he still lived) see his name appear in a Supreme Court decision, though not such a decision as he will have wished; his case was cited in 1896 as a precedent in the ruling of Plessy v. Ferguson.

70 Baltimore *Sun*, November 30, 1874.

71 New York *Times*, December 3, 1874.

dark ages of slavery and which brought them to disgrace."[72] "No 'Niggers' Need Apply!" headlined Oliver Morton's Indianapolis *Journal*. "We have this morning the first fruits of the Democratic victory. It draws its inspiration straight from the dark and poisonous fountains which colored the legislation and the judicial decisions of fifty years ago ... as manifest a party decision as the infamous Dred Scott case."[73] The Terre Haute *Express* saved its scorn for the judge:

> Jesus said, "Suffer little children to come unto me." Buskirk, Chief Justice, would like to put a new interpretation upon this, making it read, "Suffer little white children to come unto me." He has pandered to the lowest prejudices of men. Perhaps he has earned for himself a place in history, which a man of his inferior ability is not expected to secure, but it will be an infamous place, such as was earned by the execrated Taney in his Dred Scott decision, and by the supporters in Congress of the fugitive slave law.[74]

The town of Brazil lay east of Terre Haute in the countryside of Clay County, the 8th Congressional District, which had barely returned its Republican congressman Morton Hunter after a campaign rife with civil rights contention. Brazil had children. It had black children. It did not have a school for black children. Brazil's school board admitted the misfits to the white schools. White parents protested, but the upset subsided – until the Buskirk decision.[75] Then the expulsions began. (See Illustration 9)

The trustees, Democrat Dillon Bridges, Republicans Edward Hussey and William Torbert, ordered school superintendent Wilkinson to comply with the dictum of the court. Wilkinson sensed a disaster. By the time he acted the press was alert. On December 2 he notified his teachers. Sort out your students. Remove those the law had purged. Twenty-five black children were extruded into the street.[76] The Chicago *Inter Ocean* described a heartrending scene: little ones clinging to their teachers' arms, grim-faced officers pulling them away.

72 Indianapolis *Journal*, December 9, 1874.

73 Indianapolis *Journal*, November 26, 27, 1874.

74 Terre Haute *Express*, December 5, 1874. The *Express* was ahead of its time. It anticipated the argument for Affirmative Action: "There should be no favoritism under the law, but if there were any it should be in favor of the blacks, who have been so cruelly treated in the past.... We must be just to the blacks, and if possible the more just because they have been humble and poor and in some sense friendless."

75 Chicago *Inter Ocean*, December 4, 1874.

76 Terre Haute *Express*, December 5.

"SUFFER LITTLE WHITE CHILDREN TO COME UNTO ME." Page 481.

ILLUSTRATION 9 Nasby "Regulates" a School
SOURCE: THOS. NAST, "*THE STRUGGLES OF … PETROLEUM V. NASBY*," P. 461.

One teacher, Miss Jennie Worthington, refused to obey; arms folded, she bade Mr. Wilkinson do it himself if he would.

> "How can I order that bright-eyed little fellow never to return to this school?" she said, pointing to an intelligent-looking boy 12 years of age.… The little fellow, with tears in his eyes, begged to remain again and again; he walked back to his seat, hugged his books tightly, and wept as if his little heart would break.[77]

A large dose of journalistic creativity enlivened the accounts. Later information verified neither the existence of Miss Jennie Worthington nor of the weeping boy. Twenty-five castaways dwindled to only five.[78] But the public

77 Chicago *Inter Ocean*, December 22, 1874.
78 Dillon Bridges, denounced as a heartless villain, sent a card to the Terre Haute *Express*. He could not believe it. He was not even a trustee. William Torbert held that office. No one wanted to expel the children. The court left no choice. Moreover only five black students had ever existed. Another vilified official, Edward Hussey, wrote the *Inter Ocean*. He was a loyal Republican, chairman of the central committee in Clay County. "And there never

read what journalists purveyed. Papers across the country picked up the story, keening children torn from the embrace of heroic schoolmarms. Gerrit Smith fired forth an open letter: "I envy not the man who can read this extract with dry eyes and an unmoved heart ... who cares not for the grief which wrung the little breasts of these dear children. Where rests the responsibility for this outrage? On the hesitancy of the Republican party to pass the pending civil rights bill."[79]

The Indiana legislature did consider changing the law. Republican George Sleeth introduced a bill to allow black children into white schools, if no alternative existed, and provided they sat separately in the classrooms.[80] Sleeth's bill passed the State Senate but stalled in the House. Indiana politicians hoped the trouble would go away. Congressmen of the Judiciary Committee and its beleaguered sub-committee had no such hope. Butler, Poland and White, buffeted by contrary winds – the elections, the Peabody Report, the Corey-Carter decision, Brazil – sought some Solomonic wisdom to unravel the skein.

Their first idea brought into play George Frisbie Hoar's Education Fund Bill. The Education Bill could resolve simultaneously problems of inequality and denial of education. If states persisted in affording second-rate facilities for segregated schools, the Education Fund would redress the imbalance. If districts like Lawrence Township refused to pay for any schools, the Education Fund would provide them.

Conservatives hated the education bill. They feared it would become an adjunct of school desegregation.[81] Federal aid to education moreover meant dictatorship. Once education became a province of federal power, declared Congressman William O'Brien, the liberties of the people "will be swept away and a military government rise on the ruins with a Caesar at its head."[82] Now reports emerged that Republicans planned a new version of the Education Fund Bill. Money from the sale of public lands would be distributed to the states not, as Hoar had proposed, in proportion to their school-age population but in proportion to their level of illiteracy. The South, most illiterate, would receive the

---

has been more than five colored children living in our city, and only four were expelled." Terre Haute *Express*, December 6; Chicago *Inter Ocean*, December 22, 1874.

79 New Orleans *Louisianan*, January 2, 1875.

80 Terre Haute *Express*, February 12, 1875.

81 When the first education fund bill appeared in the House in 1872, West Virginia's Democrat Frank Hereford proposed an amendment: no money may be withheld from any state "for the reason that the laws thereof provide for separate schools for white children, or refuse to organize a system of mixed schools." *Cong. Globe*, 42nd Congress, 2nd Session: 882. See Kelly, "The Congressional Controversy," 544.

82 Baltimore *Sun*, October 22, 1874.

highest share.[83] The school clause of the Civil Rights Bill could be struck out. Ben Butler, it was said, favored this approach.[84]

The proposal to replace the school clause with the Education Fund Bill came to naught. Even many Republicans opposed the Education Fund. Congressmen John Kasson of Iowa and William Phillips of Kansas disliked its unequal distribution of revenues. Others worried it would lead to rampant and larcenous land speculation, or be an extravagance the treasury could ill afford in a time of fiscal austerity. Butler's subcommittee fell back on the only compromise possible. They would not cut out the school clause. They tried yet again to amend it; add the doctrine of separate-but-equal, limited to schools. True believers would object. But it might save the bill, and the school clause could still secure its primary objective. Schools would exist.

Butler knew he would face an outcry. He solicited the assent of black leaders. On the 12th, as the subcommittee began its work, he wrote to Joshua Smith, the respected black Massachusetts State Representative and friend of the late Sumner. Smith was encouraging. "I have perfect confidence in your judgment; I leave the case in your hands."[85] On the 15th Butler and Poland called upon Congressmen Rainey and Cain. They were less helpful. If it came to a choice, saving the Civil Rights Bill or saving the mixed-school clause, Cain replied, drop the clause altogether. Save the bill.[86] Butler, fingers crossed, tried to save the bill and the clause.

The subcommittee presented its ideas to the full committee that same day. The Senate bill, Butler observed, was stuck on the Speaker's table. The committee must do what it had hesitated to do in May. Substitute the text of S.1 for that of H.R.796. Then it must make changes. Strike the cemetery clause. It was the least important. Let the school clause remain, but add a proviso:

> Provided, That if any State or its authorities having control of common schools or other public institutions of learning shall establish and maintain separate schools or institutions, giving equal educational facilities in all respects to all classes entitled thereto, such schools shall be in compliance with the provisions of this section.[87]

---

83 No one denied the South's analphabetism. Compared with a national average of 10.7%, Kentucky's illiteracy came in at 30%, Tennessee's nearly 40%. For Florida, Dr. Sears estimated, more than a third of the population could neither read nor write. *Proceedings of the Peabody Trustees*, vol. 1, 422. Hambleton Tapp and James C. Klotter, *Kentucky: Decades of Discord, 1865–1900* (Frankfort: 1977), 185–197.

84 Harrisburg *Patriot*, December 2.

85 Joshua Smith to Benjamin Butler, December 15, 1874. Butler Papers, Library of Congress.

86 Cincinnati *Commercial*, December 16, 1874.

87 Washington *National Republican*, December 17, 1874.

Butler's hopes ran into a buzz-saw. "The colored people are offered a measure the proper title of which should be 'a bill to legalize wrong,'" the *Louisianian* raged. "The time has come for the black voters to look around and see who their true friends are."[88] "The proposed act will enthrone caste against republicanism," screamed George Downing's National Civil Rights Council. "It gives license to proscribe and outrage, whereas such license does not now exist.... We have not asked for increased license to proscribe."[89] Downing came around to Richard Cain's conclusion. "It seems better to have no mention made of schools in your proposed civil rights bill than to have this proviso made law."[90]

Butler's friend and supporter Wendell Phillips also berated him. An exchange of letters passed between them, Phillips writing from Boston, Butler at the capital. Phillips' replies, archived in Butler's papers, only are preserved. But we can read Butler's plea in Phillips' words. Consider the pressures he faced. Without compromise the bill was doomed. Surely his amendment presented the least bad alternative. Phillips was adamant:

> I trust you will not sully your last (for the present) appearance in those Halls by consenting to any such compromise. It is a weak, timid surrender to mere bluster. – The insertion of principle of caste – race superiority – in our laws is as disastrous as the slave compromise of'89. Defeat any Bill which does not include the schools. – Better no legislation than a wicked & weak one. – Make up your record that rather than accept half the loaf & that poisoned you kept the statute book clean.[91]

Principles, said Butler, principles were fine – grand, gaudy things. But principles must yield to practical reality. Phillips was unmoved.

> Tho' I am not called on, standing as I do outside, to have that regard to policy – (i.e. immediate practicability) that you have in office, still I say, standing in your place I should kill, if I could, all Civil Rights Bills rather than incorporate into our legislation again the idea of caste.... Half a loaf is not better than no bread when the half is poisoned.

Butler floated the idea he had drafted back in February with the help of E.C. Wines. Let separate-but-equal be, but give black students the right to transfer. Phillips refused.

88 New Orleans *Louisianian*, December 26, 1874.
89 Washington *National Republican*, January 8, 1875.
90 Washington *National Republican*, January 27, 1875.
91 Wendell Phillips to Benjamin Butler, January 6, 1875. Butler-Ames Papers, Smith College.

> Your law giving a colored boy the right to change when in school is inferior – is worth nothing. – Take a half dozen young negroes in an inland county – what is their chance of such justice? Take a hundred in a city overwhelmed by numbers & silenced by a hostile press – their chance is less.

Butler cited the Peabody Report. Phillips exploded. Damn Peabody! Damn its Report!

> Those Peabody fellows are doughfaces. Winthrop! Dr. Sears! Where were they when the Antislavery fight was going on? Why, ordinary men woke up at least when the guns fired – they have never yet waked – can't see now clearly – cannot even see men, or trees walking.... We don't expect figs from such thistles – & don't wonder at their opinions, but only at their presumption.... Crush all Bills but Sumner's.

One can almost hear Benjamin Butler's sigh. The subcommittee's solution dissolved. Friends scorned it. Enemies laughed at it. "Hamlet with the character of Hamlet omitted," quipped the Memphis *Avalanche*, "a wedding without the bridegroom."[92] By the time Phillips penned his tirades the compromise had failed. In the full Judiciary Committee it met a wall of opposition. Those stalwarts who had stood firm in June, Jeremiah Wilson, William Frye, Jasper Ward and John Cessna, refused to bend in December. Ward was furious. He would hear of no "compromise." The committee must report the Senate bill as it was, or report nothing.[93] Alexander White, for his part, revived his broad separate-but-equal amendment. The result was a train wreck.

Butler unveiled the subcommittee's suggestions. Frye declared them dead on arrival. He moved to substitute the Senate bill with all provisions intact. Wilson, Cessna and Ward backed his motion. Butler, Poland and White opposed it. Tremain joined Butler. Four Republicans confronted four Republicans. Three Democrats, Eldredge, Potter and Finck, were delighted. They cheerfully played logjam. For more than two hours the wrangle continued. First the Democrats joined Butler's side. They voted for the compromise amendments. Then, when it came time to report the amended bill to the House, they spun an elegant pirouette and voted with Cessna, Ward and company to block it.[94] Twenty fruitless

92 Quoted in Chattanooga *Times*, December 19, 1874.

93 Chicago *Tribune*, December 17, 1874.

94 New York *Tribune*, December 16; Knoxville *Press and Herald*, December 16, 1874.

votes left the stalemate unchanged. Democrats helped the amendments pass, only to block them at the door. None of the Republicans broke ranks.

Butler had a new suggestion. Let the school clause remain, but allow a local option. Should authorities opt out then fail to provide separate facilities, the bill would compel them to open up the common schools or face prosecution on federal charges.[95] This idea, too, failed. Four Republicans held firm. They wanted the Senate bill or nothing. Democrats wanted the nothing. They got their wish.

Butler reconvened his troops on December 17th. Finally the majority settled on a course. The radicals stepped back. They agreed to vote for the compromise bill, just to get it out of committee. They vowed that when it came to the floor they would oppose it. They would bring the Senate bill itself to a vote. Alexander White also agreed to report the amended bill. But he promised to bring his own comprehensive separate-but-equal proposal to the floor. Potter, Eldredge and Finck promised to oppose any bill in any form. After a prodigious effort to escape they had dug themselves deeper into the quagmire. Christmas holiday arrived. Congressmen went home to contemplate peace on earth. They got no peace. Incidents ranged from the droll to the deadly.

On December 21, the Trenifiddle affair set Washington society aflutter.[96] Miss Evangeline Trenifiddle, English poetess and Quaker, currently resident in Washington, had written verses in memory of the late Sumner. She wished her ode translated into the Haitian patois for the benefit of citizens of the black republic. For this purpose she invited to her boarding-house rooms a black man, Hon. Ebenezer Don Carlos Bassett, United States Ambassador to Haiti. Bassett, the first African American to hold ambassadorial rank, presented himself at the front door. The landlord ushered him around to the back kitchen. Other black citizens followed the ambassador. They were either driven hence or piled up indecorously on the doorstep. Finally the poetess herself, bag and baggage, was bundled down stairs and deposited upon the street. Admittedly the establishment in question, as a private boarding-house, would not have been covered under the Civil Rights Bill. But the scandal – that is, the white lady's expulsion – rose to an outrage. Miss Trenifiddle swore out an affidavit. She had friends in Congress.[97]

95 New York *Times*, December 16, 1874.

96 Atlanta *Constitution*, December 25, 1874.

97 Well might the "fair daughter of song" swear an affidavit, jeered the Wilmington, North Carolina, *Journal* (Dec. 22). "A white woman who holds social intercourse with black men upon the door steps may swear, and swear profanely too, without injury to her character."

More serious affairs struck New Orleans, another fracas over school integration. It ended in murder. Louisiana already lived with a mixed-school regime. Results lagged behind Superintendent Conway's rosy depiction. But it had achieved some success. Both sides avoided overt friction. Now, flushed with election victory, whites opened confrontation. On December 13, black girls arrived, as they had since 1870, for entrance exams at the Upper and Lower Girls High Schools. This time their white classmates decided to resent the intrusion.[98] To demonstrate their pride of race the white girls fled. They paused just long enough to compose a letter to the school directors. Then they declared themselves on holiday. They vowed their "unshakable resolve" never to return.

The next day City Superintendent of Schools Charles W. Boothby appeared at the Lower High School. He found himself confronted not by girls but by a crowd of boys who had rushed to the distressed damsels' aid. They menaced the superintendent. He had admitted blacks into the schools. Worse, he had spoken discourteously of the white girls' behavior. Boothby protested. He was only following orders. Never would he defame southern femininity, be it of the juvenile variety. Metropolitan Police arrived. They threw a cordon around the school. Black students remained inside, alone.[99]

Boothby appealed to the white girls. They exonerated him. Not he but a reporter for the New Orleans *Republican,* Arthur E. Adams, had impugned their honor. Avengers set out. They spotted Adams at 3:30 p.m., strolling on Canal Street. A horse-whip was brought to bear. Police rescued the battered reporter. "We hope," concluded the *Abeille,* "that henceforth he will not insult young women, knowing that there are men of courage to defend them."[100]

Now the white boys, not to be outdone by girls, announced their intention also to quit school. "The young rebels," so the press anointed them, issued a proclamation. They closed with a ringing phrase: "Circumstances of life may place us in contact with the Negro, but never will we consent to treat him as our equal." "Never," the *Abeille* agreed, "will a white man with any spirit within him allow his sons or daughters to be raised with negroes or negresses whose contact will pollute their minds and fill them with every notion of vice and moral filth." It concluded with a prescient declaration. Before Negroes entered those precincts the President of the United States would have to deploy soldiers at the schoolhouse doors: "Unless General Grant shall order his legions to

---

98 See Louis R. Harlan, "Desegregation in New Orleans Public Schools During Reconstruction," *American Historical Review*, 67 (1962): 667–672; Roger A. Fischer, *The Segregation Struggle in Louisiana, 1862–1877* (Urbana, 1974): 123–129.

99 New Orleans *Abeille*, December 16, 1874.

100 New Orleans *Abeille*, December 18, 1874.

guard the gates of our academies, the radicals will fail before the wrath of the sovereign people."

On December 17 the boys marched to liberate the Franklin Girls High School. They formed a guard of honor around their white sisters. Black girls ran out of the building. The boys pursued them into the streets. There they encountered none other than their arch-enemy, the school commissioner himself, Henry Dibble, late unsuccessful candidate for Congress. Commissioner Dibble, wobbling on his wooden leg, fled down a side street. More formidable opposition appeared; 120 black boys issued from a nearby colored school. Whites, outnumbered, beat a strategic retreat. They rallied passersby, refilled their ranks. Rocks and bats were employed on both sides. The black forces yielded, leaving one of their number dead upon the ground.[101]

Victorious, the boys commenced a purge of all suspect high school females. Now things turned ugly. New Orleans, with its multi-hued mix, was not the place to undertake a hasty racial cleansing founded on superficial traits. The boys, in their zeal, failed to inquire into lineage, but used an improvised judgment of the proper tint. Skeletons from closets emerged. One outraged young lady at the Webster School, dragged out as a colored intruder, was found not only to be officially white but a relative of the valiant Governor McEnery. Several Jewish girls, suspiciously olive in complexion, also underwent wrongful expulsion. At the Lower High School one undeniably black girl called out a volley of names as she was led away, thereby unmasking demurely protesting classmates (and even one of the boy crusaders) passing behind a false racial identity. Finally adults called a halt. White League commander Fred Ogden ordered the boys to desist. Henry Dibble closed the schools until after holiday.[102]

---

101 New Orleans *Abeille*, December 18, 1874.

102 New Orleans' "boy crusaders" had been preceded, at least in fiction. Petroleum Nasby, David Ross Locke's literary hero, also had trouble making proper distinctions. Nasby's imagined schoolhouse stood in southern Ohio, but it was filled with migrants from Kentucky, where amalgamation made identification tricky: "Uv course comin from Kentucky, these niggers are, many uv em, ez near white ez they can be." Protective mimicry, Nasby decided, should not be an impediment to action: "It matters not.... Put me in a dark room with one uv em, no matter how little nigger there is in em, and that unerrin instink wood betray em to me, wich, by the way, goes to prove that the dislike we hev to em is not the result uv prejoodis, but is a part uv our very nacher, and one uv its highest and holiest attriboots." Needless to say, Nasby's unerring instinct picked out the wrong schoolgirl ("Ketch hold uv that pekoolyerly disgustin one yonder, sed I") just as her outraged white father entered. The result was an epic beating with Nasby on the receiving end. Nasby remained philosophical: "When the Almighty made niggers, he ought to hev made em so that mixin with the sooperior race would have been an impossibility." Letter of November 25, 1867, "Mr. Nasby Regulates a School," David Ross Locke, *The Nasby Letters, Being the Original Nasby Letters, as Written During his Lifetime* (Toledo, 1893), 92–94.

New Orleans' troubles had not finished. The New Orleans *Bulletin,* edited by Edwin L. Jewell and his associate Daniel Byerly, relished its place as the city's most conservative newspaper. With the carnage of the Penn Rebellion still fresh, the city unsettled by juvenile revolt, the *Bulletin* chose to make a most unhelpful suggestion. Bring back the Star Cars. The star, painted on the sides of selected streetcars, served to inform black people of the proper carriages for their use. Suppression of the Star Cars under the administration of Governor Henry Clay Warmoth had removed an ever-present stigma.[103] Restoring them, the *Bulletin*'s editorial of December 23 proposed, would have a salutary effect on certain persons' pretensions.

This idea upset ex-governor Warmoth. In the ever-shifting world of Louisiana politics, Warmoth kept a foot in both camps. Once a Republican, currently a Liberal Republican, he had supported the fusion ticket of McEnery and Penn. But he accompanied Pinchback into Redwitz's saloon. His Decoration Day oration pleaded for recognition of civil rights. He wrote a letter of protest. Jewell and Byerly published Warmoth's piece. But they added a vitriolic personal attack. Warmoth replied with a sharply-worded card in the *Picayune.* Jewell sent his seconds to call at Warmoth's home. They agreed on pistols at ten paces, the rencontre to occur on the 28th. On the 26th Warmoth visited his lawyer to inspect his will. He found himself walking on Canal Street. A man approached. He raised a heavy cane. He struck it against Warmoth's head with such force that it (the cane) splintered. Warmoth fell. His assailant fell upon him. Bystanders cried out. Police Sergeant Slabowski rushed up. Too late. Warmoth drew a spring-loaded pocket knife. Daniel Byerly died that night.[104]

---

103 See Roger A. Fischer, "A Pioneer Protest: The New Orleans Street-Car Controversy of 1867," *Journal of Negro History*, 53 (1968): 219–233; Fischer, *The Segregation Struggle in Louisiana*, 30–40.

104 Daniel C. Byerly, 48 at his death, was a pre-war immigrant from Pennsylvania, but he developed a fierce attachment to the South. In his struggle with Warmoth he gained an advantage by the use of his cane. But he suffered a critical disadvantage, being unable to employ his left arm. This had been shattered while its owner served his new homeland, the Confederacy, at the battle of Kennesaw Mountain. That wound, a decade later, was his undoing. Warmoth spent a short time in jail. Pinchback among others visited him. It was clearly a case of self-defense. Henry Clay Warmoth, *War, Politics and Reconstruction: Stormy Days in Louisiana* (New York, 1930), 241–243.

CHAPTER 13

If Ruin Comes from This: A House Decided

Eight weeks remained before Speaker Blaine's gavel would fall for the last time, two months for Benjamin Butler to push a civil rights bill through the House. The final form – the Judiciary Committee's muddled modifications mired in doubt – would have to be decided on the floor, if it came to the floor in any form. Democrats, time in their favor, determined that no bill should come to the floor. Their leaders again were Samuel Randall and Charles Eldredge, James Beck and Lucius Q.C. Lamar. Their tactic was delay. The Norfolk *Virginian* wrote in February: "twenty four days are theirs; all the future is ours."[1]

Butler began the final campaign as the House reconvened on January 5. The Senate bill still sat on the Speaker's table. A pile had grown beneath it. From the gallery it could be seen, protruding from the stack of legislation. "The next bill," the Atlanta *Constitution's* reporter wrote, "so near the top that the wool can be seen by a spectator in the darkest part of the House, is supposed to be the principal mourner at the late republican funeral: the civil rights bill."[2] One last time Butler asked unanimous consent to suspend the rules and take up the Senate bill. Eldredge did not consent. A realization rose for Republicans. The minority intended to block the Senate bill. Would it, Butler inquired, filibuster even the House bill? "Sufficient unto the day," Randall recited, "is the evil thereof." Now it was clear. The opposition planned to use its parliamentary power to the fullest. It had resolved to block everything – civil rights bills, army bills, force bills, special appropriations. No part of the dying majority's agenda would pass. Total obstruction. Philadelphia's Richard Vaux urged on his friend Senator Stevenson: "Drive them into the Red Sea, where the waters of desolation and retribution may swallow them up out of sight of a long suffering people."[3]

The prospect of that watery fate terrified Republicans, especially southern Republicans. They were not of one mind on the propriety of civil rights bills. But for their very survival they required passage of other legislation, the Force Bill foremost. They demanded a caucus. On December 19 they had held a sectional caucus. Virginian Christopher Thomas took the chair. The mood

1 Norfolk *Virginian*, February 5, 1875.

2 Atlanta *Constitution*, December 4, 1874.

3 Richard Vaux to John W. Stevenson, December 12, 1874. John White Stevenson Papers, Library of Congress.

was bitter. "The Southerners declared that the Party treated them with indifference or condescension. They demanded that the Party pass the laws needed for their protection."[4] They appointed a committee of liaison to consult with colleagues in the Senate: Alexander White, Horace Maynard, Richard Whiteley and James Platt, along with Alonzo Ransier and John Roy Lynch.[5] White composed the southerners' plea:

> In large portions of the South neither life, liberty or property is protected, free opinions and free speech are not tolerated.... Assassinations, murder, whippings, threats of ostracism, calumny and detraction are the means resorted to strike down and destroy Republicans and eradicate fidelity to the Constitution and laws. Loyalty to the nation is covered with odium, and fealty to the Lost Cause is invested with the halo of martyrdom.... If we remain as we are, with arms folded, paralyzed and indifferent, embarrassed, uncertain or inactive, from any cause whatever, we are drifting on ... to certain destruction, and with us we bear "the fortunes of the Republic."[6]

Democrats found it highly entertaining. The Louisville *Courier-Journal* chuckled: "They were entrusted with the work of pilfering the Southern people and exciting the negroes to riot, and they have performed their part with unquestioning fidelity. It is ungrateful for their Northern allies to turn from them now."[7]

The full party caucus met on January 9. Horace Maynard presided. For four hours angry words echoed. Alexander White made an impassioned plea, full of "blood and thunder." They must safeguard the ballot. Without that all was lost. Henry Dawes, Cessna and Ward supported him. Jasper Ward, ever zealous, declared he would not be bound by the actions of any caucus that failed to protect the rights of all citizens. Moderates objected. The Force Bill went too far. Members called upon James Blaine. He declined to speak.[8] The caucus broke up in disarray. It appointed another caucus, a "special caucus committee for Southern affairs."

That select committee met on the 15th. White took the chair. Conferees included southerners Richard Whiteley and Horace Harrison, and northerners

---

4 New York *Times*, December 21, 1874.

5 Baltimore *Sun*, December 21, 1874.

6 Washington *National Republican*, December 21; Indianapolis *Journal*, December 24, 1874.

7 Louisville *Courier-Journal*, December 22, 1874.

8 Cincinnati *Commercial*, January 10; New York *Times*, January 10, 1875.

Cessna, Ward, Tremain, Gerry Hazelton of Wisconsin, George McCrary of Iowa.[9] The special caucus reported to the full caucus on the 22nd. It recommended force bills and army bills. That idea met an unenthusiastic response. White tried to explain his force bill. Cessna argued on behalf of Whiteley's parallel proposal. Lewis Cass Carpenter, in place of Robert Elliott, pleaded for the southern program.[10]

They tried again on the 23rd.[11] Barely six weeks remained for Republicans to control the majority. Stephen Hurlbut of Illinois called for the army bill; they must re-reconstruct the South. Butler gently raised the question of his Civil Rights Bill. He urged fellow Republicans to "help him get it up." John Ambler Smith retorted. The Force Bill was needed. The Civil Rights Bill was not. If it passed, "a year hence the number of native white republicans in the South could be counted on the fingers and toes of members."[12] Finally, an agreement: Republicans remained divided on their agenda, but they would move to suspend the rules of procedure. Bills might thus be brought to the floor, debated, and passed by simple majority, rather than the ever-elusive two-thirds. The suspension would begin immediately and continue for the rest of the session. The party could act unhindered by Democratic obstruction. It could arrange priorities later.

On the 25th Republicans acted upon this plan. Their efforts were a monumental failure, brought on by the same disunity that was to plague them to the end of the 43rd Congress. Cessna moved to suspend the rules. Catch-22: a motion to suspend the rules so as to move for continuing suspension of the rules thereby to remove the necessity of two-thirds votes required a two-thirds vote. This, as usual, was not forthcoming. Cessna's motion failed. Eighteen Republicans defected. All were northerners. They feared the oncoming Force Bill. Butler offered a new motion. Suspend the rules for one purpose only, to allow debate on the Civil Rights Bill. That motion failed. Eleven Republicans defected. All but one were southerners.

The southern bloc stood firm: John Ambler Smith and James Sener, Horace Harrison, Roderick Butler and Jacob Thornburgh, Ira Hyde and Edwin Stanard, Andrew Sloan, Charles Sheats and Lloyd Lowndes. They refused to allow a motion to facilitate the Civil Rights Bill without a compensating agreement on the Force Bill. Northerners voted willingly to suspend the rules for civil rights. But many, including Blaine, Garfield, the Hoar brothers, barred the way to

9 Cincinnati *Commercial*, January 15, 1875.
10 Cincinnati *Commercial*, January 23, 1875.
11 Baltimore *Sun*, January 23, 1875.
12 Baltimore *Sun*, January 25; Savannah *News*, January 28, 1875.

facilitation of the Force Bill. The fiasco left Democrats jubilant. "It now seems very certain," the *World* assured its readers, "that the Civil Rights bill will never become a law and that none of the high-handed legislation demanded by the Republicans will be adopted. The Southerners say that they will never support the Civil Rights bill if the Northern Republicans will not sustain their demand for more executive interference in behalf of the Party in the South."[13]

Republicans caucused again. The mood was sour, proceedings "long and excited." Doors were barred, reporters excluded, but reports leaked out. Northerners expressed exasperation at Maynard, president of the caucus. Maynard retorted that Speaker Blaine was "no longer a Republican."[14] As the *World* had predicted, the party, it seemed, would implode. Finally the caucus settled on a plan of action. Members promised to lay aside their disagreements. They would put the Democrats to the test. Let them filibuster, if they dared, and bring the people's business to a halt. If they broke the filibuster, Republicans could proceed, settling internal disputes as they went. If they failed to break it, they would justify to the country the need for an even more radical move: not a temporary suspension of the rules but a permanent change of the Rules of the House. They would bring parliamentary obstruction to an end, forever. Southerners yielded on one point. They agreed to let civil rights spearhead the new tactic. "The Civil Rights Bill was to be the pioneer," one report noted, "and if that passes, other measures will be put forward."[15] Though they disliked the priority given to civil rights, the southerners would benefit if its victory facilitated passage of the Force Bill thereafter. Moderates disliked that prospect. But they could still modify any Force Bill before it passed. Civil rights supporters took heart. "We must stay here," one member was quoted, "until the last minute of the last hour of the last day of the session, without food or raiment, rather than not to pass the bill."[16] Republicans mobilized. Democrats built barricades, formed ranks and waited.

The stage was set for the great filibuster of the House of Representatives. It began on the morning of Wednesday, January 27, 1875. Both sides knew the dance. Butler rose first. He wished to make "a privileged report from the Committee on the Judiciary." The report was in fact to reconsider the recommitment of the bill to protect all persons in their civil and political rights, H.R.796 (now amended and clothed in the form of the Senate bill S.1). Randall jumped to his feet. Eldredge followed. Point of order! A motion to reconsider could not

13 New York *World*, January 26, 1875.
14 Cincinnati *Commercial*, January 27, 1875.
15 New York *Tribune*, January 27, 1875.
16 New York *Tribune*, January 27, 1875.

take precedence over pending business. Speaker Blaine overruled their objection. In so doing he read out and defined House Rule 49. This regulation was to be, for the next four days, at the center of the storm that now descended upon the House:

> It shall be in order for any member of the majority to move for reconsideration of the recommitment of a bill, and such motion shall take precedence of all other questions, except a motion to adjourn.

Randall and Eldredge thanked the Speaker. In Rule 49 they held the weapon with which to shatter the Civil Rights Bill. They proceeded to orchestrate a most elegant filibuster, a filibuster by means of dilatory motions. One motion, said Rule 49, held higher privilege than a motion to reconsider: a motion to adjourn. They moved that the House adjourn. They preempted Butler's motion and blocked it. A motion to adjourn, however, could only be made once. If it were voted down, Butler's motion would be in order. The trick lay in prolonging the diversion. One other motion shared the highest privilege: a motion to amend a motion to adjourn – a motion to adjourn, that is, to a specified day. One needed only to alternate a motion to adjourn and a motion to adjourn to a certain day or to a different day, then again a motion to adjourn, a motion to adjourn to a day, a motion to adjourn, and so on indefinitely. These motions could follow each other directly, ceaselessly, because each was in effect an amendment to the other. No motion could interrupt them because they were part of the same motion, which carried the highest privilege. So was it possible, in politics if not in physics, to perpetuate a perpetual motion of motions. Butler's request, like Zeno's racehorse, would never arrive.

Randall began. He called the first of many motions to adjourn. He fixed a day, Friday, as the day on which the House should reconvene. Eldredge called for Saturday instead. And so they voted, as they would vote, endlessly, on meaningless motions, for forty-six hours.[17]

Eldredge's amendment to Randall's motion came first. One by one, members spoke at the call of their names: "Aye;" "Nay." The clock ticked. The amendment failed: 72 in favor, 166 against. The question recurred on Randall's motion. One by one, members spoke. The motion failed. The clock ticked. Randall called out: motion to adjourn, no particular day. Members spoke. The motion failed. Randall: motion to adjourn to Friday. So the House sank softly into a relentless routine – motion to adjourn, motion to adjourn to Friday, or Saturday, or

---

17 Filibuster, *Cong. Record*, 43rd Congress, 2nd Session: 785–829.

Monday, motion to adjourn. Each motion failed, to be succeeded by the next, which failed, and was replaced by a replacement.

Hours passed. Democrats grinned. Republicans did a slow burn. Cessna rose: Point of order; the proceeding was improper. Members sprang to their feet, voices calling to the Speaker, drowning out the gavel. To correspondents viewing the scene it was pandemonium; "a volume of unintelligible sound that came up to the galleries like the howl of a menagerie."[18] Speaker Blaine ruled the point of order out of order. The business was unbearable but not unparliamentary. Randall spoke. "I think," he said, "we had better do this thing with good nature." For two days and two nights, though they accomplished absolutely nothing else, members upheld Sam Randall's suggestion. News accounts agreed. Under the most trying circumstances, mental and physical fatigue, the House retained a spirit of camaraderie, a better spirit than often prevailed during the routine of debate.

Two days and two nights of interminable, uninterrupted roll-calling presented the nation a unique spectacle. To Democrats, who inveighed against the tyranny of a majority, it was democracy in action. To Republicans, who decried the obstructionism of a minority, it violated the essence of democracy. "This is tyranny," fumed James Garfield. "One-fifth of the House can prevent the consideration of any measure they choose."[19] The New York *Times* had no liking for the Civil Rights Bill, but it censured the filibuster. It broke with all precedent. The minority had a right to be heard, but not the right to prevent debate entirely on a matter of the people's business.

> The position assumed by the minority in this instance is entirely new, and was never taken by any party before in the American Congress. Filibustering has often been resorted to to secure time for speech-making, or to gain opportunities to offer amendments. The minority have often used dilatory motions to force a compromise in the form of a bill, but never before have they undertaken to prevent a measure from receiving consideration. They meet this Civil Rights bill on the very threshold of the House and refuse it admission. The whole proceeding is contrary to the spirit of the Constitution and the principle of government by a majority.[20]

Democrats barred the threshold. Wednesday waned. Night came on. Gaslamps flamed. Shadows moved on the House floor, a somnambulistic ritual.

18 New York *Times*, January 28, 1875.
19 Mary Hinsdale, *The Garfield-Hinsdale Letters*, 316.
20 New York *Times*, January 29, 1875.

Hapless reading clerks intoned the members' names through weary hours while members tried to stay awake sufficiently to hear their names called. Republicans managed a little fun, using the Democrats' procedures against them. The *Times'* man described the scene:

> One of the leading Democrats moves that the House adjourn; another demands the yeas and nays upon this motion. Then some member on the Republican side demands the tellers on the yeas and nays. This is where the fun comes in for the Republican side. The Speaker asks if the call for tellers is seconded, and a sufficient number of Republicans rise in their places. The tellers are then appointed and take their places beside the Speaker's desk, and the Democrats who desire the yeas and nays come marching down the aisles and pass between the tellers. The Speaker then declares that a sufficient number have voted for the yeas and nays to second that demand, and the other side is not counted, so the Republicans have the opportunity of giving the Democrats some physical labor without trouble to themselves. Gen. Butler remarked to some of the Democrats amid one of these proceedings: "Some of you Generals and Colonels that were in the Confederate Army know how to march already, and we will teach the rest of you."[21]

Eventually such amusements ceased to amuse. Wednesday became Thursday. Thursday became Thursday night. Uncle William Crutchfield, for once, was in his eccentric element. Reporters spotted him "enveloped in an old-time blanket shawl, stowed away in his chair, with his feet on the desk." From that snug roost he gazed out upon the scene. Fellow Tennessean Horace Maynard was more restless. The Narragansett, wearing oddly moccasin-shaped slippers, "wandered about like an uneasy spirit in the happy hunting grounds." Quick-thinking members appropriated sofas and easy chairs in the back of the hall. Others stretched themselves across empty desks. By tacit agreement the rule against smoking was ignored. Congressmen puffed their stogies, leaving an atmosphere suffused with the odor of tobacco.

James Garfield found a quiet refuge and a little sleep stretched across the top of a committee-room table. On the second night he paired with Randall and went home for a few hours' rest.[22] Yet the good will remained. The capitol

---

21 New York *Times*, January 29, 1875. Accounts of the filibuster: New York *Times*, January 28–30; Washington *National Republican*, January 29–30; Cincinnati *Commercial*, January 29–30, 1875.

22 James Garfield, *The Diary of James Abram Garfield* (East Lansing, 1967), vol. 3, 17.

restaurant stayed open. "Citizen Downing enjoyed a profitable harvest," reporters observed.[23] Some members obtained liquid consolation. From certain committee rooms "mysterious" sounds, popping of corks, were heard. Ben Butler, cigar in mouth, occupied a front row seat. Across the aisle Sam Randall sat in the seat of the absent Alexander Stephens.

Gradually attendance in the hall declined. Members slipped out to grab a nap, a meal, a drink. Some paired off, organized into relays and sent to rest, or simply drifted away unauthorized. The House hung suspended in time. Clocks chimed the coming of Friday. In the timeless calendar of the House it remained Wednesday morning. A third day dawned. Roll-calls droned on. Empty seats outnumbered occupied ones.

Maynard, still wandering about the floor, suggested the absence of a quorum. Sergeant-at-Arms Nehemiah Ordway and his deputies left to hunt down deserters and bring them before the bar of the House. The final act had begun. Some members were beyond recall except by Sergeant Ordway's posse. Others, still within the building, rushed to return before the doors were locked. A few found the distance difficult to navigate. Henry Barry of Mississippi in his haste stepped through the framed glass doors of the House barber shop – without having opened them. The always-dapper William Walter Phelps arrived late. He climbed to the visitors' gallery, now occupied by a handful of black men. "A white man with his hair parted in the middle," he waved for colleagues below to let him in. Food became a priority. An enterprising reporter for the *National Republican* brought free provisions. The spread was laid in the Patents Committee room. Alabama's courtly Joseph Sloss presided over the board. Republicans and Democrats came together over cold cuts and cold tea, "but turkey and not politics was the theme."[24]

Nehemiah Ordway rounded up the fugitives. They appeared, each in turn, at the bar and were excused.[25] Roll-calls recommenced. At 9:00 Ben Butler went out to breakfast. In command he left Jasper Ward. The captain having left the quarterdeck, his lieutenant surrendered the vessel. Ward himself proposed a final, Republican, motion to adjourn. By a vote of 76-60 (153 not voting) the session of Wednesday, January 27, came to an end at 10:25 a.m. on Friday, January 29. Butler rushed back. Ward, he sputtered, had "pulled down the flag in

23 Washington *Forney's Sunday Chronicle*, January 31, 1875.

24 Washington, *National Republican*, January 30, 1875.

25 Most returned unrepentant. "I left this morning at four o'clock," New Jersey's Samuel Dobbins confessed, "went to my room and took a very comfortable nap, appreciated it very highly." *Cong. Rec.*, 43rd Cong., 2nd Session: 828.

the face of the enemy."[26] Most members were simply relieved. They prepared to stagger home and into bed.

Before the liberating moment a voice was heard. John Peter Shanks, Republican of Indiana, asked unanimous consent to read a document into the Record, an extract from the platform of the Democratic Party Convention of 1872, wherein Democrats had pledged equal rights for all citizens. Cries hooted him down, "roars of laughter on all sides." James Blaine's gavel fell. The hall cleared, ventilating some of the cigar-scented cloud that hovered in the air. Sam Randall left in triumph, a bouquet of flowers in his hand.[27]

On the morning of January 29, 1875, the matter of civil rights stood thus. Democrats had beaten back every assault. Republicans had failed to move the Senate bill. They had failed to move the House bill. They had failed to break the filibuster. One chance remained: a change in Rule 49. Republicans launched that move, and failed. The party again found itself crippled by its divisions. Two versions of the rules change proposal emerged. One was the handiwork of Ben Butler and John Cessna. It modified Rule 49 to permit no dilatory motions henceforth except one, and only one, motion to adjourn. After that the House must return to pending business. Nothing could take precedence. This would apply to all measures indiscriminately. Such a change horrified Democrats. But it also disturbed many Republicans. It was a license, they feared, to a rush of expenditures, an open raid upon the Treasury.

Moderates prepared a second version of the rules change. Speaker Blaine, Chairman of the Rules Committee, called together the committee's five members. They met that evening at the Speaker's home. James Garfield arrived, "feeling very sleepy and weary." Also present was the third Republican, Horace Maynard. Democrats Sam Randall and Sunset Cox attended; being satisfied with Rule 49 they declined to be helpful.[28] Blaine, Garfield and Maynard crafted their own rules change proposal. It too restricted the use of dilatory motions. But it applied brakes to overhasty consideration of suspicious measures. Henceforth the House would consider only one motion to adjourn and one to set a day for adjournment. No bill could receive a third reading on the first day of its consideration without the consent of three-quarters (later amended to two-thirds) of the House. Blaine's proposal excluded any bill designed to

26 Springfield, Massachusetts, *Republican*, January 30, 1875.

27 New York *Tribune*, January 30, 1875. One death resulted from the filibuster. James Buffinton of Massachusetts' 1st District went home to Fall River a few weeks later, reached his bedroom, and died there promptly. His health was precarious. Sleepless nights of filibuster, it was said, had set him on a terminal decline. Cincinnati *Commercial*, March 8, 1875. Henry Crapo, *The Story of William Wallace Crapo, 1830–1926* (Boston, 1942), 120.

28 Garfield, *Diary*, vol. 3, 17–18.

expend the money, credit, or property of the United States, apart from regular appropriations.

Monday, February 1, Republicans unveiled their proposals. On the strength of this single act the hopes of the Civil Rights Bill rested. Republican weakness dashed those hopes. To change the rules they must, yet again, suspend the rules. That required a two-thirds vote, the same two-thirds vote that had eluded them in May, in June, and on every occasion. It continued to elude them. Garfield and Blaine hoped to slip their motion through during the Monday morning hour, when the House operated under temporary suspension of the rules. Democrats raised dilatory objections. In the afternoon Butler called for consideration of his rules change. He received 173 votes, short of the two-thirds required. Garfield called for a recess until the next morning. They needed to regroup. That night, before falling into exhausted sleep, Garfield advised his diary: "Tomorrow we will try to bring out our strength."[29]

Tuesday, February 2, Republicans arrayed their forces for the final battle.[30] All depended upon party discipline, heretofore in very short supply. The first motion fell to Butler. He failed. One Republican, Sener of Virginia, voted Nay. Nineteen Republicans were missing: Henry Barry and George McKee of Mississippi; Amos Clark of New Jersey; Philip Crooke, William Wheeler, and John Lawson of New York; Carlton Curtis and John Packer of Pennsylvania; William Frye and Samuel Hersey of Maine; George Frisbie Hoar of Massachusetts; Morton Hunter of Indiana; James Lofland of Delaware; David Nunn of Tennessee; William Purman and Josiah Walls of Florida; Isaac Sherwood of Ohio; John Ambler Smith of Virginia; William Smith of North Carolina. The tally was 177 in favor, four votes short. Hoar, Wheeler and Frye were beyond reach, not yet returned from Louisiana, where they had gone to serve on the committee of investigation. Sherwood was on leave and out of town. Purman had returned to Florida on January 21. Morton Hunter and Amos Clark were ill. Lawson, Nunn and Packer had gone home to attend the illness of family members. Samuel F. Hersey lay on his deathbed in Bangor, Maine; he died the next day. Henry Barry, who recently had collided with an unopened glass door, was at home and, according to Garfield, drunk.[31] His colleague McKee had gone to fetch him. Just as the roll-call ended Lofland hurried into the hall, too late, the Speaker ruled, to record his vote. Democrats had survived. But their attendance also

29 Garfield, *Diary*, vol. 3, 19.

30 *Cong. Record*, 43rd Congress, 2nd Session: 880–892.

31 Garfield's accusation may be unjust. Henry Barry imbibed, more perhaps than occasionally. He also suffered physically. Reported ill on February 5, he died just four months later, on June 7, 1875, at age 35.

remained imperfect. Four truant members – William Barnum of Connecticut, Charles Kendall of Nevada, Samuel Marshall of Illinois, Alexander Mitchell of Wisconsin – held their vote to an even 90. Marshall was delayed in Louisiana. Kendall and Mitchell had left town. Barnum was ill.

Now Garfield presented the Rules Committee's version of the rules change. Republican solidarity broke. Butler demanded the right to amend prior to the vote. Garfield refused. Butler and his allies, Cessna, Greenbury Fort, Isaac Parker and Clinton Cobb, joined the opposition. The motion failed. The end approached. The last card had been played. James Garfield refused to fold. He nodded to his friend, John Kasson of Iowa. Kasson: let the Rules Committee report. Its proposal could be amended at members' discretion after suspension of the rules: a final motion, a final vote. On that vote the fate of the Civil Rights Bill balanced.

Assuming that none of the missing Democrats would appear, four more Republican ayes needed to emerge. The vote began. "Members flocked forward and filled the space in front of the clerk's desk, all eyes turning toward the Speaker."[32] The last name: Mr. Young of Georgia. "Nay!" Chief Clerk Edward McPherson handed his count to the Speaker. James Blaine read: ayes 181; 90 opposed. By a single vote the majority was freed to pursue its agenda. The bill to secure all persons in their civil rights survived. Four tardy Republicans provided the victory. Delaware's James Lofland had barely missed the first vote. He added his voice to the last. Pennsylvanian Carlton Curtis also arrived in time. Two missing Mississippians, George McKee and Henry Barry, provided the final voices.

Suddenly tension rose. Another member had left his sickbed and hastened to the House. He asked permission to record his vote. The whole result might be overthrown, hanging as it did on a single tally. Speaker Blaine ruled the vote closed. It was a false alarm. Morton Hunter, civil rights supporter, would only have added to the margin of passage. Then new excitement. Democrat Robert Vance, bitterly opposed, declared his vote had been incorrectly recorded. The clerk examined his roll. The count stood.

Democrats laid blame on the truant William Barnum of Connecticut. The millionaire ironmonger from the Bridgeport district had done little to impress his party since he had come to the House (taking the seat by defeating his more famous cousin, Phineas T. Barnum). Congressman Barnum pleaded illness. But he seemed vigorous enough. He was, declared the New York *Tribune*, simply lazy, a chronic absentee, his election to Congress an absurdity: "He is a good citizen and an honest man no doubt; is generous, good-natured and

32 New York *Times*, February 3, 1875.

jolly … [but] why send him to Congress? Once in two years regularly he runs for Congress; all the rest of the time he runs away from it."[33] The *World* cast no blame. The Republicans' victory would turn to dust in their mouths: "All that these pettifogging pygmies have gained is to secure that their dead party shall be carted off to the knacker's yard instead of being to decent burial slowly borne."[34]

Republicans reserved their animus for James Sener. He alone had voted No, deserted his party in its moment of need. Sener protested the purity of his motives. The rules change "was sprung for the express purpose of passing the civil rights bill." He could not vote for that.[35] For Republicans the pleasant, pudgy, nearsighted congressman morphed into a figure of evil. "Judas Iscariot Sener," the *National Republican* hissed. Democrats had beaten him up. Better have left him for dead.[36]

The rules change, as proposed by Garfield and Blaine, passed. Debate on the Civil Rights Bill began, Wednesday, February 3, 1875, thirteen months after it had been recommitted for review. No one doubted its passage. Democrats, however, had not surrendered. The shape of the bill remained undecided. Would it be as the Senate proposed? Would it be amended? Would it include the mixed-school clause? Ben Butler unveiled a surprise. He set before the House not one bill but four. Officially it was the Senate bill as amended in the Judiciary Committee. Three amendments challenged the Committee's amendment.

Butler defined the options. Each amendment took the Senate bill as its basic text. Each had a sponsor: Alexander White; John Cessna; Stephen Kellogg of Connecticut. White's version restored his provisos for separate-but-equal in all clauses, public accommodations, transport and common schools included. Cessna upheld the promise he had made in the Judiciary Committee. His amendment recopied the text of the Senate bill verbatim. The third proposal found its sponsor outside the Committee. Butler had tried and failed to preserve the mixed-school clause. He must take the advice of Richard Cain and Joseph Rainey. Save the bill. Kill the clause. No one on the Judiciary Committee sponsored that move. Stephen Kellogg, bespectacled judge from New Haven, undertook the task. Butler knew him; Kellogg had served on the Committee in the past. And it may be he turned to him. His amendment struck out all reference to schools.

---

33 New York *Tribune*, February 4, 1875. Subsequently Barnum ran away from the House altogether, skipping over to the Senate as replacement for Orris Ferry who died in November.

34 New York *World*, February 3, 1875.

35 Baltimore *Sun*, February 4, 1875.

36 Washington *National Republican*, February 2, 1875.

Stark choices set before it, the House began its final debate. Galleries overflowed. Doorkeeper Otis Buxton barred the portal. A flood of disappointed spectators flowed backwards, jammed the corridors outside.[37] Inside, the camaraderie of the filibuster had disappeared amid the acrimony of the rules change confrontation. The debate began badly, and grew worse.

Butler opened proceedings innocently enough. He provoked an explosion.[38] The issue, he said, had been thoroughly reviewed and needed no repetition. But he was drawn into a colloquy with a Democrat, William Niblack of Indiana. Why, Niblack inquired, did the gentleman insist that violations of his "civil rights" statute be judged only in the federal courts? Did he not trust the integrity of state or local judicial institutions? Of course Butler did not. No advocate of the bill could rely on its enforcement by a "white jury that will not convict." Butler tried to answer tactfully. It was not that southern juries or jurors were dishonest. Southerners were good people. But they were menaced. A ruthless element, "the murderers, the horse-thieves, the night riders," intimidated them. His words lit the fire. Butler's experience might have warned him. It was unwise to juxtapose references to horse-thieves and southerners. Duels had been fought for less.

Texan William McLean stood up. "Does the gentleman call the people of the South murderers and horse-thieves?"

Not at all, Butler replied, "I said the minority, not the majority. There are as good men in the South as there are in the North."

McLean sat down. But he fired, or rather mumbled, a parting shot: "You are the only murderer I know of on this floor."[39] For a moment the remark passed unheard. Butler yielded the floor to John Roy Lynch. Then someone informed him of what had been said. Interrupting Lynch, who was beginning

37 Baltimore *Sun*, February 4, 1875.

38 Butler's remarks and confrontation with William McLean, *Cong. Record*, 43rd Congress, 2nd Session: 939–942.

39 McLean's accusation adverted to a notorious wartime incident, Butler's order, while military governor of New Orleans, to hang one man. William Mumford, a Confederate patriot, defied the occupiers and tore down the American flag set above the mint. The execution was proper; the city lay under martial law. For southerners it was a war crime. Mumford's wife had pleaded for clemency, Butler recalled. He could not yield. After the war he met the widow Mumford again, homeless and unemployed. He relieved her poverty, helped her find a government job and buy a home for her children. (Butler, *Autobiography*, 438–446) The South did not forgive. "If such crimes are passed by," the Wilmington *Journal* insisted, twelve years after the event, "there is no knowing what atrocities this fiend will commit.... The execrable wretch must be punished." Wilmington, North Carolina, *Journal*, June 20, 1874.

his oration, Butler fired back. McLean's remark was "ungentlemanly, ruffianly abuse." Lynch stopped. The House became still.

Lucius Lamar's silky voice broke the hush: "I ask if the language of the gentleman from Massachusetts is parliamentary?"

Sam Randall sensed an impending disaster: "It does not amount to shucks; let it go." Randall's warning came too late. Members leaped up, swarmed the aisles. They filled the space in front of the clerk's desk, congressmen sprinting from their seats, milling, jostling, yelling. New York's David DeWitt crowded Butler, shaking a finger in his face. Alabamian Charles Pelham screamed at DeWitt: go back to your own side of the House. (He accompanied this request, the Baltimore *Sun* reported, "with a horrible and most disgraceful oath.")[40] McLean stood twitching, his face flushed, hands agitated. To some he seemed drunk.[41] Fellow Texan John Hancock interposed his body to prevent an altercation. Lamar, ever the peace-maker, urged calm.[42] McLean, it was said, reached into his pocket for a pistol. Lamar restrained him.[43] "I am ready for him," McLean fumed, "or his son, if he has a son, to take it up for him."[44]

Speaker Blaine restored order. The House Reporter consulted his notes. He read out the words Butler had spoken. It was agreed he had applied his horse-rustling epithet only to a minority of southerners. Members sat down. But the matter was far from settled. Before he retired to his seat Ben Butler hurled a last remark: "If the gentleman said I was a murderer because I hanged a man at New Orleans, so far from taking offense I glory in it, and the trouble has been that I did not hang more then than I did." All this while, John Roy Lynch seemed forgotten. One observant newsman, George S. Merriam, reporting for the *Christian Union*, noticed him, standing aside, patient, detached. "The big, vigorous white man and his fellows, pushing their quarrel in angry tones, made a striking contrast to the slightly built, frail mulatto, who stood waiting his turn."[45] The white men subsided. Butler returned the floor to Lynch.

Lynch began again. Another interruption stopped him. John Young Brown of Kentucky scrambled to his feet. His words poured out irrepressibly: "Many years ago in England!" Cries from the floor silenced his oratory in full flight. Republicans knew the virulence of Brown's prejudices. They taunted him.

40 Baltimore *Sun*, February 4, 1875.
41 *Christian Union*, February 17, 1875, p. 131.
42 New York *Times*, February 4, 1875.
43 Washington *National Republican*, February 5, 1875.
44 Paterson *Press*, February 4, 1875.
45 *Christian Union*, February 17, 1875, 131.

If he wanted to speak let him ask for the courtesy. "Let him ask Lynch," members called out.[46] Speaker Blaine turned to Butler: to whom does the gentleman yield? "I yield to the gentleman from Mississippi," Butler replied. The incident seemed trivial. But the curious words John Young Brown began that day he would complete later.

Lynch's speech meanwhile proved memorable. Of all the black members in 1875, he exhibited the most reticence. Indeed he seemed altogether reluctant to engage in the cause of the Civil Rights Bill. Lynch's hesitancy grew from his belief that priority must go to the Force Bill. A civil rights measure alone was useless. They must safeguard the right to vote, defeat the power of the White Leagues, rather than dissipate what strength the party retained. In his memoirs Lynch barely recalled the passage of the Civil Rights Act. He did recall most pointedly the effort to pass the Force Bill. That, he said, constituted the great struggle of the Forty-Third Congress. He recounted a personal interview with James Blaine, his dismay when the Speaker deserted that measure. On the fate of the Civil Rights Bill he remembered little.[47] Once resolved to speak, however, John Roy Lynch produced words that echoed through the debate. He began with social equality. Social equality and civil rights, that seemed to distress white people. Let them not fear. He treasured their civil rights. If ever he encountered injustice or discrimination practiced against them he would oppose it – no matter how socially inferior they might be.

> I cannot believe that gentlemen on the other side of the House mean what they say when they admit as they do, that the immoral, the ignorants and the degraded of their own race are the social equals of themselves and their families. If they do, then I can only assure them that they do not put as high an estimate on their own social standing as respectable and intelligent colored people place upon theirs.... I can then assure that portion of my democratic friends on the other side of the House whom I regard as my social inferiors that if at any time I should meet any one of you at a hotel and occupy a seat at the same table with you, or the same seat in a car with you, do not think that I have thereby accepted you as my social equal.[48]

46 New York *Times*, February 5, 1875.

47 John R. Lynch, *Reminiscences of an Active Life. The Autobiography of John Roy Lynch* (Chicago, 1970), 158–162.

48 Speech of John Roy Lynch, *Cong. Record*, 43rd Congress, 2nd Session: 943–947.

Here he stood, an educated man, a cultured man, a representative of the people. Yet he was treated as an outcast.

> What a sad commentary upon our system of government, our religion, and our civilization! Think of it for a moment; here am I, a member of your honorable body, representing one of the largest and wealthiest districts in the State of Mississippi ... and yet when I leave my home to come to the capital of the nation, to take part in the deliberations of the House and to participate with you in making laws for the government of the Republic, in coming through the God-forsaken States of Kentucky and Tennessee, if I come by way of Louisville and Chattanooga, I am treated not as an American citizen, but as a brute, forced to occupy a filthy smoking-car both night and day, with drunkards, gamblers, and criminals; and for what? Not that I am unable or unwilling to pay my way; not that I am obnoxious in my personal appearance or disrespectful in my conduct; but simply because I happen to be of a darker complexion.

He addressed the point that had led Butler into his difficulties with Niblack and McLean. Why did the bill mistrust the courts and juries of the South?

> What a farce! Talk about instituting a civil-rights suit in the State courts in Kentucky, for instance, where the decision of the judge is virtually rendered before he enters the court-house, and the verdict of the jury substantially rendered before it is impaneled. The only moments of my life when I am necessarily compelled to question my loyalty to my Government or my devotion to the flag of my country is when I read of outrages having been committed upon innocent colored people and the perpetrators go unwhipped of justice.... Then I can only say with sorrow and regret that our boasted civilization is a fraud; our republican institutions a failure; our social system a disgrace; and our religion a complete hypocrisy.

He recalled, though many months had passed, William Robbins' speech, his demeaning characterizations of black men; they could not be soldiers, but they could be clowns.

> The gentleman from North Carolina admits, ironically, that the colored people, even when in bondage and ignorance, could equal, if not excel, the whites in some things – dancing, singing, and eloquence.... You could not prevent them from dancing unless you kept them continually tied;

> you could not prevent them from singing unless you kept them continually gagged.... But you could and did prevent them from becoming educated for fear that they would equal you in every other respect.

Lynch called for Cessna's amendment, the Senate bill intact. He agreed with Frelinghuysen. The mixed school clause did not require mixed schools.

> I regard this school clause as the most harmless provision in the bill. If it were true that the passage of this bill with the school clause in it would tolerate the existence of none but a system of mixed free schools, then I would question very seriously the propriety of retaining such a clause; but such is not the case. If I understand the bill correctly (and I think I do,) it simply confers upon all citizens, or rather recognizes the right which has already been conferred upon all citizens, to send their children to any public free school that is supported in whole or in part by taxation, the exercise of the right to remain a matter of option as it now is – nothing compulsory about it.

By mutual accord the House recessed at the regular hour. It reconvened at 7:30 p.m., an evening session for debate only. Missouri's Isaac Parker took the chair. Spectators filled the galleries. But most congressmen were elsewhere. James Garfield preferred a convivial and bipartisan gathering at Welcker's Restaurant. The company included the urbane Clarkson Potter, his brother General Robert Potter, Justices Swayne and Bradley of the Supreme Court, and Vice-President of the United States Henry Wilson. Conversation turned to the state of morals of public men. The vice-president opined that, despite the assertions of the daily newspapers, the virtues of politicians stood higher now than in the days of their forefathers.[49] On the House floor there was a marked absence of those virtuous politicians. Some members, including Lucius Lamar and Virginian Eppa Hunton, had come prepared with speeches. They declined to offer them to empty seats.[50] Pennsylvania Democrat John B. Storm urged Republicans to heed the voice of the people.

---

49 James Garfield, *Diary*, vol. 3: 20–21.

50 Eppa Hunton, Democrat, of Virginia's 8th District, sent his speech to be printed in the Record. Republicans, he insisted, slandered southerners, defamed their native kindness. No one oppressed black people. Black people were servile. They were docile. Northerners filled their heads with notions of civil rights. Then they became uppity: "Not until the meanest of the northern people came among us and sowed the seeds of discontent and impertinence did we see any misbehavior on the part of the colored men." Southerners wanted harmony. "It is not prejudice or a feeling of unkindness to the colored man that

> I ask our republican friends to pause. I ask them to let reason and not a wild and excited frenzy prevail in their counsels. Rest assured that if you fail to heed the lessons taught by the elections last fall, a condemnation tenfold more severe awaits you in 1876.… You will be overwhelmed by the pent-up storm of popular indignation which is now ready to burst upon you in all its violence.[51]

No one else called for the floor. Julius Burrows of Michigan observed that it cost the Treasury $50 an hour to keep alight the gas-lamps that illuminated the chamber; if no one was interested in using that time perhaps it would be better to adjourn and save the taxpayers' expense. He put his motion to a vote. The count was 2 in favor 13 against.

At last the situation changed. Democrat Thomas Whitehead entered the hall. Captain Whitehead was a knightly gentleman, 50 years old, completing his single term from Virginia's 6th District. Many grievances weighed on his mind. He determined to speak them now. Once, in happier days, Whitehead had been a Whig. His party dissolved. He had been a Confederate. His nation disintegrated. War had dealt him hard blows. Two years' service in the 2nd Virginia Cavalry ended with a severe wound at the battle of Trevillian's Station. He was not inclined to sympathize with black people who whined about wounds to their precious civil rights. Thomas Whitehead spoke ex tempore. He came closest, in all the long debate, to an expression of the unaffected, raw emotions that lay behind the orotund oratory.

> Mr. Speaker, to some of the gentlemen from States north of the Potomac, perhaps to the largest part of the audience here, it may be fun, but to us who are to be affected by this law, who are to reap its bitter fruits and bear whatever of evil there is in this pernicious legislation, it is not a matter of fun, but a matter of death.… What matters it in Massachusetts or in New York whether this civil-rights bill passes or not? Why, sir, it is almost as hard to find a real genuine black man in those States as a needle in a hay-stack.[52]

---

influences the opposition of the southern white man to this bill, but a sincere desire for the welfare of both races and a wish to live together in peace." *Cong. Record*, 43rd Congress, 2nd Session, Appendix: 119.

51 *Cong. Record*, 43rd Congress, 2nd Session: 951.

52 Remarks of Thomas Whitehead and colloquy, *Cong. Record*, 43rd Congress, 2nd Session: 952–958. See ensuing quotations.

Gauzy speeches, high-sounding principles – human rights, equality, brotherhood of man. It was nothing but hypocrisy. It ended in ridiculous farce.

> If Congress can say who shall go into a hotel licensed by the State of Virginia and who shall have what you call equal rights, then if the landlord should give my friend General Hunton turkey, and the colored man beef, under this law proposed to be passed by the Congress of the United States you would have that man arrested for making a difference between the two, discriminating against the food of the colored man.

"What is the object of this bill?" he demanded. "They say it is to give the colored man something he has not got.... But he will never be satisfied, in my opinion, because the Almighty has given him what he cannot get rid of – a black skin.... You have not the power to make him white, and he never will be satisfied short of that."

What was the true motive of the so-called Civil Rights Bill? War! "We are expected to make a row down South about it.... I know that this bill is intended to stir up bad blood, to mix the two races in the schools, so that the children may first get to fighting and then the parents, and then instantly there will be a call for bayonets." He had seen it before. History replayed itself. Northern aggressors sought to provoke the South, just as they had provoked it fifteen years ago. Slavery then was the goad. "What was the cause of that war? The continual picking at that subject of slavery ... interfering with other people's business." Robbery was the goal, the South's lawful human property lawlessly expropriated. One war did not suffice. The South was not sufficiently beaten down. Slaves were gone, slave-owners' property stolen. So the North contrived a new goad: civil rights. It began to pick again, perpetual aggression, until it reached its new goal, another bloodbath.

In the heat of his anger, Whitehead put his finger on a salient point. Northerners prated about equality. But they perpetuated inequality. Theirs was an inequality more fundamental than race: the inequality of capital and labor. Let them deny it. An underclass must exist – everybody knew it – an underclass needed to serve the interests of its masters. In the South black people provided that class. In the North all men were entitled to join: the servitude of wage labor. The lords of the loom oppressed their workers. Yet these capitalists, with palsied platitudes, preached to the gentlemen of the plantation. What if southerners went about the north agitating in the mill towns and the mines, inciting the wretched, laboring masses to rise against their exploiters?

> What would you think if I went to Pennsylvania to stir up the "Molly Maguires" against the men who own the coal mines? What would you think if I went to the manufacturing towns in New England to stir up bad blood between the manufacturers and their employees? What would you think if I told the laboring men there that they had been cheated – that they had been cheated by the manufacturers out of the just profits of their labor? ... Yet that is what your party is doing in the South. You go into our States and tell these people that we have robbed them; that we have oppressed them; that we did these things for a long series of years, and that now you intend to give them the right to put the bottom rail on top.... You cannot put a man up that way who ought to remain at the bottom.

"Perhaps you wish to make somebody mad," Whitehead fumed. "You will not make me mad.... I do not intend to get mad. I have not the least idea of getting mad," he said, as he got madder and madder. "You say you are a Christian people. We are called 'ruffians;' we are called hard names, bitter epithets are used against us; and you hug the pious delusion to your souls that you are doing God's service in all this cruelty and all this wrong. Well, there is an old man, an old client of mine down in Virginia, who had a way of drawing consolation from subjects in which to other eyes it seemed least likely to exist ... no matter what it was, and, as a final result, 'Thank God there is a Hell.' I am mighty near in this case now."

A voice interrupted Whitehead's effusion, Benjamin Harris, Republican of Massachusetts. How did the gentleman feel about the testimony he had heard from Lynch, the degradation one of his own colleagues suffered on the railroads of the South? Whitehead replied calmly. The gentleman was simply mistaken. "I take great pleasure in saying that no such degradation could occur in my own State of Virginia." He himself had traveled by rail to the present session of Congress from his home in Lynchburg. All the way there, seated in front of him, rode "a colored gentleman and his wife, very genteel persons and well behaved, and I never saw anyone interfere with them." Speaking for Virginia, no discrimination existed.

Joseph Rainey rose. He wished to correct the gentleman's understanding. The gentleman was misinformed. He, Rainey, had been in Richmond, Virginia. He, personally, had been ejected from the streetcars. Richard Cain joined in. He had experienced it. He had seen it: black women brutally expelled, dragged from "whites only" cars as soon as their trains crossed into Virginia. Yet Whitehead persisted. Black people rode freely in his state. Perhaps violations occurred. If so, no matter what Beast Butler said, Virginia's courts would treat them justly. With that, the discussion reached an impasse. Gentlemen would have to agree to disagree.[53] It was 10:10 p.m. Isaac Parker tapped his gavel. The evening session ended.[54]

Thursday, February 4, the penultimate day of debate. "An enormous crowd," wrote the Louisville *Courier-Journal's* reporter, "composed very largely of negroes, the galleries literally overflowing with negroes and blackguards."[55] On the floor a bedraggled James Sener faced his colleagues, his shattered arm cradled in a sling. Written out of his party, shunned by former friends, his newspaper bankrupt, his career in shambles, he turned to an ungrateful public. Democrats had broken his body. Republicans had broken his spirit.

> Mr. Speaker, I have been most unusually and wantonly assailed by a journal professing to represent the Executive of this Government ... assailed and denounced as a Judas Iscariot to the republican party.... Because a Representative of the people comes here and in his place on the floor of this House does that which he did before his people when he asked for their commission to represent them, he is violently assaulted and foully assailed, and the very right of the Constitution brought in peril which declares that for words spoken or for acts done here he is responsible in no other place.[56]

53 No one could agree on the reality of the situation. Even now, a reader of C. Vann Woodward's authoritative classic, *The Strange Career of Jim Crow*, a work that chooses to highlight a selection of the happier anecdotes, will not be blamed for concluding that black people, as Thomas Whitehead said, suffered practically no discrimination riding the rails with unconcerned white neighbors – that is, until the "strange" and brutal clampdown of Jim Crow laws at the end of the century. C. Vann Woodward, *The Strange Career of Jim Crow* (Oxford, 1966), 27–41. On the other hand, a contemporary eyewitness of the 1870s, travel writer Edward King, came to the opposite conclusion. He described a trip precisely from Washington, D.C. to Lynchburg, Virginia. Black travelers were distinctly segregated, confined to a single, sordid, unsanitary smoking-car. The same situation, he said, prevailed across the South. Edward King, *The Great South*, 553–554, 783. A consistent conclusion may be that there was no consistency.

54 A century later, in 1964, an eerily similar colloquy unfolded, Florida's Senator George Smathers and Rhode Island's John Pastore. Smathers: "Mr. President, it irritates me considerably to hear someone from Rhode Island ... begin to tell us what is happening in Louisiana, Florida, Georgia, and other Southern States, when he does not know what he is talking about.... I can tell the Senator that I have never in my life seen any colored person go into a drug-store who could not get anything a white person could get." Pastore: "Could he be served at the counter?" Smathers: "He could be served at most of the counters." Pastore: "Then I have been reading the wrong newspapers." Smathers: "That is the trouble with the Senator; he has been reading only the wrong newspapers." Pastore: "We have all been reading the wrong newspapers." *Cong. Record*, 88th Congress, 2nd Session: 14,439.

55 Louisville *Courier-Journal*, February 5, 1875.

56 Remarks of James Sener, *Cong. Record*, 43rd Congress, 2nd Session: 978.

Nobody offered to console Jimmy Sener. Ebenezer Rockwood Hoar resumed the discourse. Silent unto this moment, he had finally reconciled himself to Sumner's deathbed commission: don't let the Civil Rights Bill fail. Hoar addressed a significant point. Opponents scoffed at the idea of legislating civil rights. Congress would simply enact a dead letter. Perhaps they were right. That did not diminish it. It might stand for generations without effect. That did not matter. It would stand, a beacon to light the way:

> The Declaration of Independence announced that all men were created equal. That announcement stood a great many years before it became a vital truth throughout this land.... Now I have no belief that this bill, if enacted into law, is going to produce any great effect immediately for good or for evil.... I can remember the time ... when the colored sailors of Massachusetts were put into jail as soon as they arrived at southern ports; and no declaration of the unconstitutionality of that proceeding under the Constitution of the United States availed to save them from their doom. There has been a fearful retribution for that wrong. But, Mr. Speaker, the value of this act is similar to that of the Declaration of Independence. It will stand as the declaration of the American people that henceforth before the law every citizen of the country is to have equality.[57]

Robert Hale, Republican of New York, addressed the legal question. "Suppose it were true that Congress was to be limited to rectifying abuses by State legislation, does any gentleman ... deny that to-day State after State of the South does live under laws which are inconsistent with the fourteenth amendment; that practices are there permitted which are in violation of the fourteenth amendment? And if that be so, then cannot Congress interfere?"[58]

Lucius Lamar rose. "I ask the gentleman if he will indicate what legislation of what State violates the provisions of the fourteenth amendment."

Hale was taken aback. "I supposed it was a matter of absolute notoriety. I have never heard it questioned before, and I did not suppose any gentleman would question it."

"I do dispute it," Lamar purred. "If there exists in the entire range of all the statutes of all the States in the South one single act, one single provision of law inconsistent with any of the principles or provisions of any of the amendments to the Federal Constitution I am ignorant of the existence of such provision. Furthermore, I say ... *throughout the length and breadth of the southern section*

---

57 Remarks of Ebenezer Hoar, *Cong. Record*, 43rd Congress, 2nd Session: 979.

58 Remarks of Robert Hale and colloquy, *Cong. Record*, 43rd Congress, 2nd Session: 980.

there does not exist in law one single trace of privilege or of discrimination against the black race. If there is, I know nothing of it." Lamar, of course, was correct. Individuals discriminated individually. States sat back to watch.

The House heard next from a Republican opponent, Edwin Stanard of Missouri. The Civil Rights Bill would be a disaster. Black people themselves had begun to regret it.

> Living in a former slave State as I do, I am satisfied that the majority of the colored people of that State are opposed to the provisions of this bill, from the simple fact that they are of the opinion that where there is a strong prejudice in the minds of the people against the colored race, that prejudice will be increased by its passage and barriers placed in their way of progress.... They are progressing in the scale of refinement and education, and our people are anxious, as the colored people are now and must be for all time part and parcel of the government, that they should be educated and elevated. If I believed that the passage of this bill would tend to the elevation of this people without damaging anybody else, I would be in favor of all its provisions; but believing that such is not the case, I cannot support it.[59]

Richard Cain rose once more. He wished to make a final statement. If the House could not rise to the enlightenment of Charles Sumner and pass the Senate bill (Cessna's amendment), he would accept on behalf of his people a compromise. Take the amendment offered by Stephen Kellogg. Strike out the school clause. Cain's concession was critical. By now not only he but Rainey and Lynch, Downing and Langston accepted the unavoidable. Scuttle mixed schools if that would save the bill. There was a note of regret, but also of hope. Once a Civil Rights Act was in place its operation would wear down the edge of prejudice. Schoolhouse doors would open inevitably. "I am not prepared to say," John Mercer Langston declared, "that it might not be the only wise and practical thing that can be done now to pass the bill without such provision, trusting to God and the future to bring us a common school which shall be harmonious with our Declaration of Independence and Constitution."[60] Cain agreed:

> I am willing, if we cannot rally our friends to those higher conceptions entertained by Mr. Sumner – if we cannot bring up the republican party

59 Remarks of Edwin Stanard, *Cong. Record*, 43rd Congress, 2nd Session: 980.

60 Indianapolis *Journal*, December 23, 1874.

> to that high standard with regard to the rights of man as seen by those who laid the foundation of this Government – then I am willing to agree to a compromise. If the school clause is objectionable to our friends, and they think they cannot sustain it, then let it be struck out entirely. We want no invidious discrimination in the laws of this country. Either give us that provision in its entirety or else leave it out altogether, and thus settle the question.[61]

Stephen Kellogg rose. Did he understand the gentleman to support his amendment? "I offered it in the interest of your people as well as ours." Cain replied, "I agree to accept it." He concluded with one final appeal: "Spare us our liberties; give us peace; give us a chance to live; give us an honest chance in the race of life; place no obstruction in our way; oppress us not; give us an equal chance, and we ask no more of the American people."

Alexander White also spoke. The Alabamian reserved for himself all the time allotted to his amendment. He delivered his valedictory to the House. Midway through the effort he cast off his long black overcoat. ("He cast it off as easily as he did his pro-slavery principles," snapped the Montgomery *Advertiser*.[62]) He called for compromise. "We are on the line where prejudices of race, of party, and of section collide." Extremism gripped the South. God forbid it should grip Congress. He recalled Alabama's terror, the slaughter of Billings and Ivey, the night-riders who roamed the countryside. All that the North thought it had eliminated in four years of war was being reborn, save only the legal institution of slavery. Southern Republicans were freedom's last bulwark. Yet they were defamed, vilified, tarred with the epithets of carpetbagger and scalawag. They suffered ostracism, or death. The nation turned its back upon their corpses.

> Is there another government in the world, or has there ever been a government, or a thing with the name or shadow of a government, which would have quietly stood by and witnessed such violence and atrocities as these without adopting efficient means to repress them and to protect its citizens? … A few years ago the story of Uncle Tom's Cabin, with its large draughts of fancy, was sufficient to thrill the nation with sympathy for the suffering slave. Now the nation turns a deaf ear to wrongs inflicted upon the same people now free citizens of the United States, which in enormity in a single year would outweigh the sufferings of a hundred years of slavery.[63]

---

61 Remarks of Richard Cain, *Cong. Record*, 43rd Congress, 2nd Session: 980. See ensuing.

62 Montgomery *Advertiser*, February 16, 1875.

63 Speech of Alexander White, *Cong. Record*, 43rd Congress, 2nd Session, Appendix: 15–24.

Charles Eldredge gave the last major speech from the Democratic side. He deployed the most enduring thesis developed by the Civil Rights Bill's opponents. Black people must rise by their own boot-straps. Those who reach for government's hand to lift themselves up hurl themselves down. Government assistance degrades. They who seek it concede their incapacity.

> If he [the colored man] be made to feel that extraordinary provisions of law are enacted in his favor because of his weakness or feebleness as a man, the very fact weakens and enfeebles him. The consciousness that there is necessity for such legislation and protection for him must necessarily humiliate and degrade him. Such laws, too, are a constant reminder to him that he is inferior.... This bill and all such bills go upon the ground that the colored race is inferior, feebler, and less capable of taking care of itself than the weakest and most inferior white man. *This* is the very predicate of this legislation. And whether he claims the natural equality of the races or not, it is an insult to every colored man in the Republic.[64]

Eldredge yielded his remaining time to John Young Brown. Tension mounted at once. Members left their seats. They stood about in the aisles, clustered around the clerk's desk, waiting. Within minutes Young Brown brought on chaos. Hard words sounded. Sergeant-at-Arms Ordway rose to arrest a member upon the floor.

The Kentuckian drove directly into his disaster: "The Civil Rights Bill!" What is it? "It is the culminating, crowning iniquity of socialism. It is born of malignity; it will be passed in defiance and violation of the Constitution, and executed I fear in violence and bloodshed."

Robert Hale rose: point of order. Such language transcended the limits of parliamentary decency. Speaker Blaine overruled him. The gentleman had a right to express his opinions. Brown continued. He pointed his opinions at the Republican Party. "Onward and onward you go in defiance of the sentiment of the country, without pity and without justice, remorselessly determined to devote these distressed southern people to complete destruction."

Republicans squirmed. Young Brown pointed to his true target: Benjamin Butler. He had not forgotten yesterday's unbearable insult – the horse-thieves remark. It was time to insult the Beast. "That accusation against that people has come from one who is outlawed in his own home from respectable society; whose name is synonymous with falsehood; who is the champion of fraud; who is the apologist of thieves" – he launched into his climax – "who is such a prodigy of vice and meanness that to describe him would sicken imagination

64 Speech of Charles Eldredge, *Cong. Record*, 43rd Congress, 2nd Session: 982–985.

and exhaust invective." He reached for his coup de grace: "In Scotland years ago there was a man [William Burke] whose trade was murder, and he earned his livelihood by selling the bodies of his victims for gold. He linked his name to the crime, and to-day it is known throughout the world as 'Burking.'"

Speaker Blaine had been distracted. He awoke to the situation. Brown's tirade threatened to violate the House's honored rule of decorum. He attacked with personal invective a fellow member upon the floor. Blaine's hammer fell. "Does the Chair understand the gentleman to be referring in this manner to a member of the House?" Brown looked up innocently: "No, sir. I am describing an individual who is in my mind's eye." Then he proceeded, without a blink, to give the imaginary individual a material identity. "Burking" had become obsolete. A new eponym of evil had arisen. "If I wished to describe all that was pusillanimous in war, inhuman in peace, forbidden in morals, and infamous in politics, I should call it 'Butlerism.'"[65]

A thunderbolt. "Members leaped to their feet with as much suddenness as if a bomb had exploded over their heads," the New York *Times'* observer wrote.[66] Young Brown had insulted a member by name, likening him to a ghoulish body-snatcher. Worse, he had lied to the Speaker. Reporters grabbed their pencils. "There was," one noted, "a faint effort at applause, but it was drowned out in the cries of order and the banging of the Speaker's gavel."[67] A dozen members rose. The Chair recognized Robert Hale. He called for the words to be taken down and a motion of censure passed. Negley of Pennsylvania: censure did not suffice. Expel him from the House. Hale framed a motion for censure. Henry Dawes called for expulsion. Civil rights debate ceased. The House debated John Y. Brown.

The import of his act came home to Young Brown. He seemed suddenly subdued, his face flushed. He sat down, toyed with papers on his desk. Benjamin Butler was radiant. First he coolly kept his seat. Then, for no apparent reason, he walked to the cloak-room, while everyone in the galleries watched agog. Then he walked back. He strolled to the Democratic side and talked casually to members, among them Eldredge, all not far from where Brown sat fidgeting.[68] Finally he returned to his seat. His face wore an attitude of pained indifference. "Butler sat impassive," one reporter wrote, "with an expression of martyrdom, most comical to witness, on his face.... When Butler assumes to be pathetic or heroic, his expression becomes ludicrous beyond measure ... simply indescribable, and beyond the powers of caricature even of a Nast."[69]

---

65 Speech of John Young Brown, *Cong. Record*, 43rd Congress, 2nd Session: 985.
66 New York *Times*, February 5, 1875.
67 Washington *National Republican*, February 5, 1875.
68 Baltimore *Sun*, February 5, 1875.
69 Cincinnati *Commercial*, February 5, 1875.

Brown found defenders: Lamar, Eldredge, Fernando Wood. High spirits, they said, a spontaneous overflowing of resentment called forth by Butler's insufferable insult (horse-thieves). Spontaneity, however, seemed unlikely. Everyone recalled Brown's peculiar unfinished sentence of the previous day. He had meditated his phrases for twenty-four hours. He must be punished. Expulsion appeared excessive, and also counterproductive. Brown's constituents would re-elect him at once. Censure passed. Nehemiah Ordway raised the Kentuckian from his seat and led him to the Speaker's desk.

James Blaine spoke: "You are arraigned at the bar of the House, under its formal resolution, for having transgressed its rules by disorderly remarks and for having resorted to prevarication when your attention was called to your violation of decorum by the Speaker. For this duplicate offense the House has directed that you be publicly censured at its bar. No words from the Chair in the performance of this most painful duty could possibly add to the gravity of the occasion or the severity of the punishment. It remains only to pronounce in the name of the House its censure."[70]

Brown replied: "I intended no evasion or prevarication to the Speaker, and I will now add no disrespect to the House." He did not disavow disrespect to Benjamin Butler.

In the end both Brown and Butler emerged enhanced in the eyes of their partisans. As expected, Brown wore his censure at the hands of the Yankees as a badge of honor. The legislature of North Carolina introduced a resolution of thanks to John Young Brown, "for his manly defense of the South and his denunciation of that arch-fiend Benj. F. Butler."[71] The Norfolk *Virginian* regretted only one thing. Butler's natural cowardice precluded calling him out to a duel. But he should be "thrashed" soundly at any rate.[72] Springfield *Republican* editor Samuel Bowles wrote to Henry Dawes: "I am afraid that Mr. J. Young Brown of Kentucky is to-day the most popular man in America."[73]

Not quite. Butler also gained popularity. "He succeeded in advertising himself once more," the *World* grumbled, "and was supremely happy."[74] Expressions of support filled Butler's correspondence. His friends in the women's rights movement rushed to comfort him. "Pray convey to Genl. Butler my warmest sympathies," wrote Phoebe Couzins. "Many anxious eyes are watching the conflict narrowed now to the House of Representatives, and if Gen.

70 Censure of John Young Brown, *Cong. Record*, 43rd Congress, 2nd Session: 992.

71 Wilmington, North Carolina, *Journal*, February 7, 1875.

72 Norfolk *Virginian*, February 6, 1875.

73 Samuel Bowles to Henry Dawes, February 5, 1875. Henry Laurens Dawes Papers, Library of Congress.

74 New York *World*, February 5, 1875.

Butler triumphs for his people rest assured he will not be without his reward."[75] Less delicately, one anonymous correspondent wrote from Cincinnati:

> Give that scoundrel Brown your very best! ... Give those Southern traitors the same kind of treatment that you gave them at New Orleans and the North will back you. The only brother I had was shot through the head by a Southern sharp-shooter and the sons of b – shall not vaunt their treason again if my life can help check them. We want you for President and we must have you.... I hope that as John Brown the martyr started the war that freed the slaves, so may John Y. Brown the bandit start the war that makes B.F. Butler our next President.[76]

Thomas Nast pointed his poisoned pencil at Young Brown, the Kentuckian portrayed as a snarling catamount raging through the House. Comical Democrats, a starchy Fernando Wood and a pathetically diminutive Sunset Cox, tugged at his tail. Butler, for once drawn respectfully, faced the assault, in his hand a scroll: "Very Civil Rights in the House of Representatives."[77] Even the New York *Times,* hardly a Butler admirer, found Brown's escapade vexing:

> The most ridiculous feature of it all is that "Young Brown" actually wasted all his beautiful eloquence on Benjamin Butler, a man who thinks no more of being called hard names than another man does of eating his dinner. Young Brown might just as well tried to batter down the Capitol with a pea-shooter as to make old Cock-eye wince with a few barbaric phrases, cudgeled out of his own dull brain.... They even oblige *us* to appear to say a good word for Butler – an extremely painful necessity.[78]

At 5:35 p.m. the House recessed. It returned at 10 a.m. For better or worse, today the business would end. There having been no adjournment, the calendar on the floor still read February 4. In the world outside it was Friday, February 5, 1875, the day the Civil Rights Bill passed the House of Representatives. One month remained to the Forty-third Congress. Three hours remained for Benjamin Butler to conclude debate, one last chance for those who wished to put their opinions on the record. No Democrat was so inclined. Amid the theatrics of the last two days they had demonstrated the sufficiency of their

---

75 Phoebe Couzins to H. Clancey, February 5, 1875. Butler Papers, Library of Congress.
76 "Your Friend" to Benjamin Butler, February 5, 1875. Butler Papers, Library of Congress.
77 *Harper's Weekly*, February 27, 1875.
78 New York *Times*, February 6, 1875.

zeal. The galleries nevertheless remained full of spectators eager to witness an epic event. Distinguished guests added their presence: Vice-President Wilson, Senators Schurz and Logan. Ex-senator Reverdy Johnson walked down the aisle to chat with Alexander Stephens.

Two amendments still lay under discussion. Stephen Kellogg spoke on behalf of his proposal to strike out the school clause. He offered it to ensure all people the right to an education. "I do it, Mr. Speaker, in the interest of education, and especially in the interest of the education of the colored children." He also offered it, he admitted, to block the advent of separate-but-equal. The public's mood was ugly. That doctrine might triumph if the school clause remained. "Sir, in the legislation of this country I recognize no distinction of color, race, or birthplace. All ought to be equal before the law; and the children of all should have an equal right to the best education they can have in the public schools of the country."[79]

Barbour Lewis took the floor. The rotund member from Memphis was now a large lame duck. He remained defiant. Democrats called the bill superfluous. Black people, they asserted, already enjoyed equal rights. Lamar boasted it was not needed in Mississippi.

> But the gentleman from Mississippi forgot to tell the reason why. It is because the Republican legislature of that State some years ago passed a most stringent and efficient civil-rights law. Previous to that the colored man was proscribed even on the railroad car and on the steamboat. Previous to that he had to go into filthy cars and submit to indignities and wrongs. Previous to that he did not receive the rights of manhood.[80]

A national civil rights act was needed. "The result will be beneficent; great and unmixed good will follow its enactment. Let us be wise and manly and pass it promptly."

Of the remaining speeches the most elaborate was that of Michigan's Julius Caesar Burrows.[81] He advocated Cessna's amendment, the Senate bill in full. He castigated timid colleagues. How could anyone entertain prejudice against colored men when the nation had just tendered its highest honors to a colored man? The reference was to Kalakaua, King of Hawaii. The monarch of the Sandwich Islands had just paid the country a state visit, the first crowned head to tour the American republic. President Grant received him. He addressed

79 Remarks of Stephen Kellogg, *Cong. Record*, 43rd Congress, 2nd Session: 997.

80 Speech of Barbour Lewis, *Cong. Record*, 43rd Congress, 2nd Session: 998.

81 Speech of Julius Burrows, *Cong. Record*, 43rd Congress, 2nd Session: 999–1001.

both houses of Congress. In New York City Mayor Samuel B. Vance greeted him at the pier. The height of society hastened to see and be seen with this black man, for so the newspapers called him. Burrows warmed to his theme: "Will it be said that he was a king? Be this my answer, that there is not a black man, however humble ... if clothed with citizenship, that does not wear a crown of royalty that makes him the peer of any sovereign on earth."

The mixed-school clause, Burrows insisted, should remain. Too many of his colleagues inclined to accept Alexander White's amendment. In that case he agreed with Richard Cain. Cut it out. Better men, "braver and truer men," would restore it in time.

> I protest here and now against entering upon that course of legislation which draws a line of demarcation between American citizens who by your laws and your Constitution stand in absolute equality on a common soil beneath a common flag.... It is the beginning of that class legislation which, if once entered upon, will know no end until it has brought to the weaker class of every race subjection and to the country only disaster and ruin. If you cannot legislate free schools, I prefer that the bill should be altogether silent upon the question until other times and other men can do the subject justice.[82]

Colleagues crowded around Burrows, pumping his hand. For several minutes he disappeared into the "congratulating throng."[83] Time grew short. Charles Williams of Wisconsin spoke. He too called for mixed schools.

> We sit with colored men in these Halls without prejudice, but we teach our little boys and girls that they are too good to sit with these men's children in the public school-room. Now if you run a color line through the schools, where will you draw it? Shall it be the child of ebony hue that you will proscribe, or shall it be the half-blood, or the quadroon, or the octoroon, or the delicate young school-girl with a slight orange tint on her cheek? Who shall decide? Shall it be the striplings, young men of

82 As to King Kalakava, "a molasses-candy colored specimen of royalty over whom the Northern people are just now going crazy," the Montgomery *Advertiser* chuckled. "If he was not a king," wrote the Indianapolis *Journal*, "Democrats would not let him ride in a first-class railway car." Montgomery *Advertiser*, December 23; Indianapolis *Journal*, December 19, 1874. The Norfolk *Virginian* was unimpressed with the royal majesty, and foresighted on his kingdom's fate. "How long before we gobble and annex this Kickshaw King's patch of ground?" Norfolk *Virginian*, December 16, 1874.

83 *Christian Union*, February 17, 1875, 131.

> great cities, who against the law and in defiance of it drive young ladies away from school examinations? Ah, Mr. Speaker, is this the road which leads up to stability and peace?[84]

William Phillips of Kansas warned. The nation must protect the rights of all its citizens, or the nation must live with a caste of citizens debased, no better than a caste of slaves: "That is the question, whether we can have a class to look down upon; whether we can have, not slavery, but a degraded class of poor, unprotected, ignorant people."[85]

James Rapier uttered the final remarks of the African-American members. "The question resolves itself into this: either I am a man or I am not a man. If I am a man, I am entitled to all the right and privileges and immunities that any other American citizen is entitled to."[86]

William Walter Phelps got his say. Now a lame duck, he held nothing back. Republicans beware. Charles Sumner had bequeathed them a poisonous gift. "Had that great heart been steeped as was Satan's with an unconquerable will and study of revenge, he could not have left to the country which he so loved, to the party which he created and led, a legacy so full of the seeds of disintegration and decay as the measure which the majority will this day pass."

The Civil Rights Bill bred hate. "It takes to the South the only thing of which the South has a plenty – contention and strife.... Has not the South suffered enough?" The Civil Rights Bill defied the law. "It could be shown by any constitutional lawyer who was not straining the Constitution as bull-dogs strain their leash ... that this whole legislation, both in spirit and in letter, is hostile to the Constitution; hostile to the Constitution which protects the minority; hostile to the Constitution which we swore to defend." The Civil Rights Bill defied reason. "You are trying to do what it seems to me this House everlastingly tries in one form or another to do – to legislate against human nature. You are trying to legislate against human prejudice, and you cannot do it." The Civil Rights Bill defied the people's will. "Upon this issue the two great parties went to judgment. And the people last fall declared their judgment, with a thunder that shook one hundred members out of these seats. When this bill was introduced one year ago, that Representative who believed it his duty to please his constituency, whether they were right or whether they were wrong, might have found a pretext for voting for it; but now this pretext is torn to shreds by the gales which swept the country in November."[87]

---

84 Speech of Charles Williams, *Cong. Record*, 43rd Congress, Second Session: 1002–1003.

85 Speech of William Phillips, *Cong. Record*, 43rd Congress, 2nd Session: 1003.

86 Remarks of James Rapier, *Cong. Record*, 43rd Congress, 2nd Session: 1001.

87 Remarks of William Walter Phelps, *Cong Record*, 43rd Cong., 2nd Session: 1001–1002.

Republicans listened to Phelps' harangue. "A large throng" gathered at his desk. The throng dispersed. "Not a hand was offered in congratulations."[88] Cessna yielded his last minutes to John Peter Shanks of Indiana. Shanks, Chairman of the Committee on Indian Affairs, recalled that unhappy minority. "Sir, there is another race, the red people of this country, for whom I stand here to speak. Under this platform and the doctrines taught in it, broad as they are, the rights of that race are secured. I speak for those who have no friends anywhere else." Shanks also recalled the friendless Phelps.

> We heard to-day from a republican, do not forget it, a republican, that he would oppose this measure; and upon what ground? Why, that one hundred men were shaken out of their seats here because this bill was before Congress at its last session. And how did he vote upon that bill, and how was he shaken? He voted against the bill.... He was defeated.... Who have been shaken out of their seats here? Timid men have been shaken out of their seats; men who have been afraid to stand up and do right have been shaken out of their seats. But those men who are willing to indorse the principles enunciated in that platform have not been shaken out of their seats; or if they have been, they will have a good place to go to and a quiet conscience to console themselves with in their retirement.[89]

Shanks was not done. He had a final piece of business. He handed the reading clerk a paper, an excerpt from the Democratic Party platform of 1872, the same excerpt he had asked to read out during the days of the filibuster. Democrats then had laughed. Now let them listen.

> We recognize the equality of all men before the law, and hold that it is the duty of the Government in its dealings with the people to mete out equal and exact justice to all of whatever nativity, race, color, or persuasion, religious or political.

Everyone knew perfectly well the Democrats had inserted this plank into their platform during the 1872 presidential election only as a concession to their coalition partners, the Liberal Republicans. They had adopted those words to suit that occasion. They had not adopted their substance. "I want to say," William Niblack interrupted, "when the democratic party adopted that resolution it had been intimidated by the Cincinnati convention [of the Liberal Republicans]."

---

88 *Christian Union*, February 17, 1874, 131.

89 Remarks of John Peter Shanks, *Cong Record*, 43rd Congress, Second Session: 1003. See ensuing quotations and comments.

Shanks smiled: "I want to say some good things for your party." He was still not finished. He proposed those words, Democratic words, become part of the Civil Rights Bill. He moved to add them as a preamble to the text. Democrats themselves would then have written the introduction to a bill they renounced. When they voted to reject the measure, as they surely would, they would vote to reject their own professed ideals. When they spoke against it, as they would undoubtedly, they would speak against their own platform: "Equality of all men before the law." They would have to avow their complicity in that obnoxious idea, or explain why not.

Shanks succeeded in annoying the Democrats. "The most impudent thing done in the House," snarled the *World*.[90] "Like quoting Scripture to sustain the devil," hissed the Dayton *Democrat*.[91] Only Sunset Cox could still appreciate a splendid joke, even at his own expense. He rose to a point of order. The gentleman "states that equal and exact justice should be done." "Where is the point of order?" Speaker Blaine inquired. "If exact and equal justice should be done, the gentleman from Indiana should be hung like Absalom by the hair."[92]

Butler granted the penultimate speech to James Garfield. The future president relished his opportunity. He recalled it that night in his diary: "Butler yielded me fifteen minutes of his time. I made a speech answering the fears of some of our timid members that we were injuring the party by doing justice to the Negro."[93]

Garfield launched an assault on the Democrats, firing their own words against them. This time the words came not from a party platform but from a more notorious document, the Ku Klux Report, the long agonizing inventory framed by the Joint Congressional Committee of 1871. That commission had traveled across the South, compiling a record of atrocities in every state. Thirteen volumes of testimony held its findings. That evidence convinced the majority, Republicans, that a state of organized terrorism existed sufficient to require the imposition of federal force.[94] The minority, Democrats, discounted it – mere anecdotal fantasies. "A greater waste of paper and ink was never

90 New York *World*, February 6, 1875.

91 Dayton, Ohio, *Democrat*, February 6, 1875.

92 *Cong Record*, 43rd Congress, 2nd Session: 1004.

93 James Garfield, *Diary*, vol. 3: 21.

94 "Oh! a strange sad story is that which fills the thirteen volumes of testimony, documents, and conclusions, reported by that committee," wrote Albion Tourgée in 1879, "a strange commentary upon Christian civilization, a strange history of peaceful years; – bloody as the reign of Mary, barbarous as the chronicles of the Comanche!" Albion Tourgée, *A Fool's Errand: A Novel of the South during Reconstruction* (New York: 1879), 251.

perpetrated," declared North Carolina's Alfred Waddell.[95] There was no need for federal intervention, said the minority report, no need for protection from a non-existent threat. Ku Klux was a phantom conjured up by Republicans to divert attention from their own excesses. Garfield turned to the minority report's appendix. The problem, it concluded, was not the oppression of black people. It was the existence of black people.

> Man's puny statutes cannot repeal or nullify the immutable ordinances of the Almighty. Those whom God has separated let no man join together. There can be no permanent partition of power, nor any peaceable joint exercise of power among such discordant bodies of men. One or the other must have all or none.... The truly sincere and rational humanitarian looks with sorrow upon the future status of the poor deluded negro ... he sees either the exodus or the extinction of this disturbing element in the social and political condition of the more powerful race.[96]

Garfield read those words. Elections had delivered the freed people into the hands of a party that vowed them to extinction, dismissed them as a "disturbing element" in its exercise of power. Hence the absolute necessity now, before it was too late, to pass the Civil Rights Bill.

Three Democrats currently sitting in the House had served on the Ku Klux Commission. They had signed the minority report: Alfred Waddell, James Beck, and Sunset Cox. Waddell disdained to argue with Yankees.[97] Beck and Cox rose hastily. That portion of the text did not reflect their views. It did not reflect the views of their party. One member of the commission was to blame. He had written the offending appendix. Its words represented his views and none other. The offender, moreover, former Congressman Philadelph Van Trump of Ohio, was now dead. Let his words rest with him. "I did not read that report," Cox declared, "and never saw it."[98]

Garfield had made his point. "I am glad," he replied. He moved on to his peroration. The present struggle was like that of the whole anti-slavery movement.

95 Alfred M. Waddell, *Some Memories of My Life* (Raleigh, 1908), 112.

96 Speech of James Garfield, *Cong. Record*, 43rd Congress, 2nd Session: 1004–1005.

97 Subsequently Waddell responded in an active manner. As mayor of Wilmington in 1898, he oversaw one of the South's bloodiest race riots, all but depopulating the city's black population.

98 Cox caught himself in a lie, as the New York *Times* pointed out. When the Ku Klux Commission submitted its findings to the House, he had risen to speak. He read out several excerpts from the minority report, some appearing on the very pages he assured Garfield he had never seen. New York *Times*, February 8, 1875.

From the beginning and at every step timid souls called for preemptive retreat. They hesitated before the Fourteenth Amendment. They feared the Fifteenth Amendment. Now they trembled again, afraid of the Civil Rights Bill. Too many, following the apparent drift of public opinion, panicked by transitory election results, cried doom for the party that pursued justice. Republicans must stand by their principles. "For this act of plain justice we are told that ruin is again staring us in the face! If ruin comes from this, I welcome ruin."[99]

The final speech, after a year of speeches, belonged to Benjamin Butler. He turned to a theme guaranteed to enflame – social equality and sex. The argument was not new. Others had exploited it before, most recently James Flanagan in the Senate with his sly stories of gingerbread boys and old white women, canoodling behind haystacks while the moon shone. Pennsylvania's Congressman William Kelley also approached it humorously. Southerners, he remarked, need not worry about encounters with dark-skinned persons. "All men know that the sun and atmosphere of the southern states soon bleach the blackest African, both in hair and complexion, to the colors characteristic of the purest Saxon lineage."[100] The theme never failed to irk the guardians of southern honor. No one knew how to irk better than Benjamin Butler.

"Social equality," he began. That was the hobgoblin. Nothing could be farther from the truth. Equality in public places, equality in law, equality in public right, those were the objects of the bill. "In fact I am inclined to think that the only equality the blacks ever have in the South is social equality." He waved a paper in his hand. "I understand the highest exhibition of social equality is communication between the sexes, and I have here a statute of the State of Mississippi, which I propose to have read, which will show the extent to which social equality had place in that State before the war."[101]

Butler passed his document to the reading clerk, a decree of the Mississippi legislature, date, 1870, 11th June. James Anderson, planter, of Holmes County, petitioned the state to legitimize various offspring he had produced over a period of years, seven children from six mothers, all slaves, with whom the gentleman had copulated at his leisure. He began before the war, continued during it, and pursued his *droit du seigneur* even as federal forces closed in on central Mississippi. The clerk read the list – mothers, babies, birthdays – all in chronological order (one little boy, born in 1859, being very likely his father's

99 Speech of James A. Garfield, *Cong. Record*, 43rd Congress, 2nd Session: 1005.

100 Kelly, "Congressional Controversy over School Segregation," 543.

101 Speech of Benjamin Butler, *Cong. Record*, 43rd Congress, 2nd Session: 1005–1009. Did Butler troll through volumes of state and local ordinances to find his document? Nothing in his correspondence indicates the source. One may imagine, however, that the conduit was his sharp-witted son-in-law Adelbert Ames, Governor of Mississippi.

half-sister's son). The roll-call ended. Butler remarked: "If there is any greater social equality than that, I do not know what an exhibition of social equality is."[102]

Butler's finale included his revenge on John Young Brown. Here he fell short of expectations. He dusted off the old rebel statements Brown had made at the start of the war and read them again into the record. The House had heard this before, in June during Brown's altercation with Starkweather and Rainey. The Butcher of New Orleans was magnanimous. He bore no malice to the good people of the South. The responsibility lay with them. Let them repress the lawless element, suppress the Ku Klux and White Leagues, renounce the night riders. Let them honor the spirit of the Civil Rights Bill.

> I desire, sir, to assure gentlemen on the other side and to assure the men of the South that we are only trying to protect these poor men that we have taken from slavery and made citizens, and I adjure them now that they shall do it for themselves after this bill is passed, so that there shall never be an occasion to put a single provision of it into effect.[103]

The Speaker's gavel sounded. It remained only to vote. William Donnan of Iowa rose to a point of order. Would the House permit wives of members, by unanimous consent, to join them on the floor? Niblack of Indiana: he did not consent if it meant yielding his seat to a lady. Louisiana's Hale Sypher got in a last civil rights jab. "Does the gentleman from Indiana expect that some colored lady may make application for his seat?"[104] Niblack maintained his objection. Ladies remained at a distance.

---

102 If Butler had any rival in the art of irksomeness, that rival was Petroleum V. Nasby (David Ross Locke). Compulsory coitus, Nasby explained, was not social equality but social dominion. "The intercourse with em, of wich yoo see indications, bein outside uv the pale uv matrimony, is not, ez yoo wood suppose, the result uv unbridled licentiousnis, but is merely the assertion uv our superiority. When the lordly Caucashen ... bids a daughter uv Ham (wich, in the original Hebrew, signifies the hindquarter uv a hog) come to him, and she doth it not, he breaks her head, wich inculcates obedience." David Ross Locke, *The Struggles ... of Petroleum V. Nasby*, 263. Letter of April 1, 1866, "A Kentucky Tea Party."

103 A century later, Butler's place, Chairman of the House Judiciary Committee, and his privilege to speak the last word, fell to Emanuel Celler of New York. He quoted the Bible: "Congress harkens unto the voice of Leviticus, 'proclaiming liberty throughout the land to all the inhabitants thereof.'" After that final vote the House called upon its doyen, a man who had lived while the first Civil Rights Act lived and now lived long enough to see its successor. Chicago's Congressman Barratt O'Hara, born April 28, 1882, reflected: "Mr. Speaker, in the closeness we have come to the brotherhood of men with the purpose of the Divine, this has been one of the happiest and most soul-satisfying days of my life." *Cong. Record*, 88th Congress, 2nd Session: 15,894–15,896, 15,914.

104 *Cong. Record*, 43rd Congress, 2nd Session: 1005.

Voting commenced: five consecutive votes – one on each of the amendments, then the preamble, and on passage of the bill. Speaker Blaine began with the amendment of Stephen Kellogg. Strike out all reference to public schools. Kellogg's proposal passed overwhelmingly, but with no better than a plurality: 128 for, 48 opposed, 113 not voting. Nearly as many members abstained as voted in favor. Republicans passed it, or rather they let it pass, without enthusiasm.

Next came Alexander White's separate-but-equal amendment. The result justified the fears that Cain and Downing and others had felt, fears that pushed them to accept the lesser evil of Kellogg's compromise. White's amendment failed by 23 votes: 91 in favor, 114 opposed. Eighty-four members abstained.

Cessna called the question on his amendment, the Senate bill including mixed schools. Anxiety displaced itself to the Democratic side. Reporters noted Lamar and Beck huddled together, scribbling a tally as the vote progressed. Nervous colleagues peered over their shoulders.[105] The amendment failed. Yet voices called for mixed schools. They surpassed the call for separate-but-equal: 114 for, 148 against. Too many terrors – the angry specter of public opinion, Ulysses Grant's off-and-on rumblings of a veto, fear of the outright collapse of public education (Dr. Sears' nightmare, Dr. Dabney's delight), the fury of an electoral backlash – stood against the vision of integrated schoolrooms. The House settled for Stephen Kellogg's fallback position. It kicked off the mixed school dilemma to a future generation.

Shanks' preamble passed. Butler approved it: "It was a good old custom of our fathers to put a preamble before all laws in order that it may be understood what was meant by the law."[106] Democrats gave up. They let their words introduce an act they despised.

The clock stood with its hands at right angle: 3:00 p.m. Benjamin Butler stood to call for the previous question, on passage of the bill. At 3:40 the result was read. The Civil Rights Bill had passed the House. In the final tally there were 162 yeas, 99 nays. Eight members paired. Twenty failed to vote.[107] No Democrat broke ranks. Thirteen Republicans voted no. Two defectors were from the North: Phelps, as before, and newcomer Simeon Chittenden.[108] The rest were

105 Washington *National Republican*, February 6, 1875.

106 *Cong. Record*, 43rd Congress, 2nd Session: 1003.

107 *Cong. Record*, 43rd Congress, 2nd Session: 1011.

108 Chittenden echoed his friend Phelps. It was senseless to legislate against prejudice. The bill would only increase hatred. Furthermore it was unfair to the South. Northerners shared the same prejudices but indulged in sanctimony because few Negroes disturbed them: "I shall vote against this bill for two reasons, which I will briefly mention. I was born in Connecticut. I have for thirty-two years been a citizen of the State of New York, and I do not believe there is a single town in New England, or one in the State of New York, having railroads and telegraphs, whose white men would favor or vote for this bill if you were to

the usual suspects: Lowndes of Maryland, Lofland of Delaware, Crutchfield, Thornburgh, Harrison and Butler of Tennessee, James Sener (paired), Ambler Smith and Christopher Thomas of Virginia, Georgia's Andrew Sloan, Edwin Stanard of Missouri.

The 1874 elections, after all the campaign cries subsided, after the frantic alarms ceased to echo, had produced precisely no effect. Congressmen stood in 1875 exactly where they had stood in 1874. James Freeman of Georgia had waffled on the first votes. He ducked the last. (Mr. Freeman, his colleague Andrew Sloan announced, was absent; had he been present he would have voted No.) Sloan himself had pledged to vote No. He voted No. Richard Whiteley had voted Aye. He voted Aye. North Carolina's Charles Thomas promised black constituents he would vote Aye. He voted Aye. Clinton Cobb had agonized, and arranged to be silent on every earlier vote. He was silent again. Virginia's Stowell and Platt had supported the bill. They supported it again. Alexander White voted for the bill as amended, after his own amendment failed.

The Tennesseans maintained their positions. Barbour Lewis and David Nunn voted Aye. Horace Maynard was marked absent. The others persisted in saying no. Louisianans maintained their positions. Sypher, Sheldon and Smith lost their elections. They voted Aye, as they had before. Darrall and Morey won. They voted yes, as they had before. Arkansans maintained their positions. Asa Hodges, Oliver Snyder and William Hynes had voted Aye. They did so again. All the Missouri Republicans were lame ducks. Isaac Parker voted Aye, as did Ira Hyde. Edwin Stanard voted No. Harrison Havens had hesitated. He hesitated again, and chose not to vote. Lofland the Delawarean maintained his position. He voted no. Maryland's William Albert cast his vote once more in favor, his colleague Lowndes once more against. No one voted for the bill who had not voted for it already.[109] No one voted against it who had not already done so.[110]

---

reverse the ratio of population giving such towns in New England and in the State of New York the same proportion of black men that South Carolina and Louisiana now have.... I am a practical man, and believe it impolitic unnecessarily to vex white men, North and South, by passing this bill now. It will moreover, in my judgment, breed mischief, prejudice and cruelty to the weaker race in their struggle for a higher civilization.... He [the Negro] cannot be lifted after a hundred years of oppression in one decade to be in all respects on the same level with the white race in this country. He ought not to expect it. Time and patience are most needed for him." *Cong. Record,* 43rd Congress, 2nd Session: 982.

109 The exception was West Virginia's John Marshall Hagans, who had abstained previously each time.

110 Three northerners who had voted No in the past – Ray of Illinois, Strait of Minnesota, St. John of New York – abstained. California's Sherman Houghton had voted Aye then No then Yes. He voted Aye.

This observation must put to rest an old and unjust critique. Historians often have cited the lame duck-ness of the outgoing 43rd Congress as a reason to dismiss the Republicans' sincerity. Being beaten, so the theory goes, they no longer cared. They sent the public a poisoned pill for which they no longer had to bear the consequences.[111] Nothing in the final vote points to such cynicism. Lame duck or reelected, members voted as they had voted before, before elections came or went or relieved them of any sense of responsibility. They wrestled with their consciences. They acted as they thought best for the nation.

When the House met next, on Saturday, February 6, a magnificent bouquet sat on Ben Butler's desk: azaleas, fuchsias, a large calla lily. It bore a card: "Justice to all is equality before the law – The country owes you its gratitude: From a Friend in New York."[112] Butler's New York friend no doubt intended the flowers as a celebration. Not a few observers thought a funeral more appropriate. Newspapers pronounced the bill dead. It was a stillborn creature, the *World* assured its readers. No need to worry. The Senate would reject a text amended in the House. That was exactly as Republicans intended. Their whole exercise was "a stroke of parliamentary tactics."[113] Politicians knew better than the journalists. "This bill," Sam Randall said, "will go over to the Senate and of course be passed at once."[114]

---

111 E.g., Hoeveler, "Reconstruction and the Federal Courts," 613: "Significantly, 90 of the 162 Representatives who voted for the Civil Rights Bill were 'lame ducks' at the time. Already defeated, they were, in short, no longer responsible to their constituents." Likewise Brandwein, *Rethinking the Judicial Settlement of Reconstruction*, 68: "Significantly, 90 of the 162 Republicans who voted for the bill had lost their seats in the previous election. This was lame duck legislation."

112 New York *Times*, February 7, 1875. According to another account, the signature read differently: "From the Ladies of New York." This inspired caustic comment in the Savannah *News*. "As the word colored is omitted in the above, we are left to infer that in New York City among the 'women of the town who ply their vocation' Beast Butler has some admirers who presume to call themselves ladies." Savannah *News*, February 19, 1875.

113 New York *World*, February 6, 1875.

114 *Cong. Record*, 43rd Congress, 2nd Session: 1012.

CHAPTER 14

Dear Tom's Deception: Birth of the Civil Rights Act

Sam Randall's astute observation met with presidential approval. Ulysses Grant was eager to sign a civil rights bill. The school clause had gone. Southern public opinion had repudiated him. The Civil Rights Act would be the revenge of a jilted suitor. "He will be glad," wrote the Cincinnati *Enquirer,* "to get a lick at the South."[1] On February 15th the chief came up to Congress. From his desk in the President's Room, he urged George Edmunds. Get the bill to the floor. Pass it "with the least possible delay."[2]

Yet that task might be difficult. If the Senate rejected the House's amendments a compromise would have to be framed. Whether that could happen before Congress' close on March 3 seemed unlikely. So the Philadelphia *Inquirer* and the New York *Times* concluded.[3] The Cincinnati *Commercial* warned senators: "Should the political sentiment of the country remain reactionary it is possible six years would elapse before any measure half so liberal as that upon which the House has acted could be passed into law."[4]

Even if Republicans heeded that advice, Democrats doubtless would filibuster. The Atlanta *Constitution* reassured Georgians. They will "talk the bill to death ... fight it to the last; they have resolved to exhaust every expedient."[5] The Richmond *Dispatch* reported Senate Democrats prepared to offer sixty amendments which they would debate until the session ended.[6] The New York *Times* summed it up: "The impossibility of final enactment of a Civil Rights bill this session is so clear that there is no justification for the extraordinary efforts that have been attempted to secure a vote on the proposition in the House."[7] Democrats would "speak it out of time."

Time. For Republicans there was too little. For Democrats there was too much. Filibusters were fickle. Their opponents could outlast them. The *World's* Washington correspondent T.F. Maynard watched the clock tick. He peppered his boss, Editor Manton Marble in New York, with anxious updates. Republicans seemed to be plotting something, some final, fatal coup delivered with a dying hand. "There is no telling at what moment they may whip in the recalcitrants

1 Quoted in Atlanta *Constitution,* February 14, 1875.
2 Baltimore *Sun,* February 6, 1875.
3 Philadelphia *Inquirer,* February 8; New York *Times,* January 29, 1875.
4 Cincinnati *Commercial,* February 10, 1875.
5 Atlanta *Constitution,* February 7, 9, 1875.
6 Richmond *Dispatch,* February 9, 1875.
7 New York *Times,* January 30, 1875.

and then the choice comes," he wrote on February 12. Days passed. By the 22nd Maynard's nerves were shot: "The temper of the Radical majority is very bad, and I wish to God March 4th were here."[8]

Still Republicans made no move. The reporter's ulcers worsened. Democrats performed no heroic last stand. Nor would they. In fact, they had conceded passage of the Civil Rights Bill. Chairman Edmunds had reached an "arrangement" with his minority colleagues.[9] The bill would come to the floor on February 26. Democrats accepted the right to speak for one day. The vote would happen precisely at 2 p.m. on February 27. The bill would pass.

The Democrats' move, when it arrived, surprised their supporters. Why did they capitulate? After having expended frantic efforts to stop Charles Sumner's "iniquity," after having terrorized the public – mandatory miscegenation, degradation, socialism, dictatorship – now they calmly proposed to surrender. Surrender they did. They signaled their submission in a formal caucus. The architects of abdication were Allen Thurman and Thomas Bayard. Over some objections they convinced their colleagues to let the Civil Rights Bill go.[10] It was a matter of priorities. The party must choose: civil rights or force bills. Civil rights were preferable by far. The Baltimore *Sun* reported:

> Some of the democratic members of the House are indignant over what they term the surrender of their party friends in the Senate in the matter of the civil rights bill. They say they had a right to expect that the democratic Senators would refuse to make any bargains with the radicals in regard to this important bill, but would fight it out to the last.... A southern Democratic Senator telegraphed ... It was done so as to use as much time as possible to throw over the Force bill to within a day or two of the end of the session.... Passage of the civil rights bill, he said, would lose votes to the republican party. But the Force bill would certainly give the radicals the machinery to carry the next presidential election. Therefore, if there was to be any "sitting out," he thought it wiser for the minority to husband their strength for the Force bill.[11]

Many among the Democratic faithful found the explanation unconvincing. Why should there be any "sitting out?" Would not a stand against civil rights serve to delay the Force Bill even more? If the senators' intent was "to use as

8 T.F. Maynard to Manton Marble, February 12, 22, 1875. Manton Marble Papers, Library of Congress.

9 Savannah *News*, March 4, 1875.

10 Savannah *News*, March 4, 1875.

11 Baltimore *Sun*, February 27, 1875.

much time as possible to throw over the Force Bill," why not use even more time by making the majority exhaust its efforts first over the Civil Rights Bill? Why "husband their strength?" What weakness prevented Democrats from mounting resistance to more than one measure? There was in any case no need to yield on the Civil Rights Bill in order to ward off the Force Bill until "within a day or two" of the end of the session. There was as yet no Force Bill. That legislation passed the House on an extremely close vote on February 27. It arrived in the Senate on Monday, March 1, three days precisely before the end of the session. Democrats by then had helped Republicans clear the Civil Rights Bill out of its path.

A deal, almost surely, was in effect – though no one, to be sure, confirmed or denied it for the record – a deal neither side was anxious to explain to the public. Thurman, Bayard and Edmunds made their "arrangement." Democrats did not block the Civil Rights Bill. Republicans, as divided in the Senate as in the House, let the Force Bill die.[12] The Forty-third Congress faded into the sunset. That denouement fooled even the sharpest observers. Sam Randall himself failed to anticipate it. Randall, architect of victory, as his southern eulogists proclaimed, felt anything but victorious at the moment. He had failed to stop the Civil Rights Bill. He had not stopped the Force Bill. On Sunday, February 28, he scrawled a note to Thomas Bayard:

> Dear Tom, Prepare for the worst in the Senate. They may try and take snap judgment on you all. Grant will do anything in the world to secure this law [the Force Bill]. It is his continuance in office and his retiracy involved. Butler caught us on Thursday night with a small House. Have each man assigned to the necessary 24 hours debate.[13]

Bayard of course had no need to assign senators to their posts. The deal was done. "Dear Tom" had already arranged the anticlimactic climax. Republicans yielded the Force Bill. Democrats conceded the Civil Rights Bill. Despite the rabid rhetoric, Democrats were not at all sorry to let Republicans have their bill. The Civil Rights Bill had helped Democrats in the 1874 elections. It had, as the *Sun's* informant said, lost votes to the Republican Party. A Civil Rights

---

12 Republican stalwart *Harper's Weekly* expressed relief at the Senate's action, or inaction, in letting the Force Bill expire: "[It reflects] an unalterable opposition to the third term and condemnation of the use of the military power for any purpose not clearly defined in the Constitution ... a sign that the Republican party is not moribund." *Harper's Weekly*, March 27, 1875: 254.

13 Samuel Randall to Thomas Bayard, February 28, 1875. Thomas F. Bayard Papers, Library of Congress.

Act would lose more votes in 1876. If Republicans welcomed ruin, why should Democrats object? If they insisted on shooting themselves in the head, why obstruct their aim? Thus the Civil Rights Bill, that which they had cursed, condemned, reviled, received the Democrats' silent blessing as they waved it on its way. Bayard personally had promised election crowds in New Jersey he would rather be shot like a dog than live under a civil rights regime. Now he calmly proposed to live. A certain odor of cynicism perfumed the Democrats' design. But its politics smelled sweet.

The elections had hit Republicans hard in the Senate as in the House. Voters could not overturn their majority, but they dented it severely. Eight Republican seats were lost. Parson Brownlow's place would go to Andrew Johnson, as the ex-president, once again a Democrat, completed his political comeback.[14] John F. Lewis of Virginia and Arthur Boreman of West Virginia returned as lame ducks. Florida, after a long struggle in its closely-divided legislature, chose Democrat Charles Jones in place of Abijah Gilbert.[15] The colorful Flanagan of Texas prepared to depart. Indiana and Pennsylvania had gone Democratic. Joseph McDonald and William Wallace would take the seats of Daniel Pratt and John Scott.

In Connecticut Republicans swallowed a particularly bitter pill. Democrats named William W. Eaton to replace William Buckingham. To Republicans Eaton was the scaliest of Copperheads. "The old reptiles are coming to the surface," the Toledo *Daily Blade* complained.[16] "He was to New England what Vallandigham was to the west," fumed the Boston *Advertiser.*[17] "If Mr. Eaton's councils had been followed there would have been no United States – except the North," wrote the Hartford *Courant.*[18] To make matters worse, Senator

14 Johnson's reincarnation left Republicans bemused. "A devilish good joke," commented Stephen Kellogg; "Best thing under the circumstances," said John Peter Shanks, "but damned bad circumstances;" "Better than a Confederate general," Freeman Clarke of New York concluded; Ben Butler chuckled: "I like it much." Democratic reaction was less cheery. "I have not made up my mind what to think," was all Sam Randall would say. "A good thing for those who wish to listen to long speeches," Allen Thurman snapped. Comments in New York *Herald*, January 29, 1875.

15 Gilbert, the only senator not to vote on the civil rights bill, remained the Senate's silent man, surpassing in taciturnity even Tennessee's Henry Cooper. His lethargy, said the Savannah *News*, had at least one benefit. Since he did nothing he did nothing obnoxious: "One thing may be said for old man Gilbert.... He has not, like the rest of the carpet-baggers, sought every opportunity to revile and malign those upon whom he was feeding.... He sat and watched with indifferent eyes the Drama of Politics." Savannah *News*, January 20, March 5, 1875.

16 Toledo *Daily Blade*, May 15, 1874.

17 Quoted in Hartford *Courant*, May 16, 1874.

18 Hartford *Courant*, May 15, 1874.

Buckingham died unexpectedly on February 5. Democratic Governor Charles Ingersoll appointed Eaton to take his seat immediately. He would have the pleasure of beginning his service with a vote against the Civil Rights Bill.

Other Republican stalwarts fell to internal party rivalries. Michigan's Zachariah Chandler went down to defeat. His replacement, Isaac Christiancy, a Republican, owed his success to Democratic votes in the state legislature. The same fate befell Matthew Carpenter in Wisconsin and Alexander Ramsay in Minnesota. Mississippi Republicans held the seat; they replaced the outgoing Henry Pease with Blanche Bruce, the second African American to enter the United States Senate. Democrats lost one seat. It went to an Independent, albeit an Independent leaning Republican. California chose its sitting governor, Newton Booth, in place of John Hager.

Liberal Republicans were electorally annihilated. Democrats Francis Cockrell and Francis Kernan prepared to replace Carl Schurz in Missouri and Reuben Fenton in New York. Republicans Algernon Paddock in Nebraska and Ambrose Burnside in Rhode Island would succeed Thomas Tipton and William Sprague. The only survivors (whose terms had not yet expired), Connecticut's Orris Ferry and Morgan Hamilton of Texas, returned to the Republican Party from whence they had come. It was a chastened majority that took up once again the problem of civil rights in the Senate.

The House struggled through filibusters and wrestled with rules changes. Senators watched and waited. They did hear a new and original contribution to the civil rights discussion. On February 17 John Sharpenstein Hager, Democrat of California, took the floor; Princeton graduate, Regent of the University of California. The bald, bespectacled senator lectured with professorial objectivity. He offered a scientific exposition, based upon the latest models of Darwinian Theory. He relied on empirical fact: "Sir, I shall not undertake to discuss this question theologically or psychologically. I am willing to concede that Adam was the great final consummation of the works of the Almighty ... but how He arrived at this great consummation we have not been informed. Whether it was by gradual advancement or by one act of creation has not been revealed to us."

> Paleontology has revealed footsteps in the sands of time – stepping-stones – showing that much has been dropped by the wayside.... When we see the monkey sometimes dressed in our habiliments we are amused and surprised at his displays of watchfulness and intelligence. He looks something like our race, but we do not regard him as such. A step higher and we have the ourang and the chimpanzee, and the resemblance is yet greater, but we do not receive them as of the human family. Still a

> step upward and we have the gorilla, and there the resemblance is still stronger ... but we do not regard him as of the human family.... Leaving the gorilla and advancing upward we reach the savage of Australia and Borneo, the wild man of the interior of those islands, untamable and unapproachable; without a written or spoken language; uttering an unintelligible muttering gibberish, and fleeing from the face of the white man like the beasts of the forest. Does humanity commence here?[19]

Evolution molded life forms hierarchically. It applied to apes, to horses, to humans.

> When we leave the Australian savage and pursue our investigations further through the different races or species or types of mankind – place the negro where you please, I have no disposition to misplace him – through the Esquimaux and the Digger Indian, the lowest of the race on this continent, through the Kanaka, the Hottentot, the Arab, the Mongolian &c., we finally reach the last great consummation, the crowning work of the Almighty when He rested, the Caucasian Adam, the type of man I see about me here in this Chamber.... The thoroughbred, the donkey, the Shetland pony, and the zebra are different species of the same race – the *genus equus*; are they equal? I do not think the donkey is the equal of the horse; nor do I think it possible to legislate them into physical or social equality.[20]

---

19 Speech of John Hager, *Cong. Record*, 43rd Congress, 2nd Session, Appendix: 52–53. The senator's reference to a creature, the "wild man of Borneo," not now recognized by science (nor to be confused with orangutans, which Hager listed separately, or certain sideshow performers exhibited by P.T. Barnum) adverted to a story recently retailed in the press. The Cincinnati *Commercial* posted the piece on April 10. The Mobile *Register* printed it on May 14, both quoting an original headlined in the Siam *Weekly Advertiser*: "A Race of Men Who Have Not Learned to Talk – On the island of Borneo has been found a certain race of wild creatures, of which kindred varieties have been discovered in the Philippine Islands, Tierra del Fuego, and in South America. They walk, usually almost erect, on two legs, and in that attitude measure about four feet in height. They construct no habitations, form no families, scarcely associate together, sleep in caves, feed on snakes and vermin, on ant's eggs, and on each other. They can not be tamed or forced to any labor, and are hunted and shot among the trees like the great gorilla, of which they are a stunted copy. When captured alive one finds with surprise that their uncouth jabbering sounds are like articulated language. They turn up a human face to gaze at their captors, and females show instincts of modesty. In fine, these wretched beings are men and women."

20 The erudite senator abused his erudition. All non-extinct humans, he well knew, belong to a single species (*homo sapiens*) in contrast to equines, the zebra (*equus quagga*), the mule (*equus africanus*) and the horse (*equus ferus*). Whence his deliberately-obfuscated

Yield dominance to one inferior species, yield it to all.

> How long will it be before the Chinese will take the same position on the Pacific? If you recognize universal political and social equality among races and species of man, you cannot deny to him what you require shall be yielded to the negro.... It is not the part of wisdom nor does humanity require that, either by legislation or by usurpation, we should place the negro or the Mongolian in dominion over men of our own race and lineage or force them into social relations in violation of the laws of creation and the rational judgment of mankind.

Senators pondered the steppingstones of life. The Civil Rights Bill stepped back into the Senate. It went first to the Judiciary Committee. The committee, as Sam Randall had predicted, accepted the House's amendments. It had no choice. On February 15, 1875, one year and one day exactly from the day Frederick Frelinghuysen had assured Charles Sumner that his original, S.1, would soon return to the floor, it returned. S.1 had become H.R.796. The House relieved S.1 of two clauses, cemeteries and schools. Frelinghuysen found himself relieved of responsibility. George Edmunds took charge of the bill. Democrats promised not to fight. Edmunds had only to arrange a last discussion, as agreed with Tom Bayard, and call for a vote.

Another week passed. On schedule, February 26, debate opened. Allen Thurman took the floor. He focused attention on a part of the bill that had so far inspired little comment, the jury clause, Section 4: "That no citizen possessing all other qualifications which are or may be prescribed by law shall be disqualified for service as a grand or petit juror in any court of the United States, or of any State, on account of race, color, or previous condition of servitude." The House had not objected. Thurman objected. Nothing in the constitution gave Congress the right to determine the qualifications of jurymen in the courts of a sovereign state. Certainly the Fourteenth Amendment conferred no such right, restricted as it was to privileges or immunities of United States citizens. States routinely made distinctions in regulating service they imposed. They developed qualifications of age, of education, of literacy, of gender. No one presumed to say that those discriminations violated the Fourteenth Amendment. "Take the case of a person who cannot speak or understand one word of the English language. May not the State say that he shall not be a juror?"

---

phrase, "races or species or types of mankind – place the negro where you please." See Ensuing quotations.

> The mere fact that persons born within the United States or here naturalized become citizens of the United States and of the State wherein they reside, confers no right to be selected or to act as jurors.... When was it that the bare fact of citizenship of the United States deprived a State of the right to provide what should be the qualification of an individual to entitle him to sit as a juror in its own courts? It is not depriving any individual of life, or liberty, or property to refuse to seat him in the jury-box.... She [the State] does not deny to any individual within the jurisdiction of the State the equal protection of her laws when she provides what shall be the qualification of the jurors in that State.[21]

George Boutwell replied. The bill in no way interfered with a state's right to set qualifications for its jurors. It said only that those qualifications must apply to all persons regardless of race. The Fourteenth Amendment, moreover, did address discrimination in just this case. It guaranteed the privileges and immunities of citizens of the United States. "What is the first privilege of citizens of the United States? That they are citizens of the State wherein they reside. And what is the chief right of the citizen of the State? That he is the equal before the law of every other citizen." To deny a citizen the right to sit upon a jury of his peers denied him that fundamental right of equality: "You shall not in the State of Ohio or in Massachusetts or in Maryland, say that a man shall not sit upon a jury because he is a black man or because he is of the German race or because he has been held in slavery, and I might say for other reasons. If for other reasons discriminations were made by the laws of any of these States, we might under the fourteenth amendment protect men from such discriminations."[22]

Oliver Morton joined the debate. It was not a question of privileges or immunities but of equal protection of the law. There the Fourteenth Amendment applied.[23]

> I would like to submit to the judgment of the Senate and of the country this proposition: Whether the colored man enjoys the equal protection of the law, the equal benefit of the law, if colored men are not permitted to sit upon juries? Will any man pretend that where the right to sit upon juries is given exclusively to white men, the colored men of that State have the equal protection of the laws? Does a State that gives the exclusive

21 Speech of Allen Thurman, *Cong. Record,* 43rd Congress, 2nd Session: 1791–1792.

22 Remarks of George Boutwell, *Cong. Record,* 43rd Congress, 2nd Session: 1792–1793.

23 Remarks of Oliver Morton and ensuing colloquy, *Cong. Record,* 43rd Congress, 2nd Session: 1793–1797.

> right to sit upon juries to white men, give the equal protection of the laws of that State to colored men? I say no.... If the State of North Carolina by law provides that no man but a white man shall sit upon a jury ... I mean to say that the whole colored race of North Carolina does not enjoy the equal protection of the laws, and how any man of common sense can deny it I cannot understand.

Joseph Rodman West of Louisiana interjected. "Reverse the proposition and how would it do in South Carolina?" Precisely, Morton agreed. "There is the State of South Carolina with a large majority of colored men. Suppose that State should pass a law that no man should sit on a jury but a colored man.... Then we should find the white men of South Carolina coming up here and claiming the benefit of the fourteenth amendment."

Morton grew heated. "I put this bill upon a ground that is impregnable," he sputtered. "No sophistry can answer it." Leaning in his seat, Allen Thurman grinned. Morton glared. "The Senator from Ohio smiles. Let him tell the Senate first what is meant by 'the equal protection of the laws.' Let him answer this question." Thurman gazed benignly. "Has the Senator concluded? I do not want to interrupt you." Morton yielded for a response. Thurman responded. "The Senator from Indiana has very truly said that his argument cannot be answered by sophistry. But it can be answered by reason." Thurman unfolded his reason. It rested upon the majestic sophistry of the law.

> Now the first thing that I have to say to that Senator is that not one woman in all the United States or the Territories thereof, outside of Wyoming Territory, is qualified to sit in a jury-box. Are they not equally protected? Do they not receive the protection of the laws? When did it come that our mothers and wives and sisters were deprived of the equal protection of the laws? But that is not all. Do not our children under the age of twenty-one years receive the equal protection of the law? Yet not one of them is qualified to sit in a jury-box.

The equal protection clause of the Fourteenth Amendment spread its aegis over everyone. It comprehended every human being under the jurisdiction of the United States. Republicans, he was told, insisted upon that point. Equal protection of the law, "you shall not deny it to any person."

> You shall not deny it to the alien, you shall not deny it to the Chinaman ... you shall not deny it to any person within your jurisdiction, be he sane or insane, be he old or young, be he innocent or criminal, be he learned

> or be he ignorant. Every human being within the jurisdiction of the State shall be entitled to the equal protection of the laws; but is every human being in that State entitled to sit upon a jury? Do you deprive the minor of the equal protection of the law when you try his case by men of mature age? Do you deprive women of the equal protection of the laws when you try their cases by their brothers or husbands or fathers? ... The idea which the Senator says no sane man can contest is simply, with great respect to him, without the slightest foundation. "The equal protection of the laws" is one thing; political privileges are another thing; and privileges to administer the laws of the land as judges, jurors, or in any other character are another and quite a different thing.

Morton fairly burst. Allen Thurman's confounding logic left him confounded.

> My question is this, and I come right back to it ... whether the colored men of North Carolina have the equal protection of the laws when the control of their right to life, liberty, and property is placed exclusively in the hands of another race of men, hostile to them, in many respects prejudiced against them, men who have been educated and taught to believe that colored men have no civil and political rights that white men are bound to respect. And yet the Senator would tell me that that is giving them the equal protection of the laws. I say no; the common sense of mankind will revolt at that proposition. But my friend, chivalrous and bold as he is in defending the doctrine of inequality, falls back under the protection of the women. [Laughter] He gets behind the ladies. That has always been the tactic ... "do women vote; do women sit on juries?" ... I am one of those who believe in the right of women to vote, and I have always believed in that; but because that right has been withheld from them, no argument can be made on that ground.... But my friend from Ohio thought his protection in getting behind the women was not sufficient, and so he got behind the children. [Laughter] ... That is the kind of logic which defends these great wrongs and inequalities. It is the logic of prejudice.

Thurman's sly smile broadened.

> Mr. President, when I was a boy at school we had an old Scotch professor of logic who was very exigent in his rule that we should reason fairly and logically.... He was asked one day by one of the students who had found himself pinned by his adversary in a corner by the inexorable logic of the

> argument, "Professor, what must I do in this strait in which I find myself?" Said he, "My son, I do not know anything you can do but to declaim." [Laughter] Now, I think that my friend from Indiana must have taken lessons from that same old professor, for when he found himself driven in a corner by inexorable logic, his answer is to make a stump speech.

The logic was inexorable. The Fourteenth Amendment made no distinctions. If the senator wished to follow his conception, come one come all. Open the jury-box wide. Open it to all human beings – "to any person" – to the women, to the children, to everyone, to tiny infants at the breast, to babbling idiots, to the comatose and the insane. If it could be closed to one category of persons it could be closed to another. It could be closed to persons of a given race or a certain color. As to the women, Thurman rose gallantly: "I am in favor of giving the white women of this country as much protection of the laws as I give the colored man. If the Senator calls that getting behind the women, then God grant that I may always have such an array before me."

Morton said nothing, his head perhaps swimming with logical deductions, lunatic jurymen drooling in the jury-box, bawling babies wheeled to court in perambulators. Another voice joined the discussion: Augustus Merrimon of North Carolina. The honest, earnest, open-hearted senator had promised to serve all his constituents, black and white. As a matter of humanity he agreed with Oliver Morton. Black people ought not to be excluded. "If he [Morton] asks me whether I think it prudent to exclude the negro from sitting in the jury-box ... I answer no. I believe it is our duty to the colored race to do the best we can by them, to educate them, to encourage them, and to protect them everywhere, and to fit them for the rights of citizenship." But as a matter of law he agreed with Allen Thurman.

> The Senator puts this case: He says suppose in South Carolina, where the colored race have the majority and can control, the Legislature should see fit to pass a law providing that none but negroes should sit upon juries, would there not be a great outcry on the part of the white people? I admit there would be a great outcry. I think it would be a great outrage.... But if the Senator asks me whether they have the power to do so, I answer yes, they have such power. They have the constitutional power to do it.

Indeed it transcended constitutionality. It was America. It was freedom. Free people granted privileges, or denied them, save only the fundamental privileges: life, liberty and property. Free people did unto others, and others did unto them.

> If the negroes should have the ascendancy in any State, if they should compose the Legislature, if they should compose the convention of the State to form the organic law, they could provide that no white man should be governor, that no white man should hold office because he is a white man. I think that would be very unwise, very impolitic, very wrong, but still they have the power … and the white man could not say that he did not have equal protection of the law.… All he could ask would be that the negro judge should administer the law to him fairly and justly.[24]

Saturday, February 27, 1875. The Civil Rights Bill reached its decisive moment. The schedule was strictly set. Amendments were in order, but discussion fell under a five-minute rule. At 2 o'clock p.m., come what may, the Senate would vote. Chairman Edmunds reserved the last half-hour for himself. Vice-President Wilson, enjoying his final Indian summer of good health, sat in the Chair. Spectators crowded the galleries; African Americans awaited the fulfillment of their hopes. The Savannah *News'* reporter eyed them as he brooded in increasing irritation.

> During yesterday and to-day the Senate galleries have been filled with the filthy negroes who overflow this District, listening with all ears to the debate. When the bill was finally passed they could scarcely contain themselves for joy. They roamed through all the corridors of the Capitol, jostling and pushing the white people aside with the most impudent gestures and language.[25]

Senators who had not yet immortalized their thoughts sought a chance to speak. Thomas Bayard stepped up. Thanks to Dear Tom's arrangement, the Civil Rights Bill would soon become a law. Critics accused the Delaware senator of a sellout. He protested. A civil rights act would pass, yes, but it would be struck down. Meanwhile he wanted to make clear his dislike.

> [It bears] evil to every section of the country. It is not a blow directed against one section only, but from the Passamaquoddy to the Rio Grande the principles that pervade this bill and the powers that are asserted upon the face of it extend down deep into the foundations of American liberty.[26]

---

24 *Cong. Record,* 43rd Congress, 2nd Session: 1796–1797.

25 Savannah *News,* March 4, 1875.

26 *Cong. Record,* 43rd Congress, 2nd Session, Appendix: 113.

Republicans forced their will upon an unwilling American people. They would not prevail. They could not prevail, nor halt humanity's progress, nor stop the march of civilization to its destined goal: Anglo-Saxon dominion. That would be the end, reducing all races, all cultures, all languages even, to irrelevance or extinction.

> The admixture of Anglo-Saxon-Celtic blood makes a current broad enough and strong enough and deep enough to carry its civilization with the course of the sun, and, as does the reveille of the English drum keep pace with its march around the earth, so also does the English tongue.... A century hence there will be one hundred and fifty millions of English-speaking people on this continent and of the Anglo-Saxon-Celtic race – the white race of commingled blood, English, Celtic, and Germanic. The question of race is then settled; it is extinguished. The Indian will have disappeared. The African will be no stronger, if as strong; but in the aggregate a mere atom in the world of being. Time and population will settle for the aggressive race what you vainly attempt to settle by legislation. You will have equality among races.... Nature will settle a question that you cannot by law.[27]

Matthew Carpenter took the floor. The Wisconsin senator was the only Republican member of the Judiciary Committee to oppose the bill. Now he was a lame duck.[28] He wanted to explain. Democrats happily yielded him the time. His explanation did not rely on Saxon supremacy, but the law. "I entertain, as strongly as any Senator, the sentiments which have inspired this bill. But I cannot go beyond the limits of the Constitution." Carpenter reviewed the constitutional objections. The Fourteenth Amendment had no power to regulate the acts of individuals. His colleagues in the Committee nonetheless insisted on the Fourteenth Amendment. They knew it was a gamble. They did consider an alternative – the commerce clause. But they found that proposition weaker

---

27 *Cong. Record*, 43rd Congress, 2nd Session, Appendix: 116.

28 See Herman J. Deutsch, "Carpenter and the Senatorial Election of 1875 in Wisconsin," *Wisconsin Magazine of History*, 16 (1932): 26–46. The senator's defense of unpopular acts, the "press-gag" law, Credit Mobilier, rankled within the party. He had even defended the Salary Grab, committing a spectacular, though amusing, gaffe in the process. Congressmen, he argued, needed adequate compensation so they could afford to live at Washington along with their families. Otherwise they might have to find new families: "The laxity of life is restrained by the supervision of a wife, and the heart is kept alive to the better feelings of our nature by the sweet voices and the tender touch of our children. Members of Congress will have families in Washington. It is better that they should have their own."

than the amendment because the bill applied to intrastate as well as interstate commerce:

> This [bill] might be sustained as a regulation of commerce if confined to the commerce over which Congress possesses the power of regulation.... [But] it applies to every person or corporation engaged in transportation from point to point within a State as well as to those engaged in transportation among the several States.... For instance, in regulating commerce among the States, Congress might provide that every person engaged in such commerce be entitled to the accommodation of inns in the several States through which he might pass in the prosecution of his business, and perhaps, upon the theory that a cheerful mind is favorable to enterprise, might provide that he should be admitted to theaters and other places of public amusement in the States wherein he might be temporarily sojourning during the transaction of his business. Such provision ... would be somewhat fantastic as a regulation of commerce; and yet, if Congress saw fit so to provide, such provision might be sustained as relating to a subject over which Congress has jurisdiction. But the bill under consideration does not rest upon this ground, because its provisions are not confined to persons engaged in such [interstate] commerce.[29]

"I am consoled," Carpenter concluded, "if it should become a law, the judicial courts will intervene to vindicate the Constitution." Carpenter's discussion put an impressive punctuation to the opposition's case. The New York *Times* printed the speech in its entirety, advising readers to note the conclusive argument.[30]

Oliver Morton failed to find anything conclusive. Thurman's "inexorable logic" still baffled him. How could it be? Or rather, how could it not be a denial of equal protection of the law? Formerly in England laws had excluded Jews from the jury-box. "The adjudication of their rights was placed exclusively in the hands of the Christians, at that time bitterly prejudiced against the whole Jewish sect and persecuting them upon all occasions." Surely the Jews then did not enjoy equal protection of the laws.[31]

George Edmunds came to Morton's aid. Caustic as always, he looked at Allen Thurman. The gentleman from Ohio, he was sure, being noted for his humanitarian instincts, opposed the Civil Rights Bill with only the most humane

29 Speech of Matthew Carpenter, *Cong. Record*, 43rd Congress, 2nd Session: 1861.

30 New York *Times*, February 28, 1875.

31 *Cong. Record*, 43rd Congress, 2nd Session: 1864.

motives. "He and his party have shown it by their votes upon the constitutional amendments, although they were always against them; they have shown it by their votes on the civil-rights bill that Judge Trumbull first brought forward in 1866; they have shown it on subsequent bills, on reconstruction and everything." But Thurman's reasoning was flawed.

> If the Constitution of the United States does not protect the equality of rights ... then every State has the right to say, and Congress has a right to say, notwithstanding the Constitution, that no Roman Catholic shall ever sit on a jury; that no Presbyterian shall ever sit on a jury ... that no man of German nativity shall ever be authorized to stand up in a court of justice to defend his rights. Why, Mr. President, "the thing won't do," to borrow a favorite phrase of the Senator from Ohio.[32]

Two o'clock neared. Thurman tried again. It was not a matter of humanity, or of justice. It was not a matter of fairness or common sense. It was a matter of law.

> It is admitted that a State may make a discrimination upon the line of ignorance, of education, and that is perfectly right ... but it is said that when you come to the question of race, then you can make no discrimination at all... No man has been able to point out one word in the Constitution which says you shall make no discrimination on account of race but you may discriminate on any other account you see fit.[33]

Thurman called for the question, a vote on his amendment to strike out the jury clause. The jury clause remained. Thurman offered another amendment,

---

32 Speech of George Edmunds, *Cong. Record*, 43rd Congress, 2nd Session: 1866.

33 Ultimately the Supreme Court found a word. The jury clause remained the only section of the Civil Rights Act whose validity it upheld. By that time the Court had served notice it would disagree with the Senator from Ohio. It spoke in its 1880 decision in the case of Strouder v. West Virginia. The Constitution did permit states to make discriminations. But it did not, thanks to the Fourteenth Amendment, permit them to discriminate on the basis of race: "We do not say that, within the limits from which it is not excluded by the amendment, a state may not prescribe the qualifications of its jurors," said the Court, Mr. Justice Strong writing for the majority, "and in so doing, make discriminations. It may confine its selection to males, to freeholders, to citizens, to persons within certain ages, or to persons having educational qualifications. We do not believe the Fourteenth Amendment was ever intended to prohibit this. Looking at its history, it is clear it had no such purpose. Its aim was against discrimination because of race or color. As we have said more than once, its design was to protect an emancipated race, and to strike down all possible legal discriminations against those who belong to it." *Strauder v. West Virginia* 100 U.S. 303 (1880).

to reduce the fines imposed in the penalty clause. It too was rejected. Republicans could allow no changes. The bill must be as the House had handed it to them.

One more amendment nevertheless came to the floor. It provided a moment of welcome relief. A little levity broke the tension. Thomas Tipton of Nebraska, sharp-tongued plainsman, minister of the Methodist Episcopal Church, proposed to strike out the word "theaters" and insert the word "churches." Tipton's pious intention unintentionally produced mirthful consequences. Illinois' Richard Oglesby rose. "I ask the clerk to read the bill as it will stand if it shall be amended as proposed by the Senator from Nebraska." Solemnly the clerk took up the document:

> All persons within the jurisdiction of the United States shall be entitled to the full and equal enjoyment of the accommodations, advantages, facilities, and privileges of inns, public conveyances on land or water, churches, and other places of public amusement. [Laughter][34]

George Edmunds stood. After a year of speeches came the final speech. The Democratic Party, Edmunds resumed, had obstructed every advance to social justice. "There has been no measure either for repressing rebellion, carrying on the war, securing the fruits of the war, that has found any favor with that party; and so I am not surprised that when we come now in some measure ... to protect the fundamental rights of citizens of the United States under its Constitution, we find the same party occupying the same old attitude." Civil rights transcended Allen Thurman's casuistic legal exercises. It embodied basic human values.

> Senators seem to be greatly alarmed when this simple proposition of common right inherent in everybody is put into a statute-book, which carries out a constitution which declares that every privilege and every immunity of an American citizen shall be sacred and protected by the power of the nation.... The real thing, Mr. President, is that there lies in this Constitution, just as in Magna Charta and as in the bills of rights of all the States, a series of declarations that the rights of citizens shall not be invaded ... that these common rights, which belong necessarily to all men alike in the reason of things, shall not be invaded on the pretence that a man is of a particular race or a particular religion.[35]

34 *Cong. Record*, 43rd Congress, 2nd Session: 1869.

35 Speech of George Edmunds, *Cong. Record*, 43rd Congress, 2nd Session: 1869–1870.

Henry Wilson tapped his gavel. Time had expired. Lewis Bogy called out: "Is it in order to reply to the speech made by the Senator from Vermont?" Cries of "No, No!" Enough had been said. The vote commenced. Sixty-four senators responded to their name. The Civil Rights Bill – H.R.796, formerly S.1 – as amended in the House, passed the Senate.

The vote was 38 to 26. One Republican, Phineas Hitchcock of Nebraska (aye), paired with one Democrat, John Johnston of Virginia (Nay). Just as their counterparts had in the House, senators remained faithful to their positions. Only one vote changed. West Virginia's Arthur Boreman had voted no on May 23. Now he voted Aye. He offered no explanation for his change of mind. Two Republicans voted No, as they had before: Matthew Carpenter, and Lewis of Virginia. All the Democrats opposed the bill. All the Liberal Republicans opposed the bill. This time Carl Schurz stood up and voted No. The record marked seven senators absent. Stephen Dorsey, Hannibal Hamlin, and Bainbridge Wadleigh would certainly have voted aye, as they had before. Brownlow, Fenton of New York, and Morrill of Maine had made their opposition clear. Florida's Abijah Gilbert remained a blank. He neither spoke nor voted.[36]

Monday, March 1. Orville Babcock, private secretary to the president, entered the capitol to communicate a message in writing. The Chief Executive informed the House of Representatives of six legislative measures to which he had put his signature: H.R.135, a joint resolution appointing new managers of the National Homes for Disabled Veteran Soldiers (*vice* Ben Butler and Lewis Gunckel resigned); H.R.1938, settlement of railway bills; H.R.3700, 3708 and 3717, granting pensions to veteran soldier Teter Wolfgong and to veterans' survivors Eunice Wilson and Sarah McAdams; H.R.796, "an act to protect all citizens in their civil and legal rights."[37]

Wednesday, March 3, 1875, 12:00 noon, the Forty-third Congress came to an end. In the Senate disorder reigned. Vice-President Wilson's strength failed him. He handed the gavel to Senator Ingalls and retired to his private room. "The Forty-third Congress ended amid uproar and confusion indescribable," Ingalls wrote his wife. "Such tumult and turmoil I never witnessed before."[38] The chamber resembled a battle-field after a battle, the detritus of combat strewn upon the ground: "Scraps of waste paper, torn up speeches and

36 In 1964 four non-southern senators voted no, all Republicans: Norris Cotton of New Hampshire, Bourke Hickenlooper of Iowa, Milward Simpson of Wyoming, and Arizona's Barry Goldwater. Six southern senators voted yes: James Beall and Daniel Brewster of Maryland (Republican and Democrat), Republican John Sherman Cooper of Kentucky, Democrats Edward Long and Stuart Symington of Missouri and Ralph Yarborough of Texas.

37 *Cong. Record*, 43rd Congress, 2nd Session: 2013.

38 John J. Ingalls, *Essays, Addresses, and Orations*, 533.

mutilated eloquence, bills and billets-doux, duns and what not, lay scattered all over the floor in one white indistinguishable litter."[39] Democrats, basking in the elections, were jubilant; Republicans less so. Senator Chandler wept softly.

On the House side Ben Butler appeared "quiet and subdued."[40] Sunset Cox was in rarest good humor. He tried to cheer up departing Republican friends. Some did not react cheerily. "I can joke with all the defeated Republicans but two," he told reporters. "There is a tender mournfulness about old Poland and Ellis Roberts which dampens all attempts at gayety. Ellis hasn't smiled once since he has been back, and Poland glares at me whenever I speak to him, as though I were a robber of hen roosts."[41]

James Blaine called the House to order for the last time. For the last time he addressed it as Speaker. Spectators – one estimate put the crowd around the capitol at five thousand – flocked to witness the end. "The scepter has passed away from those so unworthy to wield it," wrote the Louisville *Courier-Journal*, "to safer and purer hands."[42] The gavel rapped three times. Members came to their feet, "almost breathless silence."

For a moment the acrimony of the past weeks lifted. James Blaine's final, gracious words moved all present. He thanked Republicans for the honor they had accorded him. "Gentlemen, I close with this hour a six year's service as Speaker of the House of Representatives. It would be the gravest insensibility to the honors and responsibilities of life not to be deeply touched by so signal a mark of public esteem as that which I have thrice received at the hands of my political associates." He thanked Democrats for the respect they had shown him. "To those with whom I differ in my party relations, the minority of this House, I tender my acknowledgments for the generous courtesy with which they have treated me." He offered a tribute to democracy.

> By one of those sudden and decisive changes which distinguish popular institutions, and which conspicuously mark a free people, that minority is transformed in the ensuing Congress to the governing power of the House. However it might possibly have been under other circumstances, that event necessarily renders these words my farewell to the chair.... I perform my only remaining duty in declaring that the Forty-third Congress has reached its constitutional limit and that the House of

39 Louisville *Courier-Journal*, March 5, 1875.
40 Baltimore *Sun*, March 4, 1875.
41 Norfolk *Virginian*, March 14, 1875.
42 Louisville *Courier-Journal*, March 5, 1875.

> Representatives stands adjourned without day. [Earnest and prolonged applause in all parts of the Hall][43]

"When he closed, threw down the gavel, and left the chair," wrote the New York *Tribune's* correspondent, "no such scene has been witnessed in the House by the oldest habitué of the Capitol."[44] Applause rang from the galleries and from the floor. Members crowded around the retiring Speaker. They pressed his hand and embraced him. James Blaine seemed "visibly affected." The hall began to clear. "The 43rd Congress was among the things of the past."

Much of the public remained unimpressed. Newspapers, Republican sheets and Democratic, wished a thorough good riddance to the Forty-Third Congress. "Dilatory, vacillating, timid, distracted, and inefficient," pronounced the Boston *Journal* (Republican). "If ever a Congress died unlamented the 43rd is exactly that one," wrote the Baltimore *Gazette* (Democratic).[45] Tommy Hauck, the Atlanta *Constitution's* chatty Washington correspondent, wired home: "The forty-third congress has ceased to exist. It expired to-day at noon with the thump of the speaker's gavel.... It will live in history for the evil it wrought, and for the evil it sought to do."[46] In New Orleans citizens fired off a salute of artillery, "to celebrate this happy event."[47] North Carolina's legislature introduced a resolution of rejoicing in the expiration of the Forty-Third Congress.

Not all observers appraised the work of the late legislators so unkindly. They had vacillated, distracted at times and daunted by hard choices, but in that they only mirrored the mood of the nation they represented, its people also unsure and deeply divided. "The power of public opinion has never been greater than now," concluded the Providence *Journal*. "Both in what [Congress] has done and what it has left undone is found the response to the popular will."[48] The Paterson *Press* found words of praise:

> These three hundred and sixty-six representatives in the senate and House ... have been, during a long period of business depression and political turmoil and contention, the focus of the criticism of a nation of fifty millions of people, and held by them responsible for every evil that befell, or every failure to remedy a wrong or satisfy a complaint. And this when the people themselves were radically divided or fiercely

43 *Cong. Record*, 43rd Congress, 2nd Session: 2276.
44 New York *Tribune*, March 5, 1875.
45 Boston *Journal* and Baltimore *Gazette* quoted in New York *Tribune*, March 8, 1875.
46 Atlanta *Constitution*, March 7, 1875.
47 New Orleans *Abeille*, March 6, 1875.
48 Quoted in Springfield *Republican*, March 6, 1875.

> contentious among themselves.... Justice demands that the final verdict shall not be passed even upon its controverted acts until experience has proved either their wisdom or their folly. And so *vale* the much abused, but we believe still faithful Forty-third Congress.[49]

A divided nation was left to decide: did the Forty-third Congress bequeath wisdom or folly? The Supreme Court gave it little time to decide. The Civil Rights Act died of judicial review in 1883. Its memory faded. The memory of its Congress faded too. But its ghost lingered. February 7, 1925, fifty years less one month from that day on which James Blaine's gavel fell, Isaac Sherwood of Ohio stood up. He was 89 years old, last survivor of his class still sitting as a Representative of the people. Speaker Frederick Gillett yielded him the floor. He looked about him. "Mr. Speaker, it is 52 years since I first drifted into this great body of honored citizens. I am the last leaf upon the tree."[50] His thoughts faded back to another century. He saw the House become as it had been. Gas lamps replaced electricity. Old faces materialized in their long-ago seats.

> There were historical characters in that Congress.... Just across the aisle sat in constant conflict two intellectual athletes – Gen. Benjamin Butler of Massachusetts, and S.S. Cox, of New York, formerly of Ohio – who constantly measured the strength and potency of their rasping scimitars. Halfway down the aisle sat Gen. James A. Garfield, afterward President, then chairman of the Committee on Appropriations. Right in front in his wheeled chair sat Alexander H. Stephens of Georgia, the Vice-President of the Confederacy.

The people's representatives then had to work hard. They were close to the people. "Members were allowed no secretary – we had to rent our offices out of our salary, and we had to take pen in hand to answer kicking letters from constituents." Times had changed, the old man thought, not necessarily improved. "There were no typewriting machines ... no moving pictures. Tainted actresses were not then our popular stars of the stage. We had no jazz music." Congress

49 Paterson *Press*, March 5, 1875.

50 Isaac Sherwood's farewell, *Cong. Record*, 68th Congress, 2nd Session: 3228–3229. Eight other members of the 43rd Congress remained alive. William McLean of Texas died a few weeks later, on March 13, 1925; Illinois' Joe Cannon, Ira Hyde of Missouri and Jackson Orr of Iowa died in 1926; Florida's William Purman departed in 1928; Alabamian Frederick Bromberg lived on until 1930, Henry O. Pratt of Iowa until 1931. Isaac Sherwood died eight months after his farewell speech. John Roy Lynch, truly the last leaf, drifted away in Chicago on November 2, 1939.

had contended with great issues: "We were called to deal with both ethical and fundamental questions growing out of the great war; questions that stirred the blood and commanded the most potent mental endeavor." How well had he and his departed fellows dealt with those questions? The aged congressman did not judge. They had done what they could do. The last active member of the Forty-third Congress left the stage with a joke: "My age is 90 years. I think I have reached the retiring age. I propose now to devote myself to accumulating some property to take care of me when I get old. [Laughter]"

CHAPTER 15

De Pervisions, Josiar: Civil Rights Dawn

Somewhere in the editorial offices of the Fayetteville, Tennessee, *Express* a satirist resided. He deserved to have traded barbs with Mark Twain or David Ross Locke. Fate decreed that he dwell in anonymity in a small-town newsroom. Late in May, 1874, just as the Civil Rights Bill emerged from the Senate, he invented for the amusement of Fayetteville's public a dialogue: "De Pervisions, Josiar." Editor John B. Smith published it. From a humble start "De Pervisions" went forth, printed and reprinted.

De Pervisions, Josiar

A sapient-looking Fayetteville darkey, oscillating between twenty and twenty-five summers, overtook an old negro the other day, and wedging him in the fence corner, proceeded to acquaint him with all the gorgeous provisions of the Civil Rights bill. Young Africa imparted to Old Africa a fund of valuable information, thusly:

"Well, Uncle Billy, Sumner's Swivel Rights Bill has passed de Senate ob de United States widout a murmur."

"Is dat so, Josiar?"

"Jess so, Uncle Billy. And say, Uncle Billy, we colored pussons is gwine to see whose pervisions is in de pot. We are gwine to be allowed to ride free on de railroads, smoke in de ladies' car, and put our feet on de percussions ob de seats wheneber we dam please."

"Is dat so, Josiar?"

"Jess so, Uncle Billy. And say, Uncle Billy, we's gwine to be allowed to stop at de hotels and set at de head ob de table, and hab de biggest slices ob de chickens, and lay around in de parlor and spit on de carpets, and make de white trash hustle demselves and wait on us widout grumblin'; and when de boss ob de concern shoves a bill at us we'll hab him sent to Washington and obscured in de plenipotentiary."

"Is *dat* so, Josiar?"

"Jess so, Uncle Billy. And say, Uncle Billy, we's gwine to be allowed to go to de white schools and set up on de flatform wid de teacher and learn gehography, triggermanometry, gehominy, Latin, Dutch, French, Choctaw, algeebray, rheumatics, de rule ob thrice and de diarrhea."

"Good gracious! Is dat so, Josiar?"

"Jess so, Uncle Billy. And say, Uncle Billy, we's gwine to be allowed to be buried in italic coffins wid looking glasses on top ob dem, and dey will hab to carry us on a hearse to de grabe yard and burry us on top ob de white folks, so when de day ob resurrection am arrived, and de angel Gabriel come tootin' along he'll sing out troo his trumpet, 'All ob you colored gemmen rise fust!' And say, Uncle Billy, de pervisions ob dat bill –"

"What's dat you say 'bout pervisions, Josiar?"

"Well, Uncle Billy, as I was gwine on to state, de pervisions ob dat bill –"

"Stop right dare, Josiar. You say dare's pervisions in dat bill?"

"Jess so, Uncle Billy. De pervisions ob dat bill –"

"Stop right dare, Josiar. Ef dare's pervisions in dat bill, I want a sack ob flour dis bery minnit. Dam de smokin' in the ladies car, and de gehography, and de Latin, and de italic coffins! I want de pervisions, Josiar. Dey's all dere is in de bill wuff one dam cent!"

This anonymous humorist's work, perhaps the work of Editor Smith himself, struck an immediate chord with its public, especially in the South, judging from the number of southern papers that quickly reprinted it.[1] It made its way into the North and spread until Josiar's Pervisions pervaded the country.[2] It became a staple of minstrel shows, blackface gags and exhibitions of ethnic humor.[3] By 1880 "De Pervisions" had graduated to an honored place in popular culture. Textbooks gave it as an example of the use of amusing argot.[4] By then the point of the satire had faded, leaving behind only the husk of a dialectical joke. At its birth, however, the point was sharp. Whether one found it droll or offensive, it posed a serious question. Was the Civil Rights Act the dawn of a new age? Would it transform the social code, as young Josiah dreamed? Or was it, as Uncle Billy objected, a meaningless exercise, toothless and unenforceable?

---

1 The earliest reprint appears in the Nashville *Union and American* on May 29. After that, one finds "De Pervisions" repeated far and wide: the Knoxville *Press and Herald* (June 4), Wilmington, North Carolina, *Journal* (June 6), Raleigh *Sentinel* (June 9), Norfolk *Virginian* (June 14), Alexandria *Louisiana Democrat* (June 17), Tallahassee *Floridian* (June 23), Goldsboro *Carolina Messenger* (June 29), Thomasville *Times* (July 11), the Quitman, Georgia, *Independent* (August 22). The Frederick *Maryland Union* published the piece on March 18, 1875.

2 Josiar's colloquy appeared in the enthusiastically Democratic Harrisburg *Patriot* (June 22), and in the Republican Paterson *Press* (June 16) and Wheeling *Intelligencer* (June 24). It made the pages of Chicago's quarterly magazine of miscellany *Gem of the West and Soldier's Friend*, founded by Liberal Republican C. Augustus Haviland (September issue 1874, pp. 338–339).

3 John David Smith, *Anti-Abolition Tracts and Anti-Black Stereotypes* (New York: 1993), vol. 1, 224–226.

4 Henry Marlin Soper, *Scrap-Book Recitations, No. 2* (Chicago: 1880), 34–35.

Not a few of Charles Sumner's disciples agreed with Uncle Billy. What the Senate accomplished the House had ruined. *Muscae morientes perdunt suavitatem unguenti, dixit Ecclesiastes.* Without mixed schools, said William Lloyd Garrison, there was no balm; it was "emasculated.... I would prefer to have the bill defeated as it stands."[5] A hollow shell, the Boston *Commonwealth* declared: "There is nothing left in the bill for which the colored men of the South can be very grateful, and certainly nothing which repays all the trouble, time, fretfulness and change of rules etc."[6] "We should have had the whole civil rights bill or nothing at all," demanded the Xenia *Torchlight.*[7] Pointless, the New York *Herald* decided: "Mr. Sumner would have spurned it from him with contempt.... Even the negroes are not likely to be deceived by so lame and impotent a conclusion."[8] "Bare as a beanpole in December," concluded the San Jose *Mercury.*[9]

Historians have largely concurred with these negative snap judgments. "Emasculated," one critic has repeated.[10] "Emasculated," another agrees, and also "insignificant, innocuous ... the illusion of achievement."[11] "Of little meaning," observes a third.[12] "A symbolic victory," in the view of a fourth, "doomed to impotence."[13] "Emasculated" again (a favorite refrain), and moreover "of little importance," another affirms.[14] "Little more than a shadow of Sumner's original legislation," according to yet another.[15] An intentional fraud, one historian resumes: "a dead letter, as most legislators expected it would be."[16] Minus mixed schools the act "bespoke the willingness of Republicans to carve a vast and crucial area of American life out of the rights of citizenship."[17]

5 Cincinnati *Commercial*, February 11, 1875.

6 Boston *Commonwealth*, February 13, 1875.

7 Xenia, Ohio, *Torchlight*, March 3, 1875.

8 New York *Herald*, February 28, 1875.

9 San Jose *Mercury*, March 4, 1875.

10 S.G.F. Spackman, "American Federalism and the Civil Rights Act of 1875," *Journal of American Studies*, 10 (1976): 314.

11 William Gillette, *Retreat from Reconstruction, 1869–1879* (Baton Rouge: 1979), 271–273.

12 Alfred H. Kelly, "The Congressional Controversy over School Segregation, 1867–1875," *American Historical Review*, 64 (1959): 562.

13 James McPherson, "Abolitionists and the Civil Rights Act of 1875," *Journal of American History*, 51 (1965): 493, 510.

14 Bertram Wyatt-Brown, "The Civil Rights Act of 1875," *Western Political Quarterly*, 18 (1965): 774–775.

15 Peter D. Klingman, *Josiah Walls: Florida's Black Congressman of Reconstruction* (Gainesville: 1972), 129.

16 Richard H. Abbott, *The Republican Party and the South, 1855–1877: The First Southern Strategy* (Chapel Hill: 1986), 231.

17 Stephen Kantrowitz, *More than Freedom: Fighting for Black Citizenship in a White Republic, 1829–1889* (New York: 2012), 391. Note recent scholarly volumes, the titles of which reveal the authors' interpretations of the civil rights struggle: Douglas R. Egerton, *The Wars*

In 1875 those whom the Civil Rights Act most deeply affected, the nation's black citizens, remained blissfully unaware that history would ridicule their triumph; for they considered it definitely a triumph. They went out to celebrate. A gala party of the foremost African-American leaders saluted the act's passage. James Wormley provided the banquet at his elegant hotel decorated with Charles Sumner's auctioned furniture. Col. George Butler, the congressman's nephew, paid the expenses. White men joined black men. Even Democrats, Sunset Cox and Fernando Wood, accepted invitations. Guests entered a mid-Victorian enchanted realm, "ushered from the cold and inclement street into the brilliant suite of parlors literally smothered in rare exotic flowers ... extemporized fountains playing and exhaling the sweet perfume of violets."[18]

A brilliant company inhaled those violet fumes. Frederick Douglass took the chair at the head of the table. Charles Nordhoff sat across from John Mercer Langston. Gen. Horace Porter sat beside James Rapier and across from Senator Blanche Bruce. Sunset Cox dined next to Ben Butler, opposite them, in all his glory, George Downing. We have no record of the evening's toasts or what will have been a fascinating dinner conversation. No one recalled a feeling of emasculation.

Elsewhere less opulent celebrations occurred, but no less heartfelt. At Saratoga, New York, black people expressed gratitude to Congress, to the Republican Party, and to Charles Sumner posthumously for the "great boon" they had received.[19] At Dayton, Ohio, a "jollification" enlivened the black citizenry.[20] Citizens of Newark, New Jersey, invited Pinchback to join their parade on the 30th. He sent regrets. But, said his organ the *Louisianian,* though absent in the flesh "we doubt not he [will be] present in spirit."[21] J. Henri Burch greeted the Civil Rights Act in his Baton Rouge *Grand Era.*

> At last we are free – all are equal as men in the eyes of the law. Legally, the victory is ours; morally, the fruits of the victory are sure to follow. We have

---

of Reconstruction, The Brief Violent History of America's Most Progressive Era (New York: 2014), 310–313; Mark Wahlgren Summers, *The Ordeal of the Reunion, A New History of Reconstruction* (Chapel Hill: 2014), 368–371; A.J. Langguth, *After Lincoln. How the North Won the Civil War and Lost the Peace* (New York: 2014), 323. Peter Irons, *A People's History of the Supreme Court, The Men and Women Whose Cases and Decisions Have Shaped Our Constitution* (New York: 2006), 207–215.

18 Account in Galveston *News*, March 2, 1875. Also Loren Schweninger, *James T. Rapier and Reconstruction* (Chicago: 1978), 148.

19 New York *Herald,* March 3, 1875.

20 Dayton, *Democrat,* March 25, 1875.

21 New Orleans *Louisianian,* April 3, 1875.

> but to await its development, and the time can not be far in the future. "Take care of my civil-rights bill," said the dying Sumner. His dying request has been remembered.... May God forever bless the soul of Charles Sumner, the Congress of the United States, and U.S. Grant for the same.[22]

Louisville's African-American community gathered on the evening of March 11 at the Asbury Chapel. An unrestrained and effervescent crowd – "a very undignified, noisy, demonstrative, yet good-natured meeting" – filled the hall.[23] Resolutions gave thanks to Sumner "and other noble patriots and statesmen" who had brought the Civil Rights Act to life: "We hail the passage of the civil rights bill by the Forty-third Congress, and its approval by the highest executive officer of the country as a boon that can not be too highly appreciated." They designated March 25 for a day of jubilee. In Thomasville, Georgia, black residents held a "civil rights celebration." No incidents occurred, but the enthusiasm drew a warning from the whites:

> A word to the better disposed class of colored people. You have to live here among the white people of Thomasville. They have ever treated you with kindness and consideration – They need your labor, you need a support. Let not new fangled ideas of social equality disturb these relations. If you do you will be the sufferers.... Don't go crazy over civil rights.[24]

Voices in the north also counseled restraint. Exuberance would not be wise. The New York *Times,* opposed as ever, hoped the end would come quickly. "The Supreme Court, in such instances as this, is the last hope of all who still attach any value to that somewhat despised instrument, the Constitution of the United States."[25] For Republican elder Thurlow Weed it was a stretch too far:

> The disabilities of the freedmen ... are providential, and cannot be relieved by human laws.... So far as our country is concerned, the wrongs of the subjugated race have been avenged. We have converted slavery into freedom, elevating chattels into citizens. We have extended to the freedmen all the personal and political rights we possess ourselves. Further we cannot go.[26]

---

22 Quoted in Louisville *Courier-Journal,* March 21, 1875.

23 Louisville *Courier-Journal,* March 12, 1875.

24 Thomasville *Times,* March 20, 1875.

25 New York *Times,* March 2, 1875.

26 New York *Tribune,* February 20, 1875.

Weed's words drew a retort from George Downing. The Civil Rights Act enunciated an essential principle. Whatever happened, the principle would live. Downing chose to celebrate:

> My self-respect revolts at the idea of asking any man, white or colored, to open the door of his mansion to me ... [but] I ask that this legal recognition of my civil rights shall be asserted affirmatively by national legislation, because the negation of a principle is the first step toward its final overthrow.[27]

Ben Butler returned home. Black Bostonians prepared a tribute.[28] "General B.F. Butler, our Sumner now," one correspondent wrote. "May God bless you and keep you until the perfect day and save you in the End."[29] Butler, having been voted out of Congress, consoled himself: "I sought to do my duty to the country and to my fellow-men, and await with confidence a just verdict to that effect."[30] Nonetheless he forecast a bleak future. Congress' failure to pass the Force Bill would lead to war. If it did not come now it would come in 1876, when counting of the presidential ballots began. "There has not been a darker day since I left Washington in December, 1860."[31] Black citizens of Shreveport wrote him in desperation. Major Merrill had departed. White terror had descended. Look to yourselves, Butler replied. Only God can help you now:

27 New York *Tribune*, February 27, 1875.

28 Boston *Commonwealth*, March 20, 1875.

29 Joseph H.T. Myers to Butler, February 6, 1875. Butler Papers, Library of Congress. Such effusions galled Butler's detractors. Henry Ward Beecher chided black people for their easy gullibility: "We confess our regret at seeing them running after a wily politician like Butler when they have so many better and nobler friends." (*Christian Union*, March 24, 1875: 247.) They persisted in running after Butler.

30 Benjamin Butler to N. Dumont of Springfield, November 8, 1874. Butler Papers, Library of Congress. Some Republican sheets accorded Butler the verdict he hoped for. The Chicago *Inter Ocean* praised his life and his achievements: "Who is this man Butler that the whole country should be in such a constant tumult over him? He must be more cruel than Nena Sahib, more treacherous than Captain Jack, more dishonest than Tweed, more hypocritical than Pecksniff, to merit all these attacks. Yet he is none of these. Neither is he cowardly, lecherous, brutal or ignorant. In private life Benjamin F. Butler is above reproach. In learning he is the peer of any man in either house of Congress.... The colored people owe General Butler a debt they can never repay, and his absence from the House will be a greater calamity to them than the defeat of a dozen ordinary men." Chicago *Inter Ocean*, November 6, 1874.

31 Washington *Evening Star*, quoted in Atlanta *Constitution*, March 6, 1875.

> I see at present no hope of alleviation except in themselves. So long as they will submit to be killed by every marauding white man who will do so, so long there will be no help; nor do I believe there is any aid to be looked for from the United States. All I can say to the colored men is to help yourselves and Heaven will help you. I should take to killing equally if I were a colored man.[32]

To another delegation he advised scorched earth: "If you and your friends are molested, burn the dwellings and cotton fields of your persecutors. Take it when there is a high wind, and you will not have to burn more than four or five before they will be glad to let you alone."[33]

Scorched earth – on the political battlefield it had already begun. In the South the Republican Party began to shed members even before the Civil Rights Act became official. On the night of February 8 word of the House bill's passage arrived in North Carolina. Two Republican legislators, William B. Glenn and J.H. Foote, rose to announce their defection. "I declare that I hereby forever dissolve my connection with the Republican party," Foote declaimed, "and ally myself with the great party that is now building up in the South and North for the preservation of a constitutional government and the purity and salvation of the Anglo-Saxon race." Glenn and Foote submitted a resolution calling for all white Republicans to flee the Party.[34]

On February 19 the Glenn-Foote resolution came before the North Carolina Assembly. A mass of citizenry overflowed the chamber. "We never witnessed such a general outpouring in the Legislative halls before," reported the Wilmington *Journal*.[35] Debate began at noon and continued at midnight. Republicans struggled. If they endorsed the resolution they all but dissolved their party. If they opposed it they risked the fury of their white constituents. Some braved the fury. William G. Candler of Buncombe County: "He said that he represented as a Republican on this floor a Democratic constituency; that his people had confidence in him, and that he had the nerve to stand up, even before this large audience, and declare himself a Republican and in opposition to the resolutions." Samuel Barnett of Person County stood firm. "He too was elected from a Democratic county; was a Confederate soldier, surrendered at Appomattox." R.M. Norment of Robeson County arraigned the Democrats. Their game was

32 Benjamin Butler to H. Adams, W.G. Calvin and others, November 28, 1875. Butler Papers, Library of Congress, Letterbook, Box 214: 443.

33 Blanche Butler Ames, *Chronicles from the Nineteenth Century: Family Letters of Blanche Butler and Adelbert Ames*, (Clinton, Mass., 1957), vol. 2, 245.

34 Wilmington, North Carolina, *Journal*, February 9; New York *Tribune*, February 9, 1875.

35 Wilmington *Journal*, February 20, 1875.

hypocrisy. A Democrat, Marshall H. Pinnix of Davidson County, posed a question: "I would ask the gentleman, if there was only a white man's party and a black man's party in this State, which would he adopt?" Norment hesitated: "In that shape, it is rather too hard for me to answer."

Pinnix's question pinned Republicans. The Civil Rights Act forced a rift. Cooperation became untenable, collaboration a crime. Appleton Oaksmith, Independent of Carteret County, submitted a substitute resolution. Protest the civil rights law, but reject the call for a race-based political alignment. That suggestion failed. Democrats let the resolution lie on the table. Its mere appearance spelled disaster for the dwindling ranks of white Republicans.

Such scenes preceded the Civil Rights Act's birth. After it, anxiety deepened. The New York *Herald's* reporter found a tense, smoldering anger, a "deep indignation." As yet the white masses held their hand, restrained their impulse to strike.

> Mingled with the quiet and suppressed, but nevertheless intense sentiment of indignation which pervades the white race ... there is a spirit of forbearance and of hope, a trust in that benignant future which shall, ultimately and in due season, repair and avenge all these grievous wrongs.[36]

Would that forbearance last? The *Herald* doubted it. "The ingrained, congenital, constitutional element of insolence in the negro character," under the stimulus of the Civil Rights Act, might at any moment bring on an explosion. The South sat on a volcano.

Horace Redfield set out again. He reported from Texas: an eerie calm. Whites professed unconcern. No harm would come, "except perhaps, now and then, a negro killed." The Civil Rights Act could not and would not be enforced in Texas. A few "insolent or sassy" Negroes might step beyond their proper sphere. They would soon be "settled." This was unfortunate, admitted Redfield's informant in the town of Marshall: "Texas already has a bad name for murdering."[37]

State legislatures prepared countermeasures. Virginia State Delegate William S. Gilman submitted a bill that gave managers of theaters, proprietors or managers of inns, operators of vehicles of public transportation the right to deny service to any persons they chose, so long as they informed said persons that denial was not due to racial animosity. It was not necessary to prove this assertion. A simple disclaimer sufficed. Once a manager, proprietor or operator had posted this notice to the view of an unwanted client the matter was closed.

36 New York *Herald*, March 15, 1875.

37 Cincinnati *Commercial*, March 4, 1875.

Any person who disputed the case or who insisted upon accommodations etc. was to be considered a disturber of the peace, arrested, and punished by fine and or imprisonment. Col. Gilman's final clause prohibited juries from questioning the veracity of any properly-composed informational notice.[38]

In Delaware, State Senator James H. Ray introduced a bill on March 11 permitting hotel keepers, theater owners or lessees and operators of common carriers to deny service to anyone whose presence they deemed "offensive to the major part of their customers." Ray's bill went into effect on March 25. It remained in effect until 1963.[39] Georgia State Senator B.S. Crawford produced a bill "to protect inn-keepers and common carriers, by making them private corporations, privileged to dictate who [sic] they shall accommodate."[40] In Tennessee Assemblyman J. Harvey Mathes proposed "to repeal all State, county and municipal taxes on hotels, theaters and common carriers," thereby removing their licensed status and rendering them private entities.[41]

Legislative rearguard maneuvers might delay disaster. But soon, it seemed, the reaction must come. The "spirited people" would rise up and disobey. They did not. An almost surreal serenity settled upon the scene. Gilman's bill died in Virginia; even the Norfolk *Virginian* editorialized against it.[42] Crawford's failed in Georgia.[43] Mathes's measure passed only the Tennessee House.[44] Democratic leaders called upon the people to submit. Newspapers which only recently had frothed apoplectic over the prospect of civil rights recovered their equanimity with astonishing ease. Be calm. Lay low. Let "civil rights" play itself out. The reason for this change of mind readily appeared. The elections were over. Having stoked the fires of race hatred to the point of combustion (and reaped appropriate political rewards) Democrats strove to smother the

38 "In all prosecutions under the first section of this act, if it shall appear that at the time when any demand for accommodations, advantages, facilities, or privileges specified in such action was made, the person on whom such demand was made informed the person who made the same ... that the accommodations, advantages, facilities, or privileges asked for or demanded cannot be furnished because of insufficient room or insufficient provision, or because other or more guests or patrons cannot be properly or safely cared for or accommodated, such statement shall be taken as conclusive proof of the fact so stated; and in all trials under this act the court shall so instruct the jury." Richmond *Dispatch,* March 8, 1875.

39 See John H. Gauger, "A Delaware Experiment with Reconstruction Nullification," *Delaware History*, 21 (1985): 182–185.

40 Savannah *News*, February 17, 20, 1875.

41 Memphis *Appeal,* March 4, 9, 1875.

42 Norfolk *Virginian*, March 10, 1875.

43 Savannah *News*, March 8, 1875.

44 Memphis *Appeal,* March 12, 1875.

flames. The Nashville *Banner's* pre-election columns had screamed against the "quintessence of abominations." Now it downgraded the quintessence to a non-essence. "Temporarily it may be an annoyance but will show a gradual abatement in proportion to the philosophic reticence with which the people meet it."[45] Petty irritations, agreed the Nashville *Union and American*. They could be borne in good grace:

> In car or hotel we can no longer choose our company. At theater or opera a few ambitious, odorous swells, with their dusky dulcineas, may drive us out before the first act is finished ... hard to bear, but it would prove harder to resist.[46]

The Thibodaux, Louisiana, *Sentinel*, pre-election, declared the Civil Rights Bill a mandate for home invasion, the swarming of Negroes into one's best parlor. Post-election, the *Sentinel* pooh-poohed parlor pollution. Its French language edition welcomed civil rights to the family circle. Let there be good fellowship (*un esprit de bienveillance mutuelle*); "time and patience will do more than force and violence."[47]

The Atlanta *News* spun the most dizzying about-face of all. In September, with elections in the air, its columns flamed: "Our fate is to be less merciful than that of the Trojans, less sublime than that of the Carthaginians. We are not to perish by the sword as those people perished; we are to live, and live in degradation." It called for war.

> Equality will not be tolerated.... Our only hope is in a stern, resolute resistance – a resistance to the death, if necessary with arms in our hands. Our hate must be unquenchable, our war interminable and merciless.... The Civil Rights Bill means war, and war means bloodshed, and that we are terribly in earnest.[48]

Elections ended. The *News* canceled its war. Quench the hate. Suffering was good for the soul; it built character:

> Granted even that it becomes a law, we need not fear the bill. Our duty is to ignore the bill, and to continue at present as if no such law existed.

---

45 Nashville, *Banner*, February 28, March 2, 1875.

46 Nashville *Union and American*, February 8, 1875.

47 Thibodaux *Sentinel*, April 3, 1875.

48 Quoted in Indianapolis *Journal*, September 9; Chicago *Inter Ocean*, September 14, 1874; Forty-third Congress, House Report 261, Part 2, 769.

> A principle is worth suffering for; hence, if any of our people are called upon to suffer they will do it with dignity and heroism.[49]

Politics obliged. As an attractor of votes the Civil Rights Bill served the party well. As a catalyst of conflict it served the party ill, liable to create a backlash upsetting the hard-won indulgence of the North. The party needed to keep the wound, the sense of injured racial pride, alive, yet not so lively as to inspire retaliation. Patience, forbearance, sanctifying martyrdom, those were the watchwords it enjoined upon the people. Adopt a strategy of cunning passivity:

> The South must [demonstrate] a steady front of sublime patience. Insult must be met with forbearance. The people who vanquished great odds on the battle-field are now called upon to achieve in the ruling of spirits greater triumphs than the taking of cities. Let these high resolves be made. Non-resistance, except in the courts and at the ballot-box. No triumph to our enemies by doing what they most desire us to do. No mortification for ourselves by falling into the trap they have set for us.[50]

From the halls of power came an Address: "To the People of the Southern States."

> You cannot have failed to observe the persistent efforts of some of the leaders of the Republican party to revive the animosities of the late war, which happily are fast giving place to a spirit of concord and unity in every section of our common country.... The true condition of the Southern States and the real sentiment of the Southern people are being gradually made known to our fellow-citizens of the North. We hope for their favorable decision.... With this exalted purpose in view, there is nothing inconsistent with the honor and manhood of a brave people to resolve to suffer with heroic patience, whatever be their provocations and wrongs, looking through the fearful present to a hopeful future, and repelling unjust epithets and gratuitous insults with dignity and moderation. Let every white man in every neighborhood in the whole South regard himself as a commissioner of the peace, maintaining the kindest relations towards the black man.[51]

---

49 Quoted in Louisville *Courier-Journal*, February 2, 1875.

50 Augusta. Georgia, *Chronicle and Sentinel*, quoted in Galveston *News*, February 9, 1875.

51 Text in Wilmington, North Carolina, *Journal*, February 21; Santa Clara *Argus*, March 13, 1875.

Violence played into the enemy's hands.

> Every street disturbance, every homicide of whatsoever character, by whomsoever committed ... is perverted into evidence of a spirit of lawlessness and violence.... We well know the gross injustice of such charges.... We would appeal to the wisdom and patriotism of a long-suffering people, by every hope of the future, for continued forbearance and hopeful reliance upon the virtue and sense of justice of the American people.

Signers of this irenic document comprised a who's-who of the Democrats' southern elite: ten senators, including Gordon, Merrimon, Norwood, Ransom and Bogy, forty-six members of the House, among them William Robbins, Robert Vance, James Beck, Alfred Waddell, John T. Harris and Lucius Lamar. Even John Young Brown signed on. The stakes were high. Could the excitable masses be restrained by their greater and wiser mentors? The answer, it increasingly appeared, was yes. As the first days and weeks of the civil rights age passed, expectations of explosions declined.

Democrats had long and loudly asserted that Republicans designed the Civil Rights Bill precisely to provoke unrest. That point had echoed on the House and Senate floors. Republicans wanted another civil war, Thomas Whitehead declared, so they "picked" at civil rights. James Beck forecast it at the start of the debates: Negroes will be "goaded on" to create disturbances; "arrests will be made, imprisonments will follow ... the Army and Navy called into requisition." Now, if Beck was right, the moment had arrived. Beck was wrong. Republicans had no thought of a return to military rule. The interests of both sides, though for dissimilar reasons, coincided. Black leaders too embraced conciliation. Pinchback, by deed and word, pointed the way.

On March 20 a distinguished party of black statesmen from Louisiana arrived at Louisville, stopping for the night on their way home from a visit to Washington, D.C. Pinchback led them, along with Lieutenant-Governor Caesar Caius Antoine, School Superintendent William G. Brown and State Senator J. Henri Burch. Rather than charge into the nearest first-class hotel, they repaired to a discreet, segregated location, a colored boarding-house kept by Peter Butler on Second Street between Green and Jefferson. Pinchback spent the night at the private home of friends. At nine the next morning the *Courier-Journal*'s reporter knocked at Butler's hostelry. Why, he inquired, had the gentlemen not stopped at the Galt House or some other superior establishment, as the Civil Rights Act entitled them to do? "Yes," Burch responded, "we would have availed ourselves of our legal privileges, but we have no desire to force the issue." They wanted "to refute the idea that they have any disposition whatever to make any trouble over this law." Gov. Antoine puffed on a pre-breakfast cigar: "The colored people do not design any trouble.... We are opposed to unnecessarily, merely for the purpose of testing the law, testing it at the hotels."[52]

The reporter intercepted Pinchback at the depot. He too welcomed the coming of the Civil Rights Act. He too intended to apply its privileges prudently. "I rejoice in its passage, which we have obtained after a hard struggle. We do not propose, however, to make any trouble about it. Our counsel to the people is to be perfectly quiet for four or five months and not make any unnecessary tests. By that time the country will have become accustomed to the law. I do not believe there will be any trouble, for the leading men of the colored people are opposed to precipitating any." The reporter watched his subjects catch their train. There, he noted, they did not settle for second class. They boarded Pullman coaches, without objection.

Five days later, as planned, Louisville's black citizens held their civil rights celebration. N.R. Harper, the principal speaker, urged them to follow the example Pinchback had set: "Go slow in accepting the privileges, and never push matters, but strive by good conduct to wipe out the mutual prejudice which exists between whites and blacks."[53] At Nashville, African Americans similarly abjured assertive action. Abram Smith, Alfred Menefee and William Sumner spoke. "The passage of the bill was a simple act of justice to the colored people."[54] They had no thought of thrusting themselves into unwelcome situations.

Situations, nonetheless, arose. The earliest test-incidents passed without serious incident. "Several negroes applied to some of our first-class barkeepers for drinks yesterday, and were politely refused," the Norfolk *Virginian* reported on March 5: "Nobody shot." The paper's traveling correspondent sent in a lighthearted dispatch:

> It may make them [the Negroes] a little more impudent, if that is possible, but we know how to regulate all that. One of them promptly stole my four-dollar-and-a-half umbrella yesterday, under a misapprehension, as I must in charity presume, of the new privileges conferred upon his race.[55]

---

52 Story in Louisville *Courier-Journal*, March 26, 1875.

53 Louisville *Courier-Journal*, March 26, 1875.

54 Nashville *Banner*, March 2, 1875.

55 Norfolk *Virginian*, March 10, 1875.

Two hotels were reported to have closed in Alexandria, Virginia. On the steamer *Keyport* leaving Quantico "negro passengers had sole possession of the dining saloon, the white passengers declining to eat with them."[56]

Bowling Green, Kentucky, March 8, reported all quiet. "No demonstrations have been made here by darkies, and none are anticipated from our home colored people."[57] Washington, D.C., March 5, the District's first civil rights tests were noted. Two well-dressed black men entered the bar of Willard's Hotel and ordered drinks. The barman served them. They drank. They proceeded to the barber salon and demanded shaves. The manager refused them. They left in high dudgeon, but were seen later in the street laughing about their adventure.[58]

Generally such "testers" used restraint, while their targets found ways to defuse the situation. At Richmond a black man entered the Exchange Hotel and asked for dinner. Col. Carrington, the proprietor, ushered the gentleman into the midst of the other patrons and seated him at a prominent table. The colonel set three waiters to wait upon him, to hover over him and attend his wants as he dined. He was "so surprised and outflanked" that he ate with little appetite and left his meal unfinished. Hotel employees escorted him ceremoniously to the door. Other testers tested the city's bar-rooms. At Snelling's Saloon they found a notice. All drinks now cost $5 "subject to discount" (for white customers).[59] Bars were targeted in Selma, Alabama. A gang of a dozen "impudent black scoundrels" made the rounds of every saloon in town.[60] A troop of "mulattoes" campaigned through the bars and billiard saloons of Atlanta. They were turned away.[61]

To the extent that trouble emerged, the flash point was the theater. Memphis witnessed one of the earliest events on the evening of March 3, just seventy-two hours into the civil rights law. Two black men dressed in appropriate attire, appeared at the Theater box-office. They requested dress-circle tickets. Ticket agent Brooks informed door-keeper Holland who hurried to theater manager Thomas W. Davey: "Our troubles are upon us." Davey reasoned with the civil rights testers. "Boys, you don't want to go in there." They replied, "Do you mean to refuse us admission?" Not at all, returned the manager, but it would ruin his business. After some discussion the black men agreed to leave if their money were refunded. Davey vented his frustration: "It seems hard for one man … to

56 Wilmington, North Carolina, *Journal*, March 9, 1875.
57 Louisville *Courier-Journal*, March 9, 1875.
58 Washington, D.C., *National Republican*, March 5, 1875.
59 Petersburg *Index and Appeal*, March 5, 1875.
60 Montgomery *Advertiser*, March 7, 1875.
61 Atlanta *Constitution*, March 6, 1875.

be made the scape-goat of every colored person who may see fit under the civil-rights law to claim privileges in the theater.... If I do refuse a colored man admission I become amenable to the law; if I admit him I array myself against public opinion and offend those whose patronage is valuable to me. You see I am between two fires."[62]

Playhouses at Louisville came under siege. On the night of March 5 Macauley's Theater opened for a gala event: the Soldene English Opera Bouffe presenting Offenbach's "The Grand Duchess of Gérolstein," Emily Soldene herself in the title role. The height of Louisville society lined up to attend. Three young mulattoes stormed the citadel. Ticket agent Mr. Elrod took their five-dollar bill. He counted the change, presented tickets, and waved them on. The testers were taken aback, having expected to be repulsed. One ran off, but the others "plucked up their assurance" and entered the house. The *Courier-Journal* reported:

> In a twinkling the colored twain found themselves standing in the glare of the first circle gas lights upon a level with the *crème de la crème* of Louisville's *élite.* Their momentary embarrassment gave way to the proud consciousness that they were, perhaps, the first of all Kentucky's colored population to transcend the bounds that the customs and traditions of the Commonwealth had prescribed for their race.[63]

The interlopers dropped quickly into seats 752 and 753, near the exit. "Instantly every lorgnette was raised ... and had a burning-glass intervened it is probable that they would have been cremated on the spot." They were not cremated. At intermission they left, causing speculation that they did not care about the archduchess' amorous intrigues but were playing a civil rights intrigue of their own.

Montgomery, Alabama, also on the 5th, two colored persons showed up at the theater and asked for admission to the white section. The usher "kindly" advised that their presence might occasion trouble and suggested they retire, which they did. "It speaks well for the negroes of this city," concluded the Montgomery *Advertiser*. "We sincerely hope that they will continue to show their good sense in the same way."[64]

Overall the theater incidents manifested the caution that Pinchback and others had enjoined on one side, and the forbearance Democratic leaders urged on the other. Black men backed off at Memphis and Montgomery. Whites

62 Accounts in Memphis *Appeal*, March 4; Louisville *Courier-Journal*, March 6, 1875.

63 Louisville *Courier-Journal*, March 6, 1875.

64 Montgomery *Advertiser*, March 6, 1875.

submitted in Louisville. They retaliated only with sullen stares. In other places testers achieved success. At Saint Joseph, Missouri, the Georgia Minstrels performed at the opera. Management declined to sell advance tickets, but as patrons came to the door several Negroes asked for dress circle seats. They were seated. No trouble arose.[65] In New Orleans on March 10th two prominent black men, Aristide Dejoie and T.B. Stamps, successfully integrated the St. Charles Theater.[66] They took seats in the parquet. A vanishing wave of white people left the invaders "in quiet enjoyment of the entire wing." But that was all. The show went on. Such events proved, declared the New Orleans *Republican,* the Civil Rights Act would work.[67] Charles Nordhoff, the New York *Herald's* itinerant observer, found Arkansans at ease.

> When I asked whether the Federal act made any trouble, people laughed at me.... I was told there had been but a single case under this act, in which a saloon-keeper was fined twenty-five dollars. I noticed that some drinking-saloons had two bars, one for each color; but I also saw in several cases black men and white men drinking together. The negroes have shown no disposition to make the law offensive.[68]

Despite such hopeful signs, tensions remained. For three days panic paralyzed Richmond, Virginia. Trouble began again at the theater. "Davy Crockett," with Frank Mayo in the role that made him a star, opened at the Richmond Theater on Monday, March 8. As the overture played, two non-white persons insinuated themselves into the house, "a young mulatto, quite bright, but still dark enough to be immediately recognized as not of the Caucasian race, accompanied by a mulatto boy much whiter than himself." At first they passed through unperceived. Then the discovery was made. A mob descended upon the bright mulatto in an orchestra seat.

> A fierce excitement took possession of the crowd. Some mounted chairs and cried "Put him out!" "Put him out!" Others advanced towards him with menacing gestures. In a little time he was encircled by a throng of angry men and told to "clear out," and his life seemed in imminent danger.[69]

65 Springfield, Missouri, *Patriot,* March 18, 1875.

66 New Orleans *Louisianian,* March 13; Memphis *Appeal,* March 12, 1875.

67 New Orleans *Republican,* March 12, 1875.

68 Charles Nordhoff, *The Cotton States in the Spring and Summer of 1875* (New York: 1876), 35–36.

69 Richmond *Dispatch,* March 9, 1875.

Theater manager Powell urged the intruder to leave, offering a refund of his ticket. He agreed, ungraciously. He walked up the aisle, shouldering past furious white faces. Patrons heard him remark: "You needn't make so much fuss about it – you'll have to come to it at last." His companion, the barely-black boy (who prudently chose a seat close to the exit) had already disappeared. Persons recognized the truculent invader as James Ellis, remarkably the son of old Caesar Ellis, a "highly trusted" employee of the Richmond *Whig,* a man who knew his place. Young Ellis evidently did not know his. On his seat he left a book: *Rebel Barbarities*, "filled with pictures of white men lashing negroes, and such like stuff."[70]

Davy Crockett resumed. Then at 9 o'clock came a newly-horrifying discovery. Someone, his lorgnette wandering from the direction of the stage, detected another alien presence. Full in the middle of the dress-circle, "a notorious mulatto woman, there she sat, with her son, about six years old, by her side, looking as unconcerned as the best lady present." The crowd, barely recovered from the expulsion of Ellis, was undone. Men circled around the suspect female. "There were some who declared that she was white; others who said that she might be a respectable woman, and there was some hesitation about making any movement against her." Police arrived, led by Major John Poe, chief of police himself. He was asked to determine her identity; she might, it was feared, be Ellen White, inmate of a local brothel. Major Poe could not determine. The woman became frightened. She put a cap on the little boy's head and made a break for the door. The crowd erupted.

> A hundred furious men dashed after her. They blocked up the aisles, and might have caused a panic and fearful loss of life had it not been for the prompt action of Major Poe and the police, who refused to allow them to pass close towards the woman, and kept them pent up in the vestibule until she had gotten down the steps and into the street.[71]

Intermission. Male theater patrons, as was their custom, rushed across the street to Eucker's Saloon. They needed a steadying drink. A desire was expressed to know who had purchased a ticket for the harlot intruder. A voice at the bar, belonging to a young and apparently respectable white man, spoke out: "I bought the ticket for her." He avoided death by sprinting out a back door.

---

70 James Ellis' reading material most likely was a copy of the wartime opus, *Barbarities of the Rebels, As Shown in their Cruelty to the Federal Wounded and Prisoners; in their Outrages upon Union Men; in their Murder of Negroes, and in their Unmanly Conduct throughout the Rebellion,* graphic illustrations, text by Col. Percy Howard.

71 Richmond *Dispatch,* March 9, 1875.

Manager Powell, meanwhile, promised to welcome all black patrons into top quality seats in the Family Circle, reserved for their exclusive use, just one level above the dress circle. He failed to set the panic at rest. Tuesday evening another performance arrived. White men surrounded the theater. "So large was the crowd it took the combined efforts of a dozen policemen to keep a passage-way open to the sidewalk." Theater patrons passed through the gauntlet. A few black persons approached. They looked at the lobby, looked at the white crowd, and turned away. A second crowd gathered, "seventy-five or one hundred negroes scattered over the street, keeping up evidently a menacing attitude." Major Poe's police detail maintained an uneasy peace.[72]

By the 11th all was quiet. The mob had delivered its message. Black or potentially off-tinted people were successfully intimidated. "The colored people may as well understand it first as last that, although there were fifty civil rights bills passed, the white people of Richmond will never submit to such indignities."[73]

The uproar at the Richmond Theater appears the exception. At Harrodsburg, Kentucky, on March 5 citizens gathered, white and black together, in the African Methodist Episcopal church. The black reverend G.H. Graham presided. They must meet, Rev. Graham urged, "with mutual understanding, so that all good citizens might act in concert in support of law and order, and thereby deter the reckless from provoking disturbances." They framed a resolution. Do not tolerate the Civil Rights Act. Embrace it.

> Whereas, the law commonly called the civil-rights bill has passed the Congress of the United States and received the signature of the President, and is now a part of the law of the land ... therefore, while we hail with joy and receive with gratitude the investiture of "civil rights," secured to all citizens of this land of the *free* and home of the brave, we shall strive (God helping us) to so exercise them that none may have just cause of complaint, and the nation never to regret this noble act of justice.... The Government has spoken to us and committed the future to our own hands. Our destiny will be, under God, what we choose to make it.[74]

How many citizens subscribed to these noble sentiments? How many laughed at Kumbaya? Peace prevailed in Harrodsburg. It prevailed in most places, whether motivated by conviction, resignation, self-interest, or crude political calculation, as the Civil Rights Act's days progressed.

---

72 Richmond *Dispatch,* March 10, 1875.

73 Richmond *Dispatch,* March 12, 1875.

74 Louisville *Courier-Journal,* March 10, 1875.

Clarity, on the other hand, remained elusive. How far might one pursue one's equal rights? Where precisely might Negroes penetrate without incurring justifiable expulsion? Grocery stores did not fall under the act, nor did restaurants, barber shops or saloons, unless reserved for publicly licensed facilities. Yet anxiety reigned in restaurants, groceries, saloons, barber shops and bars. Uncertainty over the scope or reach of the Civil Rights Act sowed confusion.

Those who consulted their newspapers for enlightenment found obscurity. The Nashville *Banner* informed readers, incorrectly, that their restaurants and barber-shops would be subject to civil rights assault.[75] The Philadelphia *Inquirer* sent reporters fanning out across town to ask restaurateurs how they planned to deal with the onslaught.[76] Even the well-informed New York *Times* misinformed the public; blacks would descend nightly upon Delmonico's demanding a steak dinner.[77] Civil rights testers did not devour Delmonico's steaks. But they appeared at other restaurants, bars and barber-shops.

Perplexed persons turned to the authority. Benjamin Butler fielded letters from all sides, each inquiring what rights one might presume to exercise, or what intrusions one had to fear. On March 10 he received a letter from Georgia. Richard Hale, a black man, enclosed clippings torn from the Augusta *Chronicle and Sentinel* describing a recent incident. Intending to see what force lay in the Civil Rights Act, Mr. Hale and several friends had repaired to the saloon kept by Lexius Henson, also a black man, on the corner of Ellis Street. Henson declared that his was "a white man's bar." If they persisted in imposing their patronage they would ruin his business. They persisted. He stated his prices: $1 for a glass of beer; $2.50 for a shot of whiskey; $5 for a brandy. A violent altercation ensued. The civil rights testers withdrew. They pooled their money. Two returned, deposited $2 and demanded beer. Henson refused. Consequently, Hale informed Butler, he filed suit against Henson's saloon. He found, to his surprise, that the law did not support him. "I cald on Mr. Moore U.S. Commissioner for a warent & was refused saing that the bill did not tuch bar rooms nor restaurants both of which Mr. Henderson keeps."[78] There is no record of Butler's response. It cannot have been encouraging. Two weeks later Butler heard from another frustrated black citizen. Samuel Wade of Indianapolis found the law incomprehensible.

75 Nashville *Banner*, March 10, 1875.
76 Philadelphia *Inquirer*, March 4, 1875.
77 New York *Times*, March 2, 1875.
78 Richard Hale to Butler, March 10, 1875. Butler Papers, Library of Congress; report of Hale's encounter in Henson's saloon: Louisville *Courier-Journal*, March 12, 1875.

> I see in one of your letters that the colored man had no right to go in a saloon to get a drink or to a barber shop to get shaved without leave of the proprietor. …Don't we have the same rights that any other people of this country [have]? … Is not a barber shop and a drinking saloon a public place? If not why are they open to the public, and the public are all the time going & coming? … And if we are American people of the country why is it that you exclude the places of resort such as restaurants, barber shops, drinking saloons and all other places of this kind which all American citizens have a right to go in?[79]

Questions continued. In two cases Butler's replies are preserved. In May he wrote to C.H. Mercier of Portland, Oregon. No, he explained, "ice-cream saloons, barber-shops, blacksmiths' shops, tailors' shops, restaurants," all fell outside the Act. "None of these are public places." Private enterprise remained private. The whims or prejudices of the proprietors were sacred. "The civil rights bill gives the colored man every right I have, no more, no less."[80]

Butler's most explicit response came in an exchange of correspondence with Col. Robert Harlan of Cincinnati. Harlan, formerly a favored slave of the Kentucky Harlans (James and his son John Marshall), endorsed the easy lifestyle of the southern gentlemen who had owned him, much attached to horseraces and bourbon. He wrote on March 15: "Will you be kind enough to inform me if colored men are entitled to the privileges of saloons and barber shops under its [the Civil Rights Act's] provisions?" Butler's reply appeared immediately in the press.

> To this I answer … and am happy to say that the civil rights bill does not give any right to a colored man to go into a drinking saloon without the leave of the proprietor.… In reference to barber shops, let me say that the trade of a barber is like any other trade, to be carried on by the man who is engaged in it at his own will and pleasure, and the civil rights bill has nothing to do with its exercise. A barber has a right to shave whom he pleases, as much as a jeweler has a right to repair a watch for whom he pleases, or a blacksmith to shoe such colored horses as he pleases. In other words, these are public employments but private businesses, in which the law does not interfere.[81]

79 Samuel Wade to Butler, March 24, 1875. Butler Papers, Library of Congress.

80 Benjamin Butler to C.H. Mercier, May 12, 1875. Butler Papers, Library of Congress, Letterbook, Box 214, 16.

81 Robert Harlan to Butler, March 15, 1875. Butler Papers, Library of Congress. Butler's reply, Cincinnati *Commercial*, March 22, 1875.

The distinction, Butler explained, resided in the heart of the law.

> From time immemorial all men have had equal rights at the common law in places of public amusement, in public conveyances, and in inns or licensed taverns, because all such business was for the public under special privileges granted by the government.... The civil rights bill only confirms these rights of all citizens to the colored man in consideration of the prejudice against him ... [but] it has not altered the colored man's rights at all from what they were before under the common law.

Butler's reply to Robert Harlan became the definitive word. *Harper's Weekly* accompanied it with a pictorial commentary. Its April edition featured another of Thomas Nast's distinctive designs, a tribute to the Civil Rights Act and advice to its recipients. In an upper panel a graceful white hand held out a beribboned document, "The Civil Rights Bill" (Congressman Shanks' mischievous preamble neatly lettered on its cover); a sturdy black hand reached to receive the scroll. Below, Nast drew the commentary. The scene, a seedy saloon, a staggering white man slumped over the bar, a sinister, smiling barman preparing to pour yet another libation; to his side the drunkard's forlorn family, beseeching wife, small daughter hugging his knees; overhead the barman's notice, "White-Man's Saloon $5.00 A Drink (To Niggers)." To the right Nast placed another family group: a black man, wife and son, turned away from the sorry scene. At the bottom ran the caption, the words of the drunkard's wife to her inebriated spouse: "I wish *you* were not allowed in here."[82]

Butler's statement notwithstanding, confusion continued. Barber shops became a point of contention. Barbering stood out, a quintessential black occupation, both north and south.[83] Consequently those establishments formed a point of frequent contact. For black people, breaking the barber-shop barrier became a fixation. To enter a forbidden place where so many of their fellows presided yet kept them out seemed an essential demonstration of equality.

Even as the Senate passed its first version of the bill rumors emerged that the House would add coverage of barber shops.[84] It did not – but many black people acted as though it had. The Savannah *News* found it amusing. "Told that the right to shave with perfumed soap, camel's hair brushes and gilt-edged razors is not included among the provisions of the new bill, they leave with

82 *Harper's Weekly*, April 24, 1875, 336.

83 See Gerber, *Black Ohio and the Color Line*: 80–83. In the south, the Montgomery *Advertiser* estimated, nine-tenths of all barbers were black. Montgomery *Advertiser*, March 12, 1875.

84 Cincinnati *Commercial*, May 26; Saint Louis *Republican*, May 26; Chicago *Tribune*, May 27, 1874.

a puzzled expression of countenance."[85] The Alexandria *Sentinel* chuckled. "We advise those barbers who had prepared special razors for their colored customers to put them aside, until another civil-rights bill is passed."[86] One black barber, Mr. Lem Owens of Thomasville, Georgia, consulted a lawyer to determine his obligations. Greatly to his relief, he found himself excused. He posted a sign:

> My shop is neither a stage-coach, a railroad car, a steamboat, a theater or other place of amusement, a hotel nor a cemetery, and the civil rights bill does not affect my business, in any shape or form. *My shop is open for white people and white people ALONE.*[87]

Only one black man gained uncontested use of a white man's barber. United States Senator Blanche Bruce and the United States senatorial barber shop could not be parted. The newly-elected statesman from Mississippi arrived in Washington for the Senate's special session on March 4. He developed an immediate attachment to the barber shop. Twice a day, upon arrival each morning and at the close of each session, he sat complacently while his whiskers were trimmed and his hair clipped. He prolonged his tonsorial appointments, watching as assorted white colleagues stepped up to the door then stepped back, forced to take their shave elsewhere.[88]

A handful of cases made their way to the judgment of the law. Three formal complaints came before United States Commissioners in three very different jurisdictions. None worked out well for the complainants. The first legal confrontation occurred in Wilmington, North Carolina. On Wednesday, March 3, three black men, Francis Holmes, a drayman, Jim Taylor, a shoemaker, and Scipio Hill, occupation unknown, walked into the saloon of W.H. Gerken and ordered drinks. Gerken refused. Holmes swore out an affidavit, the first petition filed under the Civil Rights Act:

> That, William H. Gerken, a keeper of a licensed public liquor saloon on Front street in the city of Wilmington, State of North Carolina, did, on the 3rd day of March, A.D. 1875, deny to him [Francis Holmes] the full and equal enjoyment of the accommodations, advantages, facilities and

85 Savannah *News*, March 11, 1875.
86 Alexandria, Virginia, *Sentinel*, quoted in Richmond *Dispatch*, March 5, 1875.
87 Thomasville *Times*, March 20, 1875.
88 Louisville *Courier-Journal*, March 29, 1875.

> privileges enjoyed by the white portion of the public, in his said saloon, by refusing to sell him a glass of liquor, called for by him, and that the only ground or cause of refusal was because he was a citizen of color, contrary to the statutes of the United States, made and provided.[89]

United States Commissioner Edgar H. McQuigg issued a warrant, the first summons recorded under the Civil Rights Act. On March 5 the matter of Holmes v. Gerken came forward. Mr. Londen, the defendant's attorney, argued that the complaint should not be admitted; saloons did not fall under the terms of the Civil Rights Act. Commissioner McQuigg dismissed the case. He intended to set a precedent. The law permitted no interference with private enterprise.

The second case arose in the north, Trenton, New Jersey. Hotels, not bars were at issue.[90] Circumstances called for a clear interpretation of the Civil Rights Act. The Trenton House Hotel, Peter Katzenbach proprietor, offered all the amenities of a first-class establishment, including a billiard room. The Trenton House Billiard Parlor faced the street, situated on the ground floor with the hotel above. On the evening of Monday, March 15, two black men, Horace Deyo and Henry Onquee, entered the pool room. They requested a table. Joseph Long, the black attendant, refused. He called for the boss. Hotelier Katzenbach "expostulated" with the unwelcome pair. They stood their ground. They were expelled. On Wednesday, March 17, Deputy Marshal Boswell placed Peter Katzenbach under arrest for violation of the civil rights of citizens Deyo and Onquee.

The case came before United States Commissioner E. Mercer Shreve. On the 25th he dismissed the suit. It was without merit. Defendant's counsel had argued that the civil rights law was unconstitutional. The commissioner refused to rule on that question; that was not his concern. The law simply could not apply to the present matter. The plaintiffs had not asked to register at the hotel. Thus the public accommodations clause had no bearing. The question became whether the hotel's billiard room constituted a "place of public amusement." Commissioner Shreve found that it did not. Entrance to the billiard parlor was on street level. Use was not reserved for hotel guests. It remained therefore, even conjoined as it was to the hotel, a separate, private business enterprise. Private enterprise could discriminate at will. Management had the right to refuse service to customers whom it disliked.

---

89 Wilmington, North Carolina, *Journal*, March 5, 1875.

90 New York *Herald*, March 17, 18, 26; Trenton *State Gazette*, March 26; New York *Times*, March 26, 1875.

> The idea that the Civil Rights bill permits or encourages a colored man to force himself into any man's private shop or house, or into any eating or boarding house, or establishment of any kind except those mentioned in the law, is unworthy of any enlightened mind.... The owner of a billiard saloon has a perfect right to say he will allow no one but Frenchmen to play, or that he will only allow Englishmen to play. No one can compel him to tell why he will not allow Germans or Spaniards or colored men or anybody else to play. He has the right to exclude any or all.... Does the peculiar situation of this billiard saloon make it one of the accommodations, advantages, facilities and privileges of the hotel in the sense in which the Civil Rights bill uses these words? I think not.... Is the defendant's billiard saloon a place of public amusement within the provisions of the Civil Rights act? I think not.[91]

Two swings, two strikes. A third attempt appeared more hopeful. Cincinnati seemed the perfect place for a test – a city on the edge of the South, white, but with a considerable black population. Newsmen were on the alert. On March 7 the Cincinnati *Commercial's* reporter pounced: "The Adventures of a Celtic Gentleman and His African Companion."[92]

"We had the pleasure," his story began, "of meeting last night a gentleman who is stopping at the Henrie House." The gentleman exuded an air of mystery. He gave an abbreviated name, J. McAuliff. Asked from whence he came, he answered evasively: "I am an Irishman." He sported natty attire. "He had his hair oiled, and wore a neat neck-tie." Nor was he alone. McAuliff introduced a young companion, whose mother, he said, had entrusted him to his safekeeping. He was a handsome fellow, the reporter found, "a nice chunk of a boy, pretty black, tolerably black, but a very decent boy, with hair rather curly than otherwise, and of the blackest hue, no doubt."

McAuliff wished, he said, "in an educational way, to open the eyes of his black boy to the sketches of life presented on the dramatic stage." Therefore he had purchased a pair of dress-circle tickets to the Grand Opera House (currently playing, the smash hit "The Two Orphans"). He applied at the door and was refused. "He could go in there, but the boy must go upstairs."

---

91 "If a hotel proprietor keeps a livery stable in connection with his house, in a sense it might be considered an accommodation, but he still ought to be allowed the right of determining to whom he will hire his horses ... and so of a telegraph office or barber shop in a hotel. Such things are separate from the hotel business, although perhaps under the same roof." Trenton *State Gazette*, New York *Times*, March 26, 1875.

92 Cincinnati *Commercial*, March 7–9, 14, 1875.

> Somebody at the door, who appeared to be in authority, said: "You come here to test the Civil Rights bill, do you?" They offered him his money back, which he declined to accept.... So he adjourned from the Grand to Wood's Theater, where he purchased two tickets of admission to the dress circle; and there they refused to admit his fine, healthy black companion. ...Mr. McAuliff then spoke pleadingly on behalf of his helpless sable companion, saying "this is a friend of mine, and he goes with me." But it was all no go, although he urged that the laws of the country guaranteed that the boy should have a seat right there. ...The Manager said, "Come and get your money for your tickets." But Mr. McAuliff responded, "No, these little tickets are receipts that are of value to me."[93]

It eluded no one that the oiled-haired Irishman and his associate were a genial biracial pair of flim-flam men. There was money to be made in the testing of civil rights. Today, said McAuliff, as it was Sunday, he would go to church. Then he hoped to take his protégé "to a sacred concert," if he could find one selling tickets. Reporters staked out the churches: no sign of the pair. "They may not," suggested the *Commercial*, "be partial to the beautiful snow" (six inches had fallen overnight). On March 9 the testers emerged. They filed an affidavit with United States Commissioner Franklin Halliday, citing manager Miles of the Grand Opera and manager Macauley of Wood's Theater for violation of the Civil Rights Act. Commissioner Halliday conferred with United States District Attorney Warner M. Bateman. Bateman was not enthusiastic. He "took occasion to say" that no "desperate effort" would be made to satisfy the complaints of two transients, and that "he will not be swift to pick up such cases as may seem to be brought for a purpose of extortion." He imposed payment of a bond as security for prosecution. That imposition undid the testers. By the 14th, the *Commercial* reported, those parties, "McAuliff and his bright colored boy," had vanished.

While the con-men slept, however, on the snowy night of March 7, another person made his way through Cincinnati's streets. He walked on to the first civil rights decision: the case of Albert A. Price v. Frank Oakes, Frank Buskirk and John Connelly.[94] Hotel accommodations formed the complaint straightforward. Price told a straightforward story. He had applied for lodging at the Crawford House Hotel, a licensed establishment owned by Capt. Frank J. Oakes. The clerk on duty, either Mr. Buskirk or Mr. Connelly, rejected him. The complaint came before United States Commissioner Henry Hooper on March 24. District

93 Cincinnati *Commercial*, March 7, 1875.

94 Account and transcript of the hearing, Cincinnati *Commercial*, March 25, 1875.

Attorney Bateman accepted it. He assigned Assistant District Attorney Richard Dyer to represent Albert Price.

Capt. Oakes also hired an attorney, a young lawyer but destined for greatness: Joseph Benson Foraker, within a decade Governor of Ohio, then United States Senator and political boss of the state. Foraker, at age 27, had recently arrived in Cincinnati. He was eager to win a high-profile decision. He offered Frank Oakes vigorous legal representation.[95]

Attorneys settled in place. Both the *Commercial* and the *Gazette* preserved a full transcript of the proceedings. Albert Price seemed to present an airtight case. Yet he did not win. He had reached Cincinnati, he said, coming down the Ohio from Gallipolis. It was between midnight and 1 o'clock when Steamboat No. 4 docked. It was snowing. He went first to a colored boarding house, Mrs. Jackson's at 196 Broadway that had been recommended to him. He rang. No one answered. He wandered on through the swirling snow and came to the Crawford House at Sixth and Walnut. (See Illustration 10) He stood a few feet inside the door. He perceived two people, a clerk standing in front of a counter, and a janitor, a black man, closer to the door, engaged in scrubbing the floor. When, he asked, would the next train leave the city? Not until morning. He requested a room. The house, he was informed, was full. He turned to the janitor, who looked up from his washtub. Were there places he might stay? The janitor mentioned another colored boarding house. Price despaired of finding his way. He left.

Such was Albert Price's story. Attorney Foraker subjected him to a sharp cross-examination. His escapade was a calculated act. He was not the innocent lost traveler he pretended to be. He was, like J. McAuliff, a scheming tester. Foraker asked aggressively: "When did you first make up your mind to bring this suit?" Price stood his ground. "I don't know whether it is essential to answer that question." Commissioner Hooper intervened. "What is your object?" "The witness seems to have a very indifferent memory; I suppose I have a right to test his memory." Hooper ruled the question immaterial.

District Attorney Dyer rose for re-direct examination. He asked the two accused clerks to stand. "Look at these gentlemen again and think which one it was you saw." Price hesitated. First he indicated Connelly. Then he said Buskirk was the man. He recalled that the clerk that night wore a moustache, like

95 In his memoirs Foraker forgot this youthful episode. Defense of civil rights violators did not help a Republican politician solicitous of black votes. Nor was he at heart unsympathetic to the grievances of black people. Thirty years later, as a senator, he stood up on their behalf, protesting the punishment of black soldiers at Brownsville, Texas, falsely accused and prosecuted by President Theodore Roosevelt.

ILLUSTRATION 10 Crawford House Hotel
SOURCE: LIBRARY OF CONGRESS

Buskirk's, not a full beard, like Connelly's. Now he had made the right choice. "About the sixth guess, you think," Foraker interjected. The prosecution rested its case.

Foraker presented the defense. Three witnesses appeared. They disputed every point Price had made. First called was Charles Brown, the night porter who had been washing the floor. Yes, he was present, standing to the right of the door. The plaintiff had asked when the Louisville train would leave. He asked for the location of a colored boarding house where he might stay until that time. "He says, 'I wonder if I can get in here.' I said, 'There is the clerk.' He went out." At no time did he speak to or attempt to speak to the clerk. He never moved from the rug in front of the door. No one refused Price accommodations because he had not asked for any.

Charles Brown related the role of his employer, Captain Oakes. Oakes had informed all his hotel staff. They must obey and observe the Civil Rights Act. It was the law. "Charley," he had said, "if any of the colored people come here at night I have a place fixed to accommodate them as good as anybody else – a place for them to sleep and a place for them to eat." That place, Charles Brown indicated, could have been had by Albert Price.

Amos Allison was called. He swore he too had been present, although Price had asserted no one was there but the clerk and the janitor. Allison identified himself as a hotel patron. Passing through the lobby, he had stopped to watch. He himself had been standing in front of the desk. The plaintiff addressed no word to him, nor to the clerk, seated behind him reading a newspaper. An employee of the Cincinnati *Enquirer*, Allison was alert for civil rights tests. He had taken note. It was 2 o'clock in the morning. Price stood near the door. He talked with the porter, and left. He asked no one, and no one refused him, accommodations.

Lastly the court heard John B. Connelly, whose testimony was allowed since the plaintiff had exonerated him. He knew nothing of what had transpired that night. But he knew that Capt. Oakes had instructed his clerks to receive all black persons courteously. He had reserved rooms for their accommodation. He warned his staff not to turn them away or to discriminate in their treatment. "The same bill of fare is extended to all." Foraker showed the court a paper. That paper, Connelly said, his boss had read to all his employees. It was a copy of the Civil Rights Act.

On March 25 Commissioner Hooper gave his decision. Two witnesses had sworn "point blank" against the plaintiff's evidence. He acquitted Frank Oakes and Frank Buskirk. Foraker urged Oakes to file a counter-suit. Oakes preferred to let it go.

Albert Price's verdict, one may imagine, was fixed; it was impossible for a humble victim to win. Witnesses could be persuaded to refute the facts. Night porter Charles Brown owed his employment to Captain Oakes. A gentle hint from his boss might induce him to forget that the plaintiff had requested accommodations. Eyewitness Amos Allison appeared miraculously, even though Price had no recollection of having seen him. But there survives from the

Crawford House case another source. It was a private communication, written not for dissembling or disinformation. It informed only the recipient. Its author was Frank Oakes. The recipient was Benjamin Butler. On March 26, the very day after his acquittal, Oakes addressed himself to the authority. He enclosed a clipping with a transcript of the trial, his business card and a brochure describing the Crawford House. He had done nothing to obstruct the Civil Rights Act. He honored its letter and spirit. Yet he found himself subject to prosecution. He wanted to follow the law. He did not know how. "My Dear Sir," he concluded, "if you can and will find time to answer my inquiry I will be under many obligations." He asked for help, "from headquarters."

> I am an American, white in color, and a law abiding citizen of the U.S., an inn-keeper by occupation, as per my business card enclosed. I have been arrested and sued in the U.S. Court under the Civil Rights law, a copy of the case, trial, reports, and results enclosed. I am happy to state that my business is good and I am very often compelled to turn away people, having no room for them, the House being full to its capacity ... and yet I was arrested and sued. What is my remedy and what am I to do in cases of this kind to avoid suit? ... I frequently refuse white men and women entertainment for reasons, viz., drunk or under the influence of drink, bad reputation or character, disorderly, noisy and boisterous, dressed in garb unclean or unbecoming gentleman or lady, sick with, as I believe, some infectious disease. Can I do the same with colored men and women and be within, and protected by the law? In my house are rooms with double beds, one man occupying the same. Am I compelled to put men in the same bed with other men before my house can be said to be full? ... I am not asking this enquiry to avoid attorney's fees; it is a desire to know I am right and have information from Head Quarters.[96]

Reading Oakes' unaffected appeal, we may conclude that Albert Price's suit, like that of J. McAuliff, was a sham. Or perhaps Price too spoke sincerely. He really did recall, exhausted and wet as he was, that the doors of hospitality had shut upon him that night. Perhaps, having come from the dark and midnight snow into the gas-lit glare of the hotel lobby, he thought he had spoken to a clerk standing in front of the desk, though it was only Amos Allison. Buskirk,

96 Frank Oakes to Benjamin Butler, March 26, 1875. Butler Papers, Library of Congress. Frank J. Oakes at this moment was 53. He had been an iron manufacturer, later a riverboat skipper on the Ohio and Mississippi (whence his nautical title). He owned, sold, and then in 1874 repurchased the Crawford House.

had he heard, might have followed his employer's instructions: misunderstandings even where well-intentioned parties desired none. Perhaps no one was to blame but civil rights.

The Crawford House incident gave a foretaste of troubles and confusion to come. The mood was unsettled. Both sides were wary. The Civil Rights Act's work ended on September 23, 1883. Eight years and seven months, minus one week, was all the time granted to change a society barely a decade removed from two and a half centuries of legalized slavery. The desultory, halting, scattershot enforcement of the law left frustrated victims – Horace Deyo and Henry Onquee, Albert Price – in its wake. Yet the civil rights law began to provoke an altered state. Legislation could not erase the prejudice of people. But it could affect the behavior of people, at least in regard to their public actions. Racism remained. But indiscreet bigotry carried the threat of vexatious personal annoyance, legal pains and penalties. The New York *Herald* still ridiculed the law. It was no better than a joke played on the ghost of the poor, misused Sumner:

> Travelers will not suffer from want of hotels, negroes will find plenty of opportunities to get drunk, colored beards will be shaved as well as white beards and the drama will survive its dangers. But how Mr. Sumner might have laughed could he have foreseen this end of his dearest measure! The revolution he proposed has ended in a farce.[97]

The *Herald's* dismissal missed the point. A change had occurred, a realization: uncivil behavior did not go unchallenged. Captain Oakes acknowledged it in his plaintive letter. He needed guidance. Even those most resistant felt the ground move. For the moment they deflected invasions of their space. But they knew those invasions would continue. Katzenbach's billiard-parlor case came closer than that of Gerken's saloon; the Crawford House case came closer still. More cases failed than succeeded. Yet over time, had time been granted, they might have worn down barriers. Theaters barred their doors in Memphis. Mobs chased black people in Richmond. They admitted them in Louisville, in New Orleans, in St. Joseph.

Another early test came even closer to success: the sad case of Happy Cal Wagner.[98] It almost broke through. The defendant was Calvin Wagner, known to his public as Happy Cal, owner and headline performer of the touring minstrel show of that name, "Happy Cal Wagner's Minstrels and Brass Band." Cal, a native of Syracuse, New York, highlighted the show with his sentimental

97 New York *Herald*, March 7, 1875.

98 Account in Montgomery *Advertiser*, March 12–14, 1875.

renditions of the old plantation songs. He also did a stand-up routine in blackface. It was, critics agreed, one of the best. His patter was perfect. His mimicry never failed the stereotype, "in every detail the same good old simple-minded ignorant plantation darkey."[99]

On March 11 Wagner's Minstrels arrived in Montgomery, Alabama. As the ticket window opened at the Montgomery Theater five black men appeared. Among them was a redoubtable agitator, Robert Whittaker, recently delegate to the Alabama Equal Rights Association. His companions were State Representative Herschel V. Cashin, State Senator John W. Jones, also Thomas Ashby, a post-office clerk, and Fred Smith, musician and Pullman porter. They asked for tickets to top-class seats. They were refused.

Whittaker filed the complaint. Before the show opened that night U.S. Marshal George B. Randolph hunted down Happy Cal. He tracked his quarry to Dotzheimer's Restaurant, whence the minstrel was rudely removed from dinner and arrested. Cal Wagner and his ticket agent, Benjamin Brown, came before United States Commissioner Joseph W. Dimmick the next day. District Attorney Nicholas McAfee represented the State.[100] A trio of lawyers rode to the minstrel's rescue. They were Montgomery's best: David Clopton, former Confederate congressman; Hilary Herbert, future U.S. Secretary of the Navy; and Col. Virgil Murphey.

The case took a harsh tone. Cal Wagner's legal team challenged Whittaker's affidavit. The defendants, he alleged, had denied him the "full enjoyment" of the theater's accommodations. That, Herbert remarked, was ridiculous. Whittaker could enjoy the show fully from the Negro seats. The civil rights statute specified "full and equal" enjoyment. Therefore the warrant was invalid. Clopton assailed the constitutionality of the Civil Rights Act. He dwelt at length on the Slaughter-House Cases. He urged the commissioner to rule against the law. District Attorney McAfee appealed to the court's sense of justice. "He spoke of the new era, the bow of promise." Commissioner Dimmick took an hour's recess. "Without delivering any opinion, he quashed the proceedings and discharged the prisoners." Thus the case ended on March 12. But it resumed on the 13th. Whittaker swore out a new complaint. This time, he specified, he had been denied "the full and equal enjoyment" of all the theater's amenities.[101]

---

99 Montgomery *Advertiser*, February 2, 1874.

100 Nicholas S. McAfee of Talladega, former State Representative, member of the Republican Executive Committee. See Sarah Wiggins, *The Scalawag in Alabama Politics, 1865–1881* (University, Ala., 1977), 144–145, 150.

101 Account of the hearing, Montgomery *Advertiser*, March 14, 1875.

Witnesses testified. Whittaker recounted the events. Ticket agent Brown informed him he had no tickets to sell except for cheap seats in the gallery. He insisted on a ticket to the parquet. Brown said they were sold out. Then, in full view, he sold such tickets to white men who requested them. The defense objected again. In the affidavit Whittaker had stated he asked for a ticket to the parquet or to the dress-circle. Now it was only the parquet. Perjury, Clopton declared. He moved to exclude Whittaker's statements. Whittaker stood by the affidavit. His testimony was allowed.

Herschel Cashin took the stand. He had asked for parquet tickets and was refused. He paid 50¢ for a ticket to the gallery. It was not true that no tickets remained for the parquet. From his place inside he could see at least fifty empty seats in that section. He had seen white men purchase tickets after Whittaker was turned away. One of those white men was lawyer Murphey.

John Jones testified. He had asked for a parquet ticket. Ticket agent Brown claimed they were sold out. Then he sold one to Col. Murphey. Jones too settled for a gallery seat. He resented it. "The seats are better in the parquette than in the gallery; you have to be scrouged up in the gallery and it is very unpleasant."

The defense attorneys played a final card. Perhaps their clients had excluded Whittaker. They had every right, not because of his race but because of his character. He was simply an undesirable person to admit to a crowded theater. Police officer Maxwell testified: "Whittaker has a bad character as to being a turbulent, rough and quarrelsome negro." Police officer Brincefield: "Whittaker was loud and turbulent; our orders were not to arrest without there was a fight."

Commissioner Dimmick ruled. Nothing implicated Cal Wagner or proved he had been present when the tickets were sold, or not sold. The charge against him was dismissed. Benjamin Brown did not escape. The commissioner concluded the evidence sufficient. He cited the ticket agent to appear in District Court, pending a grand jury indictment. It was only a scare. The grand jury declined a true bill.[102] Theaters in Montgomery continued to provide entertainment for the masses. Wagner's minstrels returned in December. Happy Cal brought down the house, singing his "touching melodies, 'Down Whar De Sugar Cane Grows,' and 'De Ole Cabin In De Lane.'"[103] Proper order prevailed. Victory once more eluded civil rights.

Victory arrived twelve weeks later. It came in an unexpected place, the Federal District Court for the Eastern District of Texas, sitting at Galveston. It found an unlikely heroine: Mary Miller. It found an unlikely hero: Judge Amos Morrill.

---

102 Montgomery *Advertiser*, May 29, 1875.

103 Montgomery *Advertiser*, December 17, 1875.

Mary Miller, an iron-willed woman, ran up against all the usual obstructions – reluctant jurymen, aggressive lawyers, challenge to the law. She even encountered a new obstacle, preemptive propaganda. She persevered. Morrill, an unflinching jurist, cut through it all. For the first time a victim emerged victorious.

Amos Morrill was 65 years old. White-whiskered, balding, an avuncular appearance belied a pugnacious nature. He had enjoyed a noteworthy career, albeit on the fringes of the frontier. A northerner, a native of Salisbury, Massachusetts, graduate of Bowdoin College, Morrill moved south. He opened his legal practice in Austin, Republic of Texas, with future Gov. Andrew Jackson Hamilton as his partner. During the war he fled the state. Governor Hamilton appointed him chief justice of the Texas Supreme Court. President Grant nominated him to the federal bench. Congress confirmed his appointment in 1872. Morrill's civil rights rulings brought upon him a storm of vituperation. He would not budge. He was a Texan: "All I have or am is located here.... I do not purpose living anywhere else except Texas."[104]

Texans received a foretaste of the judge's vexatious rulings in May, when he gave his charge to the district's newly-empaneled grand jury. His reading of the Civil Rights Act was hardly radical. He did not consider it a mandate for social equality. He saw no reason segregated accommodations could not exist, on trains, in inns or anywhere else. But, he warned, segregation did not mean exclusion. No citizen could be denied public rights or privileges. "If it shall be made to appear that any inn-keeper has refused proper facilities to any one on account of race, color, or previous condition, if a railroad conductor has failed to furnish a proper seat in his cars, or a manager of a theater has excluded from his theater any one for a similar reason, you will be authorized to find a true bill against them."[105] The grand jury delivered a true bill in Galveston.

Events had occurred on March 20, 1875. On that Saturday afternoon Mary Miller and a companion, Mrs. McGhee, approached the grand façade of the Tremont Opera House on Market Street – now playing, in a matinee performance, "Enoch Arden," a dramatic adaptation.[106] Door-keeper Edward Greenwall ushered the women in. He watched in horror as they crossed the lobby and walked straight on to sit in the middle of the parquet. That cataclysm

104 Galveston *News*, June 8, 1875.

105 Galveston *News*, May 4, 1875.

106 The Tremont, grandest playhouse of the West, was famed for its opulence. Famous players, Edwin Booth, Edwin Forrest, Adelina Patti, and Maurice Barrymore trod its boards. J.S. Gellegly, "The Tremont Opera House of Galveston: The First Years," *Rice Institute Pamphlets*, 45 (1959), 52–70.

brought Edward's father, theater manager and impresario Henry Greenwall, onto the scene at a gallop.[107]

Manager Greenwall was justly surprised. He thought he had arranged an avoidance of such difficulties. After an incident earlier that month, when some black men tested the law,[108] he sought out the city's more refined colored citizens and explained the impropriety of attempting to exercise their civil rights. They agreed to enjoy exclusive use of the dress-circle on the upper tier. Mr. Miller, as he said at trial, explained it to his wife.

Mary Miller had other ideas. She calculated the perfect moment. Matinee performances permitted open seating. Red tickets, sold on matinees only, authorized the bearers to sit anywhere in the house. Clutching thus a red ticket, Mrs. Miller entered the lobby. She turned not aside but planted herself in the parquet. Greenwall the elder remonstrated, to no avail. Finally he commanded the women to leave. According to his own account, he meant they should leave the parquet and go up to the balcony. Mary, whether through misunderstanding or willful malice, interpreted it as an order to quit the theater. She filed out. Then she filed suit.[109]

Henry Greenwall, as other early civil rights defendants, found eager lawyers. The firm of Flournoy, Sherwood and Scott took up the defense. At its head was former Texas Attorney-General George M. Flournoy. Col. Flournoy called on Judge Morrill to sustain a demurrer and quash the indictment. The Galveston *News* backed his appeal. On the day the trial began it broadcast an editorial: "Law and Higher Law." Be it known to all citizens (including all potential jurors), the Civil Rights Act was unconstitutional. Only the twisted logic of an incompetent jurist (Amos Morrill), "wrapped in the awful sanctity of judicial ignorance," could think otherwise.[110]

The *News'* pique was understandable. Judge Morrill's ruling on the demurrer gave the Civil Rights Act its first legal stamp of approval. Flournoy indeed argued the law's unconstitutionality. "Until the State of Texas passed laws abridging the rights of citizens, the Fourteenth Amendment to the Constitution was inoperative." Civil rights moreover were Socialism: "The proprietary rights of a citizen could not be taken from a citizen." Congress had passed an iniquitous law. He invited the judge to reject it. United States District Attorney J.G. Boyle represented Mary Miller. He opposed Flournoy's position but declined to rebut.

---

107 On Henry Greenwall, see Claudia Anne Beach, *Henry Greenwall, Theater Manager* (Lubbock: 1986).

108 Galveston *News*, March 13, 1875.

109 Account of the incident, trial and verdict, Galveston *News*, June 5–6, 8–10, 1875.

110 Galveston *News*, June 5, 1875.

Amos Morrill needed no rebuttal. His ruling brushed aside all objections. Flournoy's constitutional quibbles meant nothing. Perhaps the colonel was correct. Very likely the Civil Rights Act *was* unconstitutional. So be it. It didn't matter. There might be "ten points involved in the constitutional construction of the law, nine of which indicated clearly that the law was unconstitutional, and there was one doubtful." It didn't matter. Only the spirit of the law mattered. That spirit, the spirit of the constitution, he believed, animated the Civil Rights Act.

> What is the letter and spirit of the law? Is it not to carry out the idea that privileges and immunities shall not be abridged by the State, or by anybody? ... What is the spirit of the law? Did Congress act according to the spirit or the letter of the Constitution? I believe it acted according to the spirit. It might be said to be unconstitutional, if taken according to the letter of the constitution. But, according to the spirit, Congress has the right to impose appropriate legislation.... Adhering to the spirit of the law, I do not think the act of Congress was unconstitutional.[111]

The trial opened on Saturday, June 5, 1875. A searing sun, a heavy and oppressive atmosphere hung over the courtroom. Heat was stifling, ventilation insufficient. Spectators packed together, white and black, perspiring in perfect social equality. From the bench Judge Morrill looked down on an overcrowded and overheated court. He banged for order.

The court took great care in selecting a jury. District Attorney Boyle insisted all jurors take the Iron-clad Oath, never to have borne arms or encouraged armed resistance to the United States. That eliminated several upstanding gentlemen at once. Morrill charged the United States marshal to find alternates. According to some bystanders, the marshal consulted a list, taking it ready-made from his pocket. "It's a put-up job," voices whispered. Flournoy caustically proposed a recess, so the marshal would have time to locate his pre-arranged jury. Boyle objected to the imputation against an officer of the court. Another suffocating hour went by. Finally eight black citizens took seats on the panel: Johnson Reed, Anderson Chandler, J.H. Ash, Thomas Ryan, Wesley Moore, Ben

111 Galveston *News*, June 5, 1875. Eight years later John Marshall Harlan framed his lonely dissent in the Supreme Court's Civil Rights Cases decision. "It is not the words of the law, but the internal sense of it that makes the law," he wrote. "The substance and spirit of the recent amendments of the constitution have been sacrificed by a subtle and ingenious verbal criticism.... 'The letter of the law is the body; the sense and reason of the law is the soul.'" Harlan might have thanked Amos Morrill for those words. (*Civil Rights Cases* 109 U.S. 3 (1883).

Lloyd, John James (the name of one juror escaped the *News'* account). Four white men joined them: P.H. Moser, H.C. Reed, A. Brook, and Albert Somerville.

Somerville, the last juror, lent the panel distinction. One of Galveston's most dynamic merchants, he had just launched the dynamic city's most ambitious project: a new railroad, the Gulf, Colorado and Santa Fe, destined to link the port of Galveston with the wealth of the interior. Laying of track had already begun. Albert Somerville, president of the consortium, had little time for civil rights annoyances. For one long, sequestered weekend he sat, ate, and discussed the law with common black citizens. The jury chose him foreman. Foreman Somerville acquired an unwanted privilege, to deliver the first guilty verdict pronounced under the Civil Rights Act.

Jurors found their chairs. Mary Miller recounted her ordeal, her humiliation. She recalled Manager Greenwall's brusque commands. Hisses surrounded her, shouts of "Put them out!" She tried to hold her place. Ed Greenwall testified. He saw the plaintiff and her companion make for the parquet. He couldn't stop them. District Attorney Boyle concluded the prosecution's case. He reviewed black people's persecution from the time of Justice Taney to the present. He eulogized Charles Sumner. He called for a guilty verdict based on the facts.

Flournoy summed up for the defense. The colonel, one of the orators of Texas secession, was in top form. The whole proceeding, he thundered, was a farce, Negroes appropriating seats in the white section of a theater. Perhaps to accentuate the farcicality, he commenced an o-ration: "We will gnaw a file! We shall flee unto the mountains of Hepsidam where the fierce lion roareth and the whangdoodle mourneth for its first born!"

How the jurors received that effusion and what sense they made of it we do not know.[112] Flournoy, in any case, denounced the jurors. The jury was rigged. His client could not get a fair trial. He turned next upon Prosecutor Boyle, insinuating doubts about the Irishman's racial ancestry. "He found occasion to compare his physiognomy and several other features with those of the witnesses [Mr. Miller and Mr. McGhee]." Boyle jumped up. He challenged the colonel to a duel. Flournoy answered with a back-of-the-hand slap to the District Attorney's nose. Judge Morrill slammed his gavel.

Calm returned. Amos Morrill handed the jurors their charge in writing. He sent them off to deliberate. The courtroom crowd mopped its sweating brows. Eleven jurors retired, Mr. Brook having absconded during lunch break. The scorching afternoon sun declined. Stars appeared. The jury did not. At 10 p.m.

---

112 The quote, an old set-piece of humor, pretended to parody revivalist preachers, the exuberance of their apocalyptic expectations. Likewise perhaps the colonel meant to mimic utopianisms of the civil rights variety.

the jurors returned, only to announce themselves deadlocked. Morrill ordered them sequestered. They could think it over until Monday.

The jury, to its credit, wrestled with the demons of civil rights law. Evidence of the trial pointed to a guilty verdict. But some jurors had read the Galveston *News'* editorial. Was it not their duty to nullify an unconstitutional law? In the wee hours of Sunday night a messenger banged at Judge Morrill's door. Come, please, the jurors implored. Explain why they should not believe the newspaper's assertions. Morrill refrained, for fear of a mistrial.

Monday morning. Amos Morrill took care of business. Interruption of sleep had not sweetened his disposition. Before he recalled the jurors he called for the battling attorneys. Boyle apologized for the unseemly courtroom combat. He purged himself of any contempt. Flournoy did not appear. Morrill sent his case to the grand jury for indictment. Next the judge dealt with the Galveston *News*. It had cast contempt upon the honorable court. Its editorial was a calculated attempt to poison and prejudice the minds of jurors. It amounted to obstruction of justice. He cited the editors to answer charges. Then he summoned the jury.

Those weary citizens announced again that they could not reach a decision. Morrill refused to accept it. He would keep them out as long as it took. "They could not agree," foreman Somerville replied, "even if they remained out until next January." Morrill read them again his written charge. The case was extraordinarily simple; "unless they had been reading the Galveston *News* there was no reason they should not agree." If Mary Miller had purchased a ticket entitling her to sit in a seat of her choice, and if the defendant denied her the right to sit where she chose, "then you will find the defendant guilty." Satisfied at last that the jurors understood his meaning, he sent them off to reconsider. They huddled briefly. Albert Somerville handed the clerk a slip: "We the jury find the defendant guilty."

Blame lay with Judge Morrill. Everyone agreed. The judge's bullying had done the trick, white jurors told the *News*. He had frightened them into the verdict.[113] Henry Greenwall moved for a new trial. Morrill denied him.[114] The Houston *Telegraph* expressed the universal resentment.

> At last a court has been found to decide the Civil Rights law constitutional – the phenomenal tribunal at Galveston yclept the United States Court for the Eastern District of Texas. Everywhere else the decisions have been invariably adverse to the rights set up under the bastard political

113 Galveston *News*, July 3, 1875.
114 Galveston *News*, June 30, 1875.

> contrivance. What a set of sublime asses the majority of the United States District and Circuit judges must be when viewed in the light of Judge Morrill's brilliant decisions.[115]

Headlines spread: Civil Rights Act vindicated. The New York *Times* was not pleased. The Galveston *News* may have shown contempt for Judge Morrill, it wrote; contempt was justified. "Any court that could fine a white man $500 for any possible injury toward two colored women" deserved society's disapprobation.[116]

Enlightenment did not come to the New York *Times*. Yet light began to flicker. Henry Greenwall's ordeal exceeded that of Benjamin Brown, whose travail transcended that of Frank Oakes, just as Oakes' surpassed the troubles of Peter Katzenbach and William Gerken. Such cases and others to follow placed civil rights in play. It stayed there for eight years and seven months. That alone must be counted as no small success. In 1880, shortly before its demise, United States Attorney-General Charles Devens reported 158 federal prosecutions in progress under the Civil Rights Act. Most failed. Some, beginning with the case of Mary Miller, succeeded.[117]

In the course of long debates over the civil rights bill angry opinions echoed. One quiet opinion correctly anticipated the state of things to come. In the end Ebenezer Hoar had said it best. The Civil Rights Act would not deliver a society sanitized. It was bound to disappoint. It was not a sweeping cure-all for the nation's ills. It was a declaration of principle: "I have no belief that this bill, if enacted into a law, is going to produce any great effect immediately for good or for evil," he told the House, "but it will stand as the declaration of the American

115 Quoted in Galveston *News*, June 12, 1875. Previous pronouncements indeed were hostile. The most emphatic had come in March from Judge Halmer H. Emmons of the Sixth District Court at Memphis. The law, said Judge Emmons, sadly, was unconstitutional. The Supreme Court had made that clear. Still, Amos Morrill was not quite alone. One other federal judge agreed with him. Judge Rensselaer R. Nelson of the United States District Court of Minnesota was not only a veteran magistrate but a Democrat, named to the federal bench by President Buchanan. His reasoning surpassed even Judge Morrill's. He did not invoke the spirit against the letter of the law. The letter was perfectly fine. He saw no limitation in the Fourteenth Amendment: "Congress can legislate, though a State has passed no obnoxious law … to remedy the evil against which the amendment proposes to guard." New York *Times*, June 9, 1875.

116 New York *Times*, June 8, 1875.

117 See Stephen J. Riegel, "The Persistent Career of Jim Crow: Lower Federal Courts and the 'Separate but Equal' Doctrine, 1865–1896," *The American Journal of Legal History*, 28 (1984): 23–24; John Hope Franklin, "The Enforcement of the Civil Rights Act of 1875," *Prologue*, 6 (1974): 226–231.

people that henceforth before the law every citizen of the country is to have equality." [See above, 538.]

Frederick Douglass agreed with Hoar. The law might not be perfect. It might not be enforced. But it was indispensable, a banner that pointed the way, a commandment for public good. When the Supreme Court struck down the Civil Rights Act in 1883, he mourned its passing. The Court had "inflicted a heavy calamity upon seven millions of the people of this country, and left them naked and defenseless against the action of a malignant, vulgar and pitiless prejudice."

> It is said that this decision will make no difference in the treatment of colored people; that the Civil Rights Bill was a dead letter, and could not be enforced. There is some truth in all this, but it is not the whole truth. That bill, like all advance in legislation, was a banner on the outer wall of American liberty, a noble moral standard, uplifted for the education of the American people. There are tongues in trees, sermons in stones, and books in the running brooks. This law, though dead, did speak. It expressed the sentiment of justice and fair play, common to every honest heart. Its voice was against popular prejudice and meanness. It appealed to all the noble and patriotic instincts of the American people. It told the American people that they were all equal before the law; that they belonged to a common country and were equal citizens. The Supreme Court has hauled down this broad and glorious flag of liberty.[118]

Black people, Douglass conceded, had won few civil rights cases. Yet discrimination did not go unchallenged, as in the past, without fear of consequences. Now the law was gone. Oppression would return, unchallenged. "It may not be felt at the moment, and the evil may be long delayed, but so sure as there is a moral government of the universe, so sure as there is a God of the universe, so sure will the harvest of evil come."[119]

---

118 Frederick Douglass, *Life and Times of Frederick Douglass*, in: *Autobiographies, Narrative of the Life and Times of Frederick Douglass, and American Slave; My Bondage and My Freedom; Life and Times of Frederick Douglass* (New York: 1994), 967–972, 977–978.

119 Douglass, *Life and Times*, 973. See Robert J. Kaczorowski, "To Begin the Nation Anew: Congress, Citizenship, and Civil Rights after the Civil War," *American Historical Review*, 92 (1987), 68: The Supreme Court's rejection of Congress' attempt at unitary federal enforcement of civil rights led to "a reactionary resurgence of state's rights that resulted in the virtual reenslavement of Southern black Americans."

The Civil Rights Act's seasons passed in a blur – from hope to hate to discard – all in a short span of life. In the radiant days of May, 1874, when a bill first passed the Senate, the Indianapolis *Journal* proclaimed that society would emerge transformed: "Five years from now the Civil Rights law will be virtually a dead letter, for the reason that nobody will think of denying their just rights to the colored people."[120] Prejudice would follow the law, *Harper's Weekly* persuaded itself. Once the law changed society would change: "The 'instinct' of dislike is founded in legal injustice."[121] In Missouri, the Princeton *Advance* looked hopefully at the spirit of the American people: "Even if there were no principle of fair play involved, intelligent Americans have too keen a sense of the ridiculous to stand out for these caste prejudices when the question is once fairly before them."[122] Americans' sense of the ridiculous, alas, did not rise to the occasion.

Ridicule did rise. In 1878 English traveler George Campbell visited the Richmond Theater. Where once James Ellis and Ellen White had sowed panic ribaldry reigned. On stage he beheld a somewhat incomprehensible farce involving a congressman, a lady, and a foreign guest. For extra comic relief a "civil rights man" appeared. Why, Sir George asked, should he laugh? His hosts explained. The character was funny; he was "in favor of complete equality of blacks and whites." Civil rights man soliloquized on the raptures of a "civil rights barbershop." All men shall shave together: hoots of laughter.[123]

The San Jose *Mercury* summed it up: "If the Civil Rights Act cannot cope with a burnt cork artist [referring to the Cal Wagner affair] to what sad burial must it come."[124] The Supreme Court buried it in 1883. In short order eighteen states passed civil rights statutes to take its place. Some were more comprehensive than Charles Sumner's offspring on which they were based.[125] Some were the product of Democratic administrations, pursuing a "newer departure," a

120 Indianapolis *Journal*, May 28, 1874.

121 *Harper's Weekly*, April 11, 1874, p. 311.

122 Quoted in Springfield, Missouri, *Patriot*, April 1, 1875. A century later politicians again, longingly or wistfully, hoped in the American spirit. "Our children's children will probably look back on these times and wonder what all the fuss was about," Maryland Congressman Carlton Sickles mused in 1963. "They will wonder why some of their grandparents found it odd that every citizen should have the same rights and opportunities, and we will, too." *Cong. Record*, 88th Congress, 1st Session: 15,890.

123 George Campbell, *White and Black: The Outcome of a Visit to the United States* (New York: 1969), 289.

124 San Jose *Mercury*, March 18, 1875.

125 See Milton R. Konvitz and Theodore Laskes, *A Century of Civil Rights: With a Study of State Law against Discrimination* (New York: 1961), 157–168.

quest for black votes.[126] Ohio's act passed in February 1884, five months after the federal act's demise, written by a Democratic legislature urged on by a Democratic governor, George Hoadly. Additional statutes strengthened it in 1894.[127] New Jersey, which had failed to pass a civil rights law in 1873, passed one in 1884, signed by its Democratic Governor Leon Abbett. Connecticut, Illinois, Iowa, Indiana, Michigan, Minnesota, Nebraska and Rhode Island followed in 1885.[128] Pennsylvania passed its act in 1887. The old New York Civil Rights Act of 1873 soldiered on. It even marked some success in school desegregation cases.[129] It expanded in 1895, adding coverage of eating-stands, bath-houses and barber shops. It expanded again in 1918 to include hospitals, parks, saloons, and grocery stores.[130] Wisconsin enacted a bill in 1895. Retired congressman Gerry Hazelton stepped up. Twenty years before, representing Wisconsin's 2nd District, he had voted to create the national civil rights act. Now he represented the plaintiffs in the first civil rights suits brought under his own state's statute.[131]

Those state statutes also failed. Juries nullified. Judges ignored the law or ruled around it.[132] Civil rights statutes sprouted. Jim Crow sprouted alongside. The Ku Klux Klan enjoyed a new birth of freedom. The twentieth century progressed.

Writing his memoirs in 1903, a year before his death, George Frisbie Hoar looked back over a long career. He regretted only two failures of his Republican Party: the failure to secure the country honest elections; the failure to secure

126 Lawrence Grossman, *The Democratic Party and the Negro: Northern and National Politics, 1868–1892* (Urbana: 1976), 60–106.

127 Gerber, *Black Ohio and the Color Line*: 235–236.

128 Grossman, *The Democratic Party and the Negro*: 71, 77, 96–103.

129 J. Morgan Kousser, *Dead End: The Development of Nineteenth-Century Litigation on Racial Discrimination in Schools* (Oxford: 1986), 12–14.

130 David McBride, "Fourteenth Amendment Idealism: The New York State Civil Rights Law, 1873–1918," *New York History*, 71 (1990): 219, 232.

131 Leslie H. Fishel, Jr., "The Genesis of the First Wisconsin Civil Rights Act," *Wisconsin Magazine of History*, 49 (1966): 328–333.

132 See Gerber, *Black Ohio and the Color Line*: 46–47; McBride, "New York Civil Rights Act," 209–226; Riegel, "The Persistent Career of Jim Crow," 17–40; Donna A. Barnes and Catherine Connolly, "Repression, the Judicial System, and Political Opportunities for Civil Rights Advocacy during Reconstruction," *The Sociological Quarterly*, 40 (1999): 327–345; Emma Lou Thornbrough, *The Negro in Indiana before 1900: A Study of a Minority* (Bloomington: 1993), 259–266; Valeria W. Weaver, "The Failure of Civil Rights, 1875–1883, and its Repercussions," *Journal of Negro History*, 54 (1969): 373–377. Civil Rights Cases: *United States v. Stanley; United States v. Ryan; United States v. Nichols; United States v. Singleton; Robinson et ux. v. Memphis & Charleston R.R. Co.* 109 U.S. 3.

civil rights.[133] He might have recalled his brother's words. Not until human sentiment changed would change arrive. Slavery lingered as discrimination. Equal rights became an idle turn-of-phrase. Citizens of Harrodsburg, Kentucky, at the birth of the Civil Rights Act, had issued a hopeful resolution: "The Government has spoken to us and committed the future to our hands. Our destiny will be, under God, what we choose to make it." The nation chose, under God, a destiny unencumbered by commitment to civil rights.

None of that was the responsibility of those who framed the Civil Rights Act or of those who passed it. None of it invalidates Ebenezer Hoar's observation on the act's passage, or lessens the truth of Frederick Douglass' lament on its demise. None of it justifies the interpretations that historians have crafted. "If the bill could claim any significance," one authority concluded, "it lay on the bankruptcy of Republican Reconstruction principles ... a travesty of racial justice, because neither the white public nor its representatives expected or wanted the Act's enforcement."[134] Principles were not bankrupt in 1875. Those astute politicians – Butler, Edmunds, Conkling, Frelinghuysen, Jasper Ward – the men who created the Civil Rights Act, wanted its enforcement. They intended no travesty. But they understood the public's ugly temper. Change needed time. In time they hoped for a metamorphosis.[135]

Nor did they pursue Charles Sumner's dream with mocking levity, their actions guided by "political expediency and cynical partisanship."[136] Their pursuit was monumentally inexpedient. If only a hollow, cynical duplicity lay behind the resounding words of Oliver Morton, George Boutwell, Frelinghuysen and Garfield, Timothy Howe, then it was a pointless, suicidal cynicism. It cost the Republicans a dozen states and scores of congressional seats. They cannot have pursued it hoping in some Machiavellian way to perpetuate their hold on power. Yet that view persists:

> To Republican leaders of Sumner's generation the hegemony of their party was necessary to preserve the rights of freedmen, to their successors

133 George F. Hoar, *Autobiography of Seventy Years* (New York: 1903), vol. 1, 249.

134 Bertram Wyatt-Brown, "The Civil Rights Act of 1875," 775.

135 Some historians have taken a more positive view. Thus the conclusion of Kirt Wilson: "Perhaps the bill had been largely symbolic, but it was also the nation's final chance to learn how to transform the Declaration of Independence into the 'practice of everyday living.'" Kirt Wilson, *The Reconstruction Desegregation Debate. The Politics of Equality and the Rhetoric of Place, 1870–1875* (East Lansing: 2002), 16. Michael Ross speaks of the "potent" Civil Rights Act. "Justice Miller's Reconstruction: The *Slaughter-House Cases*, Health Codes, and Civil Rights in New Orleans, 1861–1873," *Journal of Southern History*, 64 (1998): 672.

136 McPherson, "Abolitionists and the Civil Rights Act of 1875," 508.

> the protection of the Negroes was required in order to assure the success of the Republican Party. Political technicians devoid of ideology ... few had any deep interest in the plight of the Negro.[137]

This volume concludes the contrary. Compromise with hard realities of political life does not reflect abandonment of principles. Republicans in 1875 did not sell their souls to the devil. Faustian congressmen, historians assure us; they acted with compassionless calculation. Yet, at the very same time they were overcome by slobbery sentiment. It was a "tribute" to Charles Sumner.[138] But no, it was a cynical dodge designed to mock that tribute. "The widely understood assumption that the measure would never operate effectively was the *reason* [emphasis added] the bill had passed."[139] Not even the most partisan Democrat in 1875 advanced that critique. As Allen Thurman might have said, the logic "just won't do." Rather, let us admit, Republicans in the Forty-third Congress guided their actions on a sincerity historians have generally not been pleased to attribute to them.[140] They protected African Americans to protect the nation. They accepted present political disaster – they welcomed ruin – for the sake of the future.

Republicans passed the Civil Rights Act of 1875 as a classic exemplar of Rights-For-Order statesmanship. They passed it over enormous public resistance, in defiance of the voters' clear desires. They did so for the sake of peace, to stabilize an unstable country. It was not a meaningless sop to black voters,

---

137 David Donald, *Charles Sumner and the Rights of Man* (New York: 1970), 350, 421, 508. Robert Kaczorowski summed up the historiography: "Most of these studies either implicitly assume or explicitly state that the Radicals, in proposing their civil rights program, had little or no regard for the Negro; rather, they were motivated by self-seeking political goals and feelings of revenge against the South. Consequently, proposals which had the ostensible purpose of benefiting the Negro were really political stratagems ... a meaningless tactic to keep the South under Radical control." *The Nationalization of Civil Rights: Constitutional Theory and Practice in a Racist Society, 1866–1883* (New York: 1987), 4.

138 Even a very recent study adopts the old idea. H.W. Brands, *The Man Who Saved the Union: Ulysses Grant in War and Peace* (New York: 2012), 552–553.

139 Gillette, *Retreat from Reconstruction*, 271.

140 Long ago, LaWanda and John Cox wondered at historians' obstinate refusal to ascribe any but "cynical" motives, self-seeking and calculation of political gain, to the Republicans' passage of the 15th Amendment. It was time for a reappraisal: "In challenge to the dominant pattern of interpretation from Braxton through Gillette ... the Republican party leadership played a crucial role in committing this nation to equal suffrage for the Negro not because of political expediency but *despite* political risk.... Why can they not be credited with an honest conviction? ... Party advantage was subordinated to principle." LaWanda and John H. Cox, "Negro Suffrage and Republican Politics: The Problem of Motivation in Reconstruction Historiography," *Journal of Southern History*, 33 (1967): 317, 330.

who could not and did not abandon the party. It was not a sentimental tribute to Sumner, some of whose best friends, Carl Schurz among them, disowned it. They did not hope for its failure. The Civil Rights Act was in essence a conservative measure. Certainly there were some, George Boutwell at their head, who urged it in pursuit of utopia. But above all they urged it to conserve peace. It would be the final act needed to settle the social conflicts of the war, to bring an end to interminable unrest. It might seem ineffective. Impatient visionaries chafed at the pace of progress. Uncle Billy's sack of flour seemed more worthwhile. Ultimately Josiar was right.

• • •

David Ross Locke, the voice of Nasby, composed his popular lecture "Cussed be Canaan" in 1867. He ridiculed the expired institution of slavery and its residue of racism. He read it publicly many times in the years that followed. Mark Twain described one performance. He recalled his friend as he strode to the stage, "raised his face slightly, flashed a glance upon the audience and bellowed" his memorable opening line: "We are all descended from grandfathers!" He went on, "tearing his ruthless way through the continuous applause and laughter."[141] Finally he paused, set aside his comic bellow, to voice a passionate conclusion:

> I want and insist upon it, that the Declaration of Independence shall no longer be a "glittering generality" … but a living robust truth, possessed of as much vitality as any other truth which has blessed the world.… Until this principle is adopted our republic is no republic, and our boasted freedom is a hollow sham. We must have no more of this inequality. We must make all men before the law equal. We must not leave the rights of a single citizen in the hands of timid legislatures, interested oligarchies, and ex-slaveholders.[142]

Locke's aspiration was, of course, the height of implausibility. No legislative act, no assemblage of injunctions and clauses, could fulfill that goal. No politician could animate it with the stroke of a pen. Yet Locke's hope took a step forward in 1875, with the stroke of a pen. The Civil Rights Act possessed in its infant limbs an insidious force. Prejudice's proud tower endured. But the law

---

141 Mark Twain, *The Autobiography of Mark Twain* (Berkeley: 2010), vol. 1: 147.

142 David Ross Locke, "Cussed be Canaan," text in *The Struggles (Social, Financial, and Political) of Petroleum V. Nasby* (Boston: 1873): 656.

set corruption at its base, an element that sapped and corroded its structure. Here and there cracks appeared. Black men sat among the "*élite*" in the Louisville Theater; a color barrier was broken. Mary Miller avenged her humiliation. Little cracks propagate. They did not breach the wall.[143] They spread softly to undermine its impregnability. Eight Supreme Court justices, with the wisdom of the law, gave it eight years to live. Eighty years later the nation redeemed its past. Or did it?

143 See Howard N. Rabinowitz, *Race Relations in the Urban South, 1865–1890* (New York, 1978): 182–197.

CHAPTER 16

Epilogue: Then and Now

The American creed, "self-evident" in the Declaration of Independence of July 4, 1776, declared that "all men are created equal." The Emancipation Proclamation of January 1, 1863, ratified this truth. The Civil Rights Act of 1875 proclaimed that ideal, yet again repeated in the Civil Rights Act of 1964. It struggles today for recognition. In this moment of Trump National Football League players kneel in protest over police brutality. The president denounces them. Marchers fill the streets demanding racial and gender equality. Violence erupts. Demands echo for the removal of Confederate monuments. In Memphis, where once they stood together in 1874 to proclaim "Indignation" at the slaughter of black people, statues of Jefferson Davis and Bedford Forrest become the focus of confrontation; are they memorials of a revered past or of racism rooted in the culture?

The idea of equality evolves over time. Each generation is encased in a time-bound set of concepts, truths, assumptions, notions, biases, experiences that form a common mental equipment, a frame of reference shared by the people of a society or a region. It is this that led Thomas Jefferson to exclaim that "every generation should write its own history." It made no sense to him to view the past through someone else's point of view. Generation X would regard an event, an idea, as important, while to Generation Y what mattered to Generation X would be irrelevant.

Voltaire, perhaps expressed the idea best when he said: "History is a pack of tricks we play on the dead." Historians seek to comprehend the past. We must consider our own times, our own frame of reference. We must know who we are. Therefore we must be active in our own moment, aware of what our own time, our own frame of reference means by "all men are created equal." The issues of Civil War and Reconstruction are very much alive today. From the prequel comes the present.

1 Prequel: 1964 to 1875

On July 2, 1964, for the third time in the nation's history, the United States Congress passed a civil rights act, perhaps, the final Civil Rights Act. That legislation was born of a long travail, an impassioned debate, a filibuster of three months in the Senate. The twentieth-century parties' positions were reversed.

A northern Democratic majority pursued social justice; conservative Republicans joined southern opposition. Yet it concluded finally through the effort of a Republican senator, Everett M. Dirksen of Illinois, whose influence brought a vote of cloture. Dramatic scenes unfolded. Senator Clair Engle of California, stricken with a brain tumor, unable to speak and carried into the Chamber, lifted a hand to his eye, signaling his affirmative vote. West Virginia's Robert Byrd spoke through the final night, standing until dawn to deliver an unheard plea against passage of (as he believed) an unjust act. Senator Hubert Humphrey of Minnesota, floor leader for the bill, handed Byrd a rose plucked from his garden, a sign of respect for those whose convictions he opposed.[1] The origin of that drama went back eight decades, to the ruling in 1883 by the Supreme Court that the Supplemental Civil Rights Act of 1875 was unconstitutional. That nineteenth-century legislation lasted but eight years. The decision in the *Civil Rights Cases* required its rebirth a century later. Had the judicial branch heeded the dissent of Justice John Marshall Harlan in 1883 the nation would have had no cause to consider a Civil Rights Act of 1964.

Congressmen in the age of Lyndon Johnson harkened back to those who had sat before them in the age of Andrew Johnson. History, Thomas Carlyle wrote, is a film stretched over the eternity of the past. Faces floated on that film. Southerners beheld figures of evil, returned from the grave to finish off the oppression they had failed to achieve in their lifetimes. "Embittered men," declared Senator John Tower of Texas, "Thaddeus Stevens and Charles Sumner, determined to impose a vindictive punishment on the southern people."[2] They lived again in this attempt to impose yet another civil rights act on a prostrate South. "The approach now is more subtle and hypocritical," noted Senator Richard Russell, "but its purposes are identical with those that prompted Charles Sumner, Thaddeus Stevens and Ben Wade."[3] For Congressman Howard Smith of Virginia a new civil rights bill inaugurated a new reign of oppression, an era "unmatched in harshness and brutality and raw dictatorship never before witnessed since the tragic days of reconstruction. The second invasion of carpetbaggers ... beatniks, misfits, and agitators from the North."[4] "There is hatred in this bill," concluded Mississippi Congressman Thomas Abernethy. "The hatred of Thad Stevens, Ben Wade, and Charles Sumner that went into

1 See Robert D. Loevy, *To End All Segregation; The Politics and Passage of the Civil Rights Act of 1964* (Lanham, 1990); *The Civil Rights Act of 1964: The Passage of the Law that Ended Racial Segregation* (Albany: 1997); Charles and Barbara Whelan, *The Longest Debate: A Legislative History of the 1964 Civil Rights Act* (Washington: 1985).

2 *Cong. Record*, 88th Congress, 2nd Session: 7,781.

3 *Cong. Record*, 88th Congress, 2nd Session: 14,301.

4 *Cong. Record*, 88th Congress, 2nd Session: 15,870.

the civil rights bills of the 1860's is handed to the South in the civil rights bill of the 1960's."[5] South Carolina's Senator Olin Johnston spoke on June 19, 1964.

> Mr. President, this is indeed the blackest day in the U.S. Senate since 1875, when Congress passed a civil rights bill similar to this one. It was 89 years ago that the Congress passed the nefarious Reconstruction era civil rights law, identical with what we are now discussing.... There is no doubt in my mind that the spirit of Thaddeus Stevens is present in this Senate Chamber.[6]

Civil rights proponents likewise saw revenants rise. "The Civil War is still with us," sighed Illinois Senator Paul Douglas. "Sometimes I wonder who won it. I sometimes wonder if we should not have the Confederate flag flying from the Capitol."[7] Pennsylvania's Joseph Clark imagined himself a civil rights warrior of the past, "some learned Senator from the North who stood up to vote for civil rights – perhaps Charles Sumner."[8] Winston Prouty of Vermont added a modern martyr. "Frederick Douglass, Abraham Lincoln, John F. Kennedy – all these are gone. How I wish that they could know that in 1964 when there was heard the cry 'freedom now,' the Congress answered 'ever more.'"[9]

Even after ninety years the debates repeated familiar themes – a record, its needle stuck in a groove, doomed to replay. Government tyranny sounded a recurrent refrain. "A piebald monster, a child of darkness," Missouri's Lewis Bogy named the Civil Rights Bill of his day in May, 1874. "The Federal Government is the sun of our political system. If we are drawn too close, we shall be burned by its central fire." Bogy's colleagues evoked the nascent menace of Communism, the International, the Paris Commune. The Civil Rights Bill, declared John Young Brown, would be "the crowning iniquity of Socialism."

Socialism! cried Senator John Sparkman of Alabama in 1964. Creeping totalitarianism, the Civil Rights Act would turn free people into automata, no better than slaves or robots.[10] "Nothing more or less than a blueprint for a police state," concluded Senator Herman Talmadge of Georgia. "If we deny 190

5 *Cong. Record*, 88th Congress, 2nd Session: 15,885.

6 *Cong. Record*, 88th Congress, 2nd Session: 14,457.

7 *Cong. Record*, 88th Congress, 2nd Session: 6,827, 11,762. Douglas' remarks elicited a cheerful response from Louisiana's Russell Long: "I ask the Senator if he is aware of the fact that when the battleship *Missouri* sailed into Tokyo Bay ... a Confederate flag was flying from the mainmast. Perhaps the admiral did not know it."

8 *Cong. Record*, 88th Congress, 2nd Session: 7,199.

9 *Cong. Record*, 88th Congress, 2nd Session: 14,508.

10 *Cong. Record*, 88th Congress, 2nd Session: 8,639.

million American citizens the right to discriminate in their private human conduct, liberty will die with that same right of discrimination."[11]

Pride of Race, the sacred right of prejudice, echoed through congressional chambers. Maryland's Ephraim Wilson spoke on June 4, 1874. By what act of hubris did Congress presume to legislate against prejudice, the natural instinct of humanity? "Prejudice now lives in all its energy, and will ever flourish as long as human nature remains unchanged." Texas Senator John Tower rose on April 13, 1964. Prejudice was just another word for freedom. "What is left of individual liberty if a man or a woman cannot choose associates in work or in play on the basis of either reason or prejudice, which are often indistinguishable?"[12] Humanity, steeped in prejudice, could not be cleansed by legislative fiat. "You are trying to legislate against human prejudice, and you cannot do it!" William Walter Phelps thundered in 1875. Just so Alabama's Congressman Armistead Selden in 1964: "The country is now beginning to pay for the gross error of seeking answers to problems in human race relations through legislation and court fiat."[13] "It is rather absurd," North Carolina's Senator Sam Ervin sputtered, "to expect Congress to pass a law controlling the minds and spirits of men and in one fell swoop to correct the imperfections in men which the Gospel has not been able to correct in 2,000 years."[14]

Nonsense, civil rights' supporters insisted. No one presumed to legislate away humanity's prejudices, only to remove them from the law. Wisconsin Senator Timothy Howe rose in 1874: "You are not required to lift him [the freedman] to his feet, but to let him get on to his feet if he can; not to lead him on his way, only not to trip him as he staggers on his way." Nevada Senator Alan Bible spoke in 1964: "Of course, we cannot legislate brotherhood and tolerance, but we can legislate equal protection and privileges under the law. I contend that this which we do legislate will foster that which we cannot."[15]

Sex. That thought obsessed civil rights' opponents in both eras. What began with pollution of public institutions, hotels, street-cars, theaters and schoolrooms would end in pollution of the domestic sanctuary. Said Kentucky's James Beck in 1874: "I suppose there are gentlemen who would arrest, imprison, and fine a young woman in any State of the South if she were to refuse to marry a Negro man on account of race in the event of his making her a proposal of marriage." Mandatory miscegenation, Senator Russell Long warned in 1964:

11 *Cong. Record*, 88th Congress, 1st Session: 12,429; 2nd Session: 8,662.
12 *Cong. Record*, 88th Congress, 2nd Session: 7,778.
13 *Cong. Record*, 88th Congress, 1st Session: 10,414.
14 *Cong. Record*, 88th Congress, 2nd Session: 11,200.
15 *Cong. Record*, 88th Congress, 2nd Session: 14,316.

"Some day they will tell us we do not have a choice in marriage.... The day will come when they will tell us, as white persons, or as Negroes, that we cannot even choose our mates in marriage."[16]

Civil rights proponents of both centuries replied: discrimination meant dehumanization. "Either I am a man or I am not a man," cried James Rapier on February 5, 1875. "If I am a man, I am entitled to all the right and privileges and immunities that any other American citizen is entitled to." Likewise Hubert Humphrey lamented on March 30, 1964, "it is heartbreaking," heartbreaking to compare the privileges of a man and those of an animal in the United States. In his hand he held out two guidebooks for the use of travelers across the South. One listed hotels willing to accommodate dogs, the other those willing in their bounty to shelter a Negro. Augusta, Georgia, he read, 5 hotels accepting of dogs, 1 that admits black people; Columbus, Georgia, 6 for dogs, 0 for black people; Charleston, South Carolina, 10 for dogs of any color, none for people of color.[17]

2 Sequel: One Step Forward, One Step Back

Looking Backward, Edward Bellamy entitled his famous novel, written in 1888. From a shining utopia envisioned in the year 2000, his protagonist looked backward to the turmoil of Gilded Age America. Bellamy's fatidic date has come and gone. A new gilded age surrounds us. Politicians look forward, unconvincingly. "We want our country to be a place where every child from every background can grow up free from fear, innocent from hatred and surrounded by love, opportunity and hope." With those utopian words President Donald J. Trump inaugurated the opening of the Mississippi Civil Rights Museum in Jackson, Mississippi, on December 9, 2017. That date marks 144 years precisely from the date, December 9, 1873, on which Frederick Douglass inaugurated the National Civil Rights Convention in Washington, D.C. These are the words Douglass' colleague and fellow civil-rights crusader George Downing spoke on that occasion to the country's then chief executive, Ulysses Grant – a different year a different president: "We begin to feel that the country has nearly arrived at that state designed by our forefathers, that all men are created equal." George Downing's feeling, despite civil rights acts in 1866, 1875 and 1964, appears more fragile today than on the day he expressed it.

It is an essentially American artifice. Laws are enacted, amendments are passed, struggling to remedy social wrongs. The reaction contrives to fight back,

16 *Cong. Record*, 88th Congress, 2nd Session: 7,909.

17 *Cong. Record*, 88th Congress, 2nd Session: 6,532.

to break down those laws, not frontally but deviously. The Thirteenth Amendment emancipated enslaved people. Black Codes eviscerated the essence of emancipation. The Fourteenth Amendment, buttressed by Civil Rights Acts, invalidated Black Codes. Jim Crow invalidated the essence of the Fourteenth Amendment. The Fifteenth Amendment guaranteed African Americans the right to vote. Poll taxes mocked the Fifteenth Amendment, though the amendment still stood. The Twenty-fourth Amendment outlawed poll taxes. Voter ID laws strive to emasculate the Twenty-fourth Amendment. End runs, to borrow a football term, reach the goal obliquely. For civil rights laws the end-run is in full progress. Nothing testifies more to that fact than that the president's fulsome words uttered at the Mississippi Civil Rights Museum were greeted with a chorus of denigration and disbelief – a chorus led not by right-wing reactionaries but by champions of the modern civil rights movement. People who marched with Dr. Martin Luther King, Congressman John Lewis of Georgia among them, refused to attend the inaugural event. They put no faith in the president or in pleasing presidential pronouncements.

Civil rights laws, laws of the nineteenth and twentieth centuries, must be seen in the context of twenty-first-century reality: end-runs, obfuscation, temporizing, outright denial. One contemporary instance offers a case in point.

The case of *Sheff v. O'Neill* is a particularly poignant reality. In April, 1989, the parents of 4th grader Milo Sheff and 16 other students sued the State of Connecticut, alleging that racial and ethnic isolation in the Hartford Schools deprived them of their educational rights guaranteed by the State Constitution. The plaintiffs were African American, Hispanic, and white students from Hartford and some surrounding districts. The case, filed by lawyers from the Connecticut Civil Liberties Union and the American Civil Liberties Union, arrived in court in 1992. In the lower court, in April 1995, Elizabeth Horton Sheff and her colleagues lost. They immediately appealed. In a stunning reversal the Connecticut Supreme Court under Chief Justice Ellen Peters ruled for the plaintiffs by a 4-3 vote. Extreme racial and ethnic isolation around the Hartford Schools, the Court held, deprived the plaintiff schoolchildren of their right to a substantially equal educational opportunity. Specifically, the Court declared, the school district boundaries separating Hartford from other towns were unconstitutional.

A civil rights victory, it seemed. The Court's ruling required the State to take remedial action. Wendell Phillips, as he wrote to Benjamin Butler 120 years before, foresaw the result. There would be no dismantling of local control, Governor John Rowland declared. There would be no busing, he vowed. There would be no meaningful remedial action. The State Attorney-General announced: "We disagree profoundly with the result [the Court's decision]." Not until 2003 did the plaintiffs and the governor reach a settlement. A new plan: it required the state to spend some $45 million per year to establish eight magnet schools in Hartford. A few were actually established. Until this moment implementation remains stalled. School desegregation in the period of Trump is rarely a priority. In the University of Michigan affirmative action cases of 2004 Justice Sandra Day O'Connor predicted that it might take 25 years for the nation to remove the racial barriers in education. Students growing up in Connecticut for more than 25 years continue to wait. Others wait elsewhere.

One need not compose any further dissertation on current events. Civil rights defended by law are in disarray. The vision of "post-racial America," a dream indulged after the election of Barack Obama, the nation's first African-American president, is fast fading. The Voting Rights Act is gutted; racial redistricting has revived in the United States Supreme Court as in the case of *Gill v. Whitford*, asserting a state's right to exercise extreme partisan gerrymandering. Voter suppression reaches rarified heights of refinement in *Husted v. A. Philip Randolph Institute*, asserting a state's right to reject and expunge from voter rolls all voters choosing to exercise their right not to vote for a period of time, a period to be determined by the state. The cry, "Black Lives Matter," reverberates in the media, not as an affirmation but as a plea. White supremacists chant racism in the streets of Charlottesville, Virginia; an American president proclaims moral parity between the racists and those who oppose them. A tradesman, averring religious scruples, asks the right to refuse service to clients of whose lifestyle he personally or piously disapproves. The Supreme Court agrees (*Masterpiece Cakeshop v. Colorado Civil Rights Commission*). Learned justices, should they scan the *Congressional Record*, might ponder the query of Maryland's Senator William Hamilton (a civil-rights-law opponent) in 1874:

> Mr. President … a colored man may go to a store and the store-keeper can say to him "I will not sell to you. To your race and color [or in today's context, to your sexual orientation] I object, and you must leave my store." Why is this?[18]

Why is this? As historians, we seek objectivity, fairness and balance. But equally we seek context. In the context of civil rights laws, nineteenth and twentieth-century endeavors – in the context of their hopes and aims – the twenty-first century presents a picture of paralysis, if not regression and retreat. That context, we submit, makes an understanding of those earlier endeavors imperative. The law of 1964, so Martin Luther King declared, was

18 Speech of William Hamilton, May 23, 1874, see below, Ch. 4.

"the child of a storm, the product of the most turbulent motion the nation has ever known in peacetime."

One may, with respect, qualify that evaluation. The storms of 1874 preceding the Civil Rights Act of 1875 lacked nothing of a dark and tempestuous nature. In 1964 substitute Emmett Till for Julia Hayden; Goodman, Chaney and Schwerner for Walter Billings and Tom Ivey. History in the early twentieth century, the time when President Woodrow Wilson entertained White House guests gaily with screenings of "Birth of a Nation" (a.k.a. "The Klansman"), viewed that Act with denigration.

History in the later twentieth century, the time of civil rights hope and flowering, looked upon it as a half-hearted deception.

The present day, the time of retreat, portends another twist, a reverse twist. It obliges us to look backward, to see how the winds blew, how they arrived at that compass point. We must allow the context. The politics of hatred live, Ohio's Governor Edward Noyes lamented, "appealing to the passions and prejudices of ignorant white men,"[19] From the era of Reconstruction we have reached the era of Trump, the state of 2018.

---

19 See above, 462.

Appendices

APPENDIX A

Chronology

1865

December 6: Ratification of the 13th Amendment.

1866

April 9: First Civil Rights Act; override of President Johnson's veto.

1868

July 9: Adoption of the 14th Amendment.

1870

February 3: Ratification of the 15th Amendment.

1871

February 28: Passage of the Second Enforcement Act.
April 20: Passage of the Third Enforcement Act (Ku Klux Klan Act).

1872

February 9: Passage of Charles Sumner's Amnesty Bill Amendment; failure of the Amnesty Bill.
February 19: Report of the Joint Select Committee on the Ku Klux (Ku Klux Klan Report).
May 9: Second passage of the Amnesty Bill Amendment; failure of the Amnesty Bill.
November 5: Reelection of President Grant; Republicans sweep the congressional elections.

1873

April 9: Passage of New York Civil Rights Act; civil rights acts in Florida, Mississippi, Arkansas.
April 13: Colfax Massacre.
April 14: Supreme Court decision in the Slaughterhouse Case.
December 2: Opening of the 43rd Congress; Charles Sumner introduces Civil Rights Bill S.1.
December 3: Sumner calls for passage of S.1; the bill is tabled.
December 9: Opening of the National Civil Rights Convention.
December 18: Benjamin Butler introduces House Civil Rights Bill H.R.796.

December 19: Debate in the House; speeches of Benjamin Butler, James Beck, Joseph Rainey.

1874

January 5: Debate resumes in the House of Representatives; speech of Alexander Stephens.
January 6: Debate continues in the House; speech of Robert Elliott.
January 7: Debate concludes; speech of Benjamin Butler; H.R.796 recommitted.
January 27: Charles Sumner moves for passage of S.1; S.1 referred to the Judiciary Committee.
March 11: Death of Charles Sumner.
April 14: Senate Judiciary Committee reports S.1 favorably.
April 29: Debate commences in the Senate; speech of Frederick Frelinghuysen.
April 30: Debate continues; speech of Thomas Norwood; debate on S.1 suspended.
May 4: Aaron Sargent introduces Army Desegregation Bill S.774.
May 8: Republican caucus; action urged on civil rights.
May 20: Debate resumes on S.1; speeches of James Flanagan and Allen Thurman.
May 21: Debate continues; speech of George Boutwell.
May 22: Marathon debate on S.1; speeches of Timothy Howe, Augustus Merrimon.
May 23: 7:10 a.m., passage of S.1; S.1 moves to the House of Representatives.
May 25: First attempt to take S.1 from the Speaker's Table fails to acquire a two-thirds vote.
June 1: Second attempt to take S.1 from the Speaker's Table blocked.
June 3: Radical members block reporting of House Bill H.R.796.
June 8: Third attempt to take S.1 from the Speaker's Table fails to acquire a two-thirds vote.
June 20: Attempt to pass S.1 from the Speaker's Table fails to acquire a two-thirds vote.
June 22: First session of the 43rd Congress ends.
August 1: Murder of Walter Billings.
August 6: Democrats sweep elections in North Carolina.
August 22: Murder of Julia Hayden.
August 25: Trenton Tennessee Massacre.
August 28: Indignation Meeting at Memphis.
August 29: Murder of Thomas Ivey; Coushatta Massacre.
September 14: Penn Rebellion in New Orleans.
September 15: Publication of the Hays-Hawley Letter.
October 13: Southern Republican Convention; Democrats sweep elections in Ohio and Indiana.
October 16: Release of the Peabody Report.
November 3: Democrats sweep elections across the nation.

November 25: Decision in the Corey-Carter Case.
December 7: Second session of the 43rd Congress opens.
December 17: House Judiciary Committee agrees to report H.R.796, amended.

1875

January 9: Republican caucus fails to agree on legislative agenda.
January 23: Republican caucus fails to agree on legislative agenda.
January 25: Republican caucus agrees to move for continuing suspension of the rules.
January 27–29: Filibuster of the House of Representatives.
February 1: Republican attempt to amend House Rule 49 fails to acquire a two-thirds vote.
February 2: Republican attempt to amend House Rule 49 succeeds by a margin of one vote.
February 3: Debate opens on the Civil Rights Bill, H.R.796, now assuming the form of the Senate Bill, amended; confrontation of Benjamin Butler and William McLean.
February 4: Debate continues; censure of John Young Brown.
February 5: Debate concludes; passage of the Kellogg Amendment removing school integration clause; 3:40 p.m., passage of H.R.796.
February 26: Debate opens in the Senate; speech of Allen Thurman and colloquy.
February 27: Debate in the Senate concludes; 2:00 p.m., passage of the Civil Rights Bill.
March 1: Ulysses Grant signs the Civil Rights Act.
March 3: End of the 43rd Congress.
Wilmington, North Carolina: William Gerken cited for violation of Civil Rights Act.
March 5: William Gerken acquitted.
June 5: Galveston, Texas: trial of Henry Greenwall begins.
June 8: Henry Greenwall convicted. Mary Miller awarded $500 for violation of her civil rights.

APPENDIX B

Civil Rights Proposals – Texts

Civil Rights/Amnesty Bill Amendment, proposed by Charles Sumner, Dec. 20, 1871 (*Cong. Globe*, 42nd Congress, 2nd Session: 244)

Sec. 1 – That all citizens of the United States without distinction of race, color, or previous condition of servitude, are entitled to equal and impartial enjoyment of any accommodation, advantage, facility, or privilege furnished by common carriers, whether on land or water; by in-keepers; by licensed owners, managers, or lessees of theaters or other places of public amusement; by trustees, commissioners, superintendents, teachers, or other officers of common schools and other public institutions of learning, the same being supported or authorized by law; by trustees or officers of church organizations, cemetery associations, and benevolent institutions incorporated by national or State authority; and this right shall not be denied or abridged on any pretense of race, color, or previous condition of servitude.

Sec. 2 – That any person violating the foregoing provision, or aiding in its violation, or inciting thereto, shall for every such offense forfeit and pay the sum of $500 to the person aggrieved thereby, to be recovered in an action on the case with full costs and such allowance for counsel fees as the court shall deem just, and shall also for every such offense be deemed guilty of a misdemeanor, and upon conviction thereof shall be fined not less than $500 nor more than $1,000, and shall be imprisoned not less than thirty days nor more than one year; and any corporation, association, or individual holding a charter or license under national or State authority violating the aforesaid provision, shall, upon conviction thereof, forfeit such charter or license; and any person assuming to use or continuing to act under such charter or license thus forfeited, or aiding in the same, or inciting thereto, shall, upon conviction thereof, be deemed guilty of a misdemeanor, and shall be fined not less than $1,000 nor more than $5,000, and shall be imprisoned not less than three nor more than seven years; and both the corporate and joint property of such corporation or association, and the private property of the several individuals composing the same, shall be held liable for the forfeitures, fines, and penalties incurred by any violation of the [first] section of this act.

Sec. 3 – That the same jurisdiction and powers are hereby conferred, and the same duties enjoined upon, the courts and officers of the United States, in the execution of this act, as are conferred and enjoined upon such courts and officers in Sections three, four, five, seven, and ten of an act entitled "An act to protect all persons in the United States in their civil rights, and to furnish the means of their vindication," passed April 9, 1866, and these sections are hereby made a part of this act; and any of the aforesaid officers failing to institute and prosecute such proceedings herein required shall, for every such offense, forfeit and pay the sum of $500 to the person aggrieved thereby, to be recovered by an action on the case, with full costs and such allowance for counsel fees as the court shall deem just, and shall on conviction thereof be deemed guilty of a misdemeanor, and be fined not less than $1,000 nor more than $5,000.

Sec. 4 – That no person shall be disqualified for service as juror in any court, national or State, by reason of race, color, or previous condition of servitude: *Provided*, That such person possesses all other qualifications which are by law prescribed; and any officer or other persons charged with any duty in the selection or summoning of jurors, who shall exclude or fail to summon any person for the reason above named, shall, on conviction thereof, be deemed guilty of a misdemeanor, and be fined not less than $1,000 nor more than $5,000.

Sec. 5 – That every law, statute, ordinance, regulation, or action, whether national or State, inconsistent with this act, or making any discriminations against any person on account of color, by the use of the word "white," is hereby repealed and annulled.

Sec. 6 – That it shall be the duty of the judges of the several courts upon which jurisdiction is hereby conferred to give this act in charge to the grand jury of their respective courts at the commencement of each term thereof.

Civil Rights Bill S.1, proposed by Charles Sumner, Dec. 2, 1873 (*Cong. Record*, 43rd Congress, 1st Session: 945)

Sec. 1, Be it enacted, &c., That no citizen of the United States shall, by reason of race, color, or previous condition of servitude, be excepted or excluded from the full and equal enjoyment of any accommodation, advantage, facility, or privilege furnished by innkeepers; by common carriers, whether on land or water; by licensed owners, managers, or lessees of theaters or other places of public amusement; by trustees, commissioners, superintendents, teachers, and other officers of common schools and public institutions of learning, the same being supported by moneys derived from general taxation or authorized by law; also of cemetery associations and benevolent associations supported or authorized in the same way; Provided, That private schools, cemeteries, and institutions of learning established exclusively for white or colored persons, and maintained respectively by voluntary contributions, shall remain according to the terms of the original establishment.

Sec. 2, That any person violating any of the provisions of the foregoing section, or aiding in their violation, or inciting thereto, shall, for every such offense, forfeit and pay the sum of $500 to the person aggrieved thereby, to be recovered in an action on the case, with full costs; and shall also, for every such offense, be deemed guilty of a misdemeanor, and upon conviction thereof, shall be fined not less than $500 nor more than $1,000, or shall be imprisoned not less than thirty days nor more than one year:

Provided, That the party aggrieved shall not recover more than one penalty; and when the offense is a refusal of burial, the penalty may be recovered by the heirs at law of the person whose body has been refused burial.

Sec. 3, That the same jurisdiction and powers are hereby conferred and the same duties enjoined upon the courts and officers of the United States in the execution of this act as are conferred and enjoined upon such courts and officers in Sections 3, 4, 5, 7 and 10 of an act entitled "An act to protect all persons in the United States in their civil rights, and to furnish the means of their vindication," passed April 9, 1866, and these sections are hereby made a part of this act; and any of the aforesaid officers failing to institute and prosecute such proceedings herein required shall, for every such offense, forfeit and pay the sum of $500 to the person aggrieved thereby, to be recovered by an action on the case, with full costs; and shall, on conviction thereof, be deemed guilty of a misdemeanor, and be fined not less than $1,000 nor more than $5,000.

Sec. 4, That no citizen possessing all other qualifications, which are or may be prescribed by law shall be disqualified for service as juror in any court, national or State, by reason of race, color, or previous condition of servitude; and any officer or other persons charged with any duty in the selection or summoning of jurors who shall exclude or fail to summon any citizen for the reason above named shall, on conviction thereof, be deemed guilty of a misdemeanor and be fined not less than $1,000 nor more than $5,000.

Sec. 5, That every discrimination against any citizen on account of color by the use of the word "white," or any other term in any law, statute, ordinance, or regulation, national or State, is hereby repealed and annulled.

Civil Rights Bill H.R. 796, proposed by Benjamin Butler, Dec. 18, 1873 (*Cong. Record*, 43rd Congress, 1st Session: 378)

A bill to protect all people in their civil and legal rights.

Be it enacted by the Senate and House of Representatives of the United States of America in Congress assembled, That whoever, being a corporation or natural person, and owner, or in charge of any public inn; or of any place of public amusement or entertainment for which a license from any legal authority is required; or of any line of stage-coaches, railroad, or other means of public carriage of passengers or freight; or of any cemetery, or other benevolent institution, or any public school supported, in whole or in part, at public expense or by endowment for public use, shall make any distinction as to admission or accommodation therein of any citizen of the United States, because of race, color, or previous condition of servitude, shall on conviction thereof, be fined not less than one hundred nor more than five thousand dollars for each offense; and the person or corporation so offending shall be liable to the citizens thereby injured in damages to be recovered in an action of debt.

Sec. 2, That the offenses under this act, and actions to recover damages, may be prosecuted before any territorial, district, or circuit court of the United States having jurisdiction of crimes at the place where the offense was charged to have been committed, as well as in the district where the parties may reside, as now provided by law.

Civil Rights Bill S.1 amended, passed by the Senate, May 23, 1874 (*Cong. Record*, 43rd Congress, 1st Session: 3451)

Sec. 1. Be it enacted &c. That all persons within the jurisdiction of the United States shall be entitled to the full and equal enjoyment of the accommodations, advantages, facilities, and privileges of inns, public conveyances on land or water, theaters, and other places of public amusement; and also of common schools and public institutions of learning or benevolence supported, in whole or in part, by general taxation; and of cemeteries so supported, subject only to the conditions and limitations established by law, and applicable alike to citizens of every race and color, regardless of any previous condition of servitude.

Sec. 2. That any person who shall violate the foregoing section by denying to any citizen, except for reasons by law applicable to citizens of every race and color, and regardless of any previous condition of servitude, the full enjoyment of any of the accommodations, advantages, facilities, or privileges in said section enumerated, or by aiding or inciting such denial, shall, for every such offense, forfeit and pay the sum of $500 to the person aggrieved thereby, to be recovered in an action on the case, with full costs; and shall also, for every such offense, be deemed guilty of a misdemeanor, and upon conviction thereof, shall be fined not less than $500 nor more than $1,000, or shall be imprisoned not less than thirty days nor more than one year; *Provided*, That the party aggrieved shall not recover more than one penalty; and when the offense is a refusal of burial, the penalty may be recovered by the heirs at law of the person whose body has been refused burial; *And, provided further*, That all persons may elect to sue for the penalty aforesaid or to proceed under their rights at common law and by State statutes; and having so elected to proceed in the one mode or the other, their right to proceed in the other jurisdiction shall be barred. But this proviso shall not apply to criminal proceedings, either under this act or the criminal law of any State.

Sec. 3. That the district and circuit courts of the United States shall have, exclusively of the courts of the several States, cognizance of all crimes and offenses against, and violations of, the provisions of this act; and actions for the penalty given by the preceding section may be prosecuted in the territorial, district, or circuit courts of the United States wherever the defendant may be found, without regard to the other party.

And the district attorneys, marshals, and deputy marshals of the United States, and commissioners appointed by the circuit and territorial courts of the United States, with powers of arresting and imprisoning or bailing offenders against the laws of the United States, are hereby specially authorized and required to institute proceedings against every person who shall violate the provisions of this act and cause him to be arrested and imprisoned or bailed, as the case may be, for trial before such court of the United States or territorial court as by law has cognizance of the offense, except in respect of the right of action accruing to the person aggrieved; and such district attorneys shall cause such proceedings to be prosecuted to their termination as in other cases; *Provided,* That nothing contained in this section shall be construed to deny or defeat any right of civil action accruing to any person, whether by reason of this act or otherwise. And any district attorney who shall willfully fail to institute and prosecute the proceedings herein required shall, for every such offense, forfeit and pay the sum of $500 to the person aggrieved thereby, to be recovered by an action on the case, with full costs, and shall, on conviction thereof, be deemed guilty of a misdemeanor, and be fined not less than $1,000 nor more than $5,000.

Sec. 4. That no citizen possessing all other qualifications which are or may be prescribed by law shall be disqualified for service as grand or petit juror in any court of the United States, or of any State, on account of race, color, or previous condition of servitude; and any officer or other person charged with any duty in the selection or summoning of jurors who shall exclude or fail to summon any citizen for the cause aforesaid shall, on conviction thereof, be deemed guilty of a misdemeanor, and be fined not more than $5,000.

Sec. 5. That all cases arising under the provisions of this act in the courts of the Unites States shall be reviewable by the Supreme Court of the United States without regard to the sum in controversy, under the same provisions and regulations as are now provided by law for the review of other causes in said court.

Civil Rights Act, signed by President Ulysses Grant, March 1, 1875.

Whereas it is essential to just government, we recognize the equality of all men before the law, and hold that it is the duty of government in its dealings with the people to mete out equal and exact justice to all, of whatever nativity, race, color, or persuasion, religious or political; and it being the appropriate object of legislation to enact great fundamental principles into law, Therefore, *Be it enacted by the Senate and House of Representatives of the United States of America in Congress assembled,* That all persons within the jurisdiction of the United States shall be entitled to the full and equal enjoyment of the accommodations, advantages, facilities, and privileges of inns, public conveyances on land or water, theaters, and other places of public amusement; subject only to the conditions and limitations established by law, and applicable alike to citizens of every race and color, regardless of any previous condition of servitude.

Sec. 2. That any person who shall violate the foregoing section by denying to any citizen, except for reasons by law applicable to citizens of every race and color, and regardless of any previous condition of servitude, the full enjoyment of any of the accommodations, advantages, facilities, or privileges in said section enumerated, or by aiding or inciting such denial, shall, for every such offense, forfeit and pay the sum of five hundred dollars to the person aggrieved thereby, to be recovered in an action of debt, with full costs; and shall also, for every such offense, be deemed guilty of a misdemeanor, and, upon conviction thereof, shall be fined not less than five hundred nor more than one thousand dollars, or shall be imprisoned not less than thirty days nor more than one year: *Provided,* That all persons may elect to sue for the penalty aforesaid or to proceed under their rights at common law and by State statutes; and having so elected to proceed in the one mode or the other, their right to proceed in the other jurisdiction shall be barred. But this proviso shall not apply to criminal proceedings, either under this act or the criminal law of any State: *And provided further,* That a judgment for the penalty in favor of the party aggrieved, or a judgment upon an indictment, shall be a bar to either prosecution respectively.

Sec. 3. That the district and circuit courts of the United States shall have, exclusively of the courts of the several States, cognizance of all crimes and offenses against, and violations of, the provisions of this act; and actions for the penalty given by the preceding section may be prosecuted in the territorial, district, or circuit courts of the United States wherever the defendant may be found, without regard to the other party; and the district attorneys, marshals, and deputy marshals of the United States, and commissioners appointed by the circuit and territorial courts of the United States, with powers of arresting and imprisoning or bailing offenders against the laws of the United States, are hereby specially authorized and required to institute proceedings against every person who shall violate the provisions of this act, and cause him to be arrested and imprisoned or bailed, as the case may be, for trial before such court of the United States, or territorial court, as by law has cognizance of the offense, except in respect of the right of action accruing to the person aggrieved; and such district attorneys shall cause such proceedings to be prosecuted to their termination as in other cases: *Provided,* That nothing contained in this section shall be construed to deny or defeat any right of civil action accruing to any person, whether by reason of this act or otherwise; and any district attorney who shall willfully fail to institute and prosecute the proceedings herein required, shall, for every such offense, forfeit and pay the sum of five hundred dollars to the person aggrieved thereby, to be recovered by an action of debt, with full costs, and shall, on conviction thereof, be deemed guilty of a misdemeanor, and be fined not less than one thousand nor more than five thousand dollars: *And provided further,* That a judgment for the penalty in favor of the party aggrieved against any such district attorney, or a judgment upon an indictment against any such district attorney shall be a bar to either prosecution respectively.

Sec. 4. That no citizen possessing all other qualifications which are or may be prescribed by law shall be disqualified for service as a grand or petit juror in any court of the United States, or of any State, on account of race, color, or previous condition of servitude; and any officer or other person charged with any duty in the selection or summoning of jurors who shall exclude or fail to summon any citizen for the cause aforesaid shall, on conviction thereof, be deemed guilty of a misdemeanor, and be fined not more than five thousand dollars.

Sec. 5. That all cases arising under the provisions of this act in the courts of the United States shall be reviewable by the Supreme Court of the United States, without regard to the sum in controversy, under the same provisions and regulations as are now provided by law for the review of other causes in said court.

Bibliography

Manuscript Sources

Allen G. Thurman, Ohio Historical Society, Columbus.

Alexander Stephens Papers, Library of Congress, Duke University Library.

Benjamin F. Butler Papers, Library of Congress.

Butler-Ames Papers, Smith College.

Charles Eldredge Papers, State Historical Society of Wisconsin.

Charles Sumner Papers, Harvard University, Houghton Library, Library of Congress, Massachusetts Historical Society, Boston.

Ebenezer Rockwood Hoar Papers, Harvard University, Houghton Library, Massachusetts Historical Society, Boston.

Edward McPherson Papers, Library of Congress.

Frederick Douglass Papers, Library of Congress.

Frederick Frelinghuysen Papers, Library of Congress.

George S. Boutwell Papers, Harvard University, Houghton Library.

George Frisbie Hoar Papers, Harvard University, Houghton Library, Massachusetts Historical Society, Boston.

Gerrit Smith Papers, Syracuse University.

Henry Laurens Dawes Papers, Library of Congress.

Henry Wilson Papers, Library of Congress.

Horace Maynard Papers, University of Tennessee, Knoxville.

James G. Blaine, Library of Congress.

John Mercer Langston Papers, Library of Congress.

John A. Logan Papers, Library of Congress.

John W. Forney Papers, Library of Congress.

John White Stevenson Papers, Library of Congress.

Joseph R. Hawley Papers, Library of Congress.

Leonidas Houk Papers, Knox County, Tennessee, Public Library.

Manton Marble Papers, Library of Congress.

Matthew Carpenter Papers, State Historical Society of Wisconsin.

Oliver Morton Papers, Indiana Historical Society/Indiana State Library, Indianapolis.

Samuel Jackson Randall Papers, University of Pennsylvania, Philadelphia.

Thomas F. Bayard Papers, Library of Congress.

Zachariah Chandler Papers, Library of Congress.

Newspapers

Alexandria, Louisiana, *Caucasian.*
Alexandria, Louisiana, *Louisiana Democrat.*
Altoona, Pennsylvania, *Morning Tribune.*
Annapolis, Maryland, *Daily Gazette.*
Atlanta *Constitution.*
Bainbridge, Georgia, *Weekly Sun.*
Baltimore *Sun.*
Boston *Commonwealth.*
Charleston, South Carolina, *News and Courier.*
Chattanooga *Times.*
Chicago *Gem of the West and Soldier's Friend.*
Chicago *Inter-Ocean.*
Chicago *Tribune.*
Cincinnati *Commercial.*
Clearfield, Pennsylvania, *Republican.*
Dayton, Ohio, *Democrat.*
Dayton, Ohio, *Journal.*
Elizabeth City, North Carolina, *North Carolinian.*
Evanston, Indiana, *Journal.*
Frederick, Maryland, *Maryland Union.*
Fredericksburg, Virginia, *Ledger.*
Galveston *News.*
Goldsboro, North Carolina, *Carolina Messenger.*
Greeneville, Tennessee, *Intelligencer.*
Harper's Weekly Magazine.
Harrisburg, Pennsylvania, *Patriot.*
Hartford, Connecticut, *Courant.*
Hollidaysburg, Pennsylvania, *Register.*
Indianapolis *Journal.*
Jackson, Mississippi, *Daily Pilot.*
Jacksonville, *Florida Union.*
Jersey City *Evening Journal.*
Kansas City *Journal of Commerce.*
Knoxville, *Press and Herald.*
Little Rock Arkansas *Daily Gazette.*
Louisville *Courier-Journal.*
Martinsburg, West Virginia, *Independent.*
Memphis *Appeal.*

Monroe, Louisiana, *Ouachita Telegraph.*
Montgomery, Alabama, *Advertiser.*
Nashville *Republican Banner.*
Nashville, *Union and American.*
Newark *Journal.*
New Orleans *Abeille.*
New Orleans *Louisianian.*
New Orleans *Republican.*
New York *Herald.*
New York *Times.*
New York *Tribune.*
New York *World.*
Norfolk *Virginian.*
Opelousas, Louisiana, *Courier.*
Paterson, New Jersey, *Press.*
Petersburg, Virginia, *Index and Appeal.*
Philadelphia *Inquirer.*
Quitman, Georgia, *Gallagher's Independent.*
Raleigh *Blasting-Powder for Democrats and Conservatives.*
Raleigh *Daily Sentinel.*
Raleigh *Evening Crescent.*
Raleigh *Republican.*
Richmond *Dispatch.*
San Diego *Union.*
San Francisco *Elevator.*
San Jose *Argus.*
San Jose *Mercury.*
Savannah *Morning News.*
Scribner's Monthly Magazine.
Shreveport *Times.*
Springfield, Massachusetts, *Republican.*
Springfield, Missouri, *Weekly Patriot.*
St. Louis *Daily Republican.*
Talladega, Alabama, *Our Mountain Home.*
Tallahassee *Floridian.*
Terre Haute, Indiana, *Express.*
Thibodaux, Louisiana, *Weekly Sentinel.*
Thomasville, Georgia, *Times.*
Toledo *Daily Blade.*
Trenton, New Jersey, *State Gazette.*

Vicksburg, Mississippi, *Daily Times.*
Washington, *Forney's Sunday Chronicle.*
Washington *National Republican.*
Washington *New National Era.*
Wheeling, West Virginia, *Intelligencer.*
Wilmington, Delaware, *Every Evening.*
Wilmington, Delaware, *Daily Commercial.*
Wilmington, North Carolina, *Journal.*
Xenia, Ohio, *Torchlight.*

United States Congress

Congressional *Globe.*
Congressional *Record.*
United States House of Representatives, Forty-Third Congress, House Report 261, Louisiana Investigative Committee, 1875.
United States House of Representatives, Forty-Third Congress, House Report 262, Alabama Investigative Committee, 1875.
United States House of Representatives, Forty-Third Congress, Judiciary Committee Papers, National Archives.
United States Senate, Senate Report 704, Louisiana Affairs, 1875.

Books and Articles in Print

Abbott, Richard H. *Cobbler in Congress: The Life of Henry Wilson, 1812–1875.* (Lexington: University Press of Kentucky, 1972).
Abbott, Richard H. *For Free Press and Equal Rights: Republican Newspapers in the Reconstruction South.* (Athens: University of Georgia Press, 2004).
Abbott, Richard H. *The Republican Party and the South, 1855–1877: The First Southern Strategy.* (Chapel Hill: University of North Carolina Press, 1986).
Adler, Selig. "The Senatorial Career of George Franklin Edmonds, 1866–1891." Diss., University of Illinois, 1934.
Alexander, Thomas B. *Political Reconstruction in Tennessee.* (New York: Russell and Russell, 1950).
Alexander, Thomas B. "Strange Bedfellows: The Interlocking Careers of T.A.R. Nelson, Andrew Johnson, and W.G. (Parson) Brownlow." *East Tennessee Historical Society Publications,* 51 (1979): 54–77.
Ames, Blanche Butler. *Chronicles From the Nineteenth Century: Family Letters of Blanche Butler and Adelbert Ames.* (Clinton: Colonial Press, 1957).

Anderson, Eric. "James O'Hara of North Carolina: Black Leadership and Local Government." in Howard N. Rabinowitz, ed., *Southern Black Leaders of the Reconstruction Era* (Urbana: University of Illinois Press, 1982): 101–125.

Anderson, Eric. *Race and Politics in North Carolina, 1872–1901.* (Baton Rouge: Louisiana State University Press, 1981).

Avins, Alfred. "Freedom of Choice in Personal Service Occupations: 13th Amendment Limitations on Antidiscrimination Legislation." *Cornell Law Quarterly* (1964): 228–256.

Avins, Alfred. "Racial Segregation in Public Accommodations: Some Reflected Light on the Fourteenth Amendment From the Civil Rights Act of 1875." *Western Reserve Law Review*, 18 (1967a): 125–183.

Avins, Alfred. *The Reconstruction Amendments' Debates. The Legislative History and Contemporary Debates in Congress on the 13th, 14th, and 15th Amendments.* (Richmond: Virginia Commission on Constitutional Government, 1967b).

Avins, Alfred. "The Civil Rights Act of 1875: Some Reflected Light on the Fourteenth Amendment and Public Accommodations. *Columbia Law Review,* 66 (1966): 873–915.

Bailey, Richard. *Neither Carpetbaggers Nor Scalawags: Black Officeholders During Reconstruction of Alabama, 1867–1878.* (Montgomery: R. Bailey, 1991).

Barnes, Donna A. and Catherine Connolly. "Repression, the Judicial System, and Political Opportunities for Civil Rights Advocacy during Reconstruction." *The Sociological Quarterly,* 40 (1999): 327–345.

Barnes, Kenneth C. *Who Killed John Clayton? Political Violence and the Emergence of the New South, 1861–1893.* (Durham: Duke University Press, 1998).

Barnes, William H. *The American Government: History of the Forty-third Congress,* 3 vols. (Washington, D.C.: W.H. Barnes Co., 1875).

Beach, Claudia Anne. *Henry Greenwall, Theater Manager.* (Lubbock: Texas Tech University Press, 1986).

Bean, W.G. "John Letcher and the Slavery Issue in Virginia's Gubernatorial Contest of 1858–9." *Journal of Southern History,* 20 (1954): 22–49.

Bean, W.G. "The Ruffner Pamphlet of 1847: An Antislavery Aspect of Virginia Sectionalism." *Virginia Magazine of History and Biography,* 61 (1953): 260–282.

Bear, James A., Jr. "Henry A. Wise and the Campaign of 1873: Some Letters from the Papers of James Lawson Kemper." *Virginia Magazine of History and Biography.* 62 (1954): 320–342.

Belz, Herman. *Emancipation and Equal Rights: Politics and Constitutionalism in the Civil War Era.* (New York: Norton, 1978).

Benedict, Michael Les. *A Compromise of Principle: Congressional Republicans and Reconstruction, 1863–1869.* (New York: Norton, 1974a).

Benedict, Michael Les. "Preserving the Constitution: The Conservative Basis of Radical Reconstruction." *Journal of American History,* 61 (1974b): 65–90.

Blackett, R.J.M. *Thomas Morris Chester, Black Civil War Correspondent: His Dispatches from the Virginia Front.* (Baton Rouge: Louisiana State University Press, 1990).

Blaine, James G. *Political Discussions, Legislative, Diplomatic, and Popular, 1856–1886.* (Norwich: Henry Bills Pub., 1887).

Blaine, James G. *Twenty Years of Congress: From Lincoln to Garfield, With a Review of the Events Which Led to the Political Revolution of 1860*, 2 vols. (Norwich: Henry Bills Publ., 1884–6).

Blair, Henry W. *Free Schools – Are They in Danger? If So, from What Source? Speech of Hon. Henry W. Blair of New Hampshire in the House of Representatives, Saturday, July 29, 1876.* (Washington: United States Government Printing Office, 1876).

Blassingame, John W. *Black New Orleans, 1860–1880.* (Chicago: University of Chicago Press, 1973).

Blum, Edward J. *Reforging the White Republic: Race, Religion, and American Nationalism, 1865–1898.* (Baton Rouge: Louisiana State University Press, 2005).

Boldrick, Charles C. "Father Abram J. Ryan, 'The Poet-Priest of the Confederacy.'" *Filson Club History Quarterly*, 46 (1972): 201–218.

Boutwell, George S. *Reminiscences of Sixty Years in Public Affairs.* (New York: Greenwood Press, 1968).

Bragg, William H. "The Junius of Georgia Redemption: Thomas M. Norwood and the 'Nemesis' Letters." *Georgia Historical Quarterly*, 77 (1993): 86–122.

Brands, H.W. *The Man Who Saved the Union: Ulysses Grant in War and Peace* (New York: Doubleday: 2012).

Brandwein, Pamela. *Rethinking the Judicial Settlement of Reconstruction.* (New York: Cambridge University Press, 2011).

Broek, Jacobus ten. *Equal Under Law.* (New York: Collier Books, 1965).

Brown, Canter, Jr. *Florida's Black Public Officials, 1867–1924.* (Tuscaloosa: University of Alabama Press, 1998).

Brown, Canter, Jr. "'Where Are the Hopes I Cherished' – The Life and Times of Robert M Brown, Canter, Jr. eacham." *Florida Historical Quarterly*, 69 (1990): 1–36.

Brown, Cecil K. *A State Movement in Railroad Development: The Story of North Carolina's First Effort to Establish an East and West Trunk Line Railroad.* (Chapel Hill: University of North Carolina Press, 1928).

Brown, Thomas M. *George Sewell Boutwell, Human Rights Advocate.* (Groton: Groton Historical Society, 1989).

Bruff, Harold H., *Untrodden Ground, How Presidents Interpret the Constitution.* (Chicago, University of Chicago Press, 2015).

Burger, Nash K. and John K. Butterworth, "L.Q.C. Lamar, Artificer of Reconciliation." in Dean Faulkner Wells and Hunter Cole eds., *Mississippi Heroes.* (Jackson: University Press of Mississippi, 1980): 107–142.

Burnside, William H. *The Honorable Powell Clayton.* (Conway: UCA Press, 1991).

Butchart, Ronald E. *Northern Schools, Southern Blacks, and Reconstruction: Freedmen's Education, 1862–1875.* (Westport: Greenwood Press, 1980).

Butler, Benjamin F. *Butler's Book. Autobiography and Personal Reminiscences of Major-General Benj. Butler.* (Boston: A.M. Thayer, 1892).

Calcott, Margaret L. *The Negro in Maryland Politics, 1870–1912.* (Baltimore: Johns Hopkins Press, 1969).

Calhoun, Charles W. *Conceiving a New Republic: The Republican Party and the Southern Question 1869–1900.* (Lawrence: University Press of Kansas, 2006).

Campbell, George. *White and Black: The Outcome of a Visit to the United States.* (New York: Negro University Press, 1969).

Capers, Gerald M. "Yellow Fever in Memphis in the 1870's." *Mississippi Historical Review,* 24 (1938): 483–502.

Carleton, Mark T. "The Politics of the Convict Lease System in Louisiana: 1868–1901." *Louisiana History: Journal of the Louisiana Historical Association,* 8 (1967): 5–25.

Carter, Dan T. "The Anatomy of Fear: The Christmas Day Insurrection Scare of 1868." *Journal of Southern History,* 42 (1976): 345–364.

Cash, William M. "Alabama Republicans During Reconstruction: Personal Characteristics, Motivations, and Political Activities of Party Activists, 1867–1880." Diss., University of Alabama, 1973.

Cheek, William F. "A Negro Runs for Congress: John Mercer Langston and the Virginia Campaign of 1888." *Journal of Negro History,* 52 (1967): 14–34.

Chernow, Ron. *Grant.* (Penguin Press, 2017).

Chidsey, Donald B. *The Gentleman from New York: A Life of Roscoe Conkling.* (New Haven: Yale University Press, 1935).

Clayton, Powell. *The Aftermath of the Civil War in Arkansas.* (New York: Negro Universities Press, 1969).

Conkling, Alfred R. *The Life and Letters of Roscoe Conkling, Orator, Statesman, Advocate.* (New York: Charles L. Webster & Co., 1889).

Conway, Alan. *The Reconstruction of Georgia* (Minneapolis: University of Minnesota Press, 1966).

Coulter, E. Merton. *William G. Brownlow: Fighting Parson of the Southern Highlands.* (Knoxville: University of Tennessee Press, 1971).

Cox, LaWanda and John H. "Civil Rights: The Issue of Reconstruction," in *Freedom, Racism and Reconstruction: The Collected Writings of LaWanda Cox,* ed. Donald G. Nieman (Athens: University of Georgia Press, 1997).

Cox, LaWanda and John H. "Negro Suffrage and Republican Politics: The Problem of Motivation in Reconstruction Historiography." *Journal of Southern History,* 33 (1967): 303–330.

Cox, LaWanda and John H. *Politics, Principles and Prejudice, 1865–1866: Dilemma of Reconstruction.* (New York: Free Press, 1963).

Cox, Samuel S. *Emancipation and its Results – Is Ohio to be Africanized? Speech of Hon. S.S. Cox of Ohio, Delivered in the House of Representatives, June 6, 1862.* (Washington: L. Towers & Co., 1862).

Cox, Samuel S. *Union – Disunion – Reunion. Three Decades of Federal Legislation, 1855 to 1885. Personal and Historical Memories of Events Preceding, During, and Since the American Civil War.* (Providence: J.A. & R.A. Reid, 1886).

Cox, Samuel S. *Why We Laugh* (New York: Benjamin Blom, 1969).

Cox, William V. *Life of Samuel Sullivan Cox, By his Nephew, William VanZandt Cox, and his Friend Milton Harlow Northrup.* (Syracuse: M.H. Northrup, 1899).

Crapo, Henry H. *The Story of William Wallace Crapo, 1830–1926.* (Boston: Thos. Todd Publ., 1942).

Crapol, Edward P. *James G. Blaine: Architect of Empire.* (Wilmington: SR Books, 2000).

Crofts, Daniel W. "The Black Response to the Blair Education Bill." *Journal of Southern History*, 37 (1971): 41–65.

Current, Richard N. "President Grant and the Continuing Civil War," in David L. Wilson and John Y. Simon, eds., *Ulysses S. Grant: Essays and Documents.* (Carbondale: Southern Illinois University Press, 1981): 71–82.

Currie-McDaniel, Ruth. *Carpetbagger of Conscience: A Biography of John Emory Bryant.* (Athens: University of Georgia Press, 1987).

Curry, Jabez L.M. *A Brief Sketch of George Peabody and A History of the Peabody Education Fund Through Thirty Years.* (Cambridge: University Press, 1898).

Dabney, Robert L. *Discussions by Robert L. Dabney, D.D., L.L.D., Recently Professor of Moral Philosophy in the University of Texas, and for Many Years Professor of Theology in Union Theological Seminary in Virginia,* ed. Clement Read Vaughan, 4 vols. (Mexico, Missouri: Crescent Book House, 1897).

Dailey, Jane. "Deference and Violence in the Postbellum Urban South: Manners and Massacres in Danville, Virginia." *Journal of Southern History*, 63 (1997): 553–590.

Davis, Hugh. *We Will Be Satisfied with Nothing Less, The African American Struggle for Equal Rights in the North during Reconstruction.* (Ithaca: Cornell University Press, 2011).

Davis, William W. *The Civil War and Reconstruction in Florida.* (Gainesville: University of Florida Press, 1964).

DeBlack, Thomas A. *With Fire and Sword. Arkansas, 1861–1874.* (Fayetteville: University of Arkansas Press, 2003).

Deutsch, Herman J. "Carpenter and the Senatorial Election of 1875 in Wisconsin." *Wisconsin Magazine of History*, 16 (1932): 26–46.

Donald, David H. *Charles Sumner and the Coming of the Civil War.* (New York: Alfred A. Knopf, 1960).

Donald, David H. *Charles Sumner and the Rights of Man.* (New York: Alfred A. Knopf, 1970).

Donald, David H. "The Scalawag in Mississippi Reconstruction." *Journal of Southern History*, 10 (1944): 447–60.

Dorgan, Howard. "Rhetoric of the United Confederate Veterans: A Lost Cause Mythology in the Making," in Waldo W. Braden, ed., *Oratory in the New South*. (Baton Rouge: Louisiana State University Press, 1979), 143–173.

Douglass, Frederick. *Autobiographies, Narrative of the Life and Times of Frederick Douglass, and American Slave; My Bondage and My Freedom; Life and Times of Frederick Douglass*. (New York: Library of America, 1994).

Downs, Gregory P. *After Appomattox: Military Occupation and the Ends of War*. (Cambridge: Harvard University Press, 2015).

Drago, Edmund L. *Black Politicians and Reconstruction in Georgia: A Splendid Failure*. (Baton Rouge: Louisiana State University Press, 1982).

Dray, Philip. *Capitol Men: The Epic Story of Reconstruction through the Lives of the First Black Congressmen*. (Boston: Houghton Mifflin, 2008).

Du Bois, W.E.B. *Black Reconstruction in America: An Essay Toward a History of the Part Which Black Folk Played in the Attempt to Reconstruct Democracy in America, 1860–1880*. (Oxford: Oxford University Press, 2007).

Duncan, Russell. *Freedom's Shore: Tunis Campbell and the Georgia Freedman*. (Athens: University of Georgia Press, 1986).

Eaton, John. *Grant, Lincoln and the Freedmen. Reminiscences of the Civil War, with Special Reference to the Work for the Contrabands and Freedmen of the Mississippi Valley*. (New York: Negro Universities Press, 1969).

Ecelbarger, Gary. *Black Jack Logan: An Extraordinary Life in Peace and War*. (Guilford: Lyons Press, 2005).

Eckert, Ralph L. *John Brown Gordon: Soldier, Southerner, American*. (Baton Rouge: Louisiana State University Press, 1989).

Egerton, Douglas R. *The Wars of Reconstruction. The Brief Violent History of America's Most Progressive Era* (New York: Bloomsbury Press, 2014).

Elliott, Mark. *Color-Blind Justice: Albion Tourgee and the Quest for Racial Equality from the Civil War to Plessy v. Ferguson*. (Oxford: Oxford University Press, 2006).

Elliott, Russell R. *Servant of Power: A Political Biography of Senator William M. Stewart*. (Reno: University of Nevada Press, 1983).

Engle, Stephen D. "Mountaineer Reconstruction: Blacks in the Political Reconstruction of West Virginia." *Journal of Negro History*, 78 (1993): 137–165.

Escott, Paul D., ed. *North Carolinians in the Era of the Civil War and Reconstruction*. (Chapel Hill: University of North Carolina Press, 2008).

Escott, Paul D. "White Republicanism and the Ku Klux Klan Terror: The North Carolina Piedmont during Reconstruction," in Jeffrey Crow, Paul D. Escott and Charles L. Flynn, eds. *Race, Class and Politics in Southern History: Essays in Honor of Robert F. Durden*. (Baton Rouge: Louisiana State University Press, 1989).

Farley, Ena L. *The Underside of Reconstruction New York: The Struggle Over the Issue of Black Equality.* (New York: Garland Publishing, 1993).

Feldman, Eugene P.R. *Black Power in Old Alabama: The Life and Stirring Times of James Rapier, Afro-American Congressman from Alabama, 1839–1883.* (Chicago: Museum of African-American History, 1968).

Felton, Rebecca Lattimer. *My Memories of Georgia Politics.* (Atlanta: Index Printing Co., 1911).

Ficker, Douglas J. 'From Roberts to Plessy: Educational Segregation and the 'Separate but Equal' Doctrine." *Journal of Negro History*, 84 (1999): 301–314.

Finkelman, Paul and Stephen C. Gottlieb, eds., *Toward a Usable Past: Liberty Under State Governments.* (Athens: University of Georgia Press, 1991).

Fischer, Roger A. "A Pioneer Protest: The New Orleans Street-Car Controversy of 1867." *Journal of Negro History,* 53 (1968): 219–233.

Fischer, Roger A. "Racial Segregation in Ante-Bellum New Orleans." *American Historical Review*, 74 (1969): 926–937.

Fischer, Roger A. *The Segregation Struggle in Louisiana, 1862–1877.* (Urbana: University of Illinois Press, 1974).

Fishel, Leslie H., Jr. "The Genesis of the First Wisconsin Civil Rights Act." *Wisconsin Magazine of History,* 49 (1966): 324–333.

Fishel, Leslie H., Jr. "The Negro in Northern Politics, 1870–1900." *Mississippi Valley Historical Review,* 42 (1955): 466–489.

Fitzgerald, Michael W. "Radical Republicanism and the White Yeomanry during Alabama Reconstruction, 1865–1868," *Journal of Southern History*, 54 (1988): 565–596.

Folk, Patrick A. "'Our Frank:' The Congressional Career of Frank Hurd." *Northwest Ohio Quarterly,* 41: 45–69; 42: 47–63; 47: 151–169; 48: 24–34, 55–79, 143–152.

Foner, Eric. *Reconstruction: America's Unfinished Revolution, 1863–1866.* (New York: Harper & Row, 1988).

Foner, Eric. "Rights and the Constitution in Black Life during the Civil War and Reconstruction." *Journal of American History*, 74 (1987): 863–883.

Foraker, Joseph B. *Notes of a Busy Life,* 2 vols. (Cincinnati: Stewart & Kidd Co., 1916).

Foulke, William Dudley. *Life of Oliver H.P.T. Morton, Including his Important Speeches*, 2 vols. (Indianapolis: Bowen-Merrill Co., 1899).

Franklin, John Hope. "The Enforcement of the Civil Rights Act of 1875." *Prologue,* 6 (1974): 225–235.

Franklin, John Hope. *Reconstruction After the Civil War.* (Chicago: University of Chicago Press, 1961).

Fraser, Walter J., Jr. "Barbour Lewis: A Carpetbagger Reconsidered." *Tennessee Historical Quarterly,* 32 (1973): 148–168.

Fraser, Walter J., Jr. "William Henry Ruffner and the Establishment of Virginia's Public School System, 1870–1874." *Virginia Magazine of History and Biography,* 79 (1971): 259–279.

Gallegly, J.S. "The Tremont Opera House of Galveston: The First Years." *Rice Institute Pamphlets*, 45 (1959): 52–70.

Gara, Larry. "A Glorious Time: The 1874 Abolitionist Reunion in Chicago." *Journal of the Illinois State Historical Society*, 65 (1972): 280–292.

Garfield, James A. *The Diary of James Abram Garfield*, 4 vols., ed. Harry J. Brown and Frederick D. Williams (East Lansing: Michigan State University Press, 1967).

Garrison, William Lloyd. *The Letters of William Lloyd Garrison*, 6 vols. (Cambridge: Harvard University Press, 1981).

Gauger, John H. "A Delaware Experiment With Reconstruction Nullification." *Delaware History*, 21 (1985): 164–185.

Gerber, David A. *Black Ohio and the Color Line, 1860–1915*. (Urbana: University of Illinois Press, 1976).

Gerber, Richard Allan and Alan Friedlander, "The Civil Rights Act of 1875: A Reexamination." *Transactions of the Connecticut Academy of Arts and Sciences*, 60 (2008): 1–50.

Gerber, Richard Allan. "Carl Schurz's Journey from Radical to Liberal Republican: A Problem in Ideological Consistency." *Mid-America*, 82 (2000): 71–99.

Gerber, Richard Allan. "Civil Rights for Freed Persons: The Issue of Private Discrimination Revisited." *Connecticut Review*, 15, no. 2 (1993): 25–33.

Gerber, Richard Allan. "Liberal Republicanism, Reconstruction, and Social Order: Samuel Bowles as a Test Case." *New England Quarterly*, (1972): 393–407.

Gerber, Richard Allan. "The Liberal Republicans of 1872 in Historiographical Perspective." *Journal of American History*, 62 (1975): 40–73.

Gerber, Richard Allan. "'Playing Tricks on the Dead': *Jones v. Alfred H. Mayer Company*, An Historical Inquiry." *Pace Law Review*, 1 (1980): 59–119.

Gerber, Richard Allan. "The Reinterpretation of the Due Process Clause of the Fourteenth Amendment in the Age of Industrialism." in Joseph R. Freese and Jacob Judd, eds., *American Industrialization, Economic Expansion, and the Law*. (Tarrytown: 1982), 143–209.

Gerber, Richard Allan. *Revolution and Union: The Dilemma of America 1763–1877*. (Chicago: Cengage, 2008).

Gerber, Richard Allan. *The System: The American Constitution in Historical Perspective, 1763–1929*. (Chicago: Cengage, 2009).

Gillette, William. *Retreat from Reconstruction, 1869–1879*. (Baton Rouge: Louisiana State University Press, 1979).

Gillette, William. *The Right to Vote: Politics and the Passage of the Fifteenth Amendment*. (Baltimore: Johns Hopkins Press, 1965).

Going, Allen J. "A Shooting Affray in Knoxville with Interstate Repercussions: The Killing of James H. Clanton by David M. Nelson, 1871." *Publications of the East Tennessee Historical Society*, 27 (1955): 39–48.

Goode, John, Jr. *Recollections of a Lifetime*. (New York: Neale Publishing Co., 1906).

Graham, W.A. *The Custer Myth: A Source Book of Custeriana.* (Mechanicsburg: Stackpole Books, 1995).

Grossman, Lawrence. *The Democratic Party and the Negro: Northern and National Politics, 1868–1892.* (Urbana: University of Illinois Press, 1976).

Grossman, Lawrence. "George T. Downing and Desegregation of Rhode Island Public Schools." *Rhode Island History*, 36 (1997): 99–105.

Grosz, Agnes. "The Political Career of Pinckney Benton Stewart Pinchback." *Louisiana Historical Quarterly*, 27 (1944): 527–623.

Gudridge, Patrick O. "Privileges and Permissions: The Civil Rights Act of 1875." *Law and Philosophy*, 83 (1989): 83–130.

Hacker, J. David. "A Census-Based Count of the Civil War Dead." *Civil War History*, 57 (2011): 307–348.

Hancock, Harold B. "Reconstruction in Delaware," in *Radicalism, Racism, and Party Realignment. The Border States During Reconstruction,* ed. Richard O. Curry (Baltimore: The Johns Hopkins Press, 1969): 188–219.

Hare, John S. "Allen G. Thurman: A Political Study," Diss., Ohio State University, 1933.

Harlan, Louis R. "Desegregation in the New Orleans Public Schools during Reconstruction." *American Historical Review*, 67 (1962): 663–675.

Harrison, Carter H., Jr. *Stormy Years: The Autobiography of Carter H. Harrison, Five Times Mayor of Chicago.* (Indianapolis: Bobbs-Merrill Co., 1935).

Harrison, John M. *The Man Who Made Nasby, David Ross Locke.* (Chapel Hill: University of North Carolina Press, 1969).

Haskins, James. *Pinkney Benton Stewart Pinchback.* (New York: Macmillan, 1973).

Haskins, James. *The First Black Governor, Pinkney Benton Stewart Pinchback.* (Trenton: Africa World Press, 1996).

Henderson, William D. *The Unredeemed City: Reconstruction in Petersburg, Virginia, 1865–1874.* (Washington, D.C.: University Press of America, 1977).

Hennessey, Melinda M. "Reconstruction Politics and the Military: The Eufaula Riot of 1874," *Alabama Historical Quarterly*, 38 (1976): 112–125.

Herbert, Hilary A. *Why the Solid South? or, Reconstruction and its Results* (Baltimore, R.H. Woodward & Co., 1890).

Herrick, Hugh M. *William Walter Phelps, His Life and Public Services.* (New York: Knickerbocker Press, 1904).

Hesseltine, William B. *Ulysses S. Grant, Politician.* (New York: Dodd, Meade & Co., 1935).

Hinsdale, Mary. *Garfield-Hinsdale Letters: Correspondence between James Abram Garfield and Burke Aaron Hinsdale.* (Ann Arbor: University of Michigan Press, 1945).

Hirshson, Stanley P. *Farewell to the Bloody Shirt: Northern Republicans and the Southern Negro, 1877–1893.* (Bloomington: Indiana University Press, 1962).

Hoar, George F. *Autobiography of Seventy Years*, 2 vols. (New York: Scribner's Sons, 1903).

Hoeveler, J. David Jr. "Reconstruction and the Federal Courts: The Civil Rights Act of 1875." *Historian*, 31 (1969): 604–617.

Holliday, Joseph E. "Daniel D. Pratt: Lawyer and Legislator." *Indiana Magazine of History*, 57 (1961): 99–126.

Holliday, Joseph E. "Daniel D. Pratt: Senator and Commissioner." *Indiana Magazine of History*, 58 (1962): 17–51.

Holt, Thomas C. *Black Over White: Negro Political Leadership in South Carolina during Reconstruction* (Urbana, University of Illinois Press, 1977).

Horton, Carol A. *Race and the Making of American Liberalism.* (New York: 2005).

House, Albert V. "Northern Congressional Democrats as Defenders of the South during Reconstruction." *Journal of Southern History*, 6 (1940): 46–71.

Hume, David L. "Membership of the Florida Constitutional Convention of 1868: A Case Study of Republican Factionalism in the Reconstruction South." *Florida Historical Quarterly*, 51 (1972): 1–21.

Hunnicutt, John L. *Reconstruction in West Alabama: The Memoirs of John L. Hunnicutt*, ed. William S. Hoole (Tuscaloosa: Confederate Publishing Co., 1959).

Hunton, Eppa. *The Autobiography of Eppa Hunton.* (Richmond: Wm. Byrd Press, 1933).

Ingalls, John J. *A Collection of the Writings of John Ingalls, Essays, Addresses, and Orations*, ed. William Connelly (Kansas City: Hudson-Kimberly Co., 1902).

Irons, Peter. *A People's History of the Supreme Court. The Men and Women Whose Cases and Decisions Have Shaped the Constitution* (New York: Viking Press, 2006).

Jackson, Luther P. *Negro Office Holders in Virginia, 1865–1895.* (Norfolk: Guide Quality Press, 1945).

Jager, Ronald B. "Charles Sumner, the Constitution, and the Civil Rights Act of 1875." *New England Quarterly*, 17 (1969): 350–372.

Johnson, Mary Rose Heilman. *William Heilman: Immigrant's Outstanding Achievements* (n.p., Tropical Press, 1982).

Jones, George L. "William H. Felton and the Independent Democratic Movement in Georgia, 1870–1890." Diss., University of Georgia, 1971.

Jones, Robert R. "James L. Kemper and the Virginia Redeemers Face the Race Question: A Reconsideration." *Journal of Southern History*, 38 (1972): 393–414.

Jordan, David M. *Roscoe Conkling: Voice in the Senate.* (Ithaca: Cornell University Press, 1971).

Kaczorowski, Robert J. *The Nationalization of Civil Rights: Constitutional Theory and Practice in a Racist Society, 1866–1883.* (New York: Garland Publ., 1987).

Kaczorowski, Robert J. *The Politics of Judicial Interpretation: The Federal Courts, Department of Justice, and Civil Rights, 1866–1876.* (Dobb's Ferry: Oceana Publications, 1985).

Kaczorowski, Robert J. "To Begin the Nation Anew: Congress, Citizenship, and Civil Rights after the Civil War." *American Historical Review*, 92 (1987): 45–68.

Kantrowitz, Stephen. *More than Freedom: Fighting for Black Citizenship in a White Republic, 1829–1889*. (New York: Penguin Press, 2012).

Kelly, Alfred H. "The Congressional Controversy over School Segregation, 1867–1875." *American Historical Review*, 64 (1959): 537–563.

Kennedy, John F. *Profiles in Courage*. (New York: Harper, 1956).

Kincaid, Larry. "Victims of Circumstance: An Interpretation of Changing Attitudes Toward Republican Policy Makers and Reconstruction." *Journal of American History*, 57 (1970): 48–66.

King, Edward. *The Great South: A Record of Journeys in Louisiana, Texas, the Indian Territory, Missouri, Arkansas, Mississippi, Alabama, Georgia, Florida, South Carolina, North Carolina, Kentucky, Tennessee, West Virginia and Maryland*. (Baton Rouge: Louisiana State University Press, 1972).

Kleppner, Paul. *The Cross of Culture: A Social Analysis of Midwestern Politics, 1850–1900*. (New York: The Free Press, 1970).

Kleppner, Paul. *The Third Electoral System, 1853–1892: Parties, Voters, and Political Cultures*. (Chapel Hill: University of North Carolina Press, 1979).

Klingman, Peter. *Josiah Walls: Florida's Black Congressman of Reconstruction*. (Gainesville: University of Florida Press, 1976).

Konvitz, Milton R. and Theodore Leskes. *A Century of Civil Rights: With a Study of State Law Against Discrimination*. (New York: Columbia University Press, 1961).

Kousser, J. Morgan. "Before Plessy, Before Brown: The Development of the Law of Racial Integration in Louisiana and Kansas," in Paul Finkelman and Stephen C. Gottlieb. *Toward a Usable Past: Liberty Under State Governments* (Athens: University of Georgia Press, 1991): 213–270.

Kousser, J. Morgan. *Dead End: The Development of Nineteenth-Century Litigation on Racial Discrimination in Schools*. (Oxford: Oxford University Press, 1986).

Kousser, J. Morgan. "Separate but *not* Equal: The Supreme Court's First Decision on Racial Discrimination in Schools." *Journal of Southern History*, 46 (1980): 17–44.

Lamson, Peggy. *The Glorious Failure: Black Congressman Robert Brown Elliott and Reconstruction in South Carolina*. (New York: Norton, 1973).

Landry, Stuart O. *The Battle of Liberty Place: The Overthrow of Carpet-Bag Rule in New Orleans, September 14, 1874*. (New Orleans: Pelican Publishing Co., 1955).

Lane, Charles. *The Day Freedom Died: The Colfax Massacre, the Supreme Court, and the Betrayal of Reconstruction*. (New York: Henry Holt & Co., 2008).

Langguth, A.J. *After Lincoln, How the North Won the Civil War and Lost the Peace*. (New York: Simon and Schuster, 2014).

Langston, John Mercer. *Freedom and Citizenship. Selected Letters and Addresses of John Mercer Langston*. (Washington: R.H. Darby, 1883).

Langston, John Mercer. *From the Virginia Plantation to the National Capitol*. (New York: Arno Press, 1969).

Leigh, Philip. *Southern Reconstruction.* (Yardley, Pa.: Westholme Publishing, 2017).

Leman, Nicholas. *Redemption: The Last Battle of the Civil War.* (New York: Farrar, Strauss and Giroux, 2006).

Lemmon, Sarah H. "Transportation Segregation in the Federal Courts since 1865." *Journal of Negro History*, 38 (1953): 174–193.

Lestage, Oscar H. "The White League in Louisiana and its Participation in Reconstruction Riots." *Louisiana Historical Quarterly*, 18 (1935): 615–695.

Lewis, Ronald L. "Cultural Pluralism and Black Reconstruction: The Public Career of Richard H. Cain." *Crisis*, 85 (1978): 57–60.

Lincove, David A. *Reconstruction in the United States. An Annotated Bibliography.* (Westport: Greenwood Press, 2000).

Lindsey, David. *"Sunset" Cox: Irrepressible Democrat.* (Detroit: Wayne State University Press, 1959).

Locke, David Ross. *The Nasby Letters. Being the Original Nasby Letters, as Written during his Lifetime, by David Ross Locke.* (Toledo: The Toledo Blade Co., 1893).

Locke, David Ross. *The Struggles (Social, Financial, and Political) of Petroleum V. Nasby … Embracing his Trials and Troubles, Ups and Downs, Rejoicings and Wailings; Likewise his Views of Men and Things, Together with the Lectures "Cussed be Canaan," "The Struggles of a Conservative with the Woman Question," and "In Search of the Sin of Man."* (Boston: L.N. Richardson & Co., 1873).

Loevy, Robert D. *The Civil Rights Act of 1964. The Passage of the Law that Ended Racial Segregation.* (Albany: State University of New York Press, 1997).

Loevy, Robert D. *To End All Segregation. The Politics of the Passage of the Civil Rights Act of 1964.* (Lanham: University Press of America, 1990).

Logan, Frenise A. *The Negro in North Carolina, 1876–1894.* (Chapel Hill: University of North Carolina Press, 1964).

Logue, Cal M. "Restoration Strategies in Gergia, 1865–1880," in Waldo W. Braden, ed., *Oratory in the New South.* (Baton Rouge: Louisiana State University Press, 1979): 38–73.

Longacre, Edward G. *A Regiment of Slaves: The 4th United States Colored Infantry, 1863–1866.* (Mechanicsburg: Stackpole Books, 2003).

Lovett, Bobby L. "Memphis Riots: White Reaction to Blacks in Memphis, May 1865 – July 1866." *Tennessee Historical Quarterly*, 37 (1979): 9–33.

Lowry, Thomas P. *Curmudgeons, Drunkards and Outright Fools: Courts-Martial of Civil War Union Colonels.* (Lincoln: University of Nebraska Press, 2003).

Luckett, Barbara. *The Civil Rights Act of 1875, a Failure Reconsidered.* (Omaha: University of Nebraska Press, 1972).

Lurie, Jonathan. "The Fourteenth Amendment: Use and Application in Selected State Court Civil Liberties Cases, 1870–1890 – A Preliminary Assessment." *The American Journal of Legal History*, 28 (1984): 295–313.

Lynch, John Roy. *The Facts of Reconstruction.* (New York: Neale Publ., 1913).

Lynch, John Roy. *Reminiscences of an Active Life: The Autobiography of John Roy Lynch,* ed. John Hope Franklin (Chicago: University of Chicago Press, 1970).

Maddex, Jack P., Jr. *Virginia Conservatives, 1867–1879: A Study of Reconstruction Politics.* (Chapel Hill: University of North Carolina Press, 1970).

Mallam, William D. "The Grant-Butler Relationship." *Mississippi Valley Historical Review,* 41 (1954): 259–276.

Maltz, Earl M. "The Civil Rights Act and the Civil Rights Cases: Congress, Courts and Constitution." *Florida Law Review,* 44 (1992): 605–635.

Maltz, Earl M. *Civil Rights, the Constitution, and Congress, 1863–1869.* (Lawrence: University of Kansas Press, 1990).

Maltz, Earl M. "Reconstruction Without Revolution: Republican Civil Rights Theory in the Era of the Fourteenth Amendment." *Houston Law Review,* 24 (1987): 221–279.

Mann, Kenneth E. "Richard Harvey Cain, Congressman, Minister and Champion for Civil Rights." *Negro History Bulletin,* 35 (1972): 64–66.

Mantell, Martin E. *Johnson, Grant, and the Politics of Reconstruction.* (New York: Columbia University Press, 1973).

Marten, James. *Texas Divided: Loyalty and Dissent in the Lone Star State, 1856–1874.* (Lexington: University Press of Kentucky, 1990).

Martis, Kenneth C. *The Historical Atlas of United States Congressional Districts, 1789–1983.* (New York: Free Press, 1982).

McAfee, Ward M. "Reconstruction Revisited: The Republican Public Education Crusade of the 1870s." *Civil War History,* 42 (1996): 133–153.

McBride, David. "Fourteenth Amendment Idealism: The New York State Civil Rights Law, 1873–1918." *New York History,* 71 (1990): 207–233.

McBride, Mary Gorton. *Randall Lee Gibson of Louisiana: Confederate General and New South Reformer.* (Baton Rouge: Louisiana State University Press, 2007).

McFeely, William S. *Grant: A Biography.* (New York: Norton, 1981).

McKinney, Gordon B. "The Rise of the Houk Machine in East Tennessee," *East Tennessee Historical Society Publications,* 45 (1973): 61–77.

McKinney, Gordon B. *Southern Mountain Republicans, 1865–1900: Politics and the Appalachian Community.* (Chapel Hill: University of North Carolina Press, 1978).

McLaughlin, James H. "John R. Lynch, the Reconstruction Politician: A Historical Perspective," Diss., Ball State University, 1981.

McPherson, James M. "Abolitionists and the Civil Rights Act of 1875." *Journal of American History,* 52 (1965): 493–510.

McVeigh, Donald R. "Charles James Faulkner: Reluctant Rebel," Diss., University of West Virginia, 1955.

Memorial Addresses on the Life and Character of Charles Sumner (A Senator from Massachusetts), Delivered in the Senate and House of Representatives, Forty-Third

Congress, First Session, April 27, 1874. (Washington: Government Printing Office, 1874).

Memorial Addresses on the Life and Character of James B. Beck (A Senator from Kentucky), Delivered in the Senate and House of Representatives, August 23 and September 13, 1890. (Washington: Government Printing Office, 1891).

Memorial Addresses on the Life and Character of Julian Hartridge (A Representative from Georgia), Delivered in the House of Representatives and in the Senate, Forty-Fifth Congress. Third Session (Washington: Government Printing Office, 1879).

Memorial Addresses on the Life and Character of Leonidas Campbell Houk (A Representative from Tennessee), Delivered in the House of Representatives and in the Senate, January 30th and February 9th 1892, Fifty-Second Congress, First Session. (Washington: Government Printing Office, 1892).

Memorial Addresses on the Life and Character of Lewis V. Bogy (A Senator from Missouri), Delivered in the Senate, January 16, 1878, and in the House of Representatives, January 23, 1878. (Washington: Government Printing Office, 1878).

Memorial Addresses on the Life and Character of Orris S. Ferry (A Senator from Connecticut), Delivered in the Senate and House of Representatives, February 8, 1876. (Washington: Government Printing Office, 1876).

Memorial Addresses on the Life and Character of Samuel J. Randall (A Representative from Pennsylvania), Delivered in the House of Representatives and in the Senate, Fifty-First Congress, First Session. (Washington: Government Printing Office, 1891).

Merrimon, Maud L. *A Memoir. Augustus Summerfield Merrimon.* (Raleigh: E.M. Uzzell & Co., 1894).

Middleton, Stephen. *Black Congressmen During Reconstruction* (Westport: Praeger, 2002).

Milnarich, Rhoda F. "The Public Career of Aaron Augustus Sargent," Diss., University of El Paso, 1961.

Moneyhon, Carl H. *Republicanism in Reconstruction Texas.* (Austin: University of Texas Press, 1980).

Montgomery, David. *Beyond Equality: Labor and the Radical Republicans, 1862–1872.* (Urbana: University of Chicago Press, 1967).

Montgomery, David. "Radical Republicanism in Pennsylvania, 1866–1873." *Pennsylvania Magazine of History and Biography,* 85 (1961): 439–457.

Morgan, John Tyler. *Radical Political Morality, Tissue Ballots in Virginia, the Bourbon Democracy.* (Washington: Government Printing Office, 1881).

Murphy, James B. *L.Q.C. Lamar: Pragmatic Patriot.* (Baton Rouge: Louisiana State University Press, 1973).

Murphy, L.E. "The Civil Rights Law of 1875." *Journal of Negro History,* 12 (1927): 110–127.

Murray, Alex L. "Harriet Beecher Stowe on Racial Segregation in the Schools." *American Quarterly,* 12 (1960): 518–519.

Nash, Howard P. *Stormy Petrel: The Life and Times of Gen. Benjamin F. Butler, 1818–1893.* (Rutherford: Fairleigh Dickinson University Press, 1975).

Nieman, Donald G., ed. *Freedom, Racism and Reconstruction: The Collected Writings of LaWanda Cox.* (Athens: University of Georgia Press, 1997).

Nordhoff, Charles. *The Cotton States in the Spring and Summer of 1875.* (New York: Burt Franklin, 1876).

Norris, James D. and Arthur H.Shaffer Politics and Patronage in the Gilded Age: The Correspondence of James A. Garfield and Charles E. Henry. (Madison: University of Wisconsin Press, 1970).

Norwood, Thomas M. *A True Vindication of the South in a Review of American History.* (Savannah: Braid & Hutton, 1917).

Norwood, Thomas M. *Plutocracy, or, American White Slavery. A Politico-Social Novel.* (New York: Metropolitan Publishing Co., 1888).

O'Connell, Robert L., *Fierce Patriot, The Tangled Lives of William Tecumseh Sherman.* (New York, Random House, 2015).

Olsen, Otto H. "North Carolina: An Incongruous Presence," in Otto H. Olsen, ed., *Reconstruction and Redemption in the South.* (Baton Rouge: Louisiana State University Press, 1980): 156–201.

O'Malley, Michael. "Specie and Species: Race and the Money Question in Nineteenth-Century America." *American Historical Review*, (1994): 369–395.

Orcutt, Dana. *Burrows of Michigan and the Republican Party.* (New York: Longmans, Green & Co., 1917).

Osthaus, Carl R. *Partisans of the Southern Press: Editorial Spokesmen of the Nineteenth Century.* (Lexington: University Press of Kentucky, 1994).

Owen, Homer L. "James Nesmith: Pioneer Judge, Legislator, Farmer, Soldier, Senator and Congressman." *Reed College Bulletin*, 24 (1950): 139–176.

Packwood, Cyril O. *Detour – Bermuda, Destination – U.S. House of Representatives: The Life of Joseph Hayne Rainey.* (Hamilton: Baxter's Ltd., 1977).

Pearson, Charles C. "William Henry Ruffner: Reconstruction Statesman of Virginia." *South Atlantic Quarterly*, 20 (1921): 25–32, 137–151.

Pereyra, Lillian A. *James Lusk Alcorn: Persistent Whig.* (Baton Rouge: Louisiana State University Press, 1966).

Perman, Michael. *The Road to Redemption: Southern Politics, 1869–1879.* (Chapel Hill: University of North Carolina Press, 1984).

Phillips, Kimberly L. "'Did the Battlefield Kill Jim Crow?' The Cold War Military, Civil Rights and Black Freedom," in Kevin M. Kruse and Stephen Tuck, eds., *Fog of War: The Second World War and the Civil Rights Movement.* (Oxford: Oxford University Press, 2012): 208–229.

Pierce, Edward L. *Memoir and Letters of Charles Sumner*, 4 vols. (Boston: Roberts Brothers, 1877–1893).

Plummer, Mark A. "'Goodbye dear Governor. You are my best friend.' The Private Letters of Robert G. Ingersoll to Richard J. Oglesby, 1867–1877." *Journal of the Illinois State Historical Society*, 73 (1980): 78–116.

Poyo, Gerald E. "Cuban Revolutionaries and Monroe County Reconstruction Politics, 1868–1876." *Florida Historical Quarterly*, 55 (1977): 408–423.

Price, James S. *The Battle of New Market Heights: Freedom Will Be Theirs By the Sword.* (Charleston: The History Press, 2011).

Proceedings of the Trustees of the Peabody Education Fund from their Original Organization on the 8th of February 1867, 6 vols. (Boston: John Wilson & Son, 1875–1916).

Queener, Verton M. "A Decade of East Tennessee Republicanism, 1867–1876." *Publications of the East Tennessee Historical Society*, 14 (1942): 59–85.

Queener, Verton M. "The Origins of the Republican Party in East Tennessee." *Publications of the East Tennessee Historical Society*, 13 (1941): 66–90.

Rabinowitz, Howard N. "From Exclusion to Segregation: Southern Race Relations, 1865–1890." *Journal of American History*, 63 (1976): 325–350.

Rabinowitz, Howard N. *Race Relations in the Urban South, 1865–1890.* (New York: Oxford University Press, 1978).

Rabinowitz, Howard N. *Southern Black Leaders of the Reconstruction Era.* (Urbana: University of Illinois Press, 1982).

Rable, George C. *But There Was No Peace: The Role of Violence in the Politics of Reconstruction.* (Athens: University of Georgia Press, 1984).

Rae, Noel. *The Great Stain, Witnessing American Slavery.* (New York, Overlook Press, 2018).

Rawley, James A. "The General Amnesty Act of 1872: A Note." *Mississippi Valley Historical Review* (1960): 480–484.

Redfield, Horace V. *Homicide, North and South. Being a Comparative View of Crime Against the Person in Several Parts of the United States.* (Columbus: Ohio State University Press, 2000).

Reid, George W. "Four in Black: North Carolina's Black Congressmen, 1874–1901." *Journal of Negro History*, 64 (1979): 229–243.

Richardson, Heather Cox. *The Death of Reconstruction. Race, Labor, and Politics in the Post-Civil War North, 1865–1901.* (Cambridge: Harvard University Press, 2001).

Riddleberger, Patrick W. "The Radicals' Abandonment of the Negro During Reconstruction." *Journal of Negro History*, 45 (1960): 88–102.

Riegel, Stephen J. "The Persistent Career of Jim Crow: Lower Federal Courts and the 'Separate but Equal' Doctrine, 1865–1896." *The American Journal of Legal History*, 28 (1984): 17–40.

Roberts, Derrell. "Social Legislation in Reconstruction Florida." *Florida Historical Quarterly*, 43 (1965): 349–361.

Roberts, William P. "The Public Career of Dr. William Harrell Felton," Diss., University of North Carolina, 1953.

Rogers, William W. and Robert D. Ward. *August Reckoning. Jack Turner and Racism in Post-Civil War Alabama.* (Baton Rouge: Louisiana State University Press, 1973).

Rogers, William W. *A Scalawag in Georgia: Richard Henry Whiteley and the Politics of Reconstruction.* (Urbana: University of Illinois Press, 2007).

Rogers, William W. *Black-Belt Scalawag: Charles Hays and Southern Republicans During Reconstruction.* (Athens: University of Georgia Press, 1993).

Rogers, William W. "'Politics is Mighty Uncertain:' Charles Hays Goes to Congress." *Alabama Review*, 30 (1977): 163–90.

Rogers, William W. "Reconstruction Journalism: The Hays-Hawley Letter, A Sensational Letter to the *Hartford Courant* Ignites a National Controversy." *American Journalism*, 7 (1989): 235–244.

Rokicky, Catherine M. *James Monroe: Oberlin's Christian Statesman and Reformer.* (Kent: Kent State University Press, 2002).

Rollins, John W. "Frederick Theodore Frelinghuysen, 1817–1885: The Politics and Diplomacy of Stewardship," Diss., University of Wisconsin, 1974.

Rosen, Hannah. *Terror in the Heart of Freedom: Citizenship, Sexual Violence, and the Meaning of Race in the Postemancipation South.* (Chapel Hill: University of North Carolina Press, 2009).

Ross, Michael A. "Justice Miller's Reconstruction: The Slaughter-House Cases, Health Codes, and Civil Rights in New Orleans, 1861–1873." *Journal of Southern History*, 64 (1998): 649–676.

Rousey, Dennis C. "Yellow Fever and Black Policemen in Memphis: A Post-Reconstruction Anomaly." *Journal of Southern History*, 51 (1985): 357–374.

Rowell, Chester H. *A Historical and Legal Digest of All the Contested Election Cases in the House of Representatives of the United States from the First to the Fifty-Sixth Congress, 1789–1901.* (Washington: House Documents, 1901).

Rowell, George P. *American Newspaper Directory, Containing Accurate Lists of all the Newspapers and Periodicals Published in the United States and Territories, and the Dominion of Canada and British Colonies of North America.* (New York: Geo. P. Rowell & Co., 1874).

Russell, William H. "Timothy O. Howe, Stalwart Republican." *Wisconsin Magazine of History*, 35 (1951): 90–99.

Ryan, James G. "The Memphis Riots of 1866: Terror in a Black Community during Reconstruction." *Journal of Negro History*, 62 (1977): 243–257.

Sanderlin, Walter S. "Arthur P. Gorman and the Chesapeake and Ohio Canal: An Episode in the Rise of a Political Boss." *Journal of Southern History*, 13 (1947): 323–337.

Scatturo, Frank J. *President Grant Reconsidered.* (Lanham: Madison Books, 1999).

Schott, Thomas E. *Alexander H. Stephens of Georgia: A Biography.* (Baton Rouge, Louisiana State University Press, 1988).

Schurz, Carl. *A Memorial of Charles Sumner.* (Boston: Wright & Potters, 1874).

Schurz, Carl. *Charles Sumner, An Essay.* (Urbana: University of Illinois Press, 1951).

Schurz, Carl. *Speeches, Correspondence and Political Papers of Carl Schurz,* ed. Frederic Bancroft, 3 vols. (New York: G.P. Putnam Sons, 1913).

Schurz, Carl. *Reminiscences,* 3 vols. (New York: McClure Co., 1907–8).

Schwartz, Bernard. *Statutory History of the United States. Civil Rights. Part I.* (New York: Chelsea House Publishers, 1970).

Schweninger, Loren. *James T. Rapier and Reconstruction.* (Chicago: University of Chicago Press, 1978.)

Schweninger, Loren "James T. Rapier and the Negro Labor Movement, 1869–1872." *Alabama Review,* 28 (1975): 185–201.

Sefton, James E. *The United States Army and Reconstruction, 1865–1877.* (Baton Rouge: Louisiana State University Press, 1967).

Seip, Terry L. *The South Returns to Congress: Men, Economic Measures, and Intersectional Relationships, 1868–1879.* (Baton Rouge: Louisiana State University Press, 1983).

Shadgett, Olive H. *The Republican Party in Georgia from Reconstruction through 1900.* (Athens: University of Georgia Press, 1964).

Sherman, John. *Recollections of Forty Years in the House, Senate, and Cabinet,* 2 vols. (New York: Greenwood Press, 1968).

Shofner, Jerrell H. *Nor Is It Over Yet: Florida in the Era of Reconstruction, 1863–1877.* (Gainesville: University of Florida Press, 1974).

Simon, John Y. ed., *The Papers of Ulysses S. Grant,* 31 vols. (Carbondale: Southern Illinois University Press, 1967–2009).

Simpson, Brooks D. "Ulysses S. Grant and the Failure of Reconstruction." *Illinois Historical Review* (1988): 269–282.

Simpson, Craig M. *A Good Southerner: The Life of Henry A. Wise of Virginia.* (Chapel Hill: University of North Carolina Press, 1995).

Sizemore, Margaret D. "Frederick G. Bromberg of Mobile: An Illustrious Character, 1837–1928." *Alabama Review,* 29 (1976): 104–112.

Sloan, John Z. "The Ku Klux Klan and the Alabama Election of 1872." *Alabama Review,* 18 (1965): 113–123.

Smith, Edward D. "The Unfortunate History of America's First Comprehensive Civil Rights Bill, 1870–1883." *Negro History Bulletin,* 47 (1984): 42–44.

Smith, John David. *Anti-Abolition Tracts and Anti-Black Stereotypes, vol. 1: Anti-Black Thought, 1863–1925; General Statements of "The Negro Problem."* (New York: Garland Press, 1993).

Smith, Samuel D. *The Negro in Congress, 1870–1901.* (Chapel Hill: University of North Carolina Press, 1940).

Smith, Theodore C. *The Life and Letters of James Abram Garfield,* 2 vols. (New Haven: Yale University Press, 1925).

Somers, Dale A. "Black and White in New Orleans: A Study in Urban Race Relations, 1865–1900." *Journal of Southern History,* 40 (1974): 19–42.

Sommers, Richard J. *Richmond Redeemed: The Siege of Petersburg.* (Garden City: Doubleday, 1981).

Soper, Henry Marlin. *Scrap-Book Recitations, No. 2.* (Chicago: T.S. Denison, 1880).

Spackman, S.G.F. "American Federalism and the Civil Rights Act of 1875." *Journal of American Studies,* 10 (1976): 313–328.

Stampp, Kenneth. *The Era of Reconstruction, 1865–1877.* (New York: Vintage, 1965).

Stewart, William M. *Reminiscences of Senator William M. Stewart of Nevada.* (New York: Neale Publishing Co., 1908).

Stone, James H. "L.Q.C. Lamar's Letters to Edward Donaldson Clark, 1868–1885." *Journal of Mississippi History,* 35 (1973): 65–73; 37 (1975): 189–201; 43 (1981): 135–164.

Storey, Moorfield, and Edward W. Emerson. *Ebenezer Rockwood Hoar, A Memoir.* (Boston: Houghton Mifflin, 1911).

Summers, Mark Wahlgren. *The Ordeal of the Reunion, A New History of Reconstruction.* (Chapel Hill: University of North Carolina Press, 2014).

Summers, Mark Wahlgren. *The Press Gang: Newspapers and Politics, 1865–1878.* (Chapel Hill: University of North Carolina Press, 1994).

Tansill, Charles F. *The Congressional Career of Thomas Francis Bayard, 1869–1885.* (Washington: Georgetown University Press, 1946).

Taylor, Joe Gray. *Louisiana Reconstructed, 1863–1877.* (Baton Rouge: Louisiana State University Press, 1974).

Temple, Oliver P. and Mary B. *Notable Men of Tennessee: From 1833 to 1875, their Times and their Contemporaries.* (New York, Cosmopolitan Press, 1912).

Thompson, C. Mildred. *Reconstruction in Georgia: Economic, Social, Political 1865–1872.* (New York: The Columbia University Press, 1915).

Thompson, E. Bruce. *Matthew Hale Carpenter, Webster of the West.* (Madison: State Historical Society of Wisconsin, 1954).

Thompson, Margaret S. "Ben Butler versus the Brahmins: Patronage and Politics in Early Gilded Age Massachusetts." *New England Quarterly,* 55 (1982): 163–186.

Thornbrough, Emma Lou. *The Negro in Indiana before 1900: A Study of a Minority.* (Bloomington: Indiana University Press, 1993).

Tipton, Thomas W. *Forty Years of Nebraska at Home and in Congress.* (Lincoln: State Journal Co., 1902).

Tourgée, Albion W. *A Fool's Errand: A Novel of the South during Reconstruction.* (New York: Harper & Row, 1961).

Trefousse, Hans L. *Ben Butler: The South Called Him Beast!* (New York: Octagon Books, 1974).

Trefousse, Hans L. *Reconstruction: America's First Effort at Racial Democracy.* (New York: Van Nostrand, 1971).

Trefousse, Hans L. *The Radical Republicans: Lincoln's Vanguard for Social Justice.* (New York: Alfred A. Knopf, 1969).

Trelease, Allen W. *White Terror: The Ku Klux Conspiracy and Southern Reconstruction.* (New York: Harper and Row, 1971).

Tuck, Stephen. "'You Can Sing and Punch ... But You Can't Be a Soldier or a Man.' African American Struggles for a New Place in Popular Culture," in Kevin M. Kruse and Stephen Tuck, eds., *Fog of War: The Second World War and the Civil Rights Movement.* (Oxford: Oxford University Press, 2012): 103–125.

Tucker, David. "Black Politics in Memphis, 1865–1875." *West Tennessee Historical Society Papers*, 26 (1972): 13–19.

Tunnell, Ted. *Crucible of Reconstruction: War, Radicalism, and Race in Louisiana, 1862–1877.* (Baton Rouge: Louisiana State University Press, 1984).

Tunnell, Ted. *Edge of the Sword: The Ordeal of Carpetbagger Marshall H. Twitchell in the Civil War and Reconstruction.* (Baton Rouge: Louisiana University Press, 2001).

Tuttle, Charles A. *Reports of Cases Determined in the Supreme Court of the State of California at the January, April, July & October Terms, 1874*, vol. 48 (San Francisco: Whitney & Bancroft, 1875).

Twain, Mark. *The Autobiography of Mark Twain*, ed. Harriet Elinor Smith (Berkeley: University of California Press, 2010).

Twain, Mark, and Charles Dudley Warner. *The Gilded Age: A Tale of To-Day*, 2 vols. (Hartford: The American Publishing Co., 1899).

Vance, Robert B. *Heart-Throbs from the Mountains.* (Nashville: Southern Methodist Publishing House, 1887).

Vandal, Gilles. "'Bloody Caddo:' White Violence against Blacks in a Louisiana Parish, 1865–1876." *Journal of Social History*, 25 (1991): 373–388.

Vaughn, William P. "Partners in Segregation: Barnas Sears and the Peabody Fund." *Civil War History*, 10 (1964): 260–274.

Vaughn, William P. "Separate and Unequal: The Civil Rights Act of 1875 and the Defeat of the School Integration Clause." *The Southwestern Social Science Quarterly*, 48 (1967): 146–154.

Waddell, Alfred M. *Some Memories of My Life.* (Raleigh: Edwards, Broughton & Co., 1908).

Walker, Barrington. "This is a White Man's Day: The Irish, White Racial Identity, and the 1866 Memphis Riots." *Left History*, 5 (1997): 31–55.

Wallace, Hettie. "The Minster, the Martyr, and the Maxim: Robert Lewis Dabney and Stonewall Jackson Biography." *Civil War History*, 49 (2003): 353–369.

Wang, Xi. *The Trial of Democracy: Black Suffrage and Northern Republicans, 1860–1910.* (Athens: University of Georgia Press, 1997).

Ward, Judson C., Jr. "Georgia under the Bourbon Democrats, 1872–1890." Diss., University of North Carolina, 1947.

Warmoth, Henry Clay. *War, Politics, and Reconstruction: Stormy Days in Louisiana.* (New York: Macmillan, 1930).

Weaver, Valeria W. "The Failure of Civil Rights, 1875–1883, and its Repercussions." *Journal of Negro History*, 54 (1969): 368–382.

Weinfeld, Daniel R. "More Courage than Discretion: Charles M. Hamilton in Reconstruction Florida." *Florida Historical Quarterly*, 84 (2006): 479–516.

Weltner, Charles H. *Southerner.* (Philadelphia: J.B. Lippincott, 1966).

Whalen, Barbara and Charles. *The Longest Debate. A Legislative History of the 1964 Civil Rights Act.* (Washington: Seven Locks Press, 1985).

Wheeler, Joanne. "Together in Egypt: A Pattern of Race Relations in Cairo, Illinois, 1865–1915," in Orville V. Burton and Robert C. McMath, *Toward a New South. Studies in Post-Civil War Southern Communities* (Westport: Praeger 1982): 103–134.

White, Ronald C. *American Ulysses: A Life of Ulysses S. Grant.* New York: Random House, 2016).

Wiggins, Sarah W. "Ostracism of White Republicans in Alabama During Reconstruction." *Alabama Review*, 27 (1974): 52–65.

Wiggins, Sarah W. *The Scalawag in Alabama Politics, 1865–1881.* (Tuscaloosa: University of Alabama Press, 1977).

Williams, Daniel B. *A Sketch of the Life and Times of Captain R.A. Paul. An Authentic and Abbreviated History of his Career from Boyhood to the Present Time: Containing a Reliable Account of the Politics of Virginia from 1874 to the Present Time.* (Richmond: Johns & Goolsby Printers, 1885).

Williams, George H. *Occasional Addresses.* (Portland: W.H. Bates & Co., 1895).

Williams, Lou Falkner. *The Great South Carolina KuKlux Trials, 1871–1872.* (Athens: University of Georgia Press, 1996).

Williams, T. Harry. "An Analysis of Some Reconstruction Attitudes." *Journal of Southern History*, 12 (1946): 469–486.

Williams, T. Harry. "The Louisiana Unification Movement of 1873." *Journal of Southern History*, 11 (1945): 349–369.

Williamson, Edward C. "The Alabama Election of 1874." *Alabama Review*, 17 (1964): 210–218.

Williamson, Joel. *The Crucible of Race: Black-White Relations in the American South since Emancipation.* (New York: Oxford University Press, 1984).

Wilson, Charles R. "Robert Lewis Dabney: Religion and the Southern Holocaust." *Virginia Magazine of History and Biography*, (1981): 79–89.

Wilson, Kirt H. *The Reconstruction Desegregation Debate: The Politics of Equality and the Rhetoric of Place, 1870–1875.* (East Lansing: Michigan State University Press, 2002).

Withers, Robert E. *Autobiography of an Octogenarian.* (Roanoke: Stone Printing, 1907).

Wood, Forrest G. *Black Scare: The Racist Response to Emancipation and Reconstruction.* (Berkeley: University of California Press, 1968).

Woodward, C. Vann. *Origins of the New South, 1877–1913.* (Baton Rouge: Louisiana State University Press, 1951).

Woodward, C. Vann. *The Strange Career of Jim Crow* (New York: Oxford University Press, 1966).

Woolfolk, Sarah V. "The Role of the Scalawag in Alabama Reconstruction," Diss., Louisiana State University, 1965.

Wyatt-Brown, Bertram. "The Civil Rights Act of 1875." *Western Political Quarterly*, 18 (1965): 763–775.

Wyatt-Brown, Bertram. *Southern Honor: Ethics and Behavior in the Old South.* (New York: Oxford University Press, 1982).

Wynes, Charles E. *Race Relations in Virginia, 1870–1902.* (Charlottesville: University of Virginia Press, 1961).

Younger, Edward E. *John A. Kasson. Politics and Diplomacy from Lincoln to McKinley.* (Iowa City: State Historical Society of Iowa, 1955).

Zilversmit, Arthur. "Grant and the Freedman," in Robert H. Abzug and Stephen E. Maizlich eds., *New Perspectives on Peace and Slavery in America: Essays in Honor of Kenneth M. Stampp.* (Lexington: University Press of America, 1986): 121–145.

Zipf, Karin L. "'The Whites shall rule the land or die:' Gender, Race, and Class in North Carolina Reconstruction Politics." *Journal of Southern History*, 65 (1999): 499–534.

Zornow, William. "Ohio Democrats and the Africanization Issue in 1862." *Negro History Bulletin*, 11 (1948): 211–214.

Index

www.ingramcontent.com/pod-product-compliance
Ingram Content Group UK Ltd.
Pitfield, Milton Keynes, MK11 3LW, UK
UKHW031635090125
453371UK00011B/82

9 781642 590746